SAINT DOMINIC'S FAMILY

GW00982525

"*Then the Lord placed His hand on the shoulder of the Blessed Virgin, and said to the blessed Dominic, 'I have given thine Order to My Mother.' Then He said again, 'And wouldst thou really see thine Order?' And he replied, 'Yea, Lord.' Then the Blessed Virgin opened the mantle in which she seemed to be dressed, and extending it before the eyes of Dominic, so that its immensity covered all the space of the heavenly country, he saw under its folds a vast multitude of his friars. The blessed Dominic fell down to thank God and the Blessed Mary, His Mother, and the vision disappeared, and he came to himself again . . .*"

From *Saint Dominic*, pp. 129 - 30
by Sister Mary Jean Dorcy, O.P.

SAINT DOMINIC'S FAMILY

THE LIVES OF
OVER 300 FAMOUS DOMINICANS

by
Sister Mary Jean Dorcy, O.P.
Dominican Sisters of the Holy Cross

> *Another parable he proposed unto them, saying:*
> *The kingdom of heaven is like to a grain of mustard*
> *seed, which a man took and sowed in his field.*
> *Which is the least indeed of all seeds; but when it is*
> *grown up, it is greater than all herbs, and becometh a*
> *tree, so that the birds of the air come, and dwell in*
> *the branches thereof.*
> —Matt. 13:31-32

THE ST. MARTIN DE PORRES
LAY DOMINICAN COMMUNITY
New Hope, Kentucky 40052

TAN BOOKS AND PUBLISHERS, INC.
Rockford, Illinois 61105

REVISORES ORDINIS: Thomas C. Donlan, O.P.
                      John A. Henry, O.P.

IMPRIMI POTEST: John E. Marr, O.P.
                      Provincial

NIHIL OBSTAT: Thomas C. Donlan, O.P.
                      Censor Librorum

IMPRIMATUR: ✛ James J. Byrne, S.T.D.
                      Archbishop of Dubuque
                      November 6, 1963

Originally published in 1964 by The Priory Press, Dubuque, Iowa.

Copyright © 1964 by The Priory Press

Copyright © 1983 by Sister Mary Jean Dorcy, O.P.

Library of Congress Catalog Card No.: 83-70219

ISBN: 0-89555-208-6

Printed and bound in the United States of America.

All rights reserved. No part of this book may be reproduced or transmitted in any form or by any means, electronic or mechanical, including photocopying, recording, or by any information storage or retrieval system, without permission in writing from TAN Books and Publishers, Inc.

2nd Printing

THE ST. MARTIN DE PORRES
LAY DOMINICAN COMMUNITY
New Hope, Kentucky 40052

TAN BOOKS AND PUBLISHERS, INC.
P.O. Box 424
Rockford, Illinois 61105
1983

This book is affectionately dedicated to
MOTHER MARY FRANCES MILLER, O.P.
*whose interest and encouragement have
made it possible.*

PREFACE

To be asked to write your family history is a work not many authors with family pride could resist, but whether it would be readable by any but equally proud members of the family is yet another thing. There is no task more booby-trapped. When loyalty, enthusiasm, and dedication set to work on family lore, tradition, and history, and when the family tree reaches back almost eight hundred years, heaven help everybody!

That Sister Mary Jean Dorcy, O.P., has nimbly danced her way through eight hundred years—less a few—of Dominicans, has avoided every one of the pitfalls and produced a collection of "lives" which is not only informative but entirely delightful, is a tribute to her balance as a scholar, her discernment as a woman, and her integrity as a Dominican. Talent, a sense of humor, and above all a mastery of the art of understatement (and where is the temptation to overstate greater than when writing of one's favorite relatives?) enhance every page of her work which, one soon discovers, it is not easy to put down.

Drawing from every available source in the history of her Order, Sister Mary Jean has culled facts and distributed emphases with the hand of an expert. Her 339 little biographies sparkle with judiciously chosen details, highlights, and decorations.

Beginning with the thirteenth century, we find not only the familiar greats—Dominic, Blessed Jordan, Peter Martyr, Margaret of Hungary, Thomas Aquinas, Raymond of Pennafort, Albert the Great—but also many other members of the Order whose stories have been eclipsed by their more impressive brothers. Here we meet the men who knew St. Dominic personally and whose recollections have created the portrait of the saint. Strangely, to know them is to draw closer to Dominic, to discern some of the magic of the man who drew so many others into the service of the Lord, and high sanctity along the way. Here are tales of the evangelizing of Europe which both map the growth of the Church in the blood of her martyrs and trace the political history of the times.

There is Moneta of Cremona who loaned Dominic a bed to die on and a tunic to die in; Blessed Isnard who drove out a devil by putting his arms around a man possessed and embracing him; Blessed Peter Gonzales who has become, for some unknown reason, St. Elmo to the sailors of the world; and Anselm and his companions who went off to the Tartars facing as fantastic an adventure as any traveler to the moon.

The forerunners of the illustrious English Dominicans appear in this century, together with Bishop Clement of Dunblane who brought the Order to Scotland and St. Ingrid of Sweden who founded that country's first Dominican convent in 1281. Blessed Santarem was a saint with a misspent youth, and Blessed Zedislava Berka is a delightful new friend for wives and mothers. Of illustrious female members there was no lack in this century—St. Helen of Hungary, novice mistress to the little girl who became St. Margaret; Constance, queen of Russia and younger sister to Margaret, whose life was one of sudden success and crushing reversal; Mechtilde of Magdeberg, a guest in the same convent as—and therefore a friend of—the great St. Gertude and her sister Mechtilde; to say nothing of the three charmers, Blessed Diana, Blessed Cecelia, and Blessed Amati.

The fourteenth century introduces us to two figures of controversy, Munio de Zamora, deposed as Master General by a pope but defended by the Order, and John Tauler, often misnamed a forerunner of the Reformation. There was the scientist, Theodore of Saxony; the vernacularist, Blessed Jordan of Pisa; the ecumenist, Bartholomew the Little; the Icelander, Bishop John Haldorsson; and the Ethiopian, Philip de Sceva. The latter, scion of the royal house, was martyred like John the Baptist for insisting that the reigning Christian monarch keep to one wife instead of several.

Among the familiar names we find St. Agnes of Montepulciano, Blessed Margaret of Castello, Blessed Imelda Lambertini, Blessed Henry Suso, Blessed Raymond of Capua, and, of course, outdazzling them all, St. Catherine of Siena.

Here also are two maidens, relatively unknown, whose stories are pure delight—Blessed Villana de Botti and Euphemia of England. Villana, worldly, witty, and pretty, as a child tried to run away like St. Catherine of Siena to become a hermit in the desert. Brought back by her amused family, she thereafter pursued a frivolous life until the day when she saw reflected in her mirror a Medusa instead of the elegant coquette. Turning to penance, she promised, like a familiar saint of the twentieth century, that after her death she would send "flowers from heaven. . . ."

Euphemia was the daughter of Edward II of England, sister to John of Gaunt and the Black Prince. Here is a tale of intrigue and suspense, with Euphemia fleeing the court and somehow managing to keep a hop, skip, and a jump ahead of her father's men. She ended her days as laundress to a convent of highborn ladies whose rank prevented them from assuming such menial tasks. One longs to have been present when they discovered that their wash lady was the daughter of the king of England.

The more one reads this book, the more one marvels at the precision of its gifted author who has ruthlessly pared down accounts which must have filled volumes without sacrificing the warm, living quality of her portraits. Brevity, rarely considered a feminine characteristic, is one of Sister Mary Jean Dorcy's outstanding virtues.

In the fifteenth century, she gives us theologians, writers, preachers, inquisitors (her accounts do much to restore that unenviable role to better focus), miracle workers, reformers, royalty, and artists—among them St. Vincent Ferrer,

Blessed John Dominici, St. Antoninus, Fra Angelico, Blesseds Margaret of Savoy and Joanna of Portugal, and Alan de la Roche, devotee of the rosary. Two child brides, Mary Mancini—wed at twelve—and Clara Gambarcorti—wed at thirteen, became friends of St. Catherine and entered the Order, and Blessed Anthony Neyrot seems a likely patron of all who have suffered brain-washing and intimidation. Fearful of death, he recanted the Faith, became an adopted son of a king, married a Turkish lady of position, commenced a translation of the Koran, and then recanting his recantation, was stoned to death proclaiming Christ and wearing once again his Dominican habit.

Blessed Sebastian Maggi, friend of Savonarola, who might have saved that friar from the stake had he lived to give him counsel, is here; and Sister Mary Jean's account of Savonarola is as precise and satisfying a summary of that tragic story as anyone could ask.

Her amusing story of Blessed Columba of Rieti reveals, oddly enough, not only this famed sixteenth century tertiary but Sister Mary Jean herself—whose quiet countenance and benign smile cloak a vixenish sense of the comic, as her friends well know. One catches half of her salty observations on life on the double-take, hidden under innocent comments about such things as love, money, or the weather.

This century for the Order of Preachers saw not only John Tetzel involved in the beginnings of the Reformation, but Dominican missionaries taking part in the great wave of exploration to the New World. The account of Tetzel, the Dominican friar who tangled with Martin Luther, points out that distortion, exaggeration, sound, fury, and bitterness had more to do with his undeserved reputation as a bad theologian than the facts bear out.

Among the Dominicans who played a part in the evangelizing of America we find Diego de Deza, champion of Columbus; Anthony of Montesino, defender of the Indians of Hispaniola; Bartholomew Mateo, convicted of cruelty to the Indians of Peru, who escaped prison to Mexico, repented, and dedicated his life to the peoples there. Especially endearing is Luis Canceri de Barbastro, who translated into Quiche rhymed couplets explaining the truths of the Faith and taught the natives by singing them to the music of flutes and occarinas.

In England martyrs were a-making, among them Blessed Adrian Fortescue, cousin to Ann Boleyn, and Richard Hargraves. Antoninus Temmermans was drawn and quartered in Antwerp by the Calvinists for refusing to break the seal of confession. Sixtus of Siena, born a Jew, was rescued from a heretic's prison by the future St. Pius V, received into the Order, and became one of the century's great Scripture scholars. Together with all these and more go the familiar names of Lucy of Narni, John of Gorkum, Louis Bertrand, Catherine de Ricci, and Venerable Louis of Granada.

Dominican history in the seventeenth century reads like a travelogue and, drawing closer to modern times, we find the lives even richer in color and detail with men and women of every race taking their place in the Order.

English and Irish Dominicans died for Christ in the British Isles; Latins died in Guadalupe, Mexico, Russia, and Turkey; Japanese Dominicans were martyred in Japan; and in China the ground was wet with blood also.

Among those called to live and serve were Lopo Cardozo, missionary to Cambodia, whom Sister Mary Jean considers the patron saint of fund raisers. Lopo barely escaped execution by elephant-trampling, collected funds to ransom his priest companion only to see the ship sink with his money aboard—with which he started collecting all over again. Here we find a tiny grandmother, Catherine Sanzo, "the grand old lady of the Chinese missions," the five Jansenboys from Holland—not a musical group, as you might expect, but pamphleteers and preachers, apostles of the Catholic press. Dominic of St. Thomas was born prince Ottoman to the empire of his father, Ibrahim, a confirmed Mohammedan before his conversion, and Marie de Combe was brought up a strict Calvinist.

As the centuries pile up and we see the followers of St. Dominic drawn from every conceivable rank and situation, land and clime, we see also the Dominican idea, "to contemplate and share the fruits of contemplation," penetrating every nook and cranny of human existence. In hermitages, cells, cloisters, monasteries, priories, prisons, ships, schoolrooms, manors, cottages, castles, universities, shops, farms, jungles, deserts, cities, towns, the sons and daughters of this questing Spaniard sewed the riches of his spiritual legacy. No place, however remote, no person, however hopeless, but existed within the orbit of divine truth, within the circle of Christ's love. Each Dominican was an extension of that first Dominican who was an extension of Christ.

The Dominican story in the eighteenth century continues on a slightly minor key. Louis Calso wanted to preach Christ to the heathen and instead was dispatched to institute a reform among his brethren. Francis of Posadas wasn't even wanted by the Order, said the prior to whom he applied. There was no room for the sons of street peddlers.

The martyrdom of Arthur MacGeogheghan, in order to discourage vocations to the Dominican priesthood, boomeranged thoroughly for it inspired swarms of stubborn young Irishmen to enter the seminary; and the martyrdom of Bishop Sanz in China reminds us of St. Thomas More and his cheery mein as he climbed the scaffold. "Rejoice . . . I am on my way to heaven," said the Bishop to his dour head-chopper. "I wish I were going with you," was the mournful reply.

Delightful as a fairy tale is the story of Benoite Rencurel, seeress, mystic, stigmatist, and charming shepherdess, while—on the other hand—Joseph Galien dwelt in the world of the scientist, studied the possibilities for man-made flight, and even drew up plans for an airplane. And high up in the firmament shone the stars of Blessed Louis Marie Grignon de Montfort and Pope Benedict XIII.

Among the great names of the nineteenth century are Pauline Jaricot, foundress of the Society for the Propagation of the Faith, the Dominican martyrs of Tonkin, and the great writer and preacher, Lacordaire. Lesser known but captivating are Catherine Jarrige, the "angel of the underground" during the French revolution, and Mother Frances Drane, gifted writer and one of the feminine converts from Anglicanism during the great Oxford movement.

Here also we find the Order putting down its roots in the American States. Maryland-born Edward Fenwick was sent from Belgium to Kentucky and ended up Bishop of Cincinnati. Mother Angela Sansbury and her companions received their habits in the Kentucky chapel of St. Mary Magdalene—a log cabin. Samuel Mazzuchelli came from Italy to the Middle West and all but lived on horseback. Visitors to Dubuque should be sure to see, outside that city, the little frame church he built and the tiny room behind the altar where this great apostle slept—now and then—and prayed. Joseph Alemany came from Spain as a young recruit and died Archbishop of San Francisco, while his traveling companion, Francis Vilarrasa became commissary general of the Order in California.

And the twentieth century finds the names of men and women within living memory added to the list. One wishes to have heard Henri Didon's great sermons on marriage. Then there was Henry Denifle, historian; Arnold Janssen, founder of the Society of the Divine Word; Doctor Agnes MacLaren, ex-Presbyterian who came into the Church in her sixties and campaigned for the work which became the Medical Mission Sisters. The fantastic story of Sister Susanna and her companions, murdered in the desert in Armenia, seems more likely to have happened in the Middle Ages than at the opening of World War I. And on and on—Mother Mary Walsh, Mother Alphonsa (Rose) Hawthorne, Father Arintero, Bede Jarrett, Father Lagrange, Eric Gill, Father Vincent McNabb, Gerald Vann, and the greatly loved American Dominican—apostle of theology for the people—Walter Farrell.

Sister Mary Jean Dorcy has written books, given lectures, cut out pictures, taught on the missions, served her Order and Christ a thousand, thousand ways. But this work is her greatest, for with it she accomplishes all these things at once. It will be an inspiration for both religious and lay people, a treasure trove for families (imagine over three hundred saint stories in one book), a priceless reference for students, but most exciting of all, to read it is to watch the parable of the mustard seed come true.

Sister Mary Jean has done the all but impossible. She has painted the portrait of an Order. We are startled to see that it is even more magnificent than we had realized.

Mary Reed Newland
Monson, Massachusetts
January, 1964

CONTENTS

CONTENTS

THIRTEENTH CENTURY

FOURTEENTH CENTURY

FIFTEENTH CENTURY

SIXTEENTH CENTURY

SEVENTEENTH CENTURY

NINETEENTH CENTURY

TWENTIETH CENTURY

THIRTEENTH CENTURY

THIRTEENTH CENTURY

ST. DOMINIC
(1170-1221)

A master of paradox was this thirteenth-century friar who established the foundations of democracy in the depressing days of feudalism, and laid out with
a globe-circling sweep the plans that would convert a world no one had yet
dreamed about. It is doubtful if any other man, saint or not, accomplished
so much in so short a lifetime, or expressed so unequivocally his faith in
the future.

Dominic de Guzman was born in Old Castile around 1170. His father
was castellan of a fort on the border of Christian Spain, and the two older
sons of the family were already studying for the priesthood when Dominic
was born. In the ordinary course of events, the boy would have been trained
to arms, but his mother's pleading and his evident talent for study determined
that he, too, would be given to the Church. Taking his studies at the
University of Palencia, he was ordained and soon afterwards joined the
chapter of Augustinian Canons at Osma. He was made prior of the canons
at this early age; a contemporary description says of him:

> Straightway he began to appear among his brother canons as a bright ray
> of sunshine, in humbleness of heart the least, in holiness the first, shedding
> around him the fragrance of quickening life, like the sweet scent of pine-
> woods in the heat of a summer's day. And advancing from strength to
> strength as does the wide-growing olive and the slender, lofty cypress, day
> and night he frequented the church, ceaselessly devoted to prayer, scarcely
> venturing beyond the cloister walls, the more to find leisure for his lone
> thoughts with God.

His whole early life is mirrored in this picture of the devout and quiet
young priest, happy in the cloister solitude with its double obligation of
choral office and teaching of the truths of God.

In 1203 his cloistered peace was disturbed by the bishop, who summoned
him to go on a diplomatic mission to "The Marches"—possibly Denmark.
Dominic could not have known it, but the peace of the Spanish cloister
was never to be his again. As they traveled through France he met the
heresy which was to be his principal adversary in life: the teaching of
the Albigensians. It had devastated the whole of the southern provinces.
Convinced that someone should preach the truth to these benighted people,
he discussed with his bishop the project of giving missions among them.

Both he and the bishop had hoped to go to Tartary as missionaries when the diplomatic journey was over, but found themselves instead involved in the troubles of France. Commissioned by the pope to assist the Cistercians in preaching against the Albigensians, Dominic and the bishop worked with a few companions. The bishop died, the Cistercians went home, discouraged, and Dominic was left with a handful of followers, linked to him only by mutual unwillingness to abandon the people of France to heresy. At this unpropitious time, Dominic decided to organize his followers into a group with papal commission to preach; he made several trips across Europe to get this permission, finally obtaining it in 1216.

By this time Dominic was the center of a great deal of action as well as prayer. A group of nine women heretics he had converted were established at Prouille in a convent; here they could assist with prayer and good works in the preaching activities of the brethren. Sixteen men, of many nationalities, had thrown in their lot with him and were willing to share with him in the business of world conquest. An unnumbered band of interested seculars, most of whom were knights and wealthy men, and their womenfolk, hovered like bees around the work of Dominic. He organized them into chapters of active religious helpers even before the Order obtained papal approval. Hence it was from the very first an Order with a multiple attack on the evils of the world: the preachers worked among the men of the schools and argued with the most learned heretics in public disputations; the nuns taught the daughters of the nobility who might otherwise fall into the clutches of the heretic teachers; and the men and women of the "Militia of Jesus Christ" pledged their swords and their fortunes to the needs of the Church.

We have today so many orders and institutes patterned on the Dominican that it is hard for us to remember that in many of its most characteristic features the Dominican Order was a startling innovation. In an age when Church and State gave no thought to any form of government except monarchy, Dominic arranged that his brethren should elect their priors, who would rule for a limited time only, and that all should have a part in the legislation of the Order. Nations which have since established democracies owe a great deal to this quiet Spanish priest who insisted on building a democracy at a time when even the word was unknown. Dominic was the first founder to insist that the rule did not bind under pain of sin, only under the penalty fixed for its violation. His rule was meant to make the way to heaven easier, not harder. He was the first to propose an order dedicated to preaching, at a time when no one but bishops regularly preached. With insight that we can bless today, he foresaw that one might preach in many ways, and in many media; so he made VERITAS the motto of the Order and did not limit the ways or means by which one might preach it. Lastly, his Order was organized to cope with problems of future centuries in lands that had not even been discovered in his day. There is nothing in the Dominican rule to prevent the evangelization of any continent, or of Mars, for that matter; its application is flexible in order to meet the problems of all times and places.

We know the story of Dominic's last years; he spent five years as head of the Order, a pitifully short time. Yet in that brief period he attracted to the Order so many of the saintly and talented men of the times that his death did not in the least menace the carrying out of his ideal; men who had heard him preach went off joyfully to die in Tartary, or to debate with heretics, or to teach in the universities, or to teach catechism to the young. Five years of his magnetic presence was enough to magnetize the whole Order, so to speak, so that in the first hundred years of its existence it would draw nearly 30,000 members from all the countries of Europe, and start on its way around the world.

St. Dominic died in Bologna on August the sixth, 1221, on his return from the Second General Chapter of the Order. He had lived long enough to see his Order established firmly enough that no persecution or trouble would shake it. Dying, he promised his weeping brethren that he would be of more use to them in heaven than he was on earth—a promise which he has kept abundantly in the seven centuries since.

The burial of St. Dominic took place, according to his wishes, in extreme simplicity. He was buried in a modest grave, "under the feet of his brethren." Here he remained until the urging of Pope Gregory IX—who was a personal friend of his—gave rise to the first translation of the relics.

This translation took place in 1233, at the time of a general chapter. Blessed Jordan presided over the ceremony, and all were filled with great emotion as the relics were exposed after twelve years' burial. Testimonials were given in writing of the sanctity of Dominic by those who had worked with him and knew him best. Pope Gregory IX had the evidence carefully preserved, and in the following year he proclaimed that Dominic de Guzman was a saint of God and entitled to the highest honors of the Church. The news reached the master general, Blessed Jordan, on August the fifth, 1234. The feast of the saint had to be transferred from the sixth, which was the day of his death, because this was the Feast of the Transfiguration. August the fourth was the feast day appointed by the pope.

BLESSED JANE OF AZA
(1140-1202)

Devotion to Our Lady was typical of medieval Spaniards, as indeed of any Christian of the time. But the devotion to Mary bequeathed by St. Dominic to his children was something more than ordinary, and in the natural course of events it could come from only one source—his own mother. Her name, the scanty records tell us, was Jane of Aza, and neither the date of her birth nor that of her death is known with certainty. Not being of great material importance, she made little impression on history; but the print of her personality will be seen for all time on the Order founded by her son. Dominic must have had a very tender love for his mother to make him turn so constantly, trustingly, instinctively to Our Lady in all the troubles and joys of his later life.

Legend relates that before the birth of Dominic, Blessed Jane beheld a vision in which she saw her son, running as a swift greyhound through the world, bearing in his mouth a torch with which he illumined the world. It was for her to fan and shelter that flame at its very kindling, and to teach this child of predilection the prayers he would say with such rich results for a lifetime of saintly action. Not only was it Jane who first taught her son the words of the Hail Mary—that key with which he unlocked heaven for so many souls—but it was she who gave to him the living example of Christian womanhood. If in later years his sons were to cherish such a chivalrous love for the gracious Queen of Heaven, much of it was due to the reverential awe and tender love with which this truly Christian lady inspired her three priest-sons. To every priest, his own mother is the personification of all that is good and lovable in woman; she is the ideal to inspire him, the lighthouse to beckon him, and the living picture of the Mother of the first Priest. It could have been no different for Dominic. Where else would he, brought up amid the scenes of war and in the man's world of the university, see in action the ideals of womanly purity, gentleness, and never-failing help that he was to cherish as the attributes of his heavenly queen?

History is silent regarding events in the life of Blessed Jane. Probably there were no great events to record. As the wife of the Castellan of Calaruega, a fortress castle on the border of Christian Spain, she would have led a life filled with the monotony of small things. Tradition relates that her two older sons, Anthony and Manez, were already preparing for the priesthood when Dominic was born. She named her youngest son for St. Dominic of Silos, at whose shrine she was a frequent pilgrim. Knowing that her soldier-husband expected their third son to carry on the family name and fortunes, Jane seems still to have cherished for him the goal of the priesthood. Very likely Dominic—and we—owe to his understanding mother the fortune that placed a book in his hand instead of a sword.

Pope Leo XII beatified Jane of Aza in 1828. Devotion to her has persisted through the centuries despite the poverty of records. The mother of three priests, one of whom died a death of heroic charity and two who were raised to the altars of the Church, can safely be judged to have been not only a valiant woman but also a saintly one. Her picture, as that of any mother, can best be seen reflected in her sons.

EVERARD OF LANGRES
(d. 1221)

Almost the same day that St. Dominic died, a venerable Dominican in France breathed his last. He was on his way to meet St. Dominic, of whom he had heard the most enthusiastic reports, but death precluded their earthly meeting. The disappointed traveler, Everard of Langres, has been known as "Blessed Everard" since pioneer days. We may hope that they met quickly in heaven.

Everard of Langres was an elderly and much esteemed canon of the chapter of Langres when he met Jordan of Saxony and was fired by his great zeal. Everard was a man of many talents. He had built a great hospital, supervised the building of the cathedral of Langres, and had successfully refused the bishopric of Lausanne. He held at the time about as much secular authority as any one priest could expect to have. In 1220, when Jordan returned to Paris from the chapter of Bologna, he found Everard of Langres ready to renounce all of his authority and throw in his lot with the new Order of Preachers.

Jordan had just received the office of provincial of Lombardy. He gave the habit to the venerable canon of Langres in the little new priory of St. Jacques in Paris. Here there is an amusing glimpse of the workings of Everard's mind. He wanted desperately to see St. Dominic, whom Jordan had described with boundless enthusiasm. As a venerable and authoritative member of the church in Langres, he was unlikely to leave France for some time, if ever. Dominic was not immediately coming to France.

But Jordan must go to Lombardy to take up his new office, and the saint would surely be there. Everard had an inspiration. He volunteered to accompany Jordan to Lombardy as a companion.

Jordan may have known what was in the back of the old priest's mind when he accepted the offer; in any case he was grateful for the company of a man with a stimulating mind and a wealth of experience. No doubt he learned a great many practical things from his venerable companion as they slowly crossed Burgundy and proceeded towards Italy.

They preached as they went. We have some record of that journey, for Jordan kept records. He threw all the credit on Everard for the success of their preaching, though perhaps if Everard had been telling the story it would have been the other way around. Jordan relates: "Through all the land of France and Burgundy which he crossed with me, Everard was esteemed by everyone, and bearing the poor and naked Christ in his heart, Everard went preaching." This friar, who only yesterday had been a wealthy churchman, was now an enthusiastic beggar for Christ's poor, and the poor flocked around him.

He had a good working-knowledge of those who, in the districts they evangelized, could be counted upon for help for the new Order. He pointed out to an interested Jordan the places where a Dominican community would be well-received, the towns where the bishop was eager for the preaching of the brethren, and the men of wealth who could be counted upon to help in building. In all, Jordan must have been very grateful for the help of this walking Baedeker of the provinces of France.

It could not have been a comfortable journey for Everard, but he made no complaints. He was much too old to begin the globe-trotting activities that younger friars took for granted. It was summer, and very hot at times. They walked from early dawn until the vesper stars appeared, with time out only for the traditional siesta. Everard, to whom the whole thing must have been startlingly unusual, took to itinerant preaching as if he had been at it all his life. He was even able to give the veteran Jordan a few pointers. And, what was even more important, he knew all the religious houses en route, so that getting hospitality was a simple thing.

Just as they started up the foothills of the Alps, Everard's strength gave out, and they realized that he was very ill. They reached Lausanne by slow stages. The doctors saw that he was going to die, but decided it would be better not to tell him so. Everard suspected the news they were hiding from him, and said, "If the doctors are of the opinion that I am going to die, why don't they tell me so? It is from those to whom the thought of

death is bitter that it must be hidden. As for me, I have no fear of death."
He died in a few days, unaware that the saint he was so anxious to meet
was even then hurrying home to die among his brethren in Bologna.

Everard has always been held in veneration, and his memory is celebrated
in the diocese of Langres on August the fifth.

HENRY OF MARBOURG
(d. 1224)

Blessed Jordan was a man of great friendships. He defined true friendship and
pointed out its place in the spiritual life. His dearest friend in life was Henry
of Marbourg, and if Henry had no other distinction than this it would make
him of very great interest to us.

Where or when Henry of Marbourg was born are not a matter of exact
record. He was one of the youngest of the students of arts in Paris when
Master Jordan was a professor there. He must have been a young man of
very attractive personality and fine character, for Jordan felt that he was
the very flower of the Order. When Reginald of Orleans died, Jordan
had a vision in which he saw in the cloister of St. Jacques a clear and
limpid fountain which ran dry. In its place a fountain sprang up, having
two heads, surging up like a great river to water the whole earth. It was
revealed to him that Henry of Marbourg was one of the fountainheads,
and the brethren easily understood that Jordan himself was the other.

Jordan had at this time fully made up his mind to abandon a promising
career in Paris and join the Order of Friars Preachers. But he could not bring
himself to leave his dearest friend behind. Often in later life he was to
say in his sermons, "You do not go to a banquet alone, but with your dear
friends; you should not go alone to heaven either!" He simply could not
imagine anyone going into the joy of the religious life without bringing
his friends along with him. So he delayed his entrance into religion until
Henry, who had not yet made up his mind, should be ready to come with
him.

Henry had completed his studies in arts and theology in Paris. He was
"handsome, reverent and virtuous, of a mind to grasp everything and with
a rare faculty for expressing himself." Jordan began to work on him because,

as he said, "I saw in him a natural disposition and a very special grace for the ministry of preaching."

The day that Jordan returned from confession to Master Reginald, shaken and exalted by the ideals that Reginald had put before him, he looked for a Scripture text to confirm his resolution. Finding one, he cut the book to find a text for Henry, and Scripture turned up the verse, "Let us stay together, let us never separate." He urged this on Henry, but the young man, who was chaste and obedient, found it difficult to accept poverty.

Henry argued with himself, prayed and meditated, but still he was unable to accept the precept of abandoning all things for the uncertainties of a mendicant life. One night, after he had prayed a long time, he saw himself at judgment, and a thunderous voice demanded of him, "And you—what have *you* given up for God?" Henry was shaken by this thought, and went to see Master Reginald, telling him that he had resolved to enter the Order as soon as it could be arranged. On Ash Wednesday of 1220, the two friends went together to the Friars' chapel to put off forever their worldly dress and don the habit of the Order.

To Jordan, who was a magnetic preacher himself, Henry was the model of preachers. We have, in fact, only a very idealized picture of Henry, because all we know of him is through the eyes of Jordan, who loved him so dearly. Jordan tried to imitate his style of preaching, as he felt that it was the most perfect type of preaching he had ever heard. In 1221, when the priory of Cologne was established, Henry was sent there as prior, and Jordan went to Lombardy. It was a sorrow to the good friends to be separated and to be left without the mutual help and inspiration that their friendship had meant to them. They wrote frequently, and what we know of those letters gives us a splendid view of a genuine friendship based on love of God and directed to the furthering of His kingdom.

In 1224, when Henry could not have been more than thirty-five years old, he died suddenly in the arms of Jordan, who happened to be visiting in Cologne. It was a terrible grief to Jordan, and his letter concerning the death of Henry is one of the saddest and most beautiful of all his eloquent writings. He writes to Blessed Diana in the newness of his sorrow, "Do not grieve too much about the death of your sister Otta . . . it is good for us to be saddened now at the same time, to go sowing our seed in tears; at the harvest we shall come carrying our sheaves in joy." Jordan confesses that he wept copiously for his friend, and, after giving a beautiful account of the last moments of Henry, he adds, "There is still a long way to go. If you are tired, your Jesus was also . . . in all humility, in all patience, He knew how to wait."

THE ABBESS EUGENIA
(1225)

We know very little about the Abbess Eugenia. She belongs to the very earliest days of the Order; in fact, it might truthfully be said that she antedated the Order. She was prioress of St. Mary's in Trastevere, in Rome, when the young Spanish priest by the name of Dominic came to her and told her he had been appointed to re-establish discipline in her community.

Mother Eugenia had been prioress for many years at this time, and she of all people could tell him that the plan was nice, but it simply would not work. She was a woman of piety and charity, and devoted herself to personal sanctification. She prayed hard for her spiritual children. Perhaps she was too easygoing to enforce her own piety upon her high-spirited daughters. Probably also she was powerless to oppose either the customs that these worldly religious had set up, or the influence of their wealthy and noble families. That Mother Eugenia could preserve *any* sense of religious life in this watered-down atmosphere is quite remarkable. Yet we know she did; she listened to the saint, and, when young Cecilia Caesarini—whose family was as wealthy and overbearing as anyone else's—threw herself on her knees at his feet and begged him to let her share in the work, the prioress knelt beside her. She warned him that he was attempting the impossible, but she promised to back him up.

The battle that followed is Dominican history. The nuns refused even to listen to the prioress' suggestion of reform. Cloister? Silence? Penance? Was she mad? But with mixed motives they sat and listened to St. Dominic, and, at the end of what must have been a very persuasive conference, all but one of the nuns pledged him their support. Then, as we know, they carried the news to their families, and the trouble began anew. When St. Dominic returned to them, all but the prioress and Sister Cecilia were wavering. He talked to them again, and finally won their promise to reform. Then they were faced with the question of leaving St. Mary's and going across the Tiber to the convent of St. Sixtus. This provoked a new argument.

To understand why this should have caused disagreement, we shall have to consider the picture of the Madonna, which was the chief glory of the convent of Trastevere. It was a very old picture, one of several supposedly painted by St. Luke, and it had been there for centuries. The tradition exists, rightly or wrongly, that this was the very picture carried by Pope Gregory the Great at the time of the plague in the seventh century. Not only the nuns, but the entire neighborhood was jealously possessive of the picture. The nuns would not consider going anywhere without it. And, someone proposed an historically-supported reason why the picture belonged right where it was; in the tenth century, Pope Sergius III had taken it to the Church of St. John Lateran, and it had come back, all by itself, to St. Mary's in Trastevere. Didn't that prove that they should stay where they were?

An obstacle like this might have stopped someone else, but not St. Dominic. Probably he ·felt that the Blessed Virgin was a friend of his and would never let him down; anyway, he told the sisters that they would, of course, take the picture with them, and if it returned by itself they would take it as a sign they should return.

On this assurance, the move was planned. The actual transfer had to be done in the middle of the night, for they did not wish to cope with a neighborhood full of devout Italians who would resent losing their beloved picture. Barefoot, and murmuring prayers for the success of the venture, the little procession wound its way from the old life to the new, and St. Sixtus became the cradle of many saints after the reform was established.

The picture never returned to St. Mary's in Trastevere, but it has had several adventures through the centuries since. Pope St. Pius V moved the sisters to "Sts. Dominic and Sixtus," a healthier location than Old St. Sixtus, in the days before the marshes were drained. In 1931, the master general moved the sisters again, to the convent in Monte Mario. Here he was up against a mightier obstacle than Italian piety: a decree from a dictator that "no historical monuments" could be removed. The sisters quite calmly had a copy made of the picture, and left it in its place when they departed with the real one. No one but themselves knew that the original Madonna, which had watched for more than a thousand years over the sisters of several convents, was still at her post in the convent of Monte Mario.

We know no more of the Abbess Eugenia; she is presumed to have died a few years after St. Dominic, having lived to see her prayers for a fervent reform more than answered.

BLESSED REGINALD OF ORLEANS
(1183?-1220)

Reginald was born in France, probably in Orleans, and received his training at the University of Paris. He taught canon law with great success and, because of his evident virtues and talents, was appointed dean of the cathedral chapter at Orleans. Here as in Paris he was renowned for the brilliance of his mind and the eloquence of his preaching, and also for a tender devotion to the Mother of God.

Since he was a very zealous young man, Reginald was not content with his life as it was. He was in truth leading a very holy life, but he yearned for more. He determined on a pilgrimage to the Holy Land, perhaps to pray for light to know his vocation, and on his way to Jerusalem he visited Rome. Here he discussed his desires with Cardinal Hugh de Segni, explaining that he felt a great call to the primitive poverty and preaching of the apostles but knew of no way to realize his hope. The cardinal replied that he knew the exact answer to his seeking, and sent him to St. Dominic, who was in Rome at the time. Reginald hastened to open his heart to the holy founder, and at St. Dominic's words he knew he had come to the end of his seeking.

Reginald had scarcely made his decision to enter the Order when he became so ill that his life was in danger. St. Dominic, who was greatly attracted to the young man and knew what an influence for good he would be in the Order, prayed earnestly for his recovery. It was said of Dominic that he never asked anything of God that he did not obtain. In any case, it was the Queen of Heaven herself who came to cure the dying man and ransom him a little time on earth.

Our Lady, accompanied by St. Cecilia and St. Catherine of Alexandria, appeared at Reginald's bedside and anointed him with a heavenly perfume. She showed him a long white scapular and told him it was to be a part of the habit of the Order. Going away, she left him completely cured and filled with great joy. The friars, who until that time, 1218, had worn the garb of the canons regular, gladly changed to the scapular especially designed for them by the Mother of God. Reginald was himself clothed with the Dominican habit, and in fulfillment of his vow proceeded to the Holy Land.

On his return, Reginald embarked on his brief but brilliant career of preaching. In Bologna and in Paris, his eloquence and the shining beauty of his life drew hundreds to follow him into the Order. Among these were not only students but many famous professors and doctors of law. One of his greatest conquests was the young German, Jordan of Saxony, who was to be like Reginald himself—a kidnaper of souls for the service of God.

The first to be given the scapular and the first to wear the Dominican habit in the Holy Land, Reginald was also the first to die in it. Consumed with the fiery zeal of his work, he died in 1220, mourned by the entire Order, when he had worn the habit scarcely two years. He displayed no fear of death—perhaps Our Lady had told him, on the occasion of the cure, that he was only loaned to life and the Order—but received the last sacraments with touching devotion.

MATTHEW OF FRANCE
(d. 1227)

The only man ever to have the title of "abbot" in the Dominican Order was Matthew of France. He is associated with the very earliest days of the Order when its government had not yet reached final form. He holds our interest for several other reasons, among which was the regard St. Dominic held for him, and the trust reposed in him by the first brethren.

Matthew was French, as we can tell from his name, but we know nothing about him until he appears in history as a student of the University of Paris. Here he attended the lectures of the young Master Reginald of Orleans who was—some fifteen years later—to become a shining light of the Dominican Order. Matthew passed his examinations with honors and was ordained.

Matthew was dean of the canons of Castres, in Languedoc, when St. Dominic came there on pilgrimage to the church of the Spanish martyr, St. Vincent. The chronicles tell us that the friars arrived soaked and hungry, having come through a rainstorm. St. Dominic sent his companions in to dry themselves by the fire while he went into the church to pray. Eventually, the dean sent someone to call him to supper, and the messenger came back completely awed, and explained that the visitor was up in the air—praying— and he did not like to disturb him. Matthew went to see for himself, and was so struck by the sight of the saint in prayer that he promptly abandoned his benefice and threw in his lot with the preachers. Let us remember that it was quite a step for a man with Matthew's education and prospects to follow an unknown Spanish priest into a life of poverty and uncertainty.

We cannot doubt that both St. Dominic and his brethren fully appreciated Matthew's natural talents: he was always called in for every decision; he was appointed to the most responsible offices in the Order; and, in the intervals when St. Dominic himself could not be at hand, he was apparently appointed to govern the brethren. At the dispersal, it was Matthew who was chosen abbot by the brethren to rule the Order in the event of St.

Dominic's death. The fact that the title "abbot" did not survive does not in any way lessen the regard of the early brethren for this saintly and solidly practical man.

Matthew's greatest contribution to the Order was probably his influence in Paris during the difficult days of their establishment there. The dispersal had sent him to his Alma Mater at the head of the band that consisted of Bertrand of Garrigua, Michael of Fabra, St. Dominic's brother, Manez, John of Navarre, and Lawrence of England. Matthew was the only one with any friends in Paris, and they needed friends very badly.

The first year was one of struggle and difficulties; people were suspicious of the new friars, unwilling to give them any chance to prove their worth and quite ready to say that the whole plan was impractical. Matthew, as superior, had to demonstrate that the Dominican way of life was feasible, and he had to do it against great odds—living in a rented house in a hostile city. Eventually, a friend of the friars gave them a little hospice which was to grow into the famous convent of St. Jacques. Another friend, a professor at the university, came into the Order, bringing with him his right to teach in this closed corporation, thus establishing the Dominican chair of theology.

It was Reginald of Orleans who brought in the first vast wave of vocations to staff the new Order, but Matthew of France likewise did his part in this important work. When St. Dominic came to St. Jacques in 1219, he found no less than thirty friars there, attracted during the first difficult year. He promptly set them to found five other houses, leaving Matthew to refill the vacant places.

On the death of St. Dominic in August, 1221, we may suppose that Matthew of France took over the government of the Order until the following May, when Jordan of Saxony was elected the master general. The months of Matthew's government were packed with business; the opening guns of the controversy between the friars and the civil authorities at Paris had already been fired. The house at St. Jacques was bulging at the seams with the crowds of young novices brought in by the preaching of Reginald. Missions needed attention. A program of studies had not fully been worked out. A new crusade against the Albigenses was imminent. One estimate places the number of young candidates admitted to the house during his time there as prior to be nearly six hundred. The disposal of this many subjects was itself a formidable task.

Matthew died in 1227, and he was buried in front of the prior's stall in the convent of St. Jacques. Over his tomb, facing the prior, was carved his likeness, so that those who followed him in office might never forget to imitate his virtues.

BLESSED BERTRAND OF GARRIGUA
(1195?-1230)

Blessed Bertrand of Garrigua was already a priest and an ardent foe of heresy when he met St. Dominic. He might even quite justly lay claim to being on the battlefield of truth earlier than Dominic himself, for he belonged to the band of missionaries under the leadership of the Cistercians who had been appointed to fight the Albigenses. His meeting with the young and zealous Spaniard in the party of Bishop Diego was full of importance for himself and for the Church. Perhaps it was Blessed Bertrand who told the true state of affairs to St. Dominic, and enlisted his interest in the heretics of France. In any case, they must have immediately understood each other, and they were to be closely related in work and ideals for the rest of their lives.

Bertrand joined the first recruits to the new Order and received the habit in Toulouse, in 1216. He was left in charge of the little community when Dominic went soon afterwards to Rome for papal approval of the Order. As one of the pioneers, considered by the others as second only to Dominic himself, Bertrand's zeal and experience played their part in the founding of the Order. When the brethren were sent out in little groups to begin the conquest of the world for Christ, Bertrand's mission was to be in Paris with Matthew of France. Here in the great university city, the intellectual center of the medieval world, he was to help in forming for all time the Dominican tradition of learning.

As prior and provincial, Bertrand did much to establish the new Order, and his advice and prayers must have played no small part in those difficult days of beginning. For this alone he would deserve our gratitude, but it is for a more personal reason, that of his close friendship with St. Dominic, that he is held in blessed remembrance by all Dominicans. He was the traveling companion of Dominic on many occasions, and the witness of miracles and heavenly favors that beset the path of his saintly friend. It is Bertrand's testimony which gives us so many vivid little glimpses into the heart and mind of St. Dominic, and lets us listen to the conversation of the man who spoke only "to God or about God."

Bertrand was himself credited with many miracles, both during his life and after his death. Others considered him a "second Dominic" in austerity and holiness, but he humbly overlooked his own claims to sanctity in his loving insistence on those of his friend.

Blessed Bertrand died at the convent of St. Mary of the Woods, near Garrigua, where he was preaching a course of sermons to the Cistercian sisters. He was buried in the sisters' cemetery until the frequency of miracles suggested a more suitable shrine. Religious wars since that time have completely destroyed his relics and even the shrine, but they could not erase the memory of the miracle worker. Pilgrimages were still made to "St. Bertrand's Cemetery" at St. Mary of the Woods until the time of the French Revolution.

SUEIRO GOMES
(d. 1233)

When Sueiro Gomes was born we do not know, nor exactly where. It is known for certain that he was Portuguese, and it is presumed that his family was wealthy and able to educate him properly. He first comes to our notice as a member of de Montfort's army in 1208. One account suggests that he had taken his early training for the priesthood, but then had become enchanted with the idea of the crusade and joined up.

We know that he met St. Dominic in Languedoc and was fired with the same apostolic zeal that inspired the saint. Dominic saw that he was zealous and capable, and had him ordained by Bishop Fouques of Toulouse. Sueiro was one of the first sixteen disciples, then, who gathered at Prouille on the Feast of the Assumption, in 1217, to conquer the world for Christ. In the allotting of missions, he was appointed to Spain with Peter of Madrid, Michael de Uzero and Dominic the Little. Since he went on almost immediately to his own country, we may presume that he was told to do so.

Arriving in Portugal, he found the country far too concerned about the new crusade against the Moors to pay much attention to a preacher whose message was penance. It is a curious picture, this, of a young man who a few years before was riding with the cheering crusaders himself, now, with his viewpoint changed to one of spiritual combat, trying to interest the volunteers in a heavenly battle. He saw that the time was simply not right for making a new foundation. At this point he met the Princess Sancia, a pious woman who would one day have the title of Blessed. She interested herself in the new Order and, for the time being, gave him a place where he could start his work, the little mountain church of Our Lady of the Snows.

Sueiro began quietly enough in his remote little church, and the people sought him out to hear his sermons and have the benefit of his direction. Soon enough he was besieged with applicants for the Order, and he built a new convent, which proved to be too small before he had it finished. Not only the young sons of Portugal's best families sought him out—he had a natural appeal for them, having been one of them himself so recently— but men of age and distinction came, too. When the archbishop of Lisbon resigned his See and put on the habit, the whole country was afire with the news.

In the midst of his activities, which must have been prodigious, Sueiro was called to attend the First General Chapter, in Bologna, in 1220, where he took part in the deliberations on the rule and various legislation that would shape the future of the Order. He returned as soon as possible to the work that awaited him in Portugal. Whether or not he attended the general chapter in 1221 we have no record, but at this time he was made provincial of Spain.

As head of the Spanish province, Sueiro Gomes accomplished much for the Order. He made many new foundations and strengthened the old ones. He established a community of Second Order sisters near Lisbon, and kept a fatherly interest in their work in all his comings and goings. He encouraged St. Raymond of Penafort to write a summary of cases of conscience, and he sponsored a life of St. Isidore written by a canon regular of Leon. The eleven years of his provincialate were a time of great activity and splendid religious spirit.

Sueiro Gomes died in 1233, and his memory is still held in veneration.

LAWRENCE OF ENGLAND
(d. 1235)

One of the curious things about the Dominican Order is the fact that its early members came from so many national backgrounds. Since St. Dominic was a Spaniard, one would expect his Order to appeal to other Spaniards. His first preaching was in France, and, therefore, it was quite natural to find Frenchmen among his early disciples. The romance languages at least linked the men who came from a common continental background. But mixed in with all these is a stranger, Lawrence the Englishman.

Legend tells us that Lawrence was one of a band of English pilgrims bound for Compostella. Their boat overturned in the river and St. Dominic performed a miracle; he brought the whole boatload safely to land. If this is true—and it very well may be—we have a good reason why an eager young pilgrim might have attached himself to the saint who had saved his life. Unfortunately, we do not really know. All we do know is that Lawrence was one of the first disciples, and that on the day of the dispersal he took his staff and set out with the little band destined for the university center of Paris. We can infer from this that he was a man with a good education, and suspect that perhaps he had been a student there, since St. Dominic was definitely putting his best foot forward with his Paris group.

The friars met nothing but reverses on first arriving in Paris. They were poor and unknown and had no powerful patron to smooth the way for them at the university which so jealously guarded its privileges. No one but Matthew of France knew anybody of consequence, and for a time it looked as if they were not going to make any impression at all. It was Lawrence the Englishman who had the prophetic dream assuring them that their work would take root there and would endure. They very much needed the encouragement.

In 1218, Lawrence was sent to Rome, reporting to St. Dominic and the pope that the friars were up against a bigoted set of professors at the university and needed some moral support. While he was in Rome, he had the unforgettable experience of being present when St. Dominic multiplied the bread for his hungry community at St. Sixtus, and again when the saint multiplied wine for the same reason. He must certainly have been present for other miracles and have been warmed and encouraged by the Italian enthusiasm for St. Dominic, which was in such contrast to the snobbery the brethren had endured in Paris. Certainly his report of these prodigies must have done wonders for the morale among the little band of French missionaries.

Lawrence the Englishman never returned to his native land, but spent the remainder of his life in securing the permanence of the community at St. Jacques in Paris. He died there in 1235. His memory in an old Dominican Martyrology gives a brief sketch of his life when it tells us: "Blessed Lawrence was renowned for his gift of prophecy, the integrity of his life, and the splendor of his miracles."

MONETA OF CREMONA
(d. 1235)

Moneta of Cremona has one distinction which he probably treasured above all others life gave to him; not the reputation for learning, which he gained by his preaching, but the joy of having loaned St. Dominic two things that he did not have himself—a bed on which to die, and a tunic in which to be buried. From this fact one can surmise quite rightly that he was both a contemporary and a friend of the saint.

Moneta was not the only professor at the University of Bologna who resented the great success of Master Reginald of Orleans in recruiting students for the new Order, but he was one who put up a notable defense against it. He did all he could to convince his students to stay away from the Dominican, using the very solid argument that if they did go to hear Reginald they might not come back. He himself made elaborate efforts to keep entirely out of Reginald's reach.

One day a group of Moneta's students laid a trap for him. They told him at the end of a lecture that they had all stayed away from the sermon of Master Reginald in order to come to class, and that the least he could do in return was to go with them to hear the next day's sermon. Moneta did his best to squirm out of the affair. He led the students to church first, and piously attended not one but three Masses. Trusting that the sermon was well over by now, he went with them to the cathedral. The preacher obviously was just getting started, but happily the cathedral was so crowded that there was not even standing room. Moneta stopped his party at the door and politely refused to push his way in.

Since it was the feast of St. Stephen, it was quite natural that the preacher should choose as his text the words about "seeing the heavens opened." It was not quite natural, however, that his words would carry out so clearly to the reluctant young man in the packed doorway, and inform him that the heavens were still opened if people would only lift up their eyes to see. Moneta could hardly wait for the end of the sermon to throw himself on his knees at Reginald's feet and beg for the habit he had avoided so skillfully.

Ironically enough, he could not be admitted to the Order until his commitments at the university were completed. To the amusement of his students, he became the friar's most persuasive recruiter during his remaining days in the classroom. One is almost tempted to believe that the university authorities released him from his obligations at the earliest possible moment in order to keep him from taking the whole student body with him. At last his obligations were fulfilled, and he received the habit from St. Dominic himself. Knowing the history of this professor, who had been so abruptly and so thoroughly converted, Dominic must have smiled to see him adjusting himself to community life.

Moneta's life was a quiet one, as professor's lives sometimes are. He spent the remaining fifteen years of his life in loyal and fruitful work for the Order, being, in the words of one chronicler, a man "conspicuous for his sanctity, wonderfully skilled in the sacred sciences, endowed with splendid judgment, a brave athlete of the faith, well-known for his miracles, and a renowned professor of theology." He died in 1235, in the convent in Bologna, after several years of blindness during which he could teach only by his example of holiness and resignation. We remember him for many reasons, one of them being his close connection with St. Dominic. For contemporary young people who may be trying to ignore the work of God, he definitely gives a demonstration of the irresistibility of God's grace, and the lengths to which God will go to call men into His elite service.

VENTURA OF VERONA
(1236)

This man was very close to St. Dominic, and he gave eloquent testimony at his canonization. We, however, know pitifully little about him.

The records tell us that he entered the Order in Bologna, in 1219, receiving the habit from St. Dominic himself. It seems almost certain that he was a priest at this time, for the saint shortened the time of his novitiate so that he could make profession, and almost immediately appointed him prior of St. Nicholas. For the rest of his life he was to occupy this position from time to time; he was in charge of the house when St. Dominic came home to die, in August of 1221, and it is from him that most of the touching details of that occasion have come down to us.

There was a close friendship between St. Dominic and Brother Ventura; they understood each other. Several times Ventura was the chosen companion on one of the journeys across the country, and they often must have discussed the aims of the Order and the needs of the Church which it was designed to fulfill. However, theirs was more than a business association. They must have been close friends. It was Ventura who heard the dying saint's confession and who held his head in his agony.

Ventura of Verona, for such an important figure, has been nearly obscured in history. We know that he took part in the first two general chapters. He held several offices under Jordan of Saxony, succeeding him as provincial of Lombardy. Also he inherited the care of the community of sisters at St. Agnes, in Bologna, and in particular the direction of Diana d'Andaló when Jordan could not be there. The most outstanding thing we know about him, however, is his testimony at the time of St. Dominic's canonization. His picture of the saint is a beautiful one, bright with the love of genuine friendship. Ventura, who knew and loved him so well, must have been much closer than many of the witnesses to the real personality of the saint.

Some time after 1236, Ventura of Verona died, most probably at St. Nicholas in Bologna. His memory has been held in benediction since the early days of the Order.

BLESSED JORDAN OF SAXONY
(1190-1237)

Men prayed for strength to resist his burning eloquence, and mothers hid their sons when Master Jordan came to town. Students and masters warned each other of the fatal magnetism of his sermons. The sweetness of his character and the holiness of his life shone through his most casual words in a flame that drew youth irresistibly to the ideal to which he had dedicated his own life. In his sixteen years of preaching, Jordan is said to have drawn more than a thousand novices to the Order, among whom were two future popes, two canonized saints, numerous blessed, and countless intellectual lights of his dazzling century.

Of Jordan's childhood nothing is known beyond the fact that he was German and of noble family. He was drawn to the Order by the preaching of Blessed Reginald, the beloved son of Dominic, brought back from death by Dominic's and Our Lady's prayers. Jordan was at that time about thirty years of age, a student at the University of Paris, and his reputation for sanctity had preceded him into the Order. He had worn the habit but two months when he was sent as a delegate to the general chapter in Bologna. The following year he was elected provincial of Lombardy, and on the death of St. Dominic, succeeded him as master general.

The Order was six years in existence when Jordan of Saxony became master general. He carried out the yet untried plans of St. Dominic, who had hurried off to heaven when many of his dreams were just beginning to open out into realization, and still more vistas beckoned beyond. Jordan will always be remembered especially for his work in increasing the manpower of the Order, but his contribution to its quality should not be forgotten. He added four new provinces to the eight already existing; he twice obtained for the Order a chair at the University of Paris and helped found the University of Toulouse; and he established the first general house of studies of the Order. He was a spiritual guide to many, including Blessed Diana d'Andalò; and somewhere in his busy lifetime he found time to write a number of books—a life of St. Dominic and several other works.

Jordan was regarded as a menace by the professors of the universities. He emptied the classrooms of their most talented students, stole their most noted professors. Young men by the hundreds beseiged the Order for admittance. Some were mere children, some famous lawyers and teachers, and some were the wealthy young bearers of the most famous names in Christendom. One and all, they were drawn to a life of perfection by this man who preached so well, and who practiced what he preached with such evident relish.

All the old writers speak of the kindness and personal charm of Jordan. He had the ability to console the troubled and to inspire the despondent with new hope. At one time, a discouraged student was busily saying the Office of the Dead when Master Jordan sat down beside him and began alternating the verses with him. When he came to the end of Psalm twenty-six, Jordan said the verse with emphasis: "Oh, wait for the Lord!" Wherewith the sorrows of the young man departed. Another student was rid of troubled thoughts merely by the imposition of Jordan's hands. To bring peace to the brothers who were being annoyed by the devil, Jordan established the beautiful custom of singing the "Salve Regina" after Compline each night.

Jordan was drowned when returning from a pilgrimage to the Holy Land in 1237.

MARGARET OF YPRES
(1216-1237)

Margaret of Ypres was wearing the Tertiary habit—whatever it was at the time—within ten years after the death of St. Dominic, in a country that he himself never visited. She gives us interesting food for thought on the growth of the Third Order in those early days.

Margaret was placed as a boarder in a monastery when she was four years old, which would have been the year before St. Dominic's death. We are not told what kind of sisters they were; however, they must ordinarily have accepted children for such education as they gave Margaret.

The little girl used to go into the chapel with the nuns and usually prayed along with them. On one occasion when they were going to receive Holy Communion, she felt strongly drawn to do likewise, but the abbess told her she was too young. She was only five years old. "But I know it is Jesus!" insisted the little girl. She persisted so that the chaplain was brought in to examine her, and he gave her permission to go to Communion three times a year, which was a liberal permission at the time. She fasted and did penance twice a week, once in honor of our Lord and once in memory of His mother. Furthermore, she shunned all seasonings in her food and sought out other ways of doing penance. She had a natural gift for quiet and reflective play which carried over into her prayer.

Perhaps her family felt she was getting too much religion; in any case, they took her away from the monastery and brought her home. Here there were few spiritual advantages and she was lonely for the nuns. She practiced so many austerities that the family finally gave up when she was about eleven, and sent her to the care of an uncle who was a priest. He, they felt, would see that she received all the religion she could accommodate.

Margaret remained in the care of her priest uncle until she was seventeen. However, instead of cultivating her spiritual life, the experience seemed to dissipate it. She developed a taste for worldly amusements and acquired a boy friend. When her uncle died, leaving her all his money, she set about having a good time in earnest, and began in a truly feminine manner by buying herself a new wardrobe.

At this point in her life, one of the new Friars Preachers, a Brother Siger, came to town. She attended a mission which he preached at her parish church, and, after one of his sermons Margaret arrived home in floods of tears and announced that she was going to enter religion. Her mother was not impressed. "You go in today, you'll be out tomorrow," she said.

The following day, Margaret met her young man on the street and was suddenly almost overcome with affection for him. She left him standing and ran to the church to kneel before the crucifix and beg for constancy in her resolution to become a religious. Then she went to Brother Siger to announce that she had had a dream—if you could call it a dream—in which she saw our Lord holding out to her three crowns. One, He told her, was the vow of chastity which she had just pronounced; the other two would be hers at death if she persevered.

Brother Siger sent her home to give away her fine wardrobe and told her that from henceforth she and her associates (there were a number of girls, including one of her sisters, who wished to follow wherever Margaret would lead) would wear only castoff clothing, and would keep almost perpetual silence. Since these two vital deprivations did not daunt the young woman, he accepted her as a spiritual disciple and a member of the secular Third Order.

The new arrangement in Margaret's life did not pass unnoticed. The devil busied himself with gossiping neighbors. Margaret's own mother was skeptical of the venture, though she made no tangible trouble for her daughter. Then, when their peculiar mode of life was just beginning to be recognized as normal, Margaret fell very ill. A doctor was called in and his diagnosis was not helpful; he declared that unless Margaret married and gave up all this nonsense she would die. Margaret, afraid of what her mother might do, prayed for a miracle and was healed.

Once during this time the Blessed Virgin appeared to Margaret and found her weeping; she asked why. Margaret told her because of the pain. Our Lady placed her hand on Margaret's heart and said, "Is this where it hurts? It will not hurt any more."

Margaret and her several companions set themselves to follow the rule of life which Brother Siger set up for them. They were allowed to receive Holy Communion every two weeks, which was very frequent for the times; they prayed and kept such silence that her mother finally complained to Brother Siger, who specified that Margaret was to talk to her mother and sisters for fifteen minutes a day after this.

The rule they followed was the primitive rule of the Brothers and Sisters of Penance, a true type of religious life, in which they took private vows and said prayers according to their education—the Office, if they were capable of it, or the prayers supplying for it. Margaret herself could read, and she said her Office from a book of hours called "The Psalter of Our Lady." They did not, apparently, say Office chorally. It is noted that Margaret and her followers wore "a simple veil with only one fold in it," to facilitate quick dressing and leave more time for prayers.

One of Margaret's special devotions was to the Holy Name. She always spoke of our Lord as "Lord and Master" rather than simply using His name. Her revelations she kept to herself and only revealed them to her spiritual father at his express wish, to be kept secret until after her death. She had many prophetic visions and was able to see the spiritual state of those who came to ask for her prayers. Once a wealthy countess came to ask her prayers, and Margaret commented sadly that they would not do any good because the woman's hands were covered with blood from the mistreatment of her servants. Many people came seeking her prayers because they had reason to believe that she was favored with heavenly visitors.

A year before her death, St. Catherine of Alexandria appeared to her and told her that she would be paralyzed and helpless for the rest of her life. This prophecy came true, and Margaret could move nothing but her tongue.

Many miracles, particularly of healing, were credited to Margaret in her last year of life. Once she saw a silver ladder going up to heaven, with Our Lady at the top, surrounded by angels and saints; she talked for hours on this beautiful vision to those gathered around her bed, though she seldom spoke of her heavenly favors.

Margaret died in 1237, when she was just twenty-one years old. Several miracles, including the healing of a withered arm, were said to have taken place at her funeral.

BLESSED MANEZ de GUZMAN
(d. 1238)

Manez de Guzman was enough older than his brother Dominic to have already begun his studies for the priesthood when Dominic was born. In company with his brother Anthony, who became a secular priest, he finished his studies and was ordained, probably while Dominic was still very young.

The fact that he was so much older than Dominic, yet so zealously and generously joined with his brother in the new and reckless venture of apostolic preaching, proves that Manez possessed the important virtues of humility and magnanimity. During the tiring years of preaching against the Albigenses, while the Order to be founded by his brother was still a dream, Manez labored, quietly and persistently, at his side. He often must have discussed it with Dominic and shared in his hopes, fears, and prayers for the undertaking. When the approval of the Order was finally given, Manez was one of the faithful group who knelt before the founder to make profession in the new way of life.

Old chronicles relate that Manez had a great charm in his preaching, and that he drew all by the kindness of his manner. He is described as a retiring and prayerful man, happiest in the seclusion of the cloister, but making no protest when sent on various difficult missions. How much of St. Dominic's success can be traced to his brother's prayers is impossible to say: however, it is encouraging to note that in the saint's ideal of religious brotherhood, family ties were not broken but made stronger. That two of the first sixteen were blood brothers gave a holy precedent to the hundreds of brothers who through the centuries were to seal the family ties of brotherhood by the strengthening ties of religious profession.

Manez was sent to Paris when the brethren were dispersed, and became one of the founders of the famous convent of St. Jacques. Then he was sent to Spain to help in the foundation of the first Dominican sisters there. He became their chaplain and looked out for their temporal welfare.

After this there is no record of his life beyond the fact that he visited Calaruega, probably soon after the canonization of St. Dominic, and urged the people to build a church there to honor his brother. He was buried with the Cistercians at Gumiel d'Izan.

Dominic was the brilliant star, the chosen one who would make the family name forever remembered. But to Manez, too, belongs the honor due to the holy ones of God. His humility and unselfish cooperation in the "great idea" of his brother is an ideal worthy of imitation by the sons and daughters of Dominic. Jealousy of a younger or more gifted person has been the disease which crippled many souls and spoiled many good plans. It might at the very outset have tarnished the beauty of the Dominican foundation had Manez not been what he was—a holy, humble, and magnanimous soul, devoted not to winning the notice of men but that of God.

BLESSED JOHN OF SALERNO
(13th Century)

John of Salerno was born in southern Italy in the latter part of the twelfth century. His people were of Norman blood and were wealthy, but more than that we do not know. John met St. Dominic when he was a student at Bologna, probably on the saint's first visit to that city. He immediately joined the friars and after a brief training was sent with a band of the brethren to pioneer the work of preaching in the city of Florence.

We reach the unavoidable conclusion that Florence was not anxious to have the friars in the city. They could find no suitable lodgings there, and finally took up residence in a convent in Ripoli which was offered to them by a wealthy man of the neighborhood. At first glance it would seem to have been a fine solution to their need for a residence, for the benefactor in question had already built a convent and a large church, and he was anxious to get a community of religious to occupy it. However, it soon appeared that there were definite drawbacks to the arrangement. The benefactor was not interested in the souls of the people of Florence, but only in his own; he wanted a community of hermits who would stay at home and pray for him unceasingly, a privilege for which he was quite willing to pay. It was John of Salerno who had to make the decision that it was time for the brethren to move, since they were apostolic preachers, not hermits.

They began by walking to Florence each day to preach, a long and tiring journey. It was principally John's talents as a preacher and his kind but firm manner that won over the Florentines and prompted them to offer the friars the small convent of St. Pancratius. This was not a permanent solution to their housing problem, but they lived there until they were eventually more suitably housed at St. Paul's.

It was John of Salerno who, in the last of many moves, established the brethren at Santa Maria Novella, a place which was to become world-famous in Dominican history. Here their work centered; they fought the Manichaeanism still rampant in the city, and built themselves into the fabric of a famous city.

John of Salerno had a great personal reputation for the reading of consciences and for casting out devils. At one time a young woman, who did not quite understand his devotion to duty, decided to entrap him into sin. She sent for him to hear her confession, on the pretext that she was very sick. He came, unsuspectingly, and soon discovered what she had in mind. The sermon he gave her must have been a vivid one, as it converted her on the spot.

John went back to his business, which at the moment entailed a visit to a church. At the time there was a priest performing an exorcism, and the devil refused to be expelled. "I won't get out unless he commands me who has walked in the flames unburned," said the devil flatly. At that moment, John of Salerno walked into the church, and the devil reacted so violently that those present knew that John was the one who had fulfilled the mysterious conditions named by the devil. John immediately finished the exorcism, though he was unwilling to explain the incident publicly.

John of Salerno died sometime between 1230 and 1240, and many miracles of healing at his tomb led to the opening of his cause. He was beatified in 1783.

CLARO OF BOLOGNA
(1240)

Claro of Bologna could rightfully claim a very early interest in the Dominicans, for he recalled walking with his father through the vineyards where the church of St. Nicholas was to stand, and hearing the sound of voices singing. His father told him they were angels, and that this was a sign that the place was to be a fountain of grace and prodigies. Claro, like all little boys, wanted to know why: "Why couldn't they be the brothers from St. Proculus, or even minstrels?" Claro the elder told him that you could always tell the difference between the singing of men and angels.

Claro was very likely born in Bologna. Certainly he was educated there. He was a man in his prime, greatly respected for his learning, occupying the chair of canon law at the university when the Dominicans first came to Bologna. Perhaps remembering the prophecy his father had made about the future holiness of the spot, he entered the new Order as soon as the brethren moved into the convent at St. Nicholas of the Vineyards. His vocation did much to help establish the brethren in the city.

Not long after Claro had become one of them, however, the brethren hit a low point in their progress. They were few and poor, almost unknown, and some of the younger members had been attracted by the chimera of greater austerity. One would think that their program of study and prayer was hard enough—it appalls us to read about it—but there are always a few who feel themselves called to higher things.

Two such zealots applied for a transfer to the Cistercians. When the dispensations came they were presented to the superior, and all the brethren were called into the chapter room to discuss the matter. As the elder fathers well knew, a movement of this sort is contagious. Now, with the Order barely getting a start in a big university city, it was not a tactful time for two of their most vocal young students to leave. Blessed Reginald addressed the chapter first, then Claro arose and spoke of the great destiny of the Order and the need for workers in the vineyard. Reginald was the more eloquent, but perhaps Claro had been their teacher; the two young students were completely convinced by his arguments that the whole affair had been an elaborate ruse of the devil. While Claro was still talking, there was a commotion at the door. It burst open to admit Master Roland of Cremona, who lost no time in throwing himself on his knees and begging for the habit. This unscheduled bit of drama seemed to give proof to the argument of Brother Claro; no more was ever heard of brethren deserting the Order.

Claro had been an eminent canonist before entering the Order, and he brought with him a prestige and a sagacity which were of tremendous help to the Dominicans. He worked in various capacities to strengthen and establish the brethren, and at the general chapter of 1221 became provincial of Rome. This brought him a second time to the notice of Cardinal Ugolino, who had known him in Bologna, and he found himself with the position of Papal Chaplain and Penitentiary.

The remainder of his life was spent in this capacity in Rome, where his poverty and humility were an edification to all. He wrote several works on canon law and theology during these years, all of which have since been lost. He died around the year 1240.

PAUL OF HUNGARY AND COMPANIONS
(d. 1241)

St. Dominic's first choice of mission was Tartary. It might be expected that as soon as he could do so he would send missionaries there. Even as late as the Second General Chapter, in 1221, he was letting his beard grow and trying to resign from the top executive position in the Order so that he himself could go to these benighted people. Instead, the fathers of the chapter appointed Paul of Hungary to lead the band into the vast uncharted land that included Russia, Mongolia, parts of Hungary, Albania and Poland—all of which went under the general name of Tartary.

Paul was a doctor of canon law from Bologna, but we do not know precisely when he joined the Order; we do know that St. Dominic himself had given him the habit. He was so anxious to begin working in Tartary that he did not even wait for the chapter to be finished, but set out for the North with Brothers Berenger and Sadoc and two others, while the fathers were still deliberating. Their path through the mountains led them to the Austrian Tyrol, where they acquired three more disciples—students who were at a Benedictine abbey there. The band accumulated more recruits as it approached the field of their labors.

On their first night in Hungary, Brother Sadoc was keeping vigil over the sleeping brethren when he was surrounded by a multitude of evil spirits. They screamed and complained, saying, "You have come to destroy our kingdom and to take away our rights! And with such children as these!"

Having the whole of the North to work in, the party decided to divide in order to cover the territory better. The Polish-speaking brothers took the right side of the Danube, and the Hungarians the left. The latter party went up the Danube as far as Raab, where there was a Benedictine abbey, and established their first convent there. Several of the Benedictines joined them, as well as some of the students of the abbey. Brother Paul founded a monastery for women in Vesprim, which was later to become famous as the home of St. Margaret of Hungary.

The two parties prepared to advance on Tartary by working among the peoples of the bordering provinces in both Hungary and Poland; there they could learn the language and establish their convents to train recruits, of which they soon had hundreds. The neighboring provinces, the strip of no man's land between Christian lands and Tartary, were a shambles of civilization and savagery. Schism and heresy had finished the work of the Tartar raiders, and the people were in a pitiable state. As hard as they could work, the friars obtained few results among the people, while the chiefs remained obdurate. It became obvious that in order to convert these people they must first convert the chiefs.

After six years they still had not penetrated Tartary. The first two preachers to try it, Albert and Dominic, had been promptly martyred. A second and a third attempt likewise failed. The friars worked in Slavonia and Moldavia, converting many Manichaeans and schismatics, and acquired hundreds of recruits for the Order. Astonished at their persistence, one of the minor Tartar princes sent for some of the preachers to explain to him why their men were so set on martyrdom. They converted him, giving them an opening wedge into his country. When he and his household of a thousand persons came into the church, under the sponsorship of Andrew, the father of St.

Elizabeth of Hungary, it was the signal for renewed enthusiasm all along the border provinces.

For awhile it seemed as though Tartary would be converted. A bishop was appointed, churches and convents were built, and a thriving religious life was functioning. Suddenly disaster struck. It came from the heart of Tibet, thousands of miles from Poland. A new migration of Tartar tribes began, and the pressure on the border states increased. Hordes of Mongol warriors poured into Central Europe like a flow of destroying lava. They devastated Transylvania and streamed into Hungary. The royal family of Hungary took flight, and made a last stand on an island in the Danube, where they promised their next child to God if he would halt this devastation. The invasion halted at that point; the Mongols being called back to Tibet to elect a new ruler. The promised child, Margaret, was to become a great Dominican saint.

When the tide had receded, the Dominican houses all over Poland and Hungary were in smouldering ruins, with not enough people left alive to tell what happened. Paul and his companions were killed in this invasion; just how many companions we do not know, though ninety is the number given in popular legends. He and his martyred band have been held in veneration since the very earliest years of the Order. It is not known exactly where the martyrdom took place.

BLESSED WILLIAM ARNAULD AND COMPANIONS, MARTYRS
(d. 1242)

One of the earliest of the many martyrs of the Dominican Order was Blessed William Arnauld. He died with eleven companions in Avignonet in 1242.

We know nothing at all of William's early life. The first date which we have for certain in his life is 1234, at which time he was appointed inquisitor for the diocese of Toulouse. With him on the preaching commission were a fellow Dominican, Bernard of Rochefort; the Franciscans, Steven of Narbonne and Raymond of Carbonier, and two others who are not named; the Benedictine, Prior Raymond; the clerks, Bernard Fortanier and Admer; the Dominican laybrother, Garcia d'Aure; and Peter the Notary. There were others who worked with him through the long and difficult years in Toulouse, but these were the ones who died in the martyrdom of Avignonet.

After the death of St. Dominic, the party of Count Raymond of Toulouse rose to power again. In a short time it regained possession of Toulouse and several armed strongholds nearby. When William Arnauld and his companions came into the vicinity, they found every gate closed against them. None of the cities under the command of Raymond's troops would allow them to come in, and, by order of the heretic commander, the citizens of Toulouse were forbidden under pain of death to supply the inquisitor's party with any food. They took refuge in a farmhouse outside of Avignonet and preached around the countryside for some time. Because they had some measure of success, the heretics intensified their efforts to entrap and kill the inquisitors.

The members of the commission realized that they were only one step from death. They might have escaped and gone safely to some other part of the country had they chosen to do so. Instead, they remained where obedience had assigned them, and at the end of May, 1242, they were given a heavenly warning that they were about to receive the crown of martyrdom. William was absent from the rest of the group when the plot was formed to kill them. Being told of a vision of martyrdom by one of the brothers, he hurried back to rejoin his group. The heretics completed their plans to massacre the entire party. Scheming carefully, they set the scene at the country home of one of the wealthy members of their group. In order to make sure of getting the inquisitors into the trap, they sent word to William that a confirmed heretic of his acquaintance wished to abjure his heresy and return to the faith.

Knowing well that it was a trap, William still could not refuse to go. He and his eleven companions went, on the evening of May the twenty-eighth, to the country house. The soldiers of Raymond were concealed in the great hall. They fell upon the helpless group and killed all but four of the members. These four were taken out by friends who had known about the plot and hurried to the church. William Arnauld and Steven of Narbonne were murdered in the sanctuary of the church. This was a crime almost unparalleled in medieval times, when the right of sanctuary was one of the few strongholds against barbarism. The bodies of the martyrs were thrown into a deep ravine, and rocks were rolled down upon them. During the night, some hours after the martyrdom, bright lights radiating from the bodies of the martyrs brought the faithful to gather up the relics.

The church of Avignonet was placed under interdict because of the sacrilege, and for forty years no Mass was said there. The doors remained closed. Finally, when the interdict was lifted, the bells rang of themselves, according to legend, to let people know that Avignonet was once more a member of the living Church.

There is a curious footnote to this story of martyrdom. Shortly after the interdict was lifted, there appeared one day on the steps of the church a fairly large statue of the Blessed Virgin. Who had put it there has never been discovered. It is difficult to see how anyone in such a small town could have successfully concealed a statue of that size, for small towns are notoriously poor places to hide secrets. The statue appeared on the steps in broad daylight, yet no one saw it being placed there. The people took it as a sign that they were forgiven for their part in the outrage, and also as a sign that they should rebuild the devotion to Our Lady which the Dominicans had preached. The statue was named "Our Lady of Miracles," and they petitioned for a special feast in honor of their own Miracle Lady.

Until very recent times, a strange little ceremony was held in the Church of Our Lady of Miracles on every May the twenty-eighth. It was a night ceremony, in memory of the night martyrdom of William Arnauld and his companions, and it was called "The Ceremony of the Vow." Carrying lighted candles, the people proceeded across the entire width of the church on their knees, praying for forgiveness for the people who committed the massacre.

Blessed William Arnauld and companions were beatified in 1866. William is invoked by people who suffer from neuralgia, in memory of a miracle of healing which he performed on one of the sisters of Prouille.

BLESSED CESLAUS
(1180-1242)

Ceslaus Odrowatz was a near relative, very probably a brother, of St. Hyacinth, and shared with him the apostolate of Northern Europe. Little is known of his early youth. He was born in the ancestral castle in Kannen, in Polish upper Silesia, and educated, with St. Hyacinth, by his uncle, a priest of Cracow. Both the young men became priests and, being well-known for their holiness, were chosen to be canons in the cathedral chapter in Cracow. When their uncle received an appointment to be made bishop of Cracow, the two young priests accompanied him on his trip to Rome, where he would be consecrated.

It was in Rome that the two zealous young priests first heard of the work of St. Dominic. The Order was then only four years old, and its eager members had penetrated to almost all parts of Christendom and were pushing into the lands of the Tartars and the Mohammedans. The new bishop strongly desired that some of the friars should come to Poland. Since St. Dominic was then in Rome, they went to him for missionaries. Dominic was deeply regretful that he had no friars who were able to speak the languages of the North. However, he was much drawn to the two young nephews of the bishop, and he promised to make them Dominican apostles if they would remain with him.

After their novitiate training, Hyacinth and Ceslaus went home to the North. Ceslaus went to Prague, and other parts of Bohemia, where he founded convents of Friars Preachers and also established a group of nuns. Then he went to Silesia, where he founded the convent of Breslau which was to become his center of activities.

The life of Blessed Ceslaus, like that of St. Hyacinth, is a record of almost countless miracles, of unbelievable distances traveled on foot through wild and warlike countries, and of miracles of grace. He cured the sick and the maimed, raised the dead to life, and accomplished wonders in building convents. His most remarkable miracle was the raising to life of a boy who had been dead for eight days.

In 1241 the Tartars swooped down upon the Christian kingdoms and laid waste the labor of centuries. Blessed Ceslaus was in Breslau at the time the Tartars laid siege to the city. He and his community fasted and prayed incessantly that the city would be saved, and when the cause looked darkest, Ceslaus mounted the ramparts with a crucifix in his hand. While the Tartars gazed in astonishment, a huge ball of fire descended from heaven and settled above him. Arrows of fire shot out from the heavenly weapon, and the Tartars fled in terror, leaving the city unmolested.

Our Lady came to receive the soul of Blessed Ceslaus, who had been tireless in preaching her glories.

BLESSED GUALA OF BERGAMO
(d. 1244)

"A man of great prudence, well acquainted with the world, and of accomplished manners." "He governed the diocese entrusted to his care with such holiness that, both during his life and after his death, he wrought many wonders through God." These two views of Blessed Guala of Bergamo, taken from writers who were his contemporaries, give a clear picture, if not an unusual one, of the man who was a close friend of St. Dominic and one of the Order's earliest and ablest administrators.

Guala was born in Bergamo, in the late twelfth century, and is variously called Guala, Walter, or William. He was attracted to the Dominican ideal in 1219, when he heard St. Dominic preach. When the friars came to open a house in Bergamo, he was one of the first applicants, and he received the habit from the hands of St. Dominic. After a short period of training under Dominic, Guala was placed in charge of the new convent of Bergamo.

Since Guala proved to be an able superior and a practical man at building, he was put on the committee for building the convent of St. Agnes, in Bologna, for the sisters. However, there was a delay on account of the opposition of the family of Blessed Diana d'Andalò, who was financing the convent, and in the interim Guala was sent to build a house in Brescia, where he was established as prior.

It was during his term in Brescia that Guala had the revelation of the glory of St. Dominic which has been often repeated in the early legends. Guala had been the saint's companion on several occasions and was an understanding friend. He did not, however, know that Dominic had returned from the chapter in a dying condition. Guala had fallen asleep with his head leaning against the belltower of the conventual church at Brescia when he had a vision in which he saw two ladders coming down from heaven. Our Lord was visible at the top of one ladder, and Our Lady at the top of the other; angels were passing up and down both of them, and, as he watched, a friar, who sat at the foot of one ladder with his face covered, was drawn up to heaven and great glory surrounded him. Guala awoke, still deeply affected by the vision, and went at once to Bologna, where he found that St. Dominic had died at the time of his vision.

In 1226, Guala was made prior of St. Nicholas' in Bologna, a convent famous for its regularity and its fervor. While he was in Bologna, Pope Honorius III appointed him as arbitrator in the war between Bologna and Modena. Guala managed to get a treaty signed, which they kept for ten years.

An even more difficult diplomatic task was given him in the following year, when Pope Gregory IX appointed him to negotiate between Frederick II and the Lombard confederacy. He was also expected to convince Frederick that he must keep his vow of going on a crusade, something no one else had managed to do. Somehow, in this deadly position between a ruthless emperor and the equally ruthless factions of the Lombard confederacy, Guala kept matters from becoming worse than they were, which was all but a miracle under the circumstances, and was made the bishop of Brescia in 1229.

As bishop, Guala arranged a number of wise and fair treaties among the cities, but Frederick II complicated his life by immediately breaking all the promises he had made, and attacking the cities which remained faithful to the pope. In 1238, Frederick's army laid siege to Brescia. Ordinarily the favor was with the besieger, but in this case the invaders had to withdraw after three months of desperate efforts to take the city. The credit for resisting such a formidable enemy went to Guala. After the supreme effort of this siege, Guala applied for permission to resign his See, and was finally permitted to do so in the following year.

On his retirement, Guala wished to go into complete seclusion where he could pray without interruption until his death, which he felt to be near. He accordingly received permission to go to the Benedictines in Astino, where he lived as a recluse until his death in 1244. He was buried in the Benedictine church, and after many miracles at his tomb had indicated his holiness, his cause was taken up by the Church. He was beatified by Pope Pius IX in 1868.

BLESSED ISNARD OF CHIAMPO
(d. 1244)

From the earliest years of the Order, that beautiful period of its springtime in Bologna, comes the story of Blessed Isnard of Chiampo, who was beatified a few years ago.

Isnard was born of a wealthy family in Chiampo, near Vicenza. We know nothing at all about his childhood. He came into history in the year 1219, when, as a student at the University of Bologna, he met St. Dominic and decided to join the new Order. He made his novitiate in Bologna, and he soon distinguished himself as a preacher. His first assignment was to Pavia, where the work of the Order was complicated by the war between the pope and the emperor.

Blessed Isnard plunged courageously into the work. He knew that he was risking death in doing so, and a less courageous man might have found some excuse for going to a more peaceful place. Our Blessed Isnard chose rather to meet the situation head-on.

One of his first encounters was with the forces of evil, quite undisguised. A possessed man had become the mouthpiece of the devil and was being used by heretics to discredit the preaching of the friar who had so recently come to Pavia to preach the faith. The devil, speaking through the lips of the possessed man, issued a challenge to the friar: "If you are from God, cast me out and cure this man."

Isnard realized that one does not lightly take up open battle with the powers of wickedness. The condition of the poor man, whose name was Martin, was enough to strike terror into the heart. The challenge came when Isnard was in the pulpit preaching. The possessed man was brought into the church, screaming, and in convulsions. The preacher realized that he must cure him or lose the interest of his audience in the cause of Christ. Stepping down from the pulpit, he approached the possessed man, put his arms around him and, in the name of the Lord Jesus Christ, demanded that the evil spirits depart. Martin was freed from his tormentor, and he ended his days, according to legend, as a laybrother in the local convent.

At another time when Isnard was preaching, a hardened heretic refused to listen to him and called out loudly, "I shall believe in the sanctity of this man only if he makes that barrel on the corner of the square come loose and strike me." Immediately, the barrel jumped from its place and struck the scoffer, breaking his leg.

Isnard spent his life preaching and working in Pavia. At his death, in 1244, it presented a quite different appearance from the godless and strife-ridden city it had been.

BLESSED PETER GONZALES
(1190-1246)

This Dominican blessed, who is popularly known in Spain as "St. Elmo," has been honored from the time of his death as a miracle worker, particularly among seafaring men.

The exact date of Peter's birth is not known, but it was near 1190, in Astorga, in Spain. Peter's parents were wealthy and evidently expected their son to become a priest so that he might in time obtain some rank. It was a period in history when this sort of thing was a trial to the Church, and Peter's worldly youth was only one of many examples. It did, however, have an unusual termination, and Peter first caught the public eye on the day when he went to claim his office, although not exactly as he had intended. Being extremely vain and very proud of his new office, Peter felt that it would be a good idea to make an entrance as public as possible so that everyone would be impressed with his fine clothes and vivid personality. Accordingly, he dressed in his finest; he rode a beautiful horse and came prancing down the street at the time the people were emerging from the High Mass. It was Christmas Day. The horse must have had a sense of the dramatic, too, for when they had sufficiently attracted the attention of everyone in town, the horse bucked and landed his fine rider wrong side up in a pile of refuse.

The Spanish people, who have a keen sense of comedy, responded with loud gusts of laughter. Peter, covered with mud and confusion, withdrew to clean up and to think over his sins.

Surprisingly enough, when his wounded feelings had healed, Peter reformed his pointless life and entered the convent of the Dominicans in Palencia. He was never to forget to weep for his sins, and his life was spent in prayer and penance to offset the wasted years of his youth. Peter's friends did not allow this to happen without protest. They had been greatly amused by his accident, but not converted by it as he was, and they did their best to talk him into leaving religious life and going back to the luxury he had left. It was probably a serious temptation to the young man, for it is not easy to reform overnight. But he did not turn back. He became, by close application to the rule, one of the shining exemplars of this difficult way of life.

After his studies were completed, Peter entered into his apostolate. It was to take him into places where his worldly background would be a help rather than a hindrance, for he could well understand the temptations and troubles of worldly people. He was first of all a military chaplain with the royal army, fighting against the Moors. His next assignment was to the court, and in both places he worked successfully to reform and spiritualize the worldly people with whom he came in contact.

When the royal army took Cordova, in 1236, it was Peter's task to moderate the conduct of the soldiers—not an easy task, for they were bent upon plundering the Moorish capital. He was showered with favors by the king, who had great confidence in him. Afraid of honors, however, he resigned from his work at the court and went into the provinces to give missions among the poorest of the people. Here he was to spend the rest of his life, working among the peasants in the mountains.

Most of the anecdotes of his life come from this period, and they have to do with miracles that he worked for these people. At his prayer, storms ceased, droughts were ended, bottles were refilled with wine, bread was found in the wilderness. The bridge which he built across the swift river Minho made his name famous throughout Spain, and it existed up to very recent times. During the time he was directing work on this bridge, he used to call the fish to come and be caught; it was a way of helping to feed the workers. Either this, or the work which he took up with sailors in the seaport towns in the last years of his life has endeared him to seafaring men and made him their patron.

Peter Gonzales died in 1246. His relics were placed in a silver shrine in the cathedral of Tuy. Peter has for several centuries been invoked by Spanish sailors during storms at sea, and he is referred to, for what reason we do not know, as "St. Elmo."

Pope Benedict XIV confirmed his cult in 1741.

ANSELM AND COMPANIONS
(d. 1247)

When the Tartar hordes first came pouring out of the East and inundated Europe it was taken for granted by Christian people that these ruthless killers came from hell. The Chronicle of Novgorod records: "We know not whence they came, nor where they hid themselves again. God knows whence He fetched them against us for our sins." Yet it is a sad commentary on human perversity that no less than twenty times in the following century did the Khans send envoys to the West, asking to be told more about Christianity. There is an ominously modern sound to the negotiations between these representatives of two widely-separated ways of life. One of the earliest of the embassies to penetrate the heart of Tartary, in answer to the Khan's request, was led by a group of Dominicans: Anselm, Simon of St. Quentin, Alexander, and Alberic.

Pope Innocent IV had sent out a Franciscan expedition in 1245, a small group headed by a remarkable man, John de Plano Carpini. The circumstances of the case made this one of the most remarkable missionary journeys in history, though no tangible results could be seen immediately. The pope decided to send a Dominican group by way of Persia and the silk route. They left in 1246. Anselm was given the powers of papal legate, and he carried letters from the pope to the Great Khan.

Guidebooks of the time informed the travelers that the country of Tartary was inhabited by folk who were only relatively human; some had the heads of dogs, and they communicated by barking; some were cyclopedes, creatures with only one arm and one leg, who must turn somersaults to walk; some had great huge ears, which were wrapped around the body for warmth; some—the small-mouthed parocitae—ate by inhaling steam. Serious discussions had been held, and left unsettled, as to whether these creatures were capable of understanding the truths of Christianity, and what language they might perhaps speak. Today's space explorers are, on the whole, better briefed on what they might find than were these friars setting out into the unknown.

It was decided to go by way of Egypt, where the embassy spent some time discussing the matter with the sultan. A sworn enemy of the Christians, the sultan was at the moment considering an alliance with the West, because he was so much more afraid of the Tartars. So he conversed amiably with them as to the best routes to follow, agreed that the Tartars were probably devils, but he politely declined to become a Christian. Refreshed but not encouraged, the embassy set out for Armenia and, at the borders of Persia, contacted the first of the Khan's troops.

Here, after so many hardships, the undertaking was doomed to founder, because of a point that is not even yet satisfactorily settled. The Khan's officers explained to the friars that all visitors to the Khan were to make three genuflections on coming into his presence, because he was the son of heaven. The envoys declined to do this, on the ground that it was idolatry.

If the envoys had been supplied with rich gifts for the Khan, it is quite possible that his officers might have overlooked the matter of protocol. They knew their master to be insatiably curious about the West. But all the friars had from the West was a letter from the pope, addressing the Tartars as his children, and asking them to refrain from killing Christians. The friars assured the Khan's officers that they would give their master the same deference they showed towards any earthly ruler. The Khan's officers, who possibly had time heavy on their hands, proposed to skin the envoys, stuff the skins with straw, and return them to the pope.

It was a woman who saved the lives of the friars. She was the wife of a prince, one of the Khan's relatives. "If you kill them," she said sensibly, "you will only bring punishment on yourselves." Unwillingly, they gave up their spectacular plan and sent the pope's letter on to the Khan by their own messengers, leaving the embassy to languish in their camp, half-starved and fearful.

The letter sent back by the Khan is a masterpiece as an example of how rumor gets around, and how magnificently wrong it can be. Out of the heart of Tartary came the Khan's question; "We hear that you Christians adore rocks and trees. Is it true?"

Anselm and his companions grasped eagerly at the show of interest and carefully explained the Christian doctrine. Their words fell on stony ground. The letter from the pope had been translated from Latin into Persian, then into. Tartar; the reply was translated in reverse order. It is possible that some of the sense of the message had been lost in all these transfers, but one still gets the same messages from the same part of the world, so perhaps they were accurate: "Those who acknowledge our arms will be safe; others will be annihilated."

The unsuccessful trip lasted two years in all. It did nothing to help matters between Tartar and Christian—a situation which after seven centuries still poses a problem—but it helped to evangelize Armenia, and it added small bits to the sketchy geographical knowledge of the time.

The Khan's reply is still to be seen in the Vatican archives, mute witness to the difficulty of dealings between peoples with different codes of behavior. Less familiar to the West is the remark of one of the Khans: "God has given the Gospel to the Christians and they do not obey it."

MICHAEL OF FABRA
(d. 1248)

A fellow countryman of St. Dominic, Michael of Fabra was one of his first disciples. This is all that we really know about the early years of a man who must have had an important part to play in the formation of the Order.

Michael of Fabra was Castilian by birth, and the records tell us that he was already a doctor of theology when he joined St. Dominic in the early days of his preaching in Toulouse. Whether he was at that time one of the chaplains with Diego de Azevedo—the most probable theory—or whether he actually bore arms in the crusade (which would hardly leave him time to earn a doctorate in theology) we are not sure. We do know that he was one of the original sixteen brethren, and that he had a voice in the shaping of the primitive rules of the Order. At the dispersal he was sent to Paris with Matthew of France. Here he became the Order's first professor of theology, a fact that was recorded in his epitaph. He apparently taught there until there were other professors prepared to take over, and then was sent to Spain, with Blessed Manez, to help with the Spanish houses.

Here he rapidly became involved in what could not have been a pleasant responsibility; he was appointed royal confessor. The only bright spot in this thankless task was that it soon led him, in company with his royal penitent, to the conquest of Majorca. The Spanish rulers were engaged in trying to drive the Moors out of the Spanish territories, and James of Aragon attacked the Moorish strongholds in Majorca. The supposedly impregnable fortress fell, after what all considered the miraculous intervention of the chaplain's prayers. The saying arose that "the Blessed Virgin and Father Michael took Majorca."

Moving in on the Moors, James laid siege to Valencia. Here, when the city finally fell, captured Moors testified that, in an apparition, they had seen Michael of Fabra hovering over the army when the fight was most bitter. He was more than life-size, shining with light, and brandishing a sword.

After the fighting was over, there was the difficult task of rebuilding the place, gathering the scattered Christians, and putting their faith on a firm footing again. Old monasteries had been serving as mosques, all Christian traditions in the place had been destroyed during the Moorish occupation, and there was little left to show that Valencia had ever been anything but a Mohammedan city. It was Michael of Fabra who brought order out of the chaos, supervised the building and repairing, and set up a Dominican convent that was to give many famous sons to the Church, including two canonized saints, Vincent Ferrer and Louis Bertrand.

It was quite to be expected that Michael would be offered the bishopric of Valencia. He refused. Shortly after this he died, in 1248, and was buried in the community cemetery in Valencia. His remains were later moved to the church, then to the chapel of St. Peter Martyr.

ANDREW OF LONGJUMEAU
(1250)

Andrew of Longjumeau has been the center of many legends, but there was nothing legendary about the fact that he was sent by St. Louis, king of France, to bring the Holy Crown of Thorns from Palestine.

Andrew was born near Paris and entered the Order there in its earliest years. He was a member of the band sent by Blessed Jordan to the Holy Land to learn oriental languages. He became fluent in several of these, principally in Arabic.

The crusades left a great deal of confusion in Palestine, and one of the sorriest features of the situation was the enmity between Latin and Greek Christians. After Constantinople was sacked by the Latin crusaders, the Greeks tried to drive them out in repeated attacks. By 1237 they were strong enough to do so, and King Baldwin II, emperor of Constantinople, turned to France for help against the Greeks. He offered the French king a most astounding bribe in return for French arms. Baldwin possessed one of the holiest relics in Christendom, the Crown of Thorns. His offer, reduced to its simplest terms, was to give this relic to the French king in exchange for troops.

King Louis of France was a saint, and Baldwin was quite sure he would rather barter for the crown than see it sold to an infidel nation, which he hinted he might have to do if the French did not cooperate. There was also the very practical question of who else might be drawn into the fight if France did not do what he asked. Louis decided to accept his terms.

There was need of someone with diplomatic experience and a good command of oriental languages to go to the Holy Land and make sure both that the transaction was honest and that the relic received due honor. Andrew of Longjumeau was chosen for the mission. Andrew and several Dominican companions set out for the Holy Land.

It is literally impossible to follow all the ramifications of this most peculiar business transaction. In 1238, when Andrew was busy negotiating, there were so many things going on at the same time that nations hardly knew who were their allies. The "Old Man of the Mountain," the dreaded chief of the assassins, had just proposed cautiously to the French that they unite against the Tartars; the Tartars, moving steadily into Moslem territory, were proposing an alliance with the West against the Mohammedans. Venetian galleys, which had profited from the plunder of Constantinople, were preying upon the Eastern ships; Genoa, in turn, set her fleet on the Venetians. When the precious relic was finally given into the hands of Andrew of Longjumeau, it had been pawned to the Venetians and captured by the Greeks, then lost to the Genoese. There then arose the question of whether the box containing the supposed relics was actually authentic.

Having identified the relics—since he had seen them before—Andrew was sent to France for the promised ransom. On the feast of St. Lawrence, in 1239, the disedifying business came to an end at last, and Andrew placed the famous relic in the hands of the king, glad that the delicate business was over. Louis carried the crown to the church of St. Stephen, walking barefoot as a sign of devotion. He later built the Sainte-Chappelle to house the famous relic.

In 1245, Andrew was appointed to the commission for the reunion of Eastern and Western Churches. Through his efforts, both the Armenian patriarch and the leader of the Jacobites made their submission to the pope.

Three years later, while the French king was resting on the Island of Cyprus, an embassy from the Tartars came to him and asked that Christian envoys be sent to the Khan. Several previous expeditions had been unsuccessful in dealing with the Tartars, though they had brought back valuable information about this curious kingdom on the other side of the world. The Khan had formed a high opinion of the French through his contact with two captive French knights, and he sent his delegation not to the pope but to the French king personally. Louis wished to reply in kind. He fitted out the expedition with rich gifts for the Khan, including a scarlet and gold chapel tent. The expedition was political rather than religious, and he required a diplomat who spoke several Eastern languages. Andrew of Longjumeau was chosen once more.

The expeditions to Tartary were uniformly uncomfortable. This one was considered to be fairly easy, as such things go; it still entailed ". . . a full year of riding ten leagues a day," after they left Antioch. There is a curiously modern ring to the plaints of the friars that the Tartars "deliberately misunderstood them." The Khan, for example, treated the famous scarlet and gold chapel tent as a tribute which King Louis had paid him, acknowledging his sovereignty; then, heaping insult upon injury, demanded a yearly tribute of gold and silver from the French king, promising to put him to the sword if he did not pay it.

When and where Andrew of Longjumeau died we do not know. It was after his return from Tartary in 1250.

ST. PETER MARTYR
(1206-1252)

St. Peter Martyr of Verona was not the first Dominican to die in the cause of truth, but so greatly was he revered for his sanctity that he was canonized the year after his death; hence he became the type of fearless apostle of the Order.

More remarkable than his death is the record of his life. Born of heretical parents, and surrounded during his whole childhood with the most harmful theories and practices, Peter preserved a purity of faith and morals which was nothing short of miraculous. Continually ridiculed and harangued by his relatives, he remained untarnished in both body and soul. Sent to Bologna to the university at the age of fifteen, he met St. Dominic, and instantly, with no backward glances at the wealth and power he was foregoing, threw himself at the saint's feet and begged admission to the Order. He was present at the death of St. Dominic, and shared in the legacy of primitive zeal and courage passed to the sons of a saint.

While still a student, Peter underwent a severe trial. He was publicly reprimanded and placed on punishment because a brother, passing Peter's cell late at night, thought he had heard women's voices in the room. The voices were those of angels, who frequently visited the saint: but in his humility he thought it better to accept the punishment and say nothing about it. He was sent to another convent to do penance, and his ordination was delayed. Peter prayed and found great strength in prayer: but, being human, he felt the disgrace keenly, and he one day complained to our Lord: "Lord, Thou knowest that I am innocent of this: why dost Thou permit them to believe it of me?" A sorrowful voice replied from the crucifix: "And I, Peter, what have I done that they should do this to Me?" Peter complained no more. The truth was eventually discovered, and Peter, reinstated in the community, resumed his studies. He prayed daily for the happiness of dying a martyr's death.

Peter soon became a celebrated preacher and engaged in disputes with the heretics all over northern Italy. Many miracles were worked through his prayers, to the rage of the heretics. In one city, a prominent man had been won to heresy, because the devil, taking the appearance of the Blessed Mother, appeared at the heretics' meetings and encouraged him to join them. Peter, determined to win the man back to the truth, went to the meeting of the heretics, and, when the devil appeared in his disguise, held up a small pyx in which he had placed a consecrated Host. "If you are the Mother of God," cried Peter, "adore your Son!" The devil fled in dismay, and many heretics were converted. Enraged by Peter's success, his enemies made plans to destroy him.

Sold like his Master for thirty pieces of silver, Peter was ambushed and killed on the road to Milan. He went to his death singing, which is the traditional Dominican way to enter heaven. Undaunted by the threats of the heretics, he walked along singing the Easter Sequence, and fell unprotesting beneath the blows of the assassins. One of his murderers, touched by grace at the sight of a saint, was converted, eventually took the Dominican habit, and was popularly known as "Blessed" Carino. To him as to us, Peter had pointed out the way to heaven when he traced on the dust of the road, in his own blood, the creed that had lighted his path: "*Credo in unum Deum.*"

BLESSED ZEDISLAVA BERKA
(1210-1252)

Born of a warrior race, Zedislava lived in a fortified castle on the borders of Christendom, in an age when the fierce Mongol hordes were the world's worst menace. Her whole life was spent within the sound of clashing arms, and the moans of the dying. The gentleness and purity of her life stand out in surprising beauty against the dark background of a warlike and materialistic people.

Zedislava learned Christian charity early in life from her mother, who taught her not only the secrets of preparing medicinal herbs but also the healing balm of prayer. Going each day to the castle gate with alms and medicines for the poor and the wretched who crowded there for help, she was soon well acquainted with human misery. Cheerful and prayerful, and alert to see the sorrows of others, the child became a light of hope to the miserable. Because of her sweetness and natural charm, she was able to teach many lessons to those about her.

At an early age, Zedislava was married to a soldier who, like her own father, was in command of a castle on the frontier. He was a good man, but a rough and battle-hardened soldier who liked nothing better than the clash of swords. He tried his young wife's patience and obedience in a thousand ways, insisting that she dress in her finest gowns and attend the long and barbarous banquets that pleased him so. Being of a retiring disposition and much given to prayer—and, moreover, having a family and a large castle to care for—she found this a real sacrifice. However, obedience and patience had been an important part of her training, and she taught herself to spiritualize the endless trials which would beset the mother of four children in a medieval fortress.

The Polish missionaries, Hyacinth and Ceslaus, brought Zedislava the first knowledge of the new religious Order which had begun but a few years before. St. Dominic, a Spaniard, had met them in Italy, where he had gone to have his Order approved. Begun in France, the Order was already international, and with the professing of Zedislava as the first Slavic Tertiary, its world-wide scope became apparent.

Enchanted with the possibilities of an Order which allowed her to share in its benefits and works while caring for her family, Zedislava threw herself into the new project with enviable zeal. She encouraged her husband to build a hostel for the many poor pilgrims who came homeless to the gate.

She visited the prisoners in the frightful dungeons, and used her influence to obtain pardons from the severe sentences meted out to them. She fed and cared for the poor, taught catechism to the children of the servants, and showed all, by the sweetness of her life, just what it meant to be a Christian lady and a Dominican Tertiary. On the occasion of a Mongol attack, when homeless refugees poured into the castle stronghold, her calm, invincible charity was a bulwark of strength to all.

With her own funds, Zedislava determined to build a church where God might be fittingly worshipped. As an act of zeal and penance, she herself carried many of the heavy beams and materials that went into the building. She did this at night so that no one would know of her hard work. Her death came soon after the completion of this church. The mourning people who knelt by her deathbed could see evidence of her strong Christian virtues in the monuments she had left: her children, her church, and the inspiration of a saintly wife and mother.

JOHN THE TEUTONIC
(d. 1252)

Most Dominicans remember John the Teutonic, if at all, for the single reason that he was the master general who placed St. Thomas in the care of St. Albert the Great, thus playing a key role in the shaping of a mighty mind. Although this is claim enough to fame, it is not the only praiseworthy accomplishment of this early Dominican. He was a remarkable person in many ways, and an ornament to the Order to which he belonged.

John's career began in an unlikely place. As a young assistant professor in the University of Bologna, he met Frederick II of Germany, the fiery and romantic character who was to keep Europe in a turmoil all his life. When John met him in 1212, Frederick was a young man of sixteen, not yet completely corrupted by the ambition and pride that later ruined him. There was then something attractive about this man who had such a fine mind, and John left his university career to follow him back to Germany. How long it took to disillusion John we are not told. But after a time he returned to Bologna and said no more about the court of Frederick II.

The evidence indicates that John was ordained a priest and was papal penitentiary in Bologna when the first friars of Master Dominic arrived and began their pious raids on the university. He received the habit from St. Dominic himself, and made profession to him in 1219. John was then past forty years of age, and a well-known preacher, not only in Latin, but also in German, French, and Italian.

John the Teutonic was sent first to the diocese of Constance, then to Austria, France, Germany, and finally to Strasbourg. From here he was sent by the pope to preach the crusade in Germany, in 1224. Perhaps because he stayed longer in Strasbourg than anywhere else, he was sometimes called "John of Strasbourg." By all the accounts, he was very successful there, and would have been quite happy to stay. But he was called, in 1227, to be provincial, then bishop, of Hungary.

Hungary, it will be recalled, was the buffer between Tartary and Christian Europe. It was in an almost constant state of turmoil, with wars, invasions, and upheavals of various kinds. Heresies came from the East and caused schisms among the faithful; the last bishop had been deposed for heresy. It was a vast battleground where the man in charge had to be a saint and a good general as well.

John the Teutonic was a man of peace, not of war. He was a college professor and a priest. There was little to recommend him for such a delicate task. Yet he did it marvelously well. Caught at one time in negotiations between the pope and the king of Hungary, he managed to bring them to agreement in what had been almost hopeless situation, and retained the friendship of each. This proved a fatal talent, indeed, for it landed him squarely in the middle of the worst feud of the time; at his own earnest request, he was relieved of the bishopric. Soon after this he was made provincial of Lombardy.

Lombardy had always been a trouble spot, and at that moment, with Frederick II there in open war against the pope, John the Teutonic was not overjoyed to be made provincial. Frederick still had a high regard for him, surprisingly enough, but it was an uncomfortable place to be.

John's attitude can best be summed up in his words: "We must always obey the orders of the pope. Yet we must refrain from criticism of the civil authority, and avoid expressing our personal opinions on thorny questions, either among ourselves or with others." He gave expression to this sentiment at three succeeding chapters, and its practical application, difficult though it was, kept the explosive situation in Lombardy from blowing up completely. So impressed were the capitular fathers with his talent for keeping both the law and the peace, they elected him master general at the chapter in 1241, when St. Raymond of Penafort resigned the office.

It was a clear case of "out of the frying pan into the fire," but John acquitted himself well. He continued the course of action laid out by the three men who had preceded him in office, giving much attention not only to the studies and to regular observance, but also to the liturgy and to preaching. He carefully supervised the establishment of the special schools in the language and customs of the East, which St. Raymond had proposed, and extended the work of the Order to new regions in the Near East.

John the Teutonic was one of the builders of the Order who helped to establish its standards of scholarship and holiness of life. He died in Strasbourg in 1252, after a life filled with apostolic pursuits, and has always been held in grateful memory by the Order.

ST. RICHARD OF CHICHESTER
(d. 1253)

St. Richard, Bishop of Chichester, canonized nine years after his death in 1253, was not a First Order Dominican; we do not have positive proof that he was a Tertiary, but a persistent legend and a large body of evidence indicates that he was. One tradition is that he was actually on the way to the Dominican convent of Orleans, where he planned to enter as a subject, when the letters came appointing him bishop.

Richard was born in Droitwich, in 1197, of a family who held property and were fairly wealthy. His parents both died when he was small, and the estates fell to his older brother, who had no gift for management and allowed the land to fall to ruin. When Richard was old enough to make himself useful, he abandoned the schools and the books he loved and threw all his energies into rebuilding his brother's estates. He actually tilled the land himself for a time, and he directed the replanting of the ruined gardens. In due time his management paid off, and the property was restored to its former value. His brother wished to make it all over to Richard's name and, furthermore, had planned for an advantageous marriage for his younger brother. Richard, however, had only one love—his books. Abandoning everything that his brother had planned for him, he went off to Oxford to finish his studies.

Franciscans and Dominicans had just come to Oxford when Richard arrived. Some of the finest teachers of both Orders were there, and Richard revelled in the intellectual atmosphere. It is true that sometimes he had to run rapidly around his freezing room to restore his circulation, and that his meals were far from regular, but he feasted on the books from which he had fasted so long. At this time he made the acquaintance of a man who was to be a lifelong friend, St. Edmund Rich, who was then chancellor of the university.

After completing his studies in Paris and Bologna, Richard returned to England and was appointed chancellor of the university at Oxford by Edmund Rich, who had become archbishop of Canterbury. Richard remained in close contact with St. Edmund during the long years of Edmund's conflict with the English king and, in fact, following him into exile in France, remained with him until Edmund's death. During these years he was ordained a priest at the Dominican Church in Orleans, and lived for some time in the community there. According to some accounts, he was a Tertiary.

It is here that the records are badly confused. There is sufficient evidence to indicate that he intended joining the community at Orleans. For some reason we do not know, he returned to England first, and shortly there-after—one record says that it was while he was on the way back to Orleans —he was appointed bishop of Chichester.

The appointment was a thorny one. It was a case in which retreat would be pure cowardice, so he accepted the unwelcome office and set about doing his best with it. At first he was all but starved out of his own diocese, because the king, angry over his appointment, forbade anyone to give him either food or shelter. No bishop dared to consecrate him and, after a year of mendicant existence, he went to Rome to receive episcopal consecration from the pope. Returning to the same life of poverty and hostility, he began the process of wearing away the rock of royal opposition by his constant goodness. In two years' time the king was forced to relent, though he never restored the revenues he had stolen from the saintly bishop.

If he was a thorn in the side of an avaricious king, Richard was a saint to his flock. Many miracles of healing and of providing for the poor were recorded during his lifetime, and many more after his death. Richard was deep in the hearts of his people, the sort of saint that anyone can recognize by his simplicity, holiness, and his endless charity to the poor.

Richard built a magnificent tomb for his friend, St. Edmund, and was himself buried there after his death in 1253. Later a separate tomb was erected for him, which became one of the most popular pilgrimage places in England. It was utterly destroyed during the Reformation.

In the early days of the Order, the name of St. Richard was inserted as a saint to be commemorated among our feasts, a fact which offers strong evidence that he himself was a member of the Order he loved.

BLESSED NICHOLAS PALAEA
(d. 1255)

Nicholas Palaea was born of noble family near Bari, in the Kingdom of Naples, and named for the great wonder-worker who had once lived there. At the age of eight he was already practicing austerities. He would not eat meat, even on feast days, because he had been favored with a vision of a young man of great majesty who told him to thus prepare for a lifetime of mortification in an Order that kept perpetual abstinence. Sent to Bologna for his studies, he met St. Dominic and was won by him to the new Order. He was the companion of St. Dominic on several of the founder's journeys to Italy, and warmed his heart at the very source of the new fire which was to mean resurrection to so many souls.

St. Nicholas of Bari had been noted for his astounding miracles, and his young namesake began following in his footsteps while yet a novice. When on a journey with several companions, he met a woman with a withered arm. Making the Sign of the Cross over her, he cured her of the affliction. At one time, as he entered his native city, he found a woman weeping beside the body of her child, who had been drowned in a well. He asked the woman the name of the child, and being told it was Andrew, he replied, "After this, it's Nicholas. Nicholas, in the name of our Lord Jesus Christ, arise!" The little one arose, alive and well. The child of his sister, Colette, mute from birth, brought her famous uncle a basket of bread. "Who sent this bread, child?" Nicholas asked her. "My mother," she replied, and from then on she was cured.

As provincial of the Roman province, Nicholas was wise, prudent, and kind. He received many novices and did much of his work among the young religious. Once he was called to the assistance of a novice who had been deceived by the devil and would not go to confession. He showed the young man the true state of his soul and undid the work of the evil one.

Nicholas earned great fame as a preacher. On one occasion, when he was preaching in the cathedral of Brescia, two irreverent young men began disturbing the congregation and soon made such a commotion that Nicholas could not make himself heard. Nicholas went out from the cathedral to a neighboring hill and there called out to the birds to come to listen to him. Like the birds in the similar story of St. Francis, flocks of feathered creatures fluttered down at his feet and listened attentively while he preached. At the end of the sermon they flew away singing.

After a lifetime of preaching and miracles, Nicholas, forewarned of his death by a visit from a brother who had been dead for many years, went happily to receive the reward of the faithful apostle. Miracles continued at his tomb and through his intercession. Among these was the miracle by which life was given to a baby born dead. His parents had promised to name the baby Nicholas if the favor were granted, and to their great joy their child lived.

CLEMENT OF DUNBLANE
(d. 1256)

One of the pioneers about whom we hear little is the colorful and resourceful Bishop Clement of Dunblane, in Scotland. The convents he founded within a few years of the beginning of the Order served the Church well, and Church annals are gemmed with the names of the people who made history in that interesting country. We read the names of Robert Bruce and Lord Douglas on the rolls of benefactors of the Blackfriars. James Beaton, archbishop of St. Andrews, fled for sanctuary to the Dominican church in 1517; and in 1554, John Knox was called to give an account of his strange doctrines in the Blackfriars Church of Edinburgh.

The man who brought the Order to Scotland was a Scotsman by birth, and he met St. Dominic at the University of Paris. Receiving the habit from the hands of Dominic, he was active and vocal in the cause of obtaining friars for his native country. Tradition holds that the Scottish king, Alexander II, in Paris on diplomatic business, made a personal appeal to St. Dominic for missionaries. It is an historical fact that this monarch was their first benefactor when the mission band at last arrived, shortly after the death of St. Dominic.

The convent of Ayr was founded in 1230, and seven other large houses soon followed. There is record of transactions with the rulers of the region at this time, and, a few years later, King Robert Bruce granted the Dominicans the privilege of grinding their grain at his mill.

Clement was appointed bishop of Dunblane in 1233, by Pope Gregory IX, a devoted friend of St. Dominic. He worked in this See for twenty-three years, and, according to an old record, he "labored with unflagging zeal to uproot superstition and destroy vice, to make true and solid piety known and practiced, and to draw the faithful entrusted to his charge to the imitation of all the virtues of Christian perfection, as he himself fulfilled all the duties of a watchful and loving pastor"—a description of a bishop that can hardly be bettered. He is described as being poor himself, and the father of the poor, and all the old writers speak of his zeal in restoring the ruined churches and the neglected rights of the Church.

According to surviving records, he must have been a busy man, this rugged missionary in a rugged land. He rebuilt the Dunblane Cathedral, visited tirelessly among the outlying regions of his diocese, setting things in order, and solicited most of the funds for reconstruction himself. He was appointed on several papal commissions, once to inquire into the heroic virtues of Margaret of Scotland, another time to determine the validity of a bishop's appointment. He was sent to collect alms for the Holy Land in 1247, at a time when he badly needed the money to rebuild his own diocese. Through his influence, the Episcopal See was transferred from the Isle of Iona, which was frequently inaccessible and always in danger from the stormy seas, to a place where it would be readily in touch with the rest of Scotland. He attended the general chapter of the Order held in London in 1250. At one time he had to pronounce a sentence of excommunication on all those who had tried to murder the king.

In spite of these varied and absorbing labors, we are interested to find that he wrote at least three books: a life of St. Dominic, a book on pilgrimages to the Holy Land, and the history of the Order in Scotland.

Clement of Scotland died in 1256, leaving a reputation for personal holiness so great that even a Protestant historian would say of him: "This man was an excellent preacher, learned above many of that time, and of singular integrity of conversation."

JOHN OF VICENZA
(d. 1256)

There are many conflicting opinions about John of Vicenza. One author asserts that he was "more Franciscan than Dominican; in fact, that he hardly represents the Dominican spirit at all." Another claims that he was literally "another St. Dominic," and that when he preached on the Rosary, roses fell from his lips in full view of his hearers. Somewhere between these two extremes the real truth must lie. At least, all agree that he was a great and important man, and that he played a vital part in the activities of a busy century.

It would help if we knew when and where he was born, but we do not. The time was without doubt the end of the twelfth century, and the place was probably Vicenza. His family name or title seems to have been de Scledo. According to tradition, his father wanted him to be a lawyer and so sent him to Padua. There he met the Dominicans and promptly joined them. He received the habit from St. Dominic, just before the saint's death in 1221.

By 1231 John was prior of the convent of Padua. In this year Pope Gregory IX appointed him as one of a committee of three to pass judgment on the heroicity of the virtues of St. Anthony of Padua. He carried out several diplomatic missions for the same pope, always with distinction. His reputation as a preacher was outstanding, even in that century of preaching giants. He seems to have been essentially a reform preacher; he inveighed against the vanities of women, against jewels and crowns of roses, and other fripperies of the age. He converted several noted sinners—one of these, a famous lawyer, went on for holy orders and ended his life as bishop of Bologna. He reconciled a Bolognese officer who had been excommunicated, and he reformed several learned citizens of the town whose hotheadedness had entangled them in difficulties with the Church and the government.

John of Vicenza is most famous for his work in evangelizing Lombardy, in the territory of the tyrant, Ezzelino. In a time and a region where tyrants were common, Ezzelino was a tyrant's tyrant, and the most accomplished of political bandits acknowledged his superiority in the field of planned violence. The damage he had done to the cause of the pope in Lombardy was immeasurable; he left the place of his operations so devastated that even the Tartars could afford to respect his thoroughness. John of Vicenza, who had begun, in 1233, a revival movement which his contemporaries called "The Great Alleluia," moved into the territory of Ezzelino. He was an accomplished preacher and had led many to penance and piety, but when the pope sent him to deal with Ezzelino everyone was convinced that he was going to certain martyrdom.

Exactly what he accomplished with this warped genius it is hard to say now—accounts differ. Some say that he converted the tyrant. Another —and probably truer—account has it that he forced him to stop preying upon the Italian towns and go back into the hills. An amusing sidelight on the affair tells us that other tyrants, not nearly so accomplished as Ezzelino—and unable to oppose him in any way themselves—were infuriated at his softness towards the preacher, and they took it upon themselves to kill John of Vicenza. They failed, and, as far as we know, John died quietly in his bed in 1256 or thereabouts.

John of Vicenza was present at the first translation of the relics of St. Dominic.

ST. HYACINTH
(1185-1257)

St. Hyacinth is called "the Polish St. Dominic," which is to say that he was the founder of the Order in Poland—the dynamo of holiness in the North that St. Dominic was in the South.

Hyacinth was born of the noble family of Odrowatz, in Polish Upper Silesia. He and Blessed Ceslaus, who was either a brother or a close relative, were carefully educated both in learning and in piety. They were greatly beloved by a priest uncle, Ivo, who sent them to the university and sponsored their education. The two young men were newly ordained priests and canons at the cathedral in Cracow when Ivo was appointed bishop of Cracow. When he went to Rome for his consecration, Ivo took his two young nephews with him.

In Rome, the Polish visitors heard much of the wonder-working Spaniard, Dominic, and were present at the miracle he performed in restoring life to the nephew of Cardinal Napoleon. They were charmed with the ideals of the newly-founded Order, and the new bishop begged St. Dominic to send friars to Poland. Dominic had no one to send, since none of the brethren spoke Polish, but his glance fell upon the two young priests in the bishop's party. He gave them the habit, trained them himself, and sent them to evangelize the North.

Hyacinth's life was henceforth an almost uninterrupted series of miracles. He walked a total of nearly twenty-five thousand miles in his apostolic travels, preaching in all the countries of the North, from Denmark and Prussia to Greece, White Russia, Tartary, and Tibet. His progress among these hostile peoples, with their barbarous customs and unknown languages, through trackless forests, in the fierce cold of the North, can be explained only by a miracle.

Early in his mission career, Our Lady appeared to Hyacinth and promised him that she would never refuse him anything. Through the years of his arduous labor she kept her promise, and his ministry was rich with a harvest of souls. He performed many astounding miracles, including countless cures. On one occasion he gave sight to two boys who had been born without eyes. He raised several dead people to life. The best known incident in his life has to do with Our Lady, which is not surprising.

During one of the Tartar invasions the convent was attacked. Hyacinth was hurrying to remove the Blessed Sacrament to hide it, when he heard Our Lady tell him not to leave her statue behind to be desecrated. It was a large statue and Hyacinth did not know how he could carry it. "I will lighten the load," said Our Lady. Carrying the Blessed Sacrament in one hand and the statue in the other, Hyacinth escaped from the burning convent and walked dry-shod across the river. On every occasion of his life, Our Lady was to lighten the load for him, and, as a last favor, she appeared to tell him that he would die on the Feast of the Assumption.

Popular devotion to St. Hyacinth has survived time and many wars in the lands where he preached. He was the first outstanding missionary apostle whose life and work shed glory on the Order at its very beginning, establishing a pattern for all the years to come.

PETER SEILA
(d. 1257)

St. Dominic's first landlord, the rich man of Toulouse who received the homeless band of preachers into his house when the city fell to De Montfort, should not be forgotten in our Dominican records. He gave us the first home for the Order at a time when that was the most pressing need, and this alone would entitle him to our gratitude.

Peter Seila was probably born in Toulouse, most likely of a wealthy family. One chronicler tries very hard to make him the innkeeper who was converted by St. Dominic in 1216, which would make him a ripe old age at the conclusion of forty-two years in the Order. The story is not, of course, impossible, but highly improbable. Peter was quite likely a young man when he opened his heart and his house to the new Order. He himself received the habit at this time and joined in the labors of the friars. At the dispersal of the brethren, he and his fellow citizen, Thomas, were sent to Toulouse, to the tiny cloister of St. Romain, which had replaced his own house as headquarters of the Order in the South.

Peter Seila may have had some previous brush with the Albigensians of Toulouse; in any case they hated him profoundly, and when De Montfort was killed, St. Dominic sent Peter to Paris. When the saint arrived in Paris, in 1219, he sent Peter at the head of a group to found a house in Limoges. Completed the following year, the convent there was soon filled with excellent religious. Peter might have remained there quite happily, doing excellent work, but when the Albigensian situation shifted again, he was sent back to Toulouse in the unhappy role of inquisitor.

Peter worked at this unpopular office with William Arnauld and a number of others, members of his own Order and of the several other Orders who had been drafted into the service of the holy office. They made their headquarters for awhile in Peter's old home, which became known as the "Convent of the Inquisition." Peter was prior of St. Romain when word came to him that William Arnauld and ten companions had been martyred in Avignonet in 1242.

Peter Seila died in 1257.

BLESSED GONSALVO OF AMARANTE
(1187-1259)

Gonsalvo of Amarante was a true son of the Middle Ages, a man right out of the pages of the "Golden Legend." His whole life reads like a mural from the wall of a church—full of marvelous things and done up in brilliant colors.

Gonsalvo Pereira was born in 1187, in the diocese of Braga, in Portugal, and his babyhood is replete with wondrous indications of his holiness. While still a small child, he was consecrated to study for the Church, and received his training in the household of the archbishop of Braga. After his ordination he was given charge of a wealthy parish, an assignment that should have made him very happy. Gonsalvo was not as interested in choice parishes as some of his companions; he went to his favorite Madonna shrine and begged Our Lady to help him in the fair administration of this office.

There was no complaint with Gonsalvo's government of the parish of St. Pelagius. He was penitential himself, but indulgent to everyone else. Revenues that might have been turned to his own use were used for the poor and the sick. The parish, in fact, was very much a going concern when he turned it over to his nephew, whom he had carefully trained as a priest, and went on pilgrimage to the Holy Land.

Gonsalvo was happy in the Holy Land. He would gladly have remained there for the rest of his life; but the archbishop of Braga had told him that he m̱ return to Portugal. Hence, after fourteen years of leisurely and fervent meditation in the holy places, he set out once more for Portugal. Arriving there, he was horrified to see that his nephew had not been the good shepherd that he had promised to be; the money left for the poor had gone to purchase a fine stable of thoroughbred horses and a pack of fine hounds. The nephew had told everyone that his old uncle was dead, and he had been appointed pastor in his place by an unsuspecting archbishop. When the uncle appeared on the scene, ragged and old, but very much alive, the nephew was not happy to see him. Gonsalvo seems to have been surprised as well as pained.

The ungrateful nephew settled the matter by turning the dogs on his inconvenient uncle. They would have torn him to pieces, but the servants called them off and allowed the ragged pilgrim to escape. Gonsalvo decided then that he had had enough of parish life, and went out into the hills to a place called Amarante. Here he found a cave and other necessities for hermit life and lived in peace for several years, spending his time building a little chapel to the Blessed Virgin. He preached to those who came to him, and soon there was a steady stream of pilgrims seeking out his retreat.

Happy as he was, Gonsalvo felt that this was not his sole mission in life, and he prayed to Our Lady to help him to know what his real vocation was. She appeared to him one night as he prayed and told him to enter the Order that had the custom of beginning the Office with "Ave Maria gratia plena." She told him that this Order was very dear to her and under her special protection. Gonsalvo set out to find out which Order she meant, and eventually came to the convent of the Friars Preachers. Here was the end of the quest, and he asked for the habit.

Blessed Peter Gonzales was the prior in the house, and he gave the habit to the new aspirant. After Gonsalvo had gone through his novitiate training, he was sent back to Amarante, with a companion, to begin a regular house of the Order. The people of the neighborhood quickly spread the news that the hermit was back. They flocked to hear him preach, and begged him to heal their sick.

One of the miracles of Blessed Gonsalvo concerns the building of a bridge across a swift river that barred many people from reaching the hermitage in wintertime. It was not a good place to build a bridge, but Gonsalvo set about it and followed the heavenly directions he had received. Once, during the building of the bridge, he went out collecting, and a man who wanted to brush him off painlessly sent him away with a note for his wife. Gonsalvo took the note to the man's wife, and she laughed when she read it. "Give him as much gold as will balance with the note

I send you," said the message. Gonsalvo told her he thought she ought to obey her husband, so she got out the scales and put the paper in one balance. Then she put a tiny coin in the other balance, and another, and another—the paper still outweighed her gold—and she kept adding. There was a sizeable pile of coins before the balance with the paper in it swung upwards.

Gonsalvo of Amarante died in 1259, after prophesying the day of his death and promising his friends that he would still be able to help them after death. Pilgrimages began coming soon, and a series of miracles indicated that something should be done about his beatification. Forty years after his death he appeared to several people who were apprehensively watching a flood on the river. The water had risen to a dangerous level, just below the bridge, when they saw a tree floating towards the bridge, and Gonsalvo was balancing capably on its rolling bulk. The friar carefully guided the tree under the bridge, preserving the bridge from damage, and then disappeared.

The cult of Gonsalvo of Amarante was approved in 1560.

ROLAND OF CREMONA
(d. 1259)

The first Dominican to teach theology at the University of Bologna, and one of the first of St. Dominic's disciples, was Master Roland of Cremona. His reputation, already great when he entered the Order, did much to establish the prestige of the new and unknown group of friars who were so soon to take the world by storm.

Roland was born in Cremona, but nothing is known of his early life. He made his studies at the University of Bologna. He was regent of the university when the Dominicans came to Bologna. He was neither attracted to them, as were so many young students, nor angered by them, as his fellow professor, Moneta. He simply paid no attention to them.

The picture drawn of him at this time is that of a gay and successful young lawyer, well-dressed and somewhat vain, given to society and good food. He was not a wicked young man; neither was he at all spiritual. He was simply worldly and quite complacent about it. His conversion to a spiritual life was as much a surprise to him as to any of his friends. He himself could never give a very clear account of what happened.

It was just that one day, like many other days, he had set out to have a thoroughly good time. He wore a dazzling new outfit of scarlet cloth, which guaranteed that every eye in the city would turn as he went by. He *had* a perfectly wonderful day—good company, good food, agreeable comments from all his friends. And that night in his room, thinking over what a wonderful day it had been, the futility of it struck him full in the face. A wonderful day, yes; and where was it now? Gone, leaving nothing behind. Tomorrow would be another such day, and the next day, and the next. Roland, sitting on the edge of his bed, facing a future of such tomorrows, began thinking seriously the same thoughts that many another young man has considered: What about eternity? Does life have to be so pointless as all this?

After a restless night, he rose with his mind made up. He went straight to the little convent of the Dominicans and sought out the famous Master Reginald, who had bewitched so many of his students. He threw himself at Reginald's feet. Reginald had dealt with such young men before. He promptly gave him the Dominican habit.

Once committed to a new way of life, Roland never looked back. He was to wear the habit with distinction for forty years, during which time he gave unstintingly of his great talents and his abounding energy.

Roland's first task was the unexpected one of master of novices. He considered himself most unfit for such a responsible post because of his unspiritual background, but obedience had placed him in the position and he discharged it with great energy and still greater humility. To make up for lost time, he prayed most of the night, after putting in a full day of teaching and preaching. St. Peter Martyr and Blessed Bartholomew of Breganza were novices during his term of office. There were many others among these early recruits who were not only nobly born or intellectually gifted, but spiritually superior. It could not have been an easy task to guide them.

In 1228 he was sent to the general chapter, representing the province of Lombardy, and remained for three years lecturing at the University of Paris. Then he was transferred to the University of Toulouse. Just when it seemed certain that he would spend the rest of his life quietly lecturing in the university, he was commissioned to go out and preach in that part of France evangelized by St. Dominic a generation before. Heresy had raised its head again and the old errors of the Cathari were receiving support from local nobles who used the confusion to their political advantage. He preached and worked among them for several years.

In 1233, Pope Gregory IX sent him back to Lombardy, where the Waldenses were active and where wars and errors were making shambles of northern

Italy. Here, in the place where Peter of Verona was eventually to die at the hands of the heretics, Roland worked and preached against their errors. He was so skillful in his work with these misguided people that he was given a commission from the pope to go in person to talk to the tyrant, Ezzelino.

Ezzelino was probably the most distinguished of a long line of landed pirates who menaced the Lombard plains. His cruelty and greed knew no bounds, and he had established a reputation for ultimates at a time and place where that called for almost inhuman talent. For a priest, and especially a Dominican—whose brothers were everywhere making life uncomfortable for the Manicheans and their political allies—to walk boldly up to Ezzelino and suggest that he make his peace with God seemed sheer madness. It was certainly not the sort of assignment that an aging professor would relish. But Roland made no complaint. He went to see Ezzelino as he had been told to do. He did not, as far as anyone could tell, accomplish much. But he walked away alive. It does not speak any less for his courage that he did not make a lamb out of the raging wolf that was Ezzelino.

At another time, too, Roland was called upon for courage above the ordinary. There was in the suite of Frederick II, who was at that time busy pillaging Italy, a heretic priest who boasted that in argumentation he could defeat any Catholic priest who would face him. Roland, who was old and tired of the incessant quarrels provoked by Frederick, heard of the boast. He set out alone for Frederick's camp, walked in unmolested, and sought out the heretic. "I've come for a disputation," he said. "Do you want to propose the questions, or shall I?" After completely routing the man, he walked out again and went quietly home.

After a colorful and useful career, Roland died in 1259, in the convent of Bologna. Perhaps no move will ever be made to raise him to the altars, but certainly his learning, his sanctity, and his personality have done a good deal to embellish the early archives of the Order and to establish the spirit for which it is known.

RUDOLPH OF FAENZA
(d. 1259)

Rudolph of Faenza was pastor of the church of St. Nicholas of the Vineyards when Bologna suddenly began to seethe with the excitement caused by the preaching of Reginald of Orleans. Like many another of the local clergy, Rudolph was nonplussed and—he says it himself—a little jealous of the way his flock went hurrying after the preaching of the dynamic friar. Rudolph was more open-minded than some of his confreres on this, but even he could not have foreseen that the time would come, and very soon, when not only his church would go to the friars, but he himself as well.

The church of St. Nicholas of the Vineyards was the property of the family of Diana d'Andalò, the strong-minded beauty who was converted to a devout life by the Dominicans, and who practically forced her father to give them the church and its revenues. The consent of the pastor was needed also for the transaction. Rudolph agreed to give up his church, and further, went himself to Reginald. Like so many talented young men who went to see Reginald, he came away wearing the Dominican habit.

Rudolph occupies a unique position in the Order, not only because he was deeply involved in the transaction which gave the friars their first convent in Bologna, but also because he was to be bursar for a lifetime, and he was always in penance because of his work. He seems to have been given the task, in the first place, because the rest of the brethren felt that, having been a pastor, he must know something about money. He is the only one of the early brethren that we know St. Dominic scolded. They were the closest of friends, and their differences of opinion regarding money never came between them. Yet it was Rudolph who received a penance for "building palaces" when he was given charge of erecting the new convent in Bologna in 1220. On several other occasions, St. Dominic chided him for being too lenient in supplying the wants of the house. Rudolph must indeed have been a man after St. Dominic's own heart, if the only thing he could find to scold him about was over-generosity.

Rudolph, according to tradition, was St. Dominic's confessor, a task for a man both saintly and humble. Once, we are told, St. Dominic came to him with a heavy heart and told him that some of his most promising novices were about to leave the Order because they could not bear its austerity. Rudolph, whose own notions of austerity were obviously more lenient than the founder's, nevertheless comforted him by relating a vision that he himself had enjoyed. In this vision he had seen our Lord and His Blessed Mother. They took him to a river where there was a great ship filled with Dominican friars, and they told him that these friars were going forth to fill and replenish the world.

It is from Rudolph that we learn some of the personal anecdotes of St. Dominic, without which our knowledge of the saint would be incomplete. He tells us, for example, that Dominic would sometimes come home so weary from a day of preaching and arguing with the heretics that, after finishing his frugal meal, he would fall asleep at the table. It is Rudolph, too, who tells us how St. Dominic went about correcting a fault: "If he saw any of the brethren commit a fault, he would act as though he did not notice it at the time, but afterwards, with serene countenance and with gentle speech, he would say, 'Brother, you have done wrong, but now repent.'" Rudolph, as we know, had personal knowledge concerning this.

We wish we knew more of this quiet, self-effacing man who managed— or possibly mismanaged—the purse for so many years, and who was so dear to St. Dominic. What we do gather from the scanty records is the picture of a warmly human and deeply pious man, a loyal friend whom the saint would always find waiting, cheerful and sensible, whenever he returned to Bologna. When he came there for the last time, on that humid sixth of August, in 1221, and the brethren knew that he had come home to die, it was Rudolph who tried to get him to go to bed. It was this faithful friend, also, who attended the dying man and listened so carefully to his words that he could repeat them verbatim at the canonization process.

Rudolph of Faenza died in 1259. He was called "Blessed Rudolph" by many of the early writers of the Order.

BLESSED SADOC AND COMPANIONS, MARTYRS
(d. 1260)

St. Dominic's dreams of converting the Tartars found realization in his sons. Missionaries did, in fact, go to the North during his lifetime, and many more were sent out by Blessed Jordan of Saxony. The more settled tribes of Poland and Hungary readily accepted the Gospel, and the North was not long in blooming with Dominican convents. But, in the thirteenth century, the restless millions of the East were riding down upon the fertile plains of Central Europe. Wild Tartar tribes soon destroyed what had been done for their more peaceful relatives, and scarcely a missionary survived to preach his message of peace to them.

Paul of Hungary and his band of ninety died as martyrs, probably in 1241. They were popularly honored as saints from earliest times. Soon to follow was the group headed by Blessed Sadoc, which had its headquarters at Sandomir, in Poland. So tragic was the early history of the Dominicans in Poland that, even in that martyred country, it is remembered: Polish Dominicans today wear a red cincture to recall the martyred hundreds who shed their blood that Poland might receive the light of faith.

Blessed Sadoc was a student at the University of Bologna when he met St. Dominic and was received into the Order. Being himself a Slav, he was eager to go to the North to preach the word of God. This he was given a chance to do when he and Paul of Hungary were given charge of the northern mission band. He soon accumulated a number of eager young students and novices, and proceeded to Poland with them. On his first night in the mission field, so say the old chronicles, the devil appeared to Sadoc and reproached him for disturbing his work: "And with such children as these," he said bitterly, pointing to the young novices. With such as these, Sadoc did make havoc with the kingdom of evil: he won many souls to God, and, in Sandomir, he soon had the satisfaction of seeing a large community working for the glory of God.

In 1260, the Tartars made a fresh invasion into Poland and attacked Sandomir. Blessed Sadoc and his community had assembled for midnight Matins when they received warning of their approaching death. A novice, reading the martyrology for the following day, was amazed to see, lettered in gold across the pages of the martyrology, the words: "At Sandomir, the passion of forty-nine martyrs." On investigation, it was discovered that it was not merely a novice's mistake, but an actual warning which they understood to be from heaven.

They spent the day in preparation for death. During the singing of the "Salve Regina," after Compline, the Tartars broke into the church and the slaughter began. One novice, terrified at the thought of death, fled to the choir loft to hide, but, hearing his brothers singing, he realized that they were going off to heaven without him, and he returned to the choir to die with the others.

From this martyrdom came the custom of singing the "Salve Regina" at the deathbed of a Dominican—priest, sister, or brother. It is fitting that a life dedicated to God and Our Lady should end thus, with the battle-cry "Hail, Holy Queen!" echoing up from this valley of tears to be joined by the voices of Dominicans in heaven, who can now see forever the clement, loving, and sweet Virgin Mary.

HUGH OF ST. CHER
(d. 1263)

The first Dominican to be made cardinal was Hugh of St. Cher, a man of many talents, besides the one for administration, which qualified him for this position. During the early days of the Order, his influence and his prestige did a great deal to help to establish the friars in the academic world.

Hugh was born before the end of the twelfth century, at St. Cher, in the diocese of Vienne. His parents were noble and wealthy, and they gave him an excellent education with the Benedictines. He was teaching at the University of Paris when he met the Dominicans, and he became interested in their work at the same time that a young student, Humbert of the Romans, decided upon his vocation. Being a professor, Hugh could not leave his work to enter the Order when Humbert did. A few months later, as soon as he could make arrangements with the university authorities, he too received the Dominican habit. That was in February of 1225.

Hugh was a talented and wise religious and, in 1227, he was appointed provincial of France. He was to occupy this position three different times. In 1233, he finished the required years of teaching for his master's degree in theology—the teaching being done under the renowned Dominican, Roland of Cremona.

By this time the question of the reunion of Eastern and Western churches was imminent, and Hugh was one of the many gifted Dominicans who worked on the cause. He began by collecting the various texts of the Bible. He issued a corrected text, with the errors of copyists omitted and a marginal commentary added. The master pattern for the Scriptures was the copy at the Convent of St. Jacques. His next step was to publish a concordance to the Bible—the first ever drawn up. These great steps in Scripture study lessened the distance between East and West and furthered the cause of acquiring accurate texts.

In 1244, Hugh of St. Cher was made a cardinal, with the title of Santa Sabina. He was the first member of the Dominicans to be so honored, and the appointment meant a great deal to the young Order.

One of the less-known works of Hugh of St. Cher was his effort to have established a feast in honor of the Holy Eucharist. While he was provincial of France, he had been told by the nun, St. Juliana, in Liege, of a revelation concerning such a feast. She had received nothing but discouragement from others who knew about her revelation, but Hugh espoused the cause, and he finally prevailed upon the bishop of Liege to establish a diocesan feast. He was called to Rome before anything more could be done. In 1252, Hugh returned to Liege as a cardinal and a papal legate. With the prestige of his office to give weight to his words, he preached ardently and often on the subject of the Eucharistic feast. In 1264, Pope Urban IV, partly due to the urging of the Dominican cardinal, established

the Feast of Corpus Christi and set its celebration on the day chosen by
Hugh of St. Cher, the Thursday after the octave of Pentecost. Making
it quite a Dominican operation, the pope requested St. Thomas Aquinas
to write the Office for the new feast. A later pope, Eugenius IV, granted
to the Dominicans the privilege of holding their processions on the Sunday
within the octave, a mark of distinction which would show the Dominican
origin of the great feast.

Hugh of St. Cher examined and revised the Carmelite rule at the time
of the transfer of the hermits from Mt. Carmel to Aylesford, and is remembered among the Carmelites as a benefactor and great friend.

Hugh of St. Cher died at Orvieto, in 1263, and was buried there. In
the following year, his body, still incorrupt, was transferred to Lyons and
buried there in the Dominican church.

JEROME OF MORAVIA
(d. 1264)

An early and very skilled master of music in the Order was Jerome of
Moravia, who, presumably, taught music in the Studium of Paris in 1255,
and who wrote down for the use of future teachers the rules necessary
for mastery of the subject.

Jerome was a Bohemian by birth, but when he was born or when he
entered the Order we do not know. We can only deduce the facts of his
life from the works he left. Music formed one of the subjects of the "quad-
rivium" in the education of that time, and his effort in transcribing the
known music theories to written copy may have been a part of the attempt
at standardizing the liturgy under Blessed Humbert. The theory in his
book is not entirely original, and he notes himself that the work is a
compilation, meant to "simplify and summarize" in textbook form, such
rules of composition, aesthetics, and liturgical chant as might be found
useful in teaching the brethren.

The book, a copy of which was chained in the Sorbonne chapel, in 1270,
as the norm by which the music of Paris should be evaluated, shows a
wide range of knowledge and a capable grasp of the field of medieval
music. He discusses both plain chant and measured music for several voices,
descant, motets, polyphony, and instrumental music; he gives advice to bell-
founders on the casting of bells, on the art of keeping bells and clocks

true, and suggests which metals to use and how to get overtones. He gives instruction for the fingering and bowing of instruments, but says nothing at all about the organ; this omission of any comments on either building or playing the organ is curious, considering how much he has to say of other instruments. He himself seems to have played the violin, or an instrument very similar to a violin.

Whereas Guido d'Arezzo wrote for children, Jerome wrote for adults, and consequently his book includes all the philosophical aspects of music that would interest scholastics. It is evident that he had studied Arabic authors and understood their theories of music as related to mathematics, and that he was thoroughly familiar with Aristotle.

Jerome thinks that the "O Lumen" should not be in the sixth mode, an obscure argument of interest only to music specialists, but it indicates the early use of the antiphon in the Order. He graded music in two directions: good, more beautiful, most beautiful; bad, worse, awful (*turpissimus*). In his chapter of advice for choir directors, he speaks authoritatively of head tones and chest tones, advising that they not be mixed.

From the study of his writings, it is possible to place Jerome of Moravia in the last half of the thirteenth century, but no definite dates can be established. That he was the acknowledged authority of the times can hardly be questioned. Researchers have assigned the years 1255-1264 as those in which he most probably compiled his music text. Possibly in the years to come, more information will be forthcoming on this interesting pioneer in a great tradition.

BLESSED GILES OF SANTAREM
(1190-1265)

The story of Blessed Giles has been so colored with romantic legends that it is nearly impossible to obtain a true picture of the man. His life, even stripped of its legend, is the story of the triumph of grace in the human soul.

Giles was born near Coimbra, in Portugal, and was from his childhood destined by his parents for the priesthood. He was ordained at an early age, but with no good intention, for he saw in the priesthood only a chance for power. His father's influence gained for him a number of rich benefices which he used sinfully for power and pleasure. Being a brilliant student, he advanced rapidly in his chosen field of medicine, an art which was at the time often linked with black magic. He neglected his priestly duties and seemed bent only on the pleasures of this life.

Legend takes up the story from here and relates that Giles, a thoroughly irreligious and pleasure-loving young man, set out for Paris to work for higher degrees in medicine and magic. According to one legend, he met the devil on the way to Paris, and signed a contract with Satan, in which he promised his soul in return for a universal knowledge of medicine. Thereupon he spent seven years in bondage to his evil master, learning all his arts. Having gained the highest degrees in medicine, Giles was at the peak of worldly success when he was treated to a horrible vision. He saw himself in the cemetery of a monastery of which he enjoyed the revenues. There he saw a specter who carried a skull and an hourglass. The specter knocked at one and then another of the tombs, calling out, "Arise, unfaithful monk!" At each summons another fearful specter appeared, until at one tomb there was no answer. "Giles!" he called. "What—not there?" He poised the hourglass and murmured, "There are yet a few sands to run!" After this fearful vision, says the legend, Giles repented of his misspent life, and set out in haste for Coimbra. At Palencia he met the friars of the newly founded Order of Preachers, and they helped him to make his peace with God. Joining them, he spent seven years in terrible penance, after which Our Lady returned to him the fateful scroll he had signed with Satan.

Such a legend adds color to the calendar of the saints, but it would be hard to tell how much of it is true. It is known that Giles had spent his youth badly, and that after entering the Order he did great penance. By nature he was witty and charming, and he found the silence hard to keep. Actual violence to his natural disposition was necessary to make him into the humble and reserved religious he afterwards became.

Blessed Giles occupied several positions of authority in the Order, and his medical skill proved a blessing in the care of the sick brethren. He made a practice of going about the dormitories, cleaning up the students' rooms while they were at class. His heroic penance did much to undo the scandal he had caused in his early years. He was sent back to Portugal after his early training in the Order, and his preaching was noteworthy, even in that age of great preachers. He founded a number of convents and did much to establish the Order in his own country. His last years were filled with visions and ecstasies. He lived to be very old, regarded by all but himself as a very great saint.

VINCENT OF BEAUVAIS
(1265)

Vincent of Beauvais was not the only Dominican who wrote extensively and authoritatively on the sum total of knowledge up to his time; it was a popular ambition during the thirteenth century to compile all this body of information and synthesize it into an orderly whole. But he was one of the first actually to attempt the gigantic task, and his work was so famous in its day and since that he merits attention as one of the builders of science and universal knowledge.

Vincent, like most medievalists, is hidden behind his work. We do not know when he was born, or where, though he was probably a Frenchman. He studied theology at Paris, and most probably entered the Order there. The only date we know for certain in connection with him is 1250, the date when he was writing his *Speculum,* or *Mirror of Knowledge.*

This work is a compilation roughly equivalent to an encyclopedia. It quotes no less than two thousand authors, stating the accomplishments of man to date, and tries to place them in relation to God. In preparing it, Vincent read and digested everything that had been written up to that time in Greek, Arabic, and Hebrew, as well as Latin. He was familiar with the use of Arabic numerals, which suggests that he was one of the first in the West to use them—a daring innovation at a time when anything of Arabic origin was suspect.

His book, or work, is roughly divided into four parts. Since it rapidly became a standard work and was copied and recopied for several centuries, it is not surprising that some alterations crept in. Scholars are now fairly certain that the fourth book is not his, but the work of someone writing later.

Part One treats of the Trinity in relation to the creation of the angels, and of light, color, and the four elements. He discusses the phenomena of heavenly bodies and their movements, and fire, rain, thunder, and wind. In his comments on the sea and the dry land, he displays a good knowledge of metals and gems, of agricultural practices, and the medicinal use of plants. He also includes household hints on gardening and cooking, and a bit of elementary budgeting.

Book Two begins with astronomy and goes on to discuss fowls and fishes, animals—wild and domesticated—and man's use of these. Book Three is doctrinal; it includes a summary of the scholastic knowledge of the age; definitions of philosophy; a Latin vocabulary; grammar, logic, rhetoric and poetry; then it proceeds to politics, medicine, physics, and mathematics, and finishes with mythology. He gives a history of the world to 1250, and apologizes for bogging down on the names of the English kings in the eighth century because, he says, his sources failed.

The title which Vincent used—the *Mirror of Nature;* the *Mirror of Doctrine;* the *Mirror of History;*—give a hint of his object, which was to relate all earthly science and development to God's plan for us.

Of Vincent himself we know practically nothing, though certainly one can tell from his work that he was a man of almost universal knowledge. He may have been the Vincent who was subprior of Beauvais in 1240; or he may have been bishop of the city. It is fairly sure that he was professor of theology at the French court. He was, apparently, just too busy to keep any personal records, and was too well-known for any of his contemporaries to keep statistics. As far as we know, he died in 1265. Whereas Vincent, the man, has managed to disappear into complete obscurity (he may have done it deliberately) Vincent, the author of the *Speculum,* has earned a lasting place in the history of man's search for knowledge.

BLESSED BARTHOLOMEW OF BREGANZA
(1201-1270)

Born of the family of the Counts of Breganza, in Lombardy, Bartholomew was sent, while still very young, to the University of Padua. He was an outstanding student and soon gained a reputation for both scholarship and sanctity. It was during his stay at the university that he met St. Dominic, and from him received the habit of the new Order which was just beginning to attract a great deal of attention in the schools. He made a fervent novitiate and continued his studies at Vicenza and Padua.

Shortly after his ordination, Bartholomew was sent to preach against heresy in the cities of Lombardy, and to make peace among the warring factions that were laying waste to the country. To this end, he founded a new military congregation. He preached so successfully in this difficult mission that he was called to Rome, and the pope appointed him master of the sacred palace. He was one of the first after St. Dominic to hold this traditionally Dominican office of the pope's theologian.

Soon after this Bartholomew was appointed bishop of a diocese on the Island of Cyprus. He journeyed there in company with St. Louis, king of France, who was on a crusade to the Holy Land. He had barely begun the administration of his diocese when he was called to Palestine by the saintly king. He was employed in many services for the king, and, because of his great assistance, was promised several valuable relics when Louis should return to France.

After some time as bishop on the Island of Cyprus, Bartholomew was appointed bishop of Vicenza. Here his first care was to suitably enshrine the relics given him by St. Louis. Under his direction was built the magnificent Church of the Crown to house these precious treasures—a relic of the true Cross and a thorn from our Lord's crown. He restored churches and rebuilt the city which had been destroyed by civil wars.

Equal to the devastation of the ruined cities was the harm done in his diocese by heresy. He set about repairing the damage and brought back many of the chief heretics to the fold. He was a peacemaker and a builder, and had to resist firmly the suggestions of the grateful people that he take over the temporal rule of the city as well as the spiritual care.

Blessed Bartholomew was present at the second translation of the relics of St. Dominic, and he was chosen to speak on the occasion.

HELEN OF HUNGARY
(d. 1270)

Helen of Hungary has a double claim on our interest; she was the first stigmatist of the Order, and she was the novice mistress of St. Margaret of Hungary.

There were several nuns named Helen at the same monastery; the one with whom we are concerned was the first of these, and had already a reputation for sanctity when Margaret entered the community. Indeed, it is probably to this reputation that we are indebted for our saint, as her parents were doubtless influenced by it when seeking a place for the education of their child.

The monastery of Vesprim was founded by Paul of Hungary in 1222. It was still in its primitive fervor when Helen entered there and joined wholeheartedly in the spirit of penance and prayer for which it was so well renowned. She had a true gift for contemplative prayer and was sometimes rapt in ecstasy. At times, God gave visible signs of her sanctity, some of which were not always understood by her companions. Once, as she prayed alone, the crucifix on the wall took on a look of life, and Christ reached down to place His hand in hers. A sister, who had been watching to see what would happen, ran to get the superior. Helen was in ecstasy for twenty-four hours, during which time everyone in the house tried to pry her hand loose from the hand of the corpus on the crucifix. No one succeeded. Another time, the large crucifix came down from the altar when she was praying, and it remained suspended in the air over her head until—at the completion of her prayer—she replaced it herself on the altar.

The principal grace—and trial—of Helen's life was the impression of the sacred wounds of our Lord. She had a special devotion to St. Francis of Assisi, the first stigmatist recorded in the Church. On his feast day, she was praying that God would give her some of Francis' intense love for heavenly things, and suddenly she was rapt in ecstasy. Her right hand began to glitter and sparkle and give off great rays of light; in the center of the palm appeared a circle of bright gold, and from this grew up a lily of dazzling brightness. The sisters watched with amazement as she remained long in ecstasy. When she regained consciousness, she prayed that God would not let the wound be visible. However, it and the wound in her left hand, which appeared some time later, were visible for many years. Only a short time before her death did they disappear.

Helen's stigmata seem to have been unique in several ways. We have no details of her receiving the wounds of feet and side, but she had all of them at some time. Seventeen years after her death, when the tomb was opened, the wound in her side, which had been closed for some time before her death, opened of itself, and rays of light shone from it. The rays of light and, even more so, the magnificent lilies of light that grew out of the wounds when she was in prayer, seem to have no counterpart in any of the other cases of stigmatization of which we have records.

In her ordinary life in the monastery, Helen was dearly loved. She was novice mistress for a time, and prioress for her last several years. She strained every effort that her monastery should remain as it had been established, a house of perfect observance and of great penance. However, this did not preclude many charming miracles of everyday life which time has attached to her name. The sisters were accustomed to see her raised in the air when she prayed. Once, all the candles lighted by themselves as she passed by the altar. There are also the "homelike" anecdotes: of her rare gift for growing plants, for in that northern land houseplants would be dear and easily damaged. Helen could (and did) merely touch a withered plant, and it would revive and bloom. One day a laysister came to her in tears; she had a little goat—a pet—and it had died. Helen went out and picked up the little animal, and it immediately sprang up, alive and active, to rejoice the heart of the laysister.

Helen was novice mistress when the king and queen of Hungary came with their four-year-old daughter to dedicate her to God. It was probably not an enviable task, being novice mistress for the princess. Helen, as we can see from the life of Margaret, did very well by her small charge.

Margaret was a favorite, and it was with a real wrench of detachment that her sisters saw her go to the new monastery her father had built under the sheltering walls of Budapest. (The monastery of Vesprim was exposed to danger on every side and was raided at least once by the Tartars.)

Helen lived for thirty years after Margaret went to her new monastery. Her life was a continued exercise of prayer and penance. After long years of praying that the stigmata would become invisible and spare her the embarrassment of publicity, they finally disappeared. Shortly afterwards, Sister Helen became seriously ill and knew that her death was near. At the moment of her death, in 1270, she was rapt in ecstasy and so radiant at the prospect of seeing God that the sisters could hardly tell that she was dead.

Helen of Hungary has long been called "Blessed" in popular terminology. She enjoys a local cult, and her cause is one which may be advanced in the next few years.

ST. MARGARET OF HUNGARY
(1242-1271)

Margaret, the daughter of King Bela IV of Hungary, was offered to God before her birth, in petition that the country would be delivered from the terrible scourge of the Tartars. The prayer having been answered, the king and queen made good their promise by placing the little girl in the Dominican convent at Vesprim. Margaret was three years old. Here, in company with other children of the nobility, she was trained in the arts thought fitting for royalty.

Margaret was not content with simply living in the house of God; she demanded the religious habit—and received it—at the age of four. Furthermore, she took upon herself the austerities practiced by the other sisters—fasting, hairshirts, the discipline, and night vigils. She soon learned the Divine Office by heart and chanted it happily to herself as she went about her play. No one but Margaret seemed to take seriously the idea that she would one day make profession and remain as a sister, for it would be of great advantage to her father if she were to make a wise marriage.

This question arose seriously when Margaret was twelve. She responded in surprise. She said that she had been dedicated to God, even before her birth, and that she intended to remain faithful to that promise. To settle the matter, she pronounced her vows to the master general of the Order, Humbert of the Romans. Again, when Margaret was eighteen, her father made an attempt to swerve her from her purpose, because the king of Bohemia had come seeking her hand. He even obtained a dispensation from the pope and approached Margaret with the permission. Margaret replied as she had previously, "I esteem infinitely more the King of Heaven and the inconceivable happiness of possessing Jesus Christ than the crown offered me by the king of Bohemia." Having established that she was not interested in any throne but a heavenly one, she proceeded with great joy to live an even more fervent religious life than she had before.

Margaret's royal parentage was, of course, a matter of discussion in the convent, but the princess managed to turn such conversation away from herself to the holy lives of the saints who were related to her by blood—St. Stephen, the king, St. Hedwig, St. Elizabeth of Hungary, and several others. She did not glory in her wealth or parentage, but strove to imitate the saints in their holiness. She took her turn in the kitchen and laundry, seeking by choice much heavy work that her rank might have excused her from doing. She was especially welcome in the infirmary, which proves that she was not a sad-faced saint, and she made it her special duty to care for those who were too disagreeable for anyone else to tend.

Margaret's austerities seem excessive to us of a weaker age. The mysteries of the Passion were very real to her and gave reason for her long fasts, severe scourgings, and other mortifications. She had a tender devotion to Our Lady, and on the eve of her feasts, Margaret said a thousand Aves.

Unable to make the long pilgrimage to the Holy Land, to Rome, or to any of the other famous shrines of Christendom, the saint developed a plan by which she could go in spirit: she counted up the miles that lay between herself and the desired shrine, and then said an Ave for every mile there and back. On Good Friday she was so overcome at the thoughts of our Lord's passion that she wept all day. She was frequently in ecstasy, and very embarrassed if anyone found her so and remarked on her holiness.

A number of miracles were performed during Margaret's lifetime and many more after her death. The island where her convent stood, called at first the "Blessed Virgin's Isle," was called "Isle of Margaret" after the saint. She is invoked against floods, in memory of a miracle she performed in stopping a flood on the Danube.

ST. THOMAS AQUINAS
(1225-1274)

Thomas the Apostle challenged the story that the Lord was risen, and his unbelief brought forth a glowing testimony of the reality of the Resurrection. Twelve centuries later, his namesake, Thomas of Aquino, questioned—without doubting—the great truths of faith, and demonstrated for all time the relationship of faith and reason. As the first Thomas found by experiment ("Except I shall see in His hands the print of the nails, and put my finger into the place of the nails, and put my hand into His side") that the Man who stood in the midst of them was none other than Jesus Christ, so Thomas, the Angelic Doctor, proved for all time that there is no quarrel between reason and revelation.

Thomas, son of the count of Aquino, was first trained at the Benedictine abbey of Montecassino, and here, even in childhood, his great mind was wrestling with theological problems. His passion for truth is expressed in his constant question, "Master, tell me—what is God?" Better to train the boy's mind, his father sent him at an early age to the University of Naples. Here he studied under Peter of Ireland and, undisturbed by the noise and wickedness of the great university city, proceeded rapidly on his quest for God. Meeting the Dominicans, he was strongly attracted by their apostolic life and petitioned to be received as one of them. While recognizing the gifts of the young student, the friars refused him admittance to the Order until he was eighteen. Acting deliberately, without a backward glance at the power and wealth he was leaving, Thomas, at eighteen, joyfully put on the habit of the new Order.

Like many a gifted young man, Thomas was bitterly opposed by his family when he attempted to become a religious. Both threats and persuasion failing, he was kidnaped by his brothers and locked in a tower for more than a year. His sisters were sent in to influence him, and he proceeded to convert them to his own way of thinking. A woman was sent in to tempt him; he drove her from the room with a burning brand from the fire; afterwards, angels came to gird him with the cincture of perpetual chastity. The captivity having failed to break the determination, his brothers relaxed their guard, and Thomas, with the help of his sisters, escaped from the tower and hurried back to his convent.

Given the finest education that his time could offer, Thomas studied first at Cologne, later at Paris, under Master Albert the Great. This outstanding

Dominican teacher and saint became his lifelong friend and loyal defender. They taught together at Cologne and became a mutual influence for good in one of the most beautiful friendships in Dominican history.

For the rest of his life, Thomas was to teach and preach with scarcely a day of rest. He traveled continually, which makes all the more remarkable the amount of writing he did. Death found him in a familiar place—on the road—where he was bound for the Council of Lyons in obedience to the pope's command. He died at the Cistercian abbey of Fossanova, in a borrowed bed—obscurity hardly fitting the intellectual light of the Order, but perfectly suited to the humble friar that Thomas had always been.

Overheard in a colloquy with the Master he served so well, with heart and mind and pen, Thomas was heard to ask as his reward, "Thyself, O Lord, none but Thyself!"

ST. RAYMOND OF PENNAFORT
(1175-1275)

St. Raymond of Pennafort is one of the Order's best examples of the quiet humility of sanctity and of the eternal youth of the Dominican ideal. Holy Church remembers him forever as a model of confessors and as a champion of law and order. But to his brothers and sisters in religion he is also patron of those faithful religious who work quietly on and on and on, years after they might have claimed the right to retire from active service, giving to God, if not their first labors, at least their last.

The life of Raymond of Pennafort spanned a century, the last half of which he spent in the Order. Elected master general of the Order, he was forced by ill health to resign in two years' time. For the remaining thirty years of his life he lived in prayerful obscurity, giving to others the fruits of his contemplation and his labors.

Of Raymond's childhood we know little. The talented son of the count of Pennafort, in Catalonia, he was at an early age sent to the cathedral school at Barcelona. Completing his education at Bologna, he soon became celebrated as a professor of canon law at the university. Here he met the Dominicans, who were beginning to attract to their ranks so many talented young men, among whom were some of Raymond's students and fellow professors. On a journey to Barcelona, he met St. Dominic. The year after the death of the founder, he was himself enrolled as one of the preachers. So greatly was Raymond revered in his university world that his entry into the

Order caused a new tidal wave of vocations to the preaching friars; among the aspirants were two bishops and several noted professors. Claro, Moneta, and Roland of Cremona had caused astonishment by their renunciation of worldly honors on entering the Order, but Raymond's profession caused even greater excitement in an already inflamed city.

Master Raymond, son of the count of Pennafort and renowned doctor of canon law, was forty-seven years of age when he donned the white habit and started as a novice to live according to a new mode of life. With the simplicity of the truly great, he fell into step with his companions and took up the work of the friars. With St. Peter Nolasco, he was cofounder of the Order of Our Lady of Ransom (for the redemption of Christian captives), a project which was carried out within a year after his profession.

Given the huge task of compiling the Decretals, Raymond did his work so thoroughly that it remains, after a period of nearly seven centuries of rapid change, a monumental tribute to his learning. He also put in permanent form the Dominican Constitutions, a document from which many democratic codes have borrowed copiously.

Elected master general on the death of Blessed Jordan of Saxony, Raymond did much for both the prestige and the striking force of the Order. He envisioned the conquest of the East by learning, as kings dreamed of conquering it by arms. To this end, he established schools in which Dominicans were trained in the languages of the East. Later, with his encouragement, St. Thomas wrote his *Summa Contra Gentiles*. Raymond had himself preached a crusade against the Moors, and his experience with the Order of Ransom gave him deep insight into the problem of converting the Eastern peoples. Begging to be released from his office because of age and infirmity, Raymond resigned after two years of intensive activity. The Fathers who accepted his resignation were severely penanced for having given up their saintly master.

It is as a wise and holy confessor that Raymond is best remembered in the Church. He was appointed, at different times, as confessor to the pope and king, and as papal penitentiary he pronounced on difficult cases of conscience. He wrote various works for the guidance of confessors and canonists, and in art he is pictured holding a key, the symbol of confession.

BLESSED INNOCENT V
(1225-1276)

Peter of Tarentaise was one of the boy-novices admitted to the Order by Blessed Jordan of Saxony. (Some of the older members of the community raised strong objections to these novices because of their youth.) He was, in fact, barely ten years old, and had been sent to Paris to study. He shared with St. Thomas Aquinas, Blessed Ambrose of Siena, and other lights of the century, the masterly teaching of St. Albert the Great.

Having received the necessary degrees, he taught for some years at Paris, where he contributed a great deal to the Order's reputation for learning. He wrote a number of commentaries on Holy Scripture, but he devoted most of his time to the classroom. As provincial of France, he began the long years of responsibility in the various offices he was to hold in his lifetime. Twice provincial, he was chosen archbishop of Lyons and administered the affairs of the diocese for some time, though he was never actually consecrated for that See.

Peter was appointed cardinal-bishop of Ostia, and with the great Franciscan, St. Bonaventure, assumed much of the labor of that Council of Lyons to which St. Thomas Aquinas was hastening when death overtook him. To the problems of clergy reform and the healing of the Greek schism the two gifted friars devoted their finest talents. Before the council was over, Bonaventure died, and Peter of Tarentaise preached the funeral sermon.

In January, 1276, Pope Gregory X died. The conclave was held in the following month, and Peter of Tarentaise received every vote except his own. With a sad heart, he left the seclusion of his religious home to ascend the Fisherman's Throne as Pope Innocent V.

The reign of the new pope, which promised so much to a harrassed people, was to be very brief. But, imbued with the spirit of the early apostles, he crowded a lifetime into the short space given him. He instigated a new crusade against the Saracens and began reforms in the matter of regular observance. He actually succeeded in solving many of the questions of the Greek schism and in establishing a short-lived truce. He restored the custom of personally assisting at choral functions with the canons of the Lateran, and he inspired all with the love which animated his own heart.

Had the measures begun by Innocent V had time to be fully carried out, he might have accomplished great good for the Church; he did at least open the way for those who were to follow him. Death stopped the hand of the zealous pope when he had reigned only five months. Like his friends, St. Thomas and St. Bonaventure, he was untouched by the honors and dignity with which he had been favored, and death found him exactly what he had been for more than forty years—a simple and humble friar.

His cult was confirmed by Pope Leo XIII in 1898.

BERNARD OF MORLAAS
(1277)

The story of Bernard of Morlaas has for so long enjoyed a place in popular legend that it is difficult to convince anybody that there was ever a real person by that name, or that he has for centuries been popularly honored as "Blessed."

The date given for Bernard's death is 1277, but this is only approximate. Some say that he was married, and had renounced the married state to enter religious life at the counsel of Blessed Giles of Portugal. It is also said that he was born of a noble family and had had a good education before entering the convent of the friars at Santarem.

It is presumed from the legend that Bernard was assigned to teach letters to the smaller children in what must have been a sort of orphanage or boarding school. Today we have no such apostolate for the members of the First Order; perhaps it was an early experiment in education.

The legend itself is consistent enough, as it invariably mentions the same details. Father Bernard, who was very fond of the children, had two friends among the small boys who always sought him out to recite their lessons to him. They were allowed to serve his Masses; if he were busy with other work, they would go into the chapel to study their lessons.

One day, as they finished their lessons and took out their lunchboxes, one of them looked up at the statue of Our Lady, which stood over the high altar. "The little Jesus has no lunch with Him," said the child. "Let's ask Him to share ours." So, the legend relates, the Christ Child came down from His Mother's arms and shared the little boys' lunch.

This went on for several days before the children got around to telling Father Bernard about it. He suggested that the next time they invited their small Heavenly Guest they remind Him that some day He must, in return, invite them to His Father's table. And, of course, the children could not go without their master, Father Bernard.

The little boys carried out his suggestion, and the Holy Infant invited them to come to His Father's house on the following day. Bernard and the children prepared well for Mass the next morning, and Bernard told his confessor about it. The confessor, understandably enough, was skeptical.

After Mass, as the priest and the two small servers knelt for their thanksgiving, the Christ Child came to conduct them to His Father's house. The confessor, coming to see how things were getting along, found that all three of them were dead, kneeling upright at the altar.

The three were buried in one tomb in the chapel and were regarded as saints by the inhabitants of Santarem. It was a story that had much popular appeal, and shortly there was a thriving cult. A large ornate tomb, with statues on it, was erected, telling the story of the legend. These legends grew with the years until people began to feel that the whole thing was the invention of a pious mind.

However, in the year 1577, which was approximately three hundred years after the event, the fathers of Santarem were making repairs on the convent and had occasion to open a door in the vault. Discovering a damaged tomb, they looked in. There were the relics of a man and two small boys, all wrapped in a shroud that—in spite of its age and the conditions—was immaculately white. Fresh impetus was given to the devotion, and the whole story was revived.

The people of the little town of Morlaas, who claim Bernard as one of their citizens, are particularly fond of the story and anxious to see him raised to the altar.

HUMBERT OF THE ROMANS
(1193-1277)

The contribution of Humbert of the Romans to Dominican life can never be overestimated. While he has never been formally beatified, he has been given the popular title of "Blessed" since his death. In all our research on the foundation of the Order and the clarification of its rule and constitutions, we find his name and the sure touch of his saintly and logical mind.

Humbert of the Romans was a Frenchman, born at Romans, in Dauphine, in 1193. He came of a large family, several of whom became religious; one of them was a Carthusian. He met the Dominicans at the University of Paris, where he was teaching on the faculty of arts and studying theology, in 1224. There is a charming legend concerning his choice of a vocation to the Dominicans which should be repeated. He was kneeling one day in the cathedral of Notre Dame, assisting at the Office of the Dead that the canons were chanting. His mind kept wandering to the choice of a vocation, for his family had been friendly with the Carthusians for many years, and his brother had already joined them. As he debated within himself, an old priest wandered down from the choir and engaged him in quiet conversation. He asked Humbert where he was from, and Humbert replied that he was a parishioner. The old priest regarded him shrewdly and said, "Do you remember what you promised at your baptism—to renounce the devil and all his pomps? Why don't you become a Friar Preacher?" Humbert could not keep his mind off the priest's words, and at the responsory for the lesson, "Where shall I fly if not to You?", he decided once and for all that he would become a friar. He went to consult with his professor of theology, Hugh of St. Cher, who was planning to become a Dominican himself as soon as he could arrange his affairs. On the feast of St. Andrew, Humbert knelt at the feet of Blessed Jordan of Saxony and asked for the habit of the Friars Preachers.

The first task of the new brother was teaching at Lyons. His profound knowledge of Scripture recommended him for the highest teaching posts in the Order. In 1240, when he was elected provincial of Lombardy, he began his administrative career.

From that time until his death, in 1277, there was scarcely an event of any importance to the Order in which he did not play a part. As provincial of France, from 1244 to 1254, he worked steadily to stabilize relations of the Order and the university, perhaps foreseeing that there would one day be a showdown between the two great forces there. He was offered the patriarchate of Jerusalem, which he refused, and at the election of Gregory IX he received nearly enough votes to be elected pope.

Humbert was a careful canonist, and he carried around a master copy of the Dominican Constitutions in order that a copy could be made in the various houses. In his time the Order had begun to feel the need for uniformity more than ever before, for its members were spreading to the far parts of the earth, and local regulations differed. This was nowhere more clearly seen than in the liturgy, which differed not only with each diocese but with each basilica. When the brethren of various provinces got together for a general chapter, it was harrowing to try to chant the office. Humbert, along with several others, was appointed to begin work on a unification of the liturgy, even before he became master general in 1254. After his election to the generalate, he intensified his efforts in this behalf.

Most of the regulations of the liturgy that have come down to us are in the words of Humbert. His principal contribution, as nearly as we can tell after all this time, was the unification of the liturgy. He set up a norm and insisted that all the varying elements conform to it, apologizing to the brethren very meekly for the fact that some of them would be disappointed in the forms chosen ("since one cannot please everyone"). Many distinguishing features of the Dominican Mass can trace their definite form to this talented and sincere man who devoted his great energies to the quiet task of building a structure that would wear through the centuries. The dignity and clarity of the Dominican Constitutions likewise owe a debt to this man who wrote so clearly and unequivocally of the spirit which Dominic had left to his children, and which was in Humbert's day just being recorded for posterity.

Humbert of the Romans died in his native city in 1277.

THE MARTYRS OF URGEL
(1242-1277)

Pons of Planedis, Bernard of Traversa, and Peter of Cadireta were the first martyrs of the province of Spain. All were martyred at different times in the same general region, the Catalan province in the north of Spain. They were among the first Dominicans appointed to the office of inquisitors in the Spanish lands. The appointment was made in 1232, eleven years after the death of St. Dominic.

Pons of Planedis was a Catalan, born at Moya, in the diocese of Vich. He received the habit at Barcelona, when the convent was first established there, and was prior at the convent of Lerida, in 1230, when Pope Gregory IX began to organize the inquisition in Spain, at the request of James of Aragon. Cathari and Waldensians had crossed the Pyrenees and were firmly established in Catalonia. They flourished in mountain strongholds along the French border, and had become a real menace to the Church of Spain. Pons was appointed inquisitor in 1232, with the office of searching out heretics and examining their doctrines. Carrying out this office in the territory of the heretic, Count de Foix, was a dangerous and discouraging business, but he carried on until he was ambushed and killed by the heretics in 1242. He was first poisoned, then savagely strangled.

In reprisal for the murder, the heretic fortress of Castelbo was razed to the ground, and the whole province was in arms. The bishop ordered that the body of the martyred inquisitor be brought to the cathedral of Urgel for burial. On the long journey this necessitated, the cortege was caught out one late afternoon, miles from any shelter, with the unhappy prospect of spending the night in the open, at the mercy of the heretics. They prayed to Pons of Planedis to help them out of the difficulty, and, according to legend, the sun did not set for hours, giving them bright daylight to complete their trip. Pons is buried in the cathedral of Urgel, where a picture shows him holding in one hand a glass of poison and in the other a shining sun. The relics were viewed in 1598, at which time they were in an almost perfect state of preservation.

His successor in the office of inquisitor was Bernard of Traversa, who was born in the mountains near the little kingdom of Andorra, and had entered the Order at Toulouse. He was a fervent preacher and renowned for the holiness of his life. He too was ambushed and killed, after long tortures by the heretics, and soon joined his predecessor in the cathedral of Urgel.

Peter of Cadireta became inquisitor in 1258. He was also a Catalan, born in Moya, and had been a companion of St. Raymond of Pennafort in Barcelona. Raymond had been especially interested in the conversion of the Moors and other infidels, and to this end founded a school of Eastern languages to train future apostles in Hebrew, Arabic, and other oriental cultures. One of the young students who gave most promise was Peter of Cadireta, and Raymond could not have been too happy when his prize pupil was sent into a position which almost guaranteed an early martyrdom.

Peter was to have the longest career of the three; he worked for twenty years before they caught him and killed him. He was stoned to death in 1277, and was laid beside his two predecessors in the cathedral, although by this time there was a Dominican convent in Urgel, of which he had been the prior.

The decree for opening the cause of these three martyrs, by way of Immemorial Cult, was published in 1915.

BLESSED ALBERT OF BERGAMO
(1214-1279)

Albert was born in the fertile valley of Serriano, in Bergamo. His father was a farmer, industrious and prayerful, and he taught his young son many practices of penance and piety which later fructified in a saintly life. At the age of seven, Albert was fasting three days a week, giving the food to the poor. Working at the heavy labor of the fields, he learned to see God in all things, and to listen for His voice in all nature. The beauty of the earth was to him a voice that spoke only of heaven. He grew up pure of heart, discreet, and humble—the edification of the entire village.

Albert married quite young, and at first his wife made no objection to his great charity and self-denial. When his father died, however, she made haste to assail his every act and word, and made his home almost unbearable with her scolding. "You give too much time to prayer and to the poor!" she charged; Albert only replied that God will return all gifts made to the poor. In testimony of this, God miraculously restored the meal Albert had given away over his wife's protests. Finally, softened by Albert's prayers, she ceased her scolding and became his rival in piety and charity. She died soon after this, and Albert, now free, gave away his farm and set out to visit the holy places of Jerusalem and Rome.

Stopping at Cremona in harvest time, Albert went to work in the fields. He soon earned the name of "the diligent worker." His guardian angel worked beside him in the fields, and, therefore, twice the work was accomplished that might be expected of one man. Weighing in his grain at the end of the day, Albert always received twice as much in wages as the other workers did. Though he gave this to the poor and kept nothing for himself, jealous companions determined to annoy him. Planting pieces of iron in the field where Albert would be working next day, they watched to see him break or dull his scythe. Miraculously, the scythe cut through iron as it did through grain, never suffering any harm.

Albert went, in all, nine times to Rome, eight times to St. James of Compostela, and once to Jerusalem. He worked his way, giving to the poor every penny he could spare. His pilgrimages were almost unbroken prayer; he walked along singing hymns and chanting psalms, or conversing on things of God with the persons he met.

Appalled at the suffering of the pilgrims who fell ill far from home and the penniless, Albert determined to build a hospital for their use. This he actually accomplished by his prayers and diligent work. In 1256, he met the Dominicans and became a Tertiary, continuing his great works of charity in his new state. He assisted the Dominican fathers in Cremona, working happily in their garden, cultivating the medicinal herbs so necessary at the time, and doing cheerfully all the work he could find that was both heavy and humble.

Falling very ill, Albert sent a neighbor for the priest, but there was a long delay, and a dove came bringing him Holy Viaticum. When he died, the bells of Cremona rang of themselves, and people of all classes hurried to view the precious remains. It was planned to bury him in the common cemetery, outside the cloister, as he was a secular Tertiary, but no spade could be found to break the ground. An unused tomb was discovered in the church of St. Mathias, where he had so often prayed, and he was buried there.

BLESSEDS DOMINIC AND GREGORY
(13th Century)

One can only suppose that Blesseds Dominic and Gregory lived very holy lives, since they have been beatified; but that fact alone is practically all that we know about them.

There is not one single date to identify these two preachers. Legend assures us that they lived and worked in Moorish Spain in the mid-thirteenth century. One infers that they were Spaniards, and tradition has it that they had preached for some time in the mountainous country of southern Spain. One day, when on their apostolic journeys from one mountain village to another, they took refuge from a storm in a large cave. The storm loosened the rocks of the cave, and a landslide buried them in the cave. The bells of the town rang loudly of themselves, indicating that something remarkable was afoot, and villagers, who ventured out after the storm, found the cave surrounded by lights and angelic music. Digging into the rubble, they found the two Dominicans crushed to death.

Wonders attended the burial and the tomb of the two Blesseds. Candles were lighted around the tomb, and people came there to pray, especially against the danger from storms. On Rogation days, and at any time of drought, the relics were carried in procession. The immemorial cult was given formal recognition by Pope Pius IX in 1854.

ST. ALBERT THE GREAT
(1207-1280)

Today in Cologne, the spires of a building begun seven centuries ago still point to heaven. It is only a legend that credits the design of this cathedral to St. Albert the Great. But it is so typical of his own life, pointing all beauty to heaven, that it is a legend very easy to believe. Albert—whom even secular history calls "the Great"—spent his life in teaching that science and faith have no quarrel, and that all earthly loveliness and order can be traced directly to God.

Albert was born in Lauingen, in Swabia, around 1207. His keen observation, which was later to show itself in his scientific works, had its initial training in the woods near his father's castle, where he and his brother, Henry—who also became a Dominican—hunted with hawks and hounds, and became experts in falconry. Sent for further studies to the University of Padua, which was queen of the natural sciences, as Paris was of theology, and Bologna of law, Albert delved happily into new fields of science. He found many new things at Padua, but his greatest find was a fellow German, Jordan of Saxony, who captured his heart for the new Order of Friars Preachers. He was received into the Order, probably in 1223.

A legend is told of this period which serves to bring out both the greatness of Albert's science and his love for Our Lady. Albert, it is related, had not worn the white habit for long when it became plain to him that he was no match for the mental wizards with whom he was studying. Anything concrete, which he could take apart and study, he could understand, but the abstract sciences were too much for him. He decided to run away from it all; planning a quiet departure, he carefully laid a ladder against the wall and waited his opportunity. As he was kneeling for one last Hail Mary before he should go over the wall, Our Lady appeared to him. She reproached him gently for his forgetfulness of her—why had he not remembered to ask her for what he wanted? Then she gave him the gift of science he so much desired, and disappeared. Whatever the truth behind the legend—and it has survived, almost unchanged, through the years—it is equally certain that Albert was a devout client of Our Lady and a master scientist.

Albert had an enquiring mind. He was an experimenter and a classifier at a time when all experimental knowledge was under suspicion. There was not a field in which he did not at least try his hand, and his keenness of mind and precision of detail make his remarks valuable, even though, because he lacked facts which we now have, his conclusions were incomplete. He wrote on botany, astronomy, chemistry, physics, biology, geography, and meteorology; he made maps and charts and experimented with plants; he studied chemical reactions; designed instruments to help with navigation; and he made detailed studies of birds and animals. He taught at both Cologne and Paris, where he had the happiness of seeing a quiet student from the Kingdom of Sicily rise like a brilliant star that would outshine all others. What must it have been to watch the mind of Thomas Aquinas develop and unfold to the wisdom of time and eternity, and to help him open the doors to profound truth?

The man for this work would need great humility and great sanctity, and these Albert had.

Albert was bishop of Ratisbon for two years, but resigned in order to return to the classroom. He outlived his beloved pupil by several years, and, in extreme old age, he walked halfway across Europe to defend a thesis of Thomas' that was challenged.

ROBERT KILWARDBY
(1280)

Robert Kilwardby was born in England early in the thirteenth century. His parents were wealthy Christians. He studied at Paris, receiving his degree there, and had been ordained for some time before entering the new Order of Friars Preachers. It is not clear whether he entered the Order at Paris or at Oxford, but in 1248 he occupied the chair of theology at Oxford. He was a diligent student, preferring to read the Fathers in the original Greek.

Robert was made provincial of the English Province in 1261, and this office he filled with distinction, enlarging the work of the friars and building up their spiritual structure. In 1272, he was summoned to be archbishop of Canterbury, an office which had been empty for twenty-nine years and in which, consequently, much was in need of doing.

On the death of Henry III, the archbishop of Canterbury was called upon to pronounce on the claim of the young Edward II to the throne. Since the young king was in the Holy Land on a crusade, it also fell to the archbishop's lot to draw up, with the queen regent, a plan of government that would suffice until the ruler came home. Archbishop Kilwardby returned from the Council of Lyons in time to crown the new king of England. These were the only official acts of his career with regard to the government. His impression on the thought of the time was far greater.

Previous to entering the Order, Kilwardby had written a number of works on grammar, philosophy, and logic. After he became a Dominican, his interests swerved to the Dominicans' first love—theology. This left him in the field with Thomas Aquinas, a much younger but very able man, who must have seemed a bit of an upstart to the staid regent of Oxford. Nevertheless, Kilwardby rallied to the defense of his brother Dominican when the Franciscans attacked Thomas' concept of poverty. It is not easy to say when he and Thomas parted company ideologically, but it was over the question of Aristotle—a thorny subject at that time. The whirlwind struck when, two years after the untimely death of Thomas, the archbishops of Paris and Canterbury condemned simultaneously thirty theses—of which several were those of Thomas. The aging St. Albert the Great, living in retirement at Cologne, was fired to defend his greatest pupil; he walked the long way to Paris and arrived, exhausted but indomitable, to fight Thomas' attackers to a finish. The Dominicans in England, undaunted by the prestige of Canterbury, took up scholastic arms in defense of Thomas there. With much effort and a certain amount of bitterness, the question was finally settled in Thomas' favor.

Whether the appointment of Archbishop Kilwardby to the post of cardinal-bishop of Porto was a case of "promote to remove" has never been completely clear. He died at Porto a year or so later, leaving the memory of a learned and courageous man who was not afraid to fight for what he believed. Legislation of the Church now makes it quite clear what one should think of St. Thomas and his works, but such issues were not so clearly drawn in Archbishop Kilwardby's day.

GERARD DE FRACHET
(d. 1281)

The man to whose diligence we are indebted for the accounts of the pioneer days of the Order and its first brethren was Gerard de Frachet. Even though, as some maintain, he was remiss in his editorial duty and allowed a rather prolix account of the early prodigies to be recounted for posterity, we would be very poor indeed if we did not have his accounts.

Gerard was born in Aquitaine, probably around 1200, and received the Dominican habit from Matthew of France at the convent in Paris, in November, 1225. He made his profession to Blessed Jordan of Saxony in the following March. In 1233, he was elected prior of Limoges, where he continued the work of preaching he had pursued at Paris.

For the next several years, Gerard occupied a number of posts of responsibility. He built the second priory in Lisbon, served a term as prior at Marseilles, and, in 1251, was elected provincial of Provence. In 1254, when the controversy centered about the privileges of religious orders began to come to a head, he went with Humbert of the Romans to the papal court at Naples to defend the privileges of the mendicants.

At the general chapter held in Paris in 1256, it was voted to appoint a writer to put on record the annals of the order: "Let every prior who has heard or known of any miracle or edifying occurrence happening in the Order, or concerning it, write diligently to the Master so that the memory of it may be preserved." The master general, Humbert of the Romans, handed over the resulting material to Gerard de Frachet to put into shape for publication.

Gerard worked on the book for four years, and for the ensuing five years he made corrections and incorporated the additional information that was sent in from the more distant provinces. The result is a sometimes repetitious account of the miraculous help of heaven in our pioneer days. From a literary standpoint, this is regrettable; but there is no reason why this should keep us from appreciating the difficulties facing such a compiler. So fluid was the state of the Order at the time, so rapid its growth and so widespread its field of operations, that the miracle is that there is any coherence to the stories at all.

Gerard continued to hold office until he was quite old, and attended several of the elective chapters as a delegate from one convent or another. He was prior of Limoges for several terms, which causes him to be referred to as "Brother Gerard, Prior of Limoges" in much of the early literature.

Gerard de Frachet died at Limoges in 1281.

INGRID OF SWEDEN
(d. 1282)

In sending the Polish brothers, Hyacinth and Ceslaus, back to Poland to begin the work of the Dominican apostolate, St. Dominic bridged the gap of language difference that might have held up preaching outside the Latin countries for many years. In 1219, he worked out the same plan by sending Simon of Sweden and Nicholas of Lund to Sweden to begin their work there. Before the death of St. Dominic, the friars were already evangelizing the North.

The first woman to wear the Dominican habit in Sweden was a near contemporary of the founder. Ingrid Elovsdotter was a child when the first Dominican friars came to Skänninge, and her father was a benefactor who helped them to build their first priory.

Ingrid lived in the shadow of the priory, attending all the services at the Dominican church, and early in life she learned to love the Order and its work. Ingrid grew up with the hope of entering religion and wearing the white habit of the new Order she loved so much. However, since she belonged to the most important family of the region, there were property settlements and family alliances to consider, and her father prevailed upon her to get married for the sake of the family. She obeyed his wish, and, for the short time of her married life, distinguished herself for charity to the poor and devotion to her husband's interests. However, her husband soon died, and she refused to make a new alliance. She had married once for the sake of her family. Now she would become a religious for the sake of her soul.

This was not simply a question of entering a nearby monastery, which would be difficult enough. She went to Peter of Dacia, the superior of the friars in Skänninge, and asked him about the possibility of building a monastery for Dominican nuns in Sweden. Peter allowed Ingrid and her sister, Christine, to wear the Dominican habit in their own home, and began forming them in the Dominican spiritual life. The practical details of building a monastery had to be delayed for a variety of reasons.

Ingrid drew about her a group of women who were interested in religious life, and, under the teaching of Peter of Dacia, they advanced in perfection and took upon themselves a number of pious works. After long discussions and meditations on the Passion of our Lord, the women decided that they wanted to go on a pilgrimage to the Holy Land and actually see the places of our Lord's Passion. Today this might be a pleasure trip. In the late thirteenth century it was a work of devotion or penance, and a definite risk of life and limb. The women secured the permission and made the tiring journey. Taking the long way home, they stopped in Rome, then went to Spain to the shrine of St. James of Compostela. Then they returned to Sweden, more determined than ever to erect a Dominican monastery where, for the rest of their lives, they could contemplate the holy places they had seen and the great mystery of our Redemption that had been accomplished there.

The convent of St. Agnes, in Denmark, was the only house for Dominican nuns in Scandinavia. Peculiarities of landholding made it difficult to get the necessary lands and permission for such a venture. Ingrid had a dream in which she saw the monastery she was to found near the church of St. Martin in her home city. It took a long time of arranging to get the necessary civil and ecclesiastical permissions. During the years of effort in this behalf, Ingrid made several trips to Rome to try to expedite the affair. It was an unlikely time to get anything done, since one period of six years saw six different popes occupying the Fisherman's Throne, and each pope had a different solution to her problem. Eventually, however, she cleared away all the legal debris and signed over her vast fortune to the costly task of building.

On the Feast of the Assumption, 1281, Ingrid's monastery was dedicated, and her community was formally affiliated with the Order. Ingrid was installed as prioress, and the regular life they had desired for so many years was begun. Ingrid was to enjoy her conventual life for only one year, for she died in 1282, leaving the memory of a saintly life.

In 1414, the request was made to canonize Ingrid of Sweden, and three years later the process was begun. In 1507, her relics were translated to a place of honor in the monastery church of Skänninge. An Office was composed for the use of the Dominicans of the diocese.

Political troubles and the Reformation delayed the canonization process, and Ingrid's relics were destroyed when the monastery was burned. However, the cause was resumed in recent years and may yet be brought to a favorable conclusion.

WILLIAM OF MOERBEKE
(1215-1282)

One of the most renowned scholars in the Order's pioneer days was William of Moerbeke, who died as archbishop of Corinth, around 1282. His greatest contributions to the Order were his careful scholarship and his gift for languages. It was he who supplied St. Thomas with the texts of Aristotle and helped to make possible the great work of his brother theologian.

William was born in Moerbeke, in Flanders, in 1215. He entered the Order at Louvain, where he was a student of oriental languages. Since there was at this time a surge of interest in the reunion of the Eastern and Western churches, the Dominicans were preparing for this reunion by various cultural means, including the language schools of the convents nearest the mission fields. The Western provinces nearly all had missionaries in the Near East, wandering preachers and teachers who would one day be organized into the *Fratres Peregrinantes*. Their work demanded books in many languages, and some of the provinces had houses with *scriptoria*, where books in various languages could be produced and copied. William of Moerbeke, with his gift of tongues, fitted perfectly into this working arm of the Order. He was sent to Greece very early, and there he worked for most of his life in one or another of the language schools.

William is described by a contemporary as being a "diligent scrutineer of all things that are," and as "a Hellenist of great style," who was in close cultural contact with the scholars of his field. He translated everything from the East that he thought would be of value to Western students, not only the works of Aristotle, for which he is best known, but also some other works of various Greek authors which are lost to us now except in his translations.

Pope Urban IV, in commissioning St. Thomas to make the works of Aristotle available to Western scholars, renewed an ancient prohibition against the use of corrupt texts. He is said to have suggested William of Moerbeke as translator for this important work of obtaining good sources. It is difficult to say exactly what William's contribution to this work was, though it was obviously very great. He made some of the classical Greek commentaries on Aristotle available to Thomas in Latin; he translated the *Politics* for the first time, and translated all of Aristotle's books on natural and moral philosophy, as well as revising an earlier work of Grosseteste. When necessary, he translated from Arabic as well as Greek. He made several works of eminent commentators available to St. Thomas for comparison.

In addition to this most memorable work, William translated the medical works of Hippocrates and Galen; tracts on mathematics and geometry; works on politics, rhetoric, zoology, meteors, and metaphysics. He was a born manuscript-hunter, and worldly-wise enough to follow the progress of battles to gather up and barter for the captured manuscripts that formed part of the plunder of war, or were in danger of being burned. In this way, he acquired, and preserved for us in translation, several valuable manuscripts.

Of William the man, we know little, for, like so many eminent scholars, he is hidden behind the very magnitude of his work. He was papal penitentiary under Popes Alexander IV and Gregory X, and attended the Council of Lyons in 1274; he was the principal adviser of the latter.

Since this council of 1274 did effect a brief and uneasy union between the East and the West, the pope sent out several Latin prelates to help maintain the union. William was made archbishop of Corinth in 1277. He died about five years later.

BLESSED JOHN OF VERCELLI
(d. 1283)

John Garbella was born early in the thirteenth century, somewhere near Vercelli. He studied at Paris and was ordained priest before 1229. He taught canon law at the University of Paris. While he was professor there, Jordan of Saxony came to Paris, and John saw one after another of his best pupils desert their careers to join the Order. He seems to have considered them quite objectively, without reference to himself, until the day an interior voice spoke to him that it was God's will for him to join the Dominicans. No one can say that John did not respond with alacrity; he dropped everything and ran down the street. ("Let me go; I am on my way to God!") Jordan received him happily and gave him the habit.

In 1232, John was sent to Vercelli to establish a convent there. He built this and several other convents in Lombardy as houses of regular observance. While provincial of Lombardy, he also became inquisitor. It was a particularly difficult moment. His brother in religion, Peter of Verona, had just been killed by the heretics in Como. The entire countryside was in a state of war, with roving bands of heretics and robbers. It was the task of the new inquisitor to try to bring order out of this chaos, and what John did was remarkable, considering the situation. In spite of his heavy labors, which included the supervision of six hundred friars in twenty-eight different cities (he reached them only by walking), John of Vercelli established the ideals of study and regular observance in all of his houses.

It was the good fortune of John of Vercelli to live in an age that was well peopled by saints. He formed a close friendship with St. Louis, the king of France. Several of his tasks in the Order, particularly the Commission on the Program of Studies, he shared with St. Albert the Great, St. Thomas Aquinas, and Peter of Tarentaise (the future Pope Innocent V). In such company one would need to have a superior set of talents; John did.

In 1264, the chapter of the Order met at Paris. Blessed Humbert had resigned as master general of the Order. John went to the chapter hoping that he could resign as provincial of Lombardy. Instead of escaping one office, he fell heir to a still more difficult one. He was elected master general. John was then a man in his sixties and was, moreover, handicapped by a crippled leg. However, he accepted the office which would require him to walk, not only all over Lombardy, but all over Europe. It took a brand of courage and obedience that was little short of heroic.

During the generalate of John of Vercelli, the relics of St. Dominic were transferred to the new tomb which had been prepared for it by Nicholas of Pisa. When the transfer was made, John of Vercelli fixed his seal on the tomb; the seals were still intact on their examination in 1946. During the translation of the relics, according to the account in the *Vitae Fratrum,* when the body of St. Dominic was exposed to view, the head was seen to turn towards John of Vercelli. John, embarrassed, moved to another part of the church and gave his place to a cardinal. Whereupon, the head of St. Dominic was seen by all to turn again in his direction.

On the death of Clement IV, John of Vercelli was very nearly elected pope. Being warned of the possibility, he fled in fright. However, his good friend, Cardinal Visconti, was elected and took the name Gregory X. He appointed John as legate on several different missions.

John was to distinguish himself for his assistance at the Council of Lyons in 1274—that council to which St. Thomas was hurrying when death found him on the road. John offered to the council the talents of his best men. At the council, he accepted for the Dominican Order the special commission of promoting reverence for the Holy Name of Jesus and fighting blasphemy, which was, in that day as in ours, a prevalent vice. He can thus be considered the founder of the Holy Name Society, even though the Confraternity was not formed until 1432.

Several precious relics were suitably enshrined by John of Vercelli. These included several thorns from the Crown of our Lord, which had been given him by St. Louis of France. The cord of St. Thomas, with which he had been girded by the angels and which he had worn until death, was given into the care of the master general, who gave it to the convent of Vercelli for safe keeping.

John's career was rapidly reaching its end. In 1279, he presided over the famous chapter of Paris at which the Order made the doctrine of St. Thomas officially its own. The following year he laid the foundations of the Church of Santa Maria Sopra Minerva. One of his last official acts was to provide for a work on the instruction of novices. He died in 1283, at Montpellier. His cult was confirmed in 1909.

BLESSED AMBROSE OF SIENA
(1220-1286)

Although his birth was attended by the prodigies also associated with Blessed James of Bevagna—that of three brilliant stars bearing the image of a friar preacher—Ambrose Sansedoni got off to a very bad start, as the world reckons. He was so badly deformed and so ugly that his own mother could hardly bear to look at him.

He was given into the care of a nurse, who daily took him with her to the Dominican church where she attended Mass. Here it was remarked that the baby, who fretted most of the time, was quiet and content when the nurse would hold him near the altar of relics, and that he cried violently when taken away. One day, as the nurse was kneeling there with the baby's face covered with a scarf, a pilgrim approached and said to her, "Do not cover that child's face. He will one day be the glory of this city." A few days later, at this same altar, a miracle was performed on the unfortunate child. He suddenly reached out his twisted limbs and quite distinctly pronounced the name of Jesus. At once, all deformity left him, and he became a normal child.

So early marked with the favor of God, it was only to be expected that Ambrose would be pious. As a child of seven he would rise at night to pray and meditate, and he daily recited the Little Office of Our Lady. While still a child, he was charitable to a heroic degree, and busied himself with the poor, the abandoned, and the sick. When he was only two or three years old, his father, who was an illuminator of books, made two little books for him. One was on secular subjects, the other on the saints. Ambrose made no hesitation about choosing the latter as his favorite, and throughout his life he was to exhibit this same choice of the things of God.

Being a handsome and talented young man, Ambrose was beset with difficulties when he expressed his intention of becoming a member of the preaching friars. Parents and friends tried to change his mind, and the devil appeared in several different forms to counsel him against such a step. Ambrose courageously overcame all the obstacles in his path and joined the friars on his seventeenth birthday.

After his profession, Ambrose was sent to Paris to study under St. Albert the Great. With his fellow pupil, St. Thomas Aquinas, he returned to Cologne with St. Albert, and thus was associated for some years with the two finest minds of the century. It is said that the humility of Ambrose, and his recognition of the true greatness of St. Thomas' writings, led him to devote his time to preaching rather than writing. He was sent on many peacemaking missions during his thirty years of preaching, and was highly regarded by both popes and members of the Order.

Despite a very active apostolate, Ambrose lived a life of almost uninterrupted prayer. He was often in ecstasy, and, shortly before his death, he was favored with several visions of great beauty. Sometimes when he preached he was raised from the ground, and a circle of glory, in which were birds of brilliant plumage, surrounded him. Many miracles were reported at his tomb, and he has been popularly called "St. Ambrose of Siena" since the time of his death.

CONSTANCE, QUEEN OF RUSSIA
(d. 1288)

Constance was the younger sister of St. Margaret of Hungary, and a daughter of Bela IV. Two other sisters are mentioned, Cunegund and Jolenta, all of whom seem to have been close in interests.

Constance was married to Prince Daniel, a Greek schismatic who, soon after his marriage, became king over a large part of Russia. His people belonged to the Ruthenian rite, but after a great deal of prayer and apostolic activity on the part of his young wife, both he and his people returned, in 1247, to Rome. The endeavors of Constance to bring her husband into the fold, together with his kingdom, was part of a movement which we have now all but forgotten, but which in its day was tremendously important. After the apostolic age itself, there was probably never a time when the fields were so ripe for the harvest.

Constance's royal husband made an effort to fulfill his part of the bargain. Innocent IV sent a legate, one Friar Henry, who anointed Daniel a Christian king, and set about Christianizing the country with two companions. They might well have asked, "What are three among so many?" for they could not hope to cope with the hordes of pagans who spoke such a medley of unmanageable tongues.

In spite of the moral support of the friars and the help of his young wife, Daniel was still bound by powerful chains to his pagan past. After a few stormy years, he abandoned the faith and returned to the barbarous practices of his people. He made no attempt to keep any semblance of Christianity, even of the schismatic variety he had once professed. The effect on a sensitive and pious wife can well be imagined.

The apostasy of Daniel left Constance in a difficult position. Most of the people of the country either went back to their schism, or followed her husband into pagan rites. Still, for many years, she persevered in her attempt to win him back. When he died, in 1266, she realized that her stay in Russia was no longer feasible. She went to her sister Cunegund, who was queen of Poland.

Cunegund was soon widowed also, and the two sisters looked about for some way of life that would satisfy their piety, and, at the same time help the great missionary movement. A younger sister, Jolenta, was just then entering the Poor Clares. Cunegund elected to go with her. Constance had not yet satisfied herself as to her vocation. She lived at the convent of the

Poor Clares, though she did not join them. Perhaps she acted as an extern sister, or simply as a pious inmate of the guest house. She was with the Poor Clares, in some capacity, at the time of the miracle for which she is best remembered.

In 1281, the Tartars made another incursion into Poland. One wonders what was left there after former invasions, for they had burned every building and killed every inhabitant in the foray that gave us the martyrs of Sandomir. However, they came again, and all Poland trembled. A generation before, the sultan of the Mohammedans had asked the Christian kings, who were fighting for Jerusalem, if they would not just forget the Holy Land for awhile and help him get rid of the Tartars. At about the same time, the Khan of the Tartars wrote to Frederick II—the scoundrelly cousin of St. Thomas—to ask if he would join him in fighting the Christians. The interior of Europe was one vast battleground. Swept by the general terror, Constance and Cunegund, and the community of Poor Clares, retired to a fortified castle.

This was a futile gesture, for the Tartars had a fiendish genius for destruction. They surrounded the castle, and the refugees knew they were doomed. This time it was Constance who saved the day, and by her prayers. At Cracow, Blessed Ceslaus had walked along the wall, turning back the Tartar arrows until the enemy became terrified and withdrew. Clare of Assisi, in the face of other invaders, had carried the Blessed Sacrament up to the highest parapet and held it high, and the invaders desisted. But there was nothing dramatic about the way Constance attacked the problem. She prayed, and she told the people that God was going to answer the prayer, and He did. The Tartars, for no reason anyone could see, simply withdrew.

After the country was at peace again, Constance retired to Lemberg, where there was a large Dominican convent. Perhaps she went to see her famous sister in Budapest; we do not know. But either Margaret's words, or her example, or the memory of the heroic Dominicans who had given their lives to the rough pagans of her husband's kingdom long ago, wakened in Constance a desire to join the Order of missionaries. Constance became first a Dominican Tertiary, then she founded in Lemberg a convent of Third Order Sisters and entered there to spend her last days in peace.

Only one more incident is recorded after this in the scant chronicles; it is said that one time when she was praying, the devil threw a rock at her. We are not even told what she did about it, or if—as one might suspect—she threw it right back at him.

At the end of a life torn by wars and sorrows, Constance died in Lemberg in 1288.

FRA RISTORO AND FRA SISTO
(d. 1283 and 1289)

Santa Maria Novella, in Florence, has been the "New St. Mary's" for seven hundred years now, and its architecture has long ceased to be a source of wonder to any but students or church builders. However, when the nave was completed, in the early fourteenth century, it was one of the wonders of the architectural world. It had been built entirely by religious, without the help of secular craftsmen, and the direction of the gigantic task lay in the hands of two Dominican laybrothers who were called simply Fra Sisto and Fra Ristoro.

Records are unfortunately meager regarding these two men. Fra Sisto was a native of Florence, and Fra Ristoro was born in nearby Campi. Both entered the Order at Santa Maria Novella after the middle of the thirteenth century, when they were young students of architecture. Floods had damaged the bridges across the Arno, and the repair of two of these bridges was confided to the talented young laybrothers. It is recorded that they built two fine bridges with stone pilings and a wooden superstructure. They were also engaged to build a cloister, which they did with great satisfaction to all. Their greatest work, however, was the designing of a new church at Santa Maria Novella, and the construction of the nave.

It is interesting to read that the enlargement of the church, and its eventual rebuilding, was called for by the popularity of Dominican preaching. The need for more space was first made evident when St. Peter Martyr came to Florence. There was not a place in town big enough to hold the crowds that flocked to hear him. The piazza of the Dominican church was the widest in the city, but on Peter's arrival the prior had to make hurried arrangements to enlarge it.

The church was first enlarged, and the friars called in Greek painters to decorate it. The Dominicans were at that time operating a school for the education of boys in Latin and the arts. One of the teachers had a nephew who was a pupil at the school. He was a dreamy child who played truant from school and hid where he could watch the Greek painters at work. The friars could hardly know that they were thus influencing the whole course of art, for the truant was Cimabue, who grew up to be the founder of the Florentine School of Art.

Rows of houses were removed and the piazza enlarged, much as today one removes houses to build a freeway. There was still no room on cold days. The answer, plainly, was to build a larger church. The two laybrothers were commissioned to build it.

Due to various disasters, it was twelve years before the new church could be begun. The cornerstone was laid on the Feast of St. Luke, in 1278, and there were still more delays before building began. The building was erected in the shape of a Latin cross, and so noted for its purity and simplicity of line that Michelangelo was one day to call it his "sweet bride." The two young architects, working at a time when many problems of weight and mass had not yet been solved, succeeded in their difficult project. The proportions are so well-chosen that the church was often to be called the fairest in the world.

The two laybrothers were called to Rome to superintend the building of some vaults. There exists a reliable tradition that while they were in Rome they laid the plans for the great Dominican church of Santa Maria Sopra Minerva, which was built shortly after this. It would seem only reasonable that they should have been consulted, as the beauty and utility of their work in Florence was well known.

Fra Sisto died in 1289, in Rome, while busy with some building for the Dominican nuns of St. Sixtus. Fra Ristoro returned to Florence, where he died in 1283. He was buried in the church that he had helped to build.

NICHOLAS OF HANAPPES
(d. 1291)

Of all the colorful characters who walk across the panoramic pages of the crusades, few stand out in finer detail than Nicholas of Hanappes, who died at the fall of Acre, in 1291. He was a Dominican and a brave and holy man, which makes him of special interest to us.

Nicholas was born early in the thirteenth century, at Hanappes, on the border of Picardy. He entered the Order at Rheims, where he distinguished himself as both theologian and linguist. The fact that he was sent to make his studies at Paris under St. Albert the Great is sufficient indication that he was a superior student. At Paris, he found himself in the company of the finest minds of the age; Thomas Aquinas, Peter of Tarentaise, and Bonaventure were his classmates. He became a popular preacher and a writer of handbooks for preachers. His best-known work was a book of sermon examples which was known as the "poor man's Bible." Some time during his early years of preaching he was called to Rome and there held various offices for several years.

In 1288, the patriarchate of Jerusalem became vacant. It was a vital post at that moment, for the crusades were at a crucial point. Pope Nicholas V and the cardinals made a unanimous choice that the important post be given to Nicholas of Hanappes. Personally consecrated by the pope, Nicholas was made bishop of Acre and legate to Syria, Cyprus, and Armenia, as well as patriarch of Jerusalem. He sailed for Jerusalem, but was never to reach it, for by the time the slow-moving ship had touched at the first port of the East, the disastrous news was waiting: Jerusalem had fallen, and all Syria was in the hands of the infidels.

The new patriarch went to Acre and tried to rally the demoralized Christian forces in the last great fortified city of the East. The outlook was more than discouraging. The past two crusades had failed, which resulted principally in setting Eastern and Western Christians at each other's throats, while the infidels plundered and burned unchecked. Letters to the kings of the West had brought no answers, and the growing panic among the remaining defenders was apt to end in disaster. Nicholas took a realistic view of the Christian chances and sent an envoy to the sultan, asking for a truce. The sultan agreed on a truce of two years' duration, and Nicholas wrote to France and Spain, begging for troops before it should be too late.

The troops came, but without a leader. The crowned heads of Europe were busy with petty jealousies and could not spare any leader of sufficient prestige to command the obedience of the enthusiastic troops who answered the call. Leaderless, and anxious above all to kill infidels, these misguided zealots violated the truce. This promptly brought all the sultan's forces down about the luckless city of Acre.

Here it is that the personality of Nicholas emerges out of the shadows of history, and he appears as a man of great stature. He was already advanced in age, and there was probably nothing in his training that would fit him to command a besieged city. Yet, Acre recognized no other leader in that panicky moment, and he was obliged to make the decisions upon which the lives of many hundreds of peoples would depend. It is an inspiration for people who dislike taking responsibility to consider him, an old man and a Churchman, assuming the dreadful burden that God had placed on his shoulders.

When the sultan died, in 1291, the Christians began to hope for reprieve. It soon became clear that the son of the sultan intended to carry out his father's wishes with a fanaticism that we find hard to credit. His troops surrounded the city on the land side, leaving only the port open. In the thirteenth century the siege of a city need only last until the water supply ran out, or became polluted; the victory was almost certainly with the attacker.

Daily scanning the sea for help, the Christians held out until the water supply was gone, and all the walls on the land side were mined and broken. The king of Cyprus took his remaining troops and sailed for home. The remaining Christians held a council to decide if it would not be better for them to go by sea, before the Moslem fleet could come and shut off their only way of escape. When it became evident that there were not enough ships to evacuate the city, they vowed to remain and fight to the last man.

There are few scenes in history to equal that of the last day in the doomed city. All but one wall had fallen. Word reached the defenders that the Moslems had climbed Mount Carmel and put to the sword the entire community of Carmelites, who were singing their evening "Salve Regina." The last night was busy with confessions and sermons in preparation for death, and in the morning Mass was sung, very early, for those who would die that day. A little after sunrise the last wall fell, and the infidels swarmed in.

The Hospitallers and the Knights Templars formed a guard around the patriarch, and fought until each man fell dying. Nicholas stood in the center of the group, crying out prayers to encourage them, holding up the cross of the patriarchate until his arms gave out, and he had to give it to another friar. Wounded by an arrow, he was carried out to the one remaining ship, but refused to let the captain pull away from the dock while any living men were left who might be got on board. At last, heavily overloaded, the ship swung out, and overturned in the harbor, drowning all on board.

No move has ever been made to promote the cause of Nicholas of Hanappes, but he is for us a shining example of courage in a warring world.

BLESSED BENVENUTA BOJANI
(1254-1292)

Companions of Blessed Benvenuta called her "the sweetest and most spiritual of contemplatives, so lovable in her holiness that her touch and presence inspired gladness and drove away temptations." When one reads about her penances, it is especially necessary to remember that they did not alienate her from her friends and relatives.

Benvenuta was born in Friuli, in Austrian territory, in 1254. There were already six daughters in the family, and Benvenuta was supposed to be a boy; no one wanted to tell her father that once again he had been disappointed. However, the good man knew from the silence of the nurse that his wife had presented him with another daughter, and he cried out, "She too shall be welcome!" Remembering this, she was named Benvenuta, the Italian word for "welcome."

The little girl was pious and good from her earliest years. An older sister, who was vain and given to dancing and fine clothes, used to try to dress her little sister in rich clothing and teach her the arts of society. Benvenuta became an expert at hiding from this sort of thing, and made her refuge in the church, where she developed a tender devotion to Our Lady. At the age of twelve she was wearing all the instruments of penance that she could obtain—a hairshirt, a rope girdle, and other forms of torture more familiar to her age than ours. As she grew, the rope became embedded in her flesh, and the day came when she realized that something would have to be done to remove it. She herself could not get it off, and she hated the thought of revealing it to anyone else; so she prayed for help—and the rope fell off at her feet. This circumstance gave rise to the symbol one usually sees in sacred art—a length of rope in Benvenuta's hands.

Benvenuta became a Third Order Dominican at the earliest opportunity, and added all the penitential practices of the sisters to those she had already developed by herself. Disciplines, fasting, abstinence, and lack of rest soon reduced her to illness. She was in bed for five years, and even when she was able to get up again she could not walk any distance. One of her sisters was kind enough to carry her to church once a week for Compline in the Dominican church. This was her favorite service, next to Mass, and most of the apparitions of her life were connected with these treasured hours in the friars' church.

One day, after she had assisted at first Vespers of the Feast of St. Dominic, the saint appeared to her, accompanied by St. Peter Martyr. St. Dominic told her that he had a wonderful surprise for her, and Benvenuta waited in great joy to see what it was. At the Salve procession, she found out. The prior was absent; but at the beginning of Compline, she saw St. Dominic go into the prior's place. He went around and gave the kiss of peace to all the brethren, then went to his own altar and disappeared. At the Salve procession, the Blessed Virgin herself came down the aisle, blessing the fathers, holding her little Son high in her arms.

Always joyful, Benvenuta had to face excruciating torture from the devil. Her penances were hard enough, but he made life even harder for her. One day, exhausted, she said to one of her sisters, "You can have paradise only once." When someone protested against the death of a promising young child, she commented, "It is much better to be young in paradise than to be old in hell." The devil appeared to her under the most horrifying forms, but Benvenuta always serenely called upon Our Lady, whose word is law, even with devils—the Blessed Virgin always protected her, and turned to nothing the schemes of the devil for upsetting the Tertiary's prayers.

GENOVESA OF SIENA
(1242-1292)

Genovesa of Siena, who was born a century before the great St. Catherine of that city, is interesting to us for several reasons. Third Order Sisters in particular should be intrigued by the details of her life, for—unless the chronicler is wrong—Tertiary Sisters were teaching in Siena even at this early time; not, of course, in schools as we know them, which did not yet exist, but as private teachers of whatever arts were taught to girls.

Genovesa was born in 1242. Her father, a Genoese, had been forced to leave his native city by an accumulation of debts and the unpleasant possibility of going to prison for them. He had come to Siena, got an excellent job as a silk maker, and—in the best American tradition—married the boss' daughter. When the little girl was born, he insisted on naming her for the city he loved, so the name was Genovesa.

Her birthday was the feast of St. Catherine of Alexandria, a saint who was to play an important part in her life. On the day of her baptism, her father saw a hideous dragon hovering over the crib of the sleeping baby, and, as he stood helpless, he saw St. Catherine of Alexandria advance upon the beast with a sword and put him to flight. Just what the vision meant he did not know, but he saw to it that the little girl was told early about the saint on whose feast day she had been born.

When Genovesa was very tiny, probably only three, she was given over to the care of the Dominican Tertiary Sisters for her education. One, by name Nera Tolomei, took special care of the little girl and taught her catechism, as well as other subjects which were thought proper for women to learn. The child was considered to have received an unusual amount of schooling for a girl.

Genovesa grew up to be a rare beauty, possessed of a sweet disposition and many talents. Besides all this, her father was well-to-do. A combination like this adds up, usually, to a husband of a higher social class. Genovesa firmly refused several wealthy and eligible young men, and surprised everyone by marrying a poor but honest workman from her father's shop, a man by the name of John.

John was very proud of his beautiful and talented wife, and for a time there was peace and happiness. Then one day a neighbor woman, jealous of the pretty young bride, made a number of sly insinuations to John that would cause him to be suspicious of his wife. Even the neighbor who started the trouble could hardly have known how far it would go, for John took a dagger and went looking for Genovesa, intending to kill her.

She did not know what was making her husband angry, as the accusations had been entirely false. She fell on her knees and pleaded with him to be reasonable. He lunged at her with the dagger—and missed. Something was standing in front of her. Puzzled, he backed away, then went out, leaving her alone. Genovesa related what had happened to her mother. Her parents then told her about the vision of the dragon. "It was St. Catherine again, protecting you," they said.

The woman who had started the mischief had the courage to go to John and tell him that she had been lying. John repented bitterly of his outburst of temper, and never ceased to marvel at the power that had saved his wife from his fury. Soon after this, he died. Her parents followed him in death, leaving the young woman alone.

Genovesa, in her loneliness, went to her old teacher, Nera Tolomei. At her suggestion, she joined the Tertiaries, receiving the habit from Blessed Ambrose of Siena.

The rest of her life was spent in prayer and in the good works of the Tertiaries. Popular tradition gives her the power of miracles, of prophecy, and of cures. She closed a holy life with an equally holy death, and was buried in the church of St. Dominic, in Siena, where—many years later— another holy Tertiary would kneel to pray, and look to her as to an older sister, for the example of holiness and perseverance to be a good Dominican.

MECHTILDE OF MAGDEBERG
(d. 1293)

Most Dominicans are familiar with the story of the great St. Gertrude and her sister, Mechtilde. However, few realize that there was a famous Dominican Mechtilde who was a close friend of the two saintly Benedictines. She was Mechtilde of Magdeberg.

Mechtilde was born in the early thirteenth century, in Germany. At the age of twelve, she left home to live as a Beguine, and for fifty years she pursued this form of life. She took private vows as a Dominican Tertiary, and under the direction of her Dominican confessor reached a very high state of mystical prayer.

In obedience to this confessor, Mechtilde wrote her revelations. Another Dominican translated her manuscript into Latin, and it had a wide circulation among the devout of several countries. However, it was this manuscript which occasioned a drastic move in Mechtilde's life. Some of her revelations tended to reprimand the faults of the clergy, and the book made many enemies for its writer. Mechtilde found it necessary to leave Magdeberg. She went to the old Benedictine monastery at Helfta, where the sisters were happy to have such a holy mystic among them. She lived with the Benedictines for the rest of her life, and she followed the rules of the house while she lived there. The evidence is, however, that she remained a Dominican Tertiary and did not become a Benedictine nun.

In the monastery at this time were two young nuns—blood sisters—who were to gain lasting fame as canonized saints; they were Gertrude and Mechtilde, who must have been little more than novices when the refugee mystic came to live with the Benedictines. They, and many others of the nuns, delighted in hearing the older Mechtilde tell them about the things of God. They valued her piety and her sagacity, and received much help from her in their pursuit of sanctity.

It is related that on one feast day, when the monastery recited special prayers for the Poor Souls, Mechtilde was taken in an ecstasy to Purgatory. She saw the souls for whom they were praying, and the results of their prayers. Her revelations on this occasion gave great impetus to their prayers for the Poor Souls.

When Mechtilde was on her deathbed, St. Gertrude, kneeling by her bed, was appalled at the spiritual anguish of her friend. She prayed that God would pierce through the darkness with which she was surrounded and give some consolation to the soul that had served him so long and so well. Our Lord answered the saint that the soul of Mechtilde was far above any need of consolation, since hers was a very superior type of sanctity. Nevertheless, when the moment came for Mechtilde to die, our Lord and His Blessed Mother came to conduct her to heaven. St. Gertrude saw our Lord bend over and give the kiss of peace to the dying woman.

Mechtilde died in 1293. Her writings, including some seven books of her revelations, enjoyed popularity long after her death. They often have been confused with the works of the Benedictine, St. Mechtilde.

CARINO OF BALSAMO
(d. 1293)

Carino of Balsamo gives us one of the most authentic mystery stories in all hagiography. It is surprising that some dramatist has not seized upon him for the central character of a play, for surely he shows—if anyone ever did—the quality of a saint's revenge.

St. Peter Martyr was the inquisitor of Lombardy at a time when his strict adherence to doctrine was an embarrassment to many wealthy and politically-important people. They determined to take care of the matter, as such people always do; first, by an attempt to buy him off, which failed; then by an attempt to scare him off, which likewise failed; lastly, by a well-planned murder.

The plotters in this evil business included a storybook array of characters: the politicians who had been offended; the hired assassin; the man who would put up the money to pay him; the men who would keep the police from interfering; the one who would buy off the judge, if it ever got to court. Carino was the hired assassin.

Carino was a field worker and a man of some talents along the line of murder, though he had never before been in such important company. He insisted upon bringing in a helper, one Albertino, who was even better on the practical details of murder than he was. They planned an ambush for the victim, and carefully studied the convent timetable to find when Peter would be most likely to be on the road. Hearing that their victim was going to Milan on the day after Easter, Carino made final plans and picked out the wooded spot where he and Albertino would wait in ambush for Peter.

Then, for a comic touch, the thieves fell out. Carino went to the man who had hired him and asked to borrow his horse. (Today it would be a get-away car.) That worthy, not wanting his name mixed up in the affair, refused. Carino departed in an angry mood for the planned ambush; he found Albertino already nervous and upset.

Peter and his companions proceeded innocently on the road to Milan. They sang the Sequence of the Easter Mass. Brother Conrad tried to sing harmony, and was told by Peter that he had better stick to the melody. All these details have come down to us, thanks to the companion of Peter, Brother Dominic of Lombardy. At noon, the friars separated to beg their dinner,

Peter and Dominic going to a nearby monastery. Just as they took the road again after lunch, the assassins fell upon them.

Carino struck first at Peter, who fell with the first blow. Albertino, the moral support, gave a cry of terror and ran. Carino turned on Brother Dominic and wounded him mortally. Then he saw that Peter was still alive and was writing on the ground in his blood. He struck the death blow and vanished into the underbrush. A farmer, plowing nearby, took after him and eventually overpowered him.

Peter was dead when the monks came running from the nearby monastery. Brother Dominic of Lombardy lingered for six days, long enough to tell in poignant detail all that had happened. When he died, the people, gathered in an ominous group around the jail, decided to break in and kill Carino. They advanced on the jail to find that the prisoner had been released. They altered their plans and decided to kill the jailor. The archbishop finally convinced them to go home in peace.

Carino did not stay to find out how the loot was divided. The thirty pieces of silver, held in a safe spot by one of the conspirators, was the occasion of a bitter quarrel on the part of the group and resulted in nearly all of them being arrested. Carino, to whom one might say the money belonged, had suddenly lost his concern about money. Knowing that he would have to leave Lombardy, he started towards Rome, working his way in the fields—the only work he knew. Whether the grass-hook he carried with him for this work was the one with which he had killed Peter, no one has ever quite determined. It was the tool of his trade, and he made a precarious living with it as he proceeded southward.

Traveling by the back roads and avoiding the towns, he became more and more obsessed with the thought of pursuit. Finally—sick, penniless, and terrified—he knocked at the door at Forli. The brothers took him in and asked no questions. When it became apparent that Carino was desperately sick, he begged for a priest. The brothers secured the nearest one, from the Dominican church nearby. The sight of the white habit was all Carino needed to break him completely.

The prior of the Dominicans had doubtless heard of the assassination of the most famous inquisitor in Lombardy. Nevertheless, he dealt in a Christ-like way with the one who had done the wicked deed. Carino, at peace with God, must have realized that the man he had killed was stronger than he, and that victory had gone to the one who died. He, Carino, could only take life away; Peter had given him eternal life. Carino, completely trans-formed, promised to enter religion if he recovered from his illness.

Carino's life was henceforth the working out of this promise. It took him forty years.

At the convent of Forli is still preserved the pruning-hook with which Carino worked, both on his desperate flight from Lombardy and during the forty years of his penance in the Dominican convent. Some claim—though it seems unlikely—that it was the same one with which he had killed St. Peter Martyr. Whether it was or not, every sight of it was a reminder to him of his crime and a great help to a spirit of humility. The convent archives picture Carino as a model of obedience, prayer, and penance, a man who sometimes spent whole nights before the Blessed Sacrament, and who never forgot the mercy of God in his behalf.

Carino died in 1293, and in his death he showed a rare humility. Known as he was for a holy and prayerful brother, no one would have taxed him with the crime of forty years ago. But on his deathbed he confessed it again, with tears, and made the request that—since he was no better than any common murderer and deserved to be treated like one—he would not be buried in consecrated ground, but in the potter's field reserved for executed criminals. When this news got about the town, the citizens of Forli took a forthright step; they *bought* the criminals' cemetery and gave it to the Dominicans.

Even this was not enough to show their feelings about the man they considered a saint. They eventually built a beautiful little chapel in which Carino was buried with full honors. In time his tomb was flanked on either side by two holy Dominicans: Blessed James of Salomonio (who had been Carino's spiritual director) and Blessed Marcolino of Forli.

BLESSEDS DIANA, CECILIA, AND AMATA

The three Sisters who are honored together on June ninth were three members of the community of St. Agnes, in Bologna. Two of them came from St. Dominic's reformed convent at St. Sixtus, and Blessed Diana was the builder of the convent of St. Agnes. All three had known St. Dominic personally.

Of Sister Amata, we know practically nothing, but that she was a good friend of St. Dominic, which should, after all, be enough to know about anybody. He, according to legend, gave her the name Amata—which means "beloved"—and very probably he either sent her to the convent in the first place or was the means of her staying there at the time of the drastic reform, when the nuns left St. Mary's beyond the Tiber and went to St. Sixtus. There was a Sister Amata from whom St. Dominic is said to have cast out seven devils, but it could hardly have been this one. The facts that he personally named her, and that she is buried with the other two, will have to be her title to honor.

Cecilia Caesarini was a high-spirited young Roman of an ancient family; she threw her considerable influence into the reform movement at the time St. Dominic was attempting to get the sisters into St. Sixtus and under a strict rule. When the saint came to speak to the sisters at St. Mary's beyond the Tiber, it was Cecilia (then seventeen, she must then have been one of the youngest in the house) who urged the prioress to support his cause. She was the first to throw herself at his feet and beg for the habit and the rule he was advocating, and her hand is evident in the eventual working out of the touchy situation. In 1224, she and three other sisters from St. Sixtus—including Blessed Amata—went to St. Agnes, in Bologna, to help with the new foundation. Sister Cecilia was the first prioress of the new house, and she proved to be a very strict one.

It is to Sister Cecilia that we are indebted for nearly all that we know of the personal appearance and habits of St. Dominic. In her extreme old age, she was asked by Theodore of Apoldia to give him all the details of the saint's personality, and all that she could recall of the early days of the Order, in order that he could record them for posterity. Sister Cecilia was nearly ninety, but her memory was keen and specific; she recalled exactly how St. Dominic had used his hands, the precise shade of his hair, the exact line of his tonsure. If she had erred, there were people still alive who could have corrected her, though there was probably no one with her descriptive power left to tell the tale. Through a woman's eyes, she saw the founder from a different angle than his fellow preachers were apt to see, and remarked on his gentleness with the sisters, and the little touches of thoughtfulness so characteristic of him. While the men who worked with him would recall his great mind and his penances, and appreciate the structural beauty of the Order he had founded, Sister Cecilia saw the glow of humanity which so many of the historians miss. Indeed, we owe a heavy debt to Sister Cecilia.

The most colorful of the three was undoubtedly Sister Diana, the spoiled and beautiful daughter of the d'Andalò family, of Bologna, who lost her heart to the ideal of the Order when listening to Reginald of Orleans preach. She espoused the cause of the friars, who were new in Bologna, and begged her father until she obtained from him the church of St. Nicholas of the

Vineyards, of which he had the patronage. Having established the brethren, she wanted a convent of Dominican Sisters in Bologna. When St. Dominic came there on his last journey, she talked to him, and all her worries departed. She knelt at his feet and made a vow to enter the Dominican Order as soon as it should be possible to build a convent in Bologna. St. Dominic, going away to Venice on a trip from which he would only return to die, made sure before leaving that the brethren understood about Diana. Four of the fathers from the community of St. Nicholas were under obedience to see that her convent was built.

In the meantime, Diana's father refused her permission to enter the convent. Stealing a leaf from the life of St. Clare, she ran away to the Augustinians, outside the city. In full armor, her brothers came after her, and Diana was returned, battered but unconvinced, to the paternal home. She nursed a number of broken ribs and several explosive ideas in silence.

The death of St. Dominic was a great grief to her, as she was still living in a state of siege in her father's house, waiting for some action on the question of the new convent. However, she soon acquired a new friend, who was to be her greatest joy in the years of her mortal life—Jordan of Saxony, master general of the Order, succeeding St. Dominic, and a future blessed of the Church. Jordan, as provincial of Lombardy, inherited the job of building the sisters' convent in Bologna, but his relations with Diana were not to be merely mundane. Their friendship, of which we have the evidence in Jordan's letters, is a tribute to the beauty of all friendship, and a pledge of its place in religious life.

Diana was nothing if not resourceful. She made another attempt to elope to the convent. This time her family gave up in despair. She remained peacefully with the Augustinians until the new convent was built in Bologna. In 1223, Diana and several other young women received the habit of the Order from Jordan of Saxony. Diana was the prioress for a time, but perhaps Jordan felt that she was too volatile for ruling others, because, as soon as the sisters came from St. Sixtus, he established Sister Cecilia as prioress. Diana, who was used to being not only her own boss, but the one who told others what to do, seems to have made no protest.

If we had the letters written by Diana, we should possess a fascinating picture of the early years of the Order and the people who made it what it is. We are indebted to Diana for what we do have of that remarkable correspondence, for she must have carefully saved all of Jordan's letters. They tell us of the progress made by the friars in various lands, and ask her to remind the sisters that they must pray for the missionaries; Jordan counts the successes when many good novices have come into the Order, begging her prayers in the low moments when promising novices leave. More than this, these are letters of spiritual direction, which should give a pattern to all such correspondence, for they infer that Diana is a willing and energetic Christian who will follow the advice she is given, not simply keep the correspondence going for the joy of it.

Diana died in 1236. She was buried in the convent of St. Agnes. Her remains were transferred when a new convent was built, and Sister Cecilia —who died sixty years later—was buried near her, along with Sister Amata. The relics were transferred several times, all three together. The head of Blessed Diana was placed in a reliquary near the tomb of St. Dominic.

Sisters Diana, Amata, and Cecilia were beatified in 1891.

ROBERT OF UZES
(1263-1296)

Robert was born in 1263, in the south of France, in the castle of his father, who was duke of Uzes. Before Robert was born, the Dominican, John the Teutonic, visited the family; most probably they gave him hospitality on one of his journeys through this heresy-ridden province. He was greatly pleased with the kindness of the young couple, and blessed their home before he left. Always afterwards, they would claim that it was his blessing which gave them two priestly sons.

The children were all piously brought up and well educated. Robert began his studies at the age of seven, under the family chaplain, and displayed a great aptitude for them. Having finished his early studies, he went to Avignon, where his uncle was bishop. Here he studied philosophy and theology. The bishop was so impressed with his nephew that on his death, in 1279, he left his entire library to Robert. This comprised quite a fortune at that time, and it was the sort of wealth that appealed to the young clerk. Robert was ordained, probably in 1287, and took up his work with great zeal.

It was an age of popular preaching; still, it is a little surprising to find a young priest setting up as an itinerant preacher. However, that is what he did, and he very soon was known for his apocalyptic preaching—which is much on the style of St. Vincent Ferrer's.

At this time, he also wrote a book concerning his visions. In Marseilles, in 1291, he had an extremely vivid vision while making his thanksgiving after Mass. He saw our Lord with St. Peter, who wore papal vestments and carried the keys in his left hand. The right hand was withered and black, and, naturally, Robert asked why. An angel told him that it was because a part of the Church was arid and useless, involved in useless quarrels between the Church and the state. "Kings cry in vain to Christian kings to save Jerusalem," he concluded. Robert knew that this was true; the Christians were not rallying to the cause of the crusade. After this vision, he gave great emphasis to penance and charity in his preaching, and to the cause of the crusade.

Robert treasured a great devotion to St. Martha, perhaps because her relics were supposed to be in the south of France. He always prayed to her to help him with his preaching, and claimed that any success he had was due to her help. Once, when he had angered a crowd of heretics so that they set upon him and tried to lynch him, he credited St. Martha with saving his life.

Robert renounced family and fortune and devoted himself to bringing the word of God to the poor. With his high personal regard for evangelical poverty and his taste for preaching, it was inevitable that sooner or later he would become interested in the Dominicans. He made an effort to study the various orders and was once imposed on by the devil, who, dressed like a monk, advised him to enter *his* Order. However, Robert discovered who his counsellor was, and lost no time in applying to the Dominicans. He received the habit in Avignon, in 1292.

In spite of his fine education and his evident preaching talents, the Dominicans were hesitant to profess a man who had such prophetic visions; this particular gift is never too popular in a community, and tends to get the prophet in trouble with civil authority sooner or later. However, on examination of his life and work, they accepted him, and he was professed in 1293.

The late thirteenth and early fourteenth centuries were the high point for prophecies of doom. The Church was in a deplorable state: civil governments were in turmoil; the Holy Land was lost with the fall of Acre in 1291. Prophets abounded. They were popular just as long as they prophesied trouble for one's enemies and criticized somebody else's sins. Robert was not always so tactful. His superiors were quite ready to admit, in private, that what he said was quite true: the Church needed reform—even the Order was not perfect. When Robert gave a thundering sermon denouncing the Dominicans for pride and for too much interest in worldly science, the prior silenced him. Robert went quietly into retirement; shortly afterwards the prior was enlightened in a vision concerning the sanctity of the preacher. He restored Robert's faculties and allowed him to resume his work.

Robert was a Dominican for only four years. He died in 1296, and has been popularly called "Blessed Robert" from the time of his death.

BLESSED JAMES OF VORAGINE
(1230-1298)

James of Voragine has been beatified by the Church for the sanctity of his life. He lives in secular history for quite a different reason—he was a creative genius of his age. His so-called *Golden Legend,* which has enjoyed a circulation of nearly seven centuries, is only one of several projects which in his time, as in ours, are a tribute to the versatility of the man and the zeal of a saint.

Little is recorded of the childhood of James. He entered the Order, in Genoa, and soon was known both for his virtue and for a singularly alert and practical mind. Tradition says that James was the first to translate the Bible into Italian. Whether this is true or not, it is ample evidence that he was a good scholar.

As prior, provincial, and later, archbishop, James gained a reputation for strict observance, heroic charity, and sound good sense. He was a builder where war had wrecked, a peacemaker where others sowed trouble. He must have had a contagious zeal, for the wealthy gave to him as readily as the poor begged from him, and under his hand ruined churches and hospitals were built again, the sick and poor were cared for, and order was restored. He was a genius at getting things done; and, fortunately, his whole heart was bent on doing for the glory of God.

Like others of his calling and training, James was first of all a preacher. For those many who could not read, one of the chief means of instruction was sermons, which took their keynote from the feast of the day. The saints, the stories of their lives and examples of their virtues, became as much a part of a Christian's life as the people around him. The collection of stories —later called *The Golden Legend*—started as a series of sermons prepared by James for the various festivals of the saints. Since he preached in Italian, rather than in Latin, his sermons had immense popular appeal, and they were rapidly copied by other preachers into all the languages of Europe. *The Golden Legend* was, next to the Bible, the most popular book of the Middle Ages.

James was rigorous in his observance of the Dominican Rule, which is of itself enough to canonize him. He had also the good sense to make use of changing trends to further the work of God. Today he would be using the radio, the press, the movies, and television; then he used what his century had to offer—sermons in the vernacular, religious drama, and music. How much present-day drama and music owe to him, it would be impossible to say. There is an amusing story told of his efforts to fight fire with fire. He organized a troop of jugglers and acrobats from the student-novices of San Eustorgio, in Milan, who were to mingle entertainment with doctrine in an effort to combat the indecency of the secular theater. This was one scheme which left no lasting effect on the Order, but it does serve to show that James was a man of his times, alert to the changing needs of a fast-moving world, and wholeheartedly determined to win the world to the truth by any honest means that came to hand.

Purity, poverty, and charity were the outstanding virtues of this man whom the Church has seen fit to enroll among her blesseds. He will always be recognized in Dominican history as a man of many and peculiar gifts, who consecrated his talents to God, and, in trading with them, gained heaven.

FOURTEENTH CENTURY

FOURTEENTH CENTURY

ANGELA TOLOMEI
(1230-1300)

Angela Tolomei is quite probably the only Dominican who was raised from the dead and lived on to profit from the experience.

Angela was born in Siena, in 1230, of a family famous in Sienese history, and one which gave members to the Order. Just when she became a Third Order Dominican we do not know, but it was most probably around 1270. She fell seriously sick and sent for her brother, who was a Dominican priest in a nearby town. When he arrived, she was in a coma, on the verge of death.

Unknown to her brother, Angela was favored with a glance at purgatory during this state of coma. She saw the frightful punishment that men have deserved for their sins—hot winds, frozen waters, wheels studded with spikes. Amid all this uncomfortable array, she was shown the place reserved for her. Regaining consciousness for one last moment before death, she begged her brother to pray that God would spare her so that she could suffer her punishment here on earth rather than in purgatory. Shortly thereafter, she died, and preparations were made for her burial.

John Baptist Tolomei, her brother, was a man of prayer and had been credited with several miracles. The most astounding one laid to his credit was the raising of his sister from the dead. He called upon Angela to come back to life, and she did.

Then Angela began a career of penance so frightening that we can hardly bear to read about it. With an insatiable thirst for suffering, roused by her sight of purgatory, she tortured her body by standing in ice-cold water, or by burning herself against a stove; by scourging and fasting; by using spiked instruments of penance. Finally she went into the mountains, where her penances would not bother anyone but herself, and there, for the remainder of her life, she lived in a cave, in continual prayer. It is a bit of an anti-climax to report that she suffered from toothache, but since the chronicler saw fit to record it, it must have been an extreme one. Her constant advice to those who shuddered at her penance was, "Weep not for me! All the pains of earth cannot compare with those of purgatory!"

Angela Tolomei died in 1300.

MUNIO DE ZAMORA
(1237-1300)

Munio de Zamora, seventh master general of the Order, will always be remembered as the man who gave definite form to the Third Order Rule and secured its approbation.

Munio de Zamora was born in 1237, in the kingdom of Leon, and entered the Order in 1257. We know little of his early life beyond the fact that it must have been exemplary, for he was first elected provincial of Spain and then, in 1285, master general.

One of his first acts in this office was to establish two distinguishing marks of Dominicanism in all the houses under his jurisdiction; the solemn cult of Our Lady, and the teaching of St. Thomas. In the first case he had no great difficulty, since devotion to the Blessed Virgin was a natural expression of the spirituality of the early friars; it needed only to be given definite form. With the second, however, there was still solid opposition to overcome. St. Albert the Great, who had fought for Thomas at Paris, was dead, and opponents of Aristotle were to be found, even among the Dominicans. The master general laid it down in no uncertain terms that the doctrine of Thomas was the doctrine of the Dominican Order, and any professor who spoke against him was to be removed from office.

It was from the French province, and, ultimately, from the French enemies of Thomas, that the opposition to the master general began to take formidable shape. He had ordained with regard to study that the members of the Order were to avoid "all vain and profane subjects," an idea which was not well received by the Parisian professors who were just beginning to taste the sweets of oriental learning.

The master general commissioned Thierry of Apoldia to write the life of St. Dominic; he himself had written the Third Order Rule, giving it definite form for the first time. It is difficult to see where he could have been criticized for lack of zeal. But when he severely penanced two professors who had gone far afield into pagan studies, they retaliated by reporting him to Pope Nicholas IV. People with a grievance can usually tell a plausible tale. The pope listened, and two Dominican cardinals were given the job of deposing the master general.

To understand the transaction, one has to remember that the whole idea of democracy was foreign and extremely suspect to a world that still believed in the absolute right of rulers. The Dominicans had no precedent for their custom of electing their superiors. No one else did things that way. Consequently the whole papal court was astounded to receive a polite letter from the Dominicans, pointing out that it was not lawful for anyone to depose a superior without making a definite charge and giving him a chance to defend himself against it. "A most rigorous examination has only served to make perfectly clear to us the merits and virtue of our Father General, who is . . . completely irreproachable, and an example to good religious. This we know and have evidence to prove. . . ." The entire weight of the Order was behind the letter; even the French province united with the rest in the common battle for a basic principle.

There was no defiance in the position of the capitular fathers who thus united to uphold Dominic's principle of justice. The idea of giving a fair trial to someone accused of a crime is not new to us, but it *was* new to the governments of the late thirteenth century. Nicholas Boccasini, the future Pope Benedict XI, was spokesman for the members of the Order, and their position was fair enough: "We are aware that Your Holiness has been given false information, and wish only to point out the truth. Let us have a direct accusation, and give our Father General an opportunity to answer the charges." The pope replied by personally deposing Munio de Zamora and all the provincials who had defended him.

Munio de Zamora retired to Spain. The king of Castile nominated him archbishop of Compostela, and he refused the honor, as he did several other bishoprics. After the death of Pope Nicholas IV, the brethren presented to the new pope, Celestine V, the case of their former master general. Pope Celestine appointed him bishop of Palencia, and the new master general compelled him to accept the honor. Six months later, Pope Celestine resigned, and the new pope deposed Munio as bishop and sent him in penance to Santa Sabina. Here he lived in retirement until his death in 1300.

Munio of Zamora, center of controversy, was buried with honors at Santa Sabina, in Rome.

BLESSED BENEDICT XI
(1240-1304)

Nicholas Boccasini was born in Treviso, in 1240, of poor parents. We know little about his family, though there are several different traditions concerning it. One claims that his father was a poor shepherd, another that he was an impoverished noble. Whichever he was, he died when Nicholas was very small, and the little boy was put in the care of an uncle, a priest in Treviso.

The child proved to be very intelligent, so his uncle had him trained in Latin and other clerical subjects. When Nicholas was ten years old, his uncle got him a position as tutor to some noble children. He followed this work until he was old enough to enter the Dominican community at Venice, which he did in 1254.

Here, and in various parts of Italy, Nicholas spent the next fourteen years, completing his education. It is quite probable that he had St. Thomas Aquinas for one of his teachers.

Nicholas was pre-eminently a teacher. He did his work well. We know this from several sources, including a testimonial from no less than St. Antoninus, who said of him that he had "a vast store of knowledge, a prodigious memory, a penetrating genius, and (that) everything about him endeared him to all." In 1295, he received the degree of master of theology.

The administrative career of Nicholas Boccasini began with his election as master general of the Order in 1296. His work in this office came to the notice of the pope, who, after Nicholas had completed a delicate piece of diplomacy in Flanders, appointed him cardinal. The Dominican hurried to Rome to protest that he should not be given the dignity of a cardinal, only to receive from the pope the mystifying prophecy that God had reserved an even heavier burden for Nicholas. Boniface VIII did not always agree with the man he had appointed cardinal-bishop of Ostia and dean of the sacred college. But they respected each other, and in the tragic affair that was shaping up with Philip the Fair of France, Cardinal Boccasini was to defend the Holy Father, even to the point of offering his life.

Philip the Fair, like several other monarchs, discovered that his interests clashed with those of the papacy. His action was particularly odious in an age when the papal power had not yet been separated completely from temporal concerns. The French monarch, who bitterly hated Boniface, besieged the pope in the Castle of Anagni, where he had taken refuge, and demanded that he resign the papacy. His soldiers even broke into the house and were met by the pope, dressed in full pontifical vestments and attended by two cardinals, one of whom was Cardinal Boccasini. For a short time it looked as though the soldiers might kill all three of them, but they refrained from such a terrible crime and finally withdrew. Cardinal Boccasini set about the difficult task of swinging public opinion to the favor of the pope. Successful in this, he stood sorrowfully by when the pontiff died, broken-hearted by his treatment at the hands of the French soldiers. At the conclave, following the death of Boniface, the prophesied burden fell upon the shoulders of the cardinal-bishop of Ostia, who took the name Benedict XI.

The reign of Benedict XI was too short to give him time to work out any of his excellent plans for settling the troubles of the Church. Most of his troubled reign was taken up with undoing the damage done by Philip the Fair. He lifted the interdict on the French people that had been laid down by his predecessor. His reign, short though it was, was noted for its leniency and kindness.

We have few personal anecdotes of Benedict, but one at least is worth telling. Once, during his pontificate, his mother came to the papal court to see him. The court attendants decided that she was too poorly dressed to appear in the presence of the Holy Father, so they dressed her up in unaccustomed finery before allowing her to see her son. Benedict, sensing what had happened, told them he did not recognize this wealthy woman, and he asked them where was the little widow, pious and poorly dressed, whom he loved so dearly.

Benedict XI died suddenly in 1304. Some people believed that he had been poisoned, but there has never been any evidence that this was the case. Many miracles were performed at his tomb, and there were several cures even before his burial. Pope Clement XII declared him blessed in 1736.

BLESSED EMILY BICCHIERI
(1238-1314)

Direct ancestor of thousands of Dominican sisters, who today are engaged in all the active charities of the Order, was Blessed Emily Bicchieri. She built the first convent for conventual Third Order Sisters in 1256.

Emily was born in 1238, the fourth of seven daughters. Before her birth, her mother was privileged to see in a dream something of the future work of her daughter. She saw a magnificent church—one that she had never seen before—and a beautiful young girl wearing white robes and a veil with a wreath of white roses. Around the young woman gathered other girls, all dressed in the same fashion, and, as the good woman watched, enthralled by the beauty of the scene, they formed into a procession and marched singing around the church. An old Dominican to whom she related the dream explained to her that it concerned the child she was bearing, and that this child, a daughter, would be a saint.

Emily grew up among her sisters and received, for that time, a good education. They were all taught to read and embroider, and Emily very early developed a talent for seeking out the poor and the troubled, using her talents to relieve their miseries. She was her father's favorite, in spite of the fact that she emptied her purse as fast as he could fill it. While her three older sisters were concerning themselves about making advantageous marriages, she was already planning her future; she would be a nun—just what kind, she did not know.

When Emily was seventeen, the first and greatest grief of her life came to her—her father died. She had been his constant companion for several years, and she had dreaded breaking the news to him that she wanted to enter a convent. However, faced with death, he had quite easily given her the permission she desired, and, after his estate was settled and her mother provided for, Emily set about accomplishing her desire. Her portion of the sizeable estate she used to build a convent for sisters of the Third Order Conventual of St. Dominic. It is not known that any such institution existed before her time, but it must have been both in the mind of St. Dominic and in the plans of his successors, because the Dominican fathers of Vercelli enthusiastically supported her in her project.

The papal brief authorizing the new foundation, the Convent of St. Margaret, bears the date of 1256. On the Feast of St. Michael, Emily and her companions—who now numbered more than thirty—were dressed for their bridal day in white gowns, with veils and wreaths of white roses. Emily's mother, coming into the church for the first time to attend the ceremony, was amazed to see the details of her dream worked out in actuality. The young aspirants were questioned concerning their intentions, and then were taken out and dressed in the Dominican habit. A Dominican nun from the Second Order had been appointed by the cardinal to train them in the tradition of the Order, and their novitiate began.

It was perhaps inevitable that the band of young novices would recognize Emily as their natural superior. She had all the qualities of leadership that one hopes for in a superior, as well as being the foundress of the convent. Consequently, when the borrowed novice mistress completed her work and saw them all professed, Sister Emily, in spite of her youth, was unanimously named superior. She was called "Mother Emily," which was a great trial to her.

We wish that we knew more about this interesting household. We know that it was designed for good works as well as prayer, which indicates that the cloister was not as strict as it was in the Second Order houses of the time, though even Second Order nuns traveled considerably in the late thirteenth century. One of the differences, and it may well be one of the principal differences, between the Convent of St. Margaret and the Second Order foundations, was that Blessed Emily's house had no lay sisters; all the sisters were of the same category and shared in the work of the house. The Divine Office was said, though we do not know whether the sisters rose for midnight Matins. Blessed Emily herself discouraged the contact with seculars which was to bring so many religious houses to ruin, and set up her horarium so that the sisters would have time and privacy for the life they were expected to lead. The rich gifts that she and the other sisters received from friends and relatives were promptly given out to those who came seeking help at the alms' gate.

Blessed Emily was not spared the agonies of spiritual doubt. Anxious as she was to receive Holy Communion frequently, the practice at the time was to go only rarely to the altar rail. Overly conscientious about her small faults, and battered about by the opinions of people less fervent than she was, she entered upon a long period of worry. Finally, our Lord Himself came to relieve her of it, and assured her that it was much more pleasing to Him for her to receive Him through love than for her to abstain from receiving through fear of unworthiness.

One of the convent tasks that Blessed Emily particularly enjoyed was that of infirmarian. This gave her the double joy of helping the sick and of mortifying herself. Once, in the exercise of this office, she had to make a difficult choice. It was Christmas Day, the time when she wanted with all her heart to receive Communion. There were three very sick sisters in the infirmary, and one of them could not be left alone. Emily had to remain with her during the Mass, only hurrying out to receive her Lord and rushing back again, without time for the long thanksgiving that she felt the occasion demanded. However, as she came back to the infirmary and glanced at the three sick sisters, she acted on divine inspiration and said to them, "I am not alone, my sisters; see, I bring Jesus to bless you." Whereupon, our Lord chose that moment to cure the three sick sisters. They promptly rose up and joined in the celebration of the feast. On another day, Emily arrived in the chapel too late for Communion. Sad and regretful, she knelt in prayer. An angel came and gave her Holy Communion, miraculously.

Emily had always been a devotee of mortification. She made use of the usual medieval methods of conquering self—fastings, disciplines, hairshirts— and added others as she thought of them. Her special devotion was to the Holy Crown of Thorns. This famous relic had been brought from the Holy Land in the year that Emily was born, and, although she could hardly have seen it, she must have heard a great deal about it. She meditated often on it and on the terrible pain that it caused our Lord. One day she bravely asked our Lord to let her share this pain, and He granted this request. The stigmata of the crown of thorns was impressed on her head for three days of intolerable suffering, and during that time she was visited by several of the saints associated with our Lord's Passion. At the end of three days the pain disappeared, but she retained her great devotion to the Crown of Thorns all her life.

Blessed Emily was a strict superior, but a beloved one. Many times she saved her sisters from grief of one kind or another by her prayers in their behalf, and her corrections were so gentle that they had great power over the culprit.

At least twice Our Lady is said to have come to see Blessed Emily, both times to teach her prayer. Miracles were worked by the prayers of the Blessed on the occasion of a disastrous flood, and also when a fire broke out inside the convent. She cured many sick people by her prayers, but she was always embarrassed at this sort of thing, as though she had somehow committed a fault.

Emily Bicchieri died in 1314, after a half-century of prayer and good works in the convent which she had founded. She was beatified in 1769.

ST. AGNES OF MONTEPULCIANO
(1268-1317)

Although St. Agnes of Montepulciano was not in any way a "child saint," like her little Roman patroness, there is about her something of the same simplicity, which makes her name appropriate. Some of the best-known legends about her concern her childhood.

Agnes was born in 1268, in a little village near Montepulciano, of the wealthy family of De Segni. Her birth was announced by great lights surrounding the house where she was born, and from her babyhood she was one specially marked out for dedication to God. By the time she was six years old she was already urging her parents to let her enter the convent. When they assured her that she was much too young to be admitted, she begged them to move to Montepulciano, where she could be near enough to the convent to make frequent visits. Since a state of armed truce existed between the cities near Montepulciano, her father was unwilling to move from his safe retreat, but he did allow the little girl to go occasionally to make visits in the convent of her choice.

On one of these visits an event occurred which all the chroniclers record as being prophetic. The little girl was traveling in Montepulciano with her mother and the women of the household, and, as they passed a hill on which stood a house of ill-fame, a flock of crows swooped down on the little girl and attacked her with beak and claw. Screaming and plunging, they managed to scratch and frighten her badly before the women drove them away. Upset by the incident, but devoutly sure of themselves, the women said that the birds must have been devils, and that they resented the purity and goodness of little Agnes, who would one day drive them from that hilltop. Agnes did, in fact, build a convent there in after years.

When she was nine years old, Agnes insisted that the time had come to let her enter the convent. She was allowed to go to a group of Franciscans in Montepulciano, whose dress was the ultimate in primitive Franciscanism; they were known, from the cut of the garment, as "Sisters of the Sack." The high-born daughter of the Segni was not at all appalled at the rude simplicity with which they followed their Father Francis; she rejoiced in it. For five years she enjoyed the only complete peace she would ever have; she was appointed bursar at the age of fourteen, and she never again was without some responsibility to others.

She reached a high degree of contemplative prayer and was favored with many visions. One of the loveliest is the one for which her legend is best known: the occasion of a visit from the Blessed Virgin. Our Lady came with the Holy Infant in her arms, and allowed Agnes to hold Him and caress Him. Unwilling to let Him go, Agnes hung on when Our Lady reached to take Him back from her. When she awakened from the ecstasy, Our Lady and her Holy Child were gone, but Agnes was still clutching tightly the little gold cross He had worn on a chain about His neck. She kept it as a precious treasure. Another time, Our Lady gave her three small stones and told her that she should use them to build a convent some day. Agnes was not at the moment even thinking about going elsewhere, and said so, but Our Lady told her to keep the stones—three, in honor of the Blessed Trinity —and one day she would need them.

Some time after this, Agnes was called upon to leave Montepulciano to help in the foundation of a new convent of the Franciscans in Proceno. Here, to her distress, she was appointed abbess. Since she was only fifteen, a special dispensation had been obtained to allow her to take the office. On the day when she was consecrated abbess, great showers of tiny white crosses fluttered down on the chapel and the people in it. It seemed to show the favor of heaven on this somewhat extraordinary situation.

For twenty years, Agnes lived in Proceno, happy in her retreat and privileged to penetrate the secrets of God in her prayer. She was a careful superior, as well as a mystic; several times she worked miracles to increase the house food supply when it was low. Once she was called back to Montepulciano for a short stay, and she went willingly enough, though she hated leaving the peace of her cloister for the confusion of traveling. She had just settled down, on her return, with the hope that she had made her last move and could now stay where she was, when obedience again called her back to Montepulciano—this time to build a new convent. A revelation had told her that she was to leave the Franciscans, among whom she had been very happy, and that she and the sisters of the house she would found should become Dominicans.

In 1306, Agnes returned to Montepulciano to put the Lord's request into action. All she had for the building of the convent were the three little stones given her by the Blessed Virgin, and Agnes—who had been bursar, and knew something about money—realized that she was going to have to rely heavily on the support of heaven in her building project. After a long quarrel with the inhabitants of the hilltop she wanted for her foundation, the land was finally secured, and the Servite prior laid the first stone, leaving her to worry about where the rest of the stones were coming from. Agnes laid hand to the project and guided it safely to completion. The church and convent of Santa Maria Novella were ready for dedication in record time, and a growing collection of aspirants pleaded with her to admit them to the new convent.

She explained that the rule was to be not Franciscan, but Dominican. All the necessary arrangements were made, and the new community settled down. They had barely established the regular life when one of the walls of the new building collapsed. It was discovered that the builders had cheated, and that the whole convent was in danger of falling on top of them. Agnes met the new problem with poise. She had many friends in Montepulciano by this time, and they rallied round to rebuild the house.

When the convent was once again completed, and had become, as hoped, a dynamo of prayer and penance, Agnes decided to go to Rome on pilgrimage. It is interesting to note that Second Order convents of the fourteenth century were so flexible in the matter of enclosure. She made the trip to Rome and visited the shrines of the martyrs. The pope was in Avignon, so she did not have the happiness of talking to him. But she returned to Montepulciano full of happiness for having seen the holy places of Rome.

At the age of forty-nine, Agnes' health began to fail rapidly. She was taken for treatment to the baths at Chianciano—accompanied, as it says in the rule, by "two or three sisters"—but the baths did her no good. She did perform a miracle while there, restoring to life a child who had fallen into the baths and drowned. But she returned to Montepulciano to die on the twentieth of April, 1317.

She died in the night, and the children of the city wakened and cried out, "Holy Sister Agnes is dead!" She was buried in Montepulciano, and her tomb soon became a place of pilgrimage.

One of the most famous pilgrims to visit her tomb was St. Catherine of Siena, who went to venerate the saint and also, probably, to visit her niece, Eugenia, who was a nun in the convent there. As she bent over the body of St. Agnes to kiss the foot, she was amazed to see Agnes raise her foot so that she did not have to stoop so far.

Agnes of Montepulciano was canonized in 1796.

BLESSED SIMON BALLACHI
(1250-1319)

A fitting patron for gardeners and all those who like to work with growing things is the Dominican laybrother, Blessed Simon Ballachi.

Simon was born of a distinguished family in San Arcangelo, in the north of Italy. Two of his uncles were bishops, and one of his brothers a priest. Since there was considerable property to be administered, it was understood that Simon would marry and take over the management of the family affairs. He was, perhaps with a view to this, trained from his earliest years as a soldier.

However, at the age of twenty-seven, the young man presented himself at the Dominican Convent of Rimini and asked to be received as a laybrother. His family was not too happy about his choice of life. They had expected him to carve out a busy and noteworthy career in the world, and they could not understand why he should want to abandon such an opportunity. Moreover, as long as he insisted on being a religious, they did not see why he would not become a priest; then, at least, there would be a chance of future preference in ecclesiastical offices.

Oblivious to the criticism and the ambitions of his family, Simon settled down happily to serve God as a laybrother. His principal work, to his great delight, was the garden. It is most unlikely that he had ever seen a garden before he entered religion, and he probably had to learn all the tiresome details by trial and error method. From what we read of him, he succeeded admirably in making a prayer of every task. He became adept at the fine art of seeing God in everything. It was written of him that he meditated on every act, "so that, while his hands cultivated the herbs and flowers of the earth, his heart might be a paradise of sweet-smelling flowers in the sight of God." He tried to find in everything he handled in the garden some lesson it could teach him about the spiritual life. When the weather was too bad for him to work out of doors, he swept and cleaned the convent. Wherever his work took him, he tried to do it well and to efface himself completely, so that no one would even notice he was there.

Under the placid exterior of the life of a gardener, Simon concealed a spiritual life of great penance and prayer. We may believe that he worked very hard at times, yet he never excused himself from rising for the night Office, nor from any of the severe penances he inflicted upon himself. For twenty years he wore an iron chain bound tightly about his waist—not exactly a comfortable device to wear when doing heavy work. In Lent, he lived on bread and water. Extra time for prayer he took from his sleep. Like St. Dominic, he scourged himself every night. A program of this sort was not apt to please the devil, who used to torment him continually, trying to distract him at prayer, or to get him to be impatient at his work.

Other visitors came to him in the silence of the night: St. Catherine of Alexandria, to whom he had a special devotion, St. Dominic and St. Peter Martyr, and sometimes our Blessed Mother herself. His little cell was radiant with heavenly lights, and sometimes angelic voices could be heard there.

At the age of fifty-seven, he lost his eyesight and sometime after this he became quite helpless. After years of suffering, Simon died on November the third, 1319. He was declared blessed in 1817.

BLESSED MARGARET OF CASTELLO
(1287-1320)

Blessed Margaret was born of poor parents, in a little mountain village of Umbria. She was born blind, an affliction which embittered her parents. When she was five years old, they made a pilgrimage to the tomb of a holy Franciscan at Castello, to pray that her eyes would be cured. No miracle being forthcoming, they abandoned the child in the church and returned to their home.

Margaret was adopted by a kindly peasant woman named Grigia, who had a large family of her own. Margaret's natural sweetness and goodness soon made themselves felt, and she more than repaid the family for their kindness to her. She was an influence for good in any group of children. She stopped their quarrels, heard their catechism, told them stories, taught them psalms and prayers. Busy neighbors were soon borrowing her to soothe a sick child or to establish peace in the house.

Her reputation for holiness was so great that a community of sisters in the town asked for her to become one of themselves. Margaret went happily to join them, but, unfortunately, there was little fervor in the house. The little girl who was so prayerful and penitential was a reproach to their lax lives, so Margaret was returned to Grigia, who gladly welcomed her home.

Some years after this, Margaret was received as a Dominican Tertiary and clothed with the religious habit. Grigia's home became the rendezvous of troubled souls who came seeking Margaret's prayers. She said the Office of the Blessed Virgin and the entire Psalter by heart, and her prayers had the effect of restoring peace of heart to those who were troubled. Denied earthly sight, Margaret was favored with heavenly visions. "Oh, if you only knew what I have in my heart!" she said often. The mysteries of the Rosary, particularly the joyful mysteries, were so vivid to her that her whole person would light up when she described the scene. She was often in ecstasy, and, despite great joys and favors in prayer, she was often called upon to suffer desolation and interior trials of frightening sorts. The devil tormented her severely at times, but she triumphed over these sufferings.

A number of miracles were performed by Blessed Margaret. On one occasion, while she was praying in an upper room, Grigia's house caught fire, and she called to Margaret to come down. The blessed, however, called to her to throw her cloak on the flames. This she did, and the blaze died out. At another time, she cured a sister who was losing her eyesight.

Beloved by her adopted family and by her neighbors and friends, Margaret died at the early age of thirty-three. From the time of her death, her tomb in the Dominican church was a place of pilgrimage. Her body, even to this century, is incorrupt.

After her death, the fathers received permission to have her heart opened. In it were three pearls, having holy figures carved upon them. They recalled the saying so often on the lips of Margaret—"If you only knew what I have in my heart!"

RICCOLDO OF MONTECROCE
(d. 1320)

Riccoldo of Montecroce stands out in a glittering company as a man of personality and distinction. His task was fantastic enough to entitle him to undying fame, but to this he added an observant mind, and a facile pen that recorded for us many of the wonders that he saw.

There is a fair amount of material concerning Riccoldo and his work, which makes it all the more surprising that we know so little of him. He was evidently born in Florence, around 1243, of the Pennini family. (The name "Montecroce" was a devotional title he added after a trip to the Holy Land.) He was professed at the convent of Santa Maria Novella, around 1268. He was the youngest of four brothers, all of whom became Dominicans. There are records of his teaching in the studium of Pisa and Prato in 1287 and 1288. He died in 1320, on the Vigil of All Saints, and was buried— with a long epitaph—at the convent where he had made profession. This is quite complete documentation for one who lived in the early days of the Order. However, it is his travels and his work that are most interesting.

His colorful career began when he sailed for the Holy Land in 1288. Acre, the great fortress of the East, was still in the hands of the Christians at the time, and Castle Pilgrim was held by the Templars; pilgrims were free to tour in the Holy Land, and the Florentine friar took full advantage of this, taking a trip through Gallilee in November of the same year, and most probably spending Christmas at Bethlehem. Not he nor anyone else could know that the sands had run clear to the end of the glass; he went on to Baghdad, unknowing that the Christian kingdom of the East would fall in another year, to be lost forever.

Riccoldo was the first man from the West to give any consideration to the racial and linguistic puzzles presented by the Mongols. Most devout Christians simply concluded that they had come from hell and were not suitable objects for Christian study. Riccoldo was fascinated by these strange mobile tribes, with their great rolling houses of felt and their peculiar customs. He had read carefully the reports of the Franciscans and the Dominicans who had gone to Tartary forty years before, and he had searched the Scriptures for evidence that these wanderers were the lost tribes of Israel. There also existed a legend that Alexander the Great had caused a mountain to fall, imprisoning a whole people between very high mountains, from whence they would emerge at the end of the world to follow anti-Christ. He noted that their language bore resemblances to both Hebrew and Chaldean, and he made a systematic effort to trace their linguistic roots and very capably traced the path of their invasions. He distinguishes three groups of Tartars and details their path of conquest surprisingly well.

He was enchanted by the sort of hats the Mongol women wore, and says: "Women are held in great honor by the Tartars, and they wear over their heads more beautiful and higher crowns than the ones any other lady of the world might have." (The Franciscan, John de Plano Carpini, had gone to great lengths to describe this towering glory, beginning rather helplessly with the remark that it was "a round thing made of bark . . . which from bottom to top grows in largeness." Both of these pious and sincere men seem not to have noticed anything else the women wore, which indicates that the hats must have been really spectacular).

Riccoldo found Baghdad very gay and interesting, populated by "over a hundred thousand Saracens". While there he wrote several works against the errors of the Saracens and a defense of the faith, which was printed in Seville, in 1500, and of which a copy still exists. Other editions were printed both in Spain and Italy, in Greek and Latin.

He was busily writing in Baghdad when the terrible news came of the fall of Acre and the loss of the Christian kingdom in the Holy Land. He was stunned and frightened at the news, and he wrote a lamentation for the fall of Jerusalem, in the form of four letters: the first to our Lord, who was seemingly siding with the Saracens in this affair; the second to Our Lady; the third to the saints; the fourth to Nicholas of Hanappes, patriarch of Jerusalem. Very shortly, the sad event came even closer to him, for some spoils from the doomed city flowed into Baghdad. Riccoldo haunted the slave markets, looking for any of his brethren who might have been captured by the Saracens. He did not find any, but in the market he found vestments and books from the religious houses, breviaries that had belonged to people he had known personally, and other tragic relics of the slaughter. Finally, he found the religious habit of Nicholas of Hanappes, covered with blood and plainly showing the slash where a spear or an arrow had pierced. He redeemed it from the market and brought it home. It seemed to him that the end of the world had arrived, and he fled into the desert.

The deserts of Arabia are not kind to Westerners, and Riccoldo soon was in trouble. Starving and dying of thirst, he was picked up by two Moslems who stripped him of his habit and tried to force him to join in their beliefs. Just what happened next is not clear, and it must have been interesting, since he turned up next in Nineveh, disguised as a cameleer. He probably found some poetic justice in finding himself in Nineveh, where long ago a clarion call for penance had been sounded. Here, too, he found evidence of the disintegrating Christian world; there were Christian gospels and lectionaries for sale in the street bazaars, and chained Christians waiting in the slave markets for their Saracen masters to carry them off to their doom.

Riccoldo is lost sight of for some time, but it is evident that he returned to Italy and that he engaged himself with the organization of the missionaries for the Near East, who had, up to that time, operated from their separate provinces. Now they would have to be welded into a more permanent form to cope with the new situation in the Holy Land. He wrote various works concerning the *Fratres Perigrinantes,* or those who would eventually come to be known by that name. In one place he says: "The Son of God was a pilgrim on earth; His life was a pilgrimage, first of all to Egypt. So shall my feet witness to Christ. If I have been willing to undertake long and laborious journeys for worldly reasons (i.e., study) I should do much more for apostolic reasons."

Riccoldo, for all his enthusiasm, was a realist. Badly as the Near East needed missionaries, he realized that not all the volunteers were missionary timber. "The hobo instinct is the principal difficulty to be dealt with," he says candidly. "If the Brethren do not arrive at their mission field within a year, they should be sent back to their own provinces. There is also a temptation in having too much association with merchants. Sometimes the Brethren are tempted to invest in commercial ventures, and in any case it is not wise for them to ally themselves too closely with merchants who enter into forbidden trading with the Saracens."

After a colorful and busy life, Riccoldo died in his home convent of Santa Maria Novella, in 1320.

AUGUSTINE OF LUCERA
(1260-1323)

Augustine was born in Dalmatia, in 1260. His people were wealthy and gave him a good education. At the age of eighteen, he and an Italian friend set out for the Dominican novitiate in France. Near Pavia, they were set upon by enemies of his friend's family, and both were left for dead in the snow beside the road. When found, his companion was dead, and Augustine was badly injured. After recovering from his injuries, he continued his journey and entered the novitiate, where he soon gave proof of the superior intellect and judgment with which he had been endowed.

Augustine spent most of his life in active battle with heresy. In his own country of Dalmatia, it was a type of Manichaean heresy; in Sicily, Mohammedan; in Hungary, a combination of both. In every situation in which he found himself, Augustine gave proof of his virtue and wisdom. When Cardinal Boccasini came to Hungary as legate, he noted the wisdom and tact of his brother Dominican, and when he himself ascended the papal throne as Benedict XI, he appointed Augustine bishop of Zagreb, in Hungary.

This diocese was in a dreadful state when Augustine took over. His three predecessors had all tried to repair the ravages of heresy, plague, and schism, which divided the diocese. The new bishop began by reforming the clergy. He finished building the cathedral and made a complete visitation of his diocese. His work was to bring him into violent conflict with the government, but, spiritually, he rebuilt the entire diocese in his years there.

Several charming miracles are related about Augustine of Lucera. One has to do with the water supply at the convent of Zagreb. The river water was unfit to drink, and the fathers asked Bishop Augustine to pray that they would find a new supply. At his prayer, a fountain sprang up in the yard of the convent, abundantly supplying all their needs. In one of the little villages he planted a tree, the leaves of which proved to have healing qualities. On one occasion, when Bishop Augustine was dining with Pope Benedict XI, the pope, feeling that a missionary bishop should eat well in order to preach well, had a dish of partridges set before Augustine. The bishop made it a practice not to eat meat, but he did not wish to offend the pope. So he prayed to find a way out of it—and the partridges, according to legend, changed into fish.

From Zagreb, Bishop Augustine was transferred to the See of Nocera, in Sicily. Here he continued his holy government, promoting devotion to St. Dominic, St. Thomas, and St. Peter Martyr in his diocese, as an aid to the spiritual advancement of his flock. Feeling that he was near death, he returned to the Dominican convent in Nocera to die among his brethren.

Under his statue in the cathedral of Nocera is the legend, "Sanctus Augustine Episcopus Lucerinus Ordinis Praedicatorum," an indication of the veneration in which he has always been held.

Pope Clement XI reconfirmed his cult in 1702.

BLESSED JANE OF ORVIETO
(1264-1306)

One of the stigmatists of the Order who deserves to be better known is Blessed Jane of Orvieto, whose marvel-filled life was the edification of Umbria in the latter half of the thirteenth century.

Jane was born near Orvieto, in 1264, and both parents died when she was very small. Left to the care of casual neighbors, the little girl grew up with special reliance on her guardian angel. She was a pious and intelligent child, spending her time in prayer, even when very young.

Since it was necessary for her to earn her living, Jane studied dressmaking and became proficient at it. For several years she worked at this trade, prayerful and happy and undisturbed about her future. However, she had a number of unhappy experiences on the street on her way to work, for young men were attracted by her beauty. It became apparent to her that she must make some public declaration of her intentions if she wanted any peace. She decided to enter the Third Order of St. Dominic. Dressed in the habit of the mantellate, she would be safe from rude remarks and from any misunderstanding.

Jane's friends opposed her plans, because they had already helpfully chosen a husband for her, and were trying to arrange a meeting of Jane and the man they had selected. Because of her youth, the Dominicans delayed in accepting her. Only after a long period of prayer and fasting was she able to win the privilege of putting on the Third Order habit and living with the other members of the Tertiary chapter. Once a member of the Order she so much desired, she set her goal at the highest sanctity and worked at attaining it. She prayed all morning and part of the afternoon, leaving herself only time to do enough work to care for her few needs and some alms to give the poor. She soon reached a remarkable state of prayer; she participated bodily in whatever she was contemplating. Her director learned not to say anything that would send her into ecstasy until he was through instructing her. Once he mentioned the martyrdom of Catherine of Alexandria and said piously, "Arise, O blessed Catherine," and Jane arose, in ecstasy, and remained suspended in the air for an hour. If he talked about the Crucifixion, her arms would go out in the form of a cross, and she would rise in the air like a figure on a crucifix. On Good Fridays she experienced the terrible agony of the Passion, and one could hear her bones cracking and see the bloody sweat. She received the stigmata, but it was not always visible.

Along with her remarkable life of prayer, Jane had to contend with physical pain. Once she was cured of a serious illness by a miraculous appearance of our Lord on the cross. He appeared to her in the midst of a bright light and gave her a cup of wine to drink. She obediently drank it, and she was instantly cured. Another time, when she was too ill to go to church to receive Communion, Our Lady came and brought the Holy Child to her.

One of Jane's principal crosses was the lack of privacy. The whole town knew about her ecstasies. As soon as she fell into one, people came running to look. Jane tried to persuade the prioress to keep them out, but the prioress was interested herself, and saw no reason why anybody should object to being watched if they were not doing anything wrong. Jane wept with embarrassment when people asked for her blessing, and assured them over and over that she was not a saint but a wicked sinner, a diagnosis which nobody believed but herself.

Blessed Jane died, in 1306, and was buried in the Third Order cemetery in Orvieto. The following year her body was transferred to the chapel of the Three Kings, and many prodigies occurred at that time, giving impetus to the process for beatification, which, however, was not completed until more than 400 years later, in 1754.

BLESSED JAMES OF BEVAGNA
(1220-1301)

Very early in life, prodigies surrounded Blessed James, for on the day of his birth three brilliant stars, each containing the image of a friar preacher, appeared in the sky over Bevagna. Children ran through the streets crying: "To the schools! To the schools! Behold the new masters heaven is sending us!" The three preachers were later understood to be James, Blessed Ambrose of Siena, and St. Thomas Aquinas.

James was given a good education and was carefully trained in the ways of holiness. The power of his prayer was seen early. When still a small child, he brought about peace between two quarreling families. At the age of sixteen, he met the Dominicans. Two friars had come to preach in his native city during Lent. Deciding, after much prayer, that God was calling him to the Dominican apostolate, he went home with the two missioners and began his novitiate.

The early promises of his great learning were well fulfilled. In an age that shone with the brilliance of Albert, Thomas, and Bonaventure, the preaching of James of Bevagna was still remarkable. He was particularly gifted at reconciling enemies and bringing peace to warring families and cities.

James was very severe with himself, particularly in the matter of poverty. On one occasion, his mother, shocked at the poor condition of the habit he was wearing, gave him money to buy a new one. As he wanted very much more to get a crucifix for his cell, he did so. His mother reminded him that the money was given to him for clothing. James replied with the text, "Put ye on the Lord Jesus Christ," assuring her that this was the garment he had bought with her gift.

At another time, praying before this same crucifix, James was overcome with a sense of his own unworthiness and begged of God some sign that his soul was to be saved. Blood gushed from the hands and side of the figure on the cross, and a voice from heaven told him that this token of God's favor would reassure him. Some of the miraculous blood was preserved for more than two centuries. Kept at the tomb of Blessed James, it worked many miracles, but it was stolen by heretics.

Forewarned of the hour of his death, James was assured that Our Lady would come to meet him, because he had often sacrificed to adorn her altars. She came at the time foretold, and James went happily with her into the presence of God.

THEODORE OF SAXONY
(1310)

This scientific-minded friar of a non-scientific age spent his life in the pursuit of the rainbow—quite literally, for he was engaged all his life in experiment with the qualities of light and the question of light refraction.

We do not know when Theodore was born, nor where; tradition says that he was a Saxon. He is variously called "of Frieburg," and several other titles, which seem to identify him, in any case, as a member of the German province. His position as German provincial, in 1293, would strengthen this theory. The chances are excellent that he studied under St. Albert the Great, who had himself evolved a theory of light refraction which he had not had time to follow up. Perhaps Theodore was the pupil who carried out the master's theory and went on to develop new theories of his own. We simply do not know.

What we do know is that Theodore wrote no less than thirty-one treatises on various phases of natural science and theology. By very good luck, twenty-one works have survived for our inspection, and they show Theodore to have been a man of talent, with that quality of persistence so necessary to a research scientist, and a certain inventiveness in carrying out his experiments.

His work, *De Iride et Radialibus Impressionibus,* is considered a remarkable advance in the science of optics and in the experimental method, both of which were in their infancy in the late thirteenth century. By coincidence, Arabic writers had worked out an almost identical theory at the same time he was working in the West; it was, in other words, a subject of much interest in those days.

Long before the well-known experiments of Descartes, Theodore of Saxony had reached some of the same conclusions. He constructed some very ingenious little glass balls, with which, filled with water, he used to show, in enlarged form, his theory about the refraction of light in drops of water. He explains with great clarity the different reflections that go to make up the first and second rainbows. He was principally concerned with the shape of the bow in its reflection of color.

At one point of his experiments, Theodore was very close to a discovery that only the nineteenth century was to conclude. In the business of projecting light through the crystal balls, he made use of an opaque screen on which the colors were projected through hexagonal crystals. The mysteries of photography were far in the future, but he did determine that the spectrum rays were always in the same order—red being nearest the line of incidence.

Aside from his scientific studies, Theodore of Saxony was employed in the regular work of a Dominican; he lectured at Paris on the *Sentences of Peter Lombard,* in 1297; six years later he was lecturing at Coblenz. In 1304, he attended the general chapter at Toulouse, at which time he presented a paper on *Rainbows,* which he had been requested to do by the master general, Aymeric of Piacenza. In 1310, he was appointed vicar-provincial of Germany.

When and where Theodore of Saxony died we do not know. Scientists, who today revel in expensive and accurate equipment and can draw upon centuries of experience, can well breathe a prayer of gratitude for this early and almost unknown scientist, for, considering his equipment, he contributed much to the vast fund of scientific knowledge.

BLESSED JORDAN OF PISA
(d. 1311)

In the study of the origins of language, the name of Blessed Jordan of Pisa deserves a high place, and students of Italian literature are careful to give him that honor. At a time when the language was poorly defined, and still under a cloud of disapproval by scholars who felt that nothing would ever replace Latin as a gentleman's language, Jordan worked to make Italian the beautiful tongue that it is today. That was not, of course, the reason he was beatified by the Church; but it is an interesting feature and is sometimes overlooked.

Jordan was born in Pisa, in the middle of the thirteenth century. He went to the University of Paris, where he met the Dominicans, in 1276. Four years later, probably after obtaining his degrees, he returned to Italy and entered the Order, at Pisa. He began a long teaching career there as soon as he was qualified to teach.

Jordan preached at Florence and, because of his excellence, was given the appointment of first lector there in 1305. He seems to have been fascinated with the whole question of preaching as an apostolic tool, and to have been one of the first to make a scientific study of it. He pointed out that the Greek church was "invaded by a multitude of errors," because the Greeks had no preachers; he could never say enough in praise of St. Dominic's farsightedness in establishing an Order specifically for preaching. He studied methods of making sermons more effective, both by using examples that would reach the people, and by the use of the vernacular. This latter was a much-disputed subject in his day; Jordan's championing of Italian as a literary language was somewhat like that of a man today stating: "Atomic power is here to stay, and we must harness it to apostolic use." Jordan was considered a daring innovator, and he was careful to be professional in the way he handled the new medium; he strove to make Italian a beautiful instrument on which he could play the melodies of the Lord.

Jordan had an extraordinary memory. He is supposed to have known the breviary by heart, as well as the missal, most of the Bible (with its marginal commentary), plus the second part of the *Summa*. This faculty of memory he used in his sermons, but he was quick to point out to young preachers that learning alone can never make a preacher. By the holiness of his own life he made this plain, and continually preached it to those he was training to preach.

Jordan of Pisa had two great devotions—to Our Blessed Mother and to St. Dominic. Once he was favored with a vision of Our Lady; she came into the fathers' refectory and served at table. Jordan, who was the only one who could see her, could barely eat for excitement. He spoke often of her in his sermons, and also of St. Dominic. He founded a number of confraternities in Pisa, one of which has lasted until the present time.

Jordan died in 1311, on his way to Paris to teach at St. Jacques. His body was returned from Piacenza, where death overtook him, to rest in the church at Pisa. He was beatified in 1838.

BLESSED JAMES SALOMONIO
(1231-1314)

In a little chapel in Forli, built as a tomb for honored dead, there are three Dominicans laid in close proximity. One side is occupied by Blessed Marcolino of Forli. The center position is held by Carino of Balsamo, the assassin of St. Peter Martyr, whose long penance and popular holiness are now under consideration for his possible beatification; the third place is that of Blessed James of Salomonio, who was the spiritual director of Carino.

James was born in Venice, in 1231, the only child of noble parents. His father died when he was very small, and his mother became a Cistercian nun, leaving him to the care of his grandmother. She did well by her orphaned grandson, and James became a good and studious boy who responded eagerly to any spiritual suggestions. Under the direction of a Cistercian monk, he learned to meditate, and on the monk's counsel, James became a Dominican at the convent of Sts. John and Paul, in Venice, as soon as he was old enough. He gave most of his money to the poor, and arrived at the convent with just enough left to buy a few books. Seeing that one of the laybrothers there was in need of clothing, he gave his small sum to the laybrother and entered empty-handed.

James wore the Dominican habit with dignity and piety, if not with any worldly distinction, for sixty-six years. He was humble and good and obedient, and there was nothing spectacular about his spirituality. He was well-known for his direction of souls, but he fled even from the distinction this work brought him.

Even his retiring habits did not protect him, for the people of Venice beat a path to his door. In self-defense, he transferred to another house, that of Forli. This was a house of strict observance and very poor. Nothing could suit him better. For the remainder of his life he worked and prayed in Forli, going out to visit the sick in the hospitals and spending long hours in the confessional. His charity to the poor and the sick gave him the name "Father of the Poor." He is represented in art surrounded by a horde of petitioners of this sort.

James Salomonio died in 1314, at the age of eighty-three. He was beatified in 1526, and has always been especially invoked against cancer.

FRANCIS OF PERUGIA
(1323)

One of the most interesting chapters in Dominican history is that which covers the vast missionary effort in the Near East in the fourteenth century. Dominican interest in the Near East took shape at the second general chapter of the Order, with the foundation of the provinces of Greece and the Holy Land. Jordan of Saxony drowned off the coast of Palestine, in 1237, while engaged in trying to set up a mission; St. Albert the Great, in 1271, was actively engaged in the same effort. Time and again, popes and kings had begged the friars to establish a permanent mission that would serve Persia and Armenia, and other vast territories of which hardly the names were known.

Over the course of the Order's first century, a great many men labored in this cause. At first, they functioned as missionaries out of one of the recognized provinces, sent out in bands, or as individual chaplains, to embassies or caravans. They were quite literally wanderers or travelers; the name, "Wandering Brethren of Christ Among the Heathen," was peculiarly apt. After the fall of Acre, in 1291, a new organization was called for, and the name, fluid for many years, became established as "Fratres Peregrinantes"; Wandering Brethren. The man who did most to bring this arm of the Order into shape was Francis of Perugia, who was made superior of the congregation in 1312.

Of Francis of Perugia's early history, we know regrettably little. Because of his name, one can infer that he was from Perugia, and most probably entered the Order there in 1270. The principal talent of this versatile man seems to have been a fluency in the Tartar language, which one would not expect to find in a Christian country at that time. He was sent to the Near East as head of a legation in 1296, which argues for his great capability both as diplomat and missionary.

In 1305, two delegations were sent out by Pope John XXII, who was concerned for the millions of unconverted pagans of the East. One delegation, bound for Peking, was under the care of the Franciscans; the other, bound for Sultaniyeh, on the caravan route to Karakorum, was led by Francis of Perugia, and it was made up principally of Dominicans. The pope, speaking of these missionary volunteers, said of them: "They have truly been placed as shining torches in the Church of God"; at the time, he had great hopes of converting the continent of Asia.

Sultaniyeh was the newly-built Tartar capital, and when the Dominicans arrived there it was at the height of its glory. Young as he was, Francis of Perugia had a reputation as a builder which he soon justified; twenty-five churches were built in the capital, and the Dominican church was said to be the most beautiful. The energetic missionary occupied himself in translating some of the works of St. Thomas into Greek, for use on the Eastern missions. In 1312, he was appointed to head the *Fratres Peregrinantes*.

Today there is little to show us how this missionary venture was organized. It was a separate province or, more properly, congregation, drawing upon all the other provinces for members, except for those of Greece and the Holy Land. These "Pilgrims for Christ" were living examples of the poverty and mobility of the apostolate. Students of all the provinces who wished to go to the missions affiliated themselves with this congregation, and they were specially trained in the language schools, established by papal order, in several of the Persian convents. Papal privilege also provided for outfitting the missionaries and prescribed penalties for provincials who tried to prevent their subjects from joining the congregation. Such students were given special courses, not only in the oriental languages, but also in the Eastern heresies, and in methods of combatting the errors of the East. Their training harked back to a solidly Dominican tradition: the *Summa Contra Gentiles* of St. Thomas, and the Eastern studies of St. Raymond of Pennafort.

Because of the vast areas covered and the constant danger of martyrdom, almost no records survive to tell us of individual accomplishment. John of Monaecorvino, who headed the Peking delegation, kept colorful and revealing records of the Franciscan work there, but the vast body of Dominican work at Sultaniyeh was unrecorded. The immense field is now covered in most books by the statement that the Dominicans and Franciscans divided Asia between them. The Franciscans were given China and the Far East; the Dominicans, the land from the Black Sea to Malacca and from Egypt to Syria.

In 1317, Francis of Perugia sent a French Dominican to the papal court at Avignon to announce that the missions of the Near East were prospering.

His messenger returned, bearing two important documents; one, the announcement of the canonization of St. Thomas Aquinas, and the other, the appointment of Francis of Perugia as archbishop of Sultaniyeh, with six suffragan bishops. He was commissioned metropolitan over ". . . all those in the Tartar empire, all those souls in the countries submitted to the Tartar emperor, and the princes and kings of Ethiopia and the Indies." John of Montecorvino, busy in far-off Peking translated the Psalms and New Testament into Tartar, was given a similar appointment, but only three of his bishops survived to reach him.

In 1320, Francis of Perugia made a list of the Dominican and Franciscan houses in Tartary, a curious and revealing document. His work makes it clear that, although the two Orders of friars worked side by side in the difficult missions of Asia, they were not a joint organization, but each had its separate government. Caffa, in the Crimea, and Pera, near Constantinople, were the largest Dominican houses, and these were the centers of linguistic studies for the missions for a century to come.

Francis of Perugia resigned his See in 1323, for what reason we do not know. There is no definite record of when or where he died.

The work of the *"Pilgrims for Christ"* continued for a little more than a century. Schools were built all over the Near East, and many members of the congregation were appointed bishops in the newly-converted lands.

The death knell sounded for the *Fratres Peregrinantes* when the plague struck the Near East, in 1347. Within a year, there were only three Dominicans left in Persia; all the others had died. Understaffed and overworked, the congregation struggled along for several years, was suppressed, revived, and finally suppressed permanently. By 1612, nothing was left but the convent of Lemberg, and even that disappeared in time, closing a glorious chapter of high adventure for thousands of brave men who were proud to call themselves Dominican *Pilgrims for Christ*.

BLESSED IMELDA LAMBERTINI
(1322-1331)

One of the most charming legends in all Dominican hagiography is that of little Imelda, who died of love on her first Communion day, and who is, by this happy circumstance, patroness of all first communicants.

Tradition says that Imelda was born in Bologna, in 1322, of the family of the counts of Lambertini. Her family was famous for its many religious, including a Dominican preacher, a Franciscan mother foundress, and an aunt of Imelda's who had founded a convent of strict observance in Bologna.

Imelda was a delicate child, petted and favored by her family, and it was no surprise to them that she should be religious by nature. She learned to read from the Psalter, and early devoted herself to attending Mass and Compline at the Dominican church. Her mother taught her to sew and cook for the poor, and went with her on errands of charity. When Imelda was nine years old, she asked to be allowed to go to the Dominicans at Val di Pietra. She was the only child of a couple old enough not to hope for any more children; it was a wrench to let her go. However, they took her to the convent and gave her to God with willing, if sorrowing, hearts.

Imelda's status in the convent is hard to discover. She wore the habit, followed the exercises of the house as much as she was allowed to, and longed for the day when she would be old enough to join them in the two things she envied most—the midnight Office and the reception of Holy Communion. Her age barred her from both. She picked up the Divine Office from hearing the sisters chant, and meditated as best she could.

It was a lonely life for the little girl of nine, and, like many another lonely child, she imagined playmates for herself—with this one difference— her playmates were saints. She was especially fond of St. Agnes, the martyr, who was little older than Imelda herself. Often she read about her from the great illuminated books in the library, and one day Agnes came in vision to see her. Imelda was delighted. Shut away from participation in adult devotions, she had found a contemporary who could tell her about the things she most wanted to know. Agnes came often after this, and they talked of heavenly things.

Her first Christmas in the convent brought only sorrow to Imelda. She had been hoping that the sisters would relent and allow her to receive Communion with them, but on the great day, when everyone except her could go to the Communion rail to receive Jesus, Imelda must remain in her place, gazing through tears at the waxen figure in the crèche. Imelda began to pray even more earnestly that she could receive Communion. When her prayer was answered, spring had come to Bologna, and the world was preparing for the Feast of the Ascension. No one paid much attention to the little girl as she knelt in prayer while the sisters prepared for the great feast. Even when she asked to remain in the chapel in vigil on the eve of the feast, it caused no comment; she was a devout child. The sisters did not know how insistently she was knocking at heaven's gates, reciting to herself, for assurance, the prayer which appears in the Communion verse for the Rogation Days: "Ask and it shall be given to you, seek and you shall find, knock and it shall be opened to you."

The door was opened for Imelda on that morning of the Vigil of the Ascension. She had asked once more for the great privilege of receiving Communion, and, because of her persistence, the chaplain was called in on the case. He refused flatly; Imelda must wait until she was older. She went to her place in chapel, giving no outward sign that she intended to take heaven by storm, and watched quietly enough while the other sisters went to Communion. After Mass, Imelda remained in her place in choir. The sacristan busied herself putting out candles and removing the Mass vestments. A sound caused her to turn and look into the choir, and she saw a brilliant light shining above Imelda's head, and a host suspended in the light. The sacristan hurried to get the chaplain.

The chaplain now had no choice; God had indicated that He wanted to be communicated to Imelda. Reverently, the chaplain took the Host and gave it to the rapt child, who knelt like a shining statue, unconscious of the nuns crowding into the chapel, or the laypeople pushing against the chapel grille to see what might be happening there.

After an interval for thanksgiving, the prioress went to call the little novice for breakfast. She found her still kneeling. There was a smile on her face, and she was dead.

The legend of Blessed Imelda is firmly entrenched in Dominican hearts, though it is difficult now to find records to substantiate it. The convent where she lived has been gone for centuries and its records with it. Several miracles have been worked through her intercession, and her cause for canonization has been under consideration for many years. As recently as 1928 a major cure was reported of a Spanish sister who was dying of meningitis. Other miracles are under consideration. The day may yet come when the lovable little patroness of first communicants can be enrolled in the calendar of the saints.

BLESSED DALMATIUS MONERIO
(1291-1331)

This Dominican blessed, who was noted particularly for his observance of poverty, lived in the early years of the Order and helped to establish the high reputation of the Spanish religious.

Dalmatius was born in Aragon, in 1291, and we know nothing else about his life before he entered the Order. He was a member of the province of

Aragon and gave a perfect example of strict observance of the rule and the spirit of religious detachment from things of earth. All that we know about him are a few anecdotes, none of which can be fixed with certainty as to date or place.

We read that his spirit of poverty was so extreme that he never wore a habit or cappa that was not in tatters. He picked up his wardrobe from thel cast-offs of his brethren, and, since the spirit of poverty was quite rigid in this province, the cast-off clothes must have looked a sight. Dalmatius seemed to make a virtue of this, since all the records we have make mention of it. As to food, he never ate fish or eggs, and lived on a diet of hard bread and unseasoned vegetables, to which he added a few ashes during Lent. The beds in the house were hard enough for most people, but not for him. He slept on the bare earth when he could not get into the church to pray and take an occasional nap, his head resting on the altar step.

Dalmatius is credited with several miracles, which included healing and spiritual assistance. At one time, a novice was tempted to leave the Order. Dalmatius, going about it without being told, sought out the novice and solved his difficulties. At another time, a mother whose small child had a serious eye disease came looking for Dalmatius to heal her child. The friar refused, because, he said, this affliction would save her child from serious sin, and that God was waiting until some time in the future to heal him.

During the last four years of his life, Dalmatius lived in the cave of St. Mary Magdalen, in the south of France, where he had gone on a pilgrimage of devotion. Here he was favored with numerous ecstasies and great spiritual insight. One time, while he was in the cave, a group of friars from his own province were lost in the woods in a bad storm. They prayed to him to help them, and a young man came with a lantern and guided them home.

Dalmatius died in his own convent in the presence of all the friars and provincials who had gathered for a chapter. He was declared blessed in 1721.

BERNARD GUI
(1261-1331)

One of the most frequently-quoted authors of the Middle Ages was Bernard Gui, or Guidonis. He possessed not only a vast fund of information but also a fluent pen.

Bernard was born in southern France, in 1261, and, after a pious child-hood, entered the Order, at Limoges, in 1280. Most of his life was spent in and around Albi, in the heart of the country evangelized by St. Dominic seventy years before. In Bernard's time, it was once more a stronghold of heresy. Most probably the inspiration of his busy pen was the very real need of his fellow preachers for working textbooks. They were thrown into constant contact with heresy and with the whole question of truth and falsehood, and it was difficult to be objective about a controversy in which much Dominican blood had already been shed.

Bernard was prior of Albi in 1290, and the next quarter-century saw him prior of the convents at Carcassonne, Castres, and Limoges—all in the heretic country. He was eventually appointed inquisitor of Toulouse by Pope John XXII.

Unpopular as this office is in secular history, Bernard brought to it a great deal of justice and practical knowledge. His writings on the sub-ject of the practices of the inquisition do not make that institution any dearer to American readers, but he is at least clear and factual rather than merely emotional. He states quite clearly the duties of the inquisitor, his instructions for the examination of suspects, and the forms of condemnation to be employed. There is no hysteria in his account, and no trace of the fanatical witch-burning language that is popularly supposed to distinguish a manual for inquisitors. We should be grateful for any writer who can discuss this delicate subject with authority and without literary embroidery. It would be difficult to question his authority to speak on the subject, since he was engaged in this work for the greater part of his life.

Bernard Gui was appointed bishop of Lodéve, an office which he exercised with vigor and justice. He died in 1331.

It is difficult to see how anyone who was regularly employed in preaching, in administration, in the work of the inquisition, and in the office of bishop, could have written as much as Bernard wrote. He wrote, besides the work on the inquisition, a number of tracts on the Blessed Virgin; an *Abridged Christian Doctrine;* histories of the kings of France, the bishops of Limoges, and the priors of Grandmont, to 1318; the bishops of Toulouse, to 1327; and the history of several old abbeys of France. He also wrote lives of the saints, a devotional *Mirror of the Saints,* a *History of the Dominican Order,* and a chronicle of the world from the time of our Lord to the year 1331. His works are quoted in all the chronicles of the Middle Ages, indicating that his immediate followers considered him a trustworthy writer.

BARTHOLOMEW THE LITTLE
(d. 1333)

In the late thirteenth and early fourteenth centuries, a great movement for the reunion of Eastern and Western Christians took place. Although it was doomed to failure, the attempt looked very hopeful for a time, and engaged the talents of some of the finest men of the two new Orders of friars. Dominicans and Franciscans were given the delicate task of resolving the differences between East and West, and they almost succeeded. One of the finest workers in this noble cause was Bartholomew the Little, patriarch of Armenia.

Bartholomew was born in Bologna, of noble parents, and, when very young, he entered the convent of St. Nicholas there. He developed a talent for preaching and, one would suppose, a gift for practical management. At any rate, these were the gifts required of anyone chosen for the oriental missions. In 1318, he was unanimously chosen by the pope and cardinals to head the mission work in the Near East, and was named patriarch of Armenia.

It is hard for us to imagine what Bartholomew faced in his new mission. His flock consisted of three main divisions: Mohammedans, pagans, and schismatics. He first had to learn the languages of the country, then convert these varying groups to orthodox Christianity. He began with the pagans. His efforts with these people were so encouraging that he soon directed his attention to the schismatics.

In the new province of the Order erected in Armenia, the schismatic monks of St. Basil had become interested in the Dominicans who worked among them. The Basilian abbot, John of Sharnak, approached Bartholomew with an astounding proposition: he and his monks would become orthodox Christians, then Dominicans. He spent six months with the Dominicans, under the direction of Bartholomew, and then returned to prepare his monks for their union with Rome. The patriarch received the entire community into the Church, placing Dominican directors over them until they should have absorbed the spirit of the reform. The new groups wished to be affiliated immediately to the great Order they admired so much, but there were practical difficulties. For one thing, the penitential practices of the Order were a stumbling block. The monks were received as Tertiaries, with permission to wear the full Dominican habit—a singular privilege. They were called "United Brethren," to indicate both their origin and their affiliation with the Order. Since the Basilians had composed almost the entire clergy of Armenia, their conversion greatly simplified the evangelization of the Near East.

Bartholomew now turned his attention to the fanatical Mohammedans. He was not to have time to do anything for them, for a martyr's death was shortly to be his. He had been metropolitan of Naksivan and had just taken up residence there when the Mohammedans attacked the Christian city. The defenders took refuge in the fort of Ararat, but the fort was captured. The patriarch was captured and tortured. When the Mohammedans withdrew, leaving him for dead, the few living Christians rescued him and tried to save his life, but he died, after ten days of agony, in the year 1333.

JORDAN OF CATALÁ
(1336)

Exactly who Jordan of Catalá was, or where he came from, is not quite clear. The French claim that his name was Jordan de Severac and that he was a Frenchman; the Portuguese also claim him, and give him the name of Jordan of Catalá. Whoever he was, he wrote vastly informative letters about the Far East in the fourteenth century, and he deserves to be remembered for these cheerful and chatty letters if for nothing else.

Wherever he came from originally, Jordan stepped into Dominican history when he was assigned to go to Armenia, which is a fair indication that he must have belonged to the "Fratres Peregrinantes," the "Wandering Brethren of Christ among the Pagans." Since this was an international province within the Order, he may have been any nationality.

He set out from a Mediterranean port—probably Venice—and arrived in Greece some time before 1312. From Armenia, he wrote that he had visited Mount Ararat, where the ark had tied up after the flood; there were relics there at that time which the natives claimed were the remains of the ark itself. He states as a known fact that St. Simon, St. Jude, and St. Bartholomew were all martyred in Armenia, that the country had been wandering in schism for many centuries, and that it just recently was making a return to Christianity, under the Dominicans and Franciscans who were working there. He goes on to say that "the Dominicans have a thriving parish at Ur of the Chaldees, where they have more than a thousand converts."

Jordan himself was stationed at the ancient city of Tauris, but he believed in side trips. One of these took him out on the silk route as far as Maragha, where the Khan had an observatory; here, too, the Dominicans and Franciscans were hard at work. He made numerous excursions, which he described as "laborious," but it is evident that he was utterly fascinated by travel, and that his sharp eyes never missed anything in this strange oriental world.

In 1320, four Franciscans stopped for hospitality at the Dominican convent at Tauris, and told him they were going to China. Would he like to come along? He hurriedly got permission and joined them. Two months later, after a long hike over the mountains and the desert, they reached Ormuz, where they could take ship for the next part of the journey. Jordan wrote a letter to go back over the land route, describing the ship. It was a model of magnificence, having "100 rooms and accommodations for 700 passengers." He described the huge sails and the hemp ropes. (The latter, he had never seen before.) With a gay, "Goodbye; we are off for Bombay," he sealed the letter and hurried aboard.

At Bombay, there was a church dedicated to St. Thomas. Christians of that region were Nestorians, but they were hospitable. Jordan set out with two Nestorian priests to visit a city where the Christians were reputedly Latins. He did not find them, but he baptized ninety people, and sailed to the end of the Gulf of Cambay. He was balked in further efforts when the ship turned of its own accord and sailed off in the other direction. As he neared the Island of Thana, where he had made his headquarters, he was horrified to hear that the four Franciscans had been martyred. He went to Thana, nevertheless, and addressed a letter to his brethren in Tauris to be sent by the next trade caravan: "Every day I have new converts; I am building a church here for the missionaries you will send, and will leave my furniture and books for them—please hurry." He told them that as soon as the relief arrived, he was going to Rome to instigate canonization procedures for the four Franciscan martyrs and to look for more missionaries.

Considering the slow-moving pace of business at that time, one is not surprised to read that two and a half years passed with no word from Tauris. Brother Nicholas of Rome had set out to relieve him, but disappeared somewhere in the vastness of mountains and desert. Jordan wrote another letter, calling himself "an orphan in this land of error." He recited a litany of woes, like that of St. Paul—he had been captured by pirates, put in prison by Saracens, beaten, cursed, starved, and treated like a criminal. He goes on to beg, "with tears in my eyes, for missionaries to help me, and for some new clothes, as mine are worn out." He gives some practical hints on travel: "If anybody prefers to come through Ethiopia, it is quite easy; let the natives know that you are Latin Christians, and they will treat you fairly." Repeating his request for friars and clean clothes, he sealed the letter and sent it off in January, 1324. This time his appeal brought abundant fruit; a band of Dominicans, headed by Francis of Pisa, and a group of Franciscans arrived in due time, and set to work inland through Travancore.

Free now to make the proposed journey, Jordan set out for Avignon. He went back through Arabia to see how things were getting on, stopped at the Isle of Chios, and finally reached Avignon, after ten months of travel. He was closely questioned by the pope and the cardinals. "If we had two or three hundred brethren for India, we could make ten thousand converts a year," he told them. "Furthermore," he said, "they are ten times better Christians than Europeans." He composed a book at this time called the *Mirabilia*, setting forth some of his reflections on the situation in the Far East. In this he gives accounts of birds, animals, and plants he has seen, of elephants and fire worshippers, and the custom of suttee. He mentions that there is "another India between India and Ethiopa," where all the natives are Christians, but heretics; it is a land where there are two volcanoes and many rough mountains. He also reports, by hearsay, of the kingdom of Prester John, gives a number of alternate routes to the Far East (with estimated mileage), and suggestions about what baggage to take.

Pope John XXII, who was tremendously interested in the missions of the Far East, appointed Jordan bishop of Colombo, which is possibly Latinized "Khoulam." Jordan set out for his new assignment and arrived there in 1331. Here he disappears into oblivion, though a legend persists that he was martyred at Thana, in 1336.

When the duke of Albuquerque arrived 150 years later, the tradition still lingered of the friars, "two men of Frangistan" (France?) who had taught the people about heaven, had healed the sick, and raised the dead to life. It should be of interest to both Dominicans and Franciscans that their friars were the first to reach India, and to work there more than 200 years before anyone else, even if they did not leave any permanent foundations.

MARGARET OF LUXEMBOURG
(1336)

Margaret was the daughter of Henry of Luxembourg, and the sister of Henry VII, who became Holy Roman Emperor in 1309. She came of a family distinguished for its benefactions to good causes, and it was no surprise to anyone when she entered the "Little Abbey" of St. Mary, at Lille, in her early youth.

St. Mary of Lille had been founded as a branch of the convent of Marienthal, and the two were still closely connected. On the accession of Henry to the throne, Margaret's mother decided to turn her dower-house at Valenciennes into a third Dominican house, connected with Marienthal. Margaret was made superior of the new house, with her mother and her sister, Felicitas, as subjects, along with some of the sisters of Lille.

Margaret's reputation for both good management and holiness soon called her to Marienthal, which was much larger than its two daughter houses. Here she was prioress, in charge of 120 choir nuns, for most of her life, and it is at Marienthal that the memory of her angelic life is treasured.

Marienthal was founded in 1232, which means that it is one of the oldest Dominican houses of women. It is situated a short distance from the city of Luxembourg, in a region that was once heavily forested. At some time before the thirteenth century, the lord of the demesne discovered a small Lady-statue in a gnarled oak tree in the forest there. He took the statue home with him, but it would not stay. After it had returned several times to the oak tree, he had a small shrine built there. Growing popularity had necessitated a larger shrine, and eventually the Dominican monastery was founded by John of Treves. The Countess of Luxembourg became the benefactress of the monastery, and for many years her family continued its help.

We wish we knew more of this angelic princess who spent most of her life at the shrine of Our Lady, when the Order was young in the world and new to her country, but there is no record even of the death of Margaret of Luxembourg.

MAURICE, PRINCE OF HUNGARY
(d. 1336)

Maurice, Prince of Hungary, and Dominican of happy memory, is quite possibly the only one of our family who was persecuted by his father-in-law for his desire to remain in the Order.

Maurice was born in the late thirteenth century, of the royal house of Hungary. There had been many heavenly signs before his birth that he was to be an unusual favorite of God, but for the first few years of his life he was so sickly that everyone despaired of his survival. By the time he was five years old, he was a delicate, dreamy child who played at saying Mass and leading family prayers. The little chapel in his father's castle was his favorite haunt, and he was always to be found there between sessions in the schoolroom.

When he was still quite small, an old Dominican came one day to visit his parents, and took a great fancy to the handsome little boy. He told the child the story of St. Alexis, which greatly impressed him. When Maurice knelt to ask the old priest's blessing, the Dominican said prophetically, "This child will one day enter our holy Order and will be one of its joys!"

In spite of the several indications that God had designs on Maurice, circumstances conspired against him. His parents died when he was still quite young, leaving him immensely wealthy and solely in charge of his father's estates. A brother, who had entered the Dominican novitiate, died very young. Relatives prevailed upon Maurice to marry. Against all his wishes, he did so. However, he and his young wife, the daughter of the Count Palatine, made a vow of chastity, and both resolved to become Dominicans as soon as it was possible to dispose of the estates. When his wife fled to the Isle of Margaret, in the Danube, and took the veil in St. Margaret's Convent, her father was furious. He went in search of the young husband and found that he, too, had gone to the Dominicans. He settled the matter in the forthright fashion of the times by kidnapping Maurice and locking him in a tower. Here, like another Thomas Aquinas, the young novice settled down to wait until someone tired of the arrangement.

After three months of unfruitful punishment, Maurice was released as incorrigible, and his relatives devoted their attention to getting hold of his estates instead. He went happily off to Bologna to make his studies, where he remained for three years.

For thirty-two years, Maurice ignored the throne and the luxuries of the world to live in obscurity and poverty. The picture of him left us by the chroniclers is an engaging one: an earnest, pious priest who made no effort to capitalize on his birth or social graces; a zealous addict of poverty, who managed, by a series of sagacious trades, to have the oldest habit in the house and the dreariest cell. He is said to have said the whole Psalter daily, plus the Penitential Psalms, and the Litany of Saints.

A number of curious stories are told about him. Once, when he was staying with a Benedictine friend, the friend noticed that he went in and out of locked doors with no trouble at all, and that the rooms lighted up by themselves when he went in. Maurice is supposed to have had the gift of prophecy. A relative of his had cheated the sisters out of some property which Maurice had left them. Maurice told him that the goods would be taken away from him, and that another man, more generous, would give it back to the sisters. The man died shortly after, and the prophecy was accomplished.

Maurice died in 1336. At least two miracles of healing were reported at his grave: one was a cure from fever, another from blindness. Butler's *Lives of the Saints* lists him as "Blessed Maurice," although his cult has never been formally approved.

BLESSED JAMES BENEFATTI
(d. 1338)

James Benefatti, Bishop of Mantua, was a famous man in his time; it is unfortunate that he is so little known in ours.

James was born in Mantua, in the latter half of the thirteenth century, and entered the Order at the convent in his native city, probably around the year 1290. He was both a learned and a holy priest, and these qualities brought him to the attention of his brother Dominican, Nicholas Boccasino, the future Pope Benedict XI. As cardinal, Nicholas chose for his companion the young Dominican from Mantua. He employed him in various offices in Rome and recommended him to other high-ranking prelates. Consequently, James found himself kept busy in diplomatic offices by several popes— Benedict XI and John XXII among them. The latter named him bishop of his home town of Mantua, and he went to take over his See in 1320.

For eighteen years, James occupied the See of Mantua and accomplished great good among the people. He rebuilt and refurnished the cathedral and worked many miracles among his flock. At his death, in 1338, many remarkable miracles occurred, and he was called "Blessed James" by people who were grateful for his favors. Nearly 150 years after his death, when repairs were being made in the church where he was buried, an accident opened his tomb, and people were startled to find that his body was completely incorrupt. Again in 1604, the same phenomenon was noted. In 1859, he was pronounced blessed by Pope Pius IX.

JON HALDORSSON
(d. 1339)

Of the early years of this interesting apostle of the Far North, we know very little. The scanty records tell us that he was Icelandic by birth, born in Bergen, Norway; Iceland was at this time a part of the Kingdom of Norway.

Tradition says that he met the Dominicans either at the University of Paris or at Bologna, and that he entered the Order at the convent of Bergen and made his first studies there.

The first definite date we have in the life of Jon Haldorsson is 1322, when he was made bishop of Skalholt, in Iceland.

In spite of the meager records we have, Jon Haldorsson emerges from the mists of history as a learned and charming person, a good and capable administrator, a firm and inspiring preacher, and a kind father to his flock. The problems facing the bishop of this isolated and frozen land must have been tremendous. We read that, four years after his arrival, there was an entire year in which no Masses could be said, for the simple reason that such storms raged around the Northern seas, no ship dared to put out for Scandinavia to obtain the necessary elements of bread and wine. The land was too far north to produce its own wheat and grapes, and all such things had to be brought by sea from Norway, after being shipped there from warmer lands. In the face of such terrible seas, the Christians could only wait and pray.

Bishop Haldorsson built many churches in his diocese and repaired the cathedral, which had been severely damaged; the building problems involved in this effort are staggering when one considers the climate and the materials he had to work with. He was a capable and busy preacher, and he found time, somehow, to write a two-volume collection of short stories to be used as sermon examples. His own sermons were lively and memorable and bore abundant fruit.

His particular devotions were to the Blessed Sacrament and to Our Lady; he introduced into Iceland the devotion of Corpus Christi.

In 1339, when on a trip to Norway for a synod, Bishop Haldorsson became ill on the road. He was carried to the nearest convent, which, providentially, turned out to be the Dominican house where he had made his novitiate and taken his vows. It soon became apparent that he was going to die.

On the Feast of Our Lady's Nativity, which was especially dear to him, he asked a young priest to say Mass in his room. During the Mass, Our Lady came into the room, carrying two lighted candles and attended by a procession of angels. She smiled at the dying bishop and pointed upwards. When the young priest turned around to give the last blessing at the end of Mass, he found that the bishop had died.

Iceland, even today, retains vestiges of the Dominican liturgy, in spite of the centuries of heresy; and the memory of this good man remains.

MARGARET EBNER
(1291-1351)

The name of Margaret Ebner is intimately connected with the spiritual renaissance in the Rhineland during the fourteenth century. She was a friend and guide to many whose names are famous in the history of mysticism, and she was in correspondence with most of the spiritual leaders of the times, including John Tauler.

Margaret was born in 1291, in Nuremberg, of a noble family, and she received a good education. At a very early age her taste for prayer became evident, and even her childhood was distinguished by remarkable spiritual favors. Her whole life was to be marked by a close intimacy with the secrets of God, and she began early to show that she considered nothing in this life comparable to the beauties of the spiritual life.

It was no surprise to anyone when, at the age of fifteen, Margaret entered a cloistered Dominican monastery, in Bavaria. Here, for five years, she lived a holy life, with increasing indications that God was calling her to a life even more rigorous. She became seriously ill and, finally, was almost completely paralyzed. For thirteen years she lived in constant pain and helplessness, offering her suffering for the souls of those who died in the war, which was then devastating the countryside.

How much Margaret knew at this time of her mission in life, she does not tell us. Many of her thoughts and revelations were later recorded by one or another of her faithful friends, but they do not say whether she knew that her sickness was part of her vocation to suffering; for the sake of the many young sisters who are struck down with illness, it would be instructive to know what she had to say about it, but this is one point on which she kept silence.

Margaret's life was to be one of expiation for the sins of others. She was to suffer intensely and for a long time. But she also shared in the mystical union with God, the greatest of joys and responsibilities. A program of this sort is not always the simplest thing to carry out in a religious community; Margaret's great gifts were the source of much trouble to her for the thirteen years that she was a helpless invalid. Around her bed, invisible to everyone but herself, the souls came crowding, begging for her prayers. It is not surprising, then, that she had a great devotion to the souls in purgatory.

At the end of the long years of suffering, she was suddenly cured, and returned to the regular life of the community. Her peace was short-lived, however. The house had to disband because of an invading army. Margaret and a laysister returned to Nuremberg to live with her family until the crisis was over. Here, her program of prayer was very much the same as it always had been. She kept an almost perpetual silence, because she was deeply engrossed in the secrets of God. One day the laysister scolded her for keeping silence so repeatedly. For one frightening minute she was given a sight of what Margaret saw all the time: the house full of souls begging for prayers. They cried out to her, "If you don't want to help us yourself, at least don't keep other people from helping us."

As soon as possible, the monastery reopened and the sisters returned. Here, for the remainder of her life, Margaret was to be both a source of blessing and a center of controversy. She was charitable and kind to all, and it was hard to find fault with her ready willingness to help the sick and the afflicted. But probably it is hard to live normally with someone who drops off into ecstasy at a moment's notice and stays that way for days. Our Lord and the saints appeared to her and instructed her in heavenly things. Holy Communion thrust her into a state of profound contemplation. In the light of these things, the rigorous silence which she kept from Thursday to Sunday, and all of Lent and Advent, do not seem excessive. She was too busy listening to the things God had to say to her to be occupied with other conversation.

It is somewhat amusing to read, in the account of her conversations with our Lord, which she wrote at her confessor's request, some of the things she wanted to know. Once she asked Him, "What did you do with the gifts of the Wise Men?" This indicates something of her childlike curiosity. Most of her conversations, however, had to do with the spiritual life and with our relationship to God. Her writings were treasured for their revelations and—it must, in all justice, be added—for their good sense. Margaret, although she often experienced consolations, realized that these did not constitute the main fabric of sanctity.

Margaret treasured an unusual love for the liturgy. For her, the chant and the changing cycle of the Church year were not only instruments by which one might praise God, but keys to unlock His spiritual treasures. Insensible to earthly conversations, she was always aware of the prayers of the Office and the Mass, and very often they gave her the clue to some obscure point of mystical theology.

Margaret died in 1351, leaving a wide variety of spiritual writings and a reputation for holiness.

HUMBERT DAUPHIN
(1312-1355)

Humbert, the last dauphin of the Duchy of Vienne, preferred a heavenly crown to an earthly one, and he made his choice rather drastically.

Humbert was the son of John II of Vienne and Beatrice of Hungary, and was born in 1312. His father died when he was seven, and Humbert and his brother were sent to be trained by their uncle. Beatrice of Hungary retired into a Cistercian convent.

Humbert was a young prince, temporarily residing at the court of Naples with his spouse, when word came that his older brother had died, leaving the Duchy of Vienne to him. He went at once to take over the management of the large estate, and began by trying to right the more obvious wrongs. He tried to reconcile Louis of Bavaria with the pope—a move which failed. The pope, who saw in Humbert the ideal Christian prince, made him leader of a crusade. Humbert pleaded successfully with him for the release of the popular preacher, Venturino of Bergamo, who had been exiled by the former pope. Led by Humbert, and preached by Venturino, the crusade got under way, and first of all captured the Turkish port of Smirna.

A number of personal tragedies came to Humbert in the East. His young wife died in Rhodes, and word was brought him that his only child, a baby son, had died in France. Venturino died on board one of the ships, in the harbor of Smirna. Christian princes turned a deaf ear to his pleading for more troops, and many of his men died of fever while they were waiting for help. When the Turkish leader asked for a truce, he gave it. Withdrawing his troops, he returned to Dauphin to settle his affairs. He ignored the suggestions of a marriage with one of the Bourbon princesses. Soon his friends began whispering in shocked tones that he wanted to be a Dominican.

They looked daggers at his Dominican confessor, but Humbert was resolute. He had had enough of worldly pomp.

There is a curious little interlude at this point. Humbert used a piece of his property to found a Dominican monastery for women at Montfleury. He had a coat of arms designed for them, in which the dolphin from his escutcheon was surrounded by a rosary; this was in 1345, a good hundred years before Alan de la Roche.

Humbert abdicated his throne to Charles, the son of the duke of Normandy, distributed his properties among various charitable organizations, and fervently hoped that he could close the door forever on the past and become a preaching friar. On July the sixteenth, 1349, he presented himself at the Dominican convent of Our Lady of Comfort in Lyons, and was given the habit of the Order. In December, 1350, Humbert took his vows in the hands of the pope at Avignon, and was ordained at the last Mass on Christmas of the same year.

For all his hopes of living a simple religious life, it soon became apparent that he would not be allowed to do so. The pope felt that a person of his prestige and virtue would be a great asset to the Church in the Near East, so he appointed Humbert patriarch of Alexandria, with his residence temporarily in Paris. Five years later, he still had not been able to reach his See city. He died in Paris, at the convent of St. Jacques. He was forty-three years old.

BLESSED VILLANA DE BOTTI
(1332-1360)

A model penitent among vain and silly companions was Villana de Botti, who sampled a wide variety of vanities before she gave them up for the pursuit of heavenly things.

Villana was born in Florence, in 1332. Her mother came of a noble family, and her father was a rich magistrate. Their large family lived in an ornate palace in a fashionable section of the city and enjoyed great prestige among the society-minded folk of Florence.

Villana was pretty, witty, and the pet of her father. While she had an instinct for piety and a precocious taste for mortification, she was easily swayed by his indulgence and the worldly circle in which the family moved. It was difficult for a girl living in such extravagant luxury to get a clear concept of poverty and penance, but somehow she did. Perhaps she was like

St. Augustine, who hoped to be converted—but not right now. She lived a very gay and noisy life, not wicked, but definitely worldly. Still, life had its other side, and she could not forget, even in the gaiety of the dance or the theater or of some other costly entertainment, that her soul was seeking a higher life.

Once, she made an attempt to break through the smothering worldliness that seemed to stifle all her good intentions. She ran away and hid in the gatehouse, waiting for darkness, when she could run to the desert and live as a proper hermit. She was caught and brought back in disgrace. Her brothers hooted with laughter at the thoughts of her becoming a hermit; her father scolded her, absent-mindedly, and gave her money to buy herself something pretty; her mother gathered up and burned all the instruments of penance that she could find, and began looking around for a solution to her problem. It was not hard to find a husband for a rich and beautiful daughter, and Villana was soon married to a wealthy merchant.

For the short years of her marriage, Villana was the complete coquette. She dressed extravagantly, danced continually, behaved as foolishly as possible. Into the midst of this comfortable and pointless life came the Black Death, which began its horrible march across Europe in 1348. Days Villana had spent in feasting and tournaments suddenly became alarmingly empty; the superfluities that had become her necessities lost all their luster. Afraid to be converted, she became more vain and foolish than before. Pretty, tepid, and unfeeling towards the suffering of the world, she drifted along, carefully turning away from unpleasant things, thinking of nothing but her own pleasure. Her awakening from this state came like a flash of lightning.

She was dressing one day for a ball, and lifting her mirror to glance at her hairdo, she saw a sight which nearly frightened her to death. Instead of a pretty, rather vapid face with high-piled hair and many jewels, she saw a hideous monster with hair of coiled serpents. Screaming a cry of horror, she threw the mirror on the floor and ran to look in the large mirror, at the side of her dressing room. There, again, was the monster— full length now. Screaming more desperately, she ran from room to room of the great palace, looking into each mirror, but seeing only the horrible monster. When every mirror in the house had told her the same story, she fled to the chapel and fell to her knees. At the age of eighteen, she had suddenly and painfully discovered that she had wasted a lot of time. Her conversion was instantaneous and complete.

Villana's first act was to remove her jewels and put on a modest and simple gown. She sent word that she would not be able to attend the ball; she went instead to Santa Maria Novella for confession. Never one to do anything halfway, she demanded of the confessor that he authorize her to go to the desert and live as an anchorite. He pointed out to her that her marriage would present certain obstacles to this plan, and he suggested that, instead of this somewhat dramatic act, she stay home and try to undo by her good life the harm she had done by her vanity. He allowed her to wear an iron chain and authorized several other penances, and received her into the Third Order, but did not give her permission to wear the habit.

Villana threw out her light literature and plunged into a study of the Bible. She gave away all her fine clothes and most of her money to the poor, and began earnestly to perform any work of charity that presented itself to her. She made rapid progress in prayer, and was favored with heavenly visits from Our Lady and various saints. A child, who came to her for an alms, once found her talking to the Blessed Virgin.

Villana's father lost most of his money in a shipwreck, and was left in a pitiful state of despair. She prayed for him, and with him, until she managed to convert him to the same way of life that she herself was leading: prayer, poverty, and penance. Villana knew the secrets in the hearts of those who talked to her, and often was able to help them through her prayers and good advice.

What attitude Villana's husband took towards her abrupt conversion we are not told. She died at the early age of twenty-eight, after a long siege of fever, and after prophesying to her friends that she would send them "flowers from heaven." Her husband seems to have made no objection to her being buried in the Tertiary habit. Miraculously, the ravages of the long fever did not show, and, in death, her face possessed a beauty it had never had in life. A Franciscan Tertiary friend, to whom she had promised to send heavenly flowers, bent over the dead woman to view the beautiful face, and great armloads of flowers fell from the sky, fulfilling Villana's prophecy.

Villana de Botti was beatified in 1829.

JOHN TAULER
(1300-1361)

Few people are so consistently misquoted and so elegantly lied about as John Tauler, who figured so prominently in the spiritual revival in the Rhineland in the fourteenth century. Protestants occasionally point to him as a harbinger of the Reformation, and people of all faiths have quoted and misquoted him in almost every cause that has arisen in the years since his death. Until the careful studies of Father Denifle, in the present century, even Dominicans looked with suspicion on this man who was such a popular preacher in his own times and such a cause of controversy after his death.

John Tauler was born in Strasbourg, in 1300, of wealthy parents. He entered the Order at the Strasbourg convent at about the time that the famous Master Eckhart was prior there. He may or may not have personally known this preacher, whose works were to undergo scrutiny by authorities of the Order and the Church. Little, in fact, is known of his early years, as it was a time of great confusion in France and Germany. Strasbourg was under interdict, because of disagreements between the emperor and the pope, and the Dominicans were several times exiled, because of their adherence to the papal cause.

In 1347, John Tauler appears in Strasbourg. At this time he was an ordained priest, and the confessor of the man who apparently started all the trouble connected with the spiritual revival in the Rhineland. His name was Rulman Merswin, and he was a pious and wealthy layman, with a desire to rule. A prominent Protestant historian of our day calls Merswin quite simply a "pious windbag"; but in his own time he managed to stir up a considerable furore. His story was that a holy layman, the "Friend of God," had come by inspiration to instruct a good priest, whom he infers was Tauler; and that the priest henceforth acted under the instructions of the "Friend of God" in leading a spiritual reform. The gist of this spiritual reform was the personal feeling of faith, and personal revelation, as opposed to Divine Revelation. Since Merswin carefully refrained from telling anyone who the "Friend of God" was, or where he lived, he gained a great notoriety from being the confidant of a saint. A country riddled by war, famine, schism, and political factions was only too ready to take up any new revelation, especially if it was personally consoling and somewhat anticlerical.

Exactly what Tauler's position was with regard to the visionary Merswin is difficult to determine from history. He was Merswin's confessor for some time, which does not mean that he was under Merswin's spiritual guidance. Tauler was a popular preacher, and he preached the sort of apocalyptic sermons that fit in well with Merswin's prophecies of imminent doom and personal justification. Unfortunately, at the time of the Reformation, zealous Protestants seized on "personal revelation" as their cue to defy papal authority. A great deal of the writing which was actually done by Merswin was credited to Tauler, and, two centuries after his death, the Dominican was firmly enthroned as a forerunner of Protestantism. The writings of the mystic Merswin and the sermons of Tauler were circulated widely in many languages.

The researches of Father Denifle have proved several points in vindication of his brother Dominican. Careful analysis weeded out sermons and works that were Merswin's, leaving the proved Tauler sermons; careful examination revealed that Tauler was a good theologian, as well as a popular preacher, and that most of the statements quoted as his were not his at all. Father Denifle further proved that the "Friend of God" never existed, except in the imagination of Merswin.

All this would seem an unnecessary digging up of old bones were it not for the impact of the aforementioned spiritual revival, which brought forth an abundant harvest of seers and mystics, particularly among religious women. Centered in Strasbourg, the movement was to reach to the furthest part of the Rhineland, involving hundreds of earnest and sometimes very holy people, all of whom seemed impelled to write their revelations. One of the Dominicans who shared in this movement, Henry Suso, has been beatified by the Church; another, Margaret Ebner, has been considered for beatification. The unfortunate Master Eckhart, on the other hand, was condemned as a heretic by the court of the inquisition. How much of personal jealousy and political intrigue went into this condemnation, historians disagree. But they all agree that the movement was important, and that the writings occasioned by the mystical revival had an effect, not only on the development of languages, but also on the spiritual writings of our own day.

John Tauler died in 1361, after twenty years of popular preaching.

BLESSED HENRY SUSO
(1290-1365)

Henry Suso is a bundle of contradictions, and a person, moreover, who has gathered legends about him like a snowball rolling downhill. He was a poet, which is not always a key to happiness in this world; a mystic of the highest order; a hard-working Dominican; and a man with a positive genius for getting into embarrassing situations. He has suffered at the hands of chroniclers who dislike his followers, or his tactics, or his poetry; he is all but canonized by those who see in him *the* Dominican mystic. It will require many years of exhaustive research to sort out the diverse elements in his personality, if, indeed, it can ever be accomplished. Poets are not easy to analyze, and Henry, before all else, was a poet.

Henry was born in Switzerland, in 1290, the son of a warlike family of counts and crusaders. His father said more than once that he wished Henry had been a girl and some of his spirited daughters had been boys; for Henry was not a type to carry a sword. Henry was a gentle, dreamy lad, who liked to accompany his mother on pilgrimages and read about heroic deeds. He had taken his mother's name of Suso, perhaps out of sheer inability to live up to the warlike title of the Count von Berg.

After a number of unsuccessful attempts to make a soldier out of Henry, his father abandoned the task and sent him, when he was barely thirteen years old, to the Dominican convent near Lake Constance. At the convent, Henry found a happy life, one that he did not know existed. Like a starved child who has had no happiness before, he revelled in the companionship of friendly people and the beauty of community prayers. For five years it did not occur to him that there was anything more to religious life than the gay and irresponsible way he lived. This brief paradise came to an abrupt end when he was eighteen. He sat one day in chapel, restless and worried, because suddenly it had dawned upon him that he was not really getting anywhere, and without warning he fell into an ecstasy that lasted more than an hour. Arousing from the ecstasy, he was a different person, and a whole new life began.

First of all Henry looked with wide-opened eyes on the lukewarm life he had been living. Considering his age, we would be inclined to suspect that it was not so much lukewarm as adolescent, but it appeared to him that he was a great sinner and should do great penance. The penance he performed for the next sixteen years became notorious, even in that age of extremes; an iron chain, and an undershirt studded with nails, were the most mentionable of the methods he used. At night, he tied his hands so that he could not slap at the mosquitoes that infested his room. Out of determination to overcome his natural taste for cleanliness, he bent over backwards in the opposite direction to torture himself into submission and to make himself ready for the grace of God, which he felt that he so little deserved. At the end of sixteen years, he was favored with another vision, telling him that the physical phase of his suffering was over, but to be prepared for mental torments.

While all this interior purification was being accomplished in his soul, Henry was busy about the ordinary work of a priest. He preached and taught and heard confessions, never absenting himself from apostolic work under the impression that pure contemplation would be better. Some of his travels got him into weird situations, and legends began building up around the strange young priest whose penances had already earned him the name of eccentric. Things happened to him that just never happened to other people.

One time he was on a journey with a laybrother who was not very bright. While Henry was looking for lodgings in a strange village, the laybrother went into a tavern, and, with the help of some of its customers, rapidly got out of hand. In order to direct attention away from himself, he told the men they should go after the priest who was with him; he said that the Jews had hired Henry to poison their wells, and that he was now out investigating how it could be done. It was possibly only the laybrother's heavy humor, but the townspeople did not think it was funny, and they went in pursuit of Henry. Seeing himself chased by men with clubs, Henry did what most people do—he ran. He hid all night in a hedge, and the next day he had to get the laybrother out of jail.

He fell into rivers and almost drowned. He became innocently involved in family feuds and was nearly killed for interfering. People tried to poison him. As prior, he ran the house finances into such a snarl that no one could untangle them. As if he did not have enough trouble, one of his penitents—at least he thought she was penitent—decided to blackmail him, and told all over town that he was the father of her child. To clean up the ensuing scandal, he stood formal trial with his superiors, and was, of course, proved innocent—but no one could stop the scandal which had by this time gone to the four winds.

As a last terrible trial, his own sister, who had gone into religion against her will, fell into serious sin and ran away from the monastery. The convent from which she had escaped was a relaxed and worldly place, but she was legally a fugitive. Henry got permission to go and look for her, and, after a long search, he found her—repentant, penniless, and terrified—in a tavern. He brought her to another monastery, where a strict rule was observed, and he stayed until she was firmly settled and living a good religious life. How any man could write poetry while trying to keep up with such events is hard to say, but some of the finest poetry in medieval German poured from the pen of this gifted man during the years when life was most difficult for him. His prose, too, was almost poetry—perhaps this is why his writings have always been so popular with women.

We are indebted to the sisters whose consciences Henry directed for all that we know of his writing. They kept careful track of all of it and made copies to circulate among a discreet circle of friends. In fact, it is from this circumstance that the unhappy charges against Suso stem. Some of the sisters, making their personal copies, took down notes indiscriminately—from Suso, Tauler, and Master Eckhart—and it was practically impossible to untangle them. Only the persistent scholarship of Father Denifle, in the past century, has identified the writings of each of these men, and exonerated both Tauler and Suso of the charges that caused Eckhart to be censured.

The best known work of Henry Suso is his *Little Book of Eternal Wisdom,* which is a classic of spiritual writing. He also composed many other short treatises on the mystical union of the soul with God, all written with the same poetic language and the same intensity of feeling. The man who had carved "the lovely name of Jesus" into the flesh over his heart was just as intense in his spiritual life. He had an outstanding devotion to the Mother of God, which he expressed very beautifully.

Henry died in 1365, in Ulm, and was buried there in the convent of St. Paul. However, in spite of the fact that his body was found intact and giving forth a sweet odor two-hundred and fifty years later, the beatification was delayed until 1831. The relics, meantime, had disappeared entirely and have never been recovered.

BLESSED PETER OF RUFFIA
(1320-1365)

Peter Cambiano was born in Chieri, in Piedmont, in 1320. His father was a city councillor and his mother was of noble birth. They were virtuous and careful parents, and they gave their little son a good education, especially in religion. Peter responded to all their care and became a fine student, as well as a pious and likeable child.

Peter was drawn to the Dominicans by devotion to the Rosary. Our Lady of the Rosary was the special patroness of the region where he lived, and he had a personal devotion to her. At the age of sixteen, therefore, he presented himself at the convent in Piedmont and asked for the habit.

Here the young student continued his study and prayer, becoming a model religious, and was ordained at the age of twenty-five. His skill as a preacher had already become evident, not the least of his talents being a loud clear voice, which in those days of open-air preaching was a real necessity.

Peter's span of active life was twenty years, most of which he spent among the heretics of northern Italy. The fathers of the Lombard province had a fine reputation to uphold. They were walking in the footsteps of martyrs, and they made a point of preparing their men carefully for controversy as well as for martyrdom. Peter's first assignment was to work among the Waldensians. These zealous and misguided folk, coming from France, had already infiltrated the Low Countries and were well established in northern Italy, by way of Switzerland. The inquisition had been set up to deal with these people in Lombardy before the death of Peter Martyr, a century before. So well did young Peter of Ruffia carry out the work of preaching among them that the Order sent him to Rome to obtain higher degrees. The pope, impressed both by his talent and his family name, appointed him inquisitor-general of Piedmont. This was a coveted appointment; to a Dominican it meant practically sure martyrdom and a carrying on of a proud tradition.

In January of 1365, Peter of Ruffia and two companions left the convent in Turin to go on a preaching tour that would take them into the mountainous country bordering Switzerland, where the heretics had done great damage. Their lives were in hourly danger. The Franciscans at Suse gave them hospitality, and they made the friary their basis of operations for a short, but very active, campaign against the Waldensians.

His preaching occasioned several notable defections from the ranks of the heretics, and it was decided that Peter must die. On the second of February, three of the heretics came to the friary and asked to see Peter of Ruffia, saying that they had an important message for him. They waited for him in the cloister, near the gate, and, when he appeared, surrounded him and killed him with their daggers. Peter died almost instantly, too soon to give any information about his assailants, and the murderers disappeared into a valley, where the heretics would protect them. All Piedmont, Switzerland, and Savoy were in an uproar over the death of Peter, who had been "a saint in his life, a martyr in his death."

The Franciscans at Suse claimed the holy relics, pointing out that it would not be safe to transport them to the nearest Dominican house, so Peter was buried among the Franciscans. Here he remained for a hundred and fifty years, until the Franciscan house was razed and desecrated by an invading army. Finally, in 1517, the relics of the great inquisitor were brought to Turin, and Peter was laid among his brethren in the convent there.

Peter of Ruffia was beatified in 1856.

PHILIP DE SCEVA
(d. 1366)

The Kingdom of Prester John has figured so long in popular legend that it has now become simply a timeworn example of medieval exaggeration, often quoted in contempt by people who dislike the religious Orders. We are quite ready to admit that the story of the convents of Plurimanos, with nine thousand monks, and the smaller convent of Alleluia, with six thousand, as well as some of the other stories of this mythical kingdom, were probably colored considerably. But it is a fact that the friars in Ethiopia were very active in the fourteenth century, and that they gave the Church many martyrs. Philip de Sceva was one of these, and we wish we had more information about him.

The eight friars who petitioned the pope for permission to make a pilgrimage to the Holy Land, in 1316, came home by way of Ethiopia, and decided to stay there. That much is history; it is the record of their early missions there. We do not know their names, though, which is not surprising. We know what they taught, and, from a few curious old books, we can discover that they worked on all levels of society. Their mission prospered, and soon they had native vocations.

Philip de Sceva was the son of the royal house of Ethiopia, and the name, obviously European, was most probably given him because no one could pronounce his native name. He is recorded to have entered the Order almost as soon as the missionaries began admitting native boys, and to have excelled in every virtue. He was a brilliant student and a good religious, and he was—remarkably enough—appointed prior soon after his ordination. A further tribute to his talent and virtue was the fact that he was, after a few years, appointed inquisitor for Abyssinia and Ethiopia.

Philip the Inquisitor was charged with keeping the purity of the faith under extraordinarily difficult conditions. The reigning monarch, who had become a Christian, had fallen back into the heathen custom of having several wives. Philip realized that unless the king kept the Christian laws in their completeness, it was hopeless to expect the people to do so. Knowing that his head would probably be forfeit for such a suggestion, he faced the king with the alternative of dismissing the extra wives or being excommunicated. As his English brothers would discover two hundred years later, this was not a popular suggestion for a priest to make to a king. Philip and the patriarch of Ethiopia were both exiled.

After a few years, the king decided that even this was not enough punishment for one who had defied him. He sent word to Philip that he had repented and would like to make his peace with God—a message that he knew would bring a priest.

Philip had been living a busy life outside the kingdom, and he knew it was healthy to stay where he was. But, like any other priest, he gave the sinner the benefit of the doubt, and went back to Ethiopia. He was not surprised when he walked into an ambush and saw the king's men descending upon him with swords.

The date of Philip's martyrdom is given as November, 1366. Little as we know about him, it is enough to demonstrate that the Christian battle is the same in any age and in any country, and that Dominicans of every color and race have fought and died for the same fundamental truths.

EUPHEMIA OF ENGLAND
(d. 1367)

Euphemia, daughter of Edward III, was the sister of John of Gaunt and the Black Prince. She was born in her father's palace, early in the fourteenth century. Being spiritually inclined, she sought out whatever there was of religious training at the court and became a model of piety at an early age. Some visiting religious attracted her attention, and she begged them to teach her how to pray properly.

The glitter and gaiety of the court made no impression on the little girl; she very early decided that she would dedicate her life to God, making a vow of virginity while she was still quite young. All this piety did not trouble the king while she was little, but, when an attractive offer for her hand was made, he told her bluntly that she had better put away her religious notions and begin making herself beautiful. Euphemia did not argue. She merely asked her father for three day's grace—because, of course, she would have to pray about such an important affair—and went to her private chapel, leaving orders that she was not to be disturbed. At the end of the three days, a disgruntled court discovered that she had dressed herself in a maid's costume and fled the country.

Euphemia was probably fourteen or fifteen years old at the time. Wearing old clothes and poorly attended, she journeyed unrecognized as far as Cologne. Here she settled down for a time, as she had great devotion to St. Ursula and her bevy of virgin-martyr companions. She secured a small room near the hospital, where she could hear Mass and spend most of the day caring for the sick poor. She changed her name to Gertrude and made no references to her old life. For some time it was wonderful; she was able to divide her day between work and prayer and—aside from having to battle with the devil now and again—had few worries. However, an old woman who lived near her, and who felt that anybody as pretty as Euphemia certainly was up to no good, decided to trap the girl into some trouble. Since she could find no evidence of her misbehavior, she carefully hunted up some and planted it in Euphemia's room. The evidence was some expensive silk that the old woman had stolen from a benefactor of the hospital. Reporting to the authorities, she led them in triumph to Euphemia's room. There, under the mattress, was the stolen silk.

Euphemia made no protest when she was arrested and put in the public stocks. After all, she was lucky not to have her ears cut off. She was quite cheerful about the whole thing—happy to suffer something for Christ. But, as she sat with her feet and hands fastened tightly in the stocks, real trouble approached, and she could see it coming—a party of her father's knights were approaching, and she knew they had been sent to find her. They stopped idly in front of the stocks and talked.

"In truth," said one, "it gets so now that every young girl we see looks like her; why, even that wicked maid in the stocks has the same color of eyes!" The other demurred, "That creature the princess? In those clothes?" "Clothes can be changed," said the first knight. "If she were properly dressed —we must talk to the jailer."

Euphemia thought fast while they got permission from the jailer to talk to a public criminal. She must also have crossed her fingers and made a very large mental reservation. When they asked her if she were not Euphemia, princess of England, she shook her head stupidly and said, "Good sir, my name is Gertrude." "And your father, is he not king of England?" they asked. Euphemia sighed and cast up her eyes. "My poor father," she told them, "was hanged as a public criminal, and eleven of my brothers died the same way. As you can see, I am a chip off the old block." (The chronicles use almost these very words, and then goes on piously to explain that of course Euphemia meant that Christ, as her Father in redemption, had been crucified, and the eleven Apostles were her brothers!)

Euphemia remained for several hours in the stocks, exposed to the jeers of passersby; as soon as she was free, she made preparations to leave Cologne. She went to Pfortzheim, where there was a large convent of the Second Order of St. Dominic, dedicated to Our Lady and St. Mary Magdalen. She knocked at the door and asked for an alms. A little judicious enquiry brought forth the information that the sisters needed a laundress, as it was a community of highborn ladies who were not accustomed to taking care of such matters. The prioress, who was a countess, allowed the wanderer to live in a little cottage, where she could easily have access to the laundry. Gertrude of Cologne did not think to mention that she was a princess as she settled down happily in the prayerful atmosphere of the monastery. Eventually, she was professed as a secular Tertiary.

In a country across the sea—the chronicles do not say what country—lived a pious anchorite who suffered from an odd sort of vanity: she pestered the Lord continually to tell her if there was anyone, anywhere in the world, who loved Him more than she did. He suggested that she go and see Euphemia. She journeyed through Germany and, finally, stopping for an alms at the monastery at Pfortzheim, came to the end of her quest. Euphemia was in the garden, washing clothes—and she was surrounded by such brilliant light that the pilgrim could hardly look at her. After a long conversation with Euphemia on spiritual things, she repaid her rather poorly by telling the whole story of her holiness to the prioress.

Immediately there was a clamor for Euphemia to enter the community as a choir sister—an offer which she politely declined. An even more awful revelation was in store for the prioress when, some time later, one of the sisters mentioned in Euphemia's hearing that the young prince of England had just been killed in battle, and Euphemia fainted on the spot. The story of her royal birth came out then, and the various shades of nobility in the house discovered that a princess royal had been doing their laundry for many years. Now they all but forced her to enter the community, but Euphemia threatened to go away if they did not leave her in peace in the little hut where she had lived so happily and so holily for all those years.

Euphemia died, in the laundress' little cottage, in February of 1367.

BLESSED SYBILLINA BISCOSSI
(1287-1367)

Blessed Sybillina has several distinguishing characteristics which make her unique in the Dominican family. She was a recluse, which is unusual enough, and she was blind.

Sybillina was born in Pavia, in 1287. Her parents died when she was tiny, and as soon as she was old enough to be of use to anyone, the neighbors, who had taken her in at the time she was orphaned, put her out to work. She must have been very young when she started to work, because at the age of twelve, when she became blind and could not work any more, she already had several years of work behind her.

We do not know what caused her blindness, but the child was left doubly destitute by the loss of her sight. The local chapter of Tertiary sisters took compassion on the child and brought her home to live with them. After a little while of experiencing their kind help, she wanted to join them. They accepted her, young though she was, more out of pity than in any hope of her being able to carry on their busy and varied apostolate. They were soon agreeably surprised to find out how much she could do. She learned to chant the Office quickly and sweetly, and to absorb their teaching about mental prayer as though she had been born for it. She imposed great obligations of prayer on herself, since she could not help them in other ways. Her greatest devotion was to St. Dominic, and it was to him she addressed herself when she finally became convinced that she simply must have her sight back so that she could help the sisters with their work.

Praying earnestly for this intention, Sybillina waited for his feast day. Then, she was certain, he would cure her. Matins came and went with no miracle; little hours, Vespers—and she was still blind. With a sinking heart, Sybillina knelt before St. Dominic's statue and begged him to help her. Kneeling there, she was rapt in ecstasy, and she saw him come out of the darkness and take her by the hand. He led her to a dark tunnel entrance, and she went into the blackness at his word. Terrified, but still clinging to his hand, she advanced past invisible horrors, still guided and protected by his presence. Dawn came gradually, and then light, then a blaze of glory. "In eternity, my dear child," he said. "Here, you must suffer darkness so that you may one day behold eternal light.'" Sybillina, the eager child, was replaced by a mature and thoughtful Sybillina who knew that there would be no cure for her, that she must work her way to heaven through the darkness.

She decided to become a recluse, and obtained the necessary permission. At the age of fifteen, she was sealed into a tiny cell next to the Dominican church. At first she had a companion, but her fellow recluse soon gave up the life. Sybillina remained, alone now, as well as blind.

The first seven years were the worst, she afterwards admitted. The cold was intense, and she never permitted herself a fire. The church, of course, was not heated, and she wore the same clothes winter and summer. In the winter there was only one way to keep from freeezing—keep moving—so she genuflected, and gave herself the discipline. She slept on a board and ate practically nothing. To the tiny window, that was her only communication with the outside world, came the troubled and the sinful and the sick, all begging for her help. She prayed for all of them, and worked many miracles in the lives of the people of Pavia.

One of the more amusing requests came from a woman who was terrified of the dark. Sybillina was praying for her when she saw her in a vision, and observed that the woman—who thought she was hearing things—put on a fur hood to shut out the noise. The next day the woman came to see her, and Sybillina laughed gaily. "You were really scared last night, weren't you?"

she asked. "I laughed when I saw you pull that hood over your ears." The legend reports that the woman was never frightened again.

Sybillina had a lively sense of the real presence and a deep devotion to the Blessed Sacrament. One day a priest was going past her window with Viaticum for the sick; she knew that the host was not consecrated, and told him so. He investigated, and found he had indeed taken a host from the wrong container.

Sybillina lived as a recluse for sixty-seven years. She followed all the Masses and Offices in the church, spending what few spare minutes she had working with her hands, to earn a few alms for the poor. She died in 1367, and was beatified in 1854.

BLESSED ANTHONY OF PAVONIO
(1326-1374)

Anthony of Pavonio was born in 1326, in Savigliano, and grew up to be a pious and intelligent youth. At the age of fifteen he was received into the convent of his native city. He was ordained in 1351, and almost immediately he was engaged in the controversy with the heretics, in which the Lombard province was so frequently embroiled.

Pope Urban V, in 1360, appointed him inquisitor-general of Lombardy and Genoa, making him one of the youngest men ever to hold that office. It was a difficult and dangerous job for a young priest of thirty-four. Besides being practically a death sentence to any man who held the office, it carried with it the necessity of arguing with the men most learned in a twisted and subtle heresy. Anthony worked untiringly in his native city, and his apostolate lasted fourteen years. During this time, he accomplished a great deal by his preaching, and even more by his example of Christian virtue. He was elected prior of Savigliano, in 1368, and given the task of building a new convent. This he accomplished without any criticism of its luxury—a charge that heretics were always anxious to make against any Catholic builders.

The consistent poverty of Anthony's life was a reproach to the heretics, who had always been able to gain ground with the poor by pointing out the wealth of religious houses. He went among the poor and let them see that he was one of them. This so discomfited the heretics that they decided they must kill him. He was preaching in a little village near Turin when they caught him.

The martyrdom occurred in the Easter octave. On the Saturday after Easter, he asked the barber to do a good job on his tonsure, because he was going to a wedding. Puzzled, the barber complied. On the Sunday after Easter, as he finished preaching, seven heretics fell upon him with their daggers, and he hurried off to the promised "wedding." He was buried in the Dominican church at Savigliano, where his tomb was a place of pilgrimage until 1827. At this time the relics were transferred to the Dominican church of Racconigi. Anthony of Pavonio was not formally beatified until 1868.

Oddly enough, Anthony takes after his Franciscan namesake. He is invoked to find lost articles.

ADELAIDE LANGMANN
(1310-1375)

One of the best known of the mystics who thrived in fourteenth-century Germany was Sister Adelaide Langmann; she died in the convent of the Second Order, at Engelthal, Bavaria, in 1375.

Adelaide was born in Engelthal, in 1310. As a little girl, she was extraordinarily pious and good, and always showed a preference for sermons on the Passion. At the age of thirteen, she was betrothed by her parents to a young man of their choice, but he died very suddenly. Adelaide was in church, praying for his soul, when she heard a voice saying, "All your fiances will die, because our Lord has reserved you for Himself." Adelaide was startled and not too pleased about it, but she conversed for some time with the mysterious voice. She was told that she should enter the cloister, and should perform certain acts of penance.

Adelaide felt that she ought to do as she had been told, but she was so attached to her friends that she could not bear the thought of going to the cloister. She took the discipline seven times a day, as she had been told to do, and her nights were a struggle with the devil. But she could not bring herself to enter the convent. One day, as she was receiving Holy Communion, she found to her distress that she could not swallow the Host. "What have I done, Lord?" she asked. The answer was very blunt, "You have gone back on your word." "But I am not strong enough to endure cloistered life," she pleaded. "Who gives you strength?" asked the Lord. "I will go to the priest," she told him hastily. "'No priest can help you in this matter," she was told sternly. "I have told you what to do, and you must do it." "Very well," said Adelaide, telling herself quietly that she could always back out of it later.

"Promise," said the Lord firmly. She promised, and suddenly felt a flood of peace and happiness in place of all the fright and indecision.

Adelaide entered the cloister, but with an ache in her heart. She wanted to do God's will, and she knew that His will was in her behalf. But she was still so fond of her friends that it was a painful wrench to go in and shut the door against them. For a year she walked uncomforted in the lonely darkness; and then the pieces of her life began to fall into place. Our Lord told her that she was to be a fruitful branch bearing many sinners to forgiveness. She turned her heart to prayer and penance, making it her special charity to pray for sinners and for the poor souls.

Only three or four times during her life in the cloister did she come into contact with anyone from outside. She prayed in seclusion for the souls who were recommended to her, and rarely saw any of them, even the ones she had saved from suicide or murder by her prayer and penance in their behalf.

Adelaide Langmann had vowed herself to a life that calls for a strong constitution, yet she was always delicate. On the morning of her profession, she reminded the Lord of her delicate health, and He replied: "That which you cannot do, I will do; I will abandon neither your body nor your soul." For five years she was bed-ridden, and her courage fell to a low point, and then the devil tempted her with thoughts of wishing to die. Our Lord came to her again and assured her, "I will give you all you need."

Our Lord was present nearly all the time in the life of Sister Adelaide, whose days and nights were full of visions, both prophetic and consoling. She saw St. Dominic and St. Thomas in visions many times, and most of the apostles and martyrs. Our Lord assured her that his greatest happiness was for people to pray for sinners.

In spite of her intensive spiritual life, Sister Adelaide was punctual at all her community exercises. Even if she were in ecstasy, she would rouse when the bell summoned her to an exercise. She avoided useless conversation at all times, and had a persistent habit of determining if everything people said was true. She had no use for uncharitable talk, made no secret of her preference for silence. She commented sadly, "There are people who, after long prayers, go out and concern themselves with impatience and uncharitable talk, thus undoing all the good they might have done."

Adelaide Langmann died in 1375. Almost her last remark was: "Avoid frivolous friendships." Though she herself had many friends among the spiritually-minded people of the country, including Christine Ebner, she was probably remembering the friendships that nearly kept her out of the convent long ago.

ST. CATHERINE OF SIENA
(1347-1380)

Fourteenth-century Italy was a land made desolate by plague, schism, and political turmoil. It was so black a time that many saints and scholars believed it heralded the end of the world. Yet, in the midst of this confusion, a person was born who was to rise above the troubles of her own time and the passing of centuries, to remain as unforgotten in our day as she was in her own. She is Catherine, Siena's—and Dominic's—best-known daughter.

Born of the rising merchant class in busy and warlike Siena, Catherine's probable future would be marriage, a home and children—a life that would be charitable and pious, but not too ascetic. Catherine, however, from babyhood was prayerful beyond all ordinary children, and, when she was six, she had a vision in which she saw our Lord enthroned among the saints. From this time on, earth had no sweetness for Catherine; she would belong to God and to Him alone. To this end, she vowed her virginity to God and strove to find more and more time to spend with Him.

In a big noisy household it was not easy for one little girl to be alone and to pray. Petted and pursued by an indulgent mother, crowded by the affairs of the family and the neighborhood, Catherine treasured each minute of solitude, because it gave her opportunity to pray. Rapt in prayer in the Dominican church near her home, she prayed and planned for the day when she would be old enough to wear the white habit herself. Threatened with marriage, she pleaded, in vain, that her heart belonged to God alone; her parents would not listen to such inconvenient desires. So Catherine, with typical firmness, cut off the wealth of her lovely hair to show that she meant what she said. Punished by having to wait on the entire family at table, she spiritualized the work by offering each serving to her beloved Jesus. Her father, seeing her in ecstasy, relented of his severity and gave her leave to live as she pleased.

For two years, Catherine dwelt in paradise, in a tiny bare room, large enough only for God and herself. She joined the Third Order, over the protests of the older members of the group, who felt it unwise to accept anyone so young. In ecstasy much of the time, she would have been content to remain forever in her little room—but God called her away from its peace and security into the full glare of publicity.

Her hand in God's, because she was terrified to go alone to the places He asked her to go, Catherine went from hospitals, prisons, and scaffolds, where she sought for straying sheep, to the papal palace, to plead with the chief shepherd himself. Nursing incurables in the public hospital, she became the "lady with the lamp," who would guide thousands of Dominican sisters to the bedsides of Christ's poor. Dictating to her followers the marvelous story of her colloquies with Christ, she was the teaching sister, giving to others the fruits of her contemplation; enduring with a prayer and a quiet smile the bitter calumnies of those for whom she had sacrificed and labored, she was the model for anyone laboring at apparently thankless tasks in the Master's vineyard.

Catherine would gladly have died a martyr, and she almost did. During one of her meditations on the Passion she received the stigmata, and the pain from this nearly crushed the frail body. But Catherine had another mission to perform before her death: to call the vacillating pope back from Avignon to Rome, which she actually did in the face of unbelievable difficulties. Catherine's life is a concrete example of the Dominican vocation of prayerful action, for it could be said that she was almost never removed from the state of prayer—and yet she accomplished, in her brief thirty-three years, more work than many lifetimes would comfortably hold.

BLESSED MARCOLINO OF FORLI
(1317-1397)

Marcolino Amanni was born at Forli and entered the Order at the age of ten. He occupies a place unique in Dominican annals, because, in a constellation of preachers who were contemplative, but men of great deeds as well, Marcolino was almost purely contemplative.

There is outwardly little to record of Blessed Marcolino, except that for seventy years he kept the Dominican rule in all its rigor. That is a claim to sanctity that can be made by very few, and is of itself enough to entitle him to canonization. He did accomplish the reform of several convents that had fallen from their primitive fervor, but this he did by his prayers and his example rather than by either teaching or preaching.

It is related that Marcolino was most at home with the laybrothers, or with the neighborhood children who enjoyed talking to him. He seldom went out of his cell, and could not have engaged in any active works; neither did he leave any writings. His work for the Order, great as it was, was the unseen work presided over by the Holy Spirit, the work of contemplation.

"To give to others the fruits of contemplation" is the Dominican motto, and one might be curious to know how Blessed Marcolino accomplished this. In order to understand the need for just such a type of holiness, it is well to remember the state of the Church in the fourteenth century. Devastated by plague and schism, divided and held up to scorn, preyed upon by all manner of evils, the Church militant was in need, not only of brave and intelligent action, but also of prayer. Consistently through the centuries, God has raised up such saints as could best avert the disasters that threatened the world in their day, and Marcolino was one answer to the need of mystics who would plead ceaselessly for the Church.

The interior life of Marcolino was not recorded by himself or by others. He lived the mystical life with such intensity that he was nearly always rapt in ecstasy and unconscious of the things around him. Some one of his brothers recorded that he seemed "a stranger on earth, concerned only with the things of heaven." Most of his brethren thought him merely sleepy and inattentive, but actually he was, for long periods, lost in converse with God. Some had heard him talking earnestly to the statue of Our Lady in his cell; some fortunate few had heard Our Lady replying to his questions, with the same simplicity.

At the death of Blessed Marcolino, a beautiful child appeared in the streets, crying out the news to the little town that the saintly friar was dead. As the child disappeared when the message was delivered, he was thought to have been an angel. Many miracles were worked at the tomb of Marcolina. One was the miraculous cure of a woman who had been bedridden for thirty years. Hearing of the death of the blessed, she begged him to cure her so that she could visit his tomb.

BLESSED RAYMOND OF CAPUA
(1330-1399)

Being spiritual adviser to a saint must have its peculiar difficulties, and, consequently, the spiritual guidance of Catherine of Siena, whose career was unprecedented in history, must have called for a great many talents, as well as virtues, on the part of her director, Blessed Raymond of Capua. As one might suspect, this was not Raymond's only claim to fame. He was a man of tremendous gifts, and his life has enriched the Order both in his day and ours.

Raymond was born in Capua, in 1330, of one of the prominent families of the city. As a student at the University of Bologna, he met the Dominicans and was received into the Order; in after years, he revealed that a vision of St. Dominic had determined him to take the step. He was a model religious and soon was entrusted with responsible work in the community.

One of his first tasks was the direction of several monasteries of nuns, at Montepulciano. He was one of the first biographers of St. Agnes of Montepulciano, who had died there less than fifty years before. In 1367, he was called to Rome to be prior of the Minerva. He was teaching at Santa Maria Novella, in Florence, when, in 1374, he was sent by the master general to Siena. Here lived the greatest woman mystic of the century, St. Catherine of Siena, in whom the authorities of the Order necessarily took great interest. Raymond was appointed her confessor and director.

This appointment was deliberate on the part of the master general, but Raymond was a stranger to Catherine. She saw him first at Mass, where she had been praying fervently for a spiritual guide who would understand the peculiar mission to which she had been called, and would direct her safely along the difficult and lonely way that God had marked out for her. As she watched him at the altar, on the Feast of St. John the Baptist, an interior voice said to her, "This is my beloved servant. This is he to whom I will entrust you." She approached him after Mass and told him her story.

Raymond was a cautious man and not overjoyed about being selected for the role of Catherine's director and confessor. He did not at first express any great enthusiasm for her mission. Further acquaintance with her convinced him that she was a very holy woman. His first move, which would make Catherine very happy, was to allow her to receive Communion as often as she wished. Further than that he could not go at that time.

It took a siege of the plague to convince him to put complete confidence in Catherine's genius. They worked together among the plague-sticken until one day Raymond collapsed with the disease himself. Catherine came to his bedside when she heard that he was already unconscious and probably dying. She did not leave until he opened his eyes and showed signs of recovery. He knew that he had been on the brink of death, and that Catherine's prayers had brought him back.

Raymond was Catherine's director and confessor for the last six years of her life, six years that are probably unparalleled in the history of any other woman. Catherine wished, first of all, to see the long-desired new crusade actually launched. The pope took several steps in the direction of initiating this project, and called for the support of all in propagandizing the crusade.

Catherine took him quite literally. She wrote a letter to the English pirate, John Hawkwood, imploring him to channel his fighting energies into the cause of God. Raymond had the delicate job of conveying this letter to the famous freebooter. In the meantime, Catherine kept sending him penitents, and he was so busy in the confessional that he barely had time to eat. Catherine possessed a tremendous power to turn people from evil to good, but she could not hear their confessions. Raymond, therefore, was kept very busy.

It is difficult, if not impossible, to follow the interplay of politics which kept the Italian peninsula in turmoil for all the years of Raymond's life. After a great many crises among the Italian cities, and a number of switches of allegiance, Catherine brought some of the leaders into line and began to hope for settlement. She persuaded the pope, Gregory VI, to go back to Rome, thereby ending the sorry situation of having the pope within reach of the French king. With a tremendous effort of will, and at great personal sacrifice, Gregory VI went back to Rome—and died.

Pope Urban VI was elected to succeed him. After a confusing series of events, the cardinals declared the first election invalid and elected Clement VII as anti-pope. The country, the Church, and the Order split in various factions over their allegiance to one or the other papal contestant. Years later, St. Antoninus was to write about these trying days:

> There were many discussions about the matter and many books were written in defense of both sides. Through all the time that the division lasted, both parts (or obediences) could count among their supporters men exceedingly learned, both in theology and canon law, and also many men of most holy life and (what is more striking still) outstanding by the miracles they wrought; yet it was never possible so to decide the question that no doubts remained in the minds of the majority of men.
>
> (Chronicorum III: Tit. 22)

Catherine and Raymond sided with Urban VI. Raymond was soon sent on an errand to the king of France, on behalf of his candidate, and was stopped and threatened by the soldiers of the anti-pope. When he reported this to Catherine, she gave him scant sympathy and hinted strongly that he was not overly brave. He tried again with no better success. When one remembers that Raymond had other work to do besides the direction of his unpredictable penitent, it becomes clear that Raymond was an exceedingly busy man. Some people broke under the load of work that Catherine so blithely distributed among her close followers.

In 1380, when Raymond was in Genoa preaching the crusade, he heard a voice in the air saying, "Tell him never to lose courage. I will be with him in every danger. If he falls, I will help him up again." A few days later he received the sorrowful news that Catherine had died in Rome on the day he heard the message.

He was soon to need all the moral support she could give him. A few weeks after her death, he was elected master general of the portion of the Order which supported Urban VI. Most superiors on taking over such a task have at least only one community to deal with; his was the unhappy task of trying to bring order out of chaos, and to promote a reform in an Order that was neatly split in half, with some of its best men on both sides. Various things have been said about his rule as master general; some claim that he saved the Order's observance, others criticize him for a seeming lack of attention to study. We, at least, can agree on the difficulty of the task facing him.

The work of reforming the Order from within was the principal work of this period. With the help of the most outstanding men of the Order, Raymond established an upward trend in observance against great obstacles. He set up several houses of strict observance to pioneer this work, and he gradually extended it until this spirit of primitive observance would predominate in the entire Order.

Raymond of Capua died in Nuremberg, while he was there promoting the reform. His body was later transferred to Naples. On the fifth centenary of his death, he was beatified by Pope Leo XIII.

FIFTEENTH CENTURY

BLESSED ANDREW FRANCHI
(1335-1401)

Andrew was born in Pistoia, in 1335, of a noble family. He entered the Order in his native city, most probably in 1351, when the Italian peninsula was still under the shadow of the plague and was deeply involved in fratricidal wars. Another theory has it that he entered at Florence, in 1348, which was the year the plague reached its peak. We do not really known which is the proper date. But he came into the Order to give attention to his immortal soul, at a time when the world around him was apparently falling to pieces.

Andrew proved to be a good religious and an able administrator. He served as prior in three convents while still quite young. In 1378, he was appointed bishop of Pistoia, an office he filled with distinction and holiness for twenty-three years.

It is written of Andrew that he devoted himself to the poor, and spent his revenues to relieve their misery and to rebuild the ruined churches. He had a great personal devotion to Our Blessed Lady, to the Holy Childhood, and to the Three Holy Kings. As bishop, he lived a life of extreme simplicity, retaining his religious habit, and as much as he could of the rule. A year before his death, he resigned his office and retired to die at his old convent of Pistoia.

Andrew Franchi died in 1401, and was beatified in 1921.

MANUEL CALECAS
(d. 1410)

Manuel Calecas, who was a celebrated Greek scholar in the late fourteenth and early fifteenth centuries, was a convert who attained great fame in the Order as theologian and writer.

Manuel was born in Greece, around the middle of the fourteenth century, of a family of Greek schismatics who were very fervent in their religion. Manuel was a scholar, and he was inquisitive to the point of exasperating his Greek masters, since he began very young to discover embarrassing loopholes in the theology of the schismatics. Finally, they quite simply threw him out of the church and told him not to come back. He went in quest of some one who would let him ask questions, and who could give him the answers he sought.

Who suggested that the Dominicans of Pera were exactly what he wanted, we do not know. He went there and studied under them for some time, and then begged to be admitted to the Order. Pera boasted a large and active unit of the "Wandering Brethren among the Pagans," and they were happy to acquire a young student with such a scholarly background in Greek. He was given the religious habit, and then he immediately set to the task of writing against the errors he knew so well. All his life, the salvation of his former companions in schism was to trouble him; he did all he could to bring them with him into the Church.

The first important work produced by Manuel Calecas was a four-part study of the errors of the Greeks. A Franciscan, returning to Rome from an embassy in the Orient, carried a copy of it to the pope, who ordered that it be copied immediately into Latin, to make it available to those who were working with Eastern peoples. It was translated by a Camaldolese abbot, and immediately took its place as a working handbook for missionaries to the Far East. The book was used at the Councils of Basle and Florence, and copyists were kept frantically busy trying to get out sufficient manuscripts for use by all those who were working to heal the schism between East and West.

Manuel Calecas remained in Pera most of his life, writing working-handbooks for the use of active missionaries. He did spend some time on the Greek islands of Chios and Lesbos, and at Crete, in active mission work among the Greeks. He stayed for a short time at the Benedictine abbey of St. Ambrose in Milan, working earnestly at the translation and exposition of the Greek position.

Manuel Calecas died in Mytilene, most probably, in 1410. Because he worked all his religious life among the "Wandering Brethren," who left so few records, it is difficult to state with any certainty the exact dates of any of his works. Like most medieval craftsmen, he was content to work unknown, if only God would reward his efforts.

ST. VINCENT FERRER
(1350-1419)

Vincent's career of miracle-working began early; prodigies attended his birth and baptism at Valencia, and, at the age of five, he cured a neighbor child of a serious illness. These gifts, and his natural beauty of person and character, made him the center of attention very early in life. Clearly, Vincent was marked for an unusual life.

He began his classical studies at the age of eight, his theological study at fourteen. Four years later, as all had expected, he entered the Dominican Order in his native city. So angelic was his appearance, and so holy his actions, that no other course seemed possible to him than to dedicate his life to God.

No sooner had he made his choice of a state in life than the devil attacked him with the most dreadful temptations. Even his parents pleaded with him to leave the convent and become a secular priest. By prayer and faith, especially prayer to Our Lady and his guardian angel, Vincent triumphed over his difficulties and finished his novitiate. He was ordained at Barcelona, in 1379.

Having made a particular study of Scripture and Hebrew, Vincent was well equipped to preach to the Jews. They were quite numerous in Spain then. During the years of his preaching, more than thirty thousand Jews and Moors were converted to Christianity. His numerous miracles, the strength and beauty of his voice, the purity and clarity of his doctrine, combined to make his preaching effective, based as it was on a firm foundation of prayer.

Two evils cried out for remedy in St. Vincent's day: the moral laxity left by the great plague, and the scandal of the papal schism. In regard to the first, he preached tirelessly against the evils of the time, bringing thousands to a better life. That he espoused the cause of the wrong man in the papal disagreement is no argument against his own sanctity; at the time, and in the midst of such confusion, it was almost impossible to tell who was right and who was wrong. The memorable thing is that he labored, with all the arts he could command, to bring order out of a chaos which has never had an equal in the history of Christianity. He worked so intensely, in fact, that he fell mortally ill, and only a miraculous visit of Sts. Francis and Dominic cured him. On this occasion, he was bidden to rise and preach —whenever and wherever he was needed.

The preaching of Vincent became a strange but marvelously effective process. He attracted to himself hundreds of people—at one time, more than ten thousand—who followed him from place to place in the garb of pilgrims. The priests of the company sang Mass daily, chanted the Office, and dispensed the sacraments to those converted by Vincent's preaching. Men and women traveled in separate companies, chanting litanies and prayers as they went barefoot along the road from one city to another. They taught catechism where needed, founded hospitals, and revived a faith that had all but perished in the time of the plague. In this way, he went through Spain, Italy, and France. Legend has it that he also went to England. The burden of his preaching was penance. Like another John the Baptist—who was also likened to an angel, as St. Vincent is in popular art—he went through the wilderness of sin, crying out to the people to make straight the paths of the Lord. Fearing the judgment, if for no other reason, sinners listened to his startling sermons, and the most obstinate were led by him to cast off sin and love God. He worked countless miracles, some of which are remembered today in the proverbs of the country. His book, *Treatise on the Spiritual Life,* is still of value to earnest souls.

He preached to St. Colette and her nuns, and it was she who told him that he would die in France. Too ill to return to Spain, he did, indeed, die in Brittany. The Breton fishermen still invoke his aid in storms. In Spain, he is also the patron of orphanages.

BLESSED CLARE GAMBACORTA
(1362-1419)

Victoria Gambacorta was born in 1362, most probably in Venice. She was the only daughter of the first family of Pisa, which was at the moment in exile, due to some political turnover unfavorable to her father. When the little girl was seven, the family returned in triumph to Pisa, and her father was installed as chief magistrate of the city, a position full of both glory and uncertainty.

Victoria was a pretty and pious child. One of her chroniclers, a contemporary, tells us that when she was still in her father's house she "used to gather the children together and recite the Rosary with them." She was a devout and penitential child, and she did not relish the marriage her father arranged for her. However, she was a dutiful daughter, and, married to her young husband, she was a dutiful and loving wife. When he died of plague, three years later, she was grief-stricken, for she had loved him. But now that she was free, she determined that no one was going to urge her to marry again.

In the first year of her marriage, when she was thirteen, Victoria had met the famous and saintly Dominican from Siena, Catherine Benincasa, who had come to Pisa to talk to her father about the league of cities. The saint had advised the lovely young bride to give her heart to God and her husband. Now that he was dead, Catherine wrote to the widow, saying: "Strip yourself of self. Love God with a free and loyal love." Victoria knew that another marriage was being arranged for her, and before it could take place she fled to the Poor Clares and took the habit. She took the name Sister Clare.

Her brothers came and removed her forcibly. They locked her up in a dark little room in her own home. She could neither talk to her friends nor receive the sacraments, but she retained the name of Clare, and she wore the Franciscan habit. The pretty young prisoner was a daughter of the times, and she managed to get errands done by her friends. One by one, her jewels were sent out and sold, and the money was given to the poor. It was the only active charity she could manage from a prison cell. Finally, on St. Dominic's day, when her father and brothers were away, her mother got her out and took her to Mass. It was the first time in months that she had been able to receive Holy Communion.

Shortly after this, a Spanish bishop came to visit the family, and Clare's father asked him to try to talk some sense into the girl. He apparently did not know that the Spaniard had been confessor to St. Brigit of Sweden, and that he was highly in sympathy with women who wished to dedicate themselves to God. The upshot of it all was that Clare's father finally relented, allowing her to make her plans to enter a convent. Her contact with St. Catherine had convinced her that she could be nothing but a Dominican, so she took refuge with the local community until she could build a convent of her own.

Due to the ravages of plague and schism, many convents, including that of the Dominicans of Pisa, were weak in observance and did not live the common life. Clare wanted a strictly religious form of life, and, in four year's time, with the help of her stepmother, the new convent was built. It was blessed for use in 1385, and a strict canonical cloister was imposed upon it, forbidding any man but the bishop and the master general to enter it. Eight years later, this strict enclosure was to cost Sister Clare a terrible loss. Her father was betrayed by a man who had always been his friend, and the volatile public turned on him and killed him in the street outside her convent. One of her brothers also fell in the fight, and a second one, wounded, begged at the convent door to be let in. Clare had to tell him, through the window, that she could not open the door to him. While she watched in horror, he was dragged away and killed.

Some time after this, Sister Clare fell seriously ill and was thought to be dying. She made a curious request: some food from the table of the man who had betrayed and killed her father and brothers. The wife of the guilty man sent a basket of bread and fruit; Sister Clare ate the bread and was cured. Shortly afterwards, the man who had seized the power unjustly was killed himself, and she offered sanctuary to his widow and daughters.

Clare's brother, Peter, who had fled from the court to become a hermit about the time she went to the Poor Clares, converted a band of highwaymen and began a community of hermits. When his father and brothers were murdered, he wished to go back to secular life and seek revenge, and Clare talked him out of it.

Clare Gambacorta died in 1419, after a holy life. Many prodigies were reported at her tomb, and there is an interesting little legend to the effect that every time a sister in her house is about to die, the bones of Blessed Clare rattle in her coffin. This gives the sister warning.

Pope Pius VIII beatified her in 1830.

BLESSED ALVAREZ OF CORDOVA
(d. 1420)

Blessed Alvarez is claimed by both Spain and Portugal. He received the habit in the convent of St. Paul, at Cordova, in 1368, and had been preaching for some time in Castile and Andalusia when St. Vincent Ferrer began preaching in Catalonia. Having gone to Italy and the Holy Land on a pilgrimage, Blessed Alvarez returned to Castile and preached the crusade against the infidels. He was spiritual advisor to the queen, and he had the work of preparing the people spiritually for the desperate effort of the crusade to drive the Moors from Spain.

Blessed Alvarez is probably best remembered as a builder of churches and convents, an activity which was symbolic of the work he did in the souls of those among whom he preached. He founded, in one place, a convent to shelter a famous image of Our Lady, which had been discovered in a miraculous manner. He built, near Cordova, the famous convent of

Scala Coeli, a haven of regular observance. It had great influence for many years. His building enterprises were often aided by the angels, who, during the night, carried wood and stones to spots convenient for the workmen.

The austerities of Alvarez were all the more remarkable in that they were not performed by a hermit, but by a man of action. He spent the night in prayer, as St. Dominic had done; he wore a hairshirt and a penitential chain; and he begged alms in the streets of Cordova for the building of his churches, despite the fact that he had great favor at court and could have obtained all the money he needed from the queen. He had a deep devotion to the Passion, and had scenes of our Lord's sufferings made into small oratories in the garden at Scala Coeli.

On one occasion, when there was no food for the community but one head of lettuce left from the night before, Blessed Alvarez called the community together in the refectory, said the customary prayers, and sent the porter to the gate. There the astonished brother found a stranger, leading a mule; the mule was loaded with bread, fish, wine, and all things needed for a good meal. The porter turned to thank the benefactor and found that he had disappeared. At another time, Blessed Alvarez was overcome with pity at a dying man who lay untended in the street. Wrapping the man in his mantle, he started home with the sufferer, and one of the brothers asked what he was carrying. "A poor sick man," replied the blessed. But when they opened the mantle, there was only a large crucifix in his arms. This crucifix is still preserved at Scala Coeli.

Blessed Alvarez died and was buried at Scala Coeli. An attempt was made later to remove the relics to Cordova, but it could not be done, because violent storms began each time the journey was resumed, and stopped when the body was returned to its original resting-place.

A bell in the chapel of Blessed Alvarez, in the convent of Cordova, rings of itself when anyone in the convent, or of special note in the Order, is about to die.

BLESSED JOHN DOMINICI
(1350-1420)

Blessed John Dominici, one of the glories of the Order in the fourteenth century, came very near not being admitted to the Dominicans, because he had such a severe speech defect that the superior felt he would never be able to preach. His life is an admirable example of the triumph of spirit over difficulty, and an indication that God can use any type of instrument He chooses, if He has a certain work to be done.

John Dominici de Banchini was born in Florence, in 1350, of a poor family. His early years were noted for piety. In fact, if anyone came looking for him, his mother would say, "Go and look in the church. He spends most of his time there." He had a special love for the Dominican church of Santa Maria Novella, and he haunted it from early morning to late at night. It was not a surprise to anyone when, at the age of seventeen, he decided to enter the Order of St. Dominic.

Here several difficulties presented themselves. John had no background of education, which was absolutely necessary in an Order of scholars. To make matters worse, he had a serious speech defect. Some of the fathers felt that he should support his parents, although they protested that this should not stand in the way of their son's vocation. It was two years before John was allowed to enter, at Santa Maria Novella, and start his novitiate. The Order was soon to discover what a treasure they had. He excelled in theology and Sacred Scripture, and so he was sent, with the other superior students, to finish his studies in Paris.

Now he was face to face with the difficulty which his superiors had seen from the beginning. An ordained priest, member of a preaching order, he must fulfill his vocation by preaching. His superiors attempted to forestall any embarrassment by assigning him to work in the house. John felt that the intervention of heaven was called for, so, with great simplicity, he prayed to St. Catherine of Siena, then recently dead, to cure him. The impediment disappeared, and John went joyfully out to preach. He was to become one of the most famous of Dominican preachers of his age and for all time.

In 1392, after years of successful missionary work in all the cities of Italy, John was appointed vicar-provincial of the Roman province. It was a task that, both intellectually and spiritually, called for a giant. The plague had cut into the Order with such devastating effect that regular life barely existed. The convent of Santa Maria Novella had lost seventy-seven friars within a few months; other convents were in even worse condition. The mortality had been higher among the friars than anywhere else, because they had gone quite unselfishly to the aid of the stricken people. However, this misfortune had left the Order perilously understaffed, and there were a good many members who believed quite sincerely that the conditions of the time called for a mitigated observance of the rule. Many of the houses were already operating in this fashion. It was to be the principal work of

Blessed John Dominici to right this condition, and bring back the Order to its first fervour.

He began his work with a foundation at Fiesole. Before he had even erected the new convent, four young men received the habit, one of whom was Antoninus—future archbishop of Florence and saint of the Church. Two years later, two of the most gifted young artists in Italy, whom history would know as Fra Angelico and his brother, Fra Benedetto, received the habit. With these and other earnest young men, John Dominici set about the difficult work of building anew an Order that had suffered a diminution of its original fervour. Soon the house at Fiesole, and others modeled upon it, could be described, as the first houses of the Order were, "the homes of angels."

Difficult days were in preparation for John Dominici. He was appointed cardinal in 1407, and chosen as confessor to the pope. Due to schism, there were two claimants to the papacy. The situation grew even worse when, after another election, no less than three powerful men claimed to have been lawfully elected pope.

Largely through the diplomacy and wise counsel of John Cardinal Dominici, the rival claimants to the papal throne agreed to withdraw their claims, and the groundwork was laid for the election of a new and acceptable candidate. At this time, John Dominici publicly renounced his cardinalate, thus indicating to the enemies who accused him of political ambition that he cared nothing for honors in this world.

Blessed John Dominici died in Hungary, in 1420, where he had been sent by the pope to preach against the heresy of John Hus. He was buried in the Church of St. Paul the Hermit, in Buda, and many miracles were worked at his tomb before it was finally destroyed by the Turks. Pope Gregory XVI beatified this great Dominican in 1837.

CONRADIN OF BRESCIA
(d. 1429)

Conradin was born in the late thirteenth century, at Brescia, of noble and wealthy parents. In a time of great uncertainty for all Christians—the time of the great Western schism—his parents were staunch adherents to the Church, and they gave their children a thorough Catholic education. Conradin was sent to the University of Padua to study civil and canon law, and, in his five years at the university, distinguished himself by his purity, charity, and devotion to study. Here he met the Dominicans, and here, in 1419, he entered the Order.

A model university student, Conradin was a'so a model Dominican. He finished his course of studies with honors and was ordained. At an early age, he was made prior of the convent in his home town of Brescia, and then of the big convent of St. Dominic, at Bologna, where he was to restore the house to primitive observance.

It is hard for us to imagine what he was up against in this task; plague and schism had laid waste to the Order, as well as the country and the Church; decimated in numbers, forced to relax discipline and shorten the time of training simply to keep the novitiate alive, the Order had reached the point where even its nobler members wondered if it would not be better to rewrite the rule and make it a little easier on people. Several times in the fourteenth and fifteenth centuries this question came up, and it was left for the more fervent members of the Order to hold the line against relaxation. In his day, Conradin of Brescia was the one who saved the primitive form of life in Bologna.

Plague had already made a shambles of law and order in the Italian peninsula, and, during Conradin's term as prior in Bologna, it struck again with savage force. The situation was especially bleak because Bologna was under papal interdict. Powerful families of the city had led the populace to rebel against papal authority and consequently had incurred the interdict, which had been duly published and was simply ignored. Conradin went into the fray on the side of papal authority, and he tried to move the fickle populace to repentance for their sins before it was too late, asking them to humble themselves so that the interdict might be lifted. Even with plague snatching its victims from their very homes, the people refused to listen to the voice of authority. Finally, they captured Conradin, beat him badly, and imprisoned him. However, in spite of this, he finally prevailed upon the people to do penance and submit to the pope.

In recognition of his work as mediator, Pope Martin V wished to make Conradin a cardinal, but the Dominican refused the honor, and he returned to his work at the Convent of St. Dominic. In 1429 a fresh outbreak of the plague called all the friars once more to the streets to assist the dying, Conradin fell victim to the plague. He is spoken of as "Blessed Conradin" in the histories of the period.

BLESSED MARY MANCINI
(1355-1431)

Catherine Mancini was born in Pisa, of noble parentage, and almost in baby-hood began enjoying the miraculous favors with which her life was filled. At the age of three, she was warned by some heavenly agency that the porch on which she had been placed by her nurse was unsafe. Her cries attracted the nurse's attention, and they had barely left the porch when it collapsed. When she was five, she beheld in an ecstasy the dungeon of a palace in Pisa in which Peter Gambacorta, one of the leading citizens, was being tor-tured. At Catherine's prayer, the rope broke and the man was released. Our Lady told the little girl to say prayers every day for this man, because he would one day be her benefactor.

Catherine would have much preferred the religious life to marriage, but she obeyed her parents and was married at the age of twelve. Widowed at sixteeen, she was compelled to marry again. Of her seven children, only one survived the death of her second husband, and Catherine learned through a vision that this child, too, was soon to be taken from her. Thus she found herself, at the age of twenty-five, twice widowed and bereft of all her children. Refusing a third marriage, she devoted herself to prayer and works of charity.

She soon worked out for herself a severe schedule of prayers and good works, fasting and mortifications. She tended the sick and the poor, bring-ing them into her own home and regarding them as our Lord Himself. She gave her goods to the poor and labored for them with her own hands. Our Lord was pleased to show her that He approved of her works by appearing to her in the guise of a poor young man, sick, and in need of both food and medicine. She carefully dressed his wounds, and she was rewarded by the revelation that it was in reality her Redeemer whom she had served.

St. Catherine of Siena visited Pisa at about this time, and the two saintly women were drawn together into a holy friendship. As they prayed together in the Dominican church one day, they were surrounded by a bright cloud, out of which flew a white dove. They conversed joyfully on spiritual matters, and were mutually strengthened by the meeting.

On the advice of St. Catherine of Siena, Catherine retired to an enclosed convent of the Second Order. In religion, she was given the name Mary, by which she is usually known. She embraced the religious life in all its primi-tive austerity, and, with Blessed Clare Gambacorta and a few other members of the convent, she founded a new and much more austere house, which had been built by Peter Gambacorta. Our Lady's prophecy of his benefactions was thus fulfilled.

Blessed Mary was favored with many visions and was in almost constant prayer. She became prioress of the house on the death of her friend Blessed Clare Gambacorta, and ruled it with justice and holiness until her death.

BLESSED PETER OF TIFERNO
(1390-1445)

Peter Capucci was born in Citta del Castello, in 1390. After a youth of innocence and devotion to study, he applied for admission to the Order. On the eve of the Feast of the Assumption, in 1405, an historic ceremony saw him clothed in the habit, in company with a frail lad by the name of Antonino, who was one day to be the great St. Antoninus of Florence. His novice master was Blessed Lawrence of Ripafratta, and his companions included Fra Angelico and Fra Benedetto, the artist-brothers who were to bring world renown to the cloisters of San Marco. The novitiate was spent at Cortona, and Peter remained there when some of the community removed to Fiesole. He was ordained at Cortona and began his apostolate there.

Peter Capucci is not a glittering character in that flamboyant century, but the virtues with which he was endowed were sufficient to bring him to the attention of the Church, even in the midst of a noisy era. He was noted for regularity, patience, and humility—virtues none too common in the fifteenth century. He took upon himself all the duties of begging that fell upon the house, as he wanted to take no satisfaction in his noble birth. Sometimes people treated him rudely, which did not disturb him, but he kept on in this humble work so that there would be food for the brethren and alms for the poor. One rich wine merchant refused him abruptly with the excuse that "the barrels down cellar are all empty." Going down a short while later, he found to his horror that they *were* all empty. He sent posthaste for the friar, apologized, and begged him to bless the barrels and restore the wine. Peter did, without any hesitation.

Other miracles testified to Peter's sanctity—cures and rescues and preservation from peril. A woman with a withered hand was cured; two men unjustly condemned were saved from execution. Some of his contacts were not so happy, however. Once, walking through the cloister, he met a young man of wicked life, and Peter prophesied to him that he would die within twenty-four hours. The young man laughed at him, but, in the middle of the night, stricken and penitent, he sent for the preacher to beg for the last sacraments.

Peter's sermons were not all sweetness and light; usually he preached holding a skull in his hands, and he was an expert at pointing out uncomfortable truths to people who would rather not hear them. He was more than a little preoccupied with the thought of death, surely not an unusual state of mind for one who lived at a time of plague and schism.

Peter Capucci died in 1445, and he was buried in a humble grave. Miracles began to occur at the grave, and his fame grew. A prominent man, who had been paralyzed for three years, received the use of his limbs at the grave, after he had promised to pay the expenses of an annual fiesta in Peter's honor. This and other miracles suggested that the relics be moved to a more suitable place, and they were finally, in 1597. Peter was beatified in 1816.

BLESSED ANDREW ABELLON
(1375-1450)

Blessed Andrew Abellon was born at St. Maximin, in France, near the world-famous shrine of St. Mary Magdalen. His entire life was centered around the shrine, and it is greatly due to his efforts that the devotion to the great penitent has become so well established.

Andrew was born in 1375, and, as a young man, may have heard the stirring sermons of St. Vincent Ferrer, who was at that time preaching in France. Perhaps the purity and penitential zeal for which this great preacher was renowned gave the young Andrew the pattern for his own life. He soon demonstrated his choice of purity and penance by joining the Friars Preachers in his native city. After a happy and holy novitiate, he made his profession and was ordained. In a few years, a finished preacher and a guide for souls, he turned his attention to the neglected shrine of St. Mary Magdalen.

This rugged and penitential region of France had been honored from the time of the Apostles as the chosen retreat of St. Mary Magdalen, who did penance there for the sins of her youth. From earliest days, it had been a place of pilgrimage, but had no definite arrangements for the care of pilgrims, nor any way of supplying their spiritual needs. In Blessed Andrew's time, Dominican fathers from St. Maximin had taken over the spiritual care of the pilgrims as a mission work, but without financial help, and in the face of great trials. Seeing the need of a permanent foundation at the shrine, Andrew set about accomplishing this worthy end. He interested the queen in his project, and obtained enough money from her to build a convent, which was a gem of architecture as well as a source of spiritual power. Andrew had studied art before his entry into the Order, and he used his talents in this field in building, beautifully and permanently, whatever he was called upon to do.

A lover of beauty in the physical order, Andrew was the same in the spiritual. He was famous as a confessor, and his wise government as prior gave great help to the spiritual growth of the new convent. A practical man as well as a deeply spiritual one, Andrew established two mills near the shrine that would provide the people with a means of earning a living while remaining there. Quite naturally, a priest who interested himself in the welfare of the people to this extent could hope for great influence with them, and this he had, both at St. Maximin and at Aix, where an altarpiece he painted may still be seen.

Blessed Andrew died in 1450, and he was buried in the Church of the Magdalen. His tomb soon became a place of pilgrimage; his help especially was sought in the cure of fevers.

BLESSED STEPHEN BANDELLI
(1369-1450)

Stephen Bandelli was born near Piacenza, in 1369, of a noble family. We know very little about his early years, except that he applied for admission at the convent of Piacenza and was received there when he was still quite young.

About all we know of Stephen Bandelli from that time on is that he took his degree in canon law and became a master in theology, and that he lectured at the University of Pavia. All of this argues that he was a man of superior intellect and a careful student. Tradition holds that he was "another St. Paul," and that his sermons were effective in bringing many Christians to a more fervent life and many sinners back into the fold. Aside from this, one reads only the traditional assurances—that he was prayerful, penitential, had a great spirit of poverty, was charitable, and was a model religious.

Stephen Bandelli died at Saluzzo, in 1450, and was buried there in the Dominican church. Many miracles were worked at his tomb, and the citizens of Saluzzo invoked him, in 1487, when the town was attacked by one of their neighbor cities. Their preservation they attributed to Stephen, as it was claimed that he had appeared in the sky above them while they were fighting. An annual feast was kept there in his honor for many years.

The cult of Stephen Bandelli was approved by Pope Pius IX, in 1856.

BLESSED PETER GEREMIA
(1381-1452)

Peter Geremia was born in Palermo, in Sicily. Unusually gifted, he was sent early to the University of Bologna, where he passed his studies brilliantly and attracted the attention and praise of all. On the brink of a successful career as a lawyer, he was brought up short by an event which changed his life.

Having retired one night, he was pleasantly dreaming of the honors that would soon come to him in his work, when he heard a knock at the window. As his room was on the third floor, and there was nothing for a human being to stand on outside his window, he sat up, in understandable fright, and asked who was there. A hollow voice responded that he was a relative who had just died, a successful lawyer who had wanted human praise so badly that he had lied to win it, and now was eternally lost because of his pride. Peter was terrified, and acted at once upon the suggestion to turn, while there was still time, from the vanity of public acclaim. He went the next day to a locksmith and bought an iron chain, which he riveted tightly about him. He began praying seriously to know his vocation.

Soon after this, God made known to him that he should enter the Order of Friars Preachers. He did so as soon as possible. His new choice of vocation was a bitter blow to his father, who had gloried in his son's achievements, hoping to see him become the most famous lawyer in Europe. He angrily journeyed to Bologna to see his son and demanded that he come home. The prior, trying to calm the excited man, finally agreed to call Peter. As the young man approached them, radiantly happy in his new life, the father's heart was touched, and he gladly gave his blessing to the new undertaking.

Peter's brilliant mind and great spiritual gifts found room for development in the Order, and he became known as one of the finest preachers in Sicily. He was so well known that St. Vincent Ferrer asked to see him, and they conversed happily on spiritual things. He always preached in the open air, because there was no church large enough to hold the crowds that flocked to hear him.

Being prior of the convent, Peter was consulted one day when there was no food for the community. He went down to the shore and asked a fisherman for a donation. He was rudely refused. Getting into a boat, he rowed out from the shore and made a sign to the fish; they broke the nets and followed him. Repenting of his bad manners, the fisherman apologized, whereupon Peter made another sign to the fish, sending them back into the nets again. The records say that the convent was ever afterwards supplied with fish.

Peter was sent as visitor to establish regular observance in the convents of Sicily. He was called to Florence by the pope, to try healing the Greek schism. A union of the opposing groups was affected, though it did not last. Peter was offered a bishopric (and refused it) for his work in this matter.

At one time, when Peter was preaching at Catania, Mount Aetna erupted, and torrents of flame and lava flowed down on the city. The people cast themselves at his feet, begging him to save them. After preaching a brief and pointed sermon on repentance, Peter went into the nearby shrine of St. Agatha, removed the veil of the saint, which was there honored as a relic, and held it towards the approaching tide of destruction. The eruption ceased and the town was saved. This and the countless other miracles he performed caused him to be revered as a saint. He raised the dead to life, healed the crippled and the blind, and brought obstinate sinners to the feet of God. Only after his death was it known how severely he had punished his own body in memory of his youthful pride.

FRA ANGELICO
(1386-1455)

Guido da Vicchio was born near Florence in 1386 or 1387, in a region of great natural beauty, which aided his innate talent for art. He studied under several artists of note in Italy just when the country was most conscious of the spirit of Giotto and Cimabue, and their influence was always to give a certain unearthly aspect to his paintings.

When he was still quite young, and already a recognized artist, he entered the Dominican convent at Fiesole with his brother, Benedetto. It is a tribute to the ability and the sanctity of both brothers that their names would stand out in such distinguished company, for some of the greatest men of the Order were housed in the same convent: Blesseds John Dominici, Peter Capucci, and Lawrence of Ripafratta, and St. Antoninus of Florence. The latter, when he was made archbishop, was to commission some of the two artists' finest work.

We have few personal details of the life of the young man from Vicchio, whose name in religion was Brother John of the Angels, and who was to be known to history as Fra Angelico. He was a priest. His painting in Florence was sufficiently well-known and admired to merit his being called to Rome to decorate the Chapel of Nicholas V at the Vatican. He was appointed prior of San Marco in 1449, holding that office for three years. He may have been recalled to Rome in 1454; he died there in 1455. In much the same way that St. Thomas was for so many centuries obscured by his writings, Fra Angelico seems to have disappeared behind his art. We know that he was the painter par excellence of the Queen of Angels and of her court.

St. Antoninus, who must have known him well, said: "No one could paint like that without first having been to heaven." One may well believe, from the sincerity of his paintings and the depth of their theological and devotional teaching, that he was, indeed, very close to heaven.

Fra Angelico and his brother, Benedetto, were both artists of skill and originality. Perhaps God wished them to work together to make Fiesole and San Marco treasure houses of art, where some innocence and beauty might remain untouched by the storm of Renaissance humanism which was soon to break. Benedetto painted and illuminated an exquisite set of choir books, reputed to be the loveliest in the world. If he had lived out his career, he might have rivalled his famous brother, but he was accidentally killed in a street battle during one of the frequent political upheavals in Florence, and his work was left unfinished.

Fra Angelico himself did some illumination; in fact, he probably began his career as an illuminator. There is in his altarpieces a definite touch of the illuminator's talent for extracting the gist of the matter and leaving out extraneous details. His work is never cluttered, which might, of course, be the result of a mind trained in theology, as well as of a hand trained in illuminating.

His frescoes were done on wet plaster, with clay colors, which means that he could not see any exact color relationship until the wall had dried, and it was too late to touch it up. This makes it all the more remarkable that his colors are so exquisitely blended, and that they still glow with such unfaded loveliness after four hundred years. Some of his best works are in the convent of San Marco, which is now a state museum.

There is in the Mellon Gallery, in Washington, D.C., an enamelled wood panel by Fra Angelico, "The Madonna of Humility," which shows, much better than the prints we are accustomed to see, the almost heavenly radiance which glowed through his paintings. The figures of the Madonna and Child have a quaint, awkward attitude; yet no one looking at them can possibly mistake the fact that he is depicting the Queen of Heaven.

Part of the "other-worldly" look of his Madonnas comes from the fact that Fra Angelico did not use models for his pictures. This alone was remarkable at a time when painters were flinging themselves into the study of anatomy, sometimes at the cost of other qualities. Perhaps he was revolted by the practice of some of his contemporary painters who chose beautiful women with bad reputations to pose for their Madonnas. Perhaps it was simply that he saw, with the clear vision of a theologian, that nothing—painting, statue, sermon, poem, or building—should obstruct one's view of God, drawing the attention away from that vision.

Fra Angelico's greatest complete work was his "Life of Christ," a series of thirty-five paintings in Fiesole. They began with the vision of the Prophet Ezechiel and ended with the lovely "Coronation of the Virgin," which we sometimes see reproduced in print. These pictures tell us what the records leave unsaid: that Brother John of the Angels was a capable theologian and a splendid Scripture scholar. He was also a devoted son of St. Dominic, whom he loved dearly and never tired of painting.

In America, we are most familiar with his paintings of the Annunciation, which was obviously one of his favorite subjects, since he painted it dozens of times. Most of his subjects were chosen from the life of Our Lord; the famous "angels," which one so often sees, are parts of much larger altar-pieces, having much more serious subjects than the colorful and joyful angels decorating them.

Some have said that Fra Angelico in art, Dante in poetry, and St. Thomas in the Summa Theologica, have each presented the same truth in three different ways. Whether or not this is completely true, it is an indication of the veneration in which history has held this man. His motto was: "To paint Christ, one must live Christ." He is the best example we have of one who preaches with a brush as eloquently as his brothers do with voice or pen. Today he still preaches, in places where no other would be heard. Perhaps his mission is still alive, to help bring into the fold those who love art but know nothing of God.

The cause of Fra Angelico was resumed on the 500th anniversary of his death and has been active since.

WILLIAM OF ORLIACO
(1404-1456)

William of Orliaco occupies a unique position among our brethren; we have few hermits, and he was one. We know very little about him, aside from the dates of his birth and death. There are some curious legends about him, but little factual material.

William was born in Bern, Switzerland, in 1404. Some authors think that "Orliaco" is simply an Italian form of his family name Orleye, pointing out that he was given his early education in Savoy, where that name can still be found. It seems obvious that he was of noble parentage. More than that we do not know.

Early in his career, William was sent to the court of Amadeus, in Savoy, as it was felt that he was destined for a fine career. He stayed for awhile at the court and tried to fit himself into its life of intrigue, romance, and petty politics, but finally gave it up as a bad job and returned to his home. His father had died, and for many years William lived quietly and piously at home, looking after his mother. In 1445, they went together to Annecy, to attend the dedication of the new church and convent of the Dominicans. He returned home in a thoughtful mood and told his mother that he had made up his mind to enter the Order. This he did in the following year, at the age of forty-two.

It is difficult to follow the religious career of William. Presumably he was ordained, though there is no record of the fact. He worked for a short time in the preaching apostolate, then he obtained permission to retire into the mountains to become a hermit.

He took up residence in an old stone fort that hung above a precipice, and he lived there for several years, eating roots and berries and drinking spring water. He followed the most extreme austerities and spent most of his time in prayer. Occasionally, curious or troubled people would make the arduous trip to see him, but he never seems to have returned to the town himself.

On Easter Monday, in 1456, a group of pilgrims decided to hunt him up. They found him in prayer, and waited until he came out of the ecstasy. When he greeted them, he was holding a little bundle of herbs in his hand, and this seemed to embarrass him. "I was just getting a good meal together," he explained. "Tomorrow Lent begins and we will all be fasting." They explained to him that Lent was over, and he seemed reluctant to say much about it. The last thing he could remember was Shrove Tuesday, and getting some herbs together for his supper.

William of Orliaco died in 1456.

BLESSED LAWRENCE OF RIPAFRATTA
(1359-1457)

One of the outstanding characters in the Dominican reform of the late fourteenth century was Blessed Lawrence of Ripafratta, who was novice-master of several saints and blesseds of our Order.

Lawrence was born in the fortified city of Ripafratta, in 1359. His noble family had the duty of guarding the outer defenses of the city of Pisa against the depredations of its powerful neighbor cities. It was a warlike place and time to come into the world, but Lawrence gave early evidence of being a man of peace. At the age of twenty, after an innocent and promising youth, he entered the convent of St. Catherine, in Pisa. He made rapid progress, both in prayer and study, and busied himself with the works of the Order for several years before being called upon to help in the reform movement that was headed by Blessed John Dominici.

In 1402, Lawrence was made novice-master in the novitiate of the reformed congregation of Tuscany, in Cortona. Here the novices were to be trained in the primitive rigor of the Order, in an attempt to by-pass the destructive elements of the past half-century, which had reduced religious observance to an alarming state of indifference. Plague and schism had taken toll both in numbers and quality of the religious orders, and the remaining houses were living under a relaxed observance of the rule, in a struggle for survival. John Dominici, under the inspiration of Raymond of Capua, felt that the time had come to tighten up the observance once more and return to the first practices of penance and silence. His suggestions were not popular among those who lived in the relaxed convents. The only alternative was to begin again, with a new novitiate, and hope that the idea would take hold gradually and effect internal reform among the other houses.

Excellent novices soon made their appearance at Cortona: St. Antoninus and Blessed Peter Capucci, and the artist brothers, Fra Angelico and Fra Benedetto. Several others who were to attain fame in the Order came under Lawrence's influence and were shaped by him into saintly and useful members of the apostolate, not all in the same fashion—St. Antoninus was to become archbishop of Florence, Fra Angelico and his brother made San Marco world-famous for its art. Blessed Lawrence is, indeed, an interesting study; a severe and exacting man when it came to keeping the rule, a man of broad vision and great resourcefulness in carrying out the work of preaching. He was obviously not at all afraid of talented people going astray if they were allowed to use their talents for God, and he displayed great insight into the development of each of his novices as individuals.

Eventually, Blessed Lawrence was appointed vicar-general of the reformed congregation and moved to the convent of St. Dominic at Pistoia. Here he preached almost continually, and had a reputation for compassion to the poor whom he tended, taught and visited, even in time of plague.

Lawrence of Ripafratta lived to be ninety-eight, and in his old age we have a touching picture of his novices—now men of distinction and authority —coming back to consult him about this or that detail of their work. He wrote often to St. Antoninus, perhaps feeling that being archbishop of Florence was a job with many worries.

Lawrence of Ripafratta died in 1457, and was beatified, after a long history of miracles at his tomb, in 1851.

ST. ANTONINUS
(1389-1459)

The life of St. Antoninus of Florence is the story of a great soul in a frail body, and of the triumph of virtue over vast and organized wickedness. The world in which he lived was engrossed with the Renaissance; it was a time of violent political upheaval, of plague, wars and injustice. The effects of the Great Schism of the West, over which St. Catherine of Siena had wept and prayed a generation before, were still tearing Christendom apart when Antoninus was born. 1389, the year of his birth, saw also the birth of Cosimo de Medici. The fortunes of Florence were largely to rest in the hands of these two men.

Of the childhood of St. Antoninus, we have few details, but they are revealing ones. He was a delicate and lovable child. His stepmother, worried over his frailty, used to give him extra meat at table. The little boy, determined to harden himself for the religious life, would slip the meat under the table to the cats. He hitched his wagon to the star of great austerity and, at the age of fourteen, discovered in the preaching of Blessed John Dominici the answer to all his questions. He went to speak to the great

preacher, who was at Santa Maria Novella, and begged to be admitted
to the Order.

Blessed John Dominici was completing plans for the building of a new
and reformed house at Fiesole, which he hoped to start again with young
and fervent subjects who would revivify the Order. It had declined under
plague and the effects of the Great Schism. As yet, he had no building
in which to house the new recruits. Even when the convent was built, it
was to be a house of rigorous observance. Antoninus looked far too frail
for such an austere program. John Dominici, looking kindly at the eager
youngster, had not the heart to explain all this. He told Antoninus to go
home and learn by heart the large and forbidding book called *The Decretum,*
supposing that its very size and appearance would discourage the lad.

Antoninus was possessed of an iron will-power. He went home and began
at the front of the book. By the end of the year he had accomplished the
all-but-impossible task, and he returned to John Dominici to recite it as
requested. There was now no further way to delay his reception of the
habit, so the frail young man donned the habit he was to wear with distinction
for fifty-four years.

Due to the unsettled state of the Church, the Order, and Italian politics,
the training of the young aspirants was carried on in several different
places, and, for a time, the regular course of studies could not be pursued.
Antoninus, nothing daunted, studied by himself. He was happily associated
during these years with several future blesseds of the Order—not only John
Dominici, but also Lawrence of Ripafratta, the novice-master; Constantius
of Fabriano; Peter Capucci; and the artist, Fra Angelico.

Ordained and set to preaching, Antoninus soon won his place in the
hearts of the Florentines. He was given consecutively several positions in
the Order, and, finally, to his horror, he was appointed archbishop of Florence.
The appointment was a genuine heartbreak to a scholar who could never
find enough time to study, but it was a blessing for the people of Florence,
and they were not slow in appreciating their good fortune.

For the remainder of his life, Antoninus combined an amazing amount
of active work with constant prayer. He wrote a great many books, all of
a practical nature, on moral theology, guidance for confessors, a chronicle
of the history of the world, and many other topics. He busied himself with
the beauty of the chant, and personally attended the Divine Office at his
cathedral. Under his guidance and encouragement, the convent of San
Marco became the center of Christian art. He called upon his old companion,
Fra Angelico, and on the miniaturist, Fra Benedetto, to do the frescoes
and the choir books which are still preserved there.

Antoninus was probably best known for his kindness to the poor, and there were many in the rich city of Florence. He took up his own garden of choice flowers to plant vegetables for the poor, and drove his housekeeper to distraction by giving away even his own tableware, food, and clothing. He kept in personal contact with the poor of the city, particularly with those who had fallen from wealth and were ashamed to beg. For their care he founded a society called the "Goodmen of St. Martin," who went about quietly doing much-needed charity work—much in the fashion of our modern Society of St. Vincent de Paul.

When the plague again came to Florence, it was the saintly archbishop who took the lead in almsgiving and care of the sick. Great numbers of the Dominican brethren died of the plague as they went about their priestly duties in the stricken city; sad but undaunted, Antoninus continued to go about on foot among the people, giving both material and spiritual aid. Cosimo de Medici, who did not always have compliments for the Dominicans, admitted frankly: "Our city has experienced all sorts of misfortunes: fire, earthquake, drought, plague, seditions, plots. I believe it would today be nothing but a mass of ruins without the prayers of our holy archbishop."

On May 2, 1459, Antoninus died, surrounded by his religious brethren from San Marco and mourned by the entire city. His whole life was mirrored in the last words he spoke: "To serve God is to reign."

BLESSED ANTONY DELLA CHIESA
(1395-1459)

Antony Della Chiesa was born in Piedmont, of a noble family. He was well educated. Showing a taste early in life for the things of God, he grew up with the hope of becoming a religious. His father, who was a man of some importance, opposed this wish. Not until Antony was twenty-two years old was he able to make the break with his family and enter the monastery at Vercelli.

Here he distinguished himself for both sanctity and learning. Being a good preacher, he was for some years the companion of the great Franciscan, Bernardine of Siena, in his missionary journeys through Italy.

Antony gives us a picture of one who followed the Dominican life perfectly, managing, most of the time, to escape public notice. There is in his life very little of the glamorous or the unusual. He kept the rule, was a good superior and a just administrator. Shunning applause, he was always serene.

The legends mention that he was particularly devoted to Our Lady, which is something one takes for granted in a Dominican, and that he conversed with her, in ecstasy, several times. He had the gift of reading hearts and was a sought-after director of souls. He also healed many sick people with his blessing. However, if any miracles are ordinary ones, these may be so described; they could be given as typical of most of our early Dominicans.

At one time, Antony was on a ship that was captured by pirates, but at his prayer, the pirates spared the passengers and brought them safely to land. One of the very few things of unusual nature which we find in his life is a legend told of him when he was prior of Savona. It makes a lovely ghost story, and it also gives us cause to think.

According to the legend, Antony was praying one night in the church. Disturbed by the sound of horses hooves clattering on the flagstones outside, he went to see who could possibly be there at such a late hour. There were several horsemen, all mounted on black horses. He addressed them, but received no answer. Thinking that they might be foreigners, he tried several languages, and still there was no response. Aware, then, that something was wrong, he commanded them in the name of our Lord to tell him who they were and where they were going. They said they were devils, and that they were on their way to meet the soul of a dying sinner, a usurer, and escort him to hell. "I will pray for him," said Antony. The demons laughed and told him he was too late. "Then at least come back and tell me whether you succeed or not," said the prior.

A short while later, the group returned, and they had succeeded. They held the unhappy usurer captive, and, while the prior watched in horror, they bore him off. The man was screaming. The next day, the usurer's relatives came to arrange an elaborate funeral. "You would do much better to have Masses said for yourselves and other poor sinners," he said.

Antony died at Como, in 1459, and was buried there in the Dominican church. Miracles at his tomb led to his beatification in 1819.

BLESSED MARGARET OF SAVOY
(1382-1464)

Margaret of Savoy is one of three royal princesses who wore the Dominican habit and was beatified. In the fifteenth century, she was the glory of a family that has given several blesseds to the Church.

Margaret was born in 1382, of the royal family of Savoy. She grew up in a household in which piety and wealth were ordinary. Her own parents died when she was small, and she was educated by an uncle, who arranged an early marriage for her. Her husband was the Marquis of Montferrat.

As queen of her fairly large domain, Margaret was the model of Christian rulers. She felt that it was her duty to exceed in charity and humility in the proportion that she was wealthier than those around her, and she devoted all of her time to God and to her neighbors. Her husband was a widower with two children, to whom she gave the greatest care. The hundreds of dependents on the large estates came in for her charity and her instructions. Disaster struck Savoy several times in the years when she was wife and mother; famine and plague came, making great demands upon her time and her courage. Unhesitatingly, she went out to nurse the plague-stricken with her own hands, and she sent out food and clothing from her husband's stores until it was doubtful if anything would be left. After this crisis had passed, war hovered over the kingdom, and she prayed earnestly that they would be delivered from the horrors of invasions.

In 1418, the Marquis of Montferrat died. His young widow was one of the most eligible women in Europe. Margaret sorrowed for her husband, but she made it clear to her relatives that they need not plan another marriage for her, as she was going to enter a convent. In order to live a life of complete renunciation, she decided to found a convent of her own that would follow the ancient rule of St. Dominic. Accordingly, she took over a cloister which had fallen into ruin, having only a few poor inhabitants, and rebuilt it for Dominican use. She dedicated the house to St. Mary Magdalen.

There is one very delightful story told about her sojourn in the convent. When she had been there many years, she one day had a young visitor; he was the son of one of her step-children. Hunting nearby, he had killed a doe, and he brought her the motherless fawn to tend. It was a pretty little animal, and it soon grew to be a great pet. The legends about the fawn have probably been exaggerated, as it was supposed to be able to go and find any sister she would name, and, for several years, the animal had free rein of the halls and cells of the sisters. Perhaps it was true, though, since the house confessor told her that the deer must go. She took it to the gate and told it to go. It fled into the forest, and returned only when Margaret was about to die.

Margaret attained a high degree of contemplative prayer. One time our Lord appeared to her and asked her whether she would rather suffer calumny, sickness, or persecution. Margaret generously accepted all three.

Her offer was taken, and for the remaining years of her life she suffered intensely from all three sorrows.

Margaret of Savoy died in 1464, and was beatified in 1669.

BLESSED BARTHOLOMEW OF CERVERIO
(1420-1466)

Carrying on the glorious tradition of death in the cause of truth, Blessed Bartholomew of Cerverio was the fourth Dominican inquisitor to win his crown in Piedmont, in the stronghold of the Catharists, who had taken the lives of Peter of Verona, Peter of Ruffia, and Anthony of Pavonio.

Bartholomew was born at Savigliano, in 1420, and, even in his early years, displayed a precocious solemnity and piety. He entered the Order in the convent of his native town, and progressed rapidly in his studies. On May the eighth, 1452, he distinguished himself by obtaining the licentiate, the doctorate and the master's degree from the University of Turin; the only time in the history of the university that anyone had acquired three degrees in one day.

Bartholomew taught for a year at the university, and then he was made prior of the convent at Savigliano. In his short apostolate of twelve years, he converted many heretics and worked steadfastly to eradicate heresy. He was appointed inquisitor in Piedmont, which made it clear to him that a martyr's death was marked out for him. Being a Dominican in Lombardy was a dangerous business, at best; to be appointed inquisitor meant that the heretics were given a target for their hatred.

In many ways the murder of Bartholomew and his companions repeats the martyrdom of Peter of Verona. Bartholomew knew beforehand that he was to die, and he made a general confession before starting out on his last trip. He remarked to his confessor, "They will call me Bartholomew of Cerverio, though I have never set foot there. Today I go there as inquisitor, and there I must die." On the road entering Cerverio, he and his party were attacked by five heretics. His companions were wounded, but escaped. Bartholomew died, riddled with dagger wounds, before they could get help.

Some people of Savigliano saw a bright light in the sky over Cerverio and surmised what had happened. They went out and brought home the relics, marveling that, despite all the wounds, the martyr had not bled. Laying him down in the church of the Dominicans, they saw his wounds bleed, and they hastily rescued the blood for relics. He was buried in the

Dominican church of Savigliano, and, later, when the church was ruined by revolution, the relics were moved to the parish church.

A chapel was built at the site of the martyrdom and richly decorated with narrative frescoes. Processions were made there several times a year by the people of Savigliano and Cerverio, invoking Bartholomew against thunder and hail especially. At the same place, a fig tree was honored for many years for its connection with Blessed Bartholomew; it was supposed to have sprung up at the time of the martyrdom, at the very place the martyr fell.

Pope Pius IX beatified Bartholomew of Cerverio in 1853.

BLESSED ANTHONY NEYROT
(d. 1469)

Blessed Anthony Neyrot occupies a unique place in Dominican history, as he is the only one among the beatified who ever renounced the faith. He expiated his sin with an act of heroism that merited heaven, washing away in his own blood the denial that might have cost him his soul.

Of the childhood of Blessed Anthony, we know nothing except that he was born at Rivoli, in Italy. He was accepted into the Order by St. Antoninus, who must have been particularly fond of the young man, since he gave him his own name. Completing his studies, Anthony was ordained and lived for a time at San Marco, the famous Dominican convent in Florence. Then, becoming restless and dissatisfied, he asked for a change of mission. He was sent to Sicily, but this did not prove to his liking either, so he set out for Naples. On this voyage, his ship was captured by pirates, and Anthony, along with the other passengers, was taken, bound, to Africa. Here the passengers were led through the streets for all to see.

The battle of Lepanto was still a hundred years in the future, but Turkish aggression, which was to bring about this great battle, was a commonplace in Anthony's time. Some captives were treated with leniency, others with great cruelty. The Mohammedan king of Tunis seems to have taken a liking to the young Dominican, as he ordered that kindness be shown to him. Anthony was not even confined to prison, until his arrogance angered his captors into more severe measures, but he was impatient and resented the very idea of captivity. Being placed in prison, living on a diet of bread and water, he soon collapsed. Then, as the Mohammedans had hoped, he denied his faith to buy his freedom.

Disaster followed upon disaster. He lost all faith in Christianity and began to translate the Koran. He was adopted by the king, married a Turkish lady of high degree, and was given the freedom of the city.

Into the false paradise he had built for himself came the news of the death of St. Antoninus. Love for his old master stirred in Anthony's heart a yearning for the Truth he had abandoned. He resolved to return to the Christian faith, although it meant certain death. In order that his return might be as public as his denial had been, he waited until the king, returning in triumph from a victory over the Christians, had a public procession. Having confessed and made his private reconciliation with God, Anthony, clothed in a Dominican habit, at that moment mounted the palace steps where all could see him. In a loud voice he proclaimed his faith, and his sorrow at having denied it. The king was at first unbelieving, then angry. Failing to change the mind of the young man, he commanded that he be stoned to death.

Anthony died under a shower of stones, proclaiming to the last his faith and his sorrow. It was Holy Thursday of 1460. His body was recovered at great expense from the Mohammedans, and brought back to Rivoli, where his tomb soon became a place of pilgrimage. Many miracles were performed here, and, until very recently, a yearly procession was held at his shrine. In the procession, all the present-day members of his family, dressed in black, walked proudly behind the statue of Blessed Anthony.

BLESSED MATTHEW CARRERI
(d. 1470)

John Francis Carreri was born in Mantua, in the late fourteenth century. He grew up a silent and prayerful child, a good student, and a great reader. These qualities seemed to recommend him to the Preaching Friars, and, at an early age, he presented himself at the convent in his home city and received the habit.

Matthew's career as a preacher began soon after his ordination, when he was sent to Lombardy to preach against the heretics. He succeeded admirably in his preaching and converted many to a spiritual way of life. Traveling from convent to convent he preached a revival of fervor and a deeper under-standing of the spirit of St. Dominic, and many of the religious of Lombardy —both Dominicans and members of other Orders—were led by him to become more fervent.

At one time, when he was preaching in Vigevano, a troupe of jugglers came into town and set up their act. They were a particularly scandalous set of people, poking ridicule at religious and at the pope. Matthew sent them word to move on, which they ignored. So he went after them with his walking-stick, and this proved more effective. They scattered and ran, but soon came back, fortified with the presence of the Duke of Milan, who scolded Matthew for being so narrow-minded and humorless. Matthew patiently pointed out to him the bad spots in their humor, and, in spite of the duke's natural aversion to friars, convinced him that he should keep the jugglers out of town.

At Lucina, there was a lady of noble birth and great talents who was wasting her time in frivolities. Never one to avoid an issue, Matthew aimed a powerful sermon in her direction, and she came to him afterwards in a torrent of tears and begged him to help her. He gave her the habit of the Third Order and outlined a stiff rule of life, which she afterwards faithfully followed. He also met and directed Blessed Stephanie Quinzanis, who proved to be an apt pupil.

Matthew was given the job of reforming the convents of the friars in Soncino, and in nearby towns, and he worked for many years in Milan. Going up and down the peninsula, he varied his approach but never his message: penance and love of God. So many were the conversions he effected that a whole group of follow-up preachers had to be appointed to carry on, as he moved rapidly from place to place. Preaching his way, he went through Tuscany, and took ship at Genoa.

The ship was soon captured by a Turkish corsair. The Mohammedan captain called on the three Dominicans for an explanation of why they were there. Matthew spoke up so fearlessly and eloquently that the captain released all three of them. Just as they were being hustled off to a rescue boat, the wail of one of the women passengers stopped them. The lady and her young daughter were not anxious to be taken to Algiers, and Matthew began pleading for them. The captain told him he had better let the affair alone and be satisfied that he had saved his own skin. Matthew thereupon volunteered to go to Algiers, in chains, if the captain would release the two women. Amazed at his courage as well as at his brashness, the captain released all of them and told them to get out of his sight quickly, before he changed his mind.

Many miracles are credited to Matthew Carreri. One day, a young father, who came to hear Matthew preach, had left his little son at home with the nurse. The baby fell into the fire and was badly burned. The distracted father brought the little one to Matthew, who cured him. The baby was well in a few days, and grew up to be a Franciscan friar. Matthew cured another man of hemorrhage, and worked many cures on the sick and possessed.

One day, while meditating on the Passion, Matthew asked our Lord to partake of His sufferings. He received the stigmata, in the form of an arrow that pierced his heart. For the remainder of his life, he suffered great pain from this wound.

Matthew Carreri died, in 1470, in a house composed entirely of religious he had rescued from a life of laxity. His cult was confirmed twelve years after his death, testifying to the great reputation for sanctity he enjoyed among the people of northern Italy.

ALAN DE LA ROCHE
(1428-1479)

Sooner or later, in any research on the Rosary, one encounters the name of Alan de la Roche. Some people credit him with inventing the Rosary, some with popularizing it, some with revising it. Some, who object to the warmth —and what they consider the extravagances—of his book of popular examples, think that he is an impostor and a teller of tall tales. He may have been a little of all these, but the records we have indicate that he was the founder of the Confraternity of the Rosary and a great promoter of that devotion.

Alan was born in Brittany, in 1428, and entered the Order there in his early youth. Religious life was at a low ebb in Brittany at the time, and he transferred to the province of Holland. Here he worked as a preacher, writer and organizer, who was extraordinarily devoted to the Blessed Virgin —a preacher who never missed an occasion to preach the Rosary.

It is now impossible to follow the career of this man with any exactness. He worked in a country that was at war, and records there, if they ever existed, could have been destroyed a dozen times over. We have evidence that he was a professor at St. Jacques, in Paris, which indicates that he must have been a capable and sound theologian. He also taught at Lille and Douai, and received his master's degree in sacred theology in 1474. His greatest and best-known work was done in the Rhineland, mostly in and around Cologne. He had traveled all over western Europe during his lifetime, and once he was visitator to Poland. By the time of his death, in Zwolle, in 1479, he was such a popular figure that legend had almost completely obscured the man. We can only do our best to sort out the traditions which seem to have basis in fact.

Alan is supposed to have had a vision of Our Lady, who encouraged him to revive the devotion of the Rosary. This is the controversial vision over which so many different opinions are held, and we need not add to it. He did become a famous preacher of the Rosary. He preached on St. Dominic and popularized the Rosary as a devotion. Let us remember that Alan worked principally in Germany, where St. Dominic's personal influence had never been felt. It is quite understandable that the people who heard him preach might have considered him the founder of the Rosary devotion.

We know that the first printed manual of the Rosary Confraternity came from his hands. It was printed in Cologne, in 1476. This was a manual of instruction explaining the method of saying the Rosary and appointing a definite set of fifteen mysteries. Whether he originated the mysteries, or their arrangement, or simply put down on paper what St. Dominic had taught, we do not know. But he did give form to it in the medium best understood at the time.

The Confraternity of the Rosary, as Alan preached it, was founded at Douai, in 1470. Other confraternities had been founded before, and some of them were Rosary Confraternities, but most of them were local and soon died out. Alan visualized an international organization and did his best to bring it about. The Rhineland was at war, and he established the Confraternity at Cologne, where it centered about the Rosary Altar, at which the faithful prayed for peace. When peace came, it was he who arranged for a feast of thanksgiving. He also petitioned the emperor to arrange with the pope for an international confraternity to be begun at that time and unified and organized, in the future, by certain obligations of prayer and penance. The feast was held on the day of Our Lady's nativity, in 1479. The emperor placed his signature first on the Register of the Confraternity, and all of his court followed. As though this were the crowning effort of his life, Alan died the day the confraternity was founded.

His work lived on. Five thousand names were signed within the first few months. By the end of the year there were fifty thousand. The confraternity was established in London as early as 1486, and in Denmark ten years later. Within a quarter of a century, it had reached every corner of Europe.

It is hard for us today to realize how much membership in the confraternity meant to people living in little isolated villages, out of touch with the great events of the world. It was their precious opportunity to share in the work and merit of a great religious Order, and it carried indulgences never before available to lay people. The obligations for membership included enrollment in the Register kept by the Dominican fathers, the saying of either the 150 psalms, or the complete Rosary, once a week, and the reception of the sacraments at stated times. There was also the opportunity to enroll deceased friends and relatives, so that they might share in the indulgences. Especially in the tremendous missionary effort of the next two hundred years was the Confraternity of the Rosary to be a great instrument for good and for the preaching of the word of God.

Today, there is a Confraternity of the Rosary in every Dominican parish, and the indulgences are still rich and obtainable. Since the time of Alan, various popes have added indulgences, particularly those of Rosary Sunday, which make it surprising that every Catholic in the world does not hasten to join such a source of spiritual reward.

JOHN BREHAL
(d. 1479)

It should be of interest to Dominicans to know that the first steps toward sainthood for Joan of Arc were made possible by the work of a Dominican theologian, John Brehal.

John Brehal was born at Evreux, in the early fifteenth century, and entered the Order there at about the same time that Joan of Arc was condemned and burned at the stake in Rouen. In common with most French Dominicans, his sympathy was entirely with the Maid and against those who had connived in her death. While one cannot say that it became the ruling interest of his life to see Joan vindicated, still, it was a subject always present in his mind.

In 1443, John Brehal received his doctorate in theology, in Caen, and two years later he was prior of the great convent of St. Jacques of Paris. Seven years later he was appointed inquisitor-general of France, and this office gave him the authority to investigate a cause that had always been close to his heart: the vindication of Joan. For fourteen years he labored over the examination of the process by which Joan had been committed to death at the stake. On July 7, 1466, thirty-five years after her death, he solemnly declared that her condemnation had been iniquitous and unjust.

Since the process of canonization is slow in any case, it was further delayed by the circumstances peculiar to the death of Joan of Arc, and the state of the French government, it was to be many years—six hundred, in fact—before the Maid, who had been called a witch and a heretic, was raised to the altars and honored as a saint of God. But, without the painstaking and devoted work of John Brehal, it might have been delayed much longer.

In 1474, John Brehal resigned his office as inquisitor-general and retired to the convent of Evreux. There he lived in retirement and prayer until his death, five years later. During these last years, he wrote several works of a practical nature. Most of his works have been lost.

BLESSED ANDREW OF PESCHIERA
(d. 1480)

Andrew Grego was born early in the fifteenth century, a time which was second only to the pioneer years of the Order for the number and variety of its beatified members. As a child, he lived on the shores of Lake Garda, in the north of Italy, and his training for a life of heroic sanctity began early, with voluntary penances and unquestioning obedience to his father.

Andrew's first desire was to be a hermit, an ambition which met with nothing but abuse and ridicule from his brothers. Failing to realize this hope, he made for himself a severe schedule of prayer and penance, and, in his own home, lived the life of one wholly given to God.

After the death of his father, it became increasingly impossible to carry out this plan, so he resolved to enter the cloister. His brothers had persecuted him without mercy, but as he was leaving home he knelt and humbly asked their prayers and their forgiveness for having annoyed them. He left them the only possession he had, a walking-stick. This stick, thrown carelessly in a corner by the brothers, was forgotten until, long afterwards, it bloomed like the legendary rod of St. Joseph, in token of Andrew's holiness.

The young man received the habit at Brescia and was sent to San Marco, in Florence. This convent was then at its peak of glory, stamped with the saintly personalities of St. Antoninus and the Blesseds Lawrence of Riprafratta, Constantius, and Antony Della Chiesa. Andrew caught from this flaming source the torch of apostolic zeal, and set forth on his mission in the mountains of north Italy.

Heresy and poverty had combined to draw almost this entire region from the Church. It was a country of great physical difficulties, and, in his travels in the Alps, he risked death from snowstorms and avalanches as often as from the daggers of the heretics. Nevertheless, he traveled tirelessly—preaching, teaching, and building—for his entire lifetime.

Churches, hospitals, schools, and orphanages were built under Andrew's direction. He would retire from time to time to these convents for periods of prayer and spiritual refreshment, so that he could return with renewed courage and zeal to the difficult apostolate. He was known as "The Apostle of the Valtelline," because of the district he evangelized.

Blessed Andrew performed many miracles. Probably his greatest miracle was his preaching, which produced such fruits in the face of great obstacles. At one time, when he was preaching to the people, the heretics presented him with a book in which they had written down their beliefs. He told them to open the book and see for themselves what their teachings amounted to. They did so, and a large viper emerged from the book.

Blessed Andrew closed a holy life by an equally holy death and was buried at Morbegno. He had labored so long among the poor and the neglected that his place in their hearts was secured. Because of the miracles worked at his tomb, and the persistent devotion of the people, his relics were twice transferred to more suitable tombs.

BLESSED CONSTANTIUS OF FABRIANO
(1410-1481)

Constantius of Fabriano was as near a "sad saint" as is possible for a Dominican; he is supposed to have had the gift of tears. However, that was not his only title to distinction.

Constantius was born in Fabriano, in the early fifteenth century. His childhood was remarkable, not only for the usual signs of piety, which all medieval chroniclers note, but for a miracle that he worked when he was a little boy. Constantius had a sister who had been a bed-ridden invalid for most of her nine years. One day, the little boy brought his parents in to her bedside and made them pray with him. The little girl rose up—well, and she remained well for a long and happy life. Naturally, the parents were amazed, and they were quite sure it had not been their prayers that effected the cure, but those of their little son.

Constantius entered the Order in Fabriano when he was fifteen. He did well in his studies; we read, among other things, that, as a student, he wrote a commentary on Aristotle. His special forte was Scripture, and he studied it avidly. After his ordination, he was sent to teach in various schools of Italy, arriving eventually at the convent of San Marco, in Florence, which had been erected as a house of strict observance and was a leading light in the reform movement. This was a work dear to his heart, and he himself became closely identified with the movement.

Several miracles and prophecies are related about Constantius during his stay in Florence. He one day told a student not to go swimming, because he would surely drown if he did. The student disregarded the warning, went swimming, and drowned. One day, Constantius came upon a man lying in the middle of the road. The man had been thrown by his horse and was badly injured; he had a broken leg and a broken arm. All he asked was to be taken to some place where care could be given him, but Constantius did better than that—he cured the man and left him, healed and astonished.

Constantius was made prior of Perugia, where he lived a strictly penitential life. Perhaps the things that he saw in visions were responsible for his perpetual sadness, for he foresaw many of the terrible things that would befall Italy in the next few years. He predicted the sack of Fabriano, which occurred in 1517. At the death of St. Antoninus he saw the saint going up to heaven, a vision which was recounted in the process of canonization.

Blessed Constantius is said to have recited the Office of the Dead every day, and often the whole one hundred and fifty psalms, which he knew by heart, and used for examples on every occasion. He also said that he had never been refused any favor for which he had recited the whole psalter. He wrote a number of books; these, for the most part, were sermon material, and some were the lives of the blesseds of the Order.

Constantius died at Ascoli, in 1481. On the day of his death, little children of the town ran through the streets crying out, "The holy prior is dead! The holy prior is dead!" On hearing of his death, the city council met and stated that it was a public calamity.

The relics of Blessed Constantius have suffered from war and invasion. After the Dominicans were driven from the convent where he was buried, his tomb was all but forgotten for a long time. Then one of the fathers put the relics in the keeping of Camaldolese monks in a nearby monastery, where they still remain.

Constantius of Fabriano was equivalently beatified in 1821.

BLESSED CHRISTOPHER OF MILAN
(d. 1484)

Nothing is known of the early years of Blessed Christopher of Milan. He received the habit in the convent of San Eustorgio, in Milan, in the early fifteenth century. He is recorded as being "holy and abstemious, humble and studious"—the ordinary virtues which we have come to take for granted in beatified Dominicans; there is nothing to indicate what sort of person he was, or what peculiar circumstances might have led him to the Order. He is noted especially for his preaching and for his gift of prophecy.

The age in which Christopher lived was a rough and dangerous one, and a time for prophets and penitents to thrive. He was himself an apostolic preacher, famous for the impact of his sermons on sinners. He had a vivid power of description and this, coupled with his gift of prophecy, made his sermons unforgettable.

Christopher of Milan worked in many parts of Italy, but his name is particularly reverenced in Taggia, where he spent many years, and where he built a monastery and church dedicated to Our Lady of Mercy. A great wave of spiritual revival was felt in Taggia during his stay there, but he was not optimistic about the future. In vision he saw that most of the population would be carried off by plague. Twenty years before anyone was paying any attention to the Turks, he told the people of Taggia that Turks would invade the city, and they did, as he had prophesied. A disastrous flood swept the area, fulfilling another of his prophesies.

Christopher of Milan wrote four volumes of sermon aids, containing scriptural examples and quotations from the Fathers of the Church.

In 1484, when he was absent from Taggia preaching a mission, Christopher fell ill and knew that he was going to die. He insisted on returning to his own convent at Taggia. He received the last sacraments and immediately died.

Pope Pius IX confirmed the cult of Christopher of Milan in 1875.

BLESSED DAMIAN OF FINARIO
(d. 1484)

One of the bright lights of the fifteenth century was Damian of Finario. Unfortunately we know very little about him, except that he lived at a time and place not noted for sanctity, and he was known as a holy man.

Damian was born in Finario, near Genoa, at the end of the fourteenth century. His people were rich and noble, and also pious. We know nothing of his youth, except the not-too-revealing fact that when he was a baby he was kidnapped by a lunatic. His parents prayed to Our Lady, and the baby was returned unharmed.

Damian entered the Order at Genoa and became a diligent student and a model Dominican. He was to be known especially for his preaching. The field of his endeavors was Italy. He seems never to have left the country.

By the force of his preaching, he inspired many hundreds of sinners to re-pentance; and, since the fifteenth century produced many sinners who needed such preaching, he was kept supplied with work for a long lifetime.

Damian died in a little village near Modena, in 1484, and immediately became the object of much pious speculation, because of the miracles worked at his tomb. He was not, however, beatified until 1848, though his relics were by that time widely distributed and his cult well known.

BLESSED BERNARD SCAMMACCA
(d. 1486)

Bernard Scammacca was born in Sicily, at the beginning of the fifteenth century. His parents were wealthy and pious, and Bernard was given a good education. In spite of this good training, he spent a careless youth. Only after he was badly injured in a quarrel was he brought back to his senses. His long convalescence gave him plenty of time to think, and once he was able to go out of the house, he went to the Dominican convent of Catania and begged to be admitted to the Order.

Bernard, as a religious, was the exact opposite of what he had been as a young man. Now he made no effort to obtain the things he had valued all his life, but spent his time in prayer and solitude. There is little recorded of his life, except that he kept the rule meticulously, and that he was particu-larly kind to sinners in the confessional. Apparently, he did not attain fame as a preacher, but was content to spend his time in the work of the confes-sional and the private direction of souls.

One legend pictures Bernard as having great power over birds and animals. When he walked outside in the garden, praying, the birds would flutter down around him, singing; but as soon as he went into ecstasy, they kept still, for fear they would disturb him. Once, the porter was sent to Bernard's room to call him, and saw a bright light shining under the door. Peeking through the keyhole, he saw a beautiful child shining with light and holding a book, from which Bernard was reading. He hurried to get the prior to see the marvel.

Bernard had the gift of prophecy, which he used on several occasions to try warning people to amend their lives. He prophesied his own death, which occurred in 1486. Fifteen years after his death, he appeared to the prior, tell-ing him to transfer his remains to the Rosary chapel. During this translation, a man was cured of paralysis by touching the relics.

BLESSED JOANNA OF PORTUGAL
(1452-1490)

Joanna, a child of many prayers, was born heiress to her father's throne, at a time when Spain and Portugal had divided the colonial wealth of the earth between them. A brother, Juan, was born three years later, and soon after this the queen died. Joanna was left to the care of a wise and pious nurse, who cultivated the child's natural piety. The little princess soon exceeded her teacher in penitential practices, and, at the age of five, was practicing great austerities. She fasted and prayed, rose at night to take the discipline, and wore a hairshirt under her glittering court apparel.

Although Joanna would not inherit the throne of Portugal while her brother was alive, a wise marriage would do much to increase the power of King Alfonso, her father. Accordingly, he began early to arrange for her marriage. Joanna, whose knowledge of court intrigue was as good as his own, skillfully escaped several proposed matches. She had treasured since childhood a desire to enter the convent, but, in view of her father's plans, her desires met with violent opposition. She was flatly refused for a long time; finally, her father gave his reluctant consent, but he withdrew it again at her brother's insistence.

Joanna and one of her ladies-in-waiting had long planned to enter the Dominican cloister at Aveiro, which was noted for its strict observance. When at last her father gave consent for her to enter religion, he did not allow her to enter the Dominican convent. She had to go to a royal abbey nearby, and here she was beseiged by weeping and worldly relatives who had only their own interests at heart. After two months of this mental torture, she returned to the court.

The rest of Joanna's life is a story of obedience and trials. Her obligations of obedience varied. She was required to obey: to a wavering father, who never seemed able to make a decision and abide by it; to bishops, swayed by political causes, who forced her to sign a paper that she would never take her solemn vows; and to doctors, who prescribed remedies that were worse than the maladies they tried to cure. The trials came from a jealous brother, from ambitious and interfering relatives, from illness, and from cares of state.

After twelve years of praying and hoping, Joanna finally received the Dominican habit. Once, she was deprived of it by an angry delegation of bishops and nobles, and, at another time, her brother tore the veil from her head. Despite the interruptions of plague, family cares, and state troubles, Joanna lived an interior and very penitential life. She became an expert at spinning and weaving the fine linens for the altar, and busied herself with lowly tasks for the love of God. Her special devotion was to the Crown of Thorns, and, in early childhood, she had embroidered this device on her crest. To the end of her life she was plagued by the ambition of her brother, who again and again attempted to arrange a marriage for her, and continually disturbed her hard-won peace by calling her back to court for state business.

On one of these trips to court, Joanna was poisoned by a woman—a person she had rebuked for leading an evil life. The princess lived several months in fearful pain, enduring all her sufferings with heroic courage. She died, as it says in an Old Chronicle, "with the detachment of a religious and the dignity of a queen," and with the religious community around her.

BLESSED JAMES OF ULM
(1407-1491)

James was born at Ulm, in Swabia, and spent a fortunate childhood. He was thoroughly instructed both in his father's trade of glass-painting and in the practices of piety. He assisted his father in the making of stained glass, which was at that time a fine art in Germany, and he passed a sinless and happy youth in his native city. Wishing to make a pilgrimage to Rome, he asked his father's blessing on the enterprise and set forth on his long journey, arriving in time to spend Lent in the holy city.

Having run out of funds, James enlisted with the army in Sicily. Here his pious nature received a rude shock from the soldiers with whom he lived. They were given to every manner of vice and resented any effort to change their lives. Disgusted with the corrupt morals and practices around him, James made haste to free himself as soon as his enlistment was up. He went into service with a lawyer, who soon entrusted him with his most important affairs and would gladly have adopted him as his own son. Having worked with this man for several years, James became anxious to return home to see his aging father, so he once more set forth on the road.

In Bologna, while he was praying before the tomb of St. Dominic, an interior voice made known to him that his vocation was to be a Dominican. He sought no further, but went immediately to the prior to beg admission as a laybrother in the Order.

James set for himself no extraordinary program of sanctity when he entered the Order, but resolved to keep the rule perfectly. He did this with great success. His humility and obedience were particularly remarkable.

James resumed his father's trade of making stained-glass windows, and all his working time was devoted to making windows for the churches and convents that desired them. At one time, when he had a particularly large and elaborate window for firing in the furnace, the prior called for him to go out begging. Without a backward glance at his precious window, he went. He was gone all day, and it was only to be expected that his window would be in ashes when he returned, but God rewarded his obedience with a miracle—the window was more beautiful than he could ever have hoped.

On another occasion, the prior, who had been telling a visiting bishop of James' virtue, called him and told him to take a letter to Paris—a journey of some three weeks. James, bowing his head, asked only that he might first go to his cell to get his walking stick. The prior did not send him; he had only wished to try his obedience.

James was silent and recollected at his work, diligent and prayerful, and always ready to leave one kind of work for another when obedience called him, even though he had a craftsman's regard for finishing his work well. His chief distinction was in keeping the rule perfectly, though he also performed a number of miracles.

Two windows made by Blessed James are still in existence; one in the chapel of the Bentivoglio palace, the other in the cathedral of St. Petronius in Bologna.

BLESSED AUGUSTINE OF BIELLA
(1430-1493)

Miracles around the tomb of Augustine of Biella led to his beatification, in 1878, after he had long been forgotten by everyone, except the residents of the little town where he lived. His is another example of a life noted for piety and regularity, but quite unremarkable for unusual events or venturesome projects.

Augustine was born at Biella, a little village at the foot of the Alps. His father was a member of the family of Fangi, who were wealthy and noble, and, because of this, he had planned a secular career for his son. But when the Dominicans came to Biella, his plans were changed, for Augustine was completely charmed by their way of life and begged to join them. He entered, while quite young, the new convent that the Dominicans had built at Biella.

Augustine's reputation for penance was great, even at a time when people were not as squeamish as they are today. Not only did he inflict great penances upon himself, he also bore with great patience whatever pain and annoyance life granted him gratuitously. At one time he was required to undergo a surgical operation without, of course, any anaesthetic. He did so without making the slightest outcry. In fact, he said afterwards that his mind was so intensely focused on something else that he hardly noticed what was being done to him. His mind was on that "something else" most of the time, for he prayed continually.

In 1464, Augustine was made prior at Soncino. Several of his best known miracles were performed there. At one time, a deformed child, who had died without baptism, was restored to life, by Augustine's prayer, long enough to be baptized. At another time, when he was passing down the street, he met a little boy who was crying bitterly, because he had broken a jug of wine. Augustine gathered up the pieces and put them back together again. Then, with a prayer, he refilled the jug and handed it back to the startled child. Another time, through his intercession, a woman was delivered from possession of five devils.

Augustine spent his last ten years in the convent at Venice, and he died there on the Feast of St. Mary Magdalen, 1493. He was buried in a damp place. Forty years later, on the occasion of some repairs to the church, his coffin, found floating in water, was opened. His body and habit were still intact. This fact did much to promote interest in his cause. Nevertheless, it was more than three centuries before he was finally beatified.

BLESSED AIMO TAPPARELLI
(1395-1495)

Blessed Aimo Tapparelli is one of the few men who occupied the office of inquisitor of Piedmont and lived to die in bed. One of his first tasks on taking over his dangerous office was to give honorable burial to two of his predecessors, who had fallen under the daggers of the heretics. This would seem to be a prophecy of his own death, but, as a matter of fact, he lived an exceedingly long life and died peacefully at the age of one hundred.

Aimo was born in Savigliano, in 1395, and entered the Order there in his early youth. He was a good student and made such rapid strides in his studies that he was asked to teach at the University of Turin. Much of his life was occupied in that staple of Dominican diet, preaching or teaching.

Aimo spent some time in the court of Amadeus of Savoy, as his confessor. He did not care for court life, but it was not a restful change that was offered him when he was finally freed from it. At the age of seventy-one he was sent as inquisitor-general to Piedmont, to replace Blessed Bartholomew Cerverio, who had just been martyred there by the heretics.

Bartholomew was a young and vigorous man of forty-six, and it had taken all his strength, as well as h:s life, to hold down such a position. Aimo went to Piedmont with understandable misgivings, but he seems to have been a great succees in the difficult office. He converted many of his listeners by the sincerity and sweetness of his preaching. His example was a beacon of hope to the Catholics of Piedmont who had sometimes been embarrassed by the affluence of Church authorities and the obvious poverty of the heretics.

One of Aimo's first acts in Piedmont was to arrange for the relics of Blessed Anthony of Pavonio to be brought home to Savigliano and interred in the friars' church there.

BLESSED SEBASTIAN MAGGI
(1414-1496)

Sebastian Maggi lived in a colorful and troubled age, the time of Savonarola; he was, in fact, a friend of the friar of Ferrara and always staunchly defended him.

Sebastian was born in Brescia, in 1414, and entered the Order there as soon as he was old enough. His early years were remarkable only for his devotion to the rule and for the purity of his life. He was superior of several houses of the Order, and, finally, he was made vicar of the reformed congregation of Lombardy, which made him the superior of Jerome Savonarola, the dynamic reformer around whom such a tragic storm was brewing.

Perhaps, if Sebastian Maggi had lived, he might have saved Savonarola from the political entanglements that sent him to his death. Sebastian was his confessor for a long time, and always testified in his favor when anyone attacked the reformer's personal life. Just where he stood politically in the long and complex series of events concerning the separation of the Lombard province from the province of Italy, it is hard to say. But all that has been written of him conveys the same impression: he was a kind and just superior, who kept the rule with rigid care, but was prudent in exacting it of others.

Several times Sebastian Maggi was sent on missions of reform, and he died on one of these. On his way to a convent for visitation, he became ill at Genoa and died there, in 1496.

Sebastian Maggi was beatified in 1760. His body is incorrupt at the present time.

BLESSED MARK OF MODENA
(d. 1498)

Mark was born in Modena and entered the convent of the Order there in young manhood. He observed the rules with great fidelity, and became noted both for his learning and his holiness, which is a sentence that would fit into nearly every Dominican biography written, and tells us nothing in particular about Mark as a person. However, when we recall the times in which he lived, it becomes clearer to us that *anyone* who kept the Dominican Rule in its entirety is truly entitled to our notice. The abuses which stirred Savonarola to thundering speech in the pulpits of Ferrara and Florence could not have been absent from all of Italy. It took solid virtue to hold out against the opulent worldliness of the times, and Mark of Modena apparently did a thorough job of it, since he has been beatified.

Mark was made prior of the convent of Pesaro, and the only miracle we have on record (he is supposed to have performed many) took place at this convent. A woman's little boy had died, and she pleaded with Mark to restore the child's life. After praying for awhile, Mark turned to her and said, "Madam, your little boy is in paradise. Do not try to get him back again, for his second loss will be worse than this one." However, she insisted on his working the miracle, and he did so. The child returned to life, and, ten years later, covered with disgrace and opprobrium, died a second time, leaving his mother in worse grief than ever.

Mark of Modena died in 1498, the year that the city of Florence burned Savonarola at the stake. It was a time of terrible happenings in Italy and all Europe. The people of Modena mourned the death of Mark, and went to pray at his tomb. Many of their needs were answered there, and a number of prodigies were reported in connection with the translation of his relics to the Rosary chapel of the church. The bells were said to have rung by themselves, and sweet perfume filled the air. Until recently, his relics were still exposed yearly for veneration during the week of Whitsunday.

JEROME SAVONAROLA
(1452-1498)

The most controversial figure in all Dominican history was Jerome Savonarola, who was burned at the stake in 1498. Even today he is a source of violent disagreement among scholars. Some regard him as a saint; others insist that he was a reprobate. So heated were the politics of the day, and so prejudiced were the people who put him to death, that it is almost hopeless to expect to get the whole truth after all these years. He cannot be omitted from any Dominican account. He played too important a role in his lifetime, and reports of his life and death have found their way into all sorts of accounts, both inimical and sympathetic.

Jerome Savonarola was born in Ferrara, in 1452, of a wealthy and socially prominent family. His father died when he was very young. His early training was calculated to give him a gloomy outlook on life—an outlook that was not hard to acquire in a century of plague and political knavery. There is a legend that the young Jerome fell in love with a beautiful young lady. She spurned his proposal of marriage, and this rebuke embittered him against women. He supposedly, also, rejected a chance to be trained at court. Whatever was his background and whatever his motives, he entered the Dominican convent in Bologna in 1475.

After his ordination, which probably took place in 1480, he was sent out to preach in his home city of Ferrara. Oddly enough, he, who was to set all Italy aflame with his preaching in a few years, made a signal failure of his trial flight. Most of his early attempts at preaching were eminent failures. It was several years before his gift of apocalyptic oratory developed sufficiently to command any attention.

At some time, not now easily identified, Savonarola began preaching in a vein of dire prophecy. The Italian peninsula was in the throes of political upheaval and death, and oppression reigned. In 1489, Savonarola—who had by now become a great popular preacher—was called to Florence, quite possibly at the request of Lorenzo de Medici, who had endowed the Dominican house in Florence, and who was also responsible for many of the dark political deeds of the day. Perhaps Lorenzo hoped to win the great preacher to his side in the political struggle that lay ahead; we do not know. Savonarola came, and shortly it became clear to the Medici that he did not recognize their authority—only the authority of God.

A growing tension between the friar and the Medici came to a head in 1491. Savonarola was elected prior at San Marco, and refused to pay a visit of homage to Lorenzo de Medici, who murmured, "A stranger has come to live in my house and will not even pay me a visit." It is not easy, now, to follow the many twisting threads that traced the involvement of Savonarola in Florentine independence, or the many small annoyances to politicians which eventually spelled out his death.

One thing that even hostile historians record of Savonarola is his effect on the morals of the city. Even while regarding his zeal as indiscreet, they admit that he must have had some tremendous power, since he brought a great and worldly city to repentance. He organized the children into bands to gather up vain objects and profane books for burning, and he publicly conducted several huge bonfires to consume the vanities. He brought a city to repentance in action, and much charity was done under his direction.

As a prophet, one has a dozen opinions to choose from. Savonarola claimed to be inspired directly by God to preach repentance, before the great tragedy of invasion would strike the country. Some of his prophecies came true and some did not. It would not take divine intervention to have foreseen some of the events that were brought about by people in high places. When the French came into Italy, much of the terror he had prophesied came to pass. With the flight of the Medici from Florence and his projected return, the whole question of the friar's political loyalty became very complex. Finally, as it was inevitable, his position was seen to run counter to that of Pope Alexander VI. There was bound to be trouble.

Alexander VI is not a pope of whom the Church can boast; he was a man of irregular personal life. Possibly if he had received a true account of Savonarola's doings and, above all, of his letters, the affair might not have ended so tragically. But between Savonarola and the pope there were a dozen grasping and interested persons who would benefit by stimulating trouble between them, and a situation that was bad enough to begin with very quickly became worse. Even so, the letters of Alexander VI—whatever may have been his personal faults—are models of fatherly discretion.

Briefly, the case can be presented in this way: Savonarola, deeply entangled in Florentine politics, opposed the League of Cities. The pope favored the League, but for reasons that the friar considered selfish. His opposition to the League inevitably found its way into his sermons, which were already inflammatory. The pope sent word for him to moderate the tone of his sermons; then he asked the friar to come to Rome. Savonarola protested, with justice on his side, that it would be suicidal to go to Rome, but that he would come as soon as it was safe. Then, it is claimed, a brief of excommunication was sent to the friar. There is a good deal of argument on this point, some claiming that the excommunication had no effect, because it was based upon false information, others, that it was never read and therefore was not effectual. It was not a time when anything could be seen clearly. The city rulers, having voted in several members who hated Savonarola for purely personal reasons, turned on him, and one of the many political parties in the city took it upon themselves to espouse the cause of the pope for the time being. They attacked the convent, and they would have burned it to the ground if the friar had not come out of his own accord and surrendered to them.

In May, 1498, after eleven days of torture, Savonarola and two of his staunchest friends were tied to the stake, and they were burned to death in the city square. Most of his brethren, who lived with him and should have known what they were talking about, claimed that he was a good religious, obedient and zealous, and that he had not disobeyed anyone, let alone the pope. His enemies rejoiced at his death, but were unhappy to find that they had made a martyr of him. Some of the Dominican saints, including St. Catherine de Ricci, who credited Savonarola with curing her of a serious illness, maintained that he had been unjustly condemned. Nearly everyone now admits that there was some juggling of documents which could bear heavily on his guilt or innocence.

SIXTEENTH CENTURY

BLESSED COLUMBA OF RIETI
(1467-1501)

One of many pious members of the Third Order who have been beatified is the mystic, Columba of Rieti, who lived in the late fifteenth century, in a convent in Perugia that she herself had founded.

Columba was born in Rieti in 1467, and, according to the legends, angels sang around the house when she was born. She was originally to be called Angelica, but a white dove appeared over the baptismal font, and it was decided that the name be changed to Columba. Her parents were too charitable to save any money, and she learned how to be hungry gracefully with them. Early in life, she learned to spin and sew, and she and her mother took upon themselves the task of doing the mending for the Dominican fathers in her native city.

Columba soon picked up the art of reading from the sisters at Rieti, and learned the Little Office from hearing it chanted. She was especially devout to Our Lady, and, as soon as she had read a life of St. Catherine of Siena, she began to model her life on that of the great Tertiary. Columba's parents seem to have had a very casual attitude towards the goods of this world, and, apparently, she and they worked only at odd times, when it was absolutely necessary. They devoted the rest of their time to prayer and good works among the poor.

Columba, at twelve, was self-supporting, and, furthermore, she had learned that charming truth: "It is better to need less than to have more." Earnestly praying to know her vocation, she was favored with a vision in which she saw our Lord on a golden throne, attended by Sts. Dominic, Jerome, and Peter Martyr. Columba interpreted the vision to mean that she was to dedicate herself to God, and she pronounced a private vow of virginity and made plans to live a solitary life. Unfortunately, she did not think to mention this to her parents, who were busy arranging a marriage for her. The night before the engagement was to be publicly announced, they suddenly told her that the young man they had arranged for her to marry was waiting in the parlor to see her. Forewarned by a vision, Columba had made up her mind what to do. She quickly cut off her hair and sent it in to him, which seems to be the accepted Dominican way of declining a suit. He took the hint and departed, to the fury of Columba's brothers, who perhaps had felt that the family finances were about to be put on a solid basis.

Columba, following St. Catherine's lead, settled down to live the life of a recluse in her father's house. She worked skillfully at whatever her mother suggested, which softened the good lady's annoyance at her daughter's peculiar choice of life. An uncle and one of her brothers persecuted her continually, and one time her brother tried to kill her. All in all, one would hardly say that these were comfortable surroundings for a mystic. In the midst of all this, Columba set sturdily about her program of spirituality: she kept five Lents a year, fasted on bread and water, and went to Mass and to Communion as often as she was allowed in those days of infrequent Communion.

Columba had a special devotion to the Holy Infancy, and she longed with a great longing to visit the Holy Land and see the places sanctified by the sacred humanity of Christ. Never able to make the trip in actuality, she made it spiritually, and once, in an ecstasy that lasted five days, she was conducted to all the holy places in Palestine. On one occasion, her confessor, who was something of an artist, had promised to make her a set of crib figures to use at Christmas time. He forgot to do so, and she was desolate until the Christ-child himself appeared to her. Then she had no need of wooden figures. Once, when she was meditating on the Passion, she was so affected by what she saw that she begged our Lord never to let her see such suffering again, for fear she would die of its intensity.

At the age of nineteen, Columba was received into the Third Order of St. Dominic. She had been favored with a vision telling her that she should join this group, and, as soon as she was clothed with the habit, she led a pilgrimage to the Dominican shrine of Our Lady of the Oak, in Viterbo.

Her fame had already begun to spread; as they went along the road, people crowded to get close to her and hailed her as a saint. Columba was embarrassed by such attention, but she proceeded to Viterbo. Here she prayed that a devil might be cast out of a young woman who had been possessed for eighteen years. When the woman was healed, the word spread all over the region that Columba was a real saint. The citizens of Narni determined to trap her and keep her as she passed through the city on her return to Rieti. Warned of their intention, Columba and her little party crept out by night and fled from those over-enthusiastic citizens, who would one day wage a bloody battle to gain custody of another saintly Dominican —Lucy of Narni.

We do not know why Columba moved to Foligno; perhaps the fame of her miracles—including the raising of a dead child to life—was beginning to press down upon her. In 1488, she went to the convent of the Poor Clares.

The bishop soon heard about her, and, unexpectedly, Columba found herself in the role of foundress for a community of Third Order Dominicans that the bishop wished to establish in Perugia. The bishop sent word for her to go to Perugia, and at the same time the master general told her to return to Rieti.

The good people of Foligno blocked all the roads, and said quite plainly that Columba was not going anywhere. When the master general's envoy came to get her, she was in ecstasy, and he had to shake her awake to give her the message. She went along very obediently. Eventually, however, the master general changed his mind, and she was sent to Perugia.

Columba took her solemn vows in the convent of Perugia on Pentecost, in 1490. She lived there happily, frequently lost in prayer, until her death eleven years later. Bishops and priests came to consult her about their various problems, and to ask her prayers. When the plague was decimating the peninsula, in 1494, she told the people to dedicate the city to St. Dominic and St. Catherine. Her request was carried out, and the plague immediately ceased.

One might think that all this heavenly activity might cause Columba to be a distracted superior. The records indicate that she was very kind to her subjects, and that she never expected of them the severe penances she herself performed. She claimed: "No sister dead to grace can remain in a convent; for either she will repent of her sins, or she will be cast out on the cold shores of the world, or, of her own free will, she will leave the blessed retreat of the cloister."

Columba of Rieti died on the eve of the Feast of the Ascension, in 1501, at the age of thirty-four. At the moment of her death, her soul appeared, radiant in glory, to her spiritual friend, Blessed Osanna of Mantua. She was beatified in 1697.

BERNARD ARNOLD
(1400-1502)

Bernard Arnold was of English blood, of the house of Arundel. His father had gone to Portugal with the Duke of Lancaster, accompanying an English princess. When the princess died, Arnold stayed on in Portugal, and his two sons were born there. Thus it came about that a man, who bore the very un-Portuguese name of "Arnold," was to bring honor to the Order in that country throughout a very long life.

Bernard was born in 1400, and, as soon as he was old enough, entered the Order there. He was a model of asceticism, performing every type of penance. He slept on a pile of twigs, and he made every situation an occasion of mortifying himself. He was given charge of the garden, and took upon himself whatever other work that was of a hard and undistinguished nature.

It is not too clear just when Bernard was ordained; from the fact that he was porter for so many years, one might infer that he was a laybrother, but we read that he always said Mass at the altar of the Holy Name, so he was evidently a priest. It is related in the legend that he almost always went into ecstasy during his Mass, and that, in the early years of this phenomenon, his server thought he was asleep and tried to wake him. However, it became apparent—when Bernard was seen raised two feet above the ground—that he was not sleeping. The belief that he was a saint was current, both among the brethren and outside the convent. Even the hard-hearted Juan II, who persecuted his sister, Blessed Juana, for her piety, used to come occasionally to watch Bernard in ecstasy. Once he noticed that the sanctuary lamp was out and that, at Bernard's prayer, it re-lighted itself.

Many miracles are credited to Bernard. On one occasion the whole country was suffering from drought. All the gardens and orchards were ruined, and vegetables withered in the fields. Yet Bernard set out a crop of cabbages and turnips in the convent garden, blessed them, and produced enough vegetables to keep the community fed throughout the time of the drought. On several occasions, he healed the sick, and he often multiplied bread for the poor, or, by prayer, obtained it outright from heaven.

Bernard would make a good patron for absent-minded folk. One day, while he was in choir singing Compline, the infirmarian rang the passing bell, to indicate that one of the brethren was dying and that the community should come to sing the *Salve*. The entire community filed out, leaving Bernard completely unaware that he had missed a cue. When they returned, he was just intoning the *"In manus tuas Domine,"* which is near the end of Compline, and he hadn't missed them at all. When questioned about it, he assured them that *someone* had been there chanting with him all the time—perhaps it was angels. Perhaps it was.

Bernard died in 1502, at the age of one hundred and two.

BLESSED MAGDALEN PANNATIERI
(1443-1503)

One hears so much about the detachment necessary for sanctity that it is refreshing to read about someone beatified who unblushingly loved her family, her country, her friends, and all little children.

Magdalen Pannatieri was born at Trino, near Vercelli, in 1443, of deeply religious parents. She was a devout child, who made a vow of virginity while she was quite young. Before she was twenty years old, she took her vows as a Dominican Tertiary, an exceptional circumstance, showing that she was held in high esteem. The Tertiary chapter was made up principally of widows and older women who centered their apostolate of active charities around the Dominican church. Magdalen fitted into this work with ease, and she brought to the chapter a spirit of penance that few of her companions could match. The delightful part of it all was that her penances never rendered her dreary; she was a cheerful, resourceful person to have around. People drew as much good from her spirit of joy as from any other feature of her spirituality.

Magdalen had a special fondness for little children, and their welfare was a large part of her apostolate. She did a good deal of what we now call baby-sitting, and used her influence with the children to bring their parents to a better way of life. Childless women won her sympathy, and several times her prayers brought the blessing of motherhood to such people. She taught catechism to children, and gradually the older folk of her acquaintance began to sit in on her classes. She was quite unaware that she had great powers of description and could make the truths of religion clear to simple people. The Dominican fathers allowed her to use a large room attached to the church for a class room, and the class grew. Not only the parents of the children and the simple folk of the neighborhood, but also a number of priests and religious were attending regularly.

When the reform movement started by Blessed Raymond of Capua got underway, Magdalen Parnatieri promoted it in Trino. Through her influence, Blessed Sebastian Maggio was invited to preach there, and he accomplished great good.

Magdalen was considered the protectress of the city of Trino. Whatever disaster threatened it, the citizens expected her to look out for their interests, and she usually did. In her life there is no mention of a "dark night of the soul," or of grim detachment from all the things of earth. Her love of God kept her from attaching herself to any illegitimate pleasures, but she thoroughly enjoyed the lawful ones—she loved her family and her townspeople and was always happy in their company. Her favorite brother was a good-for-nothing—he was always in trouble. When his conduct had gone beyond the patience of everyone but Magdalen, she threw herself on her knees in front of her crucifix, and she stayed there until our Lord assured her that He would take a hand with the black sheep: "I cannot refuse you anything," He said.

The Dominican fathers received her solicitude when they were persecuted by a wealthy man of the town. This person carried his hatred so far that he was finally excommunicated for persecuting the Church. There was, of course, a good deal of blood shed before the affair was over, and one of the reprobate's followers made the mistake of hitting Magdalen and calling her names. Before the irate townspeople could deal out justice to him, God did; the man died a violent death.

God revealed to Magdalen the coming political troubles of Italy: the French invasion of the country. She did not live to see this prophecy accomplished, but she persistently asked God's mercy for her people. During the violent quarrels and bloodshed of the time, Trino was always spared, though the villages all around were in a shambles. The townsfolk unhesitatingly gave credit to Magdalen.

Magdalen Pannatieri died in 1503, and was beatified by Pope Leo XII.

BLESSED OSANNA OF MANTUA
(1449-1505)

Osanna Andreassi was born of a wealthy family in Mantua, and her pious childhood was replete with heavenly revelations. She kept these to herself. One time she saw the Child Jesus carrying a cross and wearing a crown of thorns. He told her that He had a special love for children and for purity, and, though Osanna was only six years old, the revelation made a great impression on her; it had, in fact, the effect of determining her to consecrate her life entirely to God.

In order to be able to say the Divine Office, Osanna wanted to learn to read. She approached her father on the subject, but he refused her, because, as he said, there was no use at all in a woman learning to read and write—she was to spend her life bringing up a family. Osanna did not intend to spend her life that way, but she did not dare to explain to him. At the age of fourteen, knowing that her father was already trying to arrange a marriage for her, she went secretly to the Dominican church and received the habit of the Dominican Tertiaries. When she appeared at home in her religious garb, she explained it by saying that she had made a vow and had to wear the habit until she had fulfilled her promise.

A pious man, her father accepted this explanation, but, as the months went by, he began to suspect that she had some mysterious plan in mind. He had refused her request to enter a cloister, and he was not at all happy with her determination to remain a Dominican Tertiary in her own home. However, he eventually gave up opposing her, and Osanna settled down to the routine of prayer, penance, and works of charity. She was to follow this program the rest of her life. Although she received the habit at the age of fourteen, she did not make profession until a few months before her death, forty-two years later.

Osanna's parents died while she was still quite young. This left her mistress of her father's house, and she promptly turned it into a center for her charitable works. People could come there to discuss spiritual matters. The poor and the sick always knew where to find her and were continually in her prayers and good works. Even some of the wealthy and the noble came to her for advice or prayers.

Her desire to learn to read was granted one day during her prayers. She saw two words printed on a slip of paper and read them off quite simply; "Those words are 'Jesus' and 'Mary,'" she said. From then on she could read anything pertaining to spiritual matters. By the same sort of favor, she also learned to write.

In 1477, when she was twenty-eight years old, Osanna received the first marks of the stigmata. The first to appear was the wound in her side, caused by a long, terrible nail. From then until the following year, she received, at different times, the remainder of the sacred wounds, including the crown of thorns. These were noticeable to other people only on Wednesdays and Fridays and during Holy Week, but they were visible to her, as a source of both pain and spiritual joy, all the time.

Perhaps all stigmatists have difficulty in finding spiritual directors; certainly people so favored are in need of a director with unusual wisdom, patience, and understanding. Osanna felt this need very keenly and prayed that she would find someone who could guide her properly along her unusual path. One time, during Mass, she heard an interior voice say to her, "That's the one you need, the one who is saying Mass." Osanna took a good look and decided that he was too young. A few days later, she was surprised to meet the same priest in confession and discover that he had been divinely chosen to direct her. In spite of his youth, he was quite capable of doing so.

Shortly before Osanna's death, the soul of another Dominican Tertiary, Columba of Rieti, appeared to her. Columba told her that she was dying and that Osanna would soon follow her, so Osanna joyfully prepared for death. She died in 1505, and she was beatified in 1694.

BLESSED JOHN LICCIO
(1400-1511)

The man who holds the all-time record for wearing the Dominican habit— ninety-six years—was also a person about whom some delightful legends are told. Perhaps only in Sicily could so many wonderful things have happened to one man.

John was born in Sicily, in 1400, of a poor family. His mother died at his birth, and his father, too poor to hire a nurse for the baby, fed him on crushed pomegranates and other odds and ends. He was obliged to leave the baby alone when he went out to work in the fields, and a neighbor woman, who heard the child crying, took the baby over to her house and fed him properly. She laid the baby in bed beside her sick husband, who had been paralyzed for a long time. Her husband rose up—cured, and the woman began to proclaim the saintly quality of the baby she had taken in. When John's father came in, however, he was not only unimpressed by her pious remarks, he was downright furious that she had interfered in his household. He took the baby home again and fed it more pomegranates.

At this point, the sick man next door fell ill again, and his wife came to John's father and begged to be allowed to care for the baby. Begrudgingly, the father let the wonderful child go. The good woman took care of him for several years, and never ceased to marvel that her husband had been cured a second time, and that he had remained well.

Even as a tiny child, John gave every evidence that he was an unusual person. At an age when most children are just beginning to read, he was already reciting the daily Office of the Blessed Virgin, the Office of the Dead, and the Penitential Psalms. He was frequently in ecstasy, and was what might be called an "easy weeper"; any strong emotion caused him to dissolve in floods of tears.

At the age of fifteen, John went to Palermo on a business trip for his father, and he happened to go to confession to Blessed Peter Geremia, at the church of St. Zita. The friar suggested his becoming a religious. John believed himself quite unworthy, but the priest managed to convince him to give it a try. The habit, which he put on for the first time in 1415, he was to wear with distinction for nearly a century.

Humble, pure, and a model of every observance, Brother John finished his studies and was ordained. He and two brothers were sent to Caccamo to found a convent, and John resumed his career of miracle-working, which was to bring fame to the Order and to the convent of St. Zita. As the three friars walked along the road, a group of young men began ridiculing them and finally attacked them with daggers. One boy attempted to stab John, but his hand withered and refused to move. After the friars had gone on, the boys huddled together and decided that they had better ask pardon. They ran after the Dominicans and begged their forgiveness. John made the Sign of the Cross, and the withered hand was made whole.

The story of the building at Caccamo reads like a fairy-tale. There was, first of all, no money. Since the friars never had any, that did not deter John Liccio, but he knew it would be necessary to get enough to pay the workmen to begin the foundations. John went into the parish church at Caccamo and prayed. An angel told him to "build on the foundations that were already built." All he had to do was to find them. The next day, he went into the woods with a party of young wood-cutters and found the place the angel had described: foundations, strongly and beautifully laid out, for a large church and convent. It had been designed for a church called St. Mary of the Angels, but was never finished.

John moved his base of operations to the woods where the angel had furnished him with the foundations. One day, in the course of construction, the workmen ran out of materials. They pointed this out to John, who told them to come back tomorrow anyway. The next day, at dawn, a large wagon, drawn by two oxen, appeared with a load of stone, lime, and sand. The driver enquired politely where the fathers would like the material put; he capably unloaded the wagon, and disappeared, leaving John with a fine team of oxen—and giving us a fascinating story of an angel truck-driver.

These oxen figured at least once more in the legends of John Liccio. Near Christmas time, when there was little fodder, a neighbor insisted on taking the oxen home with him "because they were too much care for the fathers." John refused, saying that they were not much care, and that they had come a long way. The man took them anyway, and put them into a pasture with his own oxen. They promptly disappeared, and, when he went shame-facedly to report to the fathers, the man found the team contentedly munching —on practically nothing—in the fathers' yard. "You see, it takes very little to feed them," John said.

During the construction, John blessed a well and dried it up, until they were finished with the building. Whereupon, he blessed it again, and once more it began to give fine sweet water, which had curative properties. Beams that were too short for the roof, he simply stretched. Sometimes he had to multiply bread and wine to feed his workers, and once he raised from the dead a venturesome little boy who had fallen off the roof while watching his uncle setting stones.

Word of this miraculous gift got around, of course, and all the neighbors came to John with their problems. One man had sowed a field with good grain, only to have it grow up full of weeds. John advised him to do as the Scripture had suggested—let it grow until the harvest. When harvest time came, it still looked pretty bad; but it took the man ten days to thresh the enormous crop of grain that he reaped from that one field.

John never let a day pass without doing something for some neighbor. Visiting a widow whose six small children were crying for food, John blessed them, and he told her to be sure to look in the bread box after he had gone. Knowing there had been nothing in it for days, she looked anyway; it was full, and it stayed full for as long as the need lasted. Once, when a plague had struck most of the cattle of the vicinity, one of John's good friends came to him in tears, telling him that he would be ruined if anything happened to his cattle. "Don't worry," said John, "yours won't get sick." They didn't. Once a neighbor came running to tell him that his wife was dying. "Go home," said John. "You have a fine new son, and you shouldn't waste any time getting home to thank God for him."

John was never too famous as a preacher, though he did preach a good deal in the ninety years of his active apostolate. His favorite subject was the Passion, but he was more inclined to use his hands than his speech. He was provincial of Sicily for a time, and held office as prior on several occasions.

John Liccio died in 1511 and was beatified in 1733. He is especially invoked to help anyone who has been hit on the head, as he cured no less than three people whose heads were crushed in accidents.

ANNE OF ZORN
(d. 1511)

Anne of Zorn is included, not because we have a great deal of information about her personally, but because the only thing we do know about her offers us such a brilliant picture of one facet of Dominican life in her times that we seldom hear of.

Anne of Zorn was prioress of the convent of St. Agnes, in Strasbourg, in 1475, when Charles the Bold invaded Alsace and laid siege to the city. She had been prioress there for seven years. It was a convent that she had restored to regular observance, for it had fallen into a state of relaxation. Understandably, she was deeply attached to the convent of St. Agnes, and when word came that, as a military precaution, it was to be razed, she hired a lawyer and set out to defend her home.

The convent of St. Agnes was a large and sturdy building, near the city walls. Strategically, it would be a grave error to leave it there for Charles to capture and fortify for use against the city. The nuns were advised that they would have to move immediately to the convent of St. Margaret, where seventeen Dominican nuns were living in a huge convent that was much too large for them. Mother Anne and her flock declined to leave. When the engineers began tearing down the walls around them, however, it was decided that the move was inevitable, and the nuns started their packing. The scene that next ensued is almost incredible to us of another age. It moves across the dry pages of history like a glowing miniature.

Just before Christmas, in 1475, the zero hour struck for the convent of St. Agnes. The bishop and his retinue, the mayor and the city magistrates, and the Knights of St. John came in full uniform to escort the weeping nuns to their new home. The bishop carried the Blessed Sacrament; the girls who had been boarders or students at St. Agnes were there (probably in orderly lines, in their Sunday uniforms, with the youngest carrying flowers); and the ladies of the noble families—plus delegations from all the other convents in town. Specific mention is made of the Lady Abbess of St. Stephen's, who was a princess of the Holy Roman Empire. She and her ladies must have added color to the procession. All the trade guilds were there, also, with banners flying, and the canons of the Cathedral, chanting against the resonant clamor of all the church bells in the city. People of that age certainly never sinned by underrating an occasion.

As the procession moved away from the doomed convent, the nuns wept loudly, and Mother Anne fainted. They moved on, first to the church of St. Thomas, where Benediction was held. A second Benediction was at old St. Peter's Church. Then, after a long and colorful detour around the city, the procession arrived at St. Margaret's, where the nuns were to take refuge. The door was locked. They knocked long and loud, and were finally assured that if they wanted to get in they could break in. So some of the men got a large beam for a battering ram, and they broke down the door. Everyone filed into the chapel, and there was a third Benediction. Then the nuns prostrated in the chapel and prayed. The battering-ram was brought in, the cloister door smashed, and the nuns crossed over, chanting imperturbably.

Inside the cloister, the prioress of St. Margaret's waited with her community. Having made the gesture of resistance, and thus protected some ancient rights of the house of which we are ignorant today, she advanced to meet the visitors and extended to them all the hospitality at her command. She told them that she was resigning her position as prioress, since the incoming community was much larger than hers. Whereupon, Mother Anne assured her that she, too, would resign her office, and that all she wanted was hospitality for her nuns. (Her words were: "Just let us sleep in the attic.")

Mother Catherine, of the convent of St. Margaret's, died soon after this, and, in the election which followed, Anne of Zorn was elected prioress of the combined community. The house took both names, and, in the thirty-three years of Mother Anne's term of rule, reached great heights of fame as a house of saints and scholars. The Emperor Maximilian visited the convent, in 1507, and remarked on the elegant Latin spoken by the sisters.

Anne of Zorn died in 1511.

FRA BARTOLOMEO DELLA PORTA
(d. 1517)

Second only to the great Fra Angelico, of whom he was a near contemporary, was the Dominican friar-painter, Fra Bartolomeo Della Porta. As an artist, he was close to the top of the list, and, since he lived in an age of giants, it speaks well both for his skill and his personal charm that he should be remembered even today.

Bartolomeo was born in a little village not far from Florence, and was taken to the queen city of the arts as soon as it became evident that he had talent for painting. He was placed to study under an inferior painter, and, for all practical purposes, wasted years of his time with this man. Finally, in company of a fellow student named Albertinelli, who shared his disgust in the poor teacher, he set out to study elsewhere.

The two young students shared their lodgings, their purse, and their dreams, but they parted company on religious and moral questions. Albertinelli lived the fast and undisciplined life which was so soon to be condemned by Savonarola. Bartolomeo was by nature timid and pious. However, they got on well in their studies. It was Savonarola himself who broke up this strange partnership, and swept the young Bartolomeo into the Order.

The effect of the great reformer on the city of Florence is hard for us to imagine now. No earthquake nor flood could so thoroughly disturb a worldly city as this apocalyptic friar, who thundered of judgment to the richest and most powerful men of the land. Even the children joined him in gathering up the vanities of the city for burning. One of his most ardent admirers was Bartolomeo Della Porta, who came with another artist, Lorenzo di Credi, to submit their sketches to Savonarola.

Partly out of jealousy for his friend, and partly because the reformer threatened his way of life, Albertinelli joined the party that had sworn to kill Savonarola. Just what part he had in the attack on San Marco, it is hard to tell. Tradition says that Bartolomeo was among the armed friars and citizens who tried to defend Savonarola when the convent was attacked. Bartolomeo himself related that it was there, in the midst of battle, surrounded by smoke and blood and the screams of the dying, that he resolved to quit the world and enter the Dominican Order.

Certainly he must have seen Savonarola give himself up to the rabble, to spare the people from more fighting. He must have been in the crowd, watching with horrified eyes, when Savonarola and his two companions died at the stake. It was grim training for a painter of madonnas.

Bartolomeo was not the only young painter who laid down his brush in horror and fled from a city gone mad. Several of the most promising young artists did likewise. But, after his sorrow had eased, and the tumult in Florence had quieted down, he made a move that proved he had thought deeply about the eternal aspects of the affair; he put away all his art equipment, and he entered the Dominican Order in Prato.

Bartolomeo finished a happy novitiate and took his vows. Eventually he received the diaconate, though he could not go on to the priesthood because of an inferior education. Even after he had returned to Florence as a friar, there was still a dead weight on his heart that prevented him from doing any creative work. He still believed wholeheartedly in Savonarola and his reform. The great reformer had held high and pure ideals of art, which Fra Bartolomeo had espoused with great enthusiasm. But Florence had not only stoned her prophet, she had killed him. Florence, the city of art, had turned away from religion and supported only the licentious art that Savonarola had condemned. Confused, and sick at heart, Fra Bartolomeo felt he had lost faith in his city and in humanity; it was eight years before he took up his painting again.

The convent of San Marco was a treasure-house of beauty. The walls were adorned with the frescoes of Fra Angelico, and the community numbered both eminent saints and outstanding artists among its members. A nephew of Luca della Robbia was one of Fra Bartolomeo's companions. The very air must have breathed of art, yet the young man who had watched his hero die at the stake was too shattered to take up the career he had abandoned. But obedience did what he alone could not do, and, at the insistence of the prior, he began work on an altarpiece. It was, to everyone else, a magnificent piece of work. To its creator, it highlighted a number of his own weaknesses. The young friar sought permission to study with a master of the age, Leonardo da Vinci, who was, providentially, in Florence as a political exile.

Da Vinci was then engaged in an artistic contest with Michelangelo, an affair which drew all the artists of Italy to Florence to watch what was almost a battle of the gods. Two young artists, who were themselves to win immortality, came there to study the contest; they were Ghirlandaio and Raphael. Both of them met the young Dominican in the studio of Da Vinci, and Raphael, in particular, grew very fond of him. Tradition says that they worked together for some time, and that some of Raphael's madonnas were the fruit of his long discussions with the earnest young friar. Several paintings are pointed out today as the joint work of the two.

Shortly after this, Fra Bartolomeo went to Venice to study the use of color. Where Florence excelled in drawing and Siena in religious feeling, Venice was the center of color. Titian was a young student there when Fra Bartolomeo came to place himself under the instruction of Giorgione. The earnest friar saw and absorbed the beauty of color and mass, and took from Venice what that city had to give to an eternal cause. On his return to Florence, the Dominican had reached maturity in his art.

Fra Bartolomeo was singularly unlucky in a number of things. These factors influenced his painting, and probably kept him from realizing his talent to the full. First of all, there were the wasted years when an uninspired teacher held him down to worthless copying. For another thing, he was perpetually experimenting with kinds of paint and methods of delineation. Some of the experiments were disastrous, as the pictures darkened after a few years, and the designs perished through his faulty knowledge of the chemistry of paint. Then, for many years, he worked closely with Albertinelli, a talented but unprincipled and violent man, who kept his friend in a continual spiritual turmoil. In addition to these impediments, Bartolomeo seems to have been the world's worst businessman; there is hardly a painting of his over which there was not a resounding financial squabble. Usually he got nothing out of a painting but the experience— and, after it was too late to cheer him, the unquestioned glory of being listed among the immortals.

Today there are many pictures of Fra Bartolomeo's proven authorship, and many more of which he was a collaborator. From the strange little picture of Savonarola, which was to hang in the cell of St. Catherine de

Ricci, to the great canvases and altar pieces that graced the finest churches of his time, the works of the friar always show that heavenly contact that made him kin to Fra Angelico and drew the love of Raphael. As an example of a Christian artist, he is a shining light.

Fra Bartolomeo died in 1517, leaving unfinished a huge painting on which he had worked determinedly as death crept upon him. His friend, Raphael, finished several of his paintings.

DOMINIC DE SOUZA
(1518)

After the return of Vasco da Gama from the Indies, there was a concerted rush on the part of all the European rulers to make use of his discoveries. One of the first expeditions fitted out to follow his route to India was that of Alfonso, duke of Aubuquerque, who sailed with six vessels from Lisbon, in 1503. As chaplains to his fleet, and missionaries to the Indies, there were five Dominicans: Dominic de Souza, Peter de Abru, John of the Rosary, Anthony de Metta, and Rodrigo Homen.

Dominic de Souza, as leader of the mission band, sailed on the flagship with the duke, and it was his task to try to moderate the policies of the gold-hungry men who made up the expedition. He soon found that it is much easier to convert savages than to keep Christian men Christian, if they are faced with sudden wealth.

Arriving in India, the Portuguese built a fortress and laid the cornerstone of a church, which was blessed by Dominic de Souza, in a colorful ceremony, and a sermon was preached by John of the Rosary. The church was named for St. Bartholomew. Not waiting for the completion of the church, Dominic went with the duke to Coulam, the port where, one hundred and fifty years before, Jordan of Catalá, the Dominican, had preached and died. Twelve thousand Christian families had been abandoned there at the time of Jordan's death, and, through the century and a half, they had dwindled, both in number and fervor. However, they were still eager for a priest, and Dominic appointed Rodrigo Homen to work among them. He himself moved on with the fleet.

By 1505, Dominic de Souza was back in Portugal, busily recruiting missionaries for the vast untended millions of the Far East. He gathered up eleven Dominicans, and then, on his enthusiastic presentation of the case to Pope Julius II, more missionaries were sent from Rome. Dominic returned to Portugal to sail with the duke of Albuquerque, who was making a second voyage.

The story of the next few years is the story of many conquests; of insatiable greed on the part of the conquerors; of disillusionment on that of the missionaries. Dominic de Souza was called by later historians the "Las Casas of Malabar"; it must be said that he did his best to defend the natives from the effects of conquest. When Ormuz fell to Portuguese, in 1507, the Dominicans established their central house there. They worked desperately to convert the natives and to moderate the conduct of the soldiers.

In 1510, Alfonso d'Albuquerque conquered Goa and made it the capital of the Portuguese colonies. Dominic de Souza remained with him. Three years later, they sailed into the Red Sea. On the vigil of the Feast of the Finding of the Holy Cross, they, and the whole ship's company, saw a radiant cross high in the air. They took it as a sign of success, and the next day Dominic celebrated Mass on the shores of the Gulf of Aden.

However, the conqueror's star was on the wane. Alfonso d'Albuquerque fell into disgrace with the king, and he was replaced as governor of the land he had conquered. Dominic de Souza stayed with him until his death, guiding and counselling him in his sorrow, as he had in the years of success.

When Dominic de Souza died, we do not know. It was after 1518.

JOHN TETZEL
(1460-1518)

All the bitterness of the Reformation has been heaped upon the unlucky head of John Tetzel, the man who ran afoul of Martin Luther. The records indicate that he was not deserving of most of the opprobrium, but he happened to be on hand when a scapegoat was needed. The Dominican Order, at least, should uphold the reputation of this man; he did his best to testify to the truth in an impossible situation.

John Tetzel was born near Dresden in 1460, and received his bachelor's degree at Leipzig. He entered the Dominican Order after he was already known as a good scholar. He soon established a reputation as a popular preacher, of the "spellbinder" tradition. Cardinal Cajetan, the master general, made him a master in sacred theology and sent him as inquisitor to Poland, then to Frankfort.

Pope Leo X delegated the archbishop of Mainz to promulgate the indulgences for the rebuilding of St. Peter's. In order to secure the cooperation of the somewhat headstrong bishop, the pope allowed him to use some of the revenues for his church-building program in Germany. Unfortunately, the archbishop of Mainz was deeply in debt to a Jewish firm of money-lenders, and, in the settlement of the affair, there was an open scandal about the alms of the faithful being appropriated by the moneylenders. It was an unsavory situation, but one which would inevitably have been remedied by peaceful means, if there had been time. However, the Augustinian monk, Martin Luther, precipitated a tragedy that soon got out of hand. He turned his scorn and his eloquence against the archbishop of Mainz, and he was particularly bitter against the Dominican who had been appointed to preach the indulgences in Germany, the popular preacher, John Tetzel.

Tetzel, although he was a popular extempore preacher, was no mean theologian. He had written a book, *The Duties of Preachers of Indulgences*, which gives proof that he understood and promulgated the orthodox teaching on indulgences, and neither regarded them as "pardons for sin," nor as commodities for sale, both of which were Luther's accusations. He states unequivocally that "the sinner is obliged to repent and to go to confession before he can gain an indulgence," and that "the Church holds as Catholic truths a number of things not explicitly found either in the Old or the New Testament, since Tradition and oral teaching are more ancient than Scripture" . . . These two arguments brought him into head-on conflict with Luther, who had, in a few months, become a bible-thumping zealot beyond reach of reasoning.

The followers of Luther were fanatically devoted to him, and they united in the cry: "Death to Tetzel." It is hard to understand today, since the authority they were flouting was vested in the bishop, not in the man appointed to preach. But the Dominican rapidly became the butt of all their sarcasm and their insults, and threats on his life made it difficult for him to move around. In the midst of the trouble, Tetzel fell seriously ill in Leipzig. When he was summoned to go to Altenbergh by the priest that the pope had sent to settle the matter, he could not get out of bed. The priest wrote to Tetzel, repeating the accusations of Luther against him: "You have been denounced as a heretic and a blasphemer, and as having insulted the Blessed Virgin." Tetzel replied, "I know that Brother Martin is obsessed with that idea, but I am sure I can prove it to you that I am a faithful son of Holy Church and that I have sacrificed my own reputation and security in the cause of truth." His superior likewise wrote to the nuncio, attesting that Tetzel was too ill to go to Altenbergh. He added: "I do not know any other man who has done and suffered as much as Tetzel in defense of the Holy See."

The nuncio, for some reason of his own, sided against Tetzel. He went to Leipzig to see the Dominican, and denounced him to his face. The dying man felt that this was the ultimate desertion—that the Church for which he had suffered so much would turn against him. He died, in the bleakness of misunderstanding, before any decisive steps could be taken. The ensuing years have blackened his memory with a great many things that he did not say or do, though unprejudiced historians today admit that much of the opprobrium was simply the bitterness of the age; it had nothing to do with him personally.

DIEGO DE DEZA
(d. 1523)

Contemporaries of Diego de Deza very probably felt that the high point of his life was his appointment as archbishop of Seville. History has remembered him for quite another reason: he was the champion of a down-at-the-heels Italian, Christopher Columbus, who wanted to sail west and find a new route to India. By the testimony of Columbus himself, it was Diego de Deza who brought it about that Spain, and not some other country, was to open up the vast treasure box of the Indies.

Diego de Deza was professed at the convent of St. Stephen, in Salamanca, the house that was to nourish so many resourceful missionaries for the New World. Of his life before he became a religious, we know nothing except that his parents were wealthy and gave him a good education. One author makes out a quite hysterical case for Diego's being a "converso," a converted Moor. He may have been, and that would have made his appointment to the archbishopric somewhat unique; we simply do not know. He steps into history and everlasting fame as regent of studies at Salamanca.

The king of Spain, like every other monarch of the time, was anxious for a quick and easy route to the Indies. The Portuguese had been first to tap the vast stores of treasure in the Far East, and Spain wanted to get her hand in before it was too late. But the theory proposed by the shabby little sailor from Genoa was too absurd to even consider. Why should anyone sail west to go east? Furthermore, the Portuguese had turned him down. If there had been either sense or money in the plan, that would not have happened. King Ferdinand gave the adventurer some good advice, but declined the proposal; he was not interested, but he suggested that Columbus discuss the plan with the Dominicans at Salamanca, for they were very wise. That is how Columbus came into touch with Diego de Deza, who conducted discussions in which his professors quizzed the stranger. Columbus had made no converts at the court of Portugal, nor at the court of Spain. But he sold his plan completely to the Dominicans at Salamanca, and acquired the best friends of his troubled life.

De Deza's actual contribution to the expedition was very great. It was he who finally convinced the queen that Columbus should be given a hearing. She, in turn, prevailed upon the king. And he kept the flame of interest from dying during the several years that the king delayed, haggling over what money he would furnish for the expedition, and what reward he would grant Columbus, if he did find the route. When Columbus was weary of the king's niggardliness, and was preparing to go to the courts of France and England to look for help, De Deza detained him. Once, when Columbus was leaving Spain in disgust, he even sent messengers to overtake him and bring him back. It was with his blessing that the three little ships finally sailed off into the great unknown.

After the venture had proved itself, and Columbus returned to a justly-earned reward, it was De Deza again who had to comfort him, because obviously the king had no intentions of paying his just debt. After the trials of the last voyage, and Columbus was sick and penniless, he turned again to the friend, who, almost alone, had remained loyal. Diego de Deza was now archbishop of Seville, and he used the full weight of his powerful position to obtain justice for Columbus. His labors were futile; Ferdinand would not even pay the sailors, as the dying admiral begged him to do. When the man who had brought him an empire died in poverty, the king ignored it. The archbishop of Seville, a friend to the last, counselled the dying man to charity and patience, even in the face of injustice. There was nothing else he could do.

Diego de Deza wrote several short works on St. Thomas, and he gave great impetus to the founding of the college named in his honor at Seville. He died in that city in 1523. But his greatest contribution to history was his faith in Columbus—the man who went hunting a trade route and found an empire.

BLESSED STEPHANIE DE QUINZANIS
(1457-1530)

It was Blessed Stephanie's good fortune always to live with holy people and to have the edifying example of many holy friends. She was born of pious parents in a little village in the north of Italy. While she was still very small, her father became a Dominican Tertiary. On visits with him to the

Dominican convent, she met the holy stigmatic, Blessed Matthew Carrieri, whose influence was to last throughout her long life. He taught her the catechism and much of his own spirit of sanctity. In fact, he told her that one day she was to be his spiritual heiress. She did not understand this for many years.

Early trained to sanctity, Stephanie responded with the love of a true saint. She fasted and did penance from her earliest years. The visions which were to sweeten her mystical life began when she was seven, and at that time she made the vows of poverty, chastity, and obedience. She was favored with a beautiful visitation from our Lord and several of the Dominican saints, and was given a splendid ring—as a token of her espousal to Christ. From then on, her heart and mind were centered on God, and no earthly attraction had power to distract her.

When Stephanie was fourteen Blessed Matthew Carrieri died, and, shortly thereafter, appeared to her. Wounded with a terrible pain, the girl realized that she had received the sacred stigmata. This was the legacy that Blessed Matthew had promised her. Now she intensified her penances, and she meditated almost ceaselessly on the Passion. In addition to her physical endurance of the Passion, she had to undergo a spiritual desolation and dryness. This aridity lasted forty years.

Stephanie was given the Tertiary habit. Some years later, she founded a community of Third Order sisters in her native town of Soncino. As a Tertiary, she had been able to go out to nurse the sick and help the poor; as a member of a regular community, she continued her charity, dispensing both material and spiritual riches. People of all classes came to consult her and ask her prayers; St. Angela Merici and the Dominicans, Augustine of Biella and Osanna of Mantua, were among these.

The life of Blessed Stephanie is a series of marvels. Only under obedience she revealed the principal visions and ecstasies long after they happened. She lived in constant union with God, and her every action had upon it the imprint of His favors. Keeping an almost perpetual fast, she punished her body with instruments of penance. Her devotion to the Blessed Sacrament and to the Passion of our Lord was intense. She could discuss the most profound truths of mystical theology, and had the ability to read the hearts and minds of those around her, and to prophesy future events. Of the saints of the Order to whom she had great devotion, she was particularly drawn to St. Thomas Aquinas, for one time, to overcome temptation of thought against purity, she threw herself upon a cart-load of thorns. Rising exhausted from this penance, she prayed fervently to St. Thomas, and, like that great saint, she was girded by angels with a cord, which they tied so tightly around her waist that she cried out in pain.

Blessed Stephanie died, after having prephesied the day of her death and the place where she would be buried. Her tomb became a pilgrimage almost immediately. Her intercession was often felt in the convent that she had founded, where the sisters obtained both material and spiritual help through her intercession.

ANTHONY OF MONTESINOS
(d. 1530)

On the Sunday before Christmas, in 1511, a Dominican friar addressed a group of Spanish grandees in a straw-thatched church on the Island of Hispaniola. He took as his text: "I am the voice of one crying in the desert," and it was all too clear both to him and to his brethren that he—like St. John the Baptist—was being offensive to important people and might pay for his zeal in somewhat the same way.

He was Father Anthony of Montesinos, and his message to the "best people" of New Spain was blunt: "You are no better than Moors and Turks, you who starve and beat and rob and oppress the Indians! I cannot promise you salvation any more than I could promise it to the Moors and the Turks." This "first cry on behalf of human liberty in the new world" was to begin a long, bloody battle that three hundred years later would call thousands of men to the battlefields. Anthony of Montesinos did not live to see his words accomplish anything. But it is a reason for honest pride to the Dominican Order that he struck the first blow in so noble a cause, and that his brethren stood by him in the dangerous position of all brave men who must make a stand against injustice.

Where or when Anthony of Montesinos was born has not been recorded. The first we know of him is the record of his profession in the Convent of St. Stephen, in Salamanca, in 1502. He was one of the first Dominicans sent to the New World, in 1510, under the leadership of Peter of Cordova. They found an ignorant people, the Indians, who were eager converts and —they tell us earnestly—good ones. They were hemmed in on all sides by gold-hungry adventurers who had come out to the colonies, as one of them put it frankly: "Not to teach the Indian about God, but to take his gold away from him."

The policy of the king was based upon the quite common presumption that Indians, being only Indians, had no rights and should not be considered the same as other human beings. They should, in fact, be grateful to the

Spaniards for relieving them of their possessions, which could be the source of so much trouble to new Christians. It was to be the work of the Dominicans to relieve the king of this interesting opinion, and the monumental task began in the church on Hispaniola; Father Anthony of Montesinos sounded the call to arms. The preachers had worked out the sermon together, and had chosen Anthony to deliver it, perhaps because he was the best speaker, perhaps because he had better nerves. And, in the inevitable uproar that followed, when the grandees came surging out of the church, demanding to see Governor Diego Columbus, the Dominicans stood together in the affair.

At the end of an upsetting interview, the Dominican superior agreed that he would ask Father Anthony to speak again the following Sunday. Mollified, the delegation went home. The following Sunday, when the same preacher addressed them, they listened in stunned silence to his fearful words: "I speak for all my brethren; you who hold Indian slaves and mistreat them will henceforth be refused absolution in the confessional. One does not give absolution to unrepentant highway robbers. Neither shall we give it to you."

The colony was split wide open with fury. Ruthless as the conquerors were, they were men of faith, and the idea of being deprived of absolution in this violent land frightened them as nothing else could. They immediately sent ambassadors to the king, burdened with vehement protests against the stiff-necked friars. The king was inclined to agree with the grandees' case as it was presented, and even the Dominican provincial sent back the message: "The friars ought not to preach such scandalous doctrine."

But the Dominicans at Salamanca were already roused about the question. They set about studying it in the light of St. Thomas. Some of the finest theologians of that center of gifted men were to debate long and earnestly on the rights of the Indians. Out of their discussions would come the ideals that future nations would build into their constitutions: that all men have rights as men, that conquerors have obligations towards the human race itself, and that all is not fair in war and conquest. One of the most learned of the doctors to discuss the sizzling question was Francis of Vitoria, whose treatises on international law are only now beginning to be appreciated properly.

However, for the hard-pressed missionaries, the wheels of justice ground slowly. They were on the firing line, and it could not have been comfortable. It is greatly to their credit that they went ahead with their preaching without promise.

One of the men most angered by the Dominican attitude was a young priest by the name of Bartholomew de las Casas. He was himself a slave-owner, and he treated his slaves well. He insisted that it was better to have slaves and treat them well than to free them to an uncertain future, a position he could not hold against the Dominicans. Point by point, he fought the uncomfortable doctrine, and once he was refused absolution for his views. Eventually, he was to lay down his arms and ask for and receive the Dominican habit; then he himself was to become one of the greatest champions the Indians ever had.

Anthony of Montesinos was summoned to Spain to defend his position before the Council of the Indies. He and Peter of Cordova defended their actions so ably that the king himself was won over to their view. This did not, of course, stop the looting and cruelties of the colonials. But it did place on record at least a defense of these people; ten years before they were thought to have no rights as human beings.

Anthony of Montesinos was sent to found a mission in Venezuela, but, due to illness, was put off the ship, and so escaped the martyrdom which fell to the lot of his companions. On recovering his health, he was sent with a mission group to Puerto Rico. In 1526, he was sent to the mainland with an expedition bound for Florida.

Exactly where Florida was, according to these men, is hard to say. They anchored in a sheltered cove that has been variously identified as a spot off the South Carolina coast, on Pamlico Sound, which is in North Carolina, and on the James River, in Virginia. The bulk of proof seems to rest with the third possibility, which would indicate that Anthony of Montesinos said Mass on the shores of Chesapeake Bay some eighty years before the settlement of Jamestown. But the Spaniards were more than a little vague on their geography, and, without more evidence, we cannot say just where this occurred.

Anthony of Montesinos went back to Spain after the expedition to Florida. He recruited a large band of missionaries from his home convent in Salamanca, and returned to America. The last record we have of him is his departure for Venezuela, at the head of a large mission band. A tradition says that he was martyred there in 1530.

PETER OF CORDOVA
(d. 1530)

Peter of Cordova stands at the junction between the Old World and the New. "If" is a word that has little substance, but if Peter of Cordova had been a different sort of man, the New World might have had a different concept of liberty. For Peter, of whom we know nothing previous to his profession at the Convent of St. Stephen, in Salamanca, was head of the mission band sent to the Indies in the wake of Christopher Columbus, and he struck the opening blow for liberty in the new land.

His being the superior was almost accidental; the superior of St. Stephen's, Dominic of Mendoza, had been appointed to this grave responsibility. Dominic went to Rome to consult with the master general on the tremendous adventure ahead of them, and had to send back word that he would be detained indefinitely in Rome. Peter of Cordova was appointed in his place. In company with Anthony of Montesinos and Bernard of St. Dominic, Peter set out into the unknown. In 1510 they landed on Hispaniola. The task ahead of them must have seemed staggering to the twenty-eight year old superior and his two companions.

The three Dominicans were received with delight by the Spaniards. Although they were offered hospitality in the guest apartment of one of the big colonial homes, which had already been built, they chose instead to live in one of the miserable little huts designed for the slaves. From this excellent vantage point, they saw slavery in all its ugliness. The Indians were docile and eager to accept Christianity, and they made excellent Christians, but they were unfailingly gullible, and they died, literally by the thousands, at the hands of the conquering Spaniards. In the first twenty years, more than a million Indians died from disease and misery and mistreatment, all brought them by white men. Against this rising tide of horror, the Dominicans fought daily with every weapon they had.

Working together, they composed an apocalyptic sermon that Anthony of Montesinos preached to the slave holders, and as a result of their uncompromising attitude they were left in deadly peril from the enraged Spaniards. In their own land these had been Christian gentlemen, but gold had turned them into prowling beasts. Now, the only real obstacle in their path was the little knot of Dominicans under the courageous Peter of Cordova. They threatened and menaced the priests in every fashion, and wrote monstrous lies about them to the court. Peter and his men, not always receiving support from Church authorities, battled doggedly on. In a slave hut on Hispaniola, where three friars insisted stubbornly that Indians, like all men, had a native dignity and rights which should not be taken away from them, American liberty was first conceived.

The Dominicans, who constituted themselves the protectors of the Indians long before the crown appointed them such, made desperate attempts to explain the situation in Spain. The laws, as they were written, were not unjust for the times, if one concedes the whole institution of slavery. But halfway around the world from Spain, men did not keep the laws, and their greeed was making a shambles of a once-mighty nation. Pleading in vain for help, Peter finally requested that his men be given leave to withdraw entirely from Hispaniola, that they might go to a new part of the Indies, where no gold-seekers would give the lie to the Gospel.

Charles V made Peter a member of the *Audiencia of the Indies*, hoping, no doubt, that the title would appease him. Peter gathered up a new set of missionaries and set sail for the New World. He planned to send a band of missionaries to Cumaná, in Venezuela, and to the half-legendary land of Florida. In the meantime, he erected the new and magnificent Convent of the Holy Cross in Guatemala, and established a training school for missionaries there.

There was not only a diversity of languages to deal with, but an entire new way of life. Young priests, just out from old Spanish cloisters, where learning and piety had ruled for centuries, had to be taught the most elementary woodsmanship and prepared in any number of ways to meet the hazards of the tropical jungles. They had to be conditioned to a lifetime of loneliness among savages who had never heard of European culture, always aware that at any moment a poisoned arrow from the jungle might end their career. Government officials had to be dealt with, and the rights of Church and civil authorities respected. Life in the missions of Central America was as different as life on the moon. Peter had to train them to cope with this kind of apostolic life, and the glorious record of that province proves that he did a good job. The surprising feature of it is that he accomplished this without sacrificing regular observance. True enough, in a mission where there were only three priests, it was not possible to observe all the niceties of the chant and retain all the other customs that were so magnificent at Salamanca; but neither was he training up a relaxed province. The spirit remained, ready to flower into full observance at the first opportunity. In 1520, an expedition was planned for Florida. Peter sent the promised band of missionaries. All of them were lost in a shipwreck.

He also sent Fathers Francis of Cordova and John Carces to Cumaná, in 1514, but a Spanish ship captain enraged the Indians and the two missionaries were killed in reprisal for the sailor's cruelty. When the word reached Peter of Cordova that the Cumaná men had died before reaching their mission, six more preachers volunteered to take their places in Venezuela. Regretfully, he watched them set off without him. In a few years, after they had established a fine mission and built a church, Spanish cruelty again incited the Indians to reprisals, and these priests, too, fell victims for the faith. This time Peter resolved that no one would go but himself; the mission was obviously too dangerous for anyone else to be sacrificed.

Peter and one companion made a foundation on the Island of Marguerite, ten leagues from Cumaná, and it soon became a thriving mission. One day, according to local legends, they were on a routine visit on board a small boat, and the boat suddenly began to move against the current. It had no oars, and the sails had not yet been hoisted. Peter looked up, and there he saw St. Dominic, steering the ship; our Lord at the prow. The boat made away from the land, and, as they looked back, they saw smoke rising from their mission. The Indians had attacked it, killing everyone in it. In memory of their miraculous delivery from death, the province adopted as its coat of arms a ship with St. Dominic and a crucifix at the helm, and the two religious kneeling behind him.

Peter of Cordova, often threatened with martyrdom, died in his bed at Hispaniola, probably in 1530.

THOMAS DE VIO, CARDINAL CAJETAN
(1468-1534)

The battling cardinal, who faced Luther at Augsburg, was one of the most famous men of his time, but today few remember that he was a Dominican, and that he has other claims to fame.

James de Vio was born at Gaeta, in 1468, of a noble family that was prominent in civic affairs. In later years, he was to be called "Cajetan," because of the city of his birth. Early turning to the religious life, he entered the Dominican Order in his native city, taking the name Thomas in religion.

In the Order he was distinguished both for intellectual and spiritual gifts. After a successful course of studies, he taught in the Universities of Padua, Brescia, Mantua, and Milan. He held various posts of responsibility in the Order and, in 1512, was elected master general.

It was a desperate moment in the history of the Church. To lead the Order in the face of the troubles of the time called for exceptional learning, great prudence, and also great sanctity. The laxity of the clergy formed a real stumbling-block to the blocking of heretical teachings, and preaching had become the work of saints. At the chapter of 1513, the new master general exhorted his men: "Let others rejoice in their prerogatives, but unless the study of the sacred sciences commends itself to us, the Order is doomed." Going on record as an uncompromising student and a follower of strict observance, he set about his difficult task. On July the first, 1517, an even greater responsibility befell him; he was appointed cardinal.

The time was ripe for a definitive battle with heresy. Luther's attack on the doctrine of indulgences required an answer. Cardinal Cajetan, as papal legate, was appointed to deal with the matter. Had Luther been sincere in his cry for reform, and personally prepared to submit to lawful authority, the whole affair might have terminated happily. As it was, he had gone too far to turn back, and he would not submit. Cardinal Cajetan has been blamed for lack of tact at this moment of crisis. It is difficult to see how he could have taken any course other than the one he did.

Cajetan was not only a renowned theologian of his time and the counsellor of four popes, he was also a careful and scholarly writer. His *Commentary on the Summa* is a classic still in use, and he wrote other noted works in philosophy and theology. Some of this exacting writing was done during the years of extreme tension, when he was trying to deal with the Lutheran controversy.

Theologians of today are re-reading the writings of Cajetan and finding that not only was he a profound and careful theologian, but also that he was a thinker far in advance of his times. Some of his conclusions, unappreciated by his own contemporaries, are eagerly seized upon by modern students, who feel that he spoke for our century even better than for his own.

Cardinal Cajetan died on August the ninth, 1534, and was buried in the Church of the Minerva. The fact that he and his writings have been the target of bitter criticism by Protestant writers should not surprise us. Anyone who engages in such a controversy is bound to make enemies. We should be proud to claim such an uncompromising warrior as a member of the Order of Truth.

BLESSED ADRIAN FORTESCUE
(1476-1539)

Not often do we have a man who is the interesting combination of Justice of the Peace, Knight of St. John of Jerusalem, and Dominican Tertiary. Such a one, however, was Blessed Adrian Fortesque, who was beatified in 1895 by Pope Leo XIII. His feast is commemorated yearly by the Dominicans in England.

Sir Adrian Fortescue was born in Devonshire, in 1476, of a family closely related to Anne Boleyn. During the difficult years of England's apostasy, he observed the obligations of his religion and served his sovereign faithfully, as far as his conscience allowed him. He went twice to France with the armies of the king.

A man of importance in his country's affairs, he conducted himself as a Catholic gentleman. He was Justice of the Peace for the county of Oxford, and attended Queen Catherine of Aragon at her coronation. A faithful Catholic and a keen student of affairs, he must have grieved to see the destruction caused by his pretty young cousin, Anne Boleyn. At about this time, he became a Dominican Tertiary and began to set his affairs in order against the inevitable reckoning to come.

He was arrested in 1534, and for some time confined in Marshalsea prison. No charge was made, and no reason was given for his release; perhaps it was politically embarrassing to have a belted knight of blameless life locked up for no good reason. He used the little time left him to provide for his five children, and watched with a sad heart as Sir Thomas More and Bishop Fisher were executed.

Four years later, with just as little reason as before, Sir Adrian was arrested and placed in the Tower. The sentence of death was passed upon him, because of "treason and sedition . . . and having most traitorously refused his allegiance to the crown," an elegantly worded lie that was obvious to all beholders.

Sir Adrian Fortescue was beheaded on July the ninth, 1539, and was honored from the very day of his death as a martyr by the people of his own country. The Knights of Malta kept the day of his death as a special feast for centuries, and finally petitioned for his formal beatification. The petition was granted in 1895.

BLESSED DOMINIC SPADAFORA
(1450-1540)

Blessed Dominic Spadafora was one of the glories of the Church in Sicily in the fifteenth century. He had a long career in the Order, for he lived to be ninety.

Dominic was born in Sicily, of an old and noble family. His father was Baron of Miletto, and members of the family were connected with the nobility of Venice and Palermo. As a child, Dominic attended school in the Convent of St. Rita in Palermo, which had been founded some years before by Blessed Peter Geremia. Exactly when he became a member of the community there, we do not know. He was sent to Padua for his theology and received his degree there in 1479. He returned to Palermo and for some time lived quietly, conducting classes for the brethren and the secular clergy.

In 1487, Dominic, making a distinguished defense of a thesis in Venice, came to the notice of the master general. Considered one of the promising young men of the province, Dominic was made the socius of the master general and, in 1493, was sent to found a convent dedicated to Our Lady of Grace in Monte Cerigone. Here he remained in retirement until his death.

What we have considered to be the usual virtues of a Dominican friar were practiced faithfully by Dominic Spadafora, but it is difficult to find anything unusual in his life. He spent most of his Dominican life in the Convent of Our Lady of Grace, directing societies and confraternities, zealous for regular observance and scrupulously exact in his own behavior. The convent where he lived was never large nor very important, and, though he seems to have had a superior intellect, he was evidently contented with complete obscurity. This in itself is sufficiently unusual.

Dominic Spadafora died in 1540, after revealing to the community that he knew he was about to die. He attended all religious exercises up to the hour of his death, and he died as every Dominican hopes he will—the community was around him, singing the "Salve Regina." Benedict XV beatified him in 1921.

MARGARET FERNANDEZ
(d. 1540)

The singular honor of being buried at the feet of St. Dominic—or, at any rate, at the foot of his tomb—belongs not to one of his first companions, nor to a canonized saint, but to a Portuguese Tertiary who spent her life as a pilgrim. Her name was Margaret Fernandez.

Margaret was born of poor parents in Portugal, in the latter half of the fifteenth century. Her father died when she was very small, and, soon afterwards, her mother, tucking the little girl away in a convent, married again. Margaret, left to her own resources, settled down and learned to pray as the sisters did. She might have been happy to stay there, but as soon as she was old enough to marry, one of her aunts arranged a match for her and took her to Lisbon to marry a workman. The man had a disposition to wander and little ambition. After a few years, he went off to seek his fortune in Africa, leaving Margaret with their small child.

Margaret went into service in a wealthy family, and she was happy and beloved as governess to the children of the house. However, her own little girl died. Later, receiving word that her husband had died in Africa, Margaret decided to take things into her own hands. A community of Dominican

Tertiaries was just in process of formation in a convent near the gate of Lisbon. After prolonged fasting and praying, in order to know God's will, Margaret presented herself at the door of the convent and asked to be admitted. They received her, first as a servant, then as a Tertiary, with permission to wear the habit publicly.

At th:s time, the plague struck Lisbon, bringing terror to the gay and wealthy city, for on its several invasions in the past century it had left thousands dead or maimed. Nearly everyone who could get out of the city did so. Margaret might have gone away to the country, but she elected to stay and nurse the plague-stricken. She made herself the servant of the sick, and no task was too hard or repulsive for her to do.

When the plague had burned itself out, Margaret had decided what she wanted to do; she wished to go on a pilgrimage to the Holy Land. She wrote to her former employer, informing him of her intentions and asking him, for the love of God, for a mantle to wear on her journey. He sent her a pilgrim's mantle and begged her prayers for his family.

Margaret set out, in 1526, to make the journey on foot. Three pious women had joined her by the time she reached Barcelona; there she wrote a farewell letter to her employer, and she told him that she was changing her name to Paula.

Proceeding through the Midi to northern Italy, Margaret finally reached Rome, where she spent some time visiting the tombs of the Apostles. Reaching Venice, she sailed for Jerusalem. Here she remained for many years—the chronicle does not say how many—and then returned to Italy. Having reached Bologna, she had a revelation that here was the place her wandering feet would rest.

In her remaining years here, Margaret lived an extraordinary life, full of heavenly favors. Outwardly, it was a grimly penitential life. She lived in a cave just outside the city walls, where she slept on a pile of straw. At the first streak of dawn, she was up to pray, and, as soon as the gates were opened, she hurried to the Church of St. Dominic and spent the day in prayer. She attended all the Masses and all the Offices, and, in the intervening time, she prayed at the tomb of St. Dominic. When the church was locked up for the siesta hour, she would sally forth to beg a crust of bread. (This, it seems, is the only thing she ate.) Winter or summer, in stifling heat and freezing cold, she followed the same program. One bitterly cold day, her confessor begged her to put on some shoes, but she refused. As he had already had evidence of her extraordinary gifts, he did not press the point.

The winter of 1540 was exceptionally severe, and Margaret died in January, during the bitterest cold. She was buried in the church attached to the convent, in Bologna, but soon a sweet perfume began to surround the grave. They moved her then, and laid her at the foot of the tomb of St. Dominic, where she had spent so many years in prayer, and there she remained.

SANCTES PAGNINI
(1470-1541)

One of the ablest Scripture scholars, in an age devoted to that science, was the Dominican, Sanctes Pagnini. He was one of the first men in history to apply a scientific study of language to the translation of Scripture.

Sanctes Pagnini was born in Lucca, in 1470, and entered the Order at Fiesole, in 1486, under the impetus of Savonarola's reform. His piety and learning were already famous, and he soon established himself as a scholar of first rank in Scripture and in oriental languages. His excellence was so well known that he was called by the pope to occupy the first chair of oriental languages in the Oriental Academy at Rome. Here he taught Hebrew, Chaldaic, and Arabic, and built up a tradition of careful scholarship that was new to Christian students of oriental sciences.

His main work took thirty years of careful research and painstaking scholarship. He was to make a new Latin translation of the entire Bible directly from the ancient manuscripts of Hebrew and Greek, using the Hebrew pronunciation of names which others had Latinized. He had a good knowledge of the rules of Hebrew poetry, and its use enriched his translation. His work had the approval and the financial support of Popes Leo X and Clement VII, but a series of delays held up publication, and only the Psalter had seen publication at the time of his death.

On his way to Avignon, seeking funds for his life-work, Sanctes Pagnini was enough of a Christian to see that others were in need, too; he asked one of his best patrons to build a hospital for the plague-stricken in Lyons. Needing money as badly as he did, the request is indicative of his sense of values. He was not the cloistered bookworm that his great works would indicate; he preached almost continuously, in Florence, Rome, and Lyons, against the Vaudois and the Lutherans.

Sanctes Pagnini died in 1541, and was buried in the choir of the Dominican church in Lyons. Sixtus of Siena, the convert friend of Pope Pius V, wrote a glowing eulogy of the work of Pagnini, calling his death a public tragedy. Sixtus was himself a prominent Hebrew scholar and a converted Jew. He commended Pagnini on his careful scholarship in translating from Hebrew into Latin, adding that the most able Rabbis had praised his knowledge of Hebrew.

Pagnini also did a *New Testament* from the Greek, using the authority of the Vulgate. He published a number of glossaries, explaining Hebrew and Chaldaic words—an *Introduction to Sacred Scripture*, dealing with the obscure and figurative expressions used in the Bible; and a six-volume work, a *Commentary on the Hebrew, Greek, and Latin Interpreters of the Pentateuch and the Psalter*. Sacred scholars today still use his system of numbering verses. His works, often reprinted, are outdated by later studies, but are still important as the first of their kind.

YVO MAYEUX
(1462-1541)

Yvo Mayeux, bishop of Rennes, lived in a glittering age, and he himself was a colorful actor on the stage of history.

Yvo was born in Brittany, in 1462, of a family of well-to-do tradesmen. Serious, even as a small child, he grew up to be a scholar, and finished both literary and philosophical studies at Morlaix before joining the Order. The Dominican convent at Morlaix was not too fervent, and the relaxed life was not inspiring. However, the house was soon in the throes of reform, and he saw that even a few fervent brothers could raise the tone of a community, and that the rule suffered no damage from the weakness of men. He entered the Order in 1483 and became a model novice. After his ordination in 1489, he was sent to the convent of Our Lady of Good News, at Rennes, where he became a good preacher, a famous confessor, and a man with a reputation for kindness to the sick and the poor.

His fame as a confessor reached the Duchess Anne of Brittany, who came to him with a complicated problem. She was a pawn in the game of royal marriage, and her hand was sought by three men, all eligible: Maximilian, who was in love with her; Louis, duke of Orleans, whom she loved; Charles VIII of France, who had more to offer her father in a marriage settlement. Which should she marry? Yvo advised her to marry Charles—a rather unromantic settlement. But Charles soon died, and Anne was free to marry the duke of Orleans, as she had wanted to do in the first place. With that curious reasoning so often noticeable in women, she decided that Yvo had given her excellent advice, and therefore she wanted him for her chaplain at court.

For fourteen years, Yvo was court chaplain. Always humble and retiring, he kept up his religious exercises in spite of the turmoil around him, and managed to guide some of the royal alms into worthy causes. His own salary he sent intact to the prior of St. Jacques, in Paris. He was made prior of the royal convent of St. Maximin, in Provence, but had to govern it from a distance. When the See of Rennes fell vacant, he was appointed bishop. He wept bitterly, but everyone else in Brittany rejoiced. The poor and the sick realized that at last they had a friend in a place of authority.

As bishop, Yvo continued to wear his Dominican habit. He must have been a severe trial to his housekeeper, as he ate very little, kept all the Dominican fasts, and would not use linen sheets. When plague struck the city, he sent out nearly all the furnishings in the house, all the medicines, and most of the food, to help the sick. After the plague had passed, many people were penniless, and many children were homeless. To provide for those who needed help, he set up a workshop in the country where wealthy people could make clothes for the poor, to the benefit of both.

For twenty-six years, Yvo was the beloved and penitential shepherd of the flock of Rennes. The honors offered him by Anne and the court never turned his attention from the poor and the sick; sometimes he did not even go to receive the honors, which made Anne very angry.

When the master general came to Brittany to visit the tomb of St. Vincent Ferrer, he was taken ill and died there. Yvo gave him the last sacraments. He was called upon to officiate at many state affairs, but his greatest work was among the poorest of his flock. When he died, in 1541, they wailed as though the world had come to an end, because they had lost their dearest friend.

As the brothers were preparing his body for burial, they discovered a cross shining on his chest; it did not seem to be carved in, and it did not come from outside—it just shone there. Word of this got around, and thousands of people came to view the prodigy. Several cures were reported at his tomb, and when it was opened, in 1596, the body was found intact. In 1775, a new cathedral was built, and the tomb was lost in the construction.

VINCENT OF VALVERDE
(d. 1543)

Vincent was born of a family that was both rich and virtuous. His father was closely associated with Pizarro, and probably helped to finance the expedition to New Spain. Vincent studied at St. Stephen's College in Salamanca and entered the Order at Seville, after he had finished his college courses. He quietly taught philosophy and theology in various houses of the Order for some years. When the king, in arranging the expedition to Peru, asked for chaplains to accompany the army, Vincent volunteered, and left Spain in 1530 for the New World.

Once arrived in America, the chaplains were dispersed with various branches of the army. Vincent of Valverde was with the group that went to Peru from Panama. In the sorry business of the conquest, his name stands out for fairness and for mercy. He could not rescue the Inca from the Spaniards, but he fought long and hard to do so. Against the greed of the gold-hungry Spaniards, the Dominican held out for mercy and justice to the Indians. There is one scene in the life of Pizarro in which historians give a prominent place to Vincent of Valverde, and which they usually misunderstand.

It was the occasion on which an Inca stood bound before the army, and Vincent demanded that the prisoner be unbound and allowed to state his case. The Inca then asked the missionary on what he based his claims as representative of the true God. Vincent handed him his breviary. The Inca, scorning this, threw it on the ground. Pizzaro, waiting hopefully for an excuse, took this as a deadly insult to religion and had the Inca chained. What the historians do not tell is that Vincent tried to convince Pizarro to send the Inca to Spain and give him a fair trial. It was a great blow to him when the Inca was put to death.

Sickened by the injustices he had seen, Vincent determined to go back to Spain to lay the matter before the Council of the Indies, in an effort to prevent the slaughter of the Indians. The Council listened to him, but the conquerors had friends at court, and they managed to drag out the business for three years. At the end of this time, the city of Cuzco was made the Episcopal See, and Vincent was appointed the first bishop.

He returned to Peru with the title "Protector of the Indians," and, theoretically, he had the right to punish those who persecuted the Indians. His arrival in Cuzco was a signal for much activity on the part of the colonizers. We are not surprised to find that the Indians loved him. The more surprising thing is that, in the unpopular job of opposing the colonizers, he also won the love and respect of the Spaniards. It was a long and difficult struggle for justice for the Indians, and Vincent gave most of his strength to the task. When the situation seemed well in hand, he went looking for a harder job.

He found this in a mission to the Puno Indians, who had the reputation of being the most barbarous people in South America. They lived in the jungles near Quito, and they had the grisly habit of cutting the heads off white men. Even Vincent, who seems to have thought well of everybody, admitted that one would have to first make them into human beings before making them Christians. The devil was active among the savages, sometimes in visible form.

Vincent came to grips with this unpleasant situation, but he had not long to work among them. He began his work vigorously by overthrowing their idols. One morning, as he was saying Mass, they killed him. Being cannibals, they proceeded to eat him; but they, in turn, were attacked by wild lions from the jungle, killing those who had murdered the priest.

There was a tradition for many years that no crop ever grew again in the place the missionary had been killed, but a great harvest of souls was eventually reaped there.

BLESSED LUCY OF NARNI
(1476-1544)

Lucy was born in 1476, of a pious Italian family. Very early, it became evident to them that this child was set for something unusual in life, for some of her heavenly favors were visible. When Lucy was five years old, she had a vision of Our Blessed Lady; two years later, Our Lady came again, bringing St. Dominic, who gave her the scapular. At the age of twelve, she made private vows and, even at this early age, had determined to become a Dominican. However, family affairs were to make this a difficult goal. Lucy's father died, leaving her to the care of an uncle. He felt that the best way to dispose of a pretty niece was to marry her off as soon as possible.

The efforts of her uncle to get Lucy successfully married form a colorful chapter in the life of the Blessed Lucy. At one time, he arranged a big family party, and his choice of Lucy's husband was there. He thought it better not to tell Lucy what he had in mind, because she had such queer ideas, so he presented the young man to her in front of the entire assembly. The young man made a valiant attempt to place a ring on Lucy's finger, and he was thoroughly slapped for his pains.

The next time, the uncle approached the matter with more tact, arranging a marriage with Count Pietro, of Milan, who was not a stranger to the family. Lucy was, in fact, very fond of him, but she had resolved on living a religious life. The strain of the situation made her seriously ill. During her illness, Our Lady appeared to her again, accompanied by St. Dominic and St. Catherine, and told her to go ahead with the marriage as a legal contract, but to explain to Pietro that she was bound to her vow of virginity and must keep it. When Lucy recovered, the matter was explained to Pietro, and the marriage was solemnized.

Lucy's life now became that of the mistress of a large and busy household. She took great care to instruct the servants in their religion and soon became known for her benefactions to the poor. Pietro, to do him justice, never seems to have objected when his young wife gave away clothes and food, nor when she performed great penances. He knew that she wore a hair-shirt under her rich clothing, and that she spent most of the night in prayer and working for the poor. He even made allowances for the legend told him by the servants, that Sts. Catherine, Agnes, and Agnes of Montepulciano came to help her make bread for the poor. However, when a talkative servant one day informed him that Lucy was entertaining a handsome young man, who seemed to be an old friend, Pietro took his sword and went to see. He was embarrassed to find Lucy contemplating a large and beautiful crucifix, and he was further confused when the servant told him that was the young man.

When Lucy departed for the desert to become an anchorite, and returned next day, saying that St. Dominic had brought her home, Pietro's patience finally gave out. He had his young wife locked up. Here she remained for the season of Lent; sympathetic servants brought her food until Easter. Perhaps they had both decided that Lucy could not live the life God had planned for her in Pietro's house. She returned to her mother's house and put on the habit of a Dominican tertiary.

Shortly after this, Lucy went to Viterbo and joined a group of Third Order sisters. She tried very hard to hide her spiritual favors, because they complicated her life wherever she went. She had the stigmata visibly, and she was usually in ecstasy, which meant a steady stream of curious people who wanted to question her, investigate her, or just stare at her. Even the sisters were nervous about her methods of prayer. Once they called in the bishop, and he watched with them for twelve hours, while Lucy went through the drama of the Passion.

The bishop hesitated to pass judgment and called in the inquisition. From here, she was referred directly to the pope. After talking to her, the pope pronounced in her favor and told her to go home and pray for him. Here the hard-pressed Pietro had his final appearance in Lucy's life. He made a last effort to persuade Lucy to change her plans and come back to him. Finally he decided to become a Franciscan, and, in later years, he was a famous preacher.

When Lucy returned to Viterbo, she may have thought her troubles were over, but they were just getting a good start. The duke of Ferrara, in the manner of other wealthy nobles with a guilty conscience, decided to build a monastery and, hearing of the fame of the mystic of Viterbo, demanded that she come there and be prioress. Lucy had been praying for some time that a means would be found to build a new convent of strict observance, and she agreed to go to the new convent at Narni.

This touched off a two-year battle between the towns. Viterbo had the mystic and did not want to lose her; the duke of Ferrara sent his troops to take her by force, and much blood was shed before she was finally brought to Narni. The shock and grief of this violent action was a new trial for Lucy. The duke sent his daughter-in-law, Lucrezia Borgia, to find postulants for the new convent. The records say, sedately: "Many of these did not persevere."

The duke of Ferrara liked to show off the convent he had founded. He brought all his guests to see it. One time, he arrived with a troop of dancing girls, who had been entertaining at a banquet, and demanded that Lucy show them her stigmata and, if possible, go into an ecstasy. It is not surprising that such events would upset religious life, and that sooner or later something would have to be done about it. Some of the sisters, naturally, thought it was Lucy's fault.

They petitioned the bishop, and he sent six nuns from the Second Order to reform the community. Lucy's foundation was of the Third Order; exactly what the difference was, we do not know. The Second Order nuns, according to the chronicle, "brought in the very folds of their veils the seed of war"; nuns of the Second Order wore black veils, a privilege not allowed to Third Order Sisters.

The uneasy episode ended when one of the visitors was made prioress. Lucy was placed on penance. The nature of her fault is not mentioned, nor is there any explanation of the fact that, until her death, thirty-nine years later, she was never allowed to speak to anyone but a confessor, who was chosen by the prioress. The Dominican provincial, probably nervous for the prestige of the Order, would not let any member of the Order go to see her. Her stigmata disappeared, too late to do her any good, and vindictive companions said: "See, she was a fraud all the time." When she died, in 1544, people thought she had been dead for many years.

It is hard to understand how anyone *not* a saint could have so long endured such a life. Lucy's only friends during her thirty-nine years of exile were heavenly ones; the Dominican, Catherine of Racconigi, sometimes visited her—evidently by bi-location—and her heavenly friends often came to brighten her lonely cell.

Lucy was buried without honors, but miracles occurring at her tomb soon made it necessary to transfer her relics to a more accessible place. She was re-buried, first in the monastery church, later in the Cathedral. In 1720, she was beatified.

FRANCIS OF VITTORIA
(d. 1546)

> "It is not to be doubted that the world is in a certain sense a single community, and possesses the right to prescribe equitable and appropriate laws for its members, like those which constitute the law of nations."

This statement, which breathes of mid-twentieth century and the ideals of the United Nations, is from the works of a famous sixteenth-century Dominican, who can well be called the father of international law. His name is Francis of Vittoria and his reputation, though it was great in his own day, has recently had a renaissance, because of world interest in the community of nations.

The exact date of Francis of Vittoria's birth is not known. Since he was equipped to accept the chair of theology at the University of Salamanca in 1526, it would be reasonable to suppose that he was born about the time of the discovery of America.

One of the results of this event is that it raised questions which never before had needed discussion, causing a great deal of theological speculation on the subject of the colonization of the vast lands which bore the corporate title of "The Indies." The most celebrated defenders of the Indians in this vast contest were to be Dominicans: Las Casas and Anthony of Montesino are champions who will always be revered for their courageous work. Behind their battle lay carefully thought-out arguments, the solid structure of theology, and the immutable laws that govern the creatures of God. The principal thinker in this new field was Francis of Vittoria; his authority was St. Thomas Aquinas.

Francis said: "Infidels cannot be deprived of civil power or sovereignty simply because they are infidels." This was an unpopular position in Spain, a country just rising from Moslem domination, and now, apparently, determined to plunder the property of their Moslem neighbors. Regarding the New World, Francis stated, unequivocally: "The Spaniards had no more right over the Indians than the latter would have over the Spaniards if they had come to Spain." This did not set well with the great merchant princes who expected to make vast fortunes by enslaving the Indians. When we read the discouraging chronicles of the colonial period in the Indies, we can see the two opposing sides quite clearly; on the one hand, the greed of the conquerors, who justified their acts of plunder by saying: "The Indians have no rights"; and on the other hand, Las Casas and Montesinos maintaining—on the strength of the reasoning of Francis of Vittoria—that the Indians were children of God, even as the Spaniards were.

The man, Francis of Vittoria, is completely lost behind his achievements. Not only do we not know when he was born, we do not know where he entered the Order, though it was most probably at Salamanca. His reputation was so great at that university that superior students from all over Spain were sent to study the new subject of international law under him. Among his famous students were Bartholomew Medina, Martin de Ledesma, and the two Dominicans who distinguished themselves at the Council of Trent, Melchior Cano and Dominic Soto. To them, and to others of his students, we are grateful for what we know of Vittoria's work, for they wrote down the material that he presented in class. He does not seem to have written any of his lectures, nor did he seem to have any idea of their permanence. His reputation was so great that he was consulted on all affairs bearing upon international justice. In 1530, when the question of the divorce of Henry VIII of England and Catherine of Aragon was discussed, the Spanish king consulted Vittoria about it, and the answer he received was that the marriage was valid and could not be nullified.

To us there is no novelty in the idea: "It is unlawful to kill the innocent in war," but this was a world-shaking notion at the time it was proposed by Francis of Vittoria. He also stated flatly: "Slavery is not a legitimate consequence of war, that hostages cannot rightfully be put to death because of a breach of faith by an enemy," and that it is unjust to deliver up a city to be sacked without the greatest necessity. He laid down what have been called *The Three Rules of a Just War*. Since his day, his ideas have been generally adopted among the Christian nations. Both the Monroe Doctrine and the League of Nations owe a debt to this Spanish scholar of the sixteenth century.

Francis of Vittoria died in 1546. Many years after his death his works began to receive the notice they deserve. The whole sad chapter of the colonization of the Indies might have been quite different had the conquerors abided by the just principles enunciated by their famous countryman. We today, concerned with an international family of nations whose interests often conflict, would do well to study the laws laid down so clearly four hundred years ago by our own religious brother who, like St. Dominic, built for the future. It is well to remember his statement: "The violators of international law sin mortally as well in peace as in war and that . . . it is not lawful for any nation to refuse to observe the law of nations."

BLESSED CATHERINE OF RACCONIGI
(1487-1547)

Catherine de Mattei was born in Piedmont, a little village so desolated by war that most of its people were starving. Her father had been a locksmith in better days, and, left unemployed by the war, he became depressed and quarrelsome. Her mother, who worked to support the family, wove coarse cloth on a loom in her own home. When they were growing up, Catherine and her brother became accustomed to the sound of family quarrels, the endless clack of the loom, and the bitter complaints of their parents, who resented the illness and poverty that were their lot.

This is surprising soil for sanctity, but at the age of five, little Catherine began the mystical experiences which were to continue through her whole life. Our Lady appeared to her as she was praying alone in her tiny room and told the child that Jesus wished to take her for His spouse. Accompanied by many saints and angels, among whom were St. Catherine of Siena and St. Peter Martyr, Jesus appeared as a child of Catherine's own age, and Our Lady placed on her finger the ring of the espousals. The ring remained visible to Catherine for the rest of her life, although it could not be seen by others.

From this time on, Catherine was favored with frequent ecstasies. Our Lord always appeared to her as if He were her own age. He conversed with her, taught her to pray, and several times took her heart away to cleanse and purify it. One day He appeared to her carrying His cross, and she offered to help Him. He let the cross rest for a moment on her shoulder, and it inflicted a wound that lasted for the rest of her life. She received the stigmata, though it remained invisible to others and, at her request, it was only revealed by her confessor after her death.

Our Lord performed a number of miracles for His friend. He made a dish she had broken whole again, and gave her money and food when their poverty was extreme. Our Lady and the saints came to console her in times of trial. At moments of great sorrow, Catherine derived great consolation from the aspiration, "Jesus, my hope!"

Catherine desired to enter the Dominican Order, but her request met much opposition. She was finally received as a Tertiary. Her mystical experiences had roused a storm of gossip among her neighbors, who were terrified at the lights and sounds coming from her room. The devil, who feared her influence over souls, stirred up more and more trouble until actual persecution developed. Even the fathers of her own Order would have nothing to do with her, and eventually she had to leave town and go elsewhere.

In her new home, in Racconigi, Catherine soon became the counsellor of the rich and poor who flocked to her for advice, prayers, and, sometimes, material help. She was in almost continual ecstasy, and the particular object of her prayers was the salvation of soldiers dying in battle. She was often tortured by the devil, who appeared to her in many forms. Her weapon against him was the aspiration already mentioned.

Numerous miracles were performed during her life and after her death. A cult arose at her tomb almost immediately, and even those who had persecuted her bitterly were made aware of her sanctity and retracted their words.

ANTHONY OF VALDEVIESCO
(d. 1549)

One of the bright spots in the dark drama of the Spanish conquest of the New World is the story of Anthony Valdeviesco, who died for the faith in Nicaragua in 1549.

Anthony was born in Castile, and received the Dominican habit around the year 1500, when the New World fever was just beginning to grip the youth of Spain. Side by side with the adventurers, who planned to make a fortune in the Indies, were the priests, who hoped to convert the Indians. Anthony volunteered for this hazardous mission and sailed with a group bound for Peru. After arriving in the Indies, he was assigned to Nicaragua.

For some time, he fought the unequal battle against the greed of the conquerors. He studied the Indian languages, teaching most of the day and praying most of the night, as other Dominicans did. But all the power of arms and money were ranged against the missionaries, and the Dominicans fought almost alone for the rights of the vanishing Indians. At last, after several public rebukes had brought nothing but more violence from the guilty conquerors, Anthony sailed for Spain to lay the case before Charles V.

The emperor listened to Anthony, as he had listened to the other Dominicans who had begged him to save the Indians. Then he named Anthony bishop of Nicaragua, and proceeded to wash his hands of the situation.

In returning to Nicaragua, Anthony knew that he had received a death sentence; only time was necessary for carrying it out. He was met with fury by the guilty Spanish officers, who tried to keep him out of the capital city by force. He boldly came in and set himself up in the cathedral, where he preached openly, mincing no words. He established the inquisition and finally placed two cities under interdict.

To the Spanish officers, who were most intimately concerned with Nicaragua, there was only one thing to do—kill the bishop. Plans for the assassination became so openly talked about that word of the officers planning a sacrilegious murder was carried back to Spain. Charles V sent back a half-hearted reprimand, but it was already too late. The governor's son and other well-born Christians, who should have known better, plied themselves with liquor and inflammatory remarks until they were nerved up to the horrible deed. Then, drunkenly shouting that they would free the Indies from tyranny, they forced their way into the bishop's house and fell upon him.

Two other Dominicans and a secular priest were with the bishop when the assassins broke in. One was wounded, two were killed. The man who attacked the bishop fled, screaming with terror, when his dagger struck a bone and would not penetrate. The dying bishop went to confession to the only living priest, then offered his life for the salvation of the Indians and for peace. He died on February 26, 1549.

A short time after this, disaster overtook the capital city and the men who had planned the murder. A nearby volcano erupted, and fiery death rained down on the fertile valley, leaving it a desolate waste. The city that had killed its bishop never rose from the ashes, and the later capital was built seven leagues away.

DOMINIC OF BETANZAS
(1480-1549)

This most famous of Mexican missionaries was born in Leon, of noble and wealthy parents, in 1480. He was baptized Francis. His parents sent him to the University of Salamanca, where he met one Peter of Arconada, who would be a lifelong friend. The two young students did volunteer nursing in a nearby hospital, and they pursued whatever other works of piety and charity came their way. They decided to become hermits.

Francis, going to the Benedictine abbey at Monteserrat, was advised to settle in one of the near-by caves. Peter found his hermitage near Naples, and for some time they pursued this singular way to perfection. Just why they both decided that this was not God's will for them, we do not know. After three years in the cave at Naples, Peter returned to Spain and began searching for his friend. The Dominicans at Salamanca did not know where he was; Peter kept on going, inquiring in likely places. At his own home, Peter asked for alms and was not recognized—an indication of how greatly he had changed since student days. Failing to find Francis anywhere, Peter returned to Salamanca and received the Dominican habit.

In the course of time, Francis Betanzas also abandoned his cave and came to Salamanca. Because of the persuasive arguments of his friend Peter, Francis joined the Dominicans. He was given the name Dominic.

After his ordination, Dominic was sent to the Indies to join Peter of Cordova, who was always looking for likely missionaries. Dominic rapidly learned the languages of the missions and worked with great success among the Indians, although at this time he, oddly enough, shared the belief held by the conquerors, that the Indians had no rights. He was to shed many tears over this in later years, and, on his deathbed, he dictated a repudiation of his first belief.

When the first mission band was organized to go to Mexico, Dominic of Betanzas was given charge of it. The first Mexican mission had very bad luck. Five of the men died almost immediately, and four others, discouraged, returned to Hispaniola. This left only three: Dominic of Betanzas; a young deacon, whose name we do not know; and another deacon, Vincent de las Casas, nephew of the great missionary. In time, the Mexican province was to become one of the glories of the Order, and it would give the Church many scholars and saintly priests. However, the first years must have been heart-breaking. Until the two young deacons could be ordained, Dominic was the only priest. They were desperately poor. They kept the rule in its entirety, which meant that they must traverse vast distances on foot.

Dominic opened a novitiate, and soon it was filled with many Spanish and Mexican novices. He had great charm and could present the cause of the missions with an irresistible appeal. The province grew rapidly. After a few years, Dominic was obliged to go to Rome to petition that the province of Mexico should be separated from that of the West Indies.

This request, which seems reasonable enough to anyone who will look at a map of the Western hemisphere, struck the authorities in Rome as a dangerous bit of independence. They debated long and carefully. Eventually they gave the restless missionary the permission he needed.

While the question was being debated, Dominic lost no time. He made a pilgrimage to the shrine of St. Mary Magdalen, asking her help with his mission. He spent three wonderful nights there on his knees, rapt in prayer, reveling in the chance of praying in a peaceful setting. Rounding up a huge band of volunteers, he returned to Mexico—full of enthusiasm and plans to expand the mission. One of his first steps was to set up a school in which the Indian dialects could be taught to the incoming missionaries. This seems routine procedure to us now, but it was an innovation at the time.

Once more Dominic of Betanzas made the Atlantic crossing, in an attempt to escape the appointment as bishop of Guatemala. Ill and tired, he died in Spain, in 1549, leaving a reputation as one of the finest missionaries who worked on our continent.

LUIS CANCERI DE BARBASTRO
(d. 1549)

Fray Luis was most probably born in Barbastro, as his family name indicates; he was, at least, born in the province of Aragon, and his early years in the Order were spent there. The year of his birth we do not know exactly; most likely it was around 1500.

At this time Spain was primarily interested in colonizing the New World. Believing that the Christian nations had an obligation towards the savages of the new lands, the Spanish monasteries sent out a steady stream of missionaries to New Spain. At some time before 1532, Fray Luis joined one of the parties bound for the Indies and arrived in Hispaniola. After some work among the various tribes of Indians in the West Indies, he was sent to the newly-erected convent of St. Dominic, in Guatemala.

Here the ardent young missionary met at firsthand the situation that was to cause the death of so many missionaries and the eventual failure of the Spanish missions in Central America—the insatiable greed of the conquerors who had come to the New World only to make their fortunes. On every hand, the priests saw their work undone and the natives betrayed by white men. The Indians were enslaved and mistreated to the extent that, in one generation, they had become a vanishing race. In 1534, Fray Luis joined in the uneven struggle.

Guatemala was known as the "Land of War," and, even among its savage neighbors, it held a reputation for the cruelty and intractability of its people. The Spaniards had tried several times to conquer it, failing miserably. The natives would not even let the traders into their lands, for they had heard about the Spanish persuasiveness that ended in slavery. By the time of Fray Luis' arrival in Guatemala, there was an almost superstitious fear of these Indians. No one, it was said, could go into the "Land of War" and come out alive.

It is not too clear whose idea it was to conquer the Indians with song. Both Fray Luis and Fray Las Casas were involved in the plan; some authorities give the cerdit to one, some to the other. However, it was a brilliant plan. It consisted, first of all, in exacting a promise from the colonial authorities that no Spanish trader or soldier would set foot in the land of Guatemala while the friars were attempting to convert the natives; further, that the Spaniards were to promise that they would leave the Indians alone, making no move to enslave them. The friars said that they would conquer the "Land of War" if the authorities would guarantee these stipulations.

The next step was to learn the Quiche language, the native tongue of the warlike tribes they intended to reach. Fray Luis had a real gift for languages, and he and Fray Las Casas translated the principal mysteries of our faith into Quiche. They could not, of course, translate the whole Bible, but they did the story of the creation, the fall of man and his redemption, the foundation of the Church, and the Gospels. They wrote these tremendous truths into rhymed couplets which could be sung to the accompaniment of the mournful-sounding flutes and ocarinas that the Indians loved, and set to the rhythm of the native drums. It was a dazzling accomplishment. Today it would be hailed all over the world as a remarkably effective device, but these busy and fervent apostles considered it simply a means to reach the darkened minds of the savage tribes who knew nothing of salvation.

But the preparation was not finished. With a patience that could come only from heaven, the friars found four young Indians of a friendly tribe and trained them to sing the long and intricate song of salvation. The young men had excellent memories and were delighted with the ballad. When they had been coached sufficiently, the friars sent them out into the hills, giving them a supply of trade goods and a blessing. The whole venture was now up to the four young Indians.

The savage Quiches made no hostile move against the four traders; they were not afraid of other Indians. They sat and listened with great interest while the visitors sang their long narrative ballad telling about God and man. Asking questions after it was finished, they were told that no one could tell them any more but the Christian priests. There was a long, fiery discussion among the elders of the tribe, and, at last—perhaps out of pure curiosity—the savage Quiches sent delegates to the Spanish convent, asking for the friars.

The two friars who had worked out the long ballad of salvation went gladly into the deadly jungles to meet the people of the "Land of War." In a short time, they converted great numbers of these people, and the fierce warriors, who had stopped an army, knelt humbly at the feet of the friars. Yet, once again Spanish officers did not keep their word, and, in a few months, the same evils of greed and debauchery were ruining the land which the hopeful friars had renamed Vera Paz—"Land of Peace."

Luis Canceri made several voyages to Spain on behalf of the Indians. He had a distinguished career as a missionary in Central America. But our reason for remembering him is that he was the first Dominican martyr of Florida.

It had long been the dream of the Spanish colonists to send settlers to the land of Florida. Several such expeditions had ended in disaster. In 1549, a new expedition was fitted out and sent to Tampa Bay. Fray Luis was one of several missionaries in the group.

What they found in Florida was not encouraging. The natives were seething with resentment against the Spaniards. They had trouble even in getting an interpreter, and, finally—much against the better judgment of Fray Luis— they took an Indian woman to interpret for them. The woman had the Christian name Magdalen. She and three members of the expedition were landed to make contact with the natives. The three white men were promptly whisked off into the jungle. Magdalen followed the shore coastline. After several days, the captain's nerve gave out. Someone brought him word that the three men had been murdered and that Magdalen was trying to lead the ship into an ambush. The captain said that he was going back to Hispaniola in the morning.

Fray Luis sympathized with the captain's point of view, but he, personally, had been sent to evangelize the Indians; he could not go back without trying. He offered to go to shore alone and let the ship sail off without him. In preparation for whatever would happen, he spent the night writing letters to his superior and his friends, and went to confession. At daybreak, on the morning of June 24, 1549, a small boat manned by frightened sailors put in to shore with the friar. Some Indians appeared at the edge of the jungle and the sailors stopped rowing, casting anguished looks back at the ship. "Leave me here," said Fray Luis quietly. "It is shallow and I can wade in." The little boat hovered for a moment while the friar ploughed through waist-high waves, and then went hurriedly back to the ship. Just as the ship was lifting anchor, the Indians fell upon the friar at the water's edge and clubbed him to death.

The cause of Fray Luis Canceri has been open for many years; perhaps sometime it will be completed, and we can add his name to the roll of martyrs.

THOMAS OF BERLANGA
(1550)

We know little about the first bishop of Panama, Thomas of Berlanga, except one charming Lady-legend which somehow has found its way even into secular histories of the Spanish-colonial period.

Thomas was born in Berlanga, Spain, and received the habit at the convent of St. Stephen in Salamanca. He went to the New World around 1525. In Santo Domingo, he was made first superior of the province of the West Indies.

A glance at a modern map will make clear to us what such a provincial had as his theater of operations. The province included not only the Caribbean Islands and Florida, but also the whole of Central America and the vast land of Mexico. There was some understandable confusion as to where the province of Peru left off and the province of the West Indies began. When we consider that Dominican provincials of the time were expected to travel on foot, and that their duties included visitation of all the missions under their care, we can get some notion of the work laid out for a man who had half a hemisphere under his government. Thomas, even with the limited information available to him, could see that the arrangement was "inconvenient" (this is the word he uses in his report to Spain), and began negotiations to have Mexico formed into a separate province. The superiors in Spain did not understand about the inconvenience; so, in 1532, he sailed back across the Atlantic to explain to them.

He succeeded in his mission of establishing a separate province of Mexico, but promptly acquired more trouble. Charles V appointed him bishop of Panama. It is hard for us to see why, in going to his new diocese, he should have gone by way of Peru, but probably such things were dictated by the sailings of ships bound for certain ports. We know that he arrived in Peru in the midst of a bitter quarrel between the Spanish officials. There was bloodshed and confusion for a long time, and there was little chance of getting passage on a ship for Panama until peace had finally been reached.

Arriving in Panama, the new bishop found himself helpless to fight alone against the greed and savagery of the Spanish colonials. For ten years he battled unsuccessfully to save the Indians and to establish Christianity, and, finally, broken in health and spirit, he sailed for Spain with a document tendering his resignation.

Some days out at sea, the ship ran into a dense fog. This weather condition continued for several days and nights, and panic mounted with the hours.

People were still very much afraid of the ocean, and a few days of utter calm, with no visibility in the middle of nowhere, were enough to frighten the strongest. To calm the hysteria of the passengers, Thomas unpacked his episcopal robes (he had put them away when he handed in his resignation), and, dressed in full regalia, he went up on deck and led the passengers and crew in the litany of Our Lady.

While they were praying, the look-out cried that there was a clear place in the fog beside the ship, and that something was floating there in the water. They looked and saw a large box. While the sailors were getting the box out of the water, the captain approached Thomas and asked him what they should do about its contents. The bishop settled the question by saying that, if the box contained church goods, he would claim it, and, if it contained other treasure, it should be up to the captain to dispose of.

Opening the box, they found a statue of Our Lady, a lovely figure, with a sweet face and a Babe in her arms. Seeing it, the captain wanted to go back on his bargain. To settle the ownership of the statue, the captain and the bishop cast lots—three times, the legend says, and three times the bishop was victorious. Delightedly, Thomas claimed the statue, and he saw that the fog was lifting and a favorable wind was filling the slack sails.

The statue was eventually set up in a house of strict observance that Thomas founded in Spain, in 1543. Here he lived in retirement among his religious brothers until his death a few years later. No definite date of his death can be found, but it most probably occurred in 1550.

DOMINIC DeVICO AND ANDREW LOPEZ
(d. 1551)

These two missionaries, who died at the same time, came from different backgrounds. Dominic was born in Andalusia, and received the habit while he was a student at Salamanca. Before he was ordained, the famous Father Las Casas came to Spain looking for missionaries, and Dominic volunteered. He went back to Guatemala with Father Las Casas and settled himself to learn the Indian languages. He was to become almost phenomenally expert in these difficult tongues, and was one of the first Europeans to put the Indian languages into written form.

Dominic became famous as a diligent student. In fact, his companions teased him about it. They may have invented the story that he once kept on studying while crossing the lake in a little boat, even though the water rose round his feet. However, he was the key man in evangelizing the wide variety of Indians, and his books and pamphlets were a help to all those who came after him.

At one time, Dominic was out in a boat on the feast of St. Andrew; the vicar-general of the Order was his fellow-passenger. A fearful storm arose, and the ship was in great danger. Dominic promised to name his first mission for St. Andrew if the holy apostle would save their lives. Questioned afterwards, he said he had asked St. Andrew because the apostle was a fisherman and often had been out in bad weather.

Dominic had many harrowing adventures with the savages. One day, walking through the jungle, he came upon a group of Indians who were about to kill a man as a sacrifice to an idol. According to the legend, he began to pray, and at once a voice from the idol cried out, "Stop! My hour is over! No more shall blood flow for my altars. It is the hour of the new preachers." With this entrance cue, Dominic and companion emerged from the jungle and took over the instruction of the frightened natives.

Because of his success with the Indians and his firm grasp on mission problems, Dominic was appointed prior of the main convent in Guatemala, and here, for several years, he instructed the new missionaries, teaching them how to work with the most savage of the natives.

Dominic was not at home when his companion in martyrdom arrived from Spain in 1551. Andrew Lopez, born of a noble Basque family, was an amiable young caballero and a fine horseman who became interested in the religious life. He joined the Order in Spain. Newly ordained, he was sent to Guatemala. On his arrival, he went looking for the prior to ask for the traveler's blessing. Since the prior was out on a mission, he saw the sub-prior and asked for his blessing. Apparently, the sub-prior did not often have to give the blessing, for, when the young priest made the venia, he said, "Requiescat in Pace".

A few days later, when the prior had returned, he and the new young priest set out for the interior to work among the savages. The local ruler, a converted native, wished to give them an armed escort, because the Indians of the interior were so savage. Not to offend his friend, Dominic accepted a small escort, but after a few days, when they were deep into the jungle, he sent them back. The next morning, the two missionaries awoke to find themselves surrounded by warlike Indians who did not wait for any discussion. They shot Dominic in the throat with an arrow. Kneeling beside the dying prior to give him absolution, Andrew was badly wounded. The Indians withdrew, and Andrew attempted to overtake the armed escort they had recently dismissed. Before he could find them, unfriendly Indians killed him, too. The relics of both missionaries were brought back to Guatemala.

Books written by Dominic DeVico are fascinating in the light they shed on the mission work of his time. They include Bible and Church histories: *Theology for the Indians; A History of Indian Superstitions;* and a *Dictionary of Seven Indian Dialects,* with a detailed study method.

MARIE CARAFFA
(d. 1552)

The name Caraffa is famous in Italian history. Less known than her illustrious brother, Pope Paul IV, was Marie Caraffa, who was prioress of a Dominican convent in Naples when she died.

Marie was one of six children, all of whom had outstanding careers. She was a great beauty, a person of a lively and likeable disposition, a favorite of her many friends, and an ornament to a famous house. In addition, she was a person of great spiritual gifts, and she privately practiced severe penances, although exteriorly she had a gay and busy social life.

Very early, Marie decided to become a religious. Not content with giving herself to God, she devoted much time to her second brother, John Peter, in whom she discerned a similar vocation. She took charge of his education and brought him up piously. The story of their vocations is an interesting tale. It goes without saying that their wealthy and politically-prominent parents did not share Marie's enthusiasm in the idea that two of their children would become Dominicans.

John Peter, at the age of twelve, made serious attempts to get into the Dominican convent at Naples. Since he was so young, the effort was doomed; the friars refused to take him. He did not give up the idea, however. When Marie was twenty, and her parents were planning an advantageous marriage for her, brother and sister decided that it was time to act.

In an age when plotting was a fine art, one is not surprised to find that they worked out a neat little strategem for accomplishing their plans. Marie asked her mother to go with her to the Dominican convent on Christmas day, because she wanted to have some prayers said. This being an innocent request, her mother went with her and knelt quietly in the chapel, presuming that her daughter was explaining to the nuns about the forthcoming marriage. Marie, in the meantime, had gone into the cloister and put on the habit. When her mother discovered what had happened, she made the expected clamor. However, while she stood at the cloister door, loudly demanding that the nuns give back her daughter, a terrified servant brought her the news that John Peter had just entered the Dominican convent, on the other side of town. A daughter was bad enough; a son was worse. Screaming with frustration, the mother left Marie, to employ her best vocal efforts to the cause of getting her son back.

It was several months before a small army, under his father's command, forcibly took the habit from John Peter and brought him home in chains. The experience had been so exhausting, and the publicity so unpleasant, that they decided to leave Marie where she was.

In time, John Peter became a priest. He never lost his love for the religious life, and, as cardinal, he was one of the founders of the Theatines.

Quietly settled in the monastery of St. Sebastian, Marie turned her attention to being a good religious. She had always been prayerful and greatly gifted spiritually. Unfortunately, spiritual as well as temporal gifts sometimes arouse the jealousy of seemingly-pious people, and Marie was forced to go through a purgatory of persecution. At this distance, it is easy enough to blame the whole thing on the jealousy of small-minded people who were not as gifted as she. However, such misunderstandings are painful to endure, and Marie endured them for a long time. At one time, she was accused of real misconduct. For awhile she prayed bravely that God would not reveal her innocence, thus giving her a chance to suffer. But, eventually, she reached a point at which she felt she could not bear it any longer, and prayed that God would release her from the trial. Our Lord appeared to her as He was on the cross, and said, "Marie, I, too, am innocent." Having told this to her confessor, Marie was commanded in obedience to reveal it to her superior. The persecution stopped.

When the French army invaded Naples, the sisters fled for their lives. Marie took refuge in a little monastery called St. Mary of the Hermitage, where the sisters, Poor Clares, were in the throes of a new foundation. Here, among strangers, surrounded by uncertainty, she fell desperately ill and almost died. By this time her brother was a bishop, and he took a hand in the affairs of the house. The records do not say so, but it must have been embarrassing to her to have her brother decide arbitrarily that the house should be Dominican, not Poor Clare, and that Marie should be prioress.

After the first difficult adjustments were over, however, the house settled down into a pattern of regular observance—a phenomenon in the mid-sixteenth century. It became famous for the sanctity of its members and for the strict adherence to the rule.

There are many charming legends told about this monastery. It is said that the angels came every day, and that one Christmas night Our Lady appeared with the Baby Jesus and gave Him to the prioress to hold for a little while. During the chanting of None, on the Feast of the Ascension, several of the sisters saw our Lord blessing the monastery. In memory of this event, the Feast of the Ascension was always kept with great solemnity.

Falling seriously ill of fever, Marie realized that she was going to die. She called her sisters together and exhorted them to strict observance of the rule. After the sisters had gone out of the sick room, the dying prioress was left alone with a young niece, who was a boarder at the monastery. When a procession of angels came into the sick room, the little girl thought they were sisters, and she cautioned them to be very quiet, as her aunt was sleeping. They told her that they had come to take her aunt to heaven. Accompanying the angels were several sisters of the monastery who had previously died; they all looked very happy, and the whole sight quite dazzled the little girl.

Marie Caraffa died on January the fourth, 1552. Many miracles of healing were reported to have taken place at her grave, though no definite attempt has ever been made to have her raised to the honors of the altar.

DOMINICA OF PARADISO
(1473-1553)

Legends cluster around the name of this sixteenth century mystic; her cause was introduced in 1624. She was a center of controversy during her lifetime, and her process has been beset with some of the same questions that troubled her life. It is doubtful now whether she will ever be beatified, but she still holds interest for members of the Order.

Dominica was born in Paradiso, a little village near Florence, in 1473. Her parents were poor and had to work hard to make even a bare living. Her father died when she was six, leaving her mother to support the children. The mother was not too good a manager, and Dominica was sadly neglected. She rarely had enough to eat, and her education was entirely overlooked. However, she was a beautiful child and a very happy one, and when she was very small she was already associating with angels and saints, who came to her in vision. Our Lady appeared to her when she was six years old, surrounded by a troupe of angels, and advised her: "Love God, avoid sin, and do good"—a very general plan of life, indeed, but Our Lady gave her many revelations explaining it. Dominica wanted to enter a convent immediately; one time she ran away, intending to become a hermit, and angels brought her home. But since she had not yet made her First Communion and was entirely ignorant of religious life, no one took her seriously.

Dominica always lived in the presence of God, and, at the age of seven, she took a vow of virginity. The devil plagued her and her mother scolded her, but she had built a citadel of interior peace where no enemy could enter. After long pleading with her mother, she was given leave to make her First Communion, but the mother would neither instruct her nor let her go to anyone else for instructions. In this dilemma, Our Lady came and prepared the little girl. Her First Communion was to be on Easter Sunday, and the day before, as she knelt in prayer, thinking about the great privilege that was soon to be hers, our Lord Himself appeared to her, and she fell into an ecstasy that lasted until Mass the next day.

The anecdote that is most frequently remembered about Dominica is the apparition of Our Lady with the Holy Child when Dominica was still quite small. She was home alone and, apparently, was looking out the door, when she saw a ragged beggar-woman and a small child at the gate. The child had a haunting beauty, in spite of his evident suffering, and he seemed to be wounded in hands and feet. The beggar-woman asked for an alms, and Dominica turned away from the door to get some bread. Turning, she saw that the woman had come into the house with the child. "Oh," said Dominica, "you shouldn't have come in like that—Mama won't like it." The beggar-woman smiled and sat down. "Who has hurt your little boy?" asked Dominica. "It is because He loves so much," explained his mother. She looked around the room and observed that the little girl had crowned the family statues with field flowers. "Why do you crown your statues?" she asked. Dominica explained that she loved our Lord and His Blessed Mother. "Some day they will crown you with a beautiful crown in heaven," the lady assured her. Dominica coaxed the little boy to sit on her lap, and she talked to him. Before they left, the heavenly pair gave her a bouquet of roses and assured her that she was very pleasing to God.

On New Year's Day of 1485, Dominica experienced the mystical espousals. Angels clothed her with white robes and pearls, and great numbers of saints and angels filled the drab little cottage as our Lord placed a ring on Dominica's finger. Shortly after this, the girl decided to go to the shrine of St. Mary Magdalene and spend her life there as an anchorite. She set out by night on the long journey and eventually found a cave, where she spent three days in prayer. At the end of this time, our Lord appeared again and said to her, "The desert is not for you. In My wounds you will learn how to die to self." The angels brought her home again, and her mother, wearied by all these happenings, none of which she could understand, decided that her daughter should be married as soon as possible. Dominica, who probably had at least heard about St. Catherine, cut off her hair and declared that she simply would not get married.

The next ten years were a struggle to find a place where Dominica, who was no ordinary young woman, could fit into the scheme of things and serve God. She had no dowry with which to enter a cloister, but since she had a distant relative at the Monastery of Santa Maria Novella, in Florence, she was admitted there. The experience was brief and not too happy, and it ended when she fell desperately ill. She was received as a postulant in an Augustinian monastery; here, too, she was seriously ill, and though she recovered sufficiently to be offered the habit, she refused it, declaring that our Lord had revealed to her that she was not to remain there.

She returned home and was given the habit of the Sisters of St. Brigit, apparently a Tertiary habit. One can hardly blame her family if their patience had begun to wear a little thin. One of her brothers, however, went too far and beat her badly.

She left home for good, and she was employed as a governess by a family who had a small baby. It was revealed to her that the baby was going to die, and she unwisely told the child's mother of the revelation. When the baby actually died, there was a terrible family uproar, and someone tried to poison Dominica. On what recommendation we are not told, she served as governess in another family, but here she proved to be luckier. Four of the children under her care later became Dominicans.

At some time during these troubled years, Dominica received the stigmata. It was always highly visible on Fridays, though not at other times. She was revered as a saint by many, and condemned by others as a witch. In 1501, her visions took a definite Dominican trend. She saw Blessed Columba of Rieti going up to heaven at her death, and our Lord appeared to show her the Dominican habit and advised her to go to San Marco for spiritual direction. She was taken in spirit to Palestine, to limbo, to hell and purgatory, to the Indies (an interesting point, in 1501) and to all the major basilicas of Europe.

She felt that the time had come to take definite religious action, so she and several other young women moved into a small house and set up Dominican observance, although they were too poor to buy habits. Their confessor managed to get the material for them to make the habits, and Our Lady came with St. Dominic and St. Catherine to show them how the habits should be made.

Eventually a regular monastery was built, and observance established, according to the reform of Savonarola. They took possession of the house in 1513. After some preliminary troubles, Dominica was appointed superior for life, and she lived in peace and prayer. She died in 1553.

ANTONINUS TEMMERMAN
(d. 1555)

It is quite probable that the Order, in its long history, can boast of more than one priest who was a martyr for refusing to violate the seal of the confessional. Since, however, this secrecy was the sole and only reason for the death of Antoninus Temmerman, he is fittingly enough our example of this particular brand of Christian fortitude and priestly integrity.

Antoninus Temmerman was born at Antwerp, near the beginning of the sixteenth century. He entered the Order in his native city at the age of twenty, and soon became an excellent preacher.

With the accession of Philip II to the Spanish throne in 1555, the stage was set for tragedy in the Netherlands. The continual Spanish oppression of the independent Dutch people, plus the infiltration of heresy, had brought the country to the verge of open rebellion. When the Netherlands rebelled, it was under a Dutch Protestant leader, William of Orange. Calvinism was established as the official religion of the Dutch government, and priests were exiled or killed. Father Temmerman remained in Antwerp after most of the clergy had been exiled.

Philip II offered a reward of 25,000 gold ducats to anyone who would kill William of Orange. As might have been expected, there were several people willing to commit murder for that amount of money. One of the most devious of the schemers was a merchant of Antwerp by the name of Anastrus. He wanted the money badly, but he also realized that whoever did the actual killing would stand an excellent chance of being killed himself. So he hired an assassin by the name of John of Jauregui, laid his plans carefully, and fled elsewhere to establish an alibi.

There has been a lot of speculation about John of Jauregui. Some say that he was a hardened criminal who planned all along to commit the murder, and that the confession and Communion he made were sacrilegious. Others say that he weakened, after having once turned from the thought of the crime, and attempted the assassination out of cupidity. We simply do not know. All that we do know is that he went to Father Temmerman, who was in Antwerp, in disguise, and talked to him the night before the planned murder of William of Orange. He went to confession and Communion, and left some money with the priest to say several Masses for his safe journey, which would seem to indicate that he planned to flee the city rather than go through with the plans.

Whatever his thoughts and intentions in the matter, John of Jauregui did make the promised attempt on the life of William of Orange. William was struck by the bullet, but he did not die. The assassin was immediately apprehended by William's followers, and they tortured and killed him. This should have been enough for the Calvinist soldiers, but someone gave them the information that John of Jauregui had gone to see a Dominican the night before and that the priest was still in the city. It took only a short while to find him and bring him before the Calvinist court.

Antoninus Temmerman was closely questioned, and threatened with all sort of horrors if he would not tell what John of Juaregui had told him. The priest had no choice in the matter; he simply could not speak. He was cruelly scourged, and then condemned to be hanged and quartered. Two days later, the sentence was carried out in all its barbarous details.

The Calvinists realized that they had left one bridge unburned; they had not succeeded at any time in getting any information out of the Dominican. To justify their own course of action, they drew up an account of the trial, detailing what they said he had told them. They claimed that he had violated the seal of confession, a fact which they hoped would make him abhorred by Catholics and Protestants alike. They published several pamphlets that narrated their carefully-prepared story, and these were circulated widely.

The Catholics of Antwerp carefully preserved some of the relics of the martyr, and stoutly refused to believe that he had made the statement attributed to him. Nearly three hundred years later, the original documents of the trial were discovered, and they were identified beyond all doubt. They proved that the people of Antwerp were right, and that the courageous Dominican died with his lips sealed on the unhappy affair of John of Jauregui.

DOMINIC OF THE CROSS
(1480-1555)

Louis of Saavedra was born in Estramadura in 1480. His parents gave him a good Christian education and sent him to Alcalá for philosophy. Here he met a young student named Francis Soto and formed a close friendship with him. They finished their studies at Alcalá and went to Paris together. At Paris, they completed their graduate studies and then returned to Alcalá, where Louis was appointed rector.

The two friends were separated when Francis Soto became a Dominican at the Convent of St. Paul, in Burgos, receiving the name Dominic. After his profession, he was assigned to Salamanca, and Louis came to see him. It was the first opportunity they had had to visit, and they talked nearly all night. Dominic Soto must have been as persuasive as his great namesake, who converted the Albigensian innkeeper in a night of argument, for the next day Louis asked for the Dominican habit also. He entered at the convent of the Holy Cross, in Segovia, and was given the name Dominic of the Cross.

The two friends were seldom to meet again. Dominic of the Cross, after getting his master's degree in sacred theology, was sent to Ocaña. He was there when missionaries came from Mexico, begging for help, and Dominic of the Cross was assigned to recruit Mexican missionaries. Subsequently, he went to Mexico himself.

Dominic was appointed vicar-general in Mexico, although he would have liked to spend his time among the Indians. His life seemed to be a long series of extraneous tasks that had to be done before he could actually preach on the missions. He was kept teaching in the University of Mexico City, and was tied down by various offices until finally, at the age of sixty, he was elected provincial. In this office he had to spend his time walking from one mission to another, visiting the houses and fostering regular observance. Charles V wanted to make him bishop. He had refused several other Sees, and, eventually, he and two other provincials set out for Spain to try settling the very complicated business of the Mexican bishoprics.

Arriving in Spain, they found that the emperor had gone to Flanders. In Flanders, they were told that he had gone to Germany. Since the Lutherans were in arms in Germany, the friars could not wear their habits. They dressed in Spanish army uniforms and started the next section of their long walk. They were horrified by the profanations they saw in Germany. In Cologne, they rescued a box of relics, including some of St. Ursula, which they proposed to take back to Mexico.

Here occurs a strange little interlude that is a tribute to the courage of Dominic of the Cross. The powerful heretic leader, Bucer, was at Strasbourg when the tired friars came into town. Instead of keeping out of his way, which would seem only prudent, Dominic demanded to see him. Bucer, seeing the uniform of a Spanish soldier, did not suspect that he was dealing with a friar until Dominic pleaded with him to return to God. How he got away alive, no one has thought to tell us.

Having settled their business with the king, the fathers returned to Spain. Dominic of the Cross was old and tired, and he had just returned from walking half way across Europe. The master general, in all kindness, refused to let him return to Mexico and the hard life of the missions. Brokenhearted, the old missionary watched the ships sail away, and he tried to resign himself to a new life in Spain.

There are two amusing anecdotes which belong to these years in Spain. One day, while Dominic was traveling, he and his companion stopped at an inn for the night. They were quite upset by the bad language of the people in the inn, and Dominic took his staff, determined to find another lodging. His companion tried to tell him that it was two leagues to the next inn, and that they had better just overlook the language and stay where they were. Dominic kept moving, and, in a few minutes' time, they rounded a corner and came upon another inn. His companion was overcome with wonder, because he was familiar with that region and knew quite well that there simply was not another inn that nearby.

At another time, Dominic and his companion arrived in a village to beg for their dinner. They separated, and, when they rejoined one another, his companion had money and he had nothing. "God is punishing us for accepting money," he said. "You take that straight back where you got it." While he was waiting for the brother to return, someone came by and gave him food for both of them.

When a new master general was elected, Dominic of the Cross lost no time in asking to return to Mexico. Given the permission, he went back joyfully. He lived two years more, praying and counselling the younger missionaries. Finally, "filled with years, works, and infirmities," he died in November, 1555, at the age of seventy-five.

FRANCIS GARCIA
(d. 1559)

Francis was a Spaniard from Galicia, and he came to America to seek his fortune. He was only one of many young Spaniards who in those days were making this their only goal in life. He succeeded rather well in accomplishing his purpose, although nothing is said about the nature of his enterprise. At any rate, he had a nestegg that was sufficient to care for his future needs when he came to the city of Pueblo in Mexico. After he was there awhile, he became acquainted with the Dominican fathers.

We do not know much about Francis at this point in his life. All we know is that he made up his mind to be a laybrother at the Dominican convent in Pueblo. Only one thing bothered him: the gold he had crossed the seas to gain. He did not want to lose it entirely. In the event that he did not permanently remain with the Dominicans, he would certainly need it some day. After a time, he resolved his problem by lending the money out at interest. Convinced, then, that he had done all that was required of him, he entered the convent.

Although the religious life held a great attraction for him, he found that he could not keep his mind off the nice little nestegg. It was dutifully accumulating interest while he hustled around the convent in a patched habit doing menial tasks. He did not, moreover, like the sort of work he was asked to do, and, apparently, he could not quite resist, occasionally, the temptation of remarking to the other laybrothers, "Well, of course, I don't *have* to stay here; I have money." The inevitable of course happened; he returned to the world to claim his gold.

Things should have been quite happy for him, but they were not. Finally, it dawned on him that he did not possess gold; the gold possessed him. Mortified and disgusted with himself and the money, he arranged that his small fortune be used as Mass stipends for the Poor Souls. As a last bit of drama, he had a Solemn High Requiem Mass offered for his own soul. Then, free for the first time in years, he went back to the Dominicans and begged to be re-admitted. In 1559, after a period of waiting, he was allowed to receive the habit again, and he wore it with distinction for many years.

Obscurity was the life Francis sought, and he achieved it so well that we have very little to record about his years as a Dominican, except that he was, to quote the chronicles: "Humble, joyous, good, and loved by all" —a nice epitaph for a Dominican. He plunged with native enthusiasm into the lowly tasks assigned him, and became an accomplished beggar for the pious works of the Order.

At the end of his life, he was still busily begging for the charities of the house. He was on his way to the mines of Taxco when illness stopped him on the road, and he sought refuge at the nearest farm, the property of a pious and wealthy widow who had often contributed to his collections. She had him put to bed and sent for the doctor. On Good Friday night, she decided to call on the sick man and see if he were any better. Approaching the door of his room, she saw a brilliant light streaming out from under the door. A careful housewife, she hunted up the servant and asked her, "Who put the big lamp in the brother's room?" Tearfully denying that *she* had, the servant went to see, and returned very awed. "It must be angels," she reported. "There is no lamp at all."

Brother Francis died on Easter Sunday, as he had predicted that he would. Ordinarily, his funeral would have been extremely simple, for only two priests were stationed in this particular place. However, fifteen priests appeared, independently of one another, and each from a different place. Apparently no one had told them to come, but they were at the funeral.

Among those who revered him, the memory of Brother Francis lasted for many years.

DOMINIC SOTO
(1494-1560)

Dominic Soto, who was one of the theologians at the Council of Trent, was closely connected with another great Dominican, Dominic of the Cross, one of the most famous missionaries of the New World. The story of their friendship is not unique in Dominican history, because we have many instances of people of very different character mutually helping each other in the apostolate. It is a nice example of a friendship between a missionary and a scholar, who found common ground and mutual encouragement in the Dominican rule.

Francis Soto was born of poor parents, in Segovia, in 1494. His father was a gardener and expected his son to follow in his footsteps. Francis himself had a great longing for an education, and he struggled for several years to obtain one. It was not as simple in his day as in ours.

While working his way through school, one of the jobs Francis held was that of a sacristan at the Dominican church. He grew very fond of the Dominicans, respected them greatly for their scholastic excellence, but did not feel drawn to enter the Order. They encouraged him in his studies, and he went to the University of Alcalá, where he studied under St. Thomas of Villanova. Here at Alcalá he met Louis of Saavedra, the future Dominic of the Cross.

The two young men, both seeking to do the will of God, formed a close friendship and worked together at their books. Both attained to eminence in their studies and received their degrees. Francis Soto accepted the chair of philosophy at Alcalá. At the very crest of fame and fortune, the two earnest young men abandoned the university and sought out, separately, a way of life that would satisfy their need for consecration to God.

Francis at first sought admission to the Benedictine monastery at Montserrat, but he was advised to become a hermit for the time being. Louis became a hermit in a place near Naples. They pursued their solitary lives for some years, until Francis, at the suggestion of his spiritual director, went to the Dominicans at Burgos, and he received the habit there. He was given the religious name Dominic. At a later date, he was transferred to Salamanca. Here he had the happiness of seeing his old friend Louis, who also received the habit, and he was given the name Dominic of the Cross.

Their paths met, only to divide again. Dominic of the Cross was soon to go to the New World and become one of its most famous missionaries. Dominic Soto began his active career as a professor at Salamanca. In 1545, because of his great reputation as teacher and author, he was chosen by the Emperor Charles V to be the imperial theologian at the Council of Trent. The emperor also chose him as his confessor and spiritual director. The responsibility of two such positions weighed heavily on Dominic Soto. It is a tribute both to his wisdom and his virtue that history records nothing but praise of him.

Several attempts were made to elevate Dominic Soto to a bishopric. He was successful in avoiding these honors, and was to end his days as a college professor at Salamanca, the place where he was happiest and felt the most at home. The distinction for which he will be longest remembered was his prudent conduct at the Council of Trent, where his charity and wisdom were evident, not only to the members of his own party, but even to the Protestants, who found so much else to criticize. We can well be proud of this great Dominican, who carried great honors without allowing them to spoil him.

Dominic Soto died in 1560, after thirty years of distinguished service to the Order and to the Church.

BARTHOLOMEW MATEO
(d. 1562)

Bartholomew Matéo did not die a martyr, although he probably expected to. No one has even suggested that his cause be promoted for beatification. His life, however, is not without interest for us, since it demonstrates very clearly the transforming power of grace.

Bartholomew began his adventures in Spain; we do not know exactly where. He comes into the records as an officer in the army of Pizarro, which was engaged in the conquest of Peru. He was an artillery man, completely given to the fortunes and business of war. In common with other young officers of the time, Bartholomew was ruthless and greedy for gold. Naturally venturesome, and possessed of a violent temper, he was interested only in what he could get for himself. He considered the Indians as human beings beneath consideration.

At various points in the spread of her vast colonial empire, Spain had made efforts to make it a Christian conquest. She did not always succeed. One of the attempts to eradicate the cruelties to the Indians was the letter sent by Charles V to Peru in 1548, and the result of it was that a number of the high officers were put in chains while they awaited sentence for their cruel behavior.

Bartholomew Matéo was one of the officers, and he was jailed with the brother of the conqueror. Loaded with chains, they waited in prison for the death sentence they knew they would receive. Bartholomew may simply have grown tired of waiting. Nobody, no matter how guilty, likes to be chained. He was a big man, in good trim, and he broke his chains, pushed out a window, and set off for Mexico.

Most of the officers with whom he had been imprisoned were executed. Perhaps it was this sobering fact that turned Bartholomew's attention to the thought of death. In any case, shortly after he arrived in Mexico, he was overcome with remorse for the crimes of which he had been guilty, and went to confession to a Dominican father. The Dominican gave him a strict penance and kept close watch on him to see that he performed it. Bartholomew stayed close to the Dominicans, and, after a time, he made up his mind that he would like to join the Order. He applied as a laybrother at the convent in Mexico City and, after a period of trial, was received and began his training.

The convent of Mexico City, under the direction of Father Christopher of the Cross, was one of strict observance. Great penance was the ordinary fare. Silence was absolute, prayer unending. Bartholomew determined to fit himself into this strict regime. It took a good deal of reforming for a Conquistador.

As Brother Bartholomew, his new character began to emerge. His violent temper subdued, his greed and pride conquered, the new brother became a model of meekness and exactitude. The use of disciplines, chains, fasts, and other austerities, brought the body which had given him so much trouble under subjection; he now became a channel of grace to all who worked with him. Those who remembered him in the conquest of Peru would not now recognize the holy and exact religious who had become, even in that household of rigid observance, the standard of behavior.

As a final testimony of his conversion, Bartholomew worked among the Indians and became their good friend. Once he had considered them hardly human, now he saw them as children of God with an eternal destiny, and no work was too hard for him to undertake in helping them. The

Indians, in turn, loved him dearly. They wept when they heard that he was going to Florida.

Nine priests and a laybrother, Bartholomew, received the obedience—which was as good as a sentence of death—to go to Florida. They set out bravely enough, but their ship was destroyed in a storm before it reached Florida. The entire mission party was drowned.

BLESSED OSANNA OF CATTARO
(1493-1565)

Blessed Osanna of Cattaro, who was beatified in 1934, is one of the few of our members who lived as a recluse, sanctifying her life as a solitary. We are surprised to find a Dominican leading this type of life, because the Order is based on brotherhood rather than on solitude, but the peculiar mission of her life dictated this choice.

Catherine Kosic was born in the village of Kumano, on the Adriatic, in that part of Jugoslavia which used to be called Montenegro. She was baptized in her parents' church, which was that of the Greek schismatics.

Catherine's childhood was spent in the country, where she had the duty of herding the family sheep. Left to herself for the greater part of every day, she developed a habit of contemplative prayer. One day, when she was out with her sheep, she saw a beautiful Child lying asleep on the grass. Attracted by its beauty, she went to pick up the Baby, but it disappeared, leaving her with a feeling of great loneliness.

She told her mother about this experience but received little sympathy; her mother told her that God simply did not appear to such poor people, and that she had only imagined it. After several apparitions, which she prudently kept to herself, Catherine developed a great desire to go to Cattaro, for there were several churches there, and she felt it would be easier to pray in a church. This did not seem a sensible reason to her mother, but she finally arranged for the girl to go to Cattaro as the servant of a wealthy woman. She gave little thought to the fact that the woman was a pious Catholic, but the girl rejoiced at her good luck. At the age of twelve, she settled down happily as a servant to the kindly woman, who made no objection to the fact that Catherine's errands invariably led her past the church, where she would drop in for a visit.

After a few years of this pleasant but not too positive type of life, she consulted her spiritual director about becoming a recluse. He thought her

too young, but she continued to press her arguments, and, after much
discussion and prayer, it was decided she should be allowed to follow this
form of life.

We know little today of this type of religious life. It was much more
common in the Middle Ages, and nearly every church or pilgrimage place
had one or more cells in which solitaries dwelt in prayer and penance.
Such a cell was built near the Church of St. Bartholomew in Cattaro; it
had a window through which the solitary could watch the Mass and
another tiny window to which people would come occasionally to ask
for prayers or to give food. Catherine was conducted to her cell in a
solemn ceremony, and, after making her promises of stability, the door
was sealed, and she embarked on her solitary life. In response to a vision,
she was later transferred to a cell at the Church of St. Paul. Here, for
fifty-two years she followed the rule of the Tertiaries of St. Dominic, to
which she had vowed herself before entering her solitude. She chose the
religious name Osanna, because she admired Osanna of Mantua, a Dominican
Tertiary who had died a few years before.

The life of such a recluse was replete with penance and barren of
comforts. Even without the spiritual punishments she endured, it was a
rugged life. She wore the coarsest of clothes, ate practically nothing, endured
cold, and the inevitable misery of being confined in a small space, not for
a little while, but for half a century. Her tiny cell was often bright with
heavenly visitors. Our Lord appeared to her many times, usually in the
form of the beautiful Babe she had first seen in the fields. Our Lady
came too, with several of the saints. And she had visitors who were not
welcome: devils who tried to tempt her and disturb her prayer. Once the
devil appeared to her in the form of the Blessed Virgin and told her to
modify her penances. By obedience to her confessor, she managed to penetrate
this very clever disguise and vanquish her enemy.

In spite of the fact that she lived in solitude, there was nothing selfish
about the spirituality of Osanna. A group of Dominican Tertiaries, who
considered her their leader, consulted her frequently and asked her advice
and her prayers. A convent of sisters founded at Cattaro regarded her as
their foundress, because of her prayers, although she never saw the place.
When the city was attacked by the Turks, the people ran to her for help,
and they credited their deliverance to her prayers. At another time, her
prayers delivered them from the plague.

Osanna died at the age of seventy-two, after a life of solitude and prayer.

BARTHOLOMEW DE LAS CASAS
(1474-1566)

"Shepherd of the Indians" and "Protector of the Indians" are only two of the many titles to fame of this man who fought for forty years to save a people from the greed of the conquerors. He died with no hope of success.

Bartholomew de las Casas was born in Seville, in 1474. He was a young man of wealth and social position when Columbus returned, in 1492, from the New World, bringing a captive Indian as a trophy. The young Bartholomew was not impressed with the brown-skinned native, nor was he much concerned with the question of justice to a people whom the Spaniards considered to be not human enough to deserve human treatment. He took his law degree at the University of Salamanca, where the Dominicans were already troubling themselves about the problems of conquest. In 1502, Bartholomew sailed for the Indies—a typical young Spanish grandee, with rather more than the usual amount of property on the island of Hispaniola.

Bartholomew was a just man, and he was kind to his Indians, but the thought of slavery did not bother him. It seemed an eminently sensible method of colonizing a new land, and, for many years, while injustice flared on all sides of him, he paid no attention to the morality of the encomienda system.

In 1510, the Dominicans arrived in Hispaniola from Spain, and almost their first act was to preach against the entire system of slavery. Affronted and embittered, the Spanish colonials took up the cause against them and sent word to Spain that the friars must be removed. Bartholomew de las Casas, who had heard the sermon of Father Anthony of Montesinos on slavery, found himself unexpectedly rallying to the side of the Dominicans in the dispute. It was true that he himself held slaves and that he had no notion of freeing them; but he suddenly saw with a terrible clarity what the Spaniards were doing to the Indians. After a time of prayer and introspection, he gave his properties into the hand of his dearest friend and formally expressed his desire to be a priest of the diocese.

The vocation of the gay young grandee was a shock to his friends, who could not accustom themselves to seeing him in the poor clothing of a cleric. After his ordination, one of his first assignments was also one of his most heartbreaking; he was chaplain to the army invading Cuba. In spite of the promises he had exacted from the leaders, there was a horrible slaughter, and he returned a broken and disillusioned man. In the following year, 1515, he sailed for Spain and presented the case of the Indians to the Council of the Indies.

For two years he pleaded with all his eloquence that the king stop the slaughter of the conquered people. The dying King Ferdinand had a positive genius for avoiding uncomfortable subjects. Giving the title "Protector of the Indians" to Las Casas, he sent him back to Hispaniola with a sheaf of fine laws to rectify matters. In less than a year, Las Casas was once more sailing for Spain, armed with the information that the laws were fine, but the Spaniards in the colonies did not pretend to obey them. Consulting with Charles V, he learned that the king had no intention of forcing them to obey.

The Dominicans at Salamanca had debated the question of the Indians' rights and reached a decision that startled and annoyed the conquerors; Las Casas accepted their analysis and built upon it. Sometime before 1522, convinced that no other path was reasonable, Bartholomew de las Casas freed his own Indians, and, kneeling, he asked to receive the Dominican habit. For eight years thereafter he lived in retirement—praying, reflecting, and writing.

Of all the varied works of his long lifetime, his writings have probably had the greatest impact on civilization. He was an impassioned speaker, and his work among the Indians was worthy of the highest praise. For the most part, he displayed a real genius for mission work. But his *History of the Indies* remains the most complete source of correct information available of the turbulent years of the conquest in a new world. In it one sees the pleading of a man who hates cruelty, and the sober realization that gold is an unbalancing factor in all conquest.

One of the most famous of his mission conquests was the evangelization of the "Land of War," Guatemala. He conquered it bloodlessly, with the cross, and he renamed it "Vera Paz." He taught in Mexico and Peru, and, in 1544, he was appointed bishop of Chiapa, in Mexico. He was seventy years old then, and the past thirty-four years had been spent in open battle in the cause of the Indians. In place after place he had to begin afresh, only to see his work ruined by the greed of the gold-hunters. As bishop of Chiapa, he made one last attempt to build a colony among the Indians—a place where Christian principles would be observed by men who professed themselves Christian. After he failed, even in Chiapa, he resigned from his office and returned to Spain.

For the remaining years of his life he lived in retirement at the convent of Our Lady of Atocha, in Madrid. Writing filled his days here; he rarely spoke any more. At the age of ninety, he wrote his last defense of the Indians, explaining the rights of personal property of infidels and pagans. He died, broken in health and in heart, in 1566.

RICHARD HARGRAVE
(d. 1566)

At the time of the dissolution of the monasteries, there were fifty-two sizeable convents of the Order in England, and a monastery of Dominican nuns at Dartford. A few of the houses went over, in whole or in part, to the new regime of Henry VIII, but most of them remained faithful. The brothers were promptly driven into exile, and the houses were confiscated to pay the bills of a hard-pressed king. Richard Hargrave, who was the English provincial at the time, was exiled to Brussels.

The English province was thus all but annihilated. Under the reign of Mary Tudor, some few Dominicans returned. They organized at the Convent of St. Bartholomew, in Smithfield, and the nuns returned to Dartford. Father Hargrave was appointed confessor to the nuns. For the rest of his life his fortunes were to be tied up with theirs, and a sadder tale of exile would be hard to find.

Queen Mary died in 1558. Queen Elizabeth took over the throne, established the Protestant religion as the state religion, and set about removing obstacles, which in this case included a high proportion of Catholics. All religious superiors were required to take the oath of supremacy or be liable to either death or exile.

Father Richard Hargrave was a difficult man to push, and the queen's men waited for an opportunity to take him into custody. When letters came to him from the provincial in Belgium naming him prior of the house in Smithfield, the foreign appointment was used as a pretext to arrest him. Soldiers were sent to Smithfield to force him to take the oath or submit to imprisonment. On his journey there from Dartford, he was warned and went into hiding in the neighborhood.

Angry at losing their prey, the soldiers descended upon Dartford and demanded that the nuns take the oath. They met an uncompromising refusal. The nuns were forthwith given a small coin apiece, permission to pack their books, and twenty-four hours to get out of the house.

Anticipating this, Father Hargrave had arranged passage for the nuns on a Spanish ship bound for Belgium. They took ship next day with a group of Brigittine sisters bound on the same sad journey, saying goodbye to England forever.

We do not know the names of all the sisters in that little group. One we do know was Elizabeth Wright, sister of Bishop John Fisher, and, apparently, she was made of the same uncompromising material as he. She and the other sisters were all advanced in years; three were over eighty, and the youngest was fifty. A journey of this kind would be hard enough for young people, who might at least look forward to a fair chance of earning a living in a new land. It must have been heartbreaking for a group of helpless old people, who had spent their lives in the cloister and whose only crime had been the integrity of their faith.

Arriving at Antwerp, Father Hargrave tried to find them housing and some means of livelihood. The only place readily available was an ancient farmhouse in Zeeland; here the sisters starved and froze by turns. Their miseries were so great that they finally returned to Antwerp. Their hand-to-mouth existence was brought to an abrupt end when, in 1566, the Protestants drove them out of the city. For a while they lived at Bergen op Zoom. This is now a pretty little tourist town, but it meant only misery to the exiled Englishwomen. One by one, they succumbed to the hardships until, seven years later, only four were living. They clung to their shattered remnants of community life, though dressed in secular clothes and having no fixed abode. The last nun died in 1585. She was buried with the Belgian Dominicans.

Father Hargrave's part in all this must have been even worse than theirs. He felt responsible for them, and there was nothing he could do for them. Everything they suffered, he suffered more intensely. He died in exile, as they all did. A quick and bloody martyrdom is easier for us to understand. We must not underestimate the horrors of the long, slow death of a province, which was not to revive for a hundred years.

SIXTUS OF SIENA
(1520-1566)

Sixtus was born in 1520 of Jewish parents, and was brought up in the Jewish religion. In his early teens, he was converted to Christianity; later he became a Franciscan.

Before he was thirty years old, the reputation of Sixtus was tremendous. He was known all over Italy as a splendid preacher and was one of the first Franciscan masters in the study of Scripture. He devoted more and more time to this fascinating study, and somewhere became contaminated with doctrines of heresy. He was a man of great originality, and many of the ideas which seemed original and dangerous to older scholars seemed only common sense to him. Before long, he found himself badly entangled in heretical doctrines and was brought before the Holy Office. He was admonished and sent back, with a warning to beware of dangerous innovations. All too soon, he relapsed into serious heresy, was taken to Rome and imprisoned until examined by the inquisition. The court found him guilty of heresy and condemned him to die at the stake.

At this time a Dominican, Michael Ghislieri, the future Pope Pius V, was commissary-general of the Holy Office. One of his duties was to visit the prisons and talk to those who had been condemned for heresy, in the hope of winning them back to the faith. He was deeply touched by the misery of the young Franciscan, and he spent a good deal of time with him. Finally he went to the pope to beg that the sentence be reversed. Because he respected the commissary-general, Pope Julius III released the young man into his hands. Father Ghislieri promptly received the young man into the Dominican Order and set about training him.

His trust was not misplaced. Sixtus, the gifted scholar, became one of the outstanding Scripture authorities of the age. He put his great knowledge of Scripture and his talent for preaching at the service of the Church. Fifteen years later he would dedicate a book of preaching aids to his great friend and father in Christ, Pope St. Pius V.

Before his early death at the age of forty-six, Sixtus had more than made reparation for his mistakes. His last years were spent in fighting vigorously against the influx of bad books that were contaminating the students. He burned most of his own writings, but he left a concordance to the Bible and books on astronomy, geography, physics, canon law, and poetry.

THOMAS STELLA
(d. 1566)

Thomas Stella was born in Venice and spent most of his life in Italy, but his influence has reached every Christian country, for he founded the confraternity that honors the Blessed Sacrament.

Thomas entered the Order in Venice and made his studies there. The skill which was to earn him the reputation of being Italy's greatest preacher displayed itself soon after his ordination. Great crowds came to hear him preach, and people began coming to Venice simply to see him. The master-general transferred him to the Convent of Santa Maria Sopra Minerva, in Rome, where he continued the marvellous preaching. This time of his life is filled with delightful legends about his preaching. During one of his sermons a flock of swallows flew into the church and circled around, twittering. Thomas endured it for a while, but finally he stopped speaking to the congregation and asked the swallows to go outside. They did, to the great amazement of the people listening. At another time, when he was preaching on almsgiving, he so moved the people that they not only emptied their pockets, but they took off all their jewelry, giving it to the poor.

On his arrival in Rome, in 1539, Thomas observed a sad fact. The Blessed Sacrament was given no honor in the churches of Rome or anywhere else. In the early ages of the Church, the Blessed Sacrament had been reserved in a dove-shaped vessel that was suspended above the altar; this custom had passed, and the Lord of the Universe was now stored away in the sacristy or on a side altar, without lights or any marks of devotion. Thomas proposed to rectify this in two ways. He began to cultivate the solemn procession to the sick; the Blessed Sacrament was now accompanied on its way to a sick bed by lighted candles and the ringing of a bell. And he founded a confraternity of people who were pledged to take care of this solemn function, both by providing the candles and by attending the priest.

As the society developed, definite customs were established: prayers were said before the Blessed Sacrament in church, and lights and flowers offered to honor our Blessed Lord. Father Stella was fond of saying: "When the kings of this world pass through our cities, they are borne with great honor, and covered with a canopy. When our Lord, the King of kings, goes among us should he be unnoticed and unhonored?" He drew up a set of rules for the confraternity which would guarantee that the Blessed Sacrament would always have honor and solemnity, at least in the churches where the group was formed. From the Church of the Minerva, which always remained the Mother Church of the Confraternity, this excellent devotion has spread around the world, and it has given rise to several other pious associations which carry on the intentions of Father Stella.

In 1544, Father Stella was made bishop of Salpi, in Naples. He was sent from here to the Council of Trent and worked on several of its important questions. Six years later, he was transferred to Capo d'Istria, where the bishop had become a Lutheran and had taken a large part of his flock with him. He labored in this difficult field for sixteen years, trying to bring his people back and erase the traces of heresy.

Bishop Stella died suddenly in 1566. Just before he died he caught someone composing a pompous epitaph for him. He replaced it with this one: "Here lies a sinner; you who pass by, pray for him."

RENÉ OF ANGERS
(d. 1568)

René was born in Angers, in the early sixteenth century. He entered the Order there when he was young. Because he was one of their best students, he was sent to Paris to finish his studies, and he returned to Angers with a doctorate, and a reputation for his virtue and for his skill in argument.

Calvinism was just getting a firm hold in France, under the patronage of Charles IX and Catherine de Medici. With their approval, several cities had been taken over by the heretics and were already centers of needless cruelty. The Dominicans assigned their most convincing speakers and their best debaters to the centers of the trouble. In 1567, René was sent to Angoulême. He was the prior there. The house had been raided by the Calvinists five years before, and the friars were killed. It was in the heart of the heretic country and it was bound, sooner or later, to be the scene of more trouble. Here René worked to undo some of the harm of the heretic preachers. He was an indomitable debater, and they feared him.

René was sent to preach during Lent in the Cathedral of Chartres, and, while he was away from Angoulème, the Huguenots attacked the convent. They killed all the friars, profaned the altars, and left the building in flames. Receiving word of the disaster, the prior set out from Chartres, but arrived to find that he was too late to help anyone. He went sadly through the ruins, weeping and praying for the community that had perished, begging God's forgiveness for the terrible sacrilege of the altars that were still stained with blood.

News of his arrival was brought to the Huguenots. They had been taunting the Catholics to send out their best apologists to meet them in open argument, but were not prepared to meet René of Angers; he was too skillful. But they broke in on him in his temporary lodging and took him prisoner.

Dragging him into the public square, they forced him to watch the hanging of a Franciscan preacher. They offered the Dominican safety and freedom if he would abjure his faith in the Real Presence, or at least promise not to preach it any more—a proposition which met nothing but silent contempt. They put him in prison, then, with some other priests. An old Dominican died in his presence, but just out of his reach, as he lay bound and helpless. He was tortured and starved. Finally the Huguenots stripped him and put him in a cart. The destination was the scaffold. He begged to say Mass once more. The answer was a shout of derision: "Go up on the scaffold and celebrate your mysteries."

Once on the scaffold, René began to speak. Spellbound, both friend and enemy listened. Then some of the Huguenot leaders realized what had happened. "He is winning the sympathy of everyone," they cried. They quickly took René and threw him off a bridge into the river. However, the river had dried up, and, though he fell heavily on the rocky bed, he did not die. A Huguenot soldier went down and shot him, sending him to join the multitude of Dominican martyrs, on August the sixteenth, 1568.

SEBASTIAN de CANTO AND JEROME OF THE CROSS
(d. 1568)

These two missionaries, drawn from different backgrounds and thrown together almost by chance, suffered in the Kingdom of Siam in 1568 and are the protomartyrs of that country.

Jerome of the Cross, the younger in age, was born in Lisbon and studied civil and canon law at Coimbra. At the age of thirty, he renounced his family name, his inheritance, and the promise of a brilliant career in law, and entered the Order in the convent of St. Dominic in Lisbon.

While Jerome was still a student, a party of missionaries bound for the East Indies was assembling in Lisbon. One of the fathers appointed to go was taken sick suddenly, and the prior had to make a hurried replacement. After Compline, he sent for Jerome and simply told him: "The vessel is ready to sail for the Indies, and you are to take the place of the priest who cannot go." Jerome prostrated for his blessing, and then he asked if there was time to go to his cell for his cappa and breviary. "Oh," said the prior, "you won't go until tomorrow. We will ordain you first."

The following day, Jerome was ordained and sent on a hasty trip to say goodbye to his mother. The mission party set out in a small harbor boat and overtook the slower caravel that had already started on its trip into the unknown. The journey itself was an ordeal; the ship was manned by sailors who blasphemed and told frightful stories. One is led to conclude that Jerome had very little sense of humor, although the situation, at best, must have been disagreeable. He pointed out to the sailors that their conduct would only draw down the vengeance of heaven on the ship, and it needed all the help heaven could give it on the high seas. Angry at his interference, one of the sailors struck at Jerome; and soon there was a full-sized brawl in progress. In order to keep peace, the captain had Jerome transferred to another ship. The middle of the Atlantic Ocean was, he felt, no place to settle differences of opinion.

When the party arrived at Goa, in the Indies, the captain told the Dominican vicar-general that it would be wise to keep Jerome away from the sailors of his ship. As it happened, the vicar-general was looking for a companion for Sebastian de Canto, who was then leaving for Siam, and he appointed Jerome to accompany Sebastian. In such a casual chain of events, Jerome's feet were set upon the path of death.

At that time, the kingdom of Siam was anxious to hear the Christian missionaries. The king himself was favorable, and even the Portuguese traders had given the Dominicans a lot of good advertising. The fact that the Fathers immediately set about learning Siamese, which they soon spoke with an uncanny facility, increased the admiration of the pagan priests and the leaders of the people. All might have gone well had it not been for the jealousy of the Mohammedan traders, who were eager for Portuguese trade. Unknown to the Siamese, these traders laid plans for a massacre, and, on the appointed day, carried it out. Their first victim was Jerome of the Cross. It was sheer accident that they did not succeed in killing Sebastian de Canto at the same time. He was so badly injured that Portuguese traders, carrying him to safety, thought he was dead.

Sebastian de Canto, of whose beginnings we know nothing, showed in his death a true Christian courage. He lay half dead for months, and roused himself only when he heard that the king of Siam, angered at the Mohammedan traders, had caught the guilty men and was going to have them put to death. Sebastian, dragging himself painfully to the court, obtained an audience with the king. "Christ does not teach vengeance," he said. "I realize that these men have killed my companion and tried to kill me. So I have come to beg for their lives. I have forgiven them; you, too, must forgive." The king, deeply impressed, did as he was asked.

For a little while the mission prospered. Then Siam was invaded by a barbarian tribe from the North. The city in which Sebastian de Canto was preaching was under siege, and, in due time, fell to the invaders. As he knelt praying in the little mission convent, the heroic missionary was put to the sword.

GASPAR OF THE CROSS
(d. 1569)

The forbidden kingdom of China beckoned to missionaries of all nations, and it was the goal of their aspirations for centuries. After the first tentative embassies of the fourteenth century, which left no permanent remains, there was no European missionary allowed in for two hundred and fifty years. St. Francis Xavier died within sight of China, in 1552, and, thirty years later, a resourceful Jesuit, Father Mateo Ricci, came in through Macao and began a cultural association with the learned Chinese; the result of this was a tiny breach in the great wall of isolation. Twenty-eight years before Father Ricci and his ingenious clock penetrated China, a lone Portuguese Dominican, Gaspar of the Cross, made a daring journey into the long-sought mission field. Even though he established no lasting work, his courage should not go unnoticed, especially among his own.

Spain approached China from the East, and, in 1580, they established the Province of the Most Holy Rosary of the Philippines as the mission province for the conversion of China. It was based in Manila, and its history is one of the most glorious in the Order. Forty years earlier, the Portuguese, approaching from the West, had set up the Province of the Holy Cross of the East Indies; its center was in Goa. Twelve Portuguese friars from the convent of Lisbon set out, in 1548, to begin work in the vastness of the East. Gaspar of the Cross was the only one of them who actually went into China.

Gaspar was born in Portugal—probably in Evora—and received the habit in the convent of Azeiteo. Sent with the mission band to the Far East, he studied at Mozambique to master the languages (just which ones we do not know) that he would need for this perilous mission.

Gaspar's first mission assignment was Cambodia. Here he soon demonstrated that he had the qualities needed on this dangerous mission—a gift of tongues, a rare ability to get people to work with him, and an absolute fearlessness. His preaching was successful, but he failed to convince the king that he should be allowed to build a church. Retaining a friendly relationship, he was politely escorted to the borders of the kingdom and informed, once and for all, that the king did not want any permanent foundations of Christianity in his country.

The Chinese emperors, one and all, had declared that they wanted no European missionary admitted to the kingdom. Their officers stood ready at every entry to enforce the emperors' decrees. How, or even where,

Gaspar penetrated this grim line of defense we do not know. Somehow he did.

Even with his facility in languages, it was not possible to learn Chinese so perfectly in a short time that he would pass unnoticed. Gaspar, therefore, was handicapped to begin with; he traveled alone, furthermore, with no weapons, and no threat of reprisals for those who would molest him. Yet he was not molested; he traveled safely along the roads and into the cities, brashly overthrowing idols, and, at every opportunity, preaching a doctrine that was opposed in every way to the religion sacred to the celestial empire— and he emerged unscathed. We do not know why.

When soldiers were on the point of cutting him to pieces, he talked them out of it—arguing that if the idols had not harmed him, why should they? Puzzled, the soldiers kept passing him from one place to another, for someone else to handle. He must have had a charmed tongue, and a doubly-charmed life. Larger and larger crowds of people followed him, and, time after time, Gaspar was escorted to the city gates and told to move on. It was undignified, they all said, that the citizens of the emperor should be taught by foreigners. Yet (perhaps out of superstition) they were afraid to kill him. Possibly they admired this brash stranger who so coolly walked where angels feared to tread. Finally, when he had been declared *persona non grata* in every city available, someone brought him to the border of China and suggested pointedly that he go somewhere else. He had been in China seven years.

It had been a short interlude and an indecisive one. It is hard to tell if anything was actually accomplished by Gaspar's trek, but he had at least accomplished one thing—he had proved that there was a vast and hungry concourse of souls awaiting the word of God inside the walls of China. Not everyone felt as the emperor did about Christianity. Once any missionary was bold and ingenious enough to get in, there was an abundant harvest waiting him.

Gaspar was banished to Ormuz, where he preached for some time. Finally, seeing the impossibility of getting back into China, he returned to Portugal. Here he wrote a book about his visit to China, and it was published in 1570.

In 1569, when the plague was raging in Portugal, Gaspar went out as boldly among the stricken as he had among the Chinese. When he was at Setubal, nursing the sick, he received letters appointing him bishop of Malakka. He remarked that he would never be consecrated and that he would, in fact, die of the plague—being its last victim. His prophecy was fulfilled to the letter, and he died in Lisbon that same year, the last person to die of the plague.

Appearing only briefly in the records of the times is one Father Denis of the Cross, a Chinese convert of Gaspar of the Cross, who lived to be one hundred and twenty years old. The scanty records say that he made profession in the Congregation of the Holy Cross of the East Indies. The evidence indicates that he was the first citizen of China to have been professed as a Dominican, and the first to be raised to the priesthood. However, we have so little information about him that, until more is forthcoming, this honor remains the proud possession of Father Gregory Lo, who lived a hundred years later.

CHRISTOPHER OF THE CROSS
(d. 1569)

This famous missionary, who was called "the St. Dominic of the New World," could be advanced as a patron for one class of people we have always with us: those who are brilliant and lazy. Teachers who deal daily with such children might be encouraged by his story. Fortunately, Christopher received the grace to make use of his God-given intelligence.

Christopher of Lugo was born in Seville of parents who were described as poor and honest. Since he was a brilliant boy, he was early apprenticed to a professor, probably as a sort of house-boy. He studied grammar and philosophy —when the professor could catch him—and soon developed a real talent for gambling. The professor, who was genuinely fond of the boy, took him to Toledo and placed him in a school where he hoped Christopher would be kept busy. For several years there was no trouble, but, when Christopher reached his early teens, he associated with bad company again, and soon he was deep in debt.

Apparently, Christopher had great charm as well as many gifts, and the professor never could think any evil of him. Consequently, while Christopher was being pushed towards the priesthood by the doting professor, he was getting deeper into trouble. Finally, he faced a crisis. His gambling debts were beyond any hope of payment. He pawned his theology books, and, by some mental process we cannot quite follow, decided that he would use the money in one last gamble to decide his fate. If he won, he would pay his debts and reform. If he lost, he would join a band of robbers. The chronicles say piously that "the Lord ordained that he should win."

Christopher was as good as his word. He reformed, and thoroughly. He finished his studies and was ordained. Shortly after his ordination, his professor-friend was called to New Spain at the request of Las Casas. He took Christopher with him. Arriving at Guadalupe, they stayed with the Jeronymite religious, who were so edified by Christopher's behaviour and his evident piety that they tried persuading him to join their community.

They journeyed on and arrived in Mexico in the midst of an uproar over the emperor's treatment of the Indians. Here, Christopher displayed unusual gifts for bringing order out of chaos, and he soon calmed the whole situation. This brought him attention from everyone who had been involved in the whole sorry affair. Men whose lives he had saved thought that he was a saint. The Franciscan archbishop wanted to keep him in his office for further diplomatic work. The professor, who was returning to Spain, wanted him to go back with him. Christopher settled the question by entering the Dominican novitiate in Mexico City.

The Mexican province was in its infancy, and observance was rigid in the extreme. The members of the household lived in unending penance and prayer. Their preaching assignments took them over vast waterless distances on foot, and every feature of their life was difficult. This made a rugged novitiate for Christopher, the unambitious. It is a tribute to his virtue that he even survived it. He made his solemn vows in 1548. Shortly after, he was made novice-master.

The rest of Christopher's life was devoted to labors of the most difficult sort. The missions were far apart, and no allowance was made in the rule for the different conditions in the New World. Christopher displayed a great devotion to the Rosary, and was one of the greatest preachers ever to work in Mexico. Compassionate to others, he took a special joy in hearing confessions and in praying for the souls in purgatory. His reputation as a confessor drew souls of all classes to him, and it also brought down upon him the direct persecution of the devil. He had the graces of prophecy and of reading hearts. Several times, making use of these gifts, he snatched a soul from damnation at the last possible moment.

There is a curious little interlude in Christopher's life which has to do with suffering in another's place. A young woman, who came to him for confession, was obsessed with a fear of losing her soul. Fiercely vain, she was completely unable to understand his admonitions. Finally, since his advice did no good, he offered himself to God, that he might suffer in her place and accept all the bodily punishment that she deserved because of vanity. Very suddenly, she died a holy death. Christopher's offer apparently was accepted. He was covered with a skin disease, and for thirteen years it gave him no rest. No one else contracted it, and no remedies helped it. He was convinced that it was God's way of letting him expiate her punishment, and felt it was a small price to pay for a soul.

The province of Mexico was preparing a mission group for Florida, and Christopher planned to go, but, in 1562, he was elected provincial. This meant that he must stay in Mexico and make visitations on foot to the scattered convents. In 1569, on his way to Mexico City, he died on the road. His cause has never been proposed for beatification, but he will always be remembered as one of the most colorful figures ever to work in the Mexican missions.

POPE ST. PIUS V
(1504-1572)

People who do not know anything else about Pope Pius V are quite apt to remember him as the Pope of the Rosary, recalling his remarkable connection with the Battle of Lepanto.

Michael Ghislieri was born in 1504, in the tiny village of Bosco. His parents were poor and could not educate their alert little boy, who seemed far too talented to spend his life herding sheep. One day, as he was minding his father's small flock, two Dominicans came along the road and fell into conversation with him. Recognizing immediately that he was both virtuous and intelligent, they obtained permission from his parents to take the child with them and educate him. He left home at the age of twelve and did not return until his ordination, many years later.

After a preliminary course of studies, he received the Dominican habit and, as a novice, was sent to Lombardy. Here, for the first time, he met the well-organized forces of heresy which he was to combat so successfully in later life. In 1528, he went home for his first Mass, and he found that Bosco had been razed by the French. There was nothing left to tell him if his parents were living or dead. He finally found them, however, in a nearby town. After he had said Mass, he returned to a career that would keep him far from home for the rest of his life.

First as novice-master, then as prior of several convents, Michael proved to be a wise and charitable administrator. He was made inquisitor at Como, where many of his religious brethren had died as martyrs to the heretics. By the time of Michael's appointment there, the heretics' chief weapon was the printed word; they smuggled books in from Switzerland, causing untold harm by spreading them in the North of Italy. The new inquisitor set himself to fight this wicked traffic, and it was not the fault of the heretics that he did not follow his brethren to martyrdom. They ambushed him several times and laid a number of complicated plots to kill him, but only succeeded in making him determined to explain the situation more fully to the pope in Rome.

He arrived in Rome on Christmas Eve, tired, cold and hungry, and here it was not the heretics that caused him pain, but his own brethren. The prior at Santa Sabina saw fit to be sarcastic and inhospitable to the unimportant-looking friar, who said he was from Lombardy. The pope knew very well who he was, however, and immediately gave him the commission of working with the heretics in the Roman prisons.

He was a true father to these unfortunates, and he brought many of them back to the faith. One of his most appealing converts was a young Franciscan, a converted Jew of a wealthy family, who had lapsed into heresy through pride in his writing. Michael proceeded to straighten out his thinking, to give him the Dominican habit, and to assure him of his personal patronage, thus securing for the Church a splendid Scripture scholar and writer.

Michael was made bishop, then cardinal, and he continued, insofar as possible, to observe the Dominican rule.

In 1566, when the papal chair was vacant, the cardinals, chiefly through the influence of St. Charles Borromeo, elected Cardinal Ghislieri pope. With great grief, he accepted the office and chose the name Pius V. He began his reign by distributing to the poor of the city the money that he should by tradition have spent for a banquet. When someone criticized this, he observed that God would judge us more on our charity to the poor than on our good manners to the rich. Such an attitude was bound to make enemies in high places, but it endeared him to the poor, and it gave right-thinking men the hope that here was a man of integrity, and one who could help to reform the clergy and make a firm stand against the Lutheran heresy.

There were massive problems of immediate urgency during the brief reign of Pius V. From within, the peace of the Church was disturbed by the several heresies of Luther, Calvin, and the Lombards, and by the need for clergy reform. In addition, England was tottering on the brink of a break with Rome. The Netherlands were trying to break away from Spain and had embraced Protestantism. The missions across the sea needed attention. And all through the Mediterranean countries, the Turk was ravaging Christian cities, creeping closer to world conquest. In the six years of his reign, Pope Pius V had to deal with all these questions—any one of which was enough to occupy his entire time.

The unfortunate Mary Queen of Scots enjoyed the sympathy and encouragement of the pope. He sent encouraging letters to her, and once, at a time when no priest was allowed to go near her, he granted her special permission to receive Holy Communion by sending her a tiny pyx that contained consecrated Hosts. It was he who finally had to pronounce excommunication on Elizabeth of England, after he had given her every possible chance of repentance.

He encouraged the new society founded by St. Ignatius and established the Jesuits in the Gregorian University. He consecrated three Jesuit bishops for India, gave St. Francis Borgia his greatest cooperation, and helped to finance missionaries to China and Japan. He built the church of Our Lady of the Angels for the Franciscans and helped St. Philip Neri in his establishment of the Oratory. Probably the act for which he will be longest remembered is his leadership at the time of the Battle of Lepanto.

In 1565, the Knights of St. John defended Malta against a tremendous attack by the Turkish fleet and lost nearly every fighting man in the fortress. It was the pope who sent encouragement and money with which to rebuild their battered city. The pope called for a crusade among the Christian nations and appointed a leader who would be acceptable to all. He ordered the Forty Hours Devotion to be held in Rome, and he encouraged all to say the Rosary. When the Christian fleet sailed out to meet the enemy, every man on board had received the sacraments, and all were saying the Rosary. The fleet was small, and numerically it was no match for the Turkish fleet, which so far had never met defeat. They met in the Bay of Lepanto on Sunday morning, October the seventh. After a day of bitter fighting, and, on the part of the Christians, miraculous help, the Turkish fleet—what was left of it—fled in disgrace, broken and defeated, its power crushed forever.

Before the victorious fleet returned to Rome, the pope had had knowledge of the victory through miraculous means. He proclaimed a period of thanksgiving; he placed the invocation "Mary, Help of Christians" in the Litany of Loreto and established the feast in commemoration of the victory. It was almost the last act of a momentous career. He died at Easter time, and he was enrolled in the calendar of the saints in 1712.

ST. JOHN OF GORKUM
(d. 1572)

Previous to his martyrdom, all that we know of the life of St. John of Gorkum can be quickly told. He was a religious of his convent of Cologne who performed the duties of a parish priest in Holland, which was at that time engaged in a death struggle with the Spanish princes. The place and date of his birth are not known; those of his death will never be forgotten.

Anti-Spanish and Protestant soldiers banded themselves into lawless armies of pirates, and, unpaid and disillusioned, foraged for themselves in the seaports, looking for plunder. Reproached by the clergy, they turned on the Church and one band of pirates laid siege to the city of Gorkum, capturing it after a struggle. For reprisal—because of the city's determined defense—they gathered all members of the clergy in Gorkum into one miserable prison and set about taking revenge on the priests for their own grievances against the Spanish crown. Hearing of the plight of these poor priests, John left the comparative safety of his parish and entered Gorkum in disguise in order to give whatever assistance he might. Several times he entered the city to dispense the sacraments, and to bring consolation to the priests who were being cruelly tortured. Eventually, he also was taken prisoner and subjected to torture.

Angered by the endurance of the priests, the pirates increased their abuses. Some of the religious were very old and infirm, but one and all, even to an aged Augustinian who was so weak he could barely stand, they bore their martyrdom with patience and sweetness for ten terrible days and nights. They were repeatedly asked to deny the Real Presence, and just as repeatedly refused, which brought on more and more dreadful tortures. Finally they were thrown into the hold of a ship, and they were taken to another city to be killed in the presence of a Protestant nobleman, a man noted for his hatred of Catholicism.

Eleven Franciscans, a Premonstratensian, an Augustinian and four secular priests suffered with John of Cologne the long anguish of protracted martyrdom. Two of the number had been far from exemplary in their lives, but by their heroic constancy at the hour of trial blotted out the stains that might otherwise have kept them out of heaven. But, sadly, there should have been twenty martyrs of Gorkum. One, who weakened and was released after he had denied the Real Presence, lived but twenty-four hours to enjoy his wretched freedom. The other nineteen gloriously went to heaven.

The martyrs, after being exhibited to the curious townspeople (who paid to see the spectacle) and subjected to every manner of torture, were finally hanged in an old barn, amid the jeers of the mob. Stripped of their habits and made, like their Master, "the reproach of men and the outcast of the people," they benefitted by their Christ-like sufferings and detachment and died a Christ-like death.

The scene of their martyrdom soon became a place of pilgrimage, where all the Christian world did reverence to the men who were so courageously obedient unto death.

BLESSED MARY BARTOLOMEO BAGNESI
(1514-1577)

Mary Bagnesi's type of sanctity is not pleasing to today's psychiatrists, and, indeed, it is somewhat of a puzzle even to members of the Dominican family. The fact that she was so disgusted with the very thought of marriage that she became ill and had to go to bed for a lifetime seems strange to us. One has to remember that God calls his children to heaven by very diverse paths.

Marietta Bagnesi was born in 1514, in Florence. She was a beautiful and appealing child, with big eyes and a constant smile. Because she was tiny, she was always called Marietta. Her mother neglected her when she was a baby, leaving her to the casual care of others, and the little girl was often hungry and cold. She never protested, but was always gay and charming, and she was the special darling of her sister, who was a Dominican nun. The sisters made quite a pet of the little girl, and she ran through the cloisters unhampered, singing for the sisters from the throne of the community-room table. What brought about her utter disgust with marriage is hard to tell. When her father proposed that she marry an eligible young man, she reacted with horror. She had been managing the household since the death of her mother, and her father felt that having a home of her own would be the best thing in the world for her. When he suggested this, Marietta fell into a faint, and she remained in that condition for days. When she recovered, she could not stand up, and had to be put to bed.

At this point a strange interlude begins, which can only be explained by the fact that God does not operate in the same fashion we do. Marietta's father was fond of quack doctors, and quacks of the sixteenth century were really fantastic. Without protest the girl endured all the weird and frightful treatments they applied, suffering more from the treatments than she ever had from the malady. Today her ailment would probably be diagnosed as some type of spastic nerve malady. Packing her in mud and winding her in swaddling bands until she, according to her own account, "felt like a squashed raisin" could not have helped anything but the quack doctor's purse. The ailments continued unabated for thirty-four years.

Marietta had hoped to be a nun; four of her sisters were already in the convent. Because such a life was, of course, impossible for an invalid, her father attempted to better her spirits by having her accepted into the Third Order. A priest came from Santa Maria Novella and received her into the Order, but he excused her from the obligation of saying the Office because of the desperate nature of her illness. When he came the following year, she made her profession. For a little while after her profession, Marietta was able to get out of bed and could even walk a little. She could see and enjoy the beauties of the city. Then she fell ill again and went back to bed; this time she had asthma, pleurisy, and a kidney ailment.

The doctors contined their experimentations through all the years of her life. A mystic, who sometimes conversed with angels, saints, and devils, Marietta was suspected by the neighbors of being in league with the devil. Her protests that "she had seen him all right but he wasn't a friend of hers," went unheeded; they obtained permission to have her exorcised. Her confessor left her; he was afraid of becoming involved. Another priest who came to see her, mostly out of curiosity, stayed on as her confessor and directed her strange and troubled path for twenty-two years.

Marietta's little room became a sort of oratory, and troubled people came there to find peace. She had an unusually soothing effect on animals; several pet cats made her the object of their affection. One of them used to sleep on the foot of her bed, and if she became sick during the night would go out to find someone to care for her. Once, when the cat felt that Marietta was being neglected, it went out and fetched her a large cheese. The cats, according to the legend, did not even glance at the songbirds that she had in a cage beside the bed.

Marietta's spiritual life is hard to chronicle against such an odd background. In her last years, she was in almost constant ecstasy. The chaplain said Mass in her room, and she went to confession daily. She never discussed the sorrowful mysteries, because she could not do so without crying, but she often talked, with great animation and a shining face, about the glorious mysteries. Once she was raised out of her bed in an ecstasy. She shared her visions with another mystic, the Carmelite, Mary Magdalen de Pazzi. Because of her devotion to St. Bartholomew, she added his name to her own, and usually used it instead of her family name.

Mary Bartolomeo Bagnesi died in 1577 and was beatified in 1804.

JOHN SOLANO
(1504-1580)

John Solano, who succeeded the martyred Bishop Vincent of Valverde in the See of Cuzco, was born in Andalusia in 1504, and entered the Order at the Convent of St. Stephen, in Salamanca, when he was nineteen. He studied theology under Francis of Vittoria, and worked for several years in Spain, holding various offices of authority.

In 1544, he was nominated bishop of Cuzco by Charles V, and, after being consecrated, set out for the Indies. After three months of very rough crossing, he arrived in his new diocese, and he found a situation that would make any heart quail. His predecesssor had been killed by the Indians, after years of vain struggle to get just treatment for them from the Spaniards. Las Casas, the intrepid champion of the Indians, had refused the See. The Indians, as John Solano found them, were sick and wretchedly poor, slaves with no rights; at the same time the colonists, who had thrown aside the laws of the king and the Church, were reigning in small courts in luxury and idleness. John began with a sweeping move that was startling and most unpopular with the Spaniards: he took a share of the wealth that was being drained from the land, and he built a large and well-equipped hospital for the Indians.

There was little the Spanish colonials could do about this without incurring the king's anger, but they soon managed to stop the activities of the zealous new bishop. For sixteen years he worked and prayed in spite of the opposition, but, when he returned to Spain to put the case before the *Council of the Indies,* he found that the colonials had sent agents ahead of him. Nothing at all would be done by Spanish authorities to help the Indians or to stop the gold-greedy colonials. He resigned his bishopric and went to Rome, determined to stay there until he obtained some justice for the Indians. He planned to go to the Holy Land and live as a hermit after the Indian question was settled. But after twenty years there was still no hope, and justice for the Indians seemed a lost cause.

Living quietly at the Minerva, John Solano was always available for sermons or for any priestly work. Out of his family inheritance, he founded the College of St. Thomas at the Minerva and he taught there until his death in 1580.

ST. LOUIS BERTRAND
(1526-1581)

Louis Bertrand was baptized at the same font where his famous relative, St. Vincent Ferrer, had been baptized some two centuries before, and he grew up with but one thought in his mind—to imitate his saintly relative and become a Friar Preacher.

The father of Louis had at one time planned to become a Carthusian, and he was, as head of the family, undoubtedly an excellent Christian; but he bitterly opposed his eldest son's desire of renouncing his inheritance and becoming a friar. He succeeded in keeping Louis from taking the step until his son was eighteen. Louis ran away when he was fifteen, planning to become a missionary, but he was recognized by a friend of the family and brought home. He busied himself with practices of devotion far beyond his years and strength, and he attached himself to the Dominican fathers, who allowed him to serve Mass and work in the garden until he should be old enough to join them. At last, when he was eighteen, he joyfully fled from his father's house and donned the white habit he had so long desired. He was received in the convent of his native Valencia.

His troubles were not over, for his health was delicate; at every symptom of illness, his mother wept and his father entreated him to come home. He passed a troubled novitiate and thankfully made his vows. Two years later, he was raised to the priesthood, and, shortly after, he had the pleasure of seeing his two younger brothers start on their paths to the same goal. One of the brothers became a Dominican like himself, and they planned for the day when they could depart together for the missions. This dream was never to come true, for the younger brother died before he had finished his studies. It was left for Louis to become a missionary in the New World.

After several years as master of novices, where he proved himself prudent, kind, and firm, Louis volunteered for the foreign missions and was assigned to the territory of New Granada. In 1562, he left Valencia on foot, carrying staff and breviary and attended by two brothers. They set sail for the New World and arrived in their mission field. It was very unpromising. The people were devil-worshippers. They lived in country almost impossible of access, and they spoke a medley of languages that seemed impossible for Europeans to understand. Louis prayed for the gift of tongues, and he received this favor. The Indians understood him and were converted.

Louis spent seven years in New Granada, in which time he is said to have baptized nearly 25,000 Indians. He traveled from place to place, teaching the Gospel and establishing the Rosary devotion. He fought through pathless jungles, braved the hostility of the natives and the danger of wild beasts, as well as the tropical diseases and the unfriendly Spanish gold-seekers. Attempts were made on his life, and, at one time, he was threatened by a man with a gun; Louis made the Sign of the Cross and the gun was changed into a crucifix. By the Sign of the Cross and the Rosary, he marked out a path of miracles wherever he went.

Returning to Spain, Louis was once again appointed master of novices, and he inspired the young men with love of God and missionary zeal. He fell ill, and, though valiant attempts were made to save such a valuable member of the Order, he died on the day he had prophesied that he would die. In heaven he became the protector of the missions he had worked so hard to establish.

GILES GONZALES
(d. 1581)

The land of Chile had long been a temptation to the Spanish conquerors. In 1561, an expedition to that country was organized, and the king asked for chaplains to accompany it. Giles Gonzales and two other Dominicans were appointed for this important mission by the chapter of Lima.

Giles was from Seville, where he had entered the Order when he was very young. Sent to Peru soon after his ordination, he became a zealous preacher and a successful missionary. He had a frank and open disposition, and everyone liked him. He had also the happy ability of seeing things in their true perspective and was not often led astray by any pretense. This was a valuable faculty in a chaplain of such an expedition, for gold would be such a strong incentive to deceit and violence.

When the expedition arrived in Chile, Giles acquired the property for building a church and convent from a rich man who had been one of the first captains of the conquest in Peru, and who now wished to become a laybrother He was a good and faithful friend to Giles. The priest was to have the uncomfortable job of condemning the Spaniards for their injustices against the Indians.

The wealth and influence of the conquerors made a formidable citadel, and a few dauntless Dominicans attacked with the weapons of justice and charity. The Spaniards were both just and charitable at home, but they persisted in their course of savage injustice against the Indians. The natives all but worshipped Father Giles, who had spoken up so often and so boldly in their behalf. The Spaniards, on the contrary, hated him bitterly. To be rid of him, they decided upon a course which may seem amusing to us: in a report to the bishop, they accused Giles of heresy. This accusation, from men who busied themselves breaking all the Commandments seven days a week, must have had a strange sound even to their own ears.

It was a time when the charge of heresy brought an almost hysterical response from the public. Giles was promptly put in prison, and the case became tantamount to headline news. His friends, headed by the Franciscan superior, rallied to his defense. They knew only too well the intention of the bandits who had accused him, and they immediately went to the bishop. They told him that the only true charge that could be made against the Dominican was that he was killing himself with work, which was not a reflection on his orthodoxy. The whole interesting interlude ended with Giles being released from prison, and his place there was taken by the man who had accused him.

During all the twenty years that Giles Gonzales worked in Chile, the countryside was in a state of war, because of the conflicting interests of the Spaniards and the Indians. However, in spite of this, he managed to have his mission made a formal convent, to live strictly according to the rule, and to establish regular discipline in the convents of the new land.

Giles Gonzales, threatened many times with martyrdom, died in 1581, "with his boots on," trying to establish the Dominican Province of Chile.

PAULINUS OF ST. BERNARD
(1515-1585)

Paulinus was born in Lucca in 1515, of a family that was to give four members to the Order: he and his brother, Francis, and two sisters. The girls became nuns in their native city.

Paulinus gave very early evidence of a superior mind, and he displayed brilliance in his studies. When still very young in the Order he was appointed to direct the studium at Santa Maria Novella, in Florence. He obtained his doctorate in theology and began a career of preaching that was to bring him into contact with the greatest minds of the time.

In 1599, Savonarola's enemies made a last attempt to have his works condemned. He had been burned at the stake more than a half century before, yet he was still too much alive to satisfy the people whose feelings he had hurt. Knowing that the reigning Pope Paul IV disliked Savonarola, the opposition party gathered its forces and presented an array of propositions—all carefully taken out of context—for condemnation. Spearheading the party for condemnation were the famous Jesuit, Father Laynez, and the foremost theologian of the Augustinians. To the defense of their besieged brother went the best theological talent of the Dominican Order—Cardinal Ghislieri (the future Pope Pius V), and Paulinus of St. Bernard, who had just been named preacher-general at the Minerva.

The actual debate must have been an exhiliarating battle of wits. Everyone concerned in it was not only a capable apologist but was motivated by strong feeling; even today, people seem unable to view Savonarola with indifference. Cardinal Ghislieri, laboring under the difficulty that the pope was acting under strong prejudice and misinformation, managed to delay the decision until the propositions could be more completely studied. Paulinus, who was a dogged fighter, cornered the Augustinian and backed him down, bit by bit, until he was so near a conviction of heresy from his very involved statements that the Augustinian general hurriedly removed him from the arena. This left the field to Paulinus and the Jesuit, Father Laynez.

Not only were the two worthy opponents involved in the contest, and not only the two great Orders—the entire city of Rome took sides. And the city of Florence, devoted to its prophet, stormed heaven to spare Savonarola the opprobrium of condemnation. The devotion of the Forty Hours was held in churches of both cities, and the streets reverberated with the sounds of litanies. Saints and sinnners alike implored heaven's intervention; St. Philip Neri prayed earnestly for the exoneration of Savonarola, whom he admired very much. Perhaps it was his prayers and those of the saints of the day who arrested the condemnation; however, it was Paulinus who faced Father Laynez and, by means of a phonomenal memory and irrefutable logic, bested the brilliant Jesuit and brought the argument to a close. The decision finally came through in answer to the prayers of thousands—the doctrine of Savonarola were declared to be "not erroneous, not heretical, not schismatic, not scandalous." At the suggestion of Paulinus, some of his sermons were temporarily placed on the Index until they could be closely examined, but not even these were ever condemned. It was a complete victory.

The next move of Paulinus was to try to popularize the Forty Hours' devotion. Cardinal Ghislieri was strongly in favor of it, and was one day to invoke it in the hour of crisis, when the Turks threatened to conquer the world. With the encouragement of both men, the devotion was held over the weekends in Lent.

Shortly after this, Paulinus was called to pass on the sanity of St. Philip Neri, who had been turned in to the Sacred Congregation for his eccentric behavior. Paulinus not only exonerated him, but he gave the saint's persecutors some salty advice on following his example. St. Philip Neri called upon him later to help in the organization of the "Clerks Regular of the Mother of God." Paulinus subsequently made a foundation of his own: a house of regular observance at Chieti. Here he retired when he was temporarily suspended for his outspoken remarks about Church policy. During the time of his suspension, he energetically took up the work of a laybrother.

Paulinus was by this time an almost legendary character in the Order. Not all the fathers had met him personally, and he apparently had to be seen to be believed. After the pope had lifted the suspension, he was summoned to Rome for a general chapter, and the capitular fathers from the distant provinces were eagerly waiting to see who had worsted a Jesuit and an Augustinian and was as a close friend of St. Philip Neri. When a nondescript old friar in a ragged habit came limping in, driving a broken-down old donkey, they enquired of him if he had seen anything of the great Father Paulinus on the road. "Paulinus is here," he said briefly. On the same trip, a precipitous sacristan threw him out of a church, thinking that he was a beggar.

The colorful and controversial career of Paulinus of St. Bernard came to an end in 1585. He was killed by a fall down stairs.

SISTER PLAUTILLA NELLI
(1523-1587)

One hears a great deal about those who succeed, and sometimes about those who fail, if they are dramatic enough about it. But there is seldom much written about the near-misses, the people who came very near success and were frustrated by circumstances. Sister Plautilla was not—heaven forbid—a frustrated artist. That she is even mentioned in an age of great artists—when no other woman, religious or secular, is noted—indicates that she must have had extraordinary talent. But, as a nun of the Second Order of St. Dominic, she had made a choice of life that ran in a different channel from that for which she seemed naturally gifted.

Savonarola left an imprint not only on the gay and worldly folk of his day, but upon the serious religious as well. Convents of nuns were founded to follow to the letter his strict mode of life. One of the methods he suggested to offset the lure of irreligious art was the introduction of painting and sculpture into the Second Order monasteries, and also into those of the cloistered Third Order. A well-known example of this was the monastery in Prato, presided over by St. Catherine de Ricci, where the nuns became famous for the little angel figurines they molded. Another house in which his suggestions were faithfully carried out was the monastery in Florence that was founded during his lifetime. It was here that Plautilla Nelli entered the Order, and it is not unreasonable to suppose that she chose it deliberately, thinking that here she could put her talents to use for God.

Plautilla, the daughter of a Florentine patrician, was born in 1523. We know nothing else about her early years, except that she had a younger sister, Petronella, who followed her into the cloister. Petronella, who displayed some talent for writing, was asked to work on the life of Savonarola. Plautilla was trained in the art of the house, which was not art with a capital A, but, obviously, that endless treadmill of spiritual bouquets, pious pictures, and commemorative verses that so often functions in convents. One did not need a great deal of talent to carry on this work, only much patience, neatness, and piety. It soon developed that what Plautilla had was talent—a wealth of it.

One can sympathize with the superiors in the case. It might not be such a problem today to get professional training for a cloistered sister. It was an impossibility then. Women simply did not become artists. They could not be expected to take the long training—the life drawing, the travels, and the irregular hours that made up an artist's apprenticeship—and they certainly would not be admitted to the circle of master artists for discussion and mutual help. It is quite easy to discover this by checking the list of artists of that time; no woman's name appears on the lists for hundreds of years. Yet here was a talented girl, yearning to do vast canvases with great colorful groups of figures, living in a convent situated where she would paint spiritual bouquets for a lifetime. It is greatly to the credit of both Plautilla and her superiors that she courageously chose to stay where she was.

Plautilla's superiors obtained materials for her, and they secured what teachers they could. Her work received favorable comments from the artists who were consulted, though they conceded that she was handicapped beyond reason by her sex and by her vocation. Flatly refusing to give up, Plautilla painted, using the sisters as models, and she learned what she could in hearsay advice from outside the cloister.

It is hard merely to describe to someone precisely how a painter uses light and shadows, or how he solves problems of distance. Plautilla's critics observed that her men looked like women, which is hardly surprising, since she used the nuns for models. Her friends insisted that she had the qualities of greatness. She did several large altar-pieces that were commissioned by various churches in the city, and they won a good deal of favorable comment, in spite of errors in technique. Other artists faced the same problems of light and shadow and perspective as she did, but they could draw upon each other's experience to solve them. Plautilla worked alone.

Little remains today of the work of this zealous and gifted nun who might, in another time, have become one of the immortals in art. She can, however, be of considerable moral support to her sisters today. Hardly a person exists who does not feel that he is capable of great things, though in wiser moments he probably will admit that much of his ambition is pure wishful thinking. But it is a real sacrifice for a talented person to be caught in a web of mediocrity, either by policy or stupidity on someone's part, or simply because —at that time and place—great work simply is not being done.

Plautilla gives us an example of someone whose gift was not a pure delusion of grandeur, but an actuality—of someone who was frustrated by circumstances. Yet, it neither embittered her nor kept her from becoming what she obviously held as a higher ideal—a good Dominican.

Plautilla Nelli was elected superior of her monastery on several occasions in her life, and died there in 1587.

VENERABLE LOUIS OF GRANADA
(d. 1588)

Louis Sorria was the only child of a poor young couple who had recently come to Granada. His father died when Louis was a baby, leaving his mother alone to support him in a strange city. She did this by washing clothes and making the bread for the Dominican fathers, an apparently accidental circumstance which probably played an important part in giving the Order one of the most distinguished of its writers.

When he was a very small boy, Louis himself broke into public notice in a street fight. The Count Tendilla, who was passing, stopped to see the fight and finally separated the boys. He liked the looks of Louis and, since he was looking for a small boy to run errands in his household, promptly took him home. Louis was happy to get a job, since it was a way of helping his mother, and he set about learning all he could from his new environment. His duties were to accompany the Count's children to school, carry their books, and wait until they were ready to return home.

It was only a short time before the Count discovered that Louis had more of an aptitude for study than his own children did. With true Christian generosity, he arranged that Louis should be given an education. Louis responded to his kindness by becoming a noted student, and his benefactors were very proud of him when, in 1545, he entered the Dominican Convent of the Holy Cross. Here his superior intellect and his high qualities of character recommended him for the best education the Order could provide. He was sent to study under Francis of Vittoria, the most noted Spanish Dominican of the time. Under his teaching, the young Louis became one of the most promising young scholars in the Order. In 1534, he returned to Granada.

Louis' reputation had grown by leaps and bounds; he was known for his gifts of oratory, his writing, his spiritual advice in the confessional, his observance of religious life, and his outstanding intellectual brilliance. When he returned to his own land and was stationed at the church of the Scala Coeli, it was found that no one had exaggerated—Louis had more than fulfilled their hopes. It is hard to keep track of all his activities at this time, because he accomplished an incredible amount of work. He published a Spanish edition of the Imitation of Christ and a popular book of prayer and meditations. He wrote his best-known book, *The Sinners Guide,* which was translated into all the languages of Europe, and it is still in use. In all, he is credited with twenty-seven books.

Louis was selected for a number of offices in the Order. He attended several of the general chapters, and he was provincial of Portugal for a time. Ecclesiastical honors were offered him on many occasions, but he always managed to escape them. He was not so fortunate in avoiding court appointments; he was advisor to several rulers, and, for a short time, while the heir was under age, he was regent of the kingdom of Portugal.

Louis defeated the shortness of time by rising every morning at four o'clock, thus giving himself time for the poor as well as for the affairs of the kingdom. We are told that his day ended at eleven, which means nineteen hours of work and prayer a day.

Louis' sermons were always practical. They all demonstrated his love for animals, plants, and his remarkable ability to use all the things in nature to reach God. At one time, when he was preaching to a great concourse of people in Granada, he saw his mother coming up the aisle looking for a seat. The fashionable congregation, seeing the poorly-dressed woman, ignored her. Louis stopped his sermon and said very distinctly, "Give that woman place. She is my mother."

Louis was famous among the poor, the afflicted, and the troubled of heart. His mother and his Order might be very proud of his reputation as scholar and preacher, but Louis himself was more concerned with helping a poor penitent, or with sending a portion of his own meal out to some beggar at the gate. When his mother was old and could no longer work, he used to save most of his food each day for her. Unlike some public figures, Louis was always happiest when among his own brethren. He relaxed completely at recreation and he was the gayest and liveliest in the room.

Many saints were friends of Louis. St. Charles Borromeo knew and loved him, and St. Teresa wrote him a number of letters. St. Francis de Sales was an enthusiastic student of his writings.

Louis died in 1588, a stormy time for Spain. To his last days, Louis worked to refute public scandals which beset the country at that time. When his death became known, people rushed to snip off pieces of his habit for relics, because everyone revered him as a saint. He is buried in the Church of St. Dominic, in Lisbon.

The process for the beatification of Louis of Granada has reached the point at which he is designated as "venerable." Whether or not the process is ever completed, he will be remembered as one of the outstanding writers of the Order.

ST. CATHERINE DE RICCI
(1522-1589)

Alexandra de Ricci was born of a noble family in Prato, near Florence. Left motherless at an early age, the little girl took Our Lady as her mother and had for her a tender devotion. The child held familiar conversations with her guardian angel, who taught her a special manner of saying the Rosary and assisted her in the practice of virtue.

As soon as Alexandra was old enough to go away from home, she was sent to a monastery. Her aunt was the abbess there. Besides learning the lessons for which she was sent, the little girl developed a great devotion to the Passion. She prayed often before a certain picture of our Lord, and at the foot of a crucifix, which is still treasured as "Alexandra's crucifix." Returning from the monastery, when her education was completed according to the norm considered proper for girls at the time, she turned her attention to her vocation.

In her plans to enter a monastery of strict observance, she met with great opposition from her father. Allowed to go for a visit with the Dominican sisters in Prato, Alexandra begged to remain with them. However, her father took her away, promising to let her return. He did not keep his promise, and the girl fell so seriously ill that everyone despaired of her life. Frightened into agreement, her father gave his consent; Alexandra, soon recovering, entered the convent of St. Vincent.

In May, 1535, Alexandra received the habit from her uncle, who was confessor to the convent. She was given the name Catherine in religion, and she very happily set about imitating her beloved patron. Lost in celestial visions, she was quite unaware that the sisters had begun to wonder about her qualifications for the religious life: for in her ecstasies she seemed merely sleepy, and at times extremely stupid. Her companions did not suspect her of ecstasy when she dozed at community exercises, spilled food, or broke dishes. Neither did it occur to Sister Catherine that other people were not, like herself, rapt in ecstasy. She was on the point of being sent home when she became aware of the situation and told her confessor. He insisted that she tell her superiors of the heavenly favors she had received. From then on there was no question of dismissing the young novice, but fresh trials moved in upon her in the form of illness. Once more her life was endangered, and, after her recovery, she was left in frail health.

Sister Catherine was twenty years old when she began the weekly ecstasies of the Passion, which were to last for twelve years. She received the sacred stigmata, which remained with her always. In addition to the five wounds, she received, in the course of her Thursday-Friday ecstasies, many of the other wounds which our Lord suffered. Watching her face, the sisters could follow the course of the Passion, as she was mystically scourged and crowned with thorns. When the ecstasy was finished, she would be covered with wounds, and her shoulder remained deeply indented where the cross had been laid. Because of the publicity which these factors attracted, she asked our Lord to make the wounds less visible, and He did.

Despite her intense mystical life of prayer and penance, Catherine lived a busy life as prioress of the convent for several years. Material details of running a large household were well managed under her hands, and she was noted as a kind and considerate superior, particularly gentle with the sick. Troubled people, both within the convent and from the town, came to her for advice and prayer, and her participation in the Passion exerted a great influence for good among all who saw it.

After Catherine's death, in 1589, many miracles were performed at her tomb. Her cult soon spread from Prato throughout the whole of Italy and thence to the whole world.

VENERABLE BARTHOLOMEW OF THE MARTYRS
(1514-1590)

Famous both for his sagacity and his sanctity, Bartholomew of the Martyrs, archbishop of Braga in Portugal, has long been a candidate for sainthood. His cause, opened soon after his death, by 1845 had advanced to the point where he is designated as "Venerable."

Bartholomew Fernandes was born, in 1514, of poor parents in a little village near Lisbon, and baptized in the Church of the Martyrs there. By reason of the name of the church, and because of his personal devotion to the martyrs, he changed his name, while he was still quite young, to "Bartholomew of the Martyrs" and was rarely called anything else. At the age of thirteen he received the Dominican habit in Lisbon, and he made his profession in 1529. Until 1551, when he received the degrees of master of sacred theology, his career was that of many Dominican priests: preaching, and teaching philosophy and theology in the houses of the Order.

He was happily occupied in teaching theology at the monastery of Batalha when he was summoned to court to take over the education of a young prince. Disliking royal appointments as much as anyone could, he was still obliged to go, and he spent two years at the unwanted task. At the end of this time, to his great distress, the queen recommended him, in 1559, to fill the See of Braga. Bartholomew appealed to the provincial, Louis of Granada, confident that he would be supported in his refusal of the honor. Louis of Granada, however, told him, in obedience, to accept the position. There was nothing else to do about it, so he went with a heavy heart to be consecrated archbishop of Braga.

If the people of Braga had expected an archbishop who would reflect the political importance of Portugal, they were sadly mistaken. Bartholomew soon made it plain that he was himself a man of apostolic simplicity, and that he had no use for pomp and circumstance. He devoted his initial years in office to clergy reform and to the betterment of the condition of the poor—two almost hopeless problems that were plaguing the Church at the time. In 1561, he went to the Council of Trent, where his personal holiness and his keen theological insight made him a valuable member of a legislative group. One of his principal contributions to this important council was his appeal for the reform of both bishops and clergy in the matter of poverty.

He came back from the council determined to apply its regulation to his own diocese. This he did with great success, even in the face of the double disaster of plague and famine, which struck Portugal shortly thereafter.

In 1582, Bartholomew finally managed to resign his See, which he had been trying to do for years. He retired to the convent at Viana, where he died eight years later, beloved by all and popularly reverenced as a saint.

Bartholomew of the Martyrs was a busy writer, though most of his works are not available in English. With the exception of one book on the catechism, they were all on the subject of clergy reform, and have been frequently published and translated since his death.

PETER MARTINEZ
(d. 1591)

The saintly laybrother, Peter Martinez, was an early volunteer for the missions of the Philippines, and he was one of the first laybrothers to work in Manila.

Peter was born in Segovia, and his pious parents gave him a good education. He was noted for his candor, simplicity, and his spirit of prayer. He had a great devotion to Our Lady, and preferred to make gardening his life-work in order that he would have ample time to pray.

One day, while he was working in the fields, Our Lady appeared to him and told him to volunteer for the missions of the Far East, in the Order founded by her servant Dominic. She showed him the habit he was to wear, and she told him to go to Segovia and make immediate application, which he did. He received the habit of a laybrother there, and soon he was noted as a holy and hard-working brother of sweet disposition and great power of prayer. When a missionary from the Philippines came to Segovia looking for volunteers, Peter asked to go with him. Unwilling as they were to lose him, the brothers at Segovia agreed that he would be a tremendous help on the missions. He sailed for Manila in 1588.

Peter Martinez was to live only a few years in the hot climate of the Philippines before fever claimed him for heaven. He was first made porter in Manila, and he pursued his duties absorbed in prayer. The Rosary mysteries were his constant theme of meditation, and he had great gifts of contemplative prayer. He had the power of discerning spirits and could discourse with great eloquence on spiritual subjects, though he seldom spoke otherwise. Once, the governor of the Philippines asked him idly for some thoughts on the Rosary, and he stood dumbfounded while the quiet laybrother preached him a lengthy and inspiring sermon on the devotion. He was made sacristan, which gave him more time for contemplative prayer than the job of porter ordinarily did, but soon he was assigned to the mission of Pangasinan.

Here, after a few months, he caught a fever and died, in 1591, leaving a reputation for holiness in every place he had lived.

DOMINIC OF SALAZAR
(1513-1594)

The fighting first bishop of Manila was a many-sided character and, of his time, one of the most traveled men in the Order. He was also the best friend the natives of the Philippines had in the unhappy years of the conquest.

Dominic was born in 1513 in Old Castile of a distinguished and wealthy family. He went to the University of Salamanca, where he studied under Francis of Vittoria, and he entered the Order in the Convent of St. Stephen, in Salamanca, in 1545. Two years later he was sent to New Spain. One of the first people he met in the New World was the great Bartholomew de las Casas, who promptly sold him his program of protecting the Indians.

Dominic of Salazar was first made professor at the house of studies in Mexico City. Here, in his spare time, he studied various Indian dialects and soon became an expert in several of them. He was a renowned speaker in these difficult languages, and also in Spanish—which he used mainly in trying to convey ideas of justice and charity to the conquerors. In 1552, he was sent to South America, and there he learned a number of new Indian dialects, and he carried on the same program of opposition to the greed of the colonials. In 1556, he gave a spirited defense of the Indians in Mexico City. Two years later, he went to Florida with the Tristan de Luna expedition and survived almost incredible hardships. He returned to Mexico convinced that the whole idea of conquest was open to question.

In all, he spent a quarter of a century in Mexico trying to obtain justice for the natives. In 1576 he was in Spain, speaking on this subject. His bluntness landed him in jail for some time; the Spaniards did not like to hear such unpleasant things about the king's soldiers. When he was released, he went on a pilgrimage to the shrine of Our Lady of Atocha, in Madrid, where Bartholomew de las Casas was buried. Kneeling at the tomb of his old friend, he wondered whether anyone could succeed where the great "Protector of the Indians" had failed. Then, resolved to die trying, he prepared to go back to Mexico. Philip II, who perhaps thought that a change of air would be good for this outspoken critic of the Mexico conquerors, appointed him bishop of Manila.

Dominic of Salazar was now more than sixty years old, a sturdy old warrior of the Lord, but he was hardly in condition to cross two oceans and begin again. However, he went in obedience, and after a long, harrowing trip on which all of his companions died of hardship, he arrived in Manila in 1581.

He had a very real doubt as to the justice of the Spanish conquest of the Philippines; he had asked many embarrassing questions of the Council of the Indies. Word had already reached the Philippines that the new bishop was somewhat obsessed on the subject of justice to the Indians. He was threatened in the streets of Manila by Spanish officers, one of whom told him, according to accounts, to "watch his step, because he could hit a mitre at fifty paces with his arquebus." The governor himself once laid violent hands on the bishop. One is not surprised to read that Dominic of Salazar was considered a man of austerity and inflexible severity; it is not quite fair, however, to omit mentioning the provocations that shaped his attitude. In context, it was not only reasonable but inevitable.

Once more Dominic of Salazar took the long road to Spain in 1591. He pleaded with the Council of the Indies, and he gave what is considered the best theological treatment left us in writing on the vexing question of conquest. Rebuffed by men who should have been the first to help him, the old bishop struggled on in a losing fight. Addressing the Council of the Indies on December 4, 1594, he suffered a stroke and fell dead at the feet of his adversaries.

JOHN DE CASTRO
(d. 1592)

Among the men who fought for the cause of the Philippine natives against the oppression of Spanish fortune-hunters, the name of John de Castro looms large. He was the right-hand man of the indomitable Bishop Dominic of Salazar.

John was born in Burgos, of a noble and virtuous family. His mother died when he was very small, and his father, after some time, entered the Dominican convent at Burgos. John, who grew up in the household of his uncle, thought of nothing else than joining his father when he should be old enough. As soon as they would admit him, he received the habit, successfully completed his novitiate, and was ordained. When a missionary from the Philippines came to Burgos recruiting volunteers, he submitted his name. A short time later, after saying an affectionate goodbye to his father, who remained in Spain, he set out across the ocean.

Like many of those designated for the Far East, John served his mission apprenticeship in Mexico. In 1572, he was provincial of Chiapa. Finally he was sent to the Philippines, arriving there in 1587 with a band of Dominican volunteers.

Dominic of Salazar was bishop, and was struggling almost single-handed with the problems of the colonial government and the oppression of the natives. He hailed the new recruits with great joy, and told them to take a week's vacation before they settled down to work; he probably knew it was the last they would ever have time to enjoy. At the end of the brief rest, the new recruits were scattered. Some went to Bataan to begin a mission, some stayed in Manila. John de Castro was sent by the bishop to build a church and convent outside Manila.

He had no money, no land and no helpers. When he chose a site that was under water from an arm of the sea, everyone who had looked with favor on his plan deserted him. He had received a revelation that this was to be the place, and he went ahead with the building. The water receded, leaving an unexpectedly sound foundation. Money came in, in small amounts, but steadily. In four months he had built a temporary shelter and was planning a permanent church. After many vicissitudes, including fire, war, raids by pirates, hurricanes, and assorted troubles, the church was finally completed in 1599.

Building the church could have taken up all of John de Castro's time, but it did not. He mastered several of the local dialects so that he could preach to the people, and he fought steadily along with the bishop to try to keep the Spanish colonials from encroaching on the rights of the natives. He picked up Chinese from coolies in Manila, and volunteered to go to China and work for awhile, if he was needed. He was.

Going into China with a smuggler who was usually successful, they had a streak of bad luck. The boat was searched, and the missionaries were taken to prison. A kind and charitable Chinese merchant bought their freedom and took them home with him, and they stayed there for a year under house arrest, though quite happy otherwise. They preached every day to the Chinese who came to them there, and even said Mass occasionally, although they had so little bread and wine that it had to be hoarded and used sparingly. When the missionaries heard that the governor planned to punish the ship captain for bringing them in, they offered to take the prescribed hundred blows in his stead. The judge, amazed at such an offer, finally let the smuggler off without any punishment. However, the missionaries were banished from China, and they returned to Manila, after a two year round trip.

John de Castro spent the rest of his days preaching to the natives of the Philippines. He had a gift for languages, and he employed it constantly. He did not like to preach to the Spanish, always dodging such assignments if possible, but he was always available to the natives.

John de Castro died in Manila in 1592, and he was mourned by the natives and the brethren alike.

MATTHEW OF PEACE
(d. 1597)

Matthew of Peace was a curiously contradictory character, or perhaps he merely looks that way because his records are fragmentary. The situation is further confused by the fact that there were two men by this name who worked in the same part of the world, at nearly the same time (a not uncommon feature of Dominican history) and their works are sometimes transposed from one account to the other. One man by this name was a priest and a writer. Our Matthew was a laybrother.

We have no information where or when Matthew was born. He comes into our history in the year 1538, on his wedding day, when, instead of going to the altar to be married, he fled to the convent in Mexico City and received the Dominican habit. After his novitiate, he made profession for the province of Guatemala and went there almost immediately. For the next half-century, his fortunes were to be entwined with those of the big Dominican convent in what is now Guatemala City.

Matthew soon established himself as a friend of the Indians. He tirelessly went about gathering alms for them, and finally bought a piece of land on which he built a hospital for sick Indians, and a shrine of Our Lady of Candelaria. The Indians flocked to his hospital, though they would not go near the one built by the Spanish king. He carried in on his own shoulders some patients, and he cared for most of them himself. Once, when he was carrying a very sick Indian to his hospital, some benefactors of the convent stopped him in the street, and he was obliged to set the patient down momentarily while he replied to their questions. Both he and they were surprised when, turning to resume his burden, he found, not a sick Indian, but a large and very beautiful crucifix.

Matthew cleaned dormitories, weeded the garden, and took care of the refectory and chapel. He must have worked around the clock to accomplish all that the records say he did. Although many people, both Spanish and Indian, came to him for prayers and advice, it never seemed to concern him that people thought him wise. He learned three native dialects, which was quite an accomplishment, and this enabled him to help the Indians with their catechism. For nearly fifty years he lived this quiet and fruitful life, never calling attention to himself or seeking any praise. He died, after doing countless good works, in 1597. He was mourned by the poor.

PAUL OF ST. MARY
(d. 1597)

Paul of St. Mary is something of a phenomenon in an Order that prides itself on its scholars and scholarship; he was an example of the good boy who always wanted to be a religious, but who just did not seem to have the qualifications.

Paul was admitted as a laybrother in the Convent of St. Paul in Seville when he was thirty years old. He had given no indication of any sort of aptitude, but he was humble and prayerful, and the fathers felt they should give him a trial. At the end of the year of trial, when they assembled to vote on admitting him to profession, they all agreed on the decision. Paul was pious and humble and made no trouble for anyone. But he could not seem to learn anything, and, furthermore, his health was very poor. It was decided to dismiss him, so the master of laybrothers told him that he should prepare to return home.

Paul made no objection. He knew he was not very bright and that his health was bad. On looking over the situation honestly, he had to admit that there was no reason at all why they should keep him. But he threw himself on his knees in front of his crucifix and begged: "Keep me, Lord —and let me learn something—anything—that will be of value to your work here."

The religious in charge of the clothing room had gone to get secular clothes for Paul, and he found that the door was locked. He searched vainly for the key, losing a great deal of time asking other people about it. Finally he decided he would break in the door. Just as he was setting about this, the bell on the novitiate door rang, and a voice came through the grating: "Father Prior said *not* to take the habit off him tonight." The harrassed religious heaved a sigh of relief and carried the message to Brother Paul, who was waiting in his cell for the secular clothes.

The next morning the prior asked the master of laybrothers if he had dismissed Brother Paul yet. The master of laybrothers replied in some surprise: "Of course I haven't—you sent word not to." The prior, greatly surprised, investigated the story. Finally he reached a decision. "Let the boy alone," he said. "At least he can pray." With this none-too-enthusiastic beginning, Paul made his profession in 1565.

Paul of St. Mary never succeeded in developing any of the talents he might have wished for. He did, however, become an expert in the art which is the fine art of the saints—prayer. He gave himself completely to prayer and to the simple duties that were assigned to him, treasuring no illusions about his abilities and asking for nothing but the privilege of living in God's house. He did his best work—or perhaps it was just that he was least clumsy —in the infirmary, so that is where he was assigned for most of his life. Sick people, who possibly cringed at the way he handled trays, or wished he had smaller feet, at least soon learned that Paul's prayers worked wonders. A determined and devoted little stream of people began seeking him out, asking him for his prayers. He made heroic efforts to keep out of people's way, but they found him anyway.

One day Paul went into a church in which a priest had just performed an exorcism. The devil who had been cast out was still at large, and, when he saw the laybrother approaching, he cried out loudly: "There's somebody

I don't like. An old enemy of mine. And you ought to see how humble he is—how prayerful." Covered with confusion, Paul beat a hurried retreat.

Inevitably, Paul's gift for healing began to be talked about. As long as he could keep people from speaking of it, he was happy to help them. He did not like to have them praise him. One day a woman came to the door to ask his help. She had a very bad cancer on her face, and she begged the prior to have Brother Paul touch it in order that it would be cured. The prior sent for the laybrother and commanded him to heal her, which he did.

One of the jobs Paul did from time to time was manage the porter's gate and dispense food to the poor. Most of the food was begged, but Paul used to save his own food from the table, and encouraged others to do the same, so that there would be enough for the crowds who came. Sometimes, even at that, he had to stretch it—and, it was said, he could multiply food if need be. One night, after he had given out everything, a beggar came to the gate. Paul had nothing left but some fish heads he had been saving for his own supper. He wrapped them in paper and gave them to the beggar. When the beggar opened his package, he found four beautiful, fresh fish. From these incidents, it was easy to see the origin of the name, "Paul of the Poor."

One of the curious things about this laybrother is that he must have had the gift of bi-location. He often prayed for travelers and pilgrims who were exposed to danger on the road. One day he was praying for travelers in Sicily. At an isolated spot in Sicily, a wagon-driver on a lonely road ran into an ambush of bandits. He prayed for help, and, almost instantly, a man wearing the habit of a Dominican laybrother appeared at the side of the road and threw his scapular over the terrified wagon-driver. The bandits ran away, leaving the driver unhurt. The laybrother remained, and even accepted a ride for part of the journey with the puzzled wagon-driver. On being asked, he said that his name was Brother Paul, and that he lived in Seville. Some time later the wagon-driver was in Spain, and he made a special trip to Seville to see if he could find the brother. He found Brother Paul and recognized him, but the prior said it was nonsense to think that Paul had been in Sicily—he had been in charge of the door at Seville for twenty-seven years.

In 1597 Seville was visited with a mysterious plague which caused many deaths. Paul of St. Mary, who knew that he would die of this illness, went matter-of-factly about his business until he succumbed to the disease. On his deathbed, he apologized to the community for not being of any use to anyone, and he thanked them for their patience with him. His death was a signal of mourning for the poor of Seville.

MICHAEL BONELLI
(1541-1598)

A great deal has been written about the practice of nepotism in the Church during the Renaissance. One person who reaped no privileges from the fact of being a cardinal's nephew was Michael Bonelli, the protegé of Pope St. Pius V.

Anthony Bonelli was born in Bosco in 1541. Father Michael Ghislieri, the future Pope Pius V, took an interest in the lad who was his grandnephew, and brought him to Rome when he went there as inquisitor-general. He enrolled Anthony in the German College and kept a sharp eye on his grades and behavior. At the age of eighteen, Anthony entered the Order at the Convent of the Minerva, taking the name Michael in religion.

It was a difficult business trying to walk in the footsteps of a saint who was not only a near relative, but also a power in Roman politics. Greatly to the credit of the young Brother Michael, it was the religious observance of his uncle that he chose to imitate. It required giant strides, and perhaps he fell short; he did succeed, however, in being a model of regularity and obedience, a most difficult accomplishment then, or now. He was ordained in 1565.

Michael Ghislieri was elected pope in 1566. Shortly after his election, the cardinals indicated that they wanted his young grandnephew appointed to the College of Cardinals. Pope Pius demurred, because he did not believe in such appointments. The cardinals insisted, and young Michael Bonelli was given the red hat and the title of Santa Maria Sopra Minerva, succeeding his famous uncle. It soon became obvious that the appointment was no political plum; Cardinal Bonelli was expected to follow in the footsteps of the most austere man in Rome. When another cardinal, who had an independent fortune, offered to outfit him in the expensive robes of his office, he politely declined in favor of his uncle's hand-me-downs. His furniture was of the poorest, his table the most meager, outside the Vatican. If ever his tastes were attracted to something less monastic, there was always the example of the ascetic on Peter's throne.

Two years later Pope Pius appointed Cardinal Bonelli papal chamberlain, an office which brought with it an estate, which the pope promptly confiscated to help raise an army against the Turks. Since he himself gave up everything he could lay hands on for the raising of the army, his nephew could hardly protest. Bit by bit, the example reached to the other cardinals, who already had a St. Charles Borromeo to inspire them. It is interesting to see how persistently these men employed the leaven of example rather than force, but the experience must have been difficult to live through.

Michael Bonelli, who had taken the name Cardinal Alexandrin, after his uncle, was given the touchy task of organizing the league against the Turks. He went to Spain and Portugal on the mission, and dealt with such slippery characters as Philip II and Catherine de Medici, who were surprised and not too happy with this new-type Renaissance cardinal. His austerity and his stubborn determination not to collaborate with the Huguenots made Catherine de Medici particularly deadly to deal with. No one could have hoped for complete success in negotiating with such people. However, when Cardinal Alexandrin was called back to Rome by the pope's illness, it was to receive probably the only compliment of a lifetime from the dying saint; Pope Pius stated that if the league had succeeded in any measure at all, it was due to the good work of Cardinal Alexandrin.

Cardinal Alexandrin outlived his famous relative by more than a quarter of a century, serving in many capacities under six popes. He died of pleurisy, in 1598, and was buried in his titular Church of the Minerva.

MICHAEL OF ZAMORA
(16th Century)

Michael of Zamora found out, the hard way, the unpleasant truths that friends can be fickle and that money may make a difference.

Michael was born in Zamora, around the close of the fifteenth century, and, as soon as he was old enough, he sailed for the New World to make his fortune. He made it, too—just how, we are not told. However, after a few years, he returned to Spain with a promising supply of gold and jewels, and he presumed he could settle down to a prosperous and peaceful life in his own land, forgetting the hardships of colonial life.

Just what inspired him to an experiment on his relatives, we do not know; perhaps he meant it as a joke. Whatever his reason, he carefully hid his good clothes and his money and approached his ancestral home clothed in rags. He did receive a fond welcome from his old father, who had given up hope of ever seeing his son again. Making no comment on his son's poor clothes, his father fed him well and listened to his stories of far-off lands. The rest of the family were not so discreet. They made unkind remarks about his lack of initiative, hinting that they would be glad if he would just go back to the Indies and stay.

After a few days of this masquerade, Michael dressed up in his good clothes and rode in on a fine horse. He oozed prosperity, and it was extraordinary how his relatives changed their attitude. They fawned upon him and deferred to him until the whole thing sickened him. "I am the same Michael who was here yesterday," he said. "Does money matter that much?"

After a few days of this unpleasant revelation of humanity, Michael made provision for his father out of his vast fortune, and giving the rest to charity, he sailed for Mexico. His wife had died while he was in the Indies the first time, and he was left with the care of a small son. He took the boy to Mexico with him, and put him in a school in Mexico City. Then, he and a friend he had known previously in the Indies, making a retreat together, decided to become hermits. Eventually the two friends took the religious habit, Michael becoming a Dominican laybrother, his friend a Franciscan.

Michael had received training as an architect, and he was greatly in demand for supervising religious buildings. When his son had finished school, he, too, became a Dominican laybrother. The young man had a talent for languages, and becoming a specialist in Mexican languages, he contributed a great service to the missionaries.

At the end of a busy life, Brother Michael was called to Oaxaca to build an aqueduct. Old and worn by years of fasting, he had a painful illness that he had borne patiently for a long time. Becoming very ill, he died at Oaxaca and was buried there, leaving a reputation as a pious and practical man.

SEVENTEENTH CENTURY

VENERABLE ROBERT NUTTER
(d. 1600)

Most candidates coming into religion have at least the advantage of a personal interview with some member of the Order they wish to join, and have the opportunity of discussing its ideals and aims in reasonable leisure before committing themselves. Robert Nutter applied by mail for membership to an Order he know only by hearsay, because Dominicans were banned from his unhappy country at the time. To make it more interesting, there is evidence that he made this request at a time when he himself was in jail awaiting sentence, and the letter was smuggled out by friends.

Robert Nutter was born in Lancashire, around 1555, of a wealthy family which usually sent its sons to Oxford. However, when Robert and his brother were of college age, both wished to be priests. The Church in England was suffering fire and the sword, so the two young men were smuggled out across the channel to the English college at Rheims. Robert was ordained there in 1581.

Young men who studied abroad for the priesthood were marked for death if they returned to England. This did not daunt Robert and his companion, a Father Haydock, as they planned their trip home. Both of them expected to be martyred; indeed, that was part of the priesthood those days in England. Three weeks after ordination, the two young men, disguised, and using forged names and passports, returned to their country and set about the work for which they had been ordained. Robert stayed clear of the law for two years. Then he was captured and put in the Tower. Here he was tortured in several ways. One instrument of torture employed was a device called "the scavenger's daughter"; even without knowing exactly what it was, one wonders how a man could emerge from such treatment and go right back to his dangerous job again.

Robert was released from the Tower—after being presented with a bill for food and candles—and, with twenty other priests, was put on board a ship for banishment. Even though they made a loud English clamor at the injustice of being sentenced without a trial (a detail that would never have bothered a Continental), they were shipped off to Normandy and threatened with immediate death if they returned.

By 1586, Father Nutter was back in England, refreshed and full of new ideas. However, the vigilance had tightened up, and he was taken prisoner in a short time. He began a long stint at Newgate prison, one of the more infamous. After a few years, he and a number of other priests were transferred to an island prison.

Here the life was severe and lonely and frustrating, but not as desperate as it had been at Newgate. The place was not so filthy, and there was no torture. Father Nutter pointed out that many monks lived as austerely, and he, with several other of the more fervent, set up a rule of life, trying to follow a sort of monastic routine. It was during this time, if the tradition is correct, that he wrote to the French Dominican provincial and begged to be admitted to the Order as a Tertiary.

After sixteen years of prison Robert Nutter and several other priests escaped and made their way to Lancashire. One account of his life proposes that at this time he met a Dominican priest, who formally received him into the Order. We do not know. There was pitifully little time to do anything, for he was captured with three other priests at Lincoln, and the death sentence was immediately carried out.

The tradition of the sanctity of Robert Nutter, like that of the other English martyr priests, was kept by the faithful during the years of persecution. His cause was formally opened in 1929, along with that of many other priests, mostly Jesuits.

Thomas Hesketh, Attorney of the Court of Wards, and a notorious priest-chaser, wrote a curiously-spelled account of Robert Nutter in a letter to his superior officer. It gives us a vivid picture:

It appeared that the true name of one of the priestes was Robert Nutter, born in Lancashire. he departed owt of England XXIJte yeares past & after that he had bene Scholler at Rames & at Rome he was made Priest by the Busshop of Laon & then Retorned into England, before the Statute made in the XXVIJ yeare of her MAties Reigne, And was then apprehended & Banisshed. And after that havinge an Intencon to go out of ffraunce into Scotland he was taken uppon the Seas in a ffrench Shipp by Captain Burrowes & Browght into England where he Remained in Wisbich & other prisoners XJ yeares. And uppon the mondaie before Palmesondaie Last he escaped owt of Wisbich the gate beinge left open by the Porter. He wolde not Confesse wher the Porter was nor what became of him. He confessed that he was a Professed ffryar of the Order of St. dominicke duringe the tyme he was prisoner in Wisbich, where in the presence of dyver priestes he did take his vowe the wche was certified to the Provinciall of the Order at Lisbon & by him allowed . . . Your honor maie easilie discerne, and so did al men as I thincke that were at the execucon, what notable traytors these kynd of peopele are, ffor not withstanding all their Glorious Speeches yett their Opinion & their doctrine is, that her highness is but tenant at will of her crowne to the Pope . . .

MARY RAZZI
(1552-1600)

The extraordinary career of Mary Razzi should convince us, among other things, that God likes variety among his creatures, and that sanctity is never to be by-passed for a mere matter of circumstances.

Mary Razzi was born on the Greek island of Chios, in 1552. Her father was a wealthy Genoese, her mother a Greek. The little girl was baptized in the church of St. Dominic, and began to show signs of unusual spiritual gifts very early in life. She had firmly made up her mind to enter a convent, but when she reached the age of twelve she was dismayed to discover that her parents had already arranged a marriage for her. A stormy year followed, in which Mary did everything in her power to avoid the marriage. However, her most vigorous efforts were of no use, and she was finally forced into the unwelcome union.

The chronology here is a little vague. Since Mary was left, at eighteen, a widow with two children and two had died, she must have married at thirteen or fourteen. Of her husband we have no information, except that he was captured and killed by the Turks as he and his family were fleeing Chios. Mary, who had suffered the indignities of Christian slavery under the conquering Turks, was moved to flight when she heard that the Grand Vizier was planning to take her two little boys away from her and train them as Moslems. She, her husband and children, fled on a small ship which was overtaken by pirates in the Straits of Messina. The helpless young wife stood by, sheltering her two tiny boys, and saw her husband slaughtered by the Turks. Then, through some twist of fortune, she was set ashore unhurt.

The widow arrived in Sicily terrified. The sole support of two babies, she was unable to speak the language and was a complete stranger to all the customs. She was only eighteen years old, very pretty, and there were many people who felt that another marriage—almost any sort of marriage—would solve her difficulties. Mary disagreed. Her parents had forced her into marriage. Now she was determined to consecrate herself to the service of God.

She placed her two little boys, Basil and Nicholas, with kindly people who would give them a home; she could see them occasionally. Both of her boys would one day become Dominicans, so it is evident that they were given a good education by their foster parents. Mary herself went to the Dominican church and asked for the Third Order habit. She received it, after some time, in a public ceremony in Messina. After this, she retired into a little room that someone had offered her. It was in one of the large homes near the Dominican church. Here, for fourteen years, she prayed almost uninterruptedly. Her reputation for sanctity was very great, and people of all classes came to her for advice and prayers.

When her second son was sent to Rome for his studies, Mary's older son was already a Dominican student at the Minerva. Mary decided it would be a rare opportunity to see Rome and to be near her sons, so she obtained permission to travel with her son. They took passage on a ship, and it was barely out of sight of land when they were horrified to see a Turkish ship bearing down upon them. Mary knew all too well what cruelty was represented by that slanted sail. She dropped to her knees and begged God to spare them. As they watched, the Turkish ship altered its course, going away without bothering them.

In Rome, a kindly family named Marini took her in, and she resumed her life of prayer and penance. She lived in perpetual abstinence, fasting most of the time, and she slept, if at all, on boards. She seemed hardly to use any time for the needs of physical life, but to spend her energies in heavenly conversations. Her little room was lighted up by the heavenly glow of her distinguished visitors: Our Lord and His Blessed Mother, St. Dominic, St. Hyacinth, St. Catherine of Siena, and shining troops of angels. The devil came, too, under horrible shapes—once as a tiger, other times as a large snake—and sometimes threw her around and beat her. She emerged from these bouts badly battered and bleeding, but victorious.

Outwardly, Mary's life was quiet. She lived in the neighborhood of the Minerva, where she went to Mass, and where her two sons were stationed. Several times a week she went to the public hospitals to help care for the patients, and she always saved the food that was given her for the sick poor. People in trouble would seek her out in her little room, or when she was praying in the Minerva. One day a young man who had resolved to commit suicide came up to her as she was praying and explained what he was going to do. She talked with him for awhile, convinced him to go to confession, and then reached under her scapular and took out a number of gold coins. "This will tide you over until you get back to your people," she told him. How did the gold coins happen to be there? She did not know. But whenever she needed money for anyone who was in trouble she always found it in some unlikely place.

On Pentecost Sunday, 1593, while making her thanksgiving after Communion in the church of the Minerva, she was overwhelmed with pain. It centered in her head, and it was so excruciating that she fainted. She realized that she had been given the stigmata of the crown of thorns. On a later occasion, she had a vision of our Lord bound to the column of the scourging.

At this time she received several of the other wounds. She bore these marks of divine favor until her death, but she was so reticent that no one of her companions knew the full extent of her stigmata.

One time, when she was attending Compline at the Church of the Minerva, she saw the Blessed Virgin going up and down the aisle, blessing the brethren. Several times she saw angels walking in the Salve procession. These "happier" visions she revealed, but she kept the sorrowful ones to herself.

There is evidence that Mary was not very talented as a babysitter. She was left one day with little Vincent Marini, the baby of the family who had been so kind to her. She put him down on the bed and gave him a nut to play with. Naturally, he swallowed it. Mary, coming in a few minutes later, discovered that the baby had choked to death. She knew only one way to handle such a situation; she began to pray. Soon the baby coughed up the nut, and began crying in a robust manner. The child died a few days later, and he returned in a vision to thank her for her care of him. Some years later she had a vision in which she saw St. Catherine of Siena and little Vincent, shining with heavenly light.

Mary seems to have had what the missal calls the "gift of tears." Hardly an event of her life is recorded without the remark that she wept copiously over it. She shed many tears—rather futilely, one would be inclined to say—for having been married. But, fortunately, most of her tears were shed for the practical reason of man's ingratitude to God.

Mary had one interesting gift that should make her the envy of every harrassed superior in the world—she could make herself invisible. If she wanted to hear a sermon without having the preacher know she was there, she merely made herself invisible. Sometimes, when in line for confession in the church, and finding that she was not ready to go in, she became invisible, letting everyone else go ahead—a truly fascinating gift.

Mary Razzi died in 1600, and no less a person than St. Charles Borromeo remarked that he was sure she was a saint.

DOMINIC BAÑEZ
(1528-1604)

Dominic Bañez, a famous theologian, was the staunch defender of Teresa of Jesus, at a time when the great reformer of Avila badly needed defense.

Dominic Bañez was born in Valladolid in 1528. His mother was Spanish, his father Basque. Being a superior student, he was sent to the University of Salamanca, where he met the Dominicans. He studied under Melchior

Cano and Dominic Soto, and continued under these great masters after he had entered the Order, at St. Stephen's, in Salamanca. Under such excellent teachers he made great strides in sacred science, and, occasionally, even as a student, he was called to fill in for an absent professor. By the time he had acquired his degree he was already well known. He taught at Avila, Valladolid, and Alcalá. It was when he arrived to take the assignment at Avila that he met the force that was Teresa.

The young Dominican professor did not know anything about Teresa when he came to Avila; absorbed in getting his doctorate at Salamanca, he had heard little gossip. When he arrived in Avila, it was to find the whole town in a turmoil; he followed the crowd to the city hall and listened while the governor delivered an impassioned oration about "closing down the monastery and driving the women out of town." Even the bishop spoke up, saying that the situation was intolerable. Dominic enquired around until he knew what the trouble was: Teresa and three other pious women wanted to start a monastery of strict observance. At a pause for breath, the stranger stood up, and a ripple went through the audience: "Here is the new doctor from Salamanca—hear, hear."

"I have never seen Doña Teresa," he said, "and I am therefore not at all prejudiced. I should have imagined from the amount of excitement that the Moors were back at our gates. I find it is only that four poor women wish to live a life of self-denial and prayer, and that you want to stop them from doing it. Just because it is new, do you therefore feel that it must be condemned? In every religious order, was there not a time at its birth into the Church when it was new? When our Lord founded the Church, wasn't it new? Trees putting forth new leaves are doing nothing novel. If these women are establishing a reform, they should be protected and helped. I find it hard to believe that a few poor women, living in poverty and praying for us, could be a menace. Have we plague? Fire? The Moors? Let us find a foe more worthy of Avila than a poor little convent that cannot defend itself."

Strangely enough, the shouting crowd quieted down and began to drift away. Men who had torches in their hands with which to set fire to the house of Doña Teresa, hurriedly slunk off, and officials hastily tried to change the subject. Teresa's project was saved. When the news was brought to her in the little convent where she had entrenched herself, she begged the messenger to go and get Father Bañez so that she could see him and thank him. "He alone is responsible for saving our beginnings," she claimed afterwards.

Father Bañez took a deep interest in the affairs of the Carmelites, and he was confessor and advisor to Teresa for some years. His combination of learning and holiness appealed to the great reformer; she was often plagued with stupid people, and she probably found it refreshing to deal with intelligent ones. Under the direction of Father Bañez, she wrote her *Way of Perfection,* her *Book of Foundations,* and her *Third Book of Revelations.*

In 1577, Dominic Bañez returned to Salamanca and a few years later was occupying the chair of theology there. When the master general ordered him to publish his theological works, he set about the gigantic task. He had been writing for years, and his commentaries on St. Thomas were published with painstaking care; he himself read and corrected all the proofs.

After a long and distinguished career as Spain's celebrated theologian, Dominic Bañez died in his native city in 1604.

THE MARTYRS OF GUADALUPE
(d. 1604)

The six Dominicans who were killed by the Indians on the island of Guadalupe, in the Caribbean, in 1604, are listed as martyrs, though it would be a little difficult to prove whether they did or did not die *"in odium fidei."*

The six men—John of Moratella, Vincent Palau, John Martinez, John Cano, Hyacinth Cistenez, and Peter Moreno—were part of a band of missionaries en route to Manila with the Philippine provincial, Diego de Soria. The travelers had just completed the long voyage across the Atlantic and, understandably enough, were anxious to land. The provincial had a premonition of disaster, and he tried to convince the captain not to anchor in this spot. However, since there apparently was no good reason not to, a detachment of twenty-five soldiers went ashore. Their duty was to guard the passengers, who wished to wash their clothes, and the crew, who were to return with fresh water.

The twelve Dominicans were together in a sheltered spot, engaged in the homely task of washing their clothes. (One can imagine what a white habit looked like after four or five months of sea travel.) The Indians attacked without warning, showering arrows down on the hapless missionaries. Some fell dead immediately, others were wounded, but escaped to the ships. After the confusion had abated somewhat, and the ship was put out far enough from shore to be safe from Indian canoes, they took account of their injuries. Five Dominicans were dead, and three were badly wounded. Hyacinth Cistenez died of blood poisoning on board ship a week later.

The men who died had a wide variety of backgrounds. John of Moratella came from the convent of Valencia, where he had been a professor; he had the habits of a scholar and a quiet disposition. Why he had volunteered for the missions of the Far East, it would be hard to say. Vincent Palau was also a native of Valencia, but was younger and very vivacious. John Martinez was Aragonese, a placid, unruffled character, who had not protested even in the wildest storms of the Atlantic crossing. John Cano came from Osma, and he was a very old man to be going on the missions; he practiced extreme poverty, and had a childlike trust in God. Hyacinth Cistenez, the man who was to die after a week of agony on ship board, was in the prime of life, in excellent health, and he had a violent temper. He had worked for years to acquire patience, and perhaps the Lord gave him a last week to plumb its depths. It is of the sixth member of the group that most of the legends are told. He was Peter Moreno, a deacon.

Peter was a native of Segovia. He had entered the Order when he was very young, and he volunteered for the missions at the age of fifteen. Having a particularly angelic appearance, he had been a constant inspiration to the older men on the long, weary crossing. At the hour of his death, a strange thing had occurred; if it was not a miracle, it was at least very hard to explain. Wounded to death in the shower of arrows, Peter ran to the water's edge and knelt down as he collapsed with the pain. The waves carried him away, still kneeling, but his companions were too busy at the moment to do more than notice that it was odd. When they were safely in the boat, the look-out reported that one of the fathers was there in the water, coming along after the boat. They stopped to get him aboard, and, to their extreme amazement, saw that it was the deacon, Peter, still kneeling upright in the water. He was dead, and there was a peaceful look on his face. But it was the posture that bothered them—even living people cannot float on their knees on water. Taking his body aboard, they discovered, among other things, that he was wearing an iron chain deeply embedded in his flesh. Little more was required to convince them of his holiness.

The dying Hyacinth Cistenez begged the saintly deacon to help him to conquer his temper, that he might die in God's favor. He prayed to die on the feast of St. Lawrence, and his prayers were answered.

The cause of these men most probably can never be advanced, as the Indians might have killed them out of pure terror, without any relation to their Christianity. But they have a place in our history because, like other brave men, they faced the prospect of crossing two oceans to serve God in those venturesome years.

LOPO CARDOZO
(1555-1605)

The missionary efforts of every province have been met with difficulties of all sorts, not only the dangers of martyrdom and the diversity of tongues, but with that perennial bane of modern missions, lack of money. Lopo Cardozo, of whom most of us know nothing at all, deserves to go down in history as a patron of fund-raisers, if for nothing else.

Lopo was born in Portugal in 1555, and he was trained in the convent of St. Dominic in Lisbon, entering there in early youth. He was known as a model of regular observance, a capable preacher, and a man well-versed in practical matters. He was sent to the Indies around 1585, and he was made prior of one of the convents in Malakka. When the king of Cambodia asked for Christian missionaries, the Dominicans were given the task, and Lopo Cardozo headed the first mission band.

The missionaries were received with honor by the king of Cambodia, who immediately built them a church and convent. The Dominicans proved to be fluent in his language, which pleased the king, and quickly attracted many converts. For a while there was real hope that the kingdom might be converted wholesale, but this hope was dashed when the king died.

His son took over the throne and promptly thrust the Christians from the court. He re-established the old idols in the temples and forbade the Dominicans to preach. He happily would have put them to death, were it not for the pleading of his mother. Lopo Cardozo sent word to Malakka that trouble was brewing. The vicar-general came in answer to his message, bringing another priest, Father Sylvester, with him. Exactly what they hoped to accomplish is not quite clear, but perhaps they were simply increasing their manpower, in expectation of persecution.

The king received the two visitors very coldly, and he said that he would allow the Christian churches to remain open only for the use of foreigners. Since whatever business the vicar-general had hoped to conclude with the king appeared hopeless, he prepared to return to Malakka. The king asked him, as a favor, to take a group of slaves who had been sold to a buyer near Malakka, back with him. He could not very well refuse, although it soon became apparent that he had acted unwisely. His conscience dictated that he should preach to the slaves on the voyage. They listened willingly enough, making use of his leniency in their behalf to escape from the ship.

The king of Cambodia had been waiting for a good excuse to clamp down on the Christians, and this event provided it. He put the Dominicans in prison, confiscating the church goods. He was planning an elaborate execution, in which the priests would be trampled to death by elephants, but once more his mother intervened in their behalf. At her pleading, the priests were released, but they were penniless, surrounded by enemy guards, and lacking even the necessities for saying Mass. All they had was the good will of the poor. One of the new converts, having no money or property, offered to sell himself into slavery to obtain money for the needs of the priests.

Since something obviously would have to be done, Lopo Cardozo went to the king and asked if he could go to Malakka for supplies. The king granted the request, but he put Father Sylvester back in prison, and said that he would leave him there as hostage until the price of the slaves should be returned to him. Sad of heart, Lopo Cardozo sailed for Malakka alone.

For long months he worked to raise the money which would ransom his brother Dominican. Finally he had the money collected and set out for Cambodia. Within sight of the port the ship sank, and all his money was lost. He had to return to Malakka and begin all over again. This time, naturally, it took longer—and, for Brother Sylvester, time was running out. Fund-raisers of today often think they have all the troubles in the world, but it is not often that someone's life at that very moment depends on their efficiency.

When finally the money was accumulated once more, Lopo Cardozo was so broken in health that he could not go to Cambodia. Someone else had the task of ransoming Brother Sylvester, who was still alive and waiting. The Cambodian mission was in ruins.

Lopo Cardozo was sent to Goa, where there was a large convent of the Order dedicated to Our Lady of Remedies, a famous pilgrimage place in the Far East. Here he remained until his health was restored. Later, he was appointed prior of Cochin. Going from there to Goa for a provincial chapter, in 1605, he fell sick and died. He was buried at sea.

MAGDALEN ORSINI
(1534-1605)

A good patroness for those who feel that life is one long contradiction would be Magdalen Orsini, foundress of the Dominican monastery on Monte Cavallo, in Rome.

Magdalen was born in 1534. She married a noble and wealthy man when she was young. After her husband's death, she became a Dominican Tertiary, continuing the works of charity which she had begun as a wealthy matron.

Seeing in her a vocation to the contemplative life, her confessor sent her to a monastery of the Second Order, instructing the superiors there to give her the complete and rigorous course in humility.

Her superiors complied admirably. It is a little mystifying now to read of some of the things they did to try Magdalen's patience, testing whether or not she understood her nothingness. One of the "trials" encouraged by her novice-mistress was having the other novices cut and tangle the embroidery threads on her work. (This causes us to wonder, in passing, what effect such "trials" had on the other novices.) Magdalen was, according to the legend, completely unruffled by it, although she could never understand why the cat always chose her work to tear and tangle. At other times, she was publicly humiliated, and someone was appointed to contradict whatever she said. She was penanced for things she did not do, scolded for things she did not say, and, even after she was professed, the visitatrix put her on public penance and took away her black veil, for a ridiculous charge that someone had thought would embarrass her. It is hard for modern Dominicans to see the need for such trumped-up trials in a world which already has quite enough, but, whatever was the reason, Magdalen's confessor was satisfied at last, and sent her off to Rome, where she was to found a reformed convent of the Second Order.

After such a novitiate, one is not surprised to read that the sisters kept to the house horarium, even, as far as possible, when traveling. They heard Mass every morning, sang Matins, and also had reading during meals. The foundation was of the strictest observance. Sister Magdalen, as superior, was just and kind, but she allowed nothing superfluous and nothing that she felt would draw the sisters' attention away from their work. Silence was strictly enforced, and any transgressors were penanced so severely that they rarely forgot twice.

Magdalen Orsini's special devotion was to the Office. She was always happy when Office was being sung, often meditating on the various hours of Office as they were representative of the scenes of our Lord's life. Sometimes she heard angels singing in choir, and sometimes, indeed, she saw them.

There is one saying of Magdalen Orsini's which proved that she was a courageous soul in the battle of life; someone had remarked to her that the best way to fight down one's feelings was to run away from the subject. Magdalen disagreed. "That is not always enough," she said. "Sometimes you have to meet them face to face and fight it out."

At the end of a difficult life, filled with trials, but brightened by her joy in living the religious life, Magdalen Orsini died in 1605.

DIEGO OF YANGUAS
(d. 1606)

Of the several Dominicans who played a part in the life of St. Teresa of Avila, Diego of Yanguas holds the unique honor of having been present at her vision of St. Dominic.

Diego received the habit in the convent of Our Lady of Atocha in Madrid. We do not know where or when he was born. In religious life he made great progress, both spiritually and intellectually. After obtaining several academic degrees, he taught at Palencia, Burgos, Alcalá, and Valladolid. In 1594, he was prior at the convent of the Holy Cross, in Segovia, when St. Teresa, whom he had directed some years before, came to see him.

Teresa had been promulgating her reform in the Carmels of Spain, and she was in Segovia on business. However, she would not go without seeing Diego, who had been a valued guide and confessor in a difficult stage of her work. She and several companions came to the convent of the Holy Cross and were joyfully received. Diego showed her the old convent, and the cave where St. Dominic had prayed on the occasion of his first trip home to Spain, after he had founded the Order. Teresa shed tears of joy, and she expressed her wish to be left to pray in the holy cave. As she knelt there, rapt in prayer, St. Dominic himself appeared to her in vision, and he talked with her for some time. He encouraged her in the work of reform, telling her that it would succeed. During the Mass which Diego said following this vision, St. Dominic appeared again during Teresa's thanksgiving after Communion. After Mass, Teresa conversed with him again for nearly two hours. He told her that he had received many graces when he had prayed there in the cave long ago. When he finally disappeared, and Teresa realized that she must proceed on her journey, she wept, saying that it was such a holy place that she would be content to remain there the rest of her life.

When Teresa died, her admirers wished to bury her in an ornate tomb. Diego of Yanguas was convinced that Teresa would have strongly disapproved of this, but he did cooperate to the extent of composing some Latin verses for her epitaph. They paraphrased some texts of Scripture, and he thought they applied to the great reformer and mystic whom he so much admired.

Only one other incident in the life of Diego of Yanguas has come down to us. Dominic of Salazar, the saintly bishop of Manila, had sent an envoy to the king of Spain to plead for the rights of the natives. The envoy, although he was a Dominican, proved false to the ideals that his brothers were defending with their lives in all parts of the New World, and he counselled the king that the only possible way to handle the natives of the Philippines was to kill them. Diego of Yanguas, who was called in on the case, lost no time in unmasking the envoy as a tool of the Spanish officers.

Diego of Yanguas died in 1606, and he was buried in the Dominican convent in Valladolid.

ANNE BASSET
(1566-1609)

When the obituary of Sister Anne of Jesus was written in the archives of the convent of Aumale, in 1609, it was not yet safe to name the people who figured in her life. From the obituary's discreet references to people in high places, and from the general history of the times, we can reconstruct what must have been a vividly colorful life.

Anne Basset was born of a prominent Catholic family in London in 1566. The day before her baptism, Queen Elizabeth I had exiled the Spanish Dominicans who were brought in by Mary Tudor, leaving the country without any priests, except those who were in hiding. Anne's mother was in the service of the queen, although we do not know in just what capacity—perhaps before her marriage she had been a court attendant. In the light of her later actions, we can see why she absented herself from the court as much as possible, and why the family moved out into the country.

The little girl had seen violence and sacrilege in London, but her own home in the country was a haven for Catholics. Although they lived in constant danger, it was a peaceful place, and she was trained piously. Her mother made vestments and secured traveling clothes for the hunted priests. One record says that her father died in prison, others, that he was martyred. Anne made her first Communion in the tiny hidden Mass-room in her father's house, and she grew up to the sense of danger and caution that surrounded the Catholics of those days.

When the queen sent word that she would "like to see mistress Anne married to some fine Protestant lord," Anne's mother took action. The child could not have been more than ten years old, if that, but her mother would take no chances. She sent Anne off secretly in the company of "a very great English princess"—whose name we do not know—to be brought up in Rouen. We do not know what happened to her mother for this independent move; she does not appear again in the narrative.

Anne lived in Rouen with the "English princess," who was pious enough, but a little annoyed at Anne's asceticism. The child wore only very shabby clothing, refused to dress her hair elaborately, and ate practically nothing. When she fell ill, it was the personal physician of the king of Spain who gave her orders to modify her austerities, an order which her confessor encouraged.

Anne had made up her mind that she would be a nun, and she made arrangements with the Brigittines to accept her. The princess discovered her plans and forbade her to carry them out, on pain of being sent back to England. She was so closely guarded that she found it barely possible to go out for Mass. At last she agreed with the princess that she would not run away to the convent, if she were allowed freedom to practice austerities at home. Some time after this, she had a dream in which her guardian angel reproached her: "You have made a bad bargain; you are putting yourself in danger." The angel, taking the girl to the top of a high mountain, allowed her a glimpse of our Lord on the cross. When Anne awoke, she arranged a more rigorous life than she had led before.

At this time, an English gentleman by the name of Chelton, who had been banished from England on account of his faith, arrived in Rouen. He soon approached the princess, asking for Anne's hand in marriage. The princess agreed, but Anne did not. After this, a Spanish grandee of advanced age sought the same privilege and was refused. Anne was very positive about it. She had made a vow of chastity many years ago, and our Lord insisted that she keep it.

The princess went to Brussels, and Anne went with her. The husband of the princess had gone to Paris to see the English ambassador, and, while there, he was poisoned by his cousin. Anne, in Brussels, waking from a sound sleep, saw an apparition of the prince in his shroud; he asked for her prayers.

During this same visit in Brussels, the discovery was made there of three miraculous Hosts, which in an act of sacrilege had bled when pierced by a dagger. The relics had been stolen and hidden for fourteen years, and they were rediscovered while Anne was in the city. Busy at her prayers, she "felt" the Hosts passing by outside her window, and she rushed out to kneel in the street.

The princess was summoned to Paris, and again Anne accompanied her. Here they met the uncle of the princess, who had been sent by Queen Elizabeth to bring the princess back to England for a second marriage. The uncle insisted that she should go, and he wanted Anne to go with her. Anne refused to return to England, saying: "I intend to be a religious."

From this point, there is a discreet silence in the records about the princess, but they show that Anne returned to Rouen. She lived a semi-religious life, praying and performing works of charity, while waiting for our Lord to make her vocation clear to her. He had assured her that she would be a religious, but had not told her when or where. She busied herself with the sick and the poor; once, she remained six weeks with a woman who had fever; another time, six months. On the second occasion, she contracted the disease, and there was no one to take care of her. Weak with fever, she fell out of bed, and she lay untended for nearly a day. When she had recovered, she resumed her works of charity, directing her energies especially to helping exiled English priests. She collected money from wealthy people, using it to clothe and care for these fugitives.

Rouen was besieged by the English and the Dutch in 1595, and by this time Anne's reputation as a holy person was so well known that the whole city appealed to her to save them from the siege. When the besieging army withdrew without ruining the city, everyone believed that Anne's prayers were responsible for what they considered a miracle. "God has sent her in person to be another Judith for the salvation of the city." This claim was made by the people.

After the siege of Rouen, Anne had another vision. Our Lord appeared to tell her to call on the Dominican Fathers, and ask their advice about entering the Order. She went to the convent as bidden, and asked for the prior. He was busy, however, and the man he sent down to interview Anne was either stupid or prejudiced; he gave a bad report to the prior, who delayed seeing Anne for some time. When she finally managed to talk with him, he sent her to the Third Order monastery at Aumale.

There was no doubt a reason why he chose this particular monastery, aside from the fact that it was under the direction of the Dominican fathers of Rouen. Anne had acquired a reputation for charitable works among the poor, and he probably felt she would rather continue with that type of work. The sisters at Aumale had a nominal cloister, as all sisterhoods did at the time, but they did not keep it; their work—good, charitable work, it may be said—had gradually absorbed the monastic quality of their life, and the sisters were far more active than contemplative. The best of them worried about the gap between theory and practice; the worst of them gave the better members things to worry about. At first, Anne was puzzled when she encountered the situation; then she decided to do something about it. She and several of the more fervent members of the house set about bettering the observance of the rule.

A reform move is usually not very welcome, especially if a young religious starts it. Anne—whose name in religion was Sister Anne of Jesus—found herself none too popular with the sisters of Aumale. Nine of the twelve years she spent in religion were strained and uncomfortable, because of the reform, but finally it did succeed. She had been threatened with deprivation of the sacraments, even with excommunication. Gradually, the monastery returned to its stated rule, and peace was restored.

Anne's confessor told her to write her autobiography, and she did. After her death, in 1609, the document was found and destroyed. It may have been because of petty jealousy, but it could just as easily have been because the people whose names appeared in the book were still alive and in danger. The archives did not dare to be specific about any of these people either, which indictates how desperate were the times for the faithful.

FRANCESCA VACCHINI
(1589-1609)

Francesca Vacchini, a novice who died at the age of twenty, influenced a great many people in her short life, and her writing still has its place in mystical literature.

Francesca was born in Viterbo, in 1589. Her parents had been denied the blessing of children for many years when she was born, and they spoiled her badly. When she was still very tiny, she became gravely ill. Both parents besought their favorite saints to save her life, promising to name the baby after the one who saved her. St. Francis was credited with the miracle, so she became Francesca.

Spoiled though she was, the little girl displayed a taste for spiritual things very early. At the age of four she prayed for sinners and went to visit the sick, and she cried bitterly when not allowed to perform great penances. The shrine of Our Lady of the Ivy, in Viterbo, was her favorite haunt. At the age of five she was taught to read and write by her guardian angel, who appeared to her frequently, sustaining her in the attacks made by the devil. Getting nowhere with the little girl, the devil began trying to influence her mother. Suddenly the mother turned against the little girl. She no longer pampered and caressed the child; now she scolded her and beat her unreasonably. Francesca's purgatory had begun.

The family was wealthy and had great plans for Francesca's marriage. Quite naturally, they were opposed to her taking a vow of virginity. Thinking she would soon outgrow such nonsense, the mother went ahead with the matchmaking, and she had the support of both Francesca's father and her confessor. The girl herself wished only to live in obscurity—modest, charitable, and prayerful. Her piety annoyed her mother to a degree that was almost psychopathic; she screamed at the girl, struck her, and told lies about her to the confessor. One time a neighbor came in just in time to prevent her from strangling her daughter, but even after that there were people who believed her stories about Francesca. The mother denounced her daughter to the bishop, saying that she was a wicked girl, a fraud, and in league with the devil. Only her father befriended her, and supported her proposal of asking for the Third Order habit. At the age of seventeen she was received as a Dominican Tertiary, and, after one last terrible battle with the devil, and another equally bad with her mother, Francesca settled down to try living a religious life.

Francesca's way of life was extreme; she performed the most difficult penances, though always with the consent of her confessor. She slept only two hours a night, on a heap of branches; she kept continual abstinence, except on Sundays, and fasted perpetually. She made herself some penitential garments—a crown of thorns, an iron chain, and a hair-shirt with needles in it. Even people who could not pretend to follow her example had great reverence for her, and they carefully wrote down what she said. Her prayers converted many people, particularly the young. Several men, going to execution for murder, were brought to penitence and a good death by her prayers. In addition to the gift of prophecy, she could read hearts. Seeing the souls in purgatory in visions, she often spoke of them in order to stimulate prayers in their behalf. After her father's death, she prayed long and earnestly for him, and she had the happiness of seeing him ascend to heaven.

Francesca Vacchini died at the age of twenty, in 1609. Her cause for beatification is active.

SIR JOHN BURKE
(d. 1610)

The gallant and resourceful Sir John Burke, an Irish Tertiary who is deserving of much more publicity than he receives, died on the gallows in 1610 because he was a Catholic. He is a sparkling example of one who was not only a militant Catholic, but a belligerent one, and this did not endear him to the representatives of the Crown.

Sir John Burke was the son of the Baron of Castle Connell, in Limerick, and Lord of Brittas Castle. Because of his noble ancestry, abundant property, and native ingenuity, he avoided capture during the last years of the reign of Elizabeth, and he devoted his time to establishing a smooth-running underground for the fugitive priests of the area. On the death of Elizabeth, there was a short period of confusion, when people waited to see what the policy of the new ruler, James I, would be. Sir John was not one to wait. He immediately set about reorganizing the scattered Catholics, rejoicing that now, at last, one could begin to show one's faith openly. By the time Lord Montjoy,

Viceroy of James, arrived in Limerick, Sir John had been so public about his rejoicing that punishment was inevitable. He was imprisoned in Dublin on a charge of treason.

Sir John was a torment to his jailors. Not only did he pray most of the time, but he also had great gifts of oratory which he made the jailors aware of at every opportunity. Apparently he had the faculty of talking rapidly, paying no attention whatsoever to their religious exhortations; they could not make themselves heard. When they addressed him, he looked through them, and beyond them, as if they did not exist. Even the hardened agents of Montjoy found that this tactic was shattering to the nerves. When the plague struck Dublin, the terrified jailor unlocked all the cells and ran away. Sir John walked out unmolested, returning to Brittas Castle with a great many new ideas for perfecting the underground.

At this time, Sir John became a member of a group to which he had long been attracted: the Dominican Order. He brought to the Tertiary organization the same militant Catholicity that had been its hallmark in the years of its foundation under St. Dominic: an unswerving fidelity to the Church and a strong arm for its defense. Priests of the Order, nearly all of them marked for martyrdom, passed safely through his hands, enjoying the protection of his quick wit and ready sword. Even the agents of Montjoy, who bitterly longed to discover a bit of damaging evidence against him, hesitated to cross swords with him and—thanks to his fertile brain—they seldom got that close to him.

Rosary Sunday of 1608 was richly indulgenced, and when the news of the new indulgences reached Ireland, Sir John Burke laid plans to celebrate the day fittingly. The roads were crowded with prowling soldiers, all eager to get the reward for capturing him. This did not stop him from bringing in not one, but three Dominicans, for a Solemn High Mass. The great hall of the castle was cleared out and adorned as a church, and, on Rosary Sunday, the braver Catholics of the neighborhood crept in silently before daybreak. Someone had revealed the plans to Lord Montjoy, and he attacked the castle during Mass. Sir John and his companions defended the gates until Mass was over; then, by a bold stroke, he arranged that the priests could leave by a back way. One priest was unlucky—or perhaps only clumsy—and was captured. Making a dashing plunge into the lines on horseback, Sir John brought the priest back to the safety of the castle.

Such safety was only a temporary thing, for the advantage was with the besieger, who could starve out a garrison or cut off its water supply. Sir John's mother and his wife both tried to plead the offer of Montjoy, who had sent word of safe conduct if he would surrender. Sir John had an unpleasant choice to make. He was a man with a young wife and family, dependents whom he had tried unsuccessfully to get safely to Spain before the trouble started.

He did not wish to subject them to the horrors of capture, but neither would he release the one Dominican remaining in the castle to Montjoy. He laid an elaborate plan whereby the priest should be taken out a back passage through the fields. Then, in full armor, sword in hand, with the chalices and other church valuables in a sack under his arm, he went boldly out the front gate and fought his way through. The incredible plan worked. The priest escaped, and Sir John arrived safely in the woods, where he hid the church vessels and then disappeared into the underground he had so carefully organized.

The chase lasted for some time, and it must have been exciting. Angered to frenzy by having their prey slip through their fingers, the troops of Montjoy considered it a personal point of honor to catch Sir John. The reward money was doubled. Two women Tertiaries, who sheltered the fugitive, were captured and condemned to die. They were both burned to death, steadily refusing to give any clue to his whereabouts. Eventually the reward money turned the trick; a woman betrayed the hiding place, and, at long last, the elusive Sir John Burke was before the court on a charge that could be proved. There was no delay about it. He was condemned to be hanged, drawn, and quartered.

While he waited in prison for death, Sir John prayed calmly and uninterruptedly. His wife came to see him on the day before the execution, and he exhorted her to remain faithful to the Church and to get the children out of the country as soon as possible.

On the scaffold, Sir John delivered a speech which an eloquent people found irresistible. He said that it was, of course, customary for a dying man to make a will, leaving his property to his heirs. Since, however, the government had deprived him of all property, he had nothing to leave to anyone. He would particularly like to be able to leave something to the Order of St. Dominic, to which he pledged his undying love. He would, therefore, give to them the only property over which the government had no jurisdiction, namely, his unborn child. This child, be it boy or girl, he dedicated to the Order of St. Dominic, that he or she might give a life in the service of Our Lady of the Rosary. He looked out into the crowd to where a Dominican father, who was disguised as a peasant and standing in the shadows, waited to give him absolution. Smiling a tender farewell to his wife, Sir John mounted the scaffold with the steady step of a brave man.

Someone managed to beg off the sentence of mutilating the body, and he was honorably buried in the Church of St. John, in Limerick.

The dedicated child, a girl, was born a few months later. She was brought up as the child of a martyr, with the single thought of becoming a Dominican when she was old enough. At first she was given the habit as a Tertiary, and the permission to wear it at home, since there was at that time no Dominican convent in Ireland. Finally, however, she went to Portugal, to the convent founded by Father Dominic of the Rosary, and she became a member of that community. She lived long enough to see the son of the judge who had condemned her father, repent of his mistakes, and present to the Dominican fathers in Limerick a magnificent statue of Our Lady of the Rosary, and also a fine chalice. After a troubled history, the statue was placed where it is today, in the Dominican church in Limerick.

The cause of Sir John Burke has never been formally opened, which is a great pity. He would make a striking example of what St. Dominic must have had in mind when he founded this militant branch of the Order.

MARY OF JESUS
(1574-1616)

Sister Mary of Jesus was a busy superior most of her life, and she was hemmed in by details of a sort that would destroy the peace of anyone less poised than she. Yet, it was written of her: "No one ever observed any precipitation in her manner, or any movement of passion in her words; nor, in the greatest press of business, was the slightest trouble or vexation visible in any of her actions. Her continual recollection of the presence of God was visible in the exterior serenity, peace and tranquility which beamed in her countenance. Nothing ever disturbed or saddened her expression, not even when she was suffering interiorly, by reason of the entire confidence with which she abandoned herself into the hands of God."

Mary was born near Toulouse in 1574. She was married young and lived with her wealthy husband for some years, occupying herself with whatever charities came her way. She was particularly fond of doing work which would enhance the altar, and, when she discovered that the little village church near her husband's estate was neglected, she took it upon herself to take care of the altars and the linens. There was not even a lamp for the Blessed Sacrament, a situation which she quickly remedied. The lamp was to her a symbol of her own dedication to God, and she filled and trimmed it every day. She became a secular Tertiary, devoting as much time as she could to prayer and meditation.

When her husband died, Mary was free to do as she wished. Declining another marriage, she devoted herself to the sick and the abandoned. She returned to Toulouse, where she became the good angel of the poorer districts, going fearlessly into the most unsavory parts of town in order to seek out those who needed help. Gradually her work centered on rescuing young girls and ailing women who had been in prison. She established a home in Toulouse for the care of these unfortunates, giving her energies to this for several years.

Mary confided to her director that her work drew her nearer and nearer to God. No matter how noisy it was, or how frightful the surroundings were, she had so formed the habit of seeking God in everyone she met that it was impossible to forget Him. Gradually, but surely, her heart was moving from active work to a life of prayer in action. This, of course, spelled "Dominican" to her Dominican director; he told her that she should make plans to found a monastery of the Second Order in Toulouse.

This was not by any means the sort of work that Mary would have chosen for herself. Furthermore, her confessor saw to it that she suffered as much as possible from humiliations of all sorts. Yet, with the grace of God and a great humility, she managed to have the house established. Until the monastery was formally cloistered, she continued her work of teaching the poor, and, indeed, it was a work that she abandoned with great reluctance. The poor, who loved her, were unwilling to lose her, even to God; they clustered around the new convent, insisting on keeping in contact with her.

Mary of Jesus introduced into her convent a number of refreshing practices, which proved that she well understood the mind of St. Dominic. Proceeding upon the belief that no one goes to heaven alone, she suggested to her sisters that they attempt to bring three souls to heaven with them—one they had liberated from purgatory by their prayers, one they had freed from sin by their prayers, and one they had recruited from the world to the cloister.

In order to make their charity practical, she often had the sisters fast and abstain in favor of the poor. The monastery shortly became the refuge of the afflicted and the source of help to many. She kept her sisters busy about works of charity, even inside the cloister. She taught them her own practice of the presence of God amid all the distractions of her tasks. Working with them on some charitable project, she instructed them in the higher ways of the spiritual life, so that heart and hands were trained at the same time. The presence of God and the art of working for God were in fact her principal points of instruction. If there was anything she hated, it was to see one of her sisters slip into the habit of performing her daily work in a routine fashion, without any attention to the direction of the work to God.

All of Mary's biographers record the same thing: "In the midst of a crowd of visitors, the importunity of the poor and the variety of external affairs, she never relaxed in the punctual observance of all spiritual exercises, which she fulfilled as regularly and tranquilly as if living in a desert." We, who live in a shattered world, a prey to the noise and confusion of city life, can well admire her constant sense of God's presence, which made this possible.

Mary, in training her novices, was a strict mistress. She had no patience with the small-mindedness of complaining people. The idle and the cowardly got a swift retort from her, and she continually exhorted them to generosity and magnanimity. "The body murmurs sometimes," she admitted, but she submitted to the ordeal without a murmur, although she was subjected to the worst that could be designed in the way of penances and humiliations.

Her practice of the virtue of poverty was one of the things for which Mary of Jesus was especially noted. Living at a time when poverty was the forgotten virtue, when nearly all religious lived individual lives instead of the common life, she inculcated in her sisters such a dread of superfluity that it was almost impossible to get them to accept any sort of present, even a useful one. During Mary's own years as superior she acquired only two things—a reliquary and an Agnus Dei—and for these she apologized to the new superior. Her cell was a model of extreme poverty. She did not even own a crucifix; there was a poor little paper picture of one propped up on the single shelf in her cell. She should be remembered as a great "community woman," in an age when that was phenomenal.

There is no miracle at all recorded of Mary of Jesus. She lived her life vigorously and courageously, not shrinking from the disagreeable or the uncomfortable things of religious life, and not seeking extraordinary manifestations of her sanctity. She died in 1616, and she has always been highly regarded in the Order, although she has never been proposed for beatification.

SEBASTIAN MONTAGNOL
(d. 1616)

Sebastian Montagnol, martyred by the natives of Mexico in 1616, is an example of the courageous men who went to their deaths in the Indies, redeeming the reputation of Spain, in spite of the excesses of the conquistadores.

Sebastian was born in Madrid, and when he was a young man he went to Mexico City, seeking his fortune. The glittering worldliness of the Spanish capitol in the New World repelled rather than attracted him, and he entered the Dominican convent there in the opening years of the seventeenth century.

At the provincial chapter, which met in Mexico City in 1616, Sebastian asked for an assignment to Zacatecas, where the natives were savage and corrupt. It was remote mountain country that had a sinister reputation, and the fathers of the chapter pointed this out to him. Nothing daunted, Sebastian received permission, said goodbye to his friends, and set out for martyrdom.

During the interval time he spent learning the difficult language of the people he had come to teach, Sebastian preached to the Spaniards on the Rosary. The Spaniards were fond of him, and, when the time came for him to go into the mountains, the local governor sent five hundred partly-civilized Indians along to help him establish an amicable relationship with the savages of Zacatecas.

For a little while, all went well. Sebastian worked among the Indians, and the few converts he made were very good ones. The source of the trouble that developed was a tribal medicine-man, who was operating a profitable working agreement with the devil. He was able to raise himself in the air through diabolical power, as well as other amazing things. He acquired a reputation for wonder-working, and he issued a threat to the poor savages that, if they continued listening to the Christian priest, he would make the mountain open up to swallow the guilty ones. Frightened, the Indians began to desert Sebastian's classes. And they looked menacingly on the Spaniards and the Christian Indians who had come with them.

At one point, a volcano erupted, terrorizing the Indians. In a frenzy, they fell upon the Spaniards and killed all but Sebastian. They raided and burned a Jesuit mission in another tribe, stole the statue of Our Lady, which was being carried in procession, and profaned the Blessed Sacrament. Bound and beaten, Sebastian was dragged deeper into the mountains to certain martyrdom. His chief concern was the sacrilege; he was glad that they left the statue behind and brought only the litter.

The story of this sacrilege is strange in mission annals. One seldom finds anything of such sophisticated malice among pagans. Usually, only Christians ever fall so far as to profane Christian treasures. But the savages of Zacatecas, once they had arrived in the deep mountains, proved themselves adept at the diabolical art. With an irreverence that reminds us of the "Reign of Terror," they placed a wicked woman on the litter and carried her around the camp, parodying the songs of the Christian procession. Sebastian, bound in their midst, lived long enough to beg them to desist, telling them of the terrible things that would happen to them if they continued. They shot him full of arrows, a strange coincidence which Sebastian probably appreciated, if they did not; it was December the tenth, 1616. Being cannibals, they were preparing to feast on the missionary, but the volcano erupted again. This sent them cringing in terror to tell the Spaniards what they had done.

ST. ROSE OF LIMA
(1586-1617)

The first canonized saint of the New World lived in a time quite different from our own. As a matter of fact, her whole life sounds very strange to us of other days and other customs. But, if we will take the trouble to study her life, we will discover that the little saint of Lima, who died three hundred years ago, could teach us a great deal. It is well to remember that the penances Rose inflicted upon herself—which are the only things most people know about her—afflicted only herself. They were no burden to those around her. Rose lived all her life with her own family, not in a desert, far from people. It is probably her greatest genius that she worked out a program of penance almost unparalleled in history and, all the while, not prove to be a nuisance to those whom she saw every day.

Rose was born in Lima in 1585, the eleventh child of Spanish-Indian parents. Because she was very delicate, she was baptized at birth and given the name Isabel. When she was taken to the church for the solemn ceremonies of baptism, the archbishop, St. Turribius, inadvertently called her Rose. The name remained. From her earliest days, the baby seemed marked with the favors of God. When she was barely able to walk, she would be found lost in contemplation before the big crucifix in her mother's room. That she understood suffering became clear when, in a childish accident at the age of three, she endured the pain of surgery without a whimper and commented that Jesus had suffered much more. At another time she was ill with a bad earache. Asked if it hurt very much, she said: "Yes, a little; but our Lord's crown of thorns must have hurt much more."

Rose's mother, an affectionate woman with little imagination, hardly knew what to do with this child, for Rose seemed to belong more to heaven than to earth. By turns, she spoiled and scolded her. When the child was four and a half, she tried to teach her to read and gave up in disgust. A few days later Rose came to her and read for her several pages from a prayer book, and she scolded the child for her presumption. Proud of the little girl's beauty, she tried to keep her dressed in the prettiest of clothes, unable to understand why Rose was indifferent to them. She tried Rose's patience in every way, but could not disturb the child's sense of obedience. Always in the background of the life of Rose, with its dramatic glimpses of heaven and hell, and its almost completely spiritual pattern, runs the obbligato of the complaints, the protests, and the tearful pride of Rose's mother. She loved her daughter, but could not understand her.

When Rose was twelve years old, the question of her marriage was broached. Her mother was a match-maker, like many others, and she envisioned her beautiful daughter as Lima's loveliest bride. Rose hated to hurt her mother, and she actually did not know how to explain that she wished to consecrate herself to God. She had, in fact, already done so—many years ago—and she had no intention of marrying. When her mother finally accepted this, she conceived what she thought was the only sensible answer: Rose should enter a convent. Neither she nor anyone else could sympathize with the girl's intention of becoming a Dominican Tertiary, living at home. A long and difficult period ensued. Finally, however, the girl's plan became a reality, and Rose, followed by her weeping mother, went to the Dominican Church to receive the habit of St. Dominic and the Tertiary rule of life.

Rose set about scaling the heights in her own peculiar way. She and her brother Ferdinand built a tiny hermitage in her father's garden. She planned to live there. It was so small that her mother protested. "It is big enough for Jesus and myself," said Rose. Here, for the remainder of her life, she was to spend all of her days and part of her nights in contemplation, performing the penances which she devised to punish herself for the sins of the world. Reading about these penances, we are appalled at the thought of anyone deliberately inflicting such sufferings on themselves. She was very fond of fruit, but, from the age of four, she would not touch it. She never ate meat. Her ordinary fare consisted of hard crusts, water and bitter herbs; during Lent she omitted the bread.

Thus far we can follow her; other saints have done the same. But few would strew their beds with rocks and broken glass in order that the hour or two of sleep they allowed themselves were as uncomfortable as possible; deprive themselves for weeks at a time of drinking any water in that hot tropical summer, or wear a crown of thorns carefully concealed under an innocent headdress. Sometimes she pinned the crown to her head, pulled tighter the cords she had tied about her body, or walked barefoot in her father's garden at night, carrying a heavy cross. One penance she devised in her early years was to have the family servant, (who wept bitterly while doing as she was told) load the little girl with blocks of firewood until she collapsed under the weight. It seems, in reading the life of this ingenious sufferer, that there was nothing at all that Rose could not turn into a penance.

Let us remember that Rose was a working girl; she could not afford simply to go off and pray to her heart's content. She had to help support the family; ten hours of every day went into this necessary work. She was an expert needlewoman, and she made many fine embroideries which were purchased by people who probably never suspected that the one who made them was a saint. She also raised flowers for market, and it was her greatest joy to keep the Lady Altar at the Dominican church supplied with the loveliest blossoms from her garden.

Rose discovered the same thing that many another Dominican has bewailed: there are only twenty-four hours in a day, and after you take ten for work there are not too many left. She partly solved this problem by going without sleep, which most of us cannot do, and partly by making her work a means of union with God, which all of us can attempt. There was probably no time during the twenty-four hours when Rose was not closely united to her heavenly Spouse, and it made little difference to her whether her hands were busy with embroidery, with her flowers, or free to finger her Rosary. She was just as ingenious at keeping her heart united with God as she was at making everything into a penance. A good patroness for today's busy religious—our St. Rose.

We do not know as much as we would like of the visions and celestial favors of Rose. Obviously she was in a state of ecstasy a great deal of the time. The tiny cell in the garden accommodated a steady stream of heavenly guests. Sometimes, when she went down to the church to receive Holy Communion, she was rapt in ecstasy, and for hours she would be unconscious of the people who crowded around to watch her. She experienced the mystical espousals and other heavenly signs of union which belong to the highest order of mystical prayer. She was also exposed to the most terrifying temptations—to visitations of the devil who came in visible form, and to long periods of spiritual desolation. Once, at the end of a particularly gruelling encounter with the devil, she reproached our Lord: "Lord, if you had been here I would not have been exposed to such horrible temptations." To which our Lord replied: "Rose, if I had not been there, do you think you would have conquered?"

Rose prayed for martyrdom, longed for the life of a missionary. Both of these things seemed remote in Catholic Lima. She prayed incessantly for missionaries, and we wonder how many of the Japanese martyrs, who were to die at Nagasaki in the year of Rose's death, owed the grace of perseverance to the little Tertiary of Lima who never saw Japan. At one time, the chance of martyrdom seemed almost within her grasp. A fleet of Dutch pirates anchored off Callao, and Lima was in a paralysis of fear. Rose hurried to the church, planning to give up her life in defense of the Blessed Sacrament. However, the fleet sailed away without harming them, and the people of Lima credited her prayers for their deliverance.

Rose died at the early age of thirty-one, on August the twenty-fourth, 1617. The entire city mourned the death of the saint, for it seemed that the people of all classes owed her a special debt. Indians and Negroes, whom she had nursed back to health, knelt around her bier alongside of Spanish grandees, whom she had brought back to the sacraments or saved from loss of fortune.

One and all, they held the same opinion; Rose was a saint. The Church confirmed this opinion in 1671, making her the first canonized saint of the Americas.

BLESSED ALPHONSUS NAVARRETE
AND COMPANIONS
(d. 1617)

Dominicans were, according to legend, the first missionaries to Japan, and 1530 is given as the date of their martyrdom. However, no conclusive proof exists regarding their names or number, and St. Francis Xavier rightly holds the title of apostle to this island kingdom. Following in Xavier's footsteps came other missionaries, and, for about forty years, they worked with great results among the people. Then, in the closing years of the century, persecution flared, and the blood of martyrs cried out with a louder voice than that of the preachers. The first Dominican to die in the great persecution was Alphonsus Navarrete.

A native of Spain, the future martyr was born in Old Castile, in 1571. When he was very young, he gave up his inheritance to enter the Order in Valladolid and, after he had completed his studies, was sent to the Philippine missions. The great persecution has just begun in Japan; the year before Alphonsus left Spain, a group of twenty-six Christians, including many Franciscans and three Japanese Jesuits, were crucified in Nagasaki.

Despite the dangers, the Dominicans, who had been excluded from Japan for several years, yearned to go into the perilous mission field. Alphonsus in particular, after a trip to Europe to recruit missionaries in 1610, begged to be allowed to go to Japan. In the following year his offer was accepted, and he was sent as superior of the mission band. During the short interval of peace, they began their work, and, during six years of growing peril, they instructed the people and prepared them for the dreadful days to come.

The missionary career of Alphonsus was brief, and it was always overshadowed by the threat of death which beset the Christians in that unhappy country. However, in the few years of his apostolate, his accomplishment was immeasurable. Like his Divine Master, he went about teaching and baptizing the people. He is called the "Vincent de Paul of Japan," because it was he who first began the tremendous task of caring for the abandoned babies there. He anticipated the work of the Holy Childhood Society by gathering up the homeless waifs, providing for their support from money he begged of wealthy Spaniards.

The warning bell of the great persecution was sounded with the martyrdom, in Omura, of two priests, a Franciscan and a Jesuit. Alphonsus Navarrete and an Augustinian companion went to Omura with the intention of rescuing the relics of the martyrs and consoling the Christians. They were captured on the way, and, with a young native catechist, were beheaded. Their bodies were thrown into the sea.

Five years later, on the hill of the holy Martyrs at Nagasaki, more than fifty Christians sealed their faith with their blood. Some of the martyrs were beheaded, some were burned at the stake. In the group were nine Jesuits, including the famous Father Charles Spinola, nine Franciscans, and nine Dominicans, among whom were the Blesseds Alphonsus de Mena, Angelo Orsucci, and Hyacinth Orphanel. Louis Bertrand, a nephew of the saint of that name, perished in the same persecution.

Thousands of Japanese Christians, from tiny children to old grandparents, died amid terrible torments in the profession of their faith. The anger of the persecutors was turned against all priests, brothers and catechists, members of the Third Orders, and Rosarians, and they made fearful attempts to stamp all traces of the hated religion out of their country. Pope Pius IX, in 1867, solemnly beatified 205 of the martyrs, among whom were fifty-nine Dominicans of the first and third orders, and fifty-eight members of the Rosary Confraternity. Although all did not die at the same time nor place, they are listed under the name of Alphonsus Navarrete, who was the first to die.

JOHN RUEDA OF THE ANGELS
(d. 1621)

John Rueda was born in Burgos, and he joined the Dominicans there when he was young. In order to more completely cut himself away from the world, he gave up his family name and, afterwards, used only the signature "John of the Angels." In 1603 he volunteered for the missions of the Far East, and he was assigned to Japan.

Dominican missions had flourished in the Philippines prior to this time, and Manila was the center of missionary activity for the entire Orient. Consequently, the band of thirty volunteers that set out from Spain with Bishop Diego of Soria was bound for Manila. After they had arrived there, those not yet assigned would be given a definite mission.

The Atlantic crossing was one of the roughest on record, and, when the ship touched at the first Mexican port, some young Dominicans were so fearfully seasick that they could not bear the thought of crossing another ocean. Since Mexico, too, was in need of missionaries, the bishop re-assigned the young missionaries, and he went on to the Philippines with the stout-hearted seven who felt that they could survive another ocean crossing. John of the Angels was one of these, for none of the horrors of travel had shaken his enthusiasm for Japan. The majority of the band were to go to Bataan, and John was given a choice of going with them, but did not take it. Japan was still his goal.

Japan had always been unfriendly to foreign missionaries, and at the time Father John of the Angels landed in the kingdom, all foreigners were under sentence of death upon capture. Christian natives found life almost unendurable, and they sorely needed their pastors, who were risking death in ministering to them. John of the Angels stepped into this dangerous spot without a backward look. A strange picture, this—a man enduring the trials of two ocean crossings, and all the troubles of travel in those uncertain days, to spend a short and dangerous life hiding from place to place like a criminal. And he was sure only of one thing: a frightful death should he be caught.

Father John of the Angels soon became known, not alone for bravery, but for charity. It was this that won for him so many converts who might otherwise have been repelled from Christianity because of its deadly dangers. One day, as he passed over a bridge, he heard pitiful moans beneath it, and, looking down, he saw an old woman. Her ungrateful children had thrown her out to die. The young priest lifted her out and made her as comfortable as he could. He spoke a little Japanese, enough to know that she was begging to be baptized.

Another time, he rescued an old blind man who was being dragged down to the river to be drowned, because the neighbors were tired hearing him moan. Father John of the Angels took him in and cared for him until he died. Such kindness to the unfortunate bridged the gap in language and made up for what he could not tell them about Christianity; they could see in his actions what it meant to believe in Christ. People flocked to him, begging to know more about the wonderful religion of kindness.

Naturally, all the Dominican missionaries made use of the Rosary. For Father John of the Angels, it was the mainstay in his work among the hunted Christians. He organized confraternities everywhere he worked, binding the frightened people together by the same tiny chain that, on the other side of the world, at the same moment, was holding the hunted Irish Catholics together in their hour of trial. It is not at all improbable that he encouraged his beleaguered people to pray for the persecuted Catholics of Ireland and England, for he must have known all about the great persecution there, hearing of it from the exiled priests who studied in Spain.

Persecutions flared up again in Japan; 1617 saw the great martyrdom at Nagasaki. Missionaries were killed or exiled; the native Christians, dying bravely for their new-found faith, carefully guarding the few priests who were left to them. Father John of the Angels stayed on, hidden and hunted and—most of the time—cold and hungry. At last, his health was so undermined by the hardships he had endured that he was obliged to go to Manila for help.

In 1620, he gathered a few brave companions and made plans for returning to Japan. No Japanese ship would take him. Eventually, he convinced a trader to take him as far as Satsuma.

When they arrived in Satsuma, the missionaries were soon recognized and thrown into prison. They spent their prison term taking a short course in Japanese. Before long, the poor of Satsuma were crowding around the jail, risking death to listen to the men of God. John of the Angels was eventually allowed to walk outside the jail. He discovered from the people that the source of pagan superstition in Satsuma was a sacred grove. The people were terrified of it. To prove to his Christian friends that the claims of the pagan priests were false, he went to the sacred grove. Making the Sign of the Cross, he walked in the woods.

This act signed his death warrant. He was taken out into a boat and beheaded, and his body thrown into the sea. The relics were never recovered. But neither this, nor any other effort of the pagan government, could efface his memory from the hearts of the people he had taught.

PETER BEDON
(1555-1621)

High in the Andes, not far from Bogotá, there is a shrine of Our Lady built around a picture that was discovered in a cave two centuries ago. It is a very beautiful picture of Our Lady with the Child Jesus, attended by St. Dominic and St. Francis. The people who climb the steep path to pray there will tell you that the angels painted it. Perhaps they did. But it is more likely that it was painted by a little-known, but extremely talented, Dominican artist who preached in that region in the sixteenth century. His name was Peter Bedón.

Peter was born in Quito, of mixed Spanish and Indian parentage, in 1555. His father was wealthy, and both his parents were pious. After a happy childhood, Peter joined the Dominicans, in the convent of St. Peter Martyr in Quito in 1569. We are told that he took this step in response to a direct command of Our Lady, who appeared to him and told him that she wanted him to join the Order. However that may be, the young novice distinguished himself, not only for his fine intellectual talents, but also for a gift with the brush and paints—a gift that his companions regarded as little short of miraculous.

His superiors placed him under the instruction of an Italian artist who had studied under Michelangelo. Under this gifted teacher, Peter's talent expanded. He worked in a medium that we do not understand today, painting on glass from the reverse side. He was called upon to decorate many churches, chapels and convents both in Quito and in Lima, where he was sent to finish his studies. All of his life he was to paint, in various places and media, as one way of preaching.

However, painting was only one of his many activities. He was head of the house of studies in Quito and taught theology there. He organized classes in the various Indian languages, in order to train the missionaries for their work in the vast territory of Ecuador, which was still mostly without priests. He petitioned the king to found a university in Colombia for the young men of that country who had no opportunity of getting an education otherwise. Later, he made strenuous efforts to establish a university in Quito. He established the Holy Name Society in Quito, in 1599, and he worked tirelessly to better the conditions of Indians and Negroes who were ground under the wheels of conquest. He founded no less than four houses of strict observance in Ecuador, doing all that was possible to uphold the Dominican rule in a missionary country.

Peter Bedón died in February, 1621, after a long and holy life devoted to other people. At several places in Lima and Quito there are pictures known to be his. The Madonna in the Cave, near Bogotá, has never been positively identified as his work, but it possesses so many traits of similarity that experts believe it was.

AGATHA OF THE CROSS
(d. 1621)

Sister Agatha of the Cross was a famous mystic of the seventeenth century. She lived in the convent of the Third Order Regular in Toledo, spending her life in an unceasing round of action and contemplation, which seems to have been designed for this particular branch of the Order.

We do not know for certain where Agatha was born, but it was probably Toledo, where she spent most of her life. It is difficult, in fact, to assign any dates to the work of this remarkable woman, for people seemed much more impressed with what she was and did than they were with the precise time of events.

We do know that the life of Sister Agatha was an unending round of active works; in that simpler age, when professional standards were different from our own, Tertiaries did not ordinarily undergo any professional training; they did whatever needed to be done. Sister Agatha, therefore, took care of the sick, taught small children, converted sinners among their elders, and was active in the apostolate to prisoners. One of her most exacting assignments was the tutoring of the royal princesses, and the necessary traveling with the court which this entailed. We can certainly judge that Sister Agatha lived in the world, though she was not of it, and that her days were, on the surface, as full of distractions as our own. What we should try to absorb from her life is the fact that she did not allow these things to distract her from her contemplation of divine things. To accomplish union with God shut away in a cloister, free of worldly distractions, is one thing; to accomplish the same end while in front of a classroom, or in a hospital ward, is quite another. It is refreshing to find a woman attaining union with God under these conditions. The Church is seriously considering her cause for canonization.

By choice, Agatha of the Cross did the hardest work in the house; she seems to have had a fondness for the laundry; she enjoyed washing the sisters' habits. It sounds familiar to read: "She hardly knew where to begin, there was so much of it." It is also a touching note to read that the first time she did the community wash her hands chapped so badly that she cried. She appealed to Our Blessed Mother who, taking compassion on her inexperience, healed her hands and warmed her; it was apparently very cold in the wash-house.

Agatha was sent out for the Saturday marketing, and she also was responsible for seeing that the vegetables and other produce of the community garden were properly stored, and that they were used at the right time. Apparently she had had no training in such housewifely details. Many modern novices will sympathize with her for the mistakes she made and the penances she received for allowing the vegetables to spoil, or for not cooking them properly.

Yet, the reputation of Agatha of the Cross was to rest not on her housewifely skill or lack of it, or even on her good will in the matter, which must have been great. History knows her as a mystic who penetrated many of the deepest secrets of the Passion of our Lord, and one who received in her own body the stigmata of the sacred wounds. It is written of her: "She had formed the habit of shutting herself up in the bosom of God; there she lived, worked, prayed, and slept." This had the effect of making her, in spite of her absorbing activities, a serene and tranquil person, who put first things first, and who was always joyous. She acquired a peace which nothing could disturb—an invaluable asset to a sister of a community engaged in active works.

Continually living in the presence of God, Agatha was acutely aware of our Lord's sufferings, and made of every little thing a means of recalling them. In the fields, she walked on the stones and briars, and, once she was met carrying a heavy faggot on her shoulders in memory of the cross. She one time asked our Lord how it was that he granted such great favors to the souls in purgatory. He replied that to ask Him anything in the name of His Passion was to unlock the treasure house of His grace.

Agatha died in Toledo in 1621. Her cause was active as late as 1929.

MOTHER FRANCES DOROTHY
(d. 1623)

A strange, controversial figure, who has for many years been listed as a potential blessed, was Frances Dorothy of Seville, mother foundress of the reformed convent of Our Lady of the Kings. Any possible blessed is intriguing to us, but she has another claim to our interest, if not to our imitation. She devoted her life to founding a Dominican house of barefoot nuns, a singular vocation among Dominicans, who have always insisted on wearing shoes.

Frances Dorothy was born in Compostella, the fifth child of a family of impoverished nobility. What they thought of her precocious piety is not recorded, but it must have been a problem to live with; she became a Third Order Franciscan at the age of six, at which time she cut off her hair and adopted a robe of sackcloth as her only garment. Her ordinary day was one of silence, austerity, and prayer. She demanded a small oratory of her own for private prayer. It was built, and furnished with a statue of Our Lady of the Kings of the Almudena, to whom she was especially devoted.

Here, in the quiet of her own oratory, Frances Dorothy made strides to the way of contemplative prayer. St. Peter and St. Paul appeared to her there, and the Blessed Virgin frequently came to counsel her. They all warned her that she had a difficult future ahead, for God had chosen her to be the foundress of a convent of very strict observance. She begged God to spare her this cross, but she was assured that this was to be her work.

On Holy Thursday night, in 1582, when she was about twelve years old, Frances Dorothy was keeping an all-night vigil with her two sisters in the Augustinian church. She went into an ecstasy and was visibly impressed with the stigmata. One of her sisters called her Augustinian confessor, who witnessed the phenomenon. Frances Dorothy remained in acute agony until Easter. Then the pain left her, but visible marks remained in her hands and feet, and these pained intermittently during the rest of her life.

When she was in her early twenties, Frances Dorothy was told in vision that now was the time to begin on the convent of reformed nuns, which should be in Seville. She consulted a Dominican confessor, who advised her to make it a Dominican convent of the Second Order. She gathered a number of women who wished to join her in the venture. Two of them were her own sisters, and one was a wealthy widow who had a house available for the new community. It was clear sailing for some time. She made the wealthy widow superior and wrote the rule that the house would follow.

Even the confessor gasped when he saw the rules. It enjoined continual fasting, daily disciplines, hair-shirts reaching to the knees ("relaxed" hair-shirts were apparently shorter) three hours of mental prayer daily, perpetual silence, both the Divine Office and the Little Office daily, and, last but not least, bare feet. He pointed out to her that she would have trouble getting such a rule approved by the Order, because of the clause about bare feet. She insisted on the whole rule as she had written it, and her troubles began.

At one point, the superior had Frances Dorothy locked up for some time. The Dominican provincial told Frances Dorothy bluntly that the Dominicans had always worn shoes and were proud of it. The archbishop refused to let them have a chapel in the house, and, finally, the superior ejected them all —after all, it was her house—and severed her connections with the project. Frances Dorothy decided to consult the Augustinians. They offered to help her rewrite the rule if she would omit the item concerning shoes, but she insisted that her nuns would go barefoot. The Augustinians gave up.

Exactly why the insistence on shoelessness we do not know. It was most probably an echo of the Carmelite reform, then so recently active in Spain. But it rather seems, viewing the situation now, that it would have been more logical to become a Carmelite if one aspired to the practices of the Carmelite reform. However, Frances Dorothy and her companions—there were six remaining—persisted in their uncomfortable position; they would be Dominicans, and they would be barefoot.

At this juncture, a Trinitarian sister in Seville had a vision. In it she saw Frances Dorothy and her companions in a group with St. Dominic and the archbishop of Granada, all surrounded by rays of light. It was all a little confusing, since the archbishop of Granada had nothing to say about Seville, and the local archbishop would have nothing to do with the proposed community. The sister had an artist paint her vision as she had seen it. People marvelled over it. Then word came that the archbishop of Seville was being transferred elsewhere, and the archbishop of Granada was coming to Seville. Frances Dorothy took hope, approaching the new archbishop as soon as possible. Eventually, she did win his approval, but it took her eleven years.

When the monastery was founded, it was named for Our Lady of the Kings of the Almudena, just as the tiny oratory of Frances Dorothy's childhood had been. Her statue was enthroned in the chapel, and there, after so many years of trial and error, the community settled down, barefoot and happy. Frances Dorothy was appointed prioress, over her protests, and she proved to be a happy choice. Some time before her death, she became blind, and she pleaded this as an excuse to be relieved of her office. No one would listen, however, and she remained superior until her death, in 1623.

Many miracles were reported even during the lifetime of Mother Frances Dorothy. She received Communion miraculously a number of times. She had the gift of prophecy, and she healed many sick people by her prayers. After her death, her body remained flexible, and it gave off a sweet fragrance from the stigmata, which were visible.

The process for the beatification of Mother Frances Dorothy was begun in 1757, and it was active as recently as 1955. She has long been popularly invoked against fire and plague.

LOUIS AQUINAS
(1550-1623)

It must be slightly unnerving to enter the Order if you bear the name of a famous relative. It was the fate of Louis of Aquin to meet people every day of his life who said: "Aquinas? Oh, not a relative of *the* Aquinas?"

Louis was born in Crucoli, in 1550, and began his studies for the secular priesthood in Naples. He was a rather ordinary young man, who caused no comment at all among his fellow students. He himself seems to have known practically nothing about his famous relative until one day, shortly after he had received minor orders, he was looking about for a book that would help him overcome worldly temptations. The book he happened upon was a life of St. Thomas, and it completely enthralled him. He read it eagerly, and then went immediately to the Dominican convent in Naples.

Here he received the habit and the religious name of Louis, and he began his life anew, on the model of the spiritual giant who was his distant cousin.

Louis was a good student, and, if he had not deliberately stood in Thomas' shadow, he might, on his own merits, be remembered for his intellectual attainments. He is said to have been a walking encyclopedia, a master of seven languages, and he knew the Bible and the lessons in the breviary from memory. He is known to have written some poetry and several devotional works on the Rosary. But he dedicated his life to making Thomas better known, effacing himself.

Shortly after his ordination, Louis was made novice-master. He had this assignment for many years. He was severe with his novices, and even more severe with himself, practicing the most extreme poverty and the most exacting cleanliness. We read of his leading his novices to clean a part of the house every day, and of his care in keeping his old patched habits clean and presentable. We can remember him gratefully for a principle he often quoted, one which Thomas would heartily have seconded: "Poverty is always beautiful; dirt never is."

Louis was prior of the convent of St. Dominic, in Naples, when St. Thomas was made the patron and protector of the city. The city and church officials had long sought this favor from the Holy See, and, in 1604, a great celebration was planned to mark its favorable conclusion. A major relic of the saint was presented to the fathers in Naples, and it was the proud task of Louis to arrange having a silver reliquary made to hold the relic. The people enthusiastically collected jewels to be used in the work of art, and, after some trouble in casting the silver, the reliquary was finished, ready for veneration. On the day of the great celebration, Louis carried the relic, rejoicing with his countrymen that God had so exalted the humble Thomas. It never entered his mind to take any personal or family pride in the matter, a fact that gives us a clear picture of his humility.

Louis had a sister and a niece who were Poor Clares, in a convent outside Naples. After long pleading on their part, he went to see them, but the deference he received so alarmed him that he would never go again. He did not go on for his doctorate, which he might easily have done, but, for a lifetime, he was busy with his novices, with the direction of monasteries of sisters, and with endless hours in the confessional.

Louis seems to have shied away from women; perhaps even in his day the Aquino women were more than the average man could deal with. This makes it all the more amusing that the miracles recorded of him were all worked in favor of women. His own sister claimed that he had cured her of migraine headaches, merely by laying his hand on her head. Another time, at the tearful plea of a mother, he cured a sick child. One day he stuck a dead branch of jasmine in the ground, and it bloomed; this is the sort of miracle which, in the seventeenth century, would hardly happen anywhere outside a convent yard.

Louis died in Naples, in 1623, after foretelling the day of his death.

CONSTANTIUS MAGNI
(d. 1624)

Constantius Magni has been overlooked in our records; a man who tried as hard as he did for martyrdom certainly deserves more credit.

Constantius was born of a noble family, in Pistoia, probably around 1565. Given a good Christian education, he studied both the humanities and theology, although he was a layman. Interested in spiritual things, he first made private vows; then he entered the Dominican convent in his native city, where he preached and taught for several years.

On a trip to Rome, in 1593, Constantius heard of the martyrdom of four Franciscans in Morocco. Fired with zeal to go preach to the Christian captives in Barbary, he obtained permission to do so. Leaving Palermo, he went to Valencia, whence he hoped to embark for Spanish Morocco. From there he would try to slip across the border into Moorish territory. His first attempt, however, ended in failure. The ship, damaged in a storm, had to return to Valencia. The next passage he could arrange was also upset. At the last minute, he was called off the ship to give the sacraments to a dying man, and the ship sailed without him. He waited and schemed, and finally he traveled as far as Ceuta, in Spanish Morocco. The plight of the slaves there was pitiful, and he decided to stay and work among them for the time being, until he could penetrate Moorish territory.

A rich merchant of Valencia, who had discovered the delights of trading between the king of Spain and the sultan of Morocco, was the ordinary agent for bringing in contraband missionaries. Constantius employed his dubious protection, attempting to slip over the border one dark night. He was caught, put in chains, and taken to Morocco. He was delighted, since this was the place he had been trying to reach for years.

The Christian slaves in Morocco were pitifully grateful to see him. Some of them had been ten or twelve years without the sacraments. They took up a collection and bought a certain amount of freedom for the Dominican, in order that he could minister to their needs. Moslem guards, who liked to make a penny on the side, looked the other way while he said daily

Mass and heard confessions. For two-and-a-half years, while worrying scrupulously about his own salvation, Constantius ministered to the Christian slaves, and escaped the sultan's notice. Then the city was struck by a violent plague. In ten days, four thousand people were attacked by it, and the sultan fled with his court. Fifteen hundred slaves died, and we are told that Constantius reached all of them with his healing ministry, in spite of the fact that he himself was ill. After the plague had subsided, Constantius was given the administration of the properties of many rich merchants who had died. He used the funds very prudently, paying the ransom for young men and women, and for those in particular peril, or those who had no money. Eventually, of course, the sultan discovered who was doing such a business-like job of ransoming his captives, and he had Constantius imprisoned. Brought chained before the Moslem judge, Constantius managed not only to talk himself out of the chains, but to be transferred from his solitary dungeon to the prison of the Jews. Here he was kept for five years, and his work was limited to helping those who could come to him.

In 1624, the sultan died. His successor freed Constantius, who promptly went back to his ministry. Unfortunately, the long prison sentence had taken its toll, and he was seriously ill. He died two months later—a natural death—but one that the sorrowing slaves considered the death of a holy martyr.

MICHAEL RUIZ
(d. 1630)

One of the most charming Lady-legends of the Far East comes to us in connection with Michael Ruiz, an otherwise undistinguished missionary.

Michael was born in Segovia, and he received the habit there, in the convent of the Holy Cross. On finishing his studies, the young priest volunteered for the missions in the Far East and went to the Philippines in 1602. Here he occupied several positions of trust. He was vicar of Bataan, then prior in Manila, and, finally, provincial of the Philippines. This seems a hurried and inadequate description of a long and faithful apostolate, but it is nearly all that the records give us.

We do read that Michael preached almost daily, and that he performed such penances that he was finally ordered to moderate them, for it was feared that he would ruin his health. He is credited with several textbooks that were used in the missions—a book on the Rosary, some manuals of devotion, and a dictionary and grammar of the native language of Binondoc;

he finished the dictionary and grammar in great pain, just before his death there in 1630. But beyond these scanty records, we know nothing about this very zealous missionary, except that he was prior in Manila when the following Lady-miracle took place, and it is through him that we have the story.

In 1613 the Spanish governor sent out a small fleet, made up of two large galleys and several barques, to assist a neighboring Spanish settlement which was under the siege of pirates. The two galleys were named for Our Lady of Guadalupe and Our Lady of Guidance. The chief gunner on the "Guadalupe" was Francis Lopez, a man given to all kinds of wickedness. He had only one soft spot in his hard heart, and that was for Our Lady of the Rosary. Wicked as he was, he never neglected his offering to the Mother of Mercy. On the voyage in question, the "Guadalupe" struck a reef and sank, and everyone had to swim for shore. Francis reached shore safely, but promptly got embroiled in a free-for-all with the native galley-slaves, who saw an opportunity to escape from the Spaniards. The slaves entrenched themselves behind the cliffs, rolling rocks down on their former masters. When the few survivors pulled away, Francis was horribly wounded and left for dead. For two weeks he lay helpless, in a frightful state because of his wounds; he was surrounded by the dead and deserted by the living. In his lucid moments he prayed—not to be delivered, not for health, but for a priest. Francis was in no state to face God without confession, and he begged Our Lady of the Rosary to send him a priest.

Two weeks later, the other galley ran into trouble and was blown off its course. It was carried into the straits where the "Guadalupe" had gone down, and, despite all the efforts of the crew, it could not be maneuvered around the cape. Finally the captain gave up, dropped anchor, and sent the men ashore for fresh water. One of the sailors heard someone calling his name. The wounded man he found was almost too horrible to look upon, but his request was plain enough: "For the love of God, get me a priest." The Franciscan chaplain was hastily summoned, the man made his confession and died. Favorable winds filled the sails of the "Guidance," and in an hour the vessel was back on course.

Back in Manila, the sacristans were decorating the sanctuary for a feast. Dusting around the statue of Our Lady of the Rosary, one of the ladies discovered an odd fact. "His little shoes are wet and muddy," she said, pointing to the Infant. "And Our Lady's skirts are damp and full of sand, as though they had been walking on the beach."

The prior, Father Michael Ruiz, was summoned to see the phenomenon. He confirmed that the Mother's robe and the Baby's sandals showed definite signs of a journey in a wet, sandy place, although the niche wherein the statue stood was perfectly dry. He carefully noted the day and the time, and summoned a visiting Franciscan from Rome, who examined the statue. The prior finally took the Baby's sandals to his room with him, as proof of the incident. Weeks later, when the "Guidance" came home, the story was pieced together; Our Lady had obviously heard the cry of her wandering child, and no one ever doubted that the sand on her robe was from the beach where Francis Lopez died, calling on Our Lady for help.

DOMINIC OF ERIQUICIA
(d. 1633)

Dominic of Eriquicia, who died at the height of the Japanese persecution, was a man of great literary gifts. From his letters to his provincial during the short time of his apostolate in Japan, we get a clearer picture of the situation than anyone else has been able to give us.

Dominic was a Basque who made profession in the convent of St. Elmo, in San Sebastian. He volunteered for the Japanese missions and arrived in Manila at the same time that the emperor of Japan sent warning that he would attack the Philippines if they did not refrain from sending Christian missionaries into his country. Nevertheless, there were dozens who wanted to go to Japan, and superiors gave their permission and their blessing to members of the community who would promise to travel quietly.

Dominic of Eriquicia set out with three other Dominicans, four Franciscans, and two Augustinians, in a leaky ship. They were barely out of port when they met a violent storm and had to turn back to Manila. On their second attempt, they reached the shores of China before they were driven on a rocky island, where there was water, but no wood. They dismantled a wrecked ship they found and repaired their own. Back once more in the channel, they were fired upon by a Chinese galley. "We are just peaceful citizens on our way to Japan," the captain protested. The Chinese galley sent back its opinion: "You look like a warship to us." And continued firing.

After a bit, the Chinese ship pulled away, leaving the missionaries demoralized. One of the Dominicans, Diego de Riviera, had been shot in the leg, and the ship's doctor said he must amputate it. It later developed that he had never performed this type of surgery before, and Diego died in agony a few days later.

After more contrary winds, they finally landed on Kagoshima. Here the missionaries went ashore by day and worked among the people, but all of them wanted to get in touch with the superiors of their various Orders and receive a regular assignment. Clothed in the peasant garments of the country, and slumped down to avoid appearing too tall, they began their trip to Nagasaki, where the bulk of the Christians and, presumably, the few remaining priests would be found. As they advanced, they heard worse and worse news about the persecution. When they arrived in Nagasaki, a message reached them from Father Dominic Castellet, who was then the oldest missionary at liberty, and the one who best knew how to move adroitly in this strange land. He advised them to get passports to board a Portuguese galley that was leaving that night, and then to present themselves to the captain, conspicuously, who then would be able to swear that they had been aboard his ship. Once on board and outside the harbor, a little fishing boat would take them off the galley and return them secretly to the Christian community. Following his instructions faithfully, they found themselves in the Christian underground.

They were obliged to stay in country places, as none of them knew the language well enough to pass a challenge on patrolled city streets. They became accustomed to the strange clothing and the straw sandals, and to the eating at odd hours, if at all. They loved and admired the Japanese Christians and quite willingly settled down to die among them. On November 13, 1623, Dominic of Eriquicia wrote to his superior in Manila: "If you are going to send us supplies, send them through Macao . . . religious could come that way, too. We could use a little money, also wine and portable missals; chasubles should be of light material so they will fold into small bundles, as we have to move every night. We still cannot find safe lodgings in Nagasaki, and we are always on the road . . ."

In January, he wrote the sad news: "Seventy Christians have been martyred in the imperial city, including a Franciscan and a Japanese priest who were burned to death. I am making some progress with the language but not enough. If the persecution continues, I will have to go out and hear confessions with just what I have. Fathers Louis Bertrand and Luke of the Holy Ghost are my companions; Father Peter Vasquez has been arrested, Father Castellet is still free. A few days ago more than a hundred soldiers came in one party looking for him, but he got away. We had to change our dwelling in the middle of the night, and spent the rest of the night barefoot on a freezing hillside. I have never been happier."

As martyrdom drew nearer, he wrote: "Whatever you do, don't abandon these people. When we die, send more men. Perhaps today, perhaps tomorrow, we will die as the others have; but send more priests to these good people. Recruits must be strong and courageous, realists, able to work . . . We who know that we will soon die lean on your prayers and those of the community.

If you do not have the things we asked for, never mind; you do have prayers, and we need them most." He paused writing this letter, to hear the confession of a young man who had come from another village, and who was returning to it to certain capture and death. "They are wonderful Christians," wrote the priest. "Do not ever abandon them."

The emperor was ingenious in methods of torture. Men who were fathers of families, he had tied up, while their wives and children were tortured before their eyes, in an attempt to make the men apostatize. Only four did, out of the hundreds treated so, and Dominic of Eriquicia managed to get to these four and bring them back to the path of renunciation. One day, during a public judgment of Christians, a rich retinue arrived, and a man of obvious importance was let out of a sedan chair. The emperor, thinking it was someone of importance from another kingdom, halted the proceedings. The wealthy man bowed to the emperor, and then informed him that he had come to be martyred, since he and all his household were Christians. After trying to shake his resolve, and failing, the emperor had the man and thirty of his followers savagely killed. In other places, the Christians had to be driven off with sticks to prevent them from volunteering for martyrdom.

Dominic gives a clear account of the missionaries' day. "We have to be very cautious, of course, and stay in a different house every night. We hear the confessions of the sick and of those in prison during the day; the street gates close at 10:00 P.M. and we have to be indoors by then. From then until after midnight we hear the confessions of those who are able to come to us, and find out how many there are for Communion. Mass is as soon after midnight as possible, so that the people can get away quickly in the morning. Only the friends of the family and a few others can get in at one time without exciting suspicion. It has been much colder here than it is in the Philippines."

When he came to one Christian house late at night, after a tiresome day, and sat down to the first meal he had had since the day before, he found that it consisted only of hard bread and wine. "We didn't want to give you anything more," the lady of the house explained, "because we know this is a Dominican fast day; the last father who was here told us so."

On the death of the old emperor, the Christians took heart, but it soon proved that the new emperor was worse than the old. Two Dominicans, two Franciscans, and two Augustinians were caught and burned to death; two more Dominicans were caught, and one escaped only by miracle. Dominic, who had to hide out in a cistern for several days, with nothing to eat but dry bread, made a trip North with Luke of the Holy Spirit, whom he gaily dubbed "the ox of St. Luke." "I am afraid the ox will soon be sent to the butcher shop," was his rather grim joke to his companion. Apparently, the men who worked under such terrible pressure saw no point in being morbid about it.

In 1633, a small fishing-smack landed with a group of missionaries, including James of St. Mary, who was Japanese, and Jordan of St. Stephen, a Sicilian. It was a minor blunder of Jordan's that gave them away. He could not speak Japanese, and he was supposed to stay close to James of St. Mary until they met the hidden priests. They were separated somehow, and Jordan, meeting a tall Japanese on the street, shook hands with him and greeted him as "Father Dominic." The pack was after them in full cry, and the two new-comers were soon captured and condemned. Dominic of Eriquicia somehow managed to rescue them, and then he fled to hide out in the nearby villages. He was captured, however, when a Christian, under torture, revealed his whereabouts. At last, he was face to face with death.

Dominic of Eriquicia died on the nineteenth of August, 1633, after thirty hours of torture, hanging head-down in a ditch that was partly filled with water. He was forty-six years old.

FRANCIS OF ST. DOMINIC
(d. 1633)

The first martyr of Formosa was a Portuguese friar. He had made profession in the convent in Zamora, in Spain. We do not know the dates of his birth and profession.

Francis of St. Dominic became interested in the missions through Diego Advarte, who was later to be appointed bishop in one of the vast, vague dioceses, in the still more vague territory known as New Spain. He spoke on the missions in the Spanish houses when Francis was a student in Zamora, and he won Francis' sympathy for the people of the new lands, where there was such a shortage of priests.

After his ordination Francis volunteered for the Indies, and was sent to the region called New Segovia. Here he worked for some time among the natives, learning several dialects, and preaching whenever he could gather a few natives together in the forest. He was drafted for service in Formosa by Father Bartholomew Martinez, and he went eagerly to this place, which had such a sinister reputation for savagery.

The first martyr of this difficult mission had a thorough training in suffering to prepare him for the sacrifice. To begin with, he suffered from severe migraine headaches, which are bad enough under the best of circumstances, but must have been frightful under such primitive and comfortless conditions. To the everyday bodily hardships, which were abundant, he added voluntary mortifications, feeling that the evils of this people could be cast out only by fasting and disciplines. He wore a hairshirt, and he rose faithfully at midnight to say his Office, as though he were in the venerable cloisters of Zamora and not in a thatched hut in a hostile jungle. He begged his bread, and sometimes he was refused.

After working for some time among the people on Tan-Chui, Francis volunteered to go to work among the Pantao people. These were the most savage among savages—there were head-hunters, and a number of other unpleasant things. To add to the trouble, they were at war with another tribe.

Francis was not the first, nor the last, European to discover that the primitive code of justice has different roots from ours. In an attempt to bring about peace between the warring tribes, he placed himself in a position that caused his own tribe to think that he was trafficking with the enemies, and his own tribe killed him. As he fell under a rain of arrows, Francis offered his life for the salvation of the savages, and he tried to convert the leader of the murderers, whom he recognized as a man he had helped release from jail a short time before.

The savages cut off the head of the missionary and departed with it to their stronghold in the mountains. They had barely arrived there when there was a sharp tremor, and the mountains opened, spouting lava and steam. Terrified, they went to the Spanish commandant, telling him what they had done. The Spaniards reverently buried the relics, and a year later, when transferring them, they found to their surprise that the body was completely incorrupt. Because of the primitive state of the people who killed him, it is hard to tell what their motives were in doing so. Consequently, there will always be the practical question as to whether or not Francis of St. Dominic died "in odium fidei." However, he was the first to shed his blood in Formosa, and in dying he made a consecration worthy of any martyr.

HYACINTH ESQUIVEL
(d. 1633)

If Hyacinth Esquivel felt frustrated in his attempts to be an apostle, no one could blame him. His whole life seemed to be a series of frustrations.

Hyacinth was a Basque, born in Bascay, around 1600. He received the habit and the name of Hyacinth of the Rosary in Vittoria, and he completed his studies in Valladolid. Here he expressed a desire to do missionary work in Japan. His best friend, Father John Lezcano, made him promise that he would not apply to go for four years. He kept his promise, but at the end of that time, he volunteered. In 1625, he was sent to the Philippines.

His first work there was teaching in the University of Santo Tomas. He enjoyed this, as it gave him a chance to learn Japanese in his spare time. He mastered the use of chopsticks and became accustomed to a rice diet. After four years of teaching, he felt that he was ready for Japan, and he asked his superior for permission to go. The superior pointed out to him the formidable difficulty of getting into Japan, for the emperor had promised to attack the Philippines if the governor allowed any more missionaries to leave from there. The only possible way of entry, at the moment, was through Formosa. Hyacinth went there.

The night he arrived at the Convent of All Saints, in Formosa, there was a hurricane, and the house blew down around him. Surveying the wreckage next morning, he observed that the Lord had provided him with some raw material to build a chapel at Tai Peh, his destination. He actually took some of the wreckage with him to Tai Peh. Here he met his parishioners, a delightful class of people: pirates by profession, they made a precarious living murdering travelers and selling their goods. Their leader was a renegade Basque Christian. Neither he nor his followers were at all eager for a pastor. However, Hyacinth set to work learning their language. He erected a huge cross in the market place, and just as he was beginning to see daylight ahead, his superiors moved him to a region where a totally different dialect was spoken.

For the rest of his short life, this was the pattern of Hyacinth's missionary activity—to settle down among some savage tribe, learn its language, compile a dictionary and catechism, and then receive an assignment somewhere else. In one place, he founded a Confraternity of Our Lady, with a sort of seminary in which young native people were educated for the Church. This institution was to train excellent catechists in the years to come, and it greatly expedited the work of converting Japan, but Hyacinth did not live to see it.

The chance to enter Japan finally came, in 1633. Hyacinth and a Franciscan friend sneaked aboard a Chinese junk that was bound for Nagasaki. Just when it looked as if his dreams were coming true, Hyacinth awoke to the fact that they had been betrayed. Within sight of the shores he had yearned for all his life, Hyacinth and the Franciscan were beheaded. The captain tucked the relics away on board ship in order to get the bounty that was being offered for dead missionaries.

MOTHER AGNES OF JESUS
(1602-1634)

The story of Mother Agnes of Jesus is the story of God's arrangement for fraternal charity in this world. She was chosen to offer her prayers and sufferings for a man who, at the time, seemed scarcely to deserve it; but he was later to become the founder of a new society in the Church and, quite possibly, a canonized saint.

Agnes was born near Langeac in 1602. Her older sister, Mary, was a devout girl, but not, apparently, as vivid a character as the talented young Agnes, who was the pet of the household. Very early in her life, Agnes was seeking out ways of penance, and she swore Mary to secrecy, lest her parents find out what she was doing and make her give them up. She used to slip out of bed at night and sleep on the floor, and she wore an iron chain whenever it seemed likely that she could conceal it from her mother's attention. One day, in the midst of a hard winter, the two girls were standing before the fire, warming themselves, and Agnes had an inspiration. She said, severely: "Mary, you have too many clothes. I am going to give them all away to the poor if you don't. It is a shame that we are well-dressed while others are freezing." Mary obligingly handed over all her extra clothes for the young zealot to distribute among the poor. Agnes regularly talked Mary out of her allowance, which also went to the poor.

Mary never seemed to resent the dictatorial attitude of her younger sister. In fact, when Agnes left for the cloister at Langeac, at the age of sixteen, Mary made up her mind to enter also. Agnes wanted her to join her in Langeac. Instead, Mary went to Vivier, where she became a laysister.

Once in the cloister at Langeac, Agnes embraced religious life with a tremendous zeal. She prayed for suffering, but perhaps she did not expect the Lord to take her so literally. She became famous for her gift of prayer, and the sisters in the house were sure that she was a saint; but for Agnes herself, it meant terrible suffering. For years and years she did not have the satisfaction of knowing that she was pleasing to God. Then, when she received a communication from God in her prayer, she was told simply that she must offer her prayers, works, and sufferings for a young French curé who was living a gay and irresponsible life. His name was John James Olier, and God wanted him reformed and sanctified, because he was to do a great work in the Church. Agnes was to offer everything for him, and she was not assured of ever receiving any information as to whether her prayers were answered or not.

For years she prayed and suffered, and, probably, also wondered. One day, (but by what means she did not know) she was carried in spirit to a church where young Father Olier was at prayer, and she knew that he saw her. "I am praying for you," she told him. "God has asked me to pray that you may become worthy to accomplish the work he wants you to do."

Only once was she to see him in the flesh, and that when she was at death's door, and she could barely force herself to the grille to see him. He seemed shaken by the fact that she recognized him, though he had never been in Langeac before. He humbly asked her to keep on praying for him, and went away again. Mother Agnes died soon after, in 1634—twenty years too soon to see the marvelous results of Father Olier's work in founding the Society of St. Sulpice.

Mary, too, deserves a note of mention. She had entered the monastery of Our Lady of the Rhone in Vivier, because it was very poor and had great need of sisters. She worked hard, considering it her duty to save the salary of a workman around the grounds. Once she dug a well by herself, because this seemed a way to save money. She caught cold, however, and was ill for a long time. Her regular work was in the infirmary, where she did the work of several people. She managed, nevertheless, to spend most of her nights in prayer. Sometimes she experienced long periods of dryness and spiritual loneliness, and she had a skin infection that made ordinary living a misery. She outlived her more famous sister by thirty-five years. She died in 1669.

The cause of Mother Agnes of Jesus was still active as recently as 1955.

MAGDALEN OF NAGASAKI
(d. 1634)

In the accounts of the early Christian martyrs, there is one provocative story about a Christian who was thrown to the lions. His lion was more tired than hungry, and it promptly lay down at his feet and went to sleep. Anxious not to lose his crown, the Christian in question gave the beast a vigorous prod with his foot and, presumably, cried out "Benedicamus Domino." Of direct spiritual lineage with this ambitious Christian was a Japanese girl, known to us as Sister Magdalen, who died for the faith in 1634.

Magdalen's parents had perished in the great persecution, and she was left on her own resources at the age of twenty-two. The girl had been left without property, by the policy of confiscation; so, parentless, homeless and moneyless, she went into the hills and found a cave where she could live as a hermit, spending her remaining days in prayer. Christians had no illusions about their future at that time. She and her companions in the faith were well aware that they would die for Christ; it only remained to see when and where.

Magdalen placed herself under the direction of a Dominican father who was also marked for an early martyrdom, Jordan of St. Stephen. With his sanction, she pronounced private vows. Eventually she received the Dominican habit as a Tertiary. She knew that the mere possession of such a garment was enough to condemn her, and, during her brief days of peace in the hermit cave, she prayed for strength against the day of her martyrdom.

Father Jordan came to bring her the sacraments as often as possible, but one day he did not come as he had promised, and she heard that he had been taken by the soldiers and was now in jail, awaiting execution. Magdalen decided this was the time to profess the faith. Dressing carefully in the full habit, she made her way to the jail. A guard in the jail came out to investigate a clamor he heard, and he saw a young woman pounding on the door of the jail, crying out loudly: "I'm a Christian. Let me in."

The guard, who had perhaps seen too much bloodshed already, tried to get rid of her. His admonition, "Go home, little girl—this is no place for you," fell upon deaf ears. She only cried out the louder: "You have no business keeping me out. I am a Christian—let me in." To quiet the clamor, he let her come inside, and she sought out Father Jordan of St. Stephen. "I've come to make my profession of vows, Father," she said simply. Through the bars of the cage where the priest was confined, she spoke the words that bound her to the Order she loved so much. It makes a rather startling picture as we see it, back through the years: the little sister, who (according to the chronicles) was exceedingly beautiful and very frail, probably looked as fragile as a china plate. The missionary, who knew what he—and she—must face, may have wondered if she could stand the almost unspeakable tortures that awaited her. He need not have feared.

The guard managed to get her out of the jail, although with much protest on the girl's part. Insulted at such treatment, Magdalen turned up—in full habit—at a public hearing presided over by the mandarin. Choosing a conspicuous moment, she stood up and cried out her profession of faith. There was now no choice, and she had to be arrested. Offers of leniency were indignantly rejected. Following the ordinary procedure, the tortures, which had already given Japan a glorious array of martyrs, were applied.

These tortures do not make good table reading. Suffice it to say, they were thorough, calculated to break the strongest spirit. Sister Magdalen endured them calmly, and, at one point, commented—in the elegant language which her race commands so well—"You humiliate me profoundly if you think I would reject Christ after only such small inconveniences. One would think you could find something worse than that to do to me." Her torturers kept on applying the "small inconveniences" until she was a mass of wounds and broken bones. The frail little Tertiary was incredibly tough; thirteen days passed before she died. She was one of the last to be put to death for the faith in Japan, and her particular brand of Christian fortitude was a great encouragement to her companions, as it should be to us.

SISTER MARINA
(d. 1634)

The story of Sister Marina gives us a glimpse of someone who had to endure more than physical tortures. Her courage should be an encouragement for those who occasionally must face the heart-rending trial of undeserved disgrace.

Marina was a Tertiary who lived in Omura during the worst years of the Japanese persecution. She was unmarried and lived at home, making her father's home a refuge for hunted Christians. She had been received into the Order by the nephew of St. Louis Bertrand, a young missionary. He himself was to die in the persecution very shortly. And later he was beatified.

There was no secret about Marina's sympathies with the foreign priests. It was only a matter of time until she was taken into custody and brought before a hostile judge to explain her actions. It might have been possible, even then, for her to avoid the outcome, but she was completely frank. She admitted that she had sheltered the foreign priests in her father's house, had given them food and clothing and provided them with methods of escape. She had done her best to keep any and all Christians out of the hands of the soldiers.

Her frankness intrigued the judges, and they demanded to know what manner of life she was living, and why she was not afraid to court death in this way. She explained about the religious vows, as much as she thought they would understand. They were quite unfamiliar with the concept of Christian chastity, and her mentioning it gave them an idea of a good way to punish her. The judge ordered that her hair be shaved off, and that she be obliged to walk through the kingdom, barefoot and bareheaded. By so doing, she would proclaim herself an adulteress.

To us, of another day and other customs, this sentence loses its force. We cannot comprehend what this disgrace meant to an honorable Japanese woman at that time and place. Suffice it to say that there were some Japanese Christian women who endured the most terrible physical tortures, but they had apostatized when faced with the alternative of making the journey that

Marina was asked to make. However, Marina was made of sterner fabric; she steeled herself for the ordeal and set out on the journey of shame rather than deny her faith.

The point of Marina's torture was not lost on any of the beholders. Women fled, weeping, from the sight of one who had to endure so much. The account of her innocence and her punishment went ahead of her, and her constancy probably did more to stiffen the courage of Japanese Christians than the most revolting tortures, for "loss of face" is most cruel to an Oriental.

Marina proceeded on her way, and her pathway was marked by at least one incident that the Christians considered a miracle. One day she was very thirsty, and she was far from any place where she might satisfy her thirst. She endured it as long as she could. Then, speaking to the soldier who was guarding her, she told him that, if he would look in a certain place nearby, he would find a clear stream of drinking water. He said that the idea was ridiculous—there was no water within miles. She told him to look, nevertheless. She was right. There was a spring, and a stream of water flowed from it from then on. Christians immediately concluded that it had been placed there miraculously for her comforting.

Returning from the walk of shame, Marina faced the judge once more. He had already discovered that the whole thing had been a mistake, because, instead of disgracing Marina, it had made a hero of her. Everyone in the kingdom was whispering that she was the bravest woman in Japan; even the pagans, who wanted nothing of the religion that motivated her, conceded that she was brave beyond all necessity.

The whispers had to be stopped. Marina was condemned to be burned to death over a slow fire. On November 11, 1634, her soul finally was released from its misery. Her ashes were taken out to sea, to keep them from the Christians, but all over Japan small bits of her clothing and shoes were hidden away as treasures, silent witnesses—to those who must die later—that faith is stronger than human tyranny.

THOMAS OF ST. HYACINTH AND JORDAN OF ST. STEPHEN
(d. 1634)

These two men, born half-a-world away from each other, died together, in 1634. Thomas of St. Hyacinth was Japanese, born in Nagasaki, and brought up amid scenes of terror, when Christians were dying everyday. His early life was not edifying, but, after some schooling under the Jesuits, who had trained his parents as catechists, Thomas regulated his life, and he went to Manila to join the Dominicans. Studying at the University of Santo Tomas, his scholastic record was good, and he was received into the Order. He and James of St. Mary, another future martyr, were clothed in the habit on the same day.

Thomas, an able theologian, became a model of all virtues. He perfected his Spanish, and he studied everything that he thought would make him more useful in spreading the Kingdom of Christ. At this time, it was decided to use Formosa as a possible way of entering Japan. Thomas, with three others, was destined for this dangerous mission. It took them a long time to make their way from Formosa, but, finally, after great privation, they entered Japan, disguised as laymen. They worked there until each was caught and martyred. Thomas, perhaps because he knew the language so well, had a long career—four years.

Jordan of St. Stephen was born in Sicily and received the habit there. He read all that he could about the Eastern missions, and, finally, when someone came from the Philippine province looking for help, he convinced his superiors that he should be allowed to go. He had an attack of scruples; the superior succeeded in overcoming them, and, after joining the other missionaries in Seville, he sailed for the New World in 1625.

During the voyage, which we must remember took in both the Atlantic and Pacific Oceans, he occupied himself translating a biography of St. Dominic from the Spanish of Castillo into Latin. At some time on this long voyage he created one of the few puns that chroniclers have bothered to record. Someone asked him: "Didn't you ever want to turn back from the missions?" He answered: "No, I am not the Jordan that was turned back." Arriving in Manila, he was appointed infirmarian in the Chinese hospital in order that he could learn Chinese and Japanese. He also studied the religious customs and superstitions of the people he would be teaching. Eventually, in 1632, he boarded a ship bound for Japan. He passed himself off as Chinese, which must have been quite a trick for a Sicilian.

The persecution was raging then, and few priests were free to work in Japan. The Dominican, Dominic of Eriquicia, and the Franciscan, Luke of the Holy Spirit, were the senior missionaries in the vicinity. It was Dominic of Eriquicia who rescued the young Sicilian when he blundered into danger, but this reprieve was not to last long.

Thomas and Jordan, who had been hiding near Nagasaki, decided to go visit some Christians who had been eight years without a priest. They spent one beautiful day with these people. Appropriately enough, it was St. Dominic's Day. During the night, a faithful Christian warned them that the soldiers of the emperor were close by, hunting for an Augustinian who was supposed to be in the neighborhood. The priests tried to get away in order not to endanger the native Christians. To the great delight of the soldiers, who were angry at not finding the Augustinian, they captured the two Dominicans instead.

Brought to trial, the two priests played over again the drama of the passion. They were questioned by various judges and then cast into a public jail for three months. During this imprisonment, a native who spoke Portuguese came to them, pretending that he was a Christian who had apostatized. He trampled on the crucifix, and the priests, heavily chained, tried to rescue it. At last they were condemned to die in the pits. This dreadful death was preceded by the water torture. The whole tragic drama took seven days, and on November 11, 1634, the two priests died—Thomas first, and Jordan shortly after.

JAMES OF ST. MARY
(d. 1635)

James was born of Christian parents in Omura, and he was educated by the Jesuits. He progressed in piety, and, at an early age, he went to Manila, hoping to join the Augustinians. Here, for reasons we do not know, he was refused admittance to the community of his choice. Baffled, but not discouraged, he went into the mountains and lived as a hermit.

Here, in the course of time, he met a Dominican who was interested in the question of native clergy for the nations of the Far East. The intelligent Japanese boy, with his background of solid Christianity and a Jesuit education, appealed to him as a very good answer to his problem. He took James to the Dominican house in Manila, and placed him under the care of Father John of the Angels, a talented missionary who was later to give his life for the conversion of Japan. James was given the habit on the Feast of the Assumption, 1621. Because of his superior education, the time of his training was shortened, and he was ordained two years later. He spent six happy years working in Manila, and then he asked if he could return to Japan and work among his own, a mission that was equivalent to a death sentence.

It was difficult to arrange passage to Japan, for even ship captains who did not like missionaries had seen so much bloodshed that they simply would not take any more priests to certain death. Finally, James secured a small boat, hardly seaworthy for such a long trip over dangerous waters. He and two

Japanese Jesuits, along with the Sicilian Dominican, Jordan of St. Stephen, fitted out the ship for their trip to Japan. They had planned on a twenty-day voyage, which would have been bad enough. Caught in storms and driven from their course, it was five months before they arrived in Satsuma. They had run out of water, wood, and food, and they were nearly dead from exposure. James' hair had turned white during the voyage. But they were in Japan.

Christians were suffering in Japan as probably in no other place since the early Christians of Rome. Anyone who sheltered a priest risked death. All Christians were in disguise. Priests and catechists knew that their work would be brief and would end in a violent death. Even with such a price hanging over them, priests continued to come in, and Christians sheltered them. James discovered another Dominican in Satsuma, and they each had an opportunity of receiving the sacrament of penance, a luxury in those desperate days.

For three months, James managed to evade the soldiers. At the end of that time, the authorities caught his catechist and tortured him. Under torture, he revealed the hiding place of the priest, and James was captured and put in irons in Omura.

James had added the title "of St. Mary" to his name, out of devotion to Our Blessed Lady, and he was to have the honor of suffering on one of her great feasts. On the eve of the Assumption, he was taken to Nagasaki and the torture begun. One of the Japanese Jesuits, who had made the fearful voyage with him, and his catechist, Paul Saito, were tortured with him. A man and his wife, with two small children, likewise suffered martyrdom at this time. They were, after a number of other tortures, hung head down over a ditch. After three days of terrible suffering, James of St. Mary died on August the seventeenth, the anniversary day of his profession.

FABYAN BIRKOWSKI
(1566-1636)

Just before the terrible holocaust in which the Cossacks destroyed the entire Polish province, there was a great flowering of learning and preaching in the North. Great libraries had been built up since the Tartar invasions of two centuries before, and the Polish province was at a high point of development. One of the men whose preaching ability did much to raise the reputation of the province at this time was Fabyan Birkowski.

Fabyan was born in Lemberg in 1566, and became acquainted with the Dominicans when he was young. He went to the University of Cracow, where he completed his studies, and he accepted a professorship in philosophy in 1587, when he was twenty-one. Five years later, he entered the Dominican convent in Cracow.

After his ordination, Fabyan was assigned to preach a course of sermons in the Church of the Holy Trinity in Cracow. So popular was his style of preaching that for fourteeen years he drew record crowds to the church, including King Sigismund III. The king, in fact, became so attached to the brilliant young preacher that he begged him to go with him to Warsaw and become tutor to his son, as well as court preacher.

In 1617, the Poles found themselves forced to fight both the Turks and the Russians. Fabyan Birkowski was sent by the king to preach to the soldiers about this crusade against the two great enemies of the country and the Church. For the next fifteen years he was occupied in preaching, much of the time to soldiers. Few of his sermons have been published, but in his own day they were considered the model for preachers. It would be interesting to know what he said to the soldiers of his day, for he enjoyed great popularity and was considered to be one of the greatest orators ever produced by a nation which highly values oratory. A scholar of both Scripture and the classics, he had a vast fund of quotations to enrich his sermons, a characteristic quickly noted in the only works of his which have been published.

Fabyan Birkowski retired to the convent of Cracow in 1634, and lived in retirement until his death, two years later. Three volumes of his sermons for Sundays and holy days, and a volume of sermons on the Blessed Virgin remain in testimony of his preaching career.

LUIS MORO
(d. 1636)

Father Luis Moro, who died at the hands of the natives in Formosa, may never be regarded as a martyr, but his life and death still entitle him to our interest.

Luis received the habit at the Dominican convent in Valladolid, in the early years of the seventeenth century. It is not known exactly when he was born. All that is known of his early years is that he yearned to go on the missions, and that he read all he could find concerning the Orient, and he was fascinated when listening to tales of mission lands. One can find many of his counterparts in youngsters today, who devour mission magazines, dreaming of a future in faraway lands. As soon as a missionary came to Spain seeking recruits, therefore, Luis volunteeered for the missions of the Philippines, with the intention of going to Japan as soon as he had mastered the language.

Japan was, at the time, the most dangerous mission committed to the Order. To go there was virtually a death sentence. Luis settled down happily on shipboard, and he began to learn the various skills of the missions from the priest who had recruited him. But, on his arrival in Manila, he met disappointment. Japan was closed to the Dominicans for the time being, and no more missionaries were to be sent until some method could be devised whereby they would reach there safely. Luis was assigned to teach the natives of Luzon. He settled down to learn the native tongue, and he soon had a flourishing parish in Bataan. A church he built there had an unusual feature—a shrine of St. Dominic of Soriano. There were many cures here, and soon the natives of other tribes were coming on pilgrimage, bringing their sick to the healing spot.

The route to Japan began to open up, and, in preparation for the pious invasion, chosen missionaries were sent to Formosa to learn Japanese. Luis was one of these. Formosa itself was a perilous place for Spaniards because of the indiscretions of the garrison stationed there. On his arrival, Luis learned that his predecessor had been murdered by the natives, some of whom were supposed to be Christians. The soldiers, looking for trouble, were determined to punish the guilty natives. Luis managed to obtain a governor's pardon for the natives, and he also secured the promise that the soldiers would stay out of the affair and let him handle it. He then went alone into the jungle to find the erring sheep of his flock. Surprisingly enough, he found them and converted them; he also converted a horde of pagan natives living there. He was quite happy among them, living a hand-to-mouth existence. It suited his sense of poverty admirably.

He might have built up another fine parish here, except that a Spanish supply ship failed to arrive, and the garrison, faced with starvation, began to make demands on the natives for food. Luis cautioned the governor not to provoke trouble again, but the governor insisted that he must send a supply train to the natives to buy rice, or his men would starve. With sinking heart, Luis saw the soldiers set out, and, in a desperate attempt to avert tragedy, begged to go with them. On the return trip, the soldiers divided up the party. Some went on to the Spanish camp while others remained, waiting for help to carry the supplies. The natives descended upon the remaining party, killing every one.

Whether they really meant to kill Luis is debatable; he was their friend. When the attack became imminent, he knelt and held out his arms in prayer, offering himself in expiation for the sins of his people. There was an arrow through his heart when the returning soldiers found him; it may have been deliberate on the part of the natives, or it may not have been.

The records tell us that Luis' body was perfectly preserved when found, a month after the tragedy, and that the holy name of Jesus was tattooed over his heart, right where the arrow had gone through. He was venerated by all who had worked with him, Spanish or native. The provincial chapter of 1637 praised him for his virtuous life and his holy death.

ABRAHAM BZOVIUS
(1567-1637)

The historian who continued the work of Cardinal Baronius on the *Annals of Church History* appears in documents simply as "Bzovius"; few know that he was a Polish Dominican of many accomplishments.

Stanislaus Bzowski was born in Prosz, Poland, in 1567. His parents both died of plague when he was a tiny baby, and he was brought up by his grandmother, who was both wealthy and pious. The little boy proved to be a genius at arithmetic, Latin, and music composition at the age of ten, and at fifteen he was explaining a treatise of John Eyck on the errors of Protestantism to anyone who would listen. He memorized whole orations of Cicero and poems of Virgil for exercise. Falling very ill, he made a promise to St. Hyacinth that he would visit his tomb if the saint would cure him. Completely cured, he fulfilled his promise, but remained in Cracow with the Dominicans instead of returning home. He took the name of Abraham in religion, in honor of the priest who had received him into the Order.

Making great progress in his studies, Brother Abraham, ordained a deacon, was sent to study in Italy. Exactly when or where he was ordained is not clear, but there is a record of his teaching philosophy at Milan and theology at Bologna. Some time after this, he returned to Poland and established the Confraternity of the Rosary. He devoted much time and attention to building up the library in the convent in Cracow, and he built the church and convent in Warsaw, which suggests that he must have been superior there. In 1610, he arranged that the relics of Blessed Ceslaus be brought to a safe place, where there would be no danger of profanation by heretics.

By 1615, Father Bzowski—or Bzovius, as his Italian friends insisted—was back in Italy. It was at this time that he made the acquaintance of Cardinal Baronius, who was working on the compilation of Church history started by St. Philip Neri. The purpose of the work was to counteract the badly-slanted history written by Protestant historians. The learned cardinal had completed nine volumes at the time of his death, and the work fell quite naturally to the Dominican from Poland who had been helping him. All the unpublished documents and other valuable materials which the cardinal had acquired were given into his hands, and he continued the work with great zeal, if not always with much style.

Historians of other Orders usually criticize Bzovius for being prejudiced in favor of his own Order, a not unusual fault. He is not too critical in his choice of anecdotes, but neither is this an isolated fault among historians. He did as he had been told to do; he continued the annals under great difficulties, and with no great encouragement. He wrote also a short history of the Church, in two volumes, and he worked out the *Summa* of St. Thomas and the commentaries of Cajetan in syllogisms. His principal work was a history of the Order up to that time. He was a hard working and zealous priest, not buried in his books as one might suppose, for he took care to give the poor all the money pensions received from his papal commission. At his death, he left his own considerable library to the convent of the Minerva, because he wanted the schools of Rome to have the tools for writing against Protestantism.

Abraham Bzovius died in 1637.

WILLIAM COURTET AND COMPANIONS
(d. 1637)

Closing the glorious chapter of the Japanese martyrs of the sixteenth and seventeenth centuries is the story of William Courtet. The missions of the Orient were Spanish and Portuguese at that time. William Courtet was French. His life and death on the missions were a simple tribute to his perseverance, for he spent a lifetime trying to get to the missions.

William Courtet was born in 1590, in the south of France. He received the Dominican habit in Albi, in 1607, and eventually became master of novices in Toulouse. But, as Dominic had longed for Tartary, William longed for the Orient. He made numerous attempts to go to the Far East, only to be told repeatedly that the French province had no missions there. Hearing that the Dominicans of Manila were in charge of the Japanese missions, he tried to join them, but was refused.

For a good many years, William obediently did his appointed work in the south of France, as prior in Avignon, novice-master, and missionary. After nearly twenty years of persevering effort, he succeeded in attaching himself to a party of Spanish Dominicans who were sailing for Manila. With the blessings—and the regrets—of his French superiors, he sailed off to almost certain death, and he was superbly happy about it.

He spent some time in Manila, learning the Japanese language, which did not come as easily to a man of fifty as to a young priest just out of school, and then he set sail for Japan. The governor of the Philippines stopped the boat and ordered the missionaries off. He set fire to the boat and told the priests to go home. Some of them did. Four Dominicans plotted together to go on with their plans. They give us a fine cross-section of the universality of the Church. They were William, the Frenchman; Vincent of the Cross, a Japanese; Anthony Gonzales, Portuguese; Michael Ozarrazza, Basque; there were also two laymen, a Japanese and a Chinese. They finally succeeded in getting another boat, and they slipped out quietly in the dead of night.

The missionaries landed on the Island of Lion-Kion. They were immediately recognized by the harrassed Christians who gathered quickly around them for the spiritual help they needed. Such activity could not go unnoticed in a small place, and, in a few days, the missionaries were bound and taken before the tribunal, where so many saintly Christians had already chosen death for Christ.

There was nothing unusual about their trials. Like all such trials since the time of Pontius Pilate, the issues of politics and religion were hopelessly confused, and the missionaries were condemned to torture and death.

The most unspeakable tortures were practiced on the unfortunate men. Fathers William Courtet and Michael Ozarrazza submitted heroically to the horrible torments; Father Vincent of the Cross, breaking under the pain, said that he was ready to apostatize. Father Anthony Gonzales was brought in the next day and was told that all the others had apostatized. As the tortures wore on, becoming more inhuman, Vincent of the Cross loudly retracted his apostasy and proclaimed himself ready to die for Christ. The soldiers heaped more torments upon him until he was too weak to kneel upright; then they beheaded him. The voices of the martyrs' singing could be heard coming from the pits for some days, even after the fearful tortures they had endured. The last voice stopped singing on the Feast of St. Michael, in 1637.

This group of martyrs, whose cause has been taken up for consideration in recent years, were the last Dominicans to die for the faith in Japan.

ST. MARTIN DE PORRES
(1579-1639)

Martin de Porres was born in Lima, Peru, of Spanish and Negro parentage. Inheriting his mother's dark color, he was despised by his aristocratic father, and, in early childhood, he was badly neglected. An intelligent boy, he was befriended by a doctor who taught him the art of healing.

Martin learned to pray when he was very young. He had a deep devotion to our Lord's Passion, and continually prayed to know what he could do in gratitude for the immense blessings of the Redemption. Deciding upon the religious life, he applied to the Dominican Convent of the Holy Rosary and was accepted as a servant. He gave himself to the lowliest duties in the house, and, finally, after many years, he was commanded by his superiors to accept the habit of a laybrother; he had considered that this was too great an honor for himself.

The report of Martin's skill as a surgeon and healer soon spread abroad. As much by his prayers as through medical knowledge, he cured the most frightening diseases. Some of his cures were: bringing from near death a priest who had a badly infected leg; curing the fingers of a young student, who had feared that an accident had ruined his hopes for the priesthood; making whole again so many people afflicted with so many diseases that no one could attempt to count them. In addition to the gift of healing, he was endowed with that of bi-location; he was seen in Mexico, Central America, and even Japan, by people who knew him well, whereas he had never been out of Lima since entering the Order. He passed through locked doors by some means that was known only to himself and God; he appeared at the bedside of sufferers without being asked and always soothed the sick even when he did not completely cure them. Even sick animals came to him for healing.

Great as his healing faculty was, Martin is probably best remembered for the legend of the rats. It is told that the prior, who objected to rats, ordered Martin to set out poison for them. Martin did as he was told, but he was very sorry for the rats. He went out into the garden and called softly—and out came the rats. He reprimanded them for their bad habits, telling them about the poison. He further assured them that he would feed them every day in the garden, if they would refrain from annoying the prior. This agreed upon, he dismissed the rats—and forever after, so the chronicle states, there was no more trouble with rats at Holy Rosary Convent.

One time Martin was on a picnic with the novices, and they overstayed their time, suddenly realizing that, even with expending their best efforts, they could not be home in time for prayers. Martin bade them join hands, and, before they knew what had happened, they were standing in the convent yard, unable to explain how they had covered the several miles in a few seconds.

These and many other startling miracles caused Martin to be called a saint, even during his lifetime. In our own day, the miracles continue. He lived a life of almost constant prayer, and he practiced unbelievable austerities. He worked at hard and menial tasks without ever losing a moment of union with God. His charity, humility, and obedience were extraordinary.

Pope John XXIII raised Martin de Porres to the altar of the Church on May the fifth, 1962.

St. Martin is the first Negro from the New World to attain the rank of sainthood.

BLESSED FRANCIS DE CAPILLAS
(1608-1640)

The seventeenth century was a period of great missionary activity. Many martyrs shed their blood on distant shores. There were many Dominicans among these glorious companies, and Francis de Capillas has become the type and exemplar of them.

Nothing is known of the childhood of Francis de Capillas. He was born in Palencia, in 1608, and entered the Order in Valladolid. He was then seventeen. The Spain of his youth was still ringing with the missionary zeal of Louis Bertrand, Las Casas, and Francis Xavier; the report of the martyrdom of Alphonsus Navarette, in Japan, was news at the time. Perhaps the bravery of these men helped to fire the young Francis with apostolic longing, for he volunteered for the Philippine missions while he was a deacon. At the age of twenty-three he left Spain and was ordained in Manila. Here, at the gateway to the Orient, the Dominicans had had a university since 1611, and the city teemed with missionaries going and coming from various points of the East.

The young priest labored for ten years in the province of Cagayan, where heat, insects, disease, and paganism leagued against the foreigner to make life very hard. But it was not hard enough for Francis. He begged for a mission field that was really difficult; perhaps, like many of the eager young apostles of that time, he was hoping for an assignment to Japan, where the great persecution was raging. He was sent to Fukien, in China, where he worked uneventfully for some years. Then a Tartar invasion put his life in jeopardy. He was captured by a band of Tartars and imprisoned.

Francis, like the Master he served, was subjected to a mock trial. Civil, military, and religious officials questioned him, and they accused him of everything from political intrigue to witchcraft. He was charged with disregarding ancestor worship, and, finally, since they could "find no cause in him," he was turned over to the torturers.

He endured the cruel treatment of these men with great courage. Seeing his calmness, the magistrates became curious about his doctrines. They offered him wealth, power, and freedom, if he would renounce his faith, but he amazed and annoyed them by choosing to suffer instead. They varied the tortures with imprisonment, and he profitably used the time to convert his jailor and fellow prisoners. Even the mandarin visited him in prison, asking Francis if he would renounce his faith or would he prefer to suffer more. Being told that he was glad to suffer for Christ, the mandarin furiously ordered that he be scourged again "so he would have even more to be glad about."

Francis was finally condemned, as it says in the breviary, as "the leader of the traitors," these being (presumably) the rebel army that was besieging the city. The official condemnation is stated in those words: "After long suffering, he was finally beheaded and so entered into the presence of the Master, who likewise suffered and died under a civil sentence."

Francis de Capillas is honored as the protomartyr of China. He was beatified by Pope Pius X in 1909.

TIMOTHY RICCI
(1579-1643)

The Ricci family of Florence contributed quite a number of its members to the Order. St. Catherine de Ricci was to be one of the lasting glories of the family. There were two Timothys, which is a little confusing. One was "Uncle Timothy," to whom credit is given for Catherine's remaining in the Order. He was the kindly confessor of the convent, who alone seemed to understand his gifted niece. The more famous priest of the same name lived several generations later, and he has won the gratitude of the world and the Order by his work with the Perpetual Rosary.

Timothy Ricci was born in Florence in 1579, and entered the reformed convent in Fiesole in 1595. Here he distinguished himself as a brilliant student and a great preacher. He taught at various places and was made a master of sacred theology. His career as a preacher was already well established when he went to Naples, and then he began his outstanding life work.

It was a woman, oddly enough, who gave impetus to this work. Her name was Mother Paula of St. Teresa, and she lived in the Dominican convent in Naples. For some time she had enjoyed private revelations, telling her of the need for reviving the Rosary in Naples, and, on Christmas night, rapt in ecstasy, she was told that the instrument of this work was at last at hand. It is quite likely that she sent for the Dominican and told him about her revelations, though he did not need revelations to show him that Naples needed a revival. After the Mass, he chose the first twelve men for his society. They were given certain obligations of saying the Rosary, and were to form the nucleus of a confraternity. In a few years, the number of members had increased to four thousand.

At the time there was a movement in the entire Order to revive the Rosary, which had become almost a private devotion only. In this general direction, a former master general had attempted to encourage the public recitation of the Rosary in all Dominican churches by making a complete religious service out of it. That, in fact, was the flaw in the plan; the service was *too* complete, and the Rosary had acquired so many embellishments that it barely resembled the simple and forthright devotion it had been originally. Timothy, who saw the apathy of the people towards a long and tiresome exercise, felt that a return to the original simplicity would solve much of the problem. It was on this basis that he established the devotion in Naples.

The people were not too enthusiastic when first informed that the new preacher wanted them to say the Rosary aloud in church. A group of social lights in the parish pointed out to him that ladies simply do not make a show of themselves in public, and that they would certainly not join in such a vulgar project. In a short time, however, the selected groups of men, and the poorer women, shamed them into cooperation, and soon everyone in Naples was ardently involved.

At the end of twelve years, the transformation of the city was remarkable. A church had been built for the use of the Confraternity. The various groups of the parish—working men, young students, young mothers—divided up the days among them, so that the Rosary was daily recited by one group publicly, or by its members in small groups. The plan worked so well in Naples that Timothy Ricci was summoned to Rome, where he was asked to plan a large-scale revival of the Rosary in Europe.

The new campaign was to start in Rome, and here, as in Naples, the idea of public recitation of the Rosary took hold. From Rome the practice spread to other cities of Italy, and then to France, where the king was indebted to Our Lady for the cure of a serious illness. Timothy was in Rome when the plague struck. He did not know that even this circumstance was to affect the organization for which his name would be so long remembered.

As in all times of plague, gatherings of all kinds were forbidden for fear of contagion. People could not say the Rosary together, and yet, there had hardly been a time when prayer was needed more. Every hour of the day people were dying, going to face a judgment for which they frequently were ill-prepared. Some met the terror with a front of worldliness, with wild dancing and orgies of pleasure, a reaction which made the prayers of the Confraternity even more necessary. Timothy Ricci and necessity were the parents of the new idea; his plan was to divide the day into its hours, and give each person the responsibility for one hour—at one certain time—so that the prayer would be unceasing. The idea caught on faster than the plague itself. Thousands clamored for their appointed times. To answer the need, Timothy worked out a plan which time has not improved; the hours and the days were indicated on tickets, which were then drawn from a wooden box in the porter's office. You drew your ticket, and the time designated on it was your hour, appointed by heaven. Intended probably as a temporary measure, the plan worked so well that it was continued.

All the cities of Italy clamored for membership. There was a brisk business in tickets and small wooden boxes. Bologna emptied the box sixteen times in the first year, indicating a membership of 140,000 people. The pope was faithful to his hour for the Confraternity, and on every possible occasion he spoke favorably of the "Holy Militia" that had wrought such wonders in Italy, and that had now spread into Austria, Germany, France, Belgium, and England.

The plan of the hour of prayer was much the same then as it is now; one third of the time in prayer for the dying; one third for sinners, and the final third for the souls of purgatory. After the plague had disappeared, the further obligation was added of meeting once a month to say the Rosary in common, to fill in the gaps if anyone had neglected or forgotten his hour.

Timothy Ricci died a holy death in 1643, after a year of serious illness. During his last few years, no less than thirty thousand people had heard him preach, and the whole of Europe had profited by his revival of prayer. The whole world for many years would profit by the Confraternity that in all times and places would work to bring men nearer to God.

JOSEPH MORAN
(d. 1643)

Among the many martyrs of our Order, Joseph Moran occupies a unique place. Nearly all of those who shed their blood on the missions, or fell under the swords of heretics, were well aware that they were on a dangerous mission and might die as martyrs. Most of them, we may suppose, prayed for martyrdom. The subject of this sketch was taken completely by surprise.

Joseph Moran was born in Gandia, and he entered the Order in Valencia. Here he became a celebrated preacher and, if we may say so, the "complete professor," wrapped up in the business of the schools. On his way to Italy on important business, his ship was captured by Algerian pirates. The unfortunate captives were taken to the slave markets of Africa and put up for sale.

Joseph Moran probably had heard of the Moorish captives and lamented their fate. It is quite certain that he never expected to become one. However, this made no difference to his captors, who told him that he could either renounce the faith or raise the money for a ransom. In the meantime, he was chained in prison, and every day he was beaten with a device called a bastinado, which had broken the spirits of many captives.

Joseph had probably never had much to do with raising money, but now he had no choice. He went around among the Christians who were captives like himself, trying to raise the ransom. When it eventually became clear that nobody had any money at all, he tried to arrange with friends in Spain to secure the necessary amount.

Free for the time being, he was enjoying his role as missionary very much. He preached to the captives and became quite popular with them. In fact, he began to become very proud about his popularity. When the ships came from Spain, bringing no money for him, the sultan had him cast into prison again. Here, with plenty of time to meditate, the unhappy man began to despair. Taking their advantage, the Mohammedans urged him to apostatize. After a good deal of pressure, he did. Taking off his habit, and putting on the turban, he was given the freedom of the city and an ample pension.

Two things happened at this point which helped the unhappy apostate to straighten out his thinking. One was the death of a Carmelite laybrother, who chose martyrdom rather than apostasy. The other was the conversion of a young Anglican who was among the captives. This young man became a Catholic, and he gave his life for his new faith. The two deaths changed Joseph. He decided that he must not only return to the faith, but also must die to wash his sins in his own blood. He took counsel from some of the Christians, who told him to run while he had the chance. This he refused to do. He waited for the appropriate time to make a public retraction. The sultan tried to restrain him from doing this, but Joseph finally succeeded. He made public acknowledgment of his apostasy, proclaimed himself deeply grieved for ever abandoning the truth, and said that he was glad to die in reparation.

Because of the publicity attending his retraction, the death of Joseph Moran was as terrible as his captors could make it. He was tortured in various ways, crowned with hemp in mockery, and finally carried to the stake and burned. His last words were to beg the pardon of the Christian captives he had scandalized.

JOHN OF ST. THOMAS
(1588-1644)

John of St. Thomas is little known in the English-speaking world, although the translation of his work on the gifts of the Holy Ghost, in 1951, has introduced him to some.

John Poinsot was born in Portugal in 1588. His father, secretary to archduke Albert of Austria, had been sent to Portugal on diplomatic business. He married a Portuguese girl, and his two sons were born and reared in Portugal. When the father was called to Holland, they remained with their mother, attending the Jesuit school at Coimbra.

John proved to be an exceptional student. He completed his courses in arts and philosophy, and one year of theology, in the Jesuit university. Then the family moved to the Netherlands, to rejoin their father, and John and his brother attended the University of Louvain. Here, studying theology under the Dominicans, he became an ardent Thomist. He received his bachelor's degree from Louvain in company with a young man named Cornelius Jansenius, who was soon to have Europe in an uproar with the heresy that would bear his name. John, unaware of the brewing heresy, hurried to Madrid, and entered the Order at the convent of Atocha. He added "of St. Thomas" to his own name, and promptly devoted all his time to the study of the great theologian.

The teaching career of John of St. Thomas was distinguished; he taught in Piacenza and Madrid, and finally became chief confessor of Alcalá. He was appointed to the inquisition, and he helped to draw up the Index of Forbidden Books—two reasons why history has not been kind to him.

As confessor and spiritual director, John of St. Thomas was loved by rich and poor alike. He counselled kings and peasants with equal objectivity, giving sound advice, as well as a heroic example of asceticism himself.

When the storm of Jansenism broke over Europe, some of the professors at Louvain were involved in the new heresy. Zealots wished to condemn all the professors, sight unseen, and urged John of St. Thomas to take up his pen against them. He refused to do so, insisting that each should be given a chance to speak for himself before any should be condemned. He had kind memories of the professors at Louvain, and he knew they were not all heretics. His leniency in this matter may have cost him his life, as he died of poison in 1644. It was never determined who poisoned him, but it was thought that an enemy of the Louvain faculty, who had hoped for a condemnation from John, had killed him when he would not give it.

The works of John of St. Thomas are numerous and important, although little known in English. In 1640, he wrote *An Explanation of Christian Doctrine* in the vernacular, to be used in the Indies. It was translated into Italian, Gaelic, and Polish, among other tongues. His *Doctrine of a General Confession* and the *Preparation for a Happy Death* were popular works, enjoying a wide circulation. Better known to scholars are his major works; a course in logic and natural philosophy, and his great *Commentary on the Summa*, on which he spent twenty years, but which was never quite completed.

BLESSED JOHN MASIAS
(1585-1645)

John Masias was born in Ribera, in Spain, and, when very small, he was left an orphan. He was adopted by a kindly uncle who set him to herding his sheep. The little boy was naturally pious, and passed his spare time in saying the Rosary. Our Lady and the Christ Child appeared to him several times, and he was often visited by his patron, St. John the Evangelist, who once showed him a vision of heaven, telling him: "This is my country."

When John was about twenty, he went to Mass in the church of the Dominicans in a neighboring city. For the moment, it seemed to him that his vocation was joining the Friars Preachers now, but St. John appeared to him, telling him that he must go elsewhere. In 1619 he embarked for the Indies, where many Spaniards were going, either to convert the natives or to seek a fortune. After a long and hazardous journey, he arrived in Lima.

There were at the time four convents of the Friars Preachers in Lima: the College of St. Thomas; the house of St. Rose, where Sister Rose of St. Mary had died just five years before; Santo Domingo or Holy Rosary, where the holy Negro laybrother, Martin de Porres, was performing such astounding miracles; and the convent of St. Mary Magdalen, which was small and poor. John decided to enter St. Mary Magdalen and, in 1622, he received the habit of a laybrother there. On the night of his profession, devils appeared to tempt and reproach him. He was attacked bodily, and, although he called on Jesus, Mary, and Joseph for help, the demons continued what was to become twelve years of torture, by actually throwing him from one cloister to another.

John was appointed assistant to the porter, and lived in the gatehouse. There the poor came for food, and the rich for advice. He became adept at begging for the poor, always managing to find enough for the more than two hundred people who came daily for help. He had little use for the wealthy and curious, and would sometimes baffle them by simply disappearing while they were looking at him. On occasion, his friend and patron, St. John, went out collecting alms for him. Also, legend relates that he had a little burro that he would send out by itself, with a note asking for what was needed in one of the empty panniers on its back. Told where to go, the burro made his route faithfully; and if the rich man on whom he called was ungracious, or even hid himself to avoid giving alms, the little burro made quite a noise, and it quickly brought the desired results.

Rays of light streamed from the blessed's face as he taught the catechism to the poor, or prayed by himself in the gatehouse. He said an amazing number of rosaries and made no less than twenty daily visits to the Blessed Sacrament. He is said to have liberated more than a million souls from purgatory, many of whom came back, while he was at prayer, to thank him for his help.

One day a certain ship captain came to the gatehouse and asked to look around. John took him by the arm and led him to the crucifix, warning him to look well on it and think of his sin. Terrified, the captain fell to his knees, confessing that he was an apostate religious, thirty years away from the sacraments, and he begged for a priest. On another occasion, the brothers were building a flight of steps and, having measured a beam wrong, they were annoyed because it did not fit. John took the beam in his hands and stretched it to fit their needs. These, and many other miracles, led people to venerate him as a saint during his lifetime. His recreation was to talk of the things of God with the other holy laybrother, Martin de Porres.

At the time of his death, Our Lady, St. Dominic, his patron, St. John, and many other saints, came to accompany him to heaven. They were seen by some of the brothers.

CATHERINE PALUZZI
(1573-1645)

The strange career of the Tertiary Sister, Catherine Paluzzi, brought her into contact with a number of saints and sinners. It seems odd that so vivid a character should have been lost in obscurity.

Frances Paluzzi was born in Morluppo, just north of Rome, in 1573. Although her respectable parents were poor, they gave their children as good an education as possible. The oldest of seven children, Frances learned to make herself useful around the house when she was quite young. She was her father's favorite and confidante, and that relationship was especially troubling for her when, at the age of four, she started having visions and could not tell him about them. The little girl grew up with her hands busy about many things, and her heart even busier with prayer.

Sometimes, in the years of her childhood, Frances tried to explain to her father about her ecstasies. He tried to be patient, but often at the end of their discussions, he found himself slapping and scolding her, and she was left in bewilderment. Her mother scolded her every time she caught the child performing any penance. Perhaps it was this gulf of misunderstanding in her home, and the complete lack of solitude, that later drew Frances so close to St. Catherine of Siena, who had suffered similar trouble. It had the effect of isolating Frances from everyone who might have helped her, even her confessor, who disapproved of all her plans to enter a cloister.

A little girl named Bernadine, who came to do weaving in the Paluzzi home, was the first to discover the spirituality of Frances. Very soon they were close friends, through penance united in love of God. When they were both about fourteen, Frances made an attempt to enter the cloister, but she met nothing but rebuffs. "We cannot get along without you at home," said her father. "You can pray here." Her confessor supported this opinion. He was suspicious of the penances the two girls practiced, and he did not want to allow either of them into the Third Order; he told Frances that he thought she was possessed, and that all her visions and heavenly messages were open to question.

Frances had received a revelation that she would one day wear the Dominican habit—that she would, in fact, found a community herself. But for the present she received no encouragement at all. Spiritually dry and lonely, she waited and prayed, with only the moral support of the faithful Bernadine. It happened that St. Philip Neri came to the town, and her confessor consulted him about the girls. The saint declared that they should immediately be allowed to make their first Communion, and that they should be allowed frequent Communion. This was a great concession at the time, but it was the only one he made in their favor, for he was more than severe with the two aspirants. He treated them as visionaries, giving them no satisfaction at all.

Baffled by the whole affair, Frances begged God to relieve her of the strange manifestations that made her confessor distrust her. They did not cease; on the contrary, they increased. One day the confessor refused to give her Communion, and she sadly went back from the communion rail to her dark corner. As she knelt weeping, the darkness disappeared, and all was bright. A Host, shining in the midst of the brightness, came down to her; she received her Lord after all.

The priest who was her director made light of her visions, but when she told him that she had had a revelation that he would be ambushed and killed on a certain road, he was careful to travel by another way. Later, he found that he had narrowly escaped an ambush. She also gave him an account of a revelation of St. Philip Neri's death, which he ridiculed, until the word reached him that the saint actually died, in the very place and at the exact time prophesied by his penitent. At the beatification process of Philip Neri, Frances was called in to testify regarding this vision.

In the Jubilee Year of 1600, Frances went to Rome. Here at last, she found a little encouragement. It was given by a Carmelite, to whom she went to confession. He placed her in a hospice in Rome, where she could talk to the pilgrims who came in for the Jubilee. The Carmelite took a real interest in the mystic who had come so opportunely into his life. She, on her part, carried on her work of counselling and instructing pilgrims. Her fame began to increase in Rome, and eventually the pope heard of her. Seeing that she was such a force for good, he sent her to a community of nuns who were badly in need of reform. It was a fine idea, but it did not work too well; a few of the sisters reformed their lives, but not all of them by any means.

Frances herself was restless, for she had had another revelation, telling her that it was time for her to return to Morluppo and begin her foundation. Time, place, and several other vital factors were unpropitious for a foundation. In this poor little town there was small hope of supporting a Second Order monastery. She began her work humbly, with great difficulties facing her. An aunt and two nieces went with her to make the first tiny beginning, in a little house with no conveniences for monastic living. They were all given the habit of the Third Order. To support themselves, they set up a spinning and weaving business. There were four looms, five sisters. One prayed while four worked, an admirably simple system. Frances took the name of Sister Catherine, in honor of her dearly-beloved Catherine of Siena.

At about this time, a cardinal who had met Sister Catherine in Rome, was in need of prayers for his work. He had received the title of the ancient church of St. Cecilia in Rome, and he wanted the relics of the saint to enshrine there. No one knew where the relics were. He wrote to Sister Catherine, asking her to pray that he would find them. She sent back precise directions, telling him where to go for the relics, where to look, how deep to dig, and exactly how the relics would look. Following her directions to the letter, he found them. The body of the martyr was incorrupt, as the sister had said it would be. The cardinal forthwith sent help of a substantial sort to help build a new monastery.

There was a new storm brewing when Sister Catherine started her monastery. One of the high officials of the town was bitterly determined to prevent her from settling there. He sent to the pope, asking for a condemnation; the pope refused the request. The town official said: "I will beggar myself if necessary. But that fanatic shall never build a monastery in Morluppo." Catherine, hearing of this threat, replied sadly: "Indeed he will beggar himself, but it will not stop me." She proved to be right, for some time later the man killed his own brother in a quarrel, and he was banished from the city penniless.

When the monastery was nearly ready, Sister Catherine went to live for some time with the Dominican nuns in Rome, in order to study regular observance. When her own monastery was opened, it followed the pattern of strict observance of the regular monastic life. She was installed as perpetual prioress in 1620.

The remainder of Sister Catherine's life was distinguished by prayer and penance. She always had her prayers answered, so it was quite natural that many people came to ask for her prayerful intervention. Her old friend, the Carmelite who had helped her in Rome, came to her once to tell her he was worried about a band of Carmelite missionaries who had gone to Persia. She told him where and how they were, facts that he afterwards checked. The devil often tried to keep her from praying, and sometimes he pushed her or hit her. She suffered a broken knee at his hands, but he got worse treatment from hers. Her gift of prophecy remained with her all her life. She told her community exactly when she would die, and her prophecy was accurate. She died in 1645, at the age of seventy-two.

ALEXANDER BALDRATI A LUGO
(1595-1645)

If anyone ever was framed and destroyed by a tissue of lies, it was Alexander Baldrati a Lugo, who was martyred by the Mohammedans on the island of Chios, in 1644.

Alexander was born in Lugo in Italy in 1595, and baptized in the Dominican church there. Showing early signs of piety, he was carefully educated, and was received into the Order in Lugo, in 1612. He studied first in Faenza, then in Naples, in the convent of Our Lady of the Arch. After his ordination, he was sent to Bologna, where he carried on a heavy program of preaching and teaching. He devoted half of his time to God and half to his neighbor; by arithmetic, that left none for himself. Eventually his health broke completely, and he fell seriously ill. It was during his convalescence in Venice that circumstances sent him on the great adventure of his life.

Just why a sick man should embark for the Orient is not quite clear; perhaps his superiors thought a sea voyage would help him. At any rate, he arrived on the island of Chios and—like many convalescent religious—promptly began devoting a full day to preaching. He happened to incur the bitter hatred of an apostate Christian, who began planning to destroy him. When the archbishop of Edessa arrived, en route to his See, and stopped over with the Dominicans, the apostate convinced his friends that the Christians were moving in on Chios, (roughly the equivalent of the rumor that the pope is moving into the White House) and a furore of anti-Christian feeling arose among the fanatical Mohammedans. However, the target of wrath was not the archbishop of Edessa, nor the other transient archbishop staying with the Dominicans, but Alexander. The apostate, who had elected himself spokesman, went to the governor and denounced Alexander. This Dominican, he said, had secretly become a Mohammedan, and he could prove it.

Like many another brazenly false charge, this one was difficult to disprove. Alexander was haled into the Mohammedan court, and the governor praised him highly for his wisdom in coming around to the beliefs of Mohammed. He was promised great rewards as his portion, especially if he could get some of his fellow Dominicans interested in the faith of the prophet. Alexander protested indignantly that he had never been in the slightest danger of professing Mohammedanism, that he was a Christian and proud of it. The governor therefore informed him that he must be treated as an apostate from Mohammedanism. Alexander realized that he was bound for the sacrifice no matter what happened, but he wanted the record kept straight. "I have *never* believed in your prophet," he said. "I have never believed in the Koran, nor in any of its teachings!"

"This man has abandoned the faith of Mohammed," said the governor. "He has blasphemed. He is guilty of death." Without further discussion, the unhappy Dominican was taken off to prison, still protesting his orthodoxy. The governor sent soldiers to bring the Dominican prior and the two archbishops. "Why did you harbor this traitor?" he demanded of them. "Our law commands us to kill anyone who abandons the faith of Mohammed, and you had no right to shelter him from his just punishment. We could seize all of you and put you to death for this treason."

The prior and the two visiting archbishops held up stoutly under the governor's polished trickery. They protested that Alexander was an excellent Christian and never had been anything else. As soon as they were released, they sent word to Alexander to be of good courage, that everyone would pray that he could bear up through the ordeal ahead. They called the Christians of the island to keep vigil in the churches, to pray for those who were to die.

Alexander, brought once more before the court, was given three days to reflect on whether or not he would proclaim himself a faithful son of the

Prophet. "I do not need three days," he said. "I can give you a definite answer right now. I am a Christian, and have never been a Mohammedan. Your prophet is a prophet of lies, your law proceeds from the father of all lies." His bold words met a chorus of fanatical screams from the populace, already incited to murder by the apostate. "Avenge your prophet!" cried the governor, and the crowds pressed in until it was necessary to put Alexander in a dungeon to keep him alive until the governor's plans were complete.

Alexander was condemned to be burned at the stake. When he was led out to die, the maddened crowds pressed in as if they would tear him to pieces. No one listened to his protesting that he was and always had been a Christian. When he was tied to the stake, the governor said to him: "Lift one finger to show that you believe in the God of Mohammed, the one true God, and your life will be spared." Bleeding and stiff from torture, the Dominican raised three fingers and cried out: "I believe in God the Father, the Son and the Holy Spirit."

The fire would not touch the martyr as he stood suffering at the stake. Wind blew the flames away, or put them out; faggots fell and rolled away from him. With a maddened roar, the crowd broke through its guard and hacked him to pieces. Then someone tossed gunpowder on the fire, and, in the sight of 40,000 witnesses, Alexander Baldrati a Lugo gave up his valiant spirit.

FATHER RICHARD BARRY AND OTHER IRISH MARTYRS
(d. 1647)

In the Acts of the General Chapter of 1656, there is commemorated "an abundant harvest of those who in our Irish province have suffered cruel torments for the Catholic Faith and have been gathered in these days into the celestial granaries." One of the brethren remembered in this group of confessors of the faith was Father Richard Barry, who died at the storming of the Rock of Cashel, in 1647.

The Dominican Order in Ireland had been all but wiped out twice by this time. The thousand Dominicans, who had been the glory of England and Ireland before the apostasy of King Henry VIII, were reduced to four friars by the end of Elizabeth's reign. Following this desperate time, when thousands of Cromwell's soldiers were spending themselves in trying to exterminate the old faith with the sword, Dominicans were trained abroad for the English and Irish missions. Spain, Flanders, Portugal, and Italy all opened their doors to the exiles, training them for the dangerous work of keeping the faith alive in spite of the sword. At one time, a formidable army of six hundred Dominican friars who had been trained abroad were engaged, in one way or another, in the English and Irish missions. Cromwell made a fanatical effort to dispose of them, and he cut the number down to one hundred and fifty before his reign was over.

Catholics took hope when the new king ascended the throne, but their hopes were soon dashed. In Ireland, the heavy hand of Cromwell was still felt in the campaign of the Earl of Inchiquin, who, in 1647, besieged the town of Cashel.

The town was poorly fortified and soon surrendered, but not the fortress, "The Rock of St. Patrick." Here the garrison and the devout Catholics took refuge. There were only three hundred soldiers, and they could not hold out indefinitely against seven thousand, but they put up an unforgettable defense. When the "Rock" finally fell to superior numbers, it was already a tomb for more than five hundred of the attacking soldiers. Angered at the stubborn defense, the commander gave word to slaughter without mercy everyone taken. The order was grimly carried out, and everyone, from babes in arms to helpless old women, was put to the sword. Only for the priests—of whom there were nearly twenty—was a longer and more painful agony prepared.

Accounts differ with regard to Father Richard Barry's capture. A highly dramatic tale has it that he faced the invaders, sword in hand, and that the commander himself, impressed with his noble mein, offered him safety if he would take off the Dominican habit. The more probable version is that he quite simply faced them with the weapon that his brothers had used so effectually among the Irish people—the Rosary. The accounts agree that he was told: "Take off that traitor's garb." And he replied: "My dress is the emblem of Christ and His Passion, and the banner of my warfare. I have borne it from my youth and I will not put it off in death." He was accordingly tortured by being burned alive.

A Tertiary who perished at the same time was one Margaret, a woman of seventy years, who was killed with a sword. Another Tertiary, who survived the slaughter and hid for the three days that the soldiers stayed to plunder, recovered the body of the martyred Father Barry, seeing to it that he received honorable burial.

The years of bitter persecution in Ireland, when all priests and religious were under the constant danger of capture and death, were the years of true greatness for Tertiaries of the secular Third Order. Young women who could arrange it obtained the permission to take the Tertiary vows and the veil privately, and wear the habit at home—a status that would bring them quick death if discovered. This part of the Order flourished and produced countless unsung heroes during the time that the other branches of the Order could not function. Most of the Tertiaries were pledged to hospitality for fugitive priests and other Catholics. At least two women Tertiaries were burned alive for assisting in the escape of Sir John Burke and his three priest companions.

Convents of the Second Order were founded in Spain and Portugal for Irish girls. One group of nuns made a foundation in Galway, in 1651, but soon had to flee to Spain. Thirty years later, a convent founded in Dublin had to break up immediately, but the nuns, wearing secular clothes, stayed on in Ireland. They lived in a miserable mud hut, by the Boyne, and a Dominican priest, in the disguise of a fisherman, rowed across the river each morning to say Mass for them. In 1722, the nieces of Oliver Plunkett, carrying with them the relics of their martyred uncle, opened a school in Drogheda.

Irish exiles went to every friendly country, trying to gain support for their beleaguered countrymen. Father Dominic O'Daly built a convent in Portugal through the charity of the Catholics there; the Bishop of Clonfert, fleeing with no possessions but a treasured Madonna picture, stopped at last at Raab, in Hungary, and the Catholics of that land gave them refuge. On St. Patrick's Day, 1697, the picture could be seen shedding tears, and it was covered with a fine film of blood. It presaged even more trouble for hard-pressed Irish Catholics, for in that year the Act of Banishment was passed, condemning priest and layman alike to slavery in the Barbadoes.

From the fragmentary records of the time it is hard to sort out the stories of individual martyrs. One may suppose that a sense of triumph would cause the persecutors to publish widely any defections they may have found among Catholics, especially among priests. The fact that there are so few who gave up and apostatized among the thousands of persecuted people is a cause for just pride. One of the commanders went on record as complaining: "It is extremely difficult to get rid of the Dominicans." When we remember the drastic means that were used to accomplish this, we can be very proud of our brothers and sisters who, during the terrible two hundred years of persecution, kept alive the flame of truth and the love of the Rosary, which we now so casually accept as the heritage of the Irish people.

THE MARTYRS OF RUSSIA
(d. 1648-1649)

When in 1621 a group of Polish pilgrims who were visiting Rome, asked the Holy Father for relics, he told them: "Go home to your own country and pick up a handful of soil; you will hardly find one in all your land that is not red with the blood of martyrs." If this were true at the beginning of the seventeenth century, it was even more so at the end, for this period in its long and troubled history saw an entire province wiped out, almost to the last man, by the fierce onslaughts of the Cossacks.

Poland had three provinces at this time: the North, called the province of Poland; the Central, or Lithuanian province; and the South, comprising the several Russias, and named for St. Hyacinth. It is the latter which suffered most during this blood-drenched century. This province gave us a long list of martyrs who deserve to be better known.

Poland was the buffer between the heresy of the West and the schism of the East. Since the king favored the Lutheran heresy, there was great difficulty in keeping the Church orthodox. The Dominicans had the tremendous task of fighting both heresy and schism, with no help from the king. For some years there had been great disturbances, and a number of Dominicans had died; they were inquisitors or preachers. The Ruthenian provinces, which were particularly exposed to the schism of the East, had twice been reconciled by the Dominicans, and once there had been a short-lived union of the Greek Church and Rome. In 1595, Dominicans succeeded for a short time in effecting a union between East and West.

The various jealousies and factions that kept these provinces in turmoil are hard to follow now, but, basically, it was a difference between Latin and Greek, between the West and the East. There were many divisive forces at work against the union of these ancient enemies. Early in the seventeenth century, the adherents of the Greek Rite began nibbling away at the union. By the time-tried method of mixing politics and religion, and confusing political freedom with religious independence, they completely undid the efforts of the peacemakers. In 1647, the Greek Patriarch of Jerusalem, a man of great persuasive powers who thoroughly hated the West, conceived the idea of turning the Cossacks on the Latin Christians.

The Cossacks were half-savage mounted nomads, invincible warriors like their Tartar ancestors, utterly ruthless in destroying everything that stood in their path. They had no special animus towards the Latin Christians; they were for hire, at the service of anyone who would furnish them with battle and money. Under the leadership of the Greek Metropolitan, 200,000 of these professional gangsters were let loose on the Latin Christians of Poland.

The Dominican Order at that time had twenty-one large convents in Russia. One after another, they fell to the Cossacks. Those convents were in such complete destruction that even the man who had planned it was appalled at the atrocities and devastation. The pattern was the same in each convent attacked: the friars were tortured and killed, the libraries were burned, the buildings destroyed. We read in the few records that were jotted down hastily—by refugee friars, by members of neighboring communities, by hearsay from some lone survivor—of how this or that entire community was put to the sword or burned, or killed in some other frightful way. By the end of 1649, nothing was left of the Province of St. Hyacinth but the ruined shells of a few stone buildings, and a glorious roll of more than five hundred martyrs.

One might suppose that neither the Polish church, nor the Dominican Order in Poland, could ever replace itself after the attack of the Cossacks. However, less than a hundred years after the holocaust, there were seventy-two convents in Russia. Greek and Cossack alike must have marvelled at the audacity and the stubbornness of those friars who patiently came back, time after time, rebuilding where their slaughtered predecessors had rebuilt a generation before. It was not bloody persecution that finally destroyed the vigor of the Polish province, but the partition of the country. Gradually, the friars were isolated and helpless when the government confiscated their property, in 1876.

By the time of the Russian revolution, in 1918, the last vestiges of the province were wiped out, except in the valiant hearts of the people, who watch and wait for another chance to go back to the grass-grown ruins and begin again.

LUCY OF THE TRINITY
(d. 1649)

Any friend of a saint is apt to be interesting. Lucy was a friend of St. Rose of Lima, and her life gives us several glimpses of that very great saint, which otherwise we would not have.

Lucy Guerra de la Daga was born in Lima of wealthy and noble parents. She married when she was very young, and her household was exemplary. She had five small children at the time that she met St. Rose. Their meeting was startling, to say the least. Rose, who drifted in and out of the great houses of Lima looking for sinners and sick servants to care for, was attending a sick Indian in the home of a wealthy friend when Lucy came to call. Rose threw her arms about her, saying: "You are the new mother prioress of the Dominican cloister—I'm so happy to meet you." Lucy gently pointed out that she must have made a mistake—a woman with a husband and five children was not the person to be prioress, even though she might be extremely interested in the building of a Dominican cloister in Lima. Rose smiled that strange, heavenly smile she had, and said: "Oh yes. You are the one."

It was some years before the dream of building the monastery in Lima came true. In the intervening years, several wealthy women had thought of financing the project, but something always prevented them. Rose prayed for the accomplishment of the plan, and when a saint prays, things happen.

Rose was in the garden one day, working with the flowers for which she was famous. Her mother, who had a sharp nose for news, came upon her with an armful of beautiful roses, a type she had not seen before. "Rose!" she demanded, "You didn't grow those. Where did they come from?" Rose smiled and answered vaguely, which only made her mother more insistent. At this point, the priest from the parish came in to call. "Father," said the older woman, "make Rose tell me where she got those roses." To the father's question, Rose explained cheerfully, but not too lucidly: "The Infant Jesus brought them to me. See, they are the sisters in the new Monastery of St. Catherine. This one is Sister Lucy, the prioress. You, Father, will sing the first Mass when the house is opened. I will not live to see it. Here is Sister Catherine, Sister Magdalen—and this one is you, Mama." Rose's mother looked at her daughter in wild astonishment.

Lucy, in the meanwhile, had lost her husband. And then her children died, one by one. Children often died in Lima in the seventeenth century; every mother learned to expect and accept the unhappy fact. But Lucy was nearly distracted. Someone sent her to Rose for comfort and strength. We do not know what Rose said to her. Rose herself was very near death, but she had no fear of it. She told Lucy to remember what she had said about the new monastery, and left her with the conviction that somehow this was God's will for her. Heartbroken, but now resolute, Lucy set to work building a convent.

The path to the accomplishment of Lucy's project was not smooth. Rose, who could sway people to her will, or pray them into submission, was dead. Authorities passed the requests back and forth in great confusion, entangling the business so badly that when the new viceroy came he thought it better to start all over on the affair, thus wasting several years' work. Lucy and her sister, Clare, who had joined with her in the work, were very discouraged.

One day they went to the church to pray, and both of them—weary of government red tape and tiresome officials—began to cry. A priest came up to them and told them that they must take heart, for God would hear their prayers and crown their work with success. He handed them two lovely roses, a rare kind, long out of season in Lima. "Let this be a sign to you," he said.

At long last, the obstacles were cleared away, and the long-desired Monastery of St. Catherine was built. On February 10, 1625, Lucy, Clare, and thirty-three other young ladies from Spain and all the Indies received the Dominican habit in as glittering a ceremony as that age would warrant.

Here, in the cloister they had sought so long, Lucy and her sisters began practicing the austerities of the Dominican rule. They embraced the entire rule with great enthusiasm, practicing the greatest penances that health and reason would permit. Lucy was particularly severe on herself in the practice of penance. She took the discipline three times in a night, in imitation of St. Dominic, and, on Fridays, she went barefoot, crowned with thorns.

After a few years, a new postulant knocked on the door of St. Catherine's monastery; she was Maria d'Oliva, St. Rose's mother. Widowed, and free of all family obligations, she wanted to spend the rest of her life wearing the habit that Rose had loved so well. With a great deal of courage, she entered into the penitential life of the sisters. Lucy took special care of her, as the mother of her very dear friend and a saint; and, knowing the ruggedness of Maria's disposition, we can believe that both of them must have been very holy. One time, Maria became very sick. Lucy called in to see her, and said: "You tell your daughter that I command her in obedience to get you well." Maria obeyed and so, apparently, did Rose; her mother got up, well and strong.

Lucy of the Trinity closed her holy life with a long and agonizing illness, and a holy death, in the month of May, 1649. She has long been revered as a saint in Lima, a city where—one must remember—saints are not at all uncommon.

JOACHIM KO
(d. 1649)

This interesting character was born of noble pagan parents, in the province of Fukien. He was given a good education and, as a young man, held a fine position in the empire. When he heard about the missionaries from Spain, he went to Foochow to investigate their teachings. He was baptized by a Jesuit, remaining there under his instruction for some time before returning to Fukien.

When the first Dominicans arrived in the province, Joachim had already set up a scheme by which he could guard them and get them from place to place. A severe persecution had been raging for some time, and the missionaries and their native protectors were in danger of death. The young Joachim, whose future in the empire was assured because of his birth and education, freely gave up his prospects, dedicating himself to the dangerous business of helping the missionaries. He began by hiding them in his own home, and he coached them in the language and customs of the country so that they could move about safely. In 1633 he went to Formosa to meet Fathers John Baptist Morales, Francis Diaz, and Peter Chavez, two of whom were future martyrs, and bring them to Fukien.

Eventually he was driven, by the force of the persecution, to Macao. He spent a year in the Portuguese city in religious work. Then he went to Manila with a group of priests. Here he worked on the docks, searching out Chinese people to convert. He compiled a dictionary and grammar of the Chinese language to help in this work, and was highly successful with converts. Finally, he went to Bataan with Father Diaz to study methods of getting back to China. He received the Dominican Tertiary habit there, and for a little while he had the great joy of following the religious exercises with the fathers. When at last it became possible to return to China, he and Father Francis De Capillas, who was to be the protomartyr of China, set out by way of Formosa. After a long and dangerous journey, they reached Fukien, where they found the Christians in hiding and the persecution still raging.

For some time Joachim was the liaison man between Christians and the hidden priests. Because of his high family estate and a military commission, he had freedom to move around, and he used it to the advantage of the Church. He propagated the Rosary and taught catechism in various hideouts. One of the most popular hide-outs was the mandarin's graveyard.

During this time, invading Tartars had put the province in a state of war. The mandarin, in rousing an army to fight them, made Joachim the admiral of the fleet. The mandarin seems to have been very fond of Joachim; not so his viceroy, who was annoyed because Joachim had converted some of his wives to Christianity. The viceroy waited his chance to avenge himself. It was many years in coming, but eventually he had his chance. Part of the army mutinied, and it was expedient to blame the admiral. He was brought to trial and various charges were made against him. Even so, the emperor released him.

At about this time, a concerted drive was being made on the missionaries. The viceroy, who hated Christians, pointed out Joachim's activities. This time there was no escape. Joachim and his young grandson were put in prison, and, after a long and painful wait, they were led out to die. Joachim reminded the bystanders to say their Rosaries, for many Christians had come to see him die. He and the little boy were beheaded. The news of the death of their great catechist and helper reached Father Francis De Capillas and Francis Diaz, who themselves were waiting in prison for death. Joachim was one of the first Dominican Tertiaries to die in China.

JULIANA MOREL
(1594-1653)

It is no surprise to find scholars, doctors, and philosophers among Dominicans, since the Order has always proudly been a leader in scholarship. It is a little surprising, however, to read of a woman of the seventeenth century who was such an outstanding scholar that everyone remarked on it. She was a student par excellence in a century that cared little for women learning much of anything. And even in the Dominican Order, her intelligence and sanctity were noteworthy. Her name was Juliana Morel.

Juliana was born in Barcelona, in 1594, and her mother died when she was a baby. The only interest of her bereaved father from her babyhood, she was taught studies that one would have thought were far beyond her. Under the determined coaching of her father, who was resolved to make her the wonder of the age, she studied logic, the humanities, and ethics; at the age of twelve she could read Greek, Latin, Hebrew, Arabic, Chaldaic, and Italian, and could speak fluently in either French or Spanish. At this tender age, she made her first public appearance, defending theses in philosophy. Her father became more than ever determined to see her become the "Doctress" of the century, and Juliana—who would, in our times, still be a child in grade school—settled down to a stiff program that included nine hours of study and no recreation, except playing on the lute or the organ. Because she was a devout child, she added the recitation of the Divine Office to this full day.

There is no question that Juliana had a wonderful intellect, and hard study shaped it into a dazzling instrument. At thirteen, she was studying physics, metaphysics, and jurisprudence; and we are not surprised to find that she suffered agonies from temptations against faith. The nerves of a young girl would most certainly wear thin under such a regime.

When Juliana was fourteen, and the career her father had planned for her seemed about to become a reality, she felt the call to dedicate herself to God in a monastery. The effect on her father, when she told him of this resolution, was almost beyond our imagination. He raged like an insane man; he even beat the girl with a rawhide whip. Sore and miserable from the lashes, she cried herself to sleep night after night. In the midst of all her troubles, she stuck to her schedule of studies, and her father decided to take her to Avignon and have her pass the examination for "Doctress of Laws." Perhaps he thought it would take her mind off the convent.

In Avignon, she not only fulfilled her father's hopes and won the coveted degree, she also made a step in her own behalf. Securing the protection of the princess, she made her entrance, secretly, into the convent of St. Catherine of Siena and St. Praxides. She must have hoped that her father would be reconciled when he saw her there, but he was not to be won so easily. He could not take her out again, with the princess espousing her cause and the eyes of the city upon her; but he cut her off in his will, left her penniless, disowning her completely.

Word reached the pope of the unfortunate girl's struggle, and he sent a dowry for her and assured her of his personal interest. With such a stormy beginning, Juliana settled down to the realities of the novitiate. She received the Dominican habit in 1609, when she was fifteen years old.

Several times, in the remaining years of her life, the invitation came, in one form or another, to step forth into the intellectual world and give evidence of one of the finest minds of the age. Juliana resisted the efforts of all who tried. It was an accomplishment, under the circumstances, to live a hidden life. Juliana succeeded. In view of her place in the intellectual world, that took a great deal of doing.

The virtue most frequently mentioned in the religious life of Juliana Morel is charity, the queen of the virtues. As mistress of novices, prioress, or as a subject, she made her life a continual round of charitable deeds. She visited the sick, often saying the Divine Office with them. One day she found that she had said the whole day's Office three times. The only charge made against her as prioress was that she was a little too liberal with alms; the mothers of the council tried to point out to her that there were limits to what one could give. "If I cannot give alms, you had better depose me," she remarked calmly. "I cannot think of any better reason to be prioress than to be in a position to help people."

The last twenty-five years of her life were made difficult for Juliana by physical suffering. Perhaps the long childhood years of study exacted their toll; we do not know the nature of her illness, only that she was continually miserable with it. Her own suffering did not keep her from noticing the suffering of others, however. In fact, it made her more charitable to them.

One thing that we note as pleasantly remarkable about Juliana—she took orders from others without a murmur. We may as well realize that her superiors were not her equal in mental ability. None of them, probably, could have made the scholastic record that she had. Yet she was perfectly obedient to all their commands. One thing that upheld her in practicing this difficult virtue was a constant consideration of our Lord's Passion.

Juliana Morel died, quietly and without fanfare, in 1653. She had suffered a long and terrible agony after a strange and difficult life. Her reputation lives on in scholarly circles and she is mentioned—with some surprise—by most of the historians of that age as being a strange phenomenon—a scholarly woman who was noted for her humility and her great charity.

THE MARTYRED IRISH NUNS
(d. 1653)

Two Irish nuns, who died for the faith under Cromwell in 1653, are, among our many martyrs, most unusual.

The elder of the two, Sister Honoria Burke, was born in 1549, the daughter of the Burke, chieftain of Clanricard, in Mayo. At the age of thirteen, she received the habit of the Third Order of St. Dominic from the Irish provincial, and she used her own inheritance to build a small convent in Burrishoole.

The convent was undisturbed through several waves of persecution, but eventually a small troop of soldiers invaded their quiet valley and demanded the daughter of Lord Clanricard. Sister Honoria fled through the woods, the soldiers after her. Her strength gone, she fell exhausted on the ground, praying for help. Then, according to a persistent legend, the bit of land on which she was kneeling became surrounded by water, deep and black. The soldiers were afraid to cross it, and they finally went away, leaving her in peace for the time being. Around the turn of the century, when the crown soldiers were combing the country for Sir John Burke of Limerick, a little further south, they came again to Burrishoole, and Sister Honoria again had to flee for her life. At one time, she spent eight days hiding in a church, without food or warmth, waiting for the soldiers to leave the area.

In spite of the harrassed days and fearful nights of those who waited for invasion and capture, Sister Honoria did not forget the charity for which the Third Order had been founded. Hordes of starving, homeless people flocked around her gates, not because she had much to give, but because somehow she always could find something to feed them, and kind words to cheer them. Often she multiplied grain in order to have enough to go around, and once, when not a single grain was left in the bin, two young men appeared at the door with a fresh supply. They did not tell her who they were, but she always presumed they were angels. Through the terrors of persecution, when rich rewards were offered Catholics who would give up their faith, or betray another into doing so, Sister Honoria was the hard core of resistance in her part of the country. It was not surprising that she was on the "most wanted" list of the invaders.

The showdown finally came when Cromwell's army arrived to gather up what anyone else had overlooked. The sisters were all obliged to flee from Burrishoole. Sister Honoria was by this time in extreme old age—past one hundred years—and travel was difficult, but she set out for a remote place known as the "Isle of Saints," in a lake inland. Her companions were Sister Honoria MaGaen, a very young and beautiful sister, and a faithful servant, who had been with the convent for years. They reached their chosen hiding place, but they had been there only a little while when the soldiers discovered them.

Sister Honoria was too old to run any more, but she told her young companion and the maid to try escaping through the woods. The soldiers easily captured the old sister; they stripped her of her clothes and threw her into a boat, breaking her ribs in the process. It was February and freezing cold; she could not live long. The maid had hidden nearby, and, after the soldiers left, she came back and tried to revive the dying sister. Sister Honoria lived just long enough to tell the maid to go help Sister Honoria MaGaen, and she died with a prayer on her lips.

The younger sister had almost managed to escape. Caught once, she had fought free. Scratched, scarred, and bleeding, she had escaped from her tormenters permanently when the maid found her. The young sister was kneeling upright in a hollow tree, frozen to death. The maid managed to get both the bodies decently buried. Then she brought the story of the deaths of the two sisters to those who would record it.

In the Acts of the General Chapter of 1656, Sister Honoria Burke is expressly called a martyr. Whether either or both of these women will ever be listed among our blessed, we do not know, of course. But their courage is nonetheless inspiring to the members of the Order to which they belonged.

JAMES GOAR
(1601-1653)

A joy to the librarians of the Order was the scholarly and venturesome James Goar, who, in the seventeenth century, rescued some of the finest manuscripts of the Near East from destruction, and made them available to Western scholars.

James was born in Paris in 1601, and entered the Order there when he was eighteen. After acquiring his degrees in theology, it developed that he had a decided aptitude for Greek, and a taste for oriental learning, so he was sent to Greece to study the history and rites of the Greek church, in the event that his studies might be of service to the cause of unity between East and West.

James was appointed missionary apostolic, and prior of the convent in Chios, which he made his base of operations. Like today's students in Paris and Rome who haunt the old book shops, he frequented the places where old manuscripts might be found, making it his business to evaluate them and—if possible—obtain them for Dominican libraries in the West. He cultivated the acquaintance of the foremost scholars of the Greek Church, and he studied their rites avidly. On his return to Paris, in 1643, where he was called to become master of novices, he had a great fund of knowledge bearing upon the whole question of Eastern rites. He also had an invaluable collection of manuscripts with which to enrich the minds of Western scholars.

James acted as master of novices for several years, and he worked on affairs of the Order that had reference to the Eastern rites. But it was apparent that his greatest contribution to the general fund of knowledge would be to organize and catalog the materials he had brought from the East. He was left free to do this, and to make additional short trips to obtain manuscripts in France and Italy. Some of the Greek material he translated and published; some he simply identified and evaluated. He wrote a valuable treatise on the Greek rites, and others on the works of the Greek canonists. His works are of particular interest to scholars; they have not been translated into English, but present-day students of the Eastern rites find that they are both scholarly and complete.

James Goar died in Paris in 1653.

CATHERINE SANZO
(d. 1655)

The grand old lady of the Chinese missions was a little old grandmother who had been born a slave. She has counterparts in every nation, and she and her type, found in every parish, are the salt of the earth. It is, however, more than a little surprising to consider the circumstances of her apostolate, for Catherine Sanzo functioned in the midst of bloody persecution, in an age when the mere tolerance of Christianity was enough to guarantee trouble.

Catherine was born in Teng-Tu, and she married a poor workman named Sanzo. She was already a venerable grandmother when Father John Garcia came to Teng-Tu and began to preach. After listening to him, she wished to become a Catholic. When she had given satisfactory evidence that she understood his instructions, Father Garcia baptized her. He probably did not know that the Chinese church had just acquired a pillar. The strong-willed old lady set out to convert her numerous family. As soon as it was permitted, she became a Third Order Dominican and, years before the name had even been coined, a lay apostle.

Catherine not only acted as catechist among her family and friends, but she rapidly progressed to a high degree of prayer; she, in fact, reached heights of contemplation that one would expect to find in some secluded monastery rather than in the midst of a noisy household. Her guardian angel used to appear visibly, and helped her with the household tasks. Our Blessed Lady came to see her several times—informal visits, like those of a neighbor— and advised her to always love God and obey her directors. Often she saw the Child Jesus in the Host during Mass, and, on several occasions, the Host leaped from Father Garcia's hand and came to her at Communion time. She had visits from the devil, too, and she handled these with a skill that all mystics could envy. "I spit at him," she confided once to Father Garcia, "or I give him some dirty work to do. He does not like that." There is an almost comic relief in the thought of this shrewd old lady ordering the devil about as if he were a naughty schoolboy, making him mop the floor.

The missionaries sent her on catechetical journeys to other villages, and she did an enormous amount of work for them, conducting long discussion and study circles with her people. She was a keen debater and a sound theologian. One by one, her family followed her into the dangerous paths of truth, risking death to be baptized in a Church they had never heard of a few years before. She brought back a number of apostates who had been frightened away by the danger of death. Learned men came to listen to her, trying to entrap her in arguments; they failed completely. But several of them began to study Christianity seriously.

Catherine's director was well aware of her splendid spiritual gifts, and he was afraid that pride might bring the whole structure toppling. After she had been the center of every discussion circle for years, he told her to remain quietly at home. If he thought it would upset her to be deprived of her audience, he was happily mistaken. Catherine quietly retired into a corner, devoting herself to contemplative prayer. She died in 1655.

MARY OF LUMAGUE
(1599-1657)

Mary of Lumague was one of several saintly women who tried to stem the tide of sin and social neglect in Paris during the seventeenth century. She was the foundress of the Institute of the Daughters of Providence, but she is of special interest to us because she was also a Dominican Tertiary.

Mary was born in Paris in 1599. In her noble family there was an ancient tradition of charity to the poor. When she was still very small, she brought home a child who was covered with sores, and placing it in her own bed, she nursed it carefully. This is an example of the acts of charity that were only to be expected of members of the family.

Mary was married to a member of parliament when she was quite young. Her husband was a good man, and, through her constant example of Christian charity, he became even better. But he died when he was young, leaving her with one child, a girl. Free now to follow her own designs, Mary announced her intentions not to marry again, and she was received as a member of the Third Order of St. Dominic. She had read the life of St. Catherine and was completely charmed by it. She put away forever the fine clothes and the family jewels in which she had dutifully dressed to please her husband, and, dressed as a simple peasant, she went forth to see what she could do about the troubles of Paris.

One of Mary's sisters was also to become a religious, and to attain fame as the foundress of a great hospital. Her four sisters, who married and remained in the world, were noted for their charity and their good works among the unfortunate. These five allies were a great help to her during the years when she was trying to work against the indifference of Christians, and the corruption of politics, that caused the evils of the city. She aspired to remedy only one of the many ills. She wanted to found a house, called the "House of Providence," where young girls who had not fallen into sin, but who were in danger of falling, might be sheltered, and taught an honest way of life. Since Paris always has need of this sort of charity, she found many who agreed that it was a worthwhile project, but few who would do anything to help her make it a reality.

After several years of hard work, and with the aid of small amounts of money given her by friends, she found herself head of an institution sheltering one hundred and eighty girls. It was her policy never to turn anyone away, and the walls were fairly bulging with eager youngsters. When the girls did not come to her, she went looking for them—in any sort of establishment where they might be found. She walked untouched through the roughest criminal hide-outs in Paris, unconcerned with anything that did not have bearing on her own project: young girls in need of help. How she fed them became a legend. An hour before dinner there would be one loaf of bread in the house, and nearly two hundred mouths to feed. She would send someone to look in the poor-box, just in case there might be a few pennies. There would be fifty gold pieces. Or a creditor would come to the front door, demanding payment; and someone with the money would knock at the back door. The Lord looked after them.

It seemed better to organize a religious community to care for this important work. Why they were not Dominicans we do not know; perhaps the Dominican superiors would not give permission for that type of work at that time. They were finally organized as the Institute of Divine Providence, and Mary, who had been ill for some time, was relieved to know that the work would be cared for if anything happened to her.

Mary never lost her individuality, and she must have spent a good deal of time looking for girls in need of help. At times this kept her out all day, so she simply carried a piece of dry bread in her purse, and, when she remembered to eat it, she sat down on a convenient curb or park bench and ate it. She would arrive home drenched with rain or snow, her clothes muddy and wet through, and then she would have to be pulled bodily from the chapel by her companions, who wanted her to get dry and warm. The internal abscess, which had bothered her for ten years, was healed on one of her many barefoot pilgrimages to Our Lady of Aubervilliers. She seemed to be completely out of touch with most of what went on in the world, hearing only the cry of those who needed her. The praise of queens meant nothing at all to her; Anne of Austria revered her as a saint.

There are at least two well-authenticated cases of Mary of Lumague raising a dead child to life. One, a child of wealthy parents, fell into a fountain and drowned. Mary—who probably was there begging for her girls—took the dead child into a room alone and laid him in front of the big fireplace. Then she knelt down and prayed. For three hours the frantic mother waited outside the closed door, and then the door opened, and the child walked out. Another time, a poor woman met Mary on the street and told her that her little son had just died. Mary went with her to where the child was laid out for burial, and she unwound the shroud from his face. Then she took out a little bottle, put a few drops of its contents on his lips, and she prayed. He, too, rose up alive; but she would never tell what was in the little bottle. Her companions said the action was just to divert attention from her sanctity, and there was nothing at all in the bottle but water.

However, these incidents received a good deal of publicity from the mothers of the children. One of the princesses of Orleans made Mary a lady of honor and governess of her children, a job she freed herself from as soon as possible. Finally, it became evident that Mary herself was failing in health. She was on a trip to Rouen in behalf of her Institute when she fell seriously ill. She wanted to die among her own, so she had herself brought back to Paris, stopping en route to see a little granddaughter who was in school with the sisters. Reaching home, she died among her sisters at the Institute of Providence, in 1657.

Mary's grandson became a priest, and a canon of the Cathedral of Chatillon. She had inculcated in all her family a deep devotion to St. Dominic, and, when the young priest went to Bologna, he went of course to the tomb of the saint. While he was there, someone stole all his luggage out of the hotel where he was staying. The next day he returned to the tomb and addressed the saint: "You were always fond of the canons; now help me and get my luggage back." It is related that St. Dominic did just as he was asked, and the canon's property was quickly restored to him.

THE VENERABLE OLIER
(1608-1657)

John James Olier, usually called the Venerable Olier, will be remembered best as the Founder of the Society of San Sulpice, and the builder of the seminary system for the training of priests. America owes a debt to this great man who has guided the destinies of the Church in America. Dominicans should be proud to know that he was a Tertiary, and he always held the Dominican Order in the greatest respect.

John Olier was born of a well-to-do family in Paris, in 1608. His father was an officer of the king, and both his parents were connected with the royal house. The little boy was proud of this, but much more proud that he had been born on Saturday, and that his mother's name was Mary, for his devotion to Our Blessed Mother started when he was very tiny. When he was very young, he would run to Our Lady's shrine, telling her any bit of news, or showing her a suit of new clothes before anyone else should see it. He would ask her always to keep him good while he wore these clothes.

In spite of his very great piety, little John was such a high-spirited child that he was always in trouble. He was impulsive and daring, and the wonder is that he did not kill himself on some of his ventures. His mother was very severe with him, as she was something of a perfectionist. Her punishments seemed to have no effect, and, at last, when John was twelve, she took him with the other children to see St. Francis de Sales, who was then in extreme old age. She expected that the saint would give her little boy a salutary scolding, and that it might have better effect than her own. The holy bishop of Geneva did nothing of the sort; he put his arms around the naughty child, and prophesied that he would some day do great work for the Church. He suggested that the mother be more patient. Shortly after this, the boy decided that he would like to be a priest. His mother felt that this was the working out of the great bishop's prophecy, so she made every effort to help him in his studies. Already she had visions of the great ecclesiastical dignities that would await this talented and well-born child.

The young student did not follow exactly the path that his mother had laid out for him. He finished his humanities at the Jesuit College, philosophy at the University of Paris, and theology at the Sorbonne. No possible fault could be found with his intellectual progress, but some could be found with the way he conducted himself. He had been pious from early youth, but all that seemed forgotten as he, with other students of the same mind, set about entertaining themselves in ways most unbecoming to the clerical habits they wore. His mother made allowance for the fact that students are usually not very sensible, but she knew that other people were talking about her son. John, on his part, had hardly a care in the world. He had decided to become a famous Hebrew scholar. With this in mind, he went to study in Rome. He had scarcely begun his studies there when his eyes failed, and the doctor told him he was going blind.

The shock brought the young student up short. He went to the shrine of Our Lady at Loretto, humbly begging Our Blessed Mother to cure him. Very literally, she did—body and soul. The young cleric, back from Loretto, abandoned the wild life of the students, and he settled down to become a worthy priest. Let us remember in this connection that he had many bad examples on all sides of him. John's mother had been praying for his reform, but she did not expect that he would go to such extremes.

She was almost beside herself with embarrassment to hear that her son was preaching to the poor of Paris; that was something which no French aristocrat had yet thought of doing. She argued with him about it, pointing out that he was making himself ridiculous. Since he would not give up his apostolate to the poor, she angrily rejected him. Stung with sorrow, the young man went to pray at the shrine of the Blessed Virgin. "My mother has rejected me," he said. "After this, you will have to be my Mother."

Just before his ordination, in 1633, John Olier had a dream, or a revelation, which he did not then understand, but which was to shape his activities for the rest of his life. He saw a vision of the heavens opened, with St. Gregory and St. Ambrose and a number of Carthusians enthroned. There was an empty throne, which John understood should belong to the parish priest. Anyone who lived in the France of that day was painfully aware that the secular priesthood was not what it should be. Benefices and poor control, plus the ravages of heresy, had given it a bad repute. It had not occurred to John Olier that he could some day do something about this. It was to be many years before he would see the work accomplished, and his efforts would bring him into contact with some of the finest men of the age, including the great St. Vincent de Paul.

The conversion and subsequent holiness of Venerable Olier came about in a singular way. Two women, strangers to him, had been given the apostolate of praying and suffering for him that he might be shaped into God's instrument. One of these was a secular named Marie Rousseau, who had several visions of his future greatness, and who, on several occasions, met him on the street and reprimanded him. The other was the prioress of the Dominican Monastery of Langeac, who appeared to him in a vision, and whom he recognized from this vision on the only occasion that he ever met her. She told him at this time that she had been given the mission to pray and suffer for him. The prayers of these holy women made a great impression on this young priest; they were decisive factors in his perseverance.

Father Olier began his work with a mission band that was made up of young clerics like himself, who regretted the low state of French spirituality. They had varying successes in their country missions. Gradually they grew closer to the idea of training priests to care for the country parishes. Preparation for the priesthood then was at the almost irreducible minimum of spiritual training: a short retreat before ordination. Father Olier and his associates felt that there must be some way of making the training more thorough and more lasting. To this end, they eventually were to found the seminary system, which today we take so much for granted. Before this, however, Father Olier was to pass through a time of cruel suffering. At the height of his missionary fame, when he was a recognized leader of the missionary band, his eloquence suddenly left him. He would "blank out" in the middle of a sermon, or, well prepared, he would begin, and then find he had completely forgotten the sequence of his arguments. At first, his companions thought it was rather a joke, but eventually he was left more and more out of the mission work, and he felt that he was not capable of doing anything at all for the missions. Once again it was Our Lady who rescued him, after two years of this painful and puzzling trial.

The seminary, when finally founded, had its first permanent home in the parish of St. Sulpice. The house was Mary's; her monogram was engraved on the silver, wrought in the iron work, and marked on the linens, so that no one would ever forget that it was her house. Her statue was in the courtyard, facing the door. The founder had delivered to her the keys of the house, with the prayer: "Herein I trust that the holy name of Mary will be blessed forever; all my desire is to imprint it deeply on the hearts of our brethren, for Mary is our Counsellor and President, our Treasurer, our Princess, our Queen and our all."

The trials were not over for the founder of the seminary. Jansenism was rife in France, and the clergy was infiltrated with this heresy. At one time, a mob attacked the church and seminary, driving Father Olier away. He returned, of course, and battled until his ideal was soundly established. We see in every country today the results of his care.

When the gentlemen founding the city of Montreal were organizing for their great colonial venture, Father Olier was the moving spirit. The city we know as Montreal was first named Ville-Marie, and Father Olier's ideal, as much as anything else, held it together during the difficult pioneer years. Money from his personal fortune helped to found the city. Later, priests who followed his rule were to die there, martyred by the Indians.

At exactly what point Father Olier became a Dominican Tertiary, we do not know, but he was very proud of this affiliation. After suffering several strokes, he died on March 26, 1657, in the arms of St. Vincent de Paul.

SISTER CATHERINE HOWARD
(d. 1661)

The first English girl to enter the Order after the dispersal of the religious of England was Antonia Howard, a cousin of the English cardinal. Planning to help in re-building the Order in England, she did not live to do so, for she died at the age of sixteen.

Several countries had offered refuge to the English Catholics; Belgium was one. Father Thomas Howard, the future cardinal, established a small convent for priests of the Order in Bornhem, and, as soon as it was possible, he opened a little convent for nuns in Vilvorde. Two Dutch choir sisters and a laysister came to open the house, bringing with them his young cousin, Antonia, who had been with the sisters for a year, in preparation for religious life. On the eleventh of June, 1661, the young postulant was given the Dominican habit and the name Sister Catherine.

The earthly course of this courageous young woman was run in a few short months. Delicate to begin with, she soon collapsed under the poverty and strain of exiled life, and she contracted a fever which proved fatal. On the Feast of St. Michael, it became apparent that the young novice was going to die, so she was allowed to make her profession, and she received the last sacraments. In her remaining ten days of life, she edified the sisters so much by her conduct and her resignation that her memory was to remain for centuries. On the eighth of October, seeing that she could not live more than a few hours, the sisters summoned her confessor, who witnessed her last hours and holy death. It is from him that we have the account of it.

Sister Catherine had received the last rites of the Church, and was holding a blessed candle and the Rosary. Suddenly, she roused from a coma and began to smile. The confessor tried to discover the cause of her joy, but he could not attract her attention. Finally he commanded her, in virtue of holy obedience, to tell him what made her so happy. She answered him: "I see it, father." "But what do you see?" he insisted. "I see Our Blessed Lady with a crown in one hand and a rosary in the other—oh, a fine crown. I do not want to see any more of this world." Very shortly thereafter, she died.

Although the life of Sister Catherine was short, it is still of interest to us, as it was in Bornhem that she was buried. The tradition still lingers there of the brave little English girl who planned to return to her country as a nun, but did not live to do so.

At least four more members of the Howard family entered the convent in Vilvorde in the half-century following Antonia's death. One of them carried on a sprightly business in underground correspondence between the exiled James Stuart and sympathetic Jacobites, as one might expect a member of a politically-minded family to do. But the memory that has remained longest is that of the girl who died as a novice, reaching for the crown held out to her by the Blessed Virgin.

CATHERINE GUILLEMARD
(1627-1663)

Catherine Guillemard began her education most unpropitiously; her teacher dabbled in black magic. Her early life was shadowed by diabolical powers and manifestations, which did not prevent her from becoming an eminent member of the Order.

Catherine, baptized Philiberte, was born in 1627 in Autun. Her father was a judge, and he insisted that his children be given a good education. It annoyed him, therefore, when little Philiberte flatly refused to attend the classes of the most eminent master in Autun because—she said—he had a hideous black face like soot, with eyes of burning coals, and a pair of business-like horns. Her father tried every method of persuasion he knew, as there was no exterior evidence against the schoolmaster, and the whole thing seemed to be the creation of an over-active childish imagination. However, Philiberte was more obstinate than he, and, since she had never opposed him before, her father decided to humor her and hired a private tutor.

The devil, who was in league with the schoolmaster, resented this slur on his professional talents, and he began a persecution of the family which is harrowing to even read about. He especially vented his rage on Philiberte. He sent a book to the house with instruction to the messenger to give it into the hands of the judge himself; but the judge was away, and one of Philiberte's sisters took the package. She was immediately possessed by the devil, and a frightful week ensued. The heretofore peaceful house was full of demoniac howls, crashing furniture, and other uncomfortable manifestations. At the end of the week, Philiberte found the book and threw it outside; the manifestations ceased, but her sister died of the effects of the terror.

With this unpromising beginning, one might suppose that the little girl's nerves would be permanently damaged. However, she proved to be remarkably durable. The experience had given her a horror of sin that was to color all her spirituality, and a distrust of spiritual manifestations that was not always to be found in seventeenth-century pious women. She was sent to school to the Dominicans in Autun. At the age of sixteen, she was received as a novice in the convent, on the Feast of St. Catherine of Siena, in whose honor she took the name Catherine.

Small and delicate in body, Catherine was a giant in prayer. Retreat, silence, and prayer were her ordinary fare, and she performed all the mortifications that she was allowed. She recited the Office of the Blessed Virgin out of devotion, in addition to the Divine Office that the community recited. At an early age, she was made novice mistress, an office which she filled capably, in spite of her youth.

In 1662, when she was still novice mistress, Sister Catherine made a bargain with God. She had in her charge a very talented and spiritually gifted girl. But the girl's health was poor. When it became evident that she was failing in strength and might have to give up her vocation and return home, Sister Catherine begged God to let her take on the girl's infirmities, allowing the girl to remain as an ornament to the house. "Just give me one year," she asked.

God took her at her word. She lived just a year—a year of continual prayer and patient suffering—and died in 1663, leaving her protégé in excellent health—a long life before her.

CATHERINE MIEOU
(d. 1663)

This valiant Chinese Tertiary lived in extremely troubled times, and, if we read the records properly, she must have been one of the first to try living a regular religious life in a country that was still largely pagan.

Catherine's father was a powerful and learned mandarin. His name was John. A fervent Christian, he died a martyr at the end of an inspiring life. Catherine was baptized in childhood by one of the Dominicans who was in hiding from the persecutions. Like her father, she became a staunch Christian, and, when she was old enough, she begged for the Tertiary habit. Here she had difficulty with her father, because he, in accordance with Chinese custom, had arranged her marriage when she was still a baby. Good Christian though he was, it had never occurred to him that Catherine might want to do anything as surprising as remain unmarried.

The young man in question was painfully surprised by her attitude. It took him a while to digest Catherine's statement, that she had found a spouse more noble, wealthier, and more powerful; the young man was not a Christian, and he had never heard of Agnes and Cecilia, who had given the same testimony fifteen hundred years before. He discussed the matter with Catherine's father, and he finally persuaded John to let him talk with the girl personally. He appeared at the house of the unwilling girl and presented his case, pointing out that both he and her father had quite a large sum of money tied up in the arrangement. Catherine cut off her hair and sent it out by one of the servants. This was her way of informing him that he was wasting his time.

The criticism Catherine received from friends and relatives, pagans and Christians, was almost beyond belief. She had defied a custom so ancient that they could only think that she was acting without full control of her sanity. Catherine herself seemed to be the only one who was not much perturbed. At this tense moment, the emperor chose to arrest her father for his religion; he had John put to death in Fukien. This caused Catherine to worry. She wondered whether or not her actions had had anything to do with her father's death.

The young man made another demand for marriage, now that her father was no longer there to protect her; he said that he would force her to keep her contract. Catherine slipped away in the night and fled to the mountains, where she took refuge with a group of Tertiaries.

We wish we knew more about these women who lived together in a "pious congregation," wearing the habit, and fulfilling all the requirements of religious life. Most of the records are lost, but we can at least imagine the life of these brave women, who gave up security and risked death to live the religious life.

Catherine died in 1663, and most of her records were lost in the persecution.

THE JANSENBOYS
(d. 1634-1663)

Brotherhood is one of the strongest characteristics of the Dominican Order. St. Dominic and his brother Manez set the precedent of blood brotherhood consecrated by religious profession. But one may safely say that the five Jansenboys—Nicholas, Dominic, Cornelius, Leonard, and Ambrose—who worked together in Holland in the seventeenth century, have set a record for Dominican brotherhood that would be difficult to surpass. These five interesting characters, sons of a well-to-do merchant, were born at Zierikzee, in Zeeland, by the Zuyder Zee.

The Netherlands had been under Spanish domination and at this time were breaking away. In gaining control, the Dutch party established Protestantism and abolished Catholic schools. The elder Jansenboys, with his large family, moved to a part of the country where the children could have a Catholic education. Five of his sons would become Dominicans in the province of the Netherlands, working for Christ during the period of persecution.

Nicholas, the oldest son, took his degree at Louvain, where he studied Greek, oriental languages, and methods of refuting the errors of Protestantism.

All of his brothers were to be engaged in this particular apostolate of refuting errors, both by preaching and by use of the press. Nicholas seems to have been the first of the brethren to become a pamphleteer. While he was still very young, he was sent to Denmark, where Protestantism was becoming a serious problem. He preached in Denmark, Holstein, and Norway, and then he reported to Rome on the mission conditions of those countries. He returned to Denmark, accompanied by two of his brothers, Cornelius and Dominic. They were well liked by the Danish king, who granted them freedom to preach. They worked there against Lutheranism, and it was in answer to a Lutheran attack on our Blessed Mother that Nicholas wrote his first pamphlet. He died in 1634, leaving a definite pattern of preaching for his brothers to follow.

Cornelius and Leonard entered the Order together, receiving their degrees from Louvain. They were sent together to Italy for further study, and they peached in Lombardy and Bologna. Cornelius was assigned to work with their brother Nicholas, and remained with him in the Scandinavian countries until Nicholas' death. They preached for many years in Lower Saxony, then returned to Flanders, where the Church was still in hiding. They became ardent apostles of the press against Calvinism and Lutheranism. Both wrote a great many works, mostly of a short and controversial nature, concerned with the refutation of error.

Dominic entered the Order some time after his brothers, and he was educated in Antwerp. He preached in Denmark and northern Germany, sometimes with his brother, sometimes by himself. He was appointed apostolic preacher of Hamburg, a big commercial city that was badly infected with Lutheranism. Here, for several years, he narrowly escaped death at the hands of the heretics. He ran a Catholic press in Hamburg for eleven years, distributing pamphlets to the faithful and Protestants alike. He was eventually recalled to Antwerp. While there he translated into Flemish the account of the miraculous image of St. Dominic of Soriano, and he wrote other works of an apologetic nature. He built the Dominican church in Amsterdam, and, in 1647, he died there.

Ambrose was educated at Bois-le-Duc, where he probably entered the Order. After the country fell to the Dutch under William of Orange, he was exiled for some time. He obtained permission from his superiors to wear secular clothes and work among the persecuted Catholics in the cities held by 'the Dutch. He did this work for thirty-four years, exposed constantly to danger of death at the hands of the Protestants, and to possible betrayal by weak Catholics. Unperturbed by this perilous existence, he wrote several books of devotion, an *Abridged History of the Holy Persons of the Order*, and a number of other books that were designed for use in the apostolate against error. He probably expected martyrdom daily, but he was spared. He died peacefully in 1663, after a long career which had been a glory to God, and a continual source of annoyance to the Protestant masters of his country.

Because of the disturbed state of the time, and the similarity of the work done by these five brother-priests, their records have been intermingled to a certain extent, and it is now difficult to sort them out with any degree of exactitude. One may suppose that many legends would grow up about five such dynamic brothers, and that their reputations would not be allowed to diminish in the popular memory.

CATHERINE OF ST. MARTHA
(d. 1664)

Catherine was born in Brittany; she was the daughter of a seneschal. From early infancy she had displayed signs of a taste for prayer and works of charity. With her father's consent, she began helping the poor when she was quite young. He was very proud of the little daughter who saved all her sweets for the poor and the sick. When she was still very tiny, she made herself a rule of life, meditated daily on the Passion of Christ, and ate no meat at all. After reading the life of St. Catherine of Siena, she decided to be a Dominican as soon as she was old enough.

When the time came for Catherine to leave home, her father protested strongly. The parish priest had arranged for her to become a laysister in a monastery of strict observance, but her old father simply could not bear to let her go. Finally he sent her off with one of her brothers, but, as soon as they were gone, he sent the rest of her brothers to overtake her and bring her back. The rescue party failed to find her, and she rode unmolested to the doors of an Ursuline convent. The pastor had arranged for her to stop there on the way to her destination.

Here a curious interruption of plans occurred; the Ursulines tried to keep her in their community. They made elaborate arrangements for her novitiate, but she politely refused to stay, and finally she was allowed to go on her way. Upon arrival at the Dominican monastery, there was a question at first of her physical fitness; she looked very delicate. Because of her obvious frailty, they insisted on her making a longer novitiate than usual. Like many frail people, she lived to a venerable age and was never ill.

Everyone was astonished at the amount of work that Sister Catherine could do in a day. She took care of the hard work of the monastery for twenty-nine years, never letting it interrupt her meditations. She performed great penances, fasted, and prayed long hours; yet she was always on hand to care for the sick or do anything asked of her. Her special devotion was to the Blessed Virgin, and she claimed, with reason, that she received whatever she prayed for. Two of her own relatives were near death one time, and both were in danger of losing their souls. She prayed without ceasing until she had Our Lady's promise to look after them. She prayed constantly for the souls in purgatory.

Like many such people, Sister Catherine gave no evidence of illness until she collapsed. Serving soup in the refectory one day, she suddenly set the soup tureen down on the table, and fell unconscious. The doctor was called, and he promptly scolded everyone; Sister Catherine was in an advanced stage of tuberculosis, and must have been suffering for months. The doctor prescribed a diet of eggs, meat, and other delicacies for her that she had never allowed herself. She was so distressed at the idea of eating these things that she asked the prioress to pray that she would get well, so there would be no need for dispensations. The prioress, who had great devotion to St. Dominic of Soriano, prayed for her cure. After a fervent retreat, and a request that everyone in the house pray for her, Sister Catherine of St. Martha died in 1664.

JOHN BAPTIST DE MORALES
(1597-1664)

Father John Baptist de Morales helped to lay the foundation of Christianity in the forbidden kingdom of China. He was born in Andalusia in 1597. When he was very young he had planned to be a Franciscan and a foreign missionary. However, he became a Dominican instead, and was sent on the missions while he was still a deacon. He was ordained a priest in Mexico, while his party of missioners was making the land lap of their journey to the Orient. Apparently it had been planned to have him work in Mexico, but one of the older priests of the Chinese band fell ill, and he was sent to replace him. Sometime near 1627, they arrived in Manila. Here he began learning the Chin-chea dialect of Chinese—a dialect so difficult that it was supposed to require a special grace from heaven to learn it. Having mastered it, he was assigned to a part of China where a different dialect altogether was spoken.

The province of the Holy Rosary in the Philippines had been organized for the evangelization of China. In fifty years of hard work they had not even been able to get a foothold in the forbidden land. They had no permanent buildings, no organized congregations; they had only a long history of hard work and suffering. In 1631, a party of priests went in with a diplomatic embassy, but barely escaped with their lives. Through his knowledge of science, the famous Jesuit, Father Matthew Ricci, penetrated the court circle, and he had a great following of learned men; but even he was not allowed to preach religion freely, nor to lay any foundations of Christianity in this pagan land. Throughout the years since Father Ricci's death, a few Jesuits and Franciscans and Dominicans had managed to get in and work for a time. When finally, in 1633, word was received in Manila that Father Angelo Cocchi had penetrated China and started a mission there, many volunteered for the dangerous post. Fathers John Baptist de Morales, Francis Diez, and Peter Chavez were chosen to go. They went with the intention of joining forces with the Jesuits and Franciscans.

They found an insurmountable difference of opinion almost immediately. The Jesuits had been allowing their converts to continue their customary rites of ancester worship, maintaining that this was a purely civil ceremony and did not prejudice their Christianity. The Dominicans insisted that these were religious rites and therefore superstitious. As the Holy See has since decided at different times in favor of both opinions, it is obvious that the question was debatable. But, in the pioneer years of the Chinese missions, it caused great embarrassment to have the few European Christians definitely divided on such an important point. It is a temptation, from this distance, to suppose that the two Orders were just carrying on a feud. But such a suspicion would be unjust. Men who are walking hourly in danger of violent death are not apt to quarrel over petty issues.

In the midst of all this, a persecution started. A pagan idol had been mutilated, and some Christians were accused of the crime. The situation was so combustible that only this was needed to turn the emperor against the missionaries. He first sent out an edict ordering all missionaries into exile. Fathers Morales and Diez were on the road in the mountains, and they did not hear the news. Ignorant of the persecution, they came into Fo-gan and were thrown into jail.

The next few months were confused, and we can see why. Writing from Macao, after they had been banished from China, Father Morales reported: "Since our arrest . . . until we arrived in Macao, we were twenty-one times dragged before the judges, whipped, scourged, locked up, kicked, trampled upon, and had our beards pulled out." They had spent uncounted weeks in jail, and each wearing a cangue, they were pelted with stones and refuse as they walked. Their stay at Macao, however, was business, not pleasure; they were on their way to Manila to report on the situation in China. Arriving in Manila, the provincial decided that it would be best if Father Morales went to

Rome and, once and for all, settled the vexing question of the Chinese rites. While he was in Europe, he also could gather up more missionaries. He returned to Macao to make the trip by way of Arabia and the trade routes, thus completing his trip around the globe.

An amusing incident that happened on this boat trip up the Tigris river has been recorded. One might think that being captured by Dutch pirates and spending several months on a refugee ship that was full of plague victims would have dimmed his enthusiasm for travel. However, he seemed to be thoroughly enjoying the boat trip on the river until Friday came along, and meat was served by the Arabian boatmen. Father Morales, who had an apostolic simplicity, said aloud, "Oh, if only we had a fish!" Instantly—to the terror of the Arabs—a large fish leaped out of the water and into the lap of the Dominican who had prayed for it. Gingerly, the Arabian cook prepared the "fish from heaven," and he regarded the priest as a miracle worker.

Two and a half years later, Father Morales reached Rome. In 1643, Pope Urban VIII took up the matter of the Chinese rites and laid it before the Propaganda for settlement. "You really should have let us know about this sooner," he chided the missionary. The theologians went to work on the question, and, after their discussions had been going on for nearly a year, Father Morales went to Spain to recruit missionaries. When the decision was finally reached, two years later, and the matter was settled in favor of the Dominicans, Father Morales had a party of thirty young Dominicans ready to return with him to China.

In 1646, he arrived in Mexico—the halfway point. He recruited more missionaries: three Franciscans and some Mexican Dominicans joined him, and, all the way across the Pacific, he drilled them in the Chinese language. When once more he reached Manila, at least six of his protégés were showing great promise in speaking it. But the trip had taken six and a half years, Fathers Francis de Capillas and Francis Diez had been martyred, and only one Dominican—Father John Garcia—was alive in China.

In spite of all obstacles, the missionary went to work with his customary energy. The besieged Christians were more than happy to see him, and they made heroic sacrifices to help him establish a church as a center for their work. One of the most willing helpers was a cheerful and hardworking lad by the name of Gregory Lo, who had been trying to get into the Dominican Order since his baptism some years before. He carried messages for the fathers, worked on the church with his own hands, and proved invaluable in many ways. One Christian sold himself into slavery, giving the money he was paid to Father Morales for the church. Certainly there was no lack of good will. In 1651, the Christians finally had the great joy of seeing their church of Teng-tu blessed, and the Dominican fathers settled in a little convent. Three months later, the pagans burned it to the ground. The Christians were saddened, but not discouraged, and they began work again with brick and mortar. Three years later, the church was finished again.

Amid all the trials, travels, and persecutions, it is hard to see how Father Morales had time for any writing. But, with the help of a brilliant young scholar, Bernard of Teng-tu, he translated the decrees regarding the Chinese rites into the language of the people, as well as several other documents that would be of interest to the new Christians. He himself wrote a *Dictionary and Grammar of Chinese* and a *Religious History of China* for the use of the missionaries, and he translated a biography of St. Dominic into Chinese for the edification of the natives. He promulgated devotion to St. Dominic, particularly under the recently popularized apparition of St. Dominic in Soriano. He encouraged the faithful Gregory Lo, and he had the great happiness of seeing him ordained in 1554—the first native of China to be raised to the priesthood. Father Morales was procurator of the missions, and, in this capacity, he distinguished himself with a lack of business ability that was truly phenomenal, but no one ever seemed to resent it.

Three years before his death in 1664, John Baptist de Morales was stricken with paralysis. After thirty-one years on the missions, risking his life daily, and probably having had no other expectation than that of martyrdom, he was compelled to lie helpless, seeing others go to their death, while he remained behind. These years were probably the hardest penance of all for the veteran missionary; they brought out a docility and sweetness of disposition in him that the busy years had never shown. As he lay dying, two missionaries came to bid him goodbye; they were his old friend Father John Garcia, and a young priest who had recently come from Spain. He roused himself to exhort them not to compromise on the question of the new Christians and the ancestor worship. Then he fell back and died.

DOMINIC CORONADO
(d. 1664)

We do not know if Dominic Coronado was related to the more famous bearer of his family name; it is quite likely he was. One of the phenomena of this curious age was the way in which priest and conqueror existed side by side in all the great families of Spain.

Dominic was born near Salamanca, and he was left an orphan early in his life. The uncle who had care of him sent him to the Dominicans at Salamanca, and here he received the Dominican habit as soon as he was old enough. In 1656, John Baptist de Morales came to Salamanca, begging for missionaries for the Far East. He went through the studium like a Pied Piper, and one of those who joyfully followed him off to the ends of the earth was young Dominic Coronado.

Arriving in Manila after two years of hard travel, Dominic was assigned to China. He and several other young missioners were destined for Cambodia, where many of the older priests had been martyred. The infusion of young blood could save the missions there, and Dominic and his companions were eager to get into the battle. But they could not penetrate the land where foreigners were banned. After a number of futile attempts, he returned with Father Gregory Lopez to Manila, and was re-assigned to Amoy.

They arrived in Amoy in 1635, utterly destitute, for their ship was wrecked, and they were brought into port by strangers. Five Dominicans made their way from Amoy to Fukien, where they took up temporary residence with a Christian family and tried to organize their campaign. Lacking even the most elementary mission supplies, and surrounded by enemies, it was not an easy task.

Nevertheless, for nearly thirty years they did a remarkable piece of mission work. People of the region, without a priest for years, were glad to see them and work with them. The Dominicans built a church, trained catechumens, baptized converted pagans, and prepared for the wrath to come. In 1664, the persecution opened with war. A Jesuit missionary, Father Ricci, had disappeared, and it was feared that he had been killed. Dominic Coronado offered to go look for him, and, after a long search in hostile country, found him safe but starving. He was with Gregory Lo, the Dominican, and another Jesuit. They escaped to another province where they carried on their work for a little while. Dominic wrote to the superiors in Manila that "twenty preachers would not be enough for the job I have here." At this juncture there was a shift in the government, and the persecution started afresh. Dominic Coronado was taken prisoner, and he was led in chains to Peking. There he was thrown into prison with a group of Jesuits and Franciscans.

After a long imprisonment and an agony of doubt, Dominic was brought to judgment, chained between a Franciscan and a Jesuit. Then, unexpectedly, the three were set free and told not to leave the city. We of the twentieth century have read what it means to be under "house arrest"; it could not have been any more pleasant three centuries ago. The priests, sick and miserable from their prison experience, were spied upon and harried and denied food, and called out at odd hours of the night for stupid questionings. When it became obvious that the Dominican was going to die, the Jesuits carried him to what they thought would be a more comfortable spot, and they bribed some of the Chinese petty crooks to get him food.

At some time in 1664, Dominic Coronado died in his temporary infirmary in a pagan temple, where he had been fed by stray pick-pockets and thieves. When death came, he was surrounded by sorrowing Jesuits who claimed that he was a genuine martyr for the faith. The surviving Jesuit wrote a letter to the Dominicans in Manila, stating the facts of the imprisonment, and the provincial chapter of 1671 commended his memory.

JOHN OF CONCA
(1613-1666)

John of Conca was one of the most interesting missionaries of the seventeenth century who worked in the Philippines. His name will always be identified with the devotion to the Rosary, particularly with the naval victory of "La Naval," the Philippine Lepanto.

John was born in the city of Los Angeles, in Mexico, in 1613, of a Spanish father and an Indian mother. His father was wealthy and pious, and a special devotion to St. Dominic prompted him to have a chapel in his own home dedicated to the saint; he also was a member of the Rosary Confraternity. A man of great charity, he was closely connected with the Dominican fathers in their apostolic work. It is not surprising, then, that his son should enter the Dominican novitiate, in Pueblo, at the age of fifteen.

When John was half-way through his novitiate, an event occurred which might well have disturbed his vocation. The provincial arrived for a visitation, and, shocked at the idea that the community was accepting novices of mixed parentage, he made the arbitrary condition that all such novices should start their novitiate over again. Four novices went home, but John remained. He made his solemn profession in 1611. He rapidly gained popularity as a teacher and preacher.

Shortly after his ordination, a band of Spanish missionaries passed through Mexico with Father John Baptist de Morales on the way to the Orient. Some of the Spanish novices and preachers had been badly battered in crossing the Atlantic, and they lacked the courage to face another ocean. John, who volunteered to replace someone, set out by ship soon afterward.

The ship ran into several bad storms. Sixty-four people on board were very ill with plague, and some of them died. They were all very glad to see Manila. John was not too happy to stay there, however, when he was appointed novice-master, for this office forced him to remain in the city instead of going on the missions.

Eventually, a call came from China for missionaries. John volunteered, and, after spending some time in the Chinese colony of Manila trying to learn the language, he ran up against an embarrassing fact: he simply could *not* learn Chinese. With the thought that perhaps he could learn it on the missions, he was sent to China. On arriving at his post, he was happy to hear that the natives there spoke a different dialect. But, after a period of trial, he discovered that he could not learn that one either. There was nothing for him to do but return to Manila.

Crossing the China Sea, the boat ran into a storm and sank. For several days John floated about on a plank, paralyzed with cold and nearly dead from exposure. He called on Our Lady of the Sea for help, and he was finally washed up on shore. While at the homely task of drying his clothes, he was captured by unfriendly natives. After several perilous days, they took him to the Augustinians, who had a mission on another island.

Shortly after this, John appeared as chaplain on one of the ships which the Philippine people devoutly call "the galleons of the miracle." These were two old commercial vessels that had been hastily fitted out to defend the Philippines, when five Dutch warships had appeared in their waters in 1648, and had menaced both freedom and religion. Humanly speaking, there was no reason at all to hope for victory when the two battered old galleons faced the Dutch guns. Yet, in several months, under circumstances that would have hindered even a well-appointed battleship, the creaking old ships put the Dutch to flight five different times. They had a secret weapon which the Dutch despised—the Rosary was said aboard each ship, and the men had promised to make a barefoot pilgrimage to the church of St. Dominic, in Manila, if victory were theirs. We do not know which of the two galleons, "The Rosary," or "The Incarnation," was John's ship, but tradition says that he sailed on one of them during the five engagements.

There is a brief and rather terrifying episode at this time in which John was pitted against the devil, who presided over some of the native rites on the less Christianized islands. The implication is that John had worn himself out fighting these dreadful battles with the devil and that at last he asked to go home to Mexico. He returned to Acapulco only to find that devotion to the Rosary had declined. Since it was in need of revival, John had a job cut out for him. He organized a Perpetual Rosary Society and set up a beautiful statue of Our Lady of the Rosary.

Shortly after this, he was made provincial, but his life was almost finished. After a long venturesome life, he died of fever, in 1666.

AGNES OF THE HOLY GHOST
(1612-1668)

The process of canonization of Agnes was introduced some years ago, and it is still alive. Agnes was born on January the twentieth, 1612, in Valencia. Her family was illustrious, and had long been known for its piety and for benefactions to the Church. She and her older brother and sister were piously brought up, and they were practicing prayer and penance at an early age. When Agnes was eight years old, her parents died, leaving the children orphans.

The brother was sent to a school where he met the Trinitarians, and he soon became one of them. Agnes and her sister lived with a pious aunt, and she sent them to live as boarders in the Dominican Monastery of St. Mary Magdalen. Here they were allowed to wear the habit, and eventually they entered the community.

Agnes made her solemn profession in 1629. Known as a model of observance, she lived happily with the community there for ten years. At the end of this time, she felt moved by an interior voice to found a community of stricter observance. She called upon a holy priest of Valencia to assist her, and he chose a site for her called Villareale, outside of Valencia. With his help, the Monastery of the Blessed Sacrament was built here. After a great many difficulties, Sister Agnes moved in with her sister, Angela, and several others, in 1639. The sisters wished to make her prioress, but she managed to avoid this by taking on the office of novice mistress. In this position she was well able to deal with the spiritual lives of those she was training. Gradually, the Monastery of the Blessed Sacrament became a model Dominican monastery—a standard by which others could judge themselves.

After fifteen years in this work, Mother Agnes felt called to establish another monastery. This time she found great opposition from both clergy and city officials. Nevertheless, she laid the foundation and moved to the monastery, leaving her sister in Villareale. Agnes was prioress of the monastery for ten years, and her wisdom, justice, and holiness were a guide to sanctity for all her sisters.

At an age when one might think that she would be glad to retire from active work, Mother Agnes had a vision in which she was called to return to Valencia "to suffer." The sisters in Valencia were glad to have her back, but they were surprised to hear that she was planning another foundation. It took her three years to found the Monastery of Our Lady of Bethlehem and firmly establish the complete religious life there.

Mother Agnes' life was purified by twenty-five years of physical suffering, either endured or ignored; she had granted herself no dispensations on account of these. She had founded three monasteries of perfect observance, battling against the inevitable red tape and civil indifference—and sometimes the opposition of the sisters and the clergy. It was a type of work that could give one little personal satisfaction, but a wealth of opportunities for humiliation and sufferings. She died in 1668.

The difficulties in the way of the beatification of Mother Agnes of the Holy Ghost are not insuperable. We should pray that they may be overcome.

MOTHER MARY VILLANI
(1583-1670)

Prioresses who feel that they have an unnecessary amount of this world's troubles should consider the life of Mother Mary Villani. She was prioress for fifty-four years, and, during that time, she was in a condition of partial deafness, complete blindness, and a paralysis which bound her to her bed.

Beatrice Villani was born near Naples in 1583, of a noble and wealthy family. When she was three years old her mother died, and she was sent to the convent of the Franciscans for her education. Rapidly developing a taste for spiritual things, she was seriously looking for a hair-shirt when she was five years old. She already slept on boards, fasted most of the time, and wore rocks in her shoes. It may have been these austerities which brought about the serious illness which attacked her at the age of six. She hovered near death for several days, and one day she was gladdened by the sight of her own mother, in company with the Blessed Virgin and St. Catherine Martyr. They cured the child and encouraged her in her way of life.

It is a little terrifying for ordinary mortals to consider the rule of life set up by this unusual child. At the age of nine, she was a veteran at using the standard equipment of asceticism—fastings, vigils, disciplines. She kept perpetual silence and meditated on the Passion most of the time. Full of charity for her neighbors, she took in sewing in order that she would have more to give the poor than even her father's generous alms allowed. She was the dispenser of these goods. During the plague and famine which struck the city, she became the guardian angel of the unfortunate.

After the plague was over, her father took her to Naples for a round of fun that he hoped would distract her from the sights of horror which had been so common during the plague. In Naples, she had many cousins near her own age, and most of them were frivolous and worldly enough to distract anyone. They were *too* frivolous for Beatrice. She entered a Dominican monastery there, and her father could not stop her. She took the name Sister Mary of Divine Love.

Here Beatrice set about practicing her usual austerities in what she thought would be better surroundings. She discovered to her sorrow, however, that the plague had damaged regular life here, as it was to do in so many convents. No one was eager to follow in her extreme rigours, and they looked askance as she divided the year into seven Lents, each with its own penitential practices. They were probably not bad religious, but they felt that one Lent in the year was quite enough. Sister Mary rapidly became unpopular. The confessor obliged her to moderate her penances, but he did not object when she told him that in a vision our Lord had told her to found a new monastery. The sisters made it difficult for her, however; it took her some time to obtain the necessary land, the permissions, and to find some companions.

At last she and her sisters were settled in a small, poor house on the outskirts of Naples. Sister Mary had changed her status from choir sister to that of laysister, but this did not prevent the sisters from electing her prioress.

The office of prioress was the one austerity, evidently, that Sister Mary was not prepared to endure. She begged the sisters to change their minds, and they gave her no satisfaction. The next time our Lord appeared to her, she frantically begged Him to let her die, but not to make her prioress. What our Lord answered was not recorded, but Sister Mary received her answer: she was stricken with an almost complete paralysis. Now she not only had to govern the house, but she had to do it from flat on her back, which is an inconvenient position. Nevertheless, she did as God apparently wanted her to do, and she did it for more than half a century.

Mother Mary Villani died in 1670, at the age of eighty-seven, leaving a reputation for sanctity both among her own sisters and among the people of the town. The troubled and the tempted came to her for counsel; priests and bishops asked for her prayers. She instituted a circle of spiritual discussion called the "Oratory of Divine Love," which guided the spiritual lives of dozens of people. At one time, she directed the drawing up of plans for a monastery; these plans were later submitted to the critical inspection of the finest architects in Naples, and they were considered perfect. She read the secrets of the heart, and she had the gift of prophecy. Her little cell was never lonely, for, besides the troubled folk of earth, it often harbored the citizens of heaven.

Mother Mary Villani is listed among the stigmatists of the Order.

DOMINIC OF ST. THOMAS
(1641-1676)

One of the most intriguing characters in all Dominican history is a simple friar whose religious name was Dominic of St. Thomas. He was born Prince Ottoman, heir to the empire of his father, Ibrahim. Had circumstances decreed otherwise, he might have been on the Ottoman throne at a time when all Christians feared the very name of his people.

Prince Ottoman was born in the harem of the Sultan Ibrahim in 1641. Although he was the eldest son, and heir to a vast empire, his mother—Zaphira—and his father's mother made early plans for smuggling the baby out of the country in order to protect him from the cruelty of Ibrahim. They sailed for Rhodes in a ship manned by sympathetic servants, but they were soon attacked by a fleet of Maltese vessels. These vessels belonged to the Knights of St. John of Jerusalem. The Turkish vessel was not well armed, and soon it fell to the knights, who took the passengers aboard and sank the ship. When they reached Malta, Zaphira died, leaving the baby to the care of his grandmother and the servants. Although they did not know who he was, the knights realized that the child was a person of consequence. When the emissaries of the sultan of Tunis arrived with ransom for the young prince, the knights discovered his identity. They refused the ransom money, but they allowed some of his servants to go free.

Soon after this, Ibrahim was killed by his own people, and the throne was vacant. Since the knights refused to release their prisoner, the throne descended to the second son. The young prince was left in the care of his Turkish tutors until he was thirteen years old. Then the grand master of the knights decided to put the boy in a school. He was placed in the care of the Dominican fathers in Malta. The priests found that the boy was endowed with a brilliant mind and fine qualities of character, but he was a confirmed Mohammedan, and he had no intention of deserting the faith of his people.

The young prince was in reality a fanatical zealot in his own faith; he made up his mind that he would die before he would accept the teaching of the Christian fathers. However, after two years of working with them every day, he changed his mind, finally deciding to take the great step that would separate him forever from the throne. He was baptized at the Rosary altar of the Dominican church in Malta, in 1656, in the presence of all the dignitaries of the Knights of St. John.

Two years later, the young man entered the Dominican novitiate. He was given the name Brother Dominic. Much as he would have preferred to be left to a quiet course of studies, his affairs were the concern of the grand master of the knights, the master general of the Order, and of all the high-ranking churchmen of the vicinity. After much discussion, he was sent to Naples for his studies, at the special request of the pope. Brother Dominic, who had hoped to go to Salamanca, where he would be out of reach of court ceremonies, went obediently to Naples—stopping only for a devotional visit at the Church of St. Dominic in Soriano. In two years he was called to Rome and assigned to the convent of the Minerva.

War between France and Turkey was imminent at this time. A delegation of papal officials journeyed to Paris; they wished to take the young prince with them to discuss international policies. Making a desperate effort to retain his identity as a simple Dominican friar, Brother Dominic begged to be allowed to travel in company with the other Dominicans instead of with the legate. Most of his caution went for nothing; in Florence, he was hailed with tremendous pomp as a reigning prince. In Venice, the Doge promptly blamed him for the war. In Turin, the archbishop displayed the holy shroud for his benefit, explaining that this was done only for reigning monarchs. In Paris, the jewelled carriages of the king came out to meet the tired friars, and—as a last touch of irony—the Turkish ambassador reprimanded Brother Dominic for appearing at a state function in such poor clothing.

For several years the young Dominican strained every effort to stay out of state business and attend to the affairs of his soul. He was not ordained, and, when the question of his ordination came up, there was a long delay; a diplomat with an original turn of mind was trying to convince the pope that it would be to the advantage of Christendom to send Prince Ottoman to claim his rightful throne. It was not too practical a plan, but it held up his ordination for some time. During his stay in Paris, a group of Armenian merchants, whose ships had been captured by the English, begged him to seek restitution for them. He wrote to the king of England and managed to arrange the affair. It was also during this time that the Greeks sent a delegation, begging him to take the throne.

Pope Clement IX arranged for him to sail with the papal fleet that was being assembled to fight against the Turks. Brother Dominic, at the pope's request, wrote to the Christians of the Pelopponesus and Albania, suggesting that they revolt against the Turks. Their answer was not consoling; they agreed to do so on the condition that he would lead them. Brother Dominic, whose only hope at the moment was to arrange a negotiated peace, sailed with the fleet, praying—quite probably—that its objective would soon be accomplished, so that he could return to the cloister and prepare for ordination.

Understandable confusion reigned among the Turkish ranks when it was known that the eldest son of Ibrahim—their hereditary ruler—was on the papal ship. Peace was eventually arranged, and the papal fleet sailed for home. Stormbound on the coast of Dalmatia, they found that the people of that country were suffering intensely the aftermath of an earthquake. The entire coast had been shattered and burned. Brother Dominic, taking the pension which had been forced on him by the grand master, gave it to the refugees, and he solicited all the other help he could for the unfortunate people.

On his return to Malta, the young prince was ordained, and he looked forward to the only glory he had ever sought—preaching the Gospel of Christ. He was assigned to the missions of Armenia, but, before he could depart for his new field of labors, the plague struck Malta. The Dominicans from the convent at Valetta went out among the plague-stricken and did what they could.

Brother Dominic, after weeks of heroic work in this difficult apostolate, came down with the plague, and he died in a day's time, in the year 1676. He was thirty-five years old. Informed of his death, the captains of the Turkish galleys ordered a salute from the guns in his honor. The fortress guns replied with a reverent salute, marking the passing of a Turkish prince.

JEANNE OF ST. MARTHA
(1590-1678)

Any Dominican who spends forty years in the community kitchen is entitled to the gratitude of the rest of the Dominican household. In such a prosaic setting, Sister Jeanne of St. Martha, a laysister, sought the perfection of charity.

Jeanne was born in Toulouse in 1590. Since her mother was a widow with a large family, Jeanne learned to work when she was a child. She also displayed great gifts of prayer at an early age, and, when still quite young, she had a chance to prove her fidelity to her religion. A wealthy uncle offered to take her and give her an education, but the uncle was a heretic, and the little girl would not go with him. She preferred to live in poverty and be allowed to pray when she wished.

As soon as she was old enough, Jeanne went out to work. She was fortunate in her choice of employers, for they were exemplary Catholics who were very kind to her. The family had close connections with the Dominicans of Toulouse. Since Jeanne was the governess of the children, she encouraged them in friendship with the Dominicans. When the eldest daughter was old enough, she entered the monastery of the Second Order in Toulouse, and she gave a large share of the credit for her vocation to the piety and kindness of her governess.

When Jeanne had made some provision for her mother, she applied for admittance as a laysister in the monastery of Toulouse, and she was received. The life of silence, mortification, and prayer was exactly what she had always wanted, and her early years had well prepared her for it. She was so exactly the model of a good religious that the prioress took her to Paris to help her establish a new foundation. Jeanne remained in Paris, happy and devout, the rest of her life.

Jeanne of St. Martha did not have time to write about her thoughts and her interior lights; cooks seldom do. It was known that she suffered for years from sciatica, which had the effect of making her patient with others who suffered; and her suffering intensified her devotion to the mysteries of the Passion, particularly the scourging of Christ. Sometimes, when she was at prayer, our Lord appeared to her, carrying His cross; but, being very humble, she presumed that other people, too, had visions, so she did not talk about hers until she was closely questioned by the prioress. The vision of the Crucified always remained very clear to her, and, as a consequence, she was never bored with the routine of her work.

When she was too old and infirm to bear the burden any longer, Jeanne of St. Martha graduated from the kitchen to the chapel, spending her last year in peaceful communion with the Lord she had served all her life. She died around 1678.

GEORGETTE VERRIER
(d. 1681)

Georgette Verrier's life is a testimony of the triumph of spirit over circumstances. Georgette was born in the Faubourg St. Germain, one of the poorest and most densely-populated sections of Paris. She must have been what modern psychologists call "accident prone"; things always happened to her. At the age of two, she was hit in the head, and, as a result, she suffered all her life from headaches. Her home was a bedlam of quarreling and misery. Her mother, who was a widow, thought that she would improve her situation by marrying a second time. The second husband, however, was a brute who beat the children, and he was especially cruel to Georgette. He finally drove her out of the house when she was eleven. She went to work in order to live away from home until he died.

One would think that Georgette had seen enough of an unhappy marriage to make her realize the need of serious thought before marrying. However, she married when she was very young, and she soon discovered that her husband was no better than her stepfather. She tried to reform him, and, although her efforts were futile, at least she learned to pray. Out of her misery she emerged as a woman of unwavering faith and prayer. Her efforts in her husband's behalf were of little help. He drank until it was impossible for him to hold a job, he beat her because he had no job, and then he worried himself insane because of the state he was in. He was finally jailed, and perhaps she should have left him in prison, but she worked until he was released. He promptly repaid her by beating her until she almost died. She endured this sort of thing for twenty years, and, finally, on the advice of her confessor, she obtained a separation and left the man to take care of himself.

She went to work as a governess and took up residence near the convent of the Third Order sisters. The sisters soon became interested in her. She ran errands for them, and she spent all of her spare time praying in their chapel. They recognized that she had reached a high degree of prayer, and they probably would have received her into the community if they could. Since that was not practical, they encouraged her to become a secular Tertiary, and she did, with great joy. Apparently she was allowed to live in some part of the convent that was reserved for externs, and here she spent the rest of her life.

The life of this pious Tertiary in the convent of St. Catherine of Siena is not unique; the devoted service to the sisters, the readiness to go on any sort of errand, the kindness to the poor and the afflicted—these are typical of such good people. But Georgette was possessed of great gifts of contemplation, and her spirit of penance was so extreme that her confessor felt obliged to make her modify her austerities. She got up at midnight for Matins of Our Lady. She kept perfect silence and always attended all the Masses. One might think she had suffered enough, but for ten years she fought with terrible temptations against faith, and she experienced a prolonged spiritual dryness. This spiritual trouble corresponded with a physical illness which gradually grew worse; the last three years of her life were an extreme of agony. This did not in any way curtail her penances, however. She continued those as long as she could move.

Georgette Verrier died in 1681. She was buried in the church in which she had spent so many hours during her last years. At the time of her death, people began reporting that she had cured their ills—migraine headaches, infected wounds—all the various maladies that afflicted the poor of the Faubourg St. Germain. The sisters and the poor, who knew her best, maintained that she was a saint, but no definite attempt has ever been made to propose her cause for beatification.

GREGORY LO
(d. 1687)

Gregory Lo was the first native of China to be raised to the priesthood. He further distinguished the Order in being the first Chinese bishop.

Gregory Lo was born of pagan parents, in Fukien, and he was converted by the Franciscan, Father Anthony of St. Mary. He worked as a catechist with the Franciscans, and he traveled with them when they were forced out of China. They went to the Philippines when it became obvious that China was closed to missionaries for a time, and Gregory enrolled at the Dominican University of Santo Tomas for courses in Latin and Spanish.

After his conversion, apparently there was no time at which Gregory Lo did not plan to be a priest. There were several reasons, however, why his plans were impractical. At that time, no native of China had been allowed to go on for Holy Orders, although the missionaries were persistent in urging Rome to consider the need of a native clergy. A greater difficulty, however, was the fact that Gregory simply was not a student. He was diligent, good, resourceful, and loyal, but the studies required for the priesthood—especially under these circumstances—seemed more than Gregory could cope with. He won his prize the hard way—by a long, devoted, and prayerful service to the missionaries. His first job was to take the mission funds into China to Father John Garcia, who was in hiding somewhere among the pagan millions. This needle-in-a-haystack assignment only whetted his appetite for more, and he attached himself to the missionaries in Fukien.

Many years later, Father John Baptist de Morales was to write that the pioneer work in China might easily have been delayed many years if it had not been for Gregory Lo. Cheerful and resourceful, if he were sent on any errand, he could be relied on to return safely; a European could not. He was an excellent catechist, and his flair for organization soon had the scattered mission posts in order. He gathered alms for the building of the church of Teng-tu, carried wood and stones, mixed cement, and led the new Christians in their prayers. Finally, the Dominicans unanimously voted that the only thing to do with Gregory was receive him into the Order. On the strong recommendation of Father John Garcia, he was presented at the Dominican house in Manila. There, at the age of thirty, he was given the Dominican habit and began his studies for the priesthood.

He had a hard time with theology, but he finally managed to pass his examinations. China was desperate, and, immediately after his ordination, in 1654, he was sent back. The priests there were in hiding in Canton, unable even to go out to give the sacraments to the hard-pressed Christians. Into the tense situation stepped the new apostle—the same cheerful, practical Gregory as before, but now enabled to offer Mass and administer the sacraments to his suffering people. The good he did is incalculable.

Father Dominic Navarrete, a future martyr, wrote of him: "In thirteen months, Lo went through ten provinces of China, strengthening the faith. In the midst of bitter persecution, he baptized 2500 people and made converts everywhere he went." We must recall this work was done at a time when baptism was practically a death sentence. In the year 1666, he converted more than a hundred adult Chinese in Fukien, and he baptized 566 on one of the islands off the coast. When Father John Baptist de Morales was dying, he took time to record that Father Lo had great power over the devils, and that he had cured many possessed people. It was inevitable that reports of his work would reach Rome. In 1675, the vicars of Cochin-China and Tonkin wrote to Pope Clement X, requesting some dignity for Father Lo as an encouragement to the persecuted Church of China. After some deliberation in Rome on the unprecedented question of a Chinese bishop, the pope sent letters to Father Lo, appointing him vicar-apostolic of six provinces and bishop of Basileus.

Father Lo was panic-stricken. All on earth he wanted to do was work as a priest among his people. The very thought of official dignity appalled him. He somehow managed to decline the honor, escaping into a part of China where even the stoutest heart could not follow him. It was five years before the papal letters caught up with him again, and this time he could not avoid the honor. His provincial, on advice from the master general, had put him under obedience to accept; the provincial also appointed a skilled theologian as the companion of the new bishop.

Busy as a pastor of souls to his last day, Gregory Lo died in Nankin, in 1687, after a lifetime of incredible hardships he had undertaken in the name of Christ.

LOUISE MARIE OF ST. CATHERINE
(1680-1687)

It would seem that the Dominican Order does not have a place for children. With the exception of some of the Japanese martyrs who died with their parents, and, of course, Blessed Imelda, our members tend to be older people. It was not the fault of Louise Marie of St. Catherine that she never made profession to the Order. She tried hard enough. But, unfortunately, she died at the age of seven.

Louise Marie was a child of prayer. She was frail from her birth. Her mother had made a pilgrimage to the shrine of Our Lady of Virtues in Aubervilliers, begging for a child, and she promised that, in honor of the Blessed Virgin, she would dress the child in white until its first Communion. Louise Marie, the answer to these prayers, was accordingly dressed in honor of Our Lady from babyhood, and she grew up in a truly Christian atmosphere. Like many children who are marked for an early death, she displayed amazing signs of piety at an early age. When she was two years old she broke her arm. She made no protest at all during the painful process of setting the bone. At the age of three and one-half years, she made her first confession.

Like many children she loved to go to church to "see Jesus." She carried a crucifix around in her apron pocket and made little altars and cribs in her play. Like St. Catherine, of whom she heard very early, she liked to say a Hail Mary on each step of the stairs. When she was four years old, someone wanted her to be godmother at a baptism. On examination, the priest decided she knew as much about her responsibility as she needed to know, and he let her be the godmother.

When Louise Marie was five years old, her mother went to the convent of the Third Order Dominicans to make a retreat. The sisters took a great fancy to the little girl, and one of them made her a religious habit. This she wore all the time her mother was at the convent, and no one could take it away from her when it was time to go home. The mother begged them to let her have the habit, because she was a delicate child. They told Louise Marie that she could come back and wear it in the convent some day, but this did not quite satisfy her.

On returning home, it developed that the little girl was very sick. She quite probably had tuberculosis. We do not know how, but she managed to talk the Dominican fathers into giving her the Tertiary habit. She was dying, and perhaps they thought that this circumstance would supply for the necessary age. At any rate, on the feast of St. Catherine of Siena, in 1687, the little girl received the habit, and she took upon herself prayers and penances that were far beyond her years.

There was very little to be done about her disease, and some of the treatments seemed cruel. Burning with thirst, she was not allowed to drink anything. She offered this suffering in memory of the Passion. She promised Our Lady never to take food or medicine without saying a Hail Mary first.

Louise Marie died after a long suffering, and she was buried in the chapel of the Second Order Sisters at St. Honoré, in Paris. She has long been venerated as a holy child. among those who remember her story.

JOHN FRANCIS DE GARCEVAL
(1643-1692)

The way of life that is represented by John Francis de Garceval has almost vanished from the earth. He is included among our Dominican personalities because this way shows one more facet of the many-sided Third Order.

John Francis de Garceval was born of a noble family in Languedoc in 1643. His family was noted for its long history of fighting heretics, and probably it had been closely connected with the Order for centuries. John was a spoiled son in a wealthy house, and he denied himself no pleasure that youth and wealth could provide. At twenty, he was engaged to a pious young lady of the nobility. She apparently was candid and firm with him about his careless life, for he made a general confession at the time of his marriage, and he promised to settle down. His young wife was a Dominican Tertiary, and, while he would not go quite that far in his reform, he did make a serious effort to live a Christian life.

Gradually, the influence of his wife won him over to a complete reversal of his former worldliness. He attended daily Mass in the private chapel of the house, said the Office, conducted family prayers night and morning, and forbade any gambling or carnival buffoonery on his estate. He saw to it, moreover, that the servants were instructed in their religion and that they attended prayers.

More than this, he became the benevolent patriarch of the huge establishment under his care. His large family, a staff of servants, and a floating population of widows and orphans who took advantage of his hospitality, all shared in his interest. The poor flocked to his door for alms, and his home was an asylum for the troubled and the afflicted. From time to time, in order to maintain a high spiritual tone on the estate, he called in missionary preachers to speak to his vast household.

John eventually made his profession in the Third Order of St. Dominic, and after that he intensified his spiritual practices. He gave up hunting, horse-back riding, and visiting that was of a merely social nature. He fasted almost continually, wore an iron chain around his waist, and took the discipline daily. Now it was the pious wife's duty to see that he ate enough to keep himself alive, for, left to himself, he would live on bread and water. He got up at midnight to recite Matins, and he added two hours of mental prayer to an already full day. He went to confession and Communion much more frequently than the custom of the times decreed.

As might be expected, he had a great devotion to St. Mary Magdalen, and near the end of his life made a pilgrimage to her shrine in southern France. His other great devotion was the Rosary, which he said faithfully and often had preached among his people.

John Francis de Garceval had made plans to enter a Trappist monastery when he fell ill of a fever and died. He was forty-nine.

MARIE DE COMBE
(1656-1692)

Marie was born in Leiden, Holland, in 1656. She was one of six children, all of whom were carefully brought up in Calvinism. Though reared in the bosom of heresy, Marie had an instinct for Catholicity, and, as a young girl, she met a priest who was in hiding in Leiden and began to take instructions in the Catholic religion. Her parents made no objections when she spent her time in charitable works among the poor, nor even when she made herself a little oratory in one of the rooms of the family home. But when they discovered that she was on the verge of being baptized a Catholic, they turned on her and began a real persecution. She was given no peace and no chance to see the priest, and, finally, to get a little rest, she went to England to stay with friends.

England in 1672 was not much better than Holland for the practice of Catholicity. Marie was happy with her friends there, but she drifted away from the Catholic practices which were hard to observe in such a situation. At the age of nineteen, she was recalled to Holland to be married to Adrian de Combé, who was a friend of her father's. He was a violent man, and he gave his young wife a hard life. After a year and a half, Marie left him and went home. He died shortly after this, and negotiations were begun for a second marriage. Marie fled to France, where she had a sister and brother-in-law who were not Catholic, but who—at least she hoped—would let her alone in her practices of religion.

Here the battle for Marie's soul began in earnest. She was pretty and popular, and fond of worldly company; but the still small voice of conscience would not let her alone. Friends suggested that she should become a Lutheran; there was her own Calvinist background, and—always—there was the steady pull of Catholic teaching and the need for certainty. One day she was in her room praying desperately: "Lead me. You are my God—tell me which way to go—without you I cannot choose!" Exhausted, she feel asleep. She awoke to hear the tinkle of a bell in the street below. Looking down, she saw a priest on his way to a sick call. Pulling herself to her knees, she recognized the Real Presence, and she also realized that she could no longer delay her baptism. She went immediately to look for a priest to whom she could make her profession of faith.

Her family began a fresh persecution. Relatives threatened to have her disinherited, would not let her alone to pray, heckled her with petty annoyances. At last she fell violently sick, and it was thought that she had been poisoned. A priest from St. Sulpice, Father de la Barmondiere, came to receive her into the Church on her deathbed. When she recovered instead of dying, he made arrangements for her to leave her sister's home and take up residence with a community of virtuous girls who lived a sort of semi-religious life in the parish of St. Sulpice.

Marie entered into her new life with the exuberant enthusiasm of many new converts. She made a retreat under a Capuchin father, and, on returning home, she designed a habit for herself. Made of rough burlap, it had a capuce like that of the retreat master. It bothered her not in the least that people laughed at her, but Father de la Barmondiere advised her to modify her dress to something less singular. He allowed her to spend her time in solitude and prayer in a little hut outside the house where she lived, and he authorized the instruments of penance she made for herself, and her regime of prayer and works of charity. Her influence began to reach others with whom she associated casually. One of these was a bitter, old woman who spoke a language Marie could not understand. In a mixture of French and Dutch, she chatted with the woman, and, though they rarely understood each other's words, Marie induced the woman to return to the sacraments. One day, as she was hurrying to Mass, an old woman stopped her in the street and told her that she had seen Marie in a dream the night before. She had seen our Lord, she said, building a new world in which justice would dwell, and Marie was in charge of a group of penitent women. She told Marie various curious details about the work that she would accomplish in rescuing homeless girls who were in danger of sin. Marie told her confessor about the dream, and he suggested that she read the life of St. Catherine of Siena and pray to her for help. Some months later, he sent her the first of the hundreds of girls that she was to shelter.

Marie poured all her energy into the new work. She had no money and few friends, but she shortly remedied at least one of these needs when she met a priest who was a Third Order Dominican. He promptly had her received into the Third Order, and someone gave her money to rent a house in which she could begin her refuge. It is a strange thing that in 1688, a century before St. Euphrasia Pelletier, Marie was wearing a white habit and managing a refuge for delinquent girls which she called "The House of the Good Shepherd."

There was never any money, and one wonders how the work kept going. When the household was on the point of being evicted, someone always came along with just enough money to pay the rent, or to buy a day's meals. Marie refused a number of endowed houses, because she insisted that "God feeds the birds, and He would not like it if I did not trust Him as much." The archbishop sent her money several times, and the king bought her a house. There were many suspicious people who told lies about her, but the archbishop, realizing what her work meant to the city, stoutly defended her. He gave her permission to have the Blessed Sacrament reserved in her house, which was one more step in the direction of her house becoming a convent.

Regrettably, most of the foundations made before the eighteenth century in France were swept away with the Revolution, and some left no records. The account of Marie's work mentions that there were "Sisters, Penitents, and girls" in her household, and that the sisters appointed the youngest of themselves to succeed Marie as superior when she was dying. We do not know just how these sisters were organized, but, apparently, Marie and the sisters wore the Dominican habit of the Third Order; possibly the penitents did also.

After two years of intense suffering, Marie died in 1692, at the age of thirty-six. As she was dying, she said to her weeping companions: "The Good Shepherd has carried me from Holland on His shoulders, and now He will carry me to Heaven." Her old friend, Father de la Barmondiere, gave her the last sacraments, and she died peacefully, surrounded by those she had helped.

THOMAS CARDINAL HOWARD
(1629-1694)

One of the most famous men of the troubled seventeenth century in England was Philip Thomas Howard, "the English Cardinal." It is a pity that later centuries have all but forgotten him, or do not honor the memory of this man who was, among other things, the founder of the English College in Rome.

Philip Howard was born in 1629, at Arundel House. Both his family name and the name of the house should strike receptive chords in anyone who reads English history. He was one of twelve children—the third of nine sons. His grandfather, Thomas, earl of Arundel, and the possessor of several other illustrious titles, took a patriarchal interest in the education of his son's family. He himself was a member of the Church of England (probably for the sake of policy), but he made no objections when the children were brought up in the care of Catholic tutors and in adulthood became members of the ancient faith that he had given up. Philip was his favorite of all the children.

Because of the disturbed state of England, the Howard family moved to the Continent, and it was in Holland that Philip first felt that he was called to the life of a religious. He made an attempt to enter the Carmelite Order, but he was prevented by his family, on the plea that he was too young. Partly to distract him, the earl of Arundel took Philip and several of his brothers on a trip to Italy. In Milan, Philip met the Dominicans, and the struggle began in earnest.

With the exception of his namesake, St. Thomas Aquinas, there is possibly no one who made a more desperate effort to receive—and keep—the Dominican habit than Philip Howard. He took the name Thomas on his reception in Cremona in 1645, when he was sixteen years old. To say that his grandfather opposed him with all the weapons of wealth and influence is to badly understate a program of determined persecution. The grandfather had been a benefactor to many Catholic causes, and the name of the earl of Arundel was powerful enough to bring tremendous pressure on officials of Church and State. Priors, archbishops, cardinals, and, at last, the pope himself were requested to oppose Philip's vocation. One by one, they engaged the young novice in conversation, determined to put an end to the disturbance. One by one, they reached the same conclusion: Philip Thomas Howard, scion of England's noblest house, and heir to a vast fortune, had chosen the better part. They did not, after talking with him, have the slightest doubts that he had a genuine religious vocation. It was not pleasant explaining this to the earl of Arundel. After the pope himself had pledged his faith in the vocation of the young man, the defeated earl went back to England, leaving his obstinate grandson happily pursuing the course of studies in Naples, where—300 years before—another young man named Thomas had fought and won the same battle to follow the call of God.

In 1650, Brother Thomas Howard was chosen from among the students to address the chapter then gathered in Rome for an election. The subject he chose, and which he delivered with eloquence and strong emotion, was a surprise to the capitular fathers; he spoke on the restoration of the Dominican Order to England. So strikingly did he point out the needs of the English Church that interest was revived in a nearly lost cause. Brother Thomas was sent to finish his studies in Brittany, where refugees from England were often sheltered, and from which any help for the English missions must come. He was ordained there in 1652.

The young Dominican enthusiastically began the work that was to occupy him for the rest of his life—the return of the faith to England. He eventually established himself in a crumbling ruin of a castle in Bornhem, where, in time, he founded a Dominican community of strict observance that was dedicated to the needs of the English mission. Here he was plagued with a thousand small details, from leaking roofs and eccentric laybrothers, to a duchess who demanded the right to stroll through the cloisters whenever she wished. The house was in continual danger, either of falling on top of the brethren, or being summarily taken away from them by the touchy duchess. Not all the Dominicans interested in the English mission were a help to the cause. Laybrothers and students came and went—sometimes doing great good and sometimes great harm. The young English priest grew old watching small details interfere with the great mission.

The year of jubilee, 1675, arrived, and England was still in a desperate state. Father Howard was planning a trip to Rome. One day a traveler drew up at the gate of the forlorn convent. He did not seem pleased, and looked again to see that he was not mistaken. Making no effort to conceal his disapproval, the stranger presented his papers from the pope. Clement X, mindful of England, had made a move towards her conversion by making Philip Thomas Howard a cardinal.

After long years of persecution, English Catholics rejoiced in the thought that a Catholic sovereign, James II, sat once more on the throne. Unfortunately, James was rash and unpredictable. The unhappy task of guiding him was given to Cardinal Howard, who took up residence at the court—under orders from Rome—to try helping the English Church. In many ways, it was a heart-breaking task, for kings are difficult to guide, and the throne of England had drawn its power from bloody oppression for generations; it seeemed impossible to get beyond the intrigue and the personalities that dominated the best families and most powerful men in England. The fact that so little bitterness has attached itself to the memory of the great cardinal is a tribute to his tact, his true charity, and his unworldliness.

In the midst of trying circumstances, in the face of little obvious gain, Cardinal Howard and his few faithful followers struggled to save the English Church. He lived to see his Flemish foundations submerged by war, but he did not live to know that, many years later, his ruined old castle in Bornhem would send out the first of many missionaries to the United States of America —where a great English-speaking apostolate would one day flourish in a land where religion was unfettered. He founded the English College at Rome, but he never knew the glorious future of the house. In 1794, fleeing before the French Revolution, the nuns—refugees from the convents he had founded in Flanders for the purpose of praying for England—came back to an England now at peace, and found refuge at Gloucester. It was the cardinal's part to sow what others would some day reap.

Cardinal Howard died in Rome, in 1694, and was buried at the Dominican Church of Santa Maria Sopra Minerva.

JOHN ANDREW CARGA
(d. 1697)

John Andrew Carga was one of a multitude of Dominicans martyred by the Turks in the seventeenth century. He was prefect-apostolic of Constantinople.

John Andrew Carga was born in Italy, around the middle of the seventeenth century, and entered the Order, probably in Venice, when he was very young. He was a model religious, and his early religious life was spent in preaching in Italy. He was appointed archbishop of the island of Siros, in the Aegean Sea, and spent some years there before his martyrdom. The Turks hated him because of his unrelenting war against vice and his repeated efforts to better the moral conditions of his diocese.

Most of the process of his martyrdom has been lost, but we know the main details. Some of the Knights of Malta came to the island for the simple reason that one of them had been born there, and he wanted to visit his relatives. He was a man of great wealth, and, as a parting gift, he presented Archbishop Cargo with a magnificent chalice to use in his cathedral. The Moslems stole the chalice, and then, when the Christians protested, they raided the cathedral for other treasures, and began pillaging Catholic homes. The Christians fled with their belongings to hide in the hills.

The Turkish governor told the archbishop to call his people back, but Carga refused unless he was given some assurance of their safety. The governor had been waiting for some pretext to seize the archbishop, and this did as well as any.

Archbishop Carga and three other Dominicans were arrested and taken on board a Turkish ship. They were hanged from the mast of the ship, and then the mast was cut down and thrown into the sea. The martyrs were still attached to it. As it floated away, a light began to shine around the mast. A passing ship slowed, and the captain looked in amazement at the shining mast with its strange burden. He took it on board his ship, and, later, the bodies of the martyrs were brought to the island of Siros, where they were buried in the cathedral church of St. George.

Many miracles occurred then, and they occasioned the opening of the process of canonization. A good deal of material was amassed towards completing the case, but the material was lost in a shipwreck, and the process cannot be reopened unless new material is found.

GABRIELLE DE MONTFORT
(d. 1699)

It would be pleasant to assume that the convent of Our Lady of Prouille always remained the model of religious observance that it was in St. Dominic's time. As a matter of fact, however, it fell into decadence. Like all other

French convents of such size and revenues, it was a royal temptation. After the Concordat of 1516, when the crown acquired the right to appoint the abbesses of royal abbeys, only a short step was necessary for the king to confiscate the monastery of Prouille. Our Lady of Prouille was not included in the royal benefices, and—to do them justice—the Dominicans fought a long, tiresome fight to keep their rights. They punctually elected a prioress each time the rule said to do so; and just as regularly the crown appointed the daughter of some royal favorite or creditor to fill the office and receive the revenues. Liberty and religious observance were approaching the nadir when a young lady, Gabrielle de Montfort, applied for entrance there as a postulant in 1644.

Gabrielle de Montfort was born of the noble and charitable Vivier family, and she had shown early signs of piety. The year Gabrielle was born, a perpetual royal abbess had been appointed to govern Prouille. She was a Benedictine of noble birth, a woman who devoted herself to the nicer things of life (perhaps she was somewhat like Chaucer's prioress, with her "little dogges"). When the pretty young daughter of the Count de Vivier entered the novitiate, she rejoiced, for, obviously, here was a girl with beauty and family background who would add lustre to her salon. It was some little time before an irritating fact began asserting itself—Gabrielle had come to the convent fully intending to keep the rule in its entirety. No one knew where she had acquired her old-fashioned ideas, but a fact is a fact. She actually felt obliged to go to community exercises—all of them—and she accepted with embarrassed reluctance the dispensations that the abbess scattered with a lavish hand.

Gabrielle should go down in history as the patroness of those who have no ascetic ambitions to "out-fast or out-vigil the hermits, but only to keep the rule." In our day, thank God, it is not such a task. In hers, it required heroic virtue. And she was up against that most baffling of all enemies—sweet reasonableness. The abbess showered her with dispensations that she did not want, but did not know how to refuse. She gave Gabrielle gifts that were far too extravagant, and she invited her to all sorts of cozy little gatherings that were the exact antithesis of community life. Gabrielle endured it until she had been professed for several years. Then, finally, she was overwhelmed with the futility of such a life, and began working her way out of the maze. Perseveringly, she was steadfast in her program of attending all the community exercises and denying herself all that was superfluous. The abbess was indulgent about it—after all, she loved Gabrielle, and if it was her whim to act piously, well, no one would stop her. However, one by one, the other sisters awakened to the small revolution that silently was going on in their midst.

Without any preaching on Gabrielle's part, it became obvious to them that she was nearer to the ideal of a religious than the graceful and worldly abbess. One after another sought out the copy of the rule and read it thoughtfully, and they began appearing regularly at community exercises and avoiding relaxations.

The abbess followed a time-tested treatment of Gabrielle. She first had made a pet of her, and showered her with favors. When the girl's peculiar aberration first manifested itself, she tried kindness and the argument of her love. When that did not deter her, she tried ridicule—delicate at first, then unmistakably merciless. Finally, when it was obvious that Gabrielle was stubbornly insistent upon her course of life, she arranged to have her transferred to another convent. The abbess sent a note to the new superior to treat Gabrielle kindly because she was somewhat mentally deranged but not dangerous—it was just that she insisted on eating in the refectory, wearing no jewels, and saying all her prayers.

Gabrielle spent two years in exile in a convent in Bordeaux. Puzzled and embarrassed, the sisters there had reported her condition to Cardinal Mazarin, who, surprisingly enough, defended her. When she returned to Prouille on the abbess' death, the sisters welcomed her with open arms. For the remainder of her life, she lived, quietly and unobtrusively, according to the rule, just as she had hoped to do when dedicating herself to God in the first place.

Gabrielle died in 1699, but she left no impression on the life of religious women in France. It would take the Revolution and the saints that followed it to clear away the debris of the decadent centuries, and Prouille was not to rise from the ashes until the time of Lacordaire.

EIGHTEENTH CENTURY

CHAPTER NINE

LOUIS CALCO
(1669-1709)

Reformers are never the most popular members of an Order, but they are sometimes necessary. Fortunately, the Dominican Order has never needed to have a reform enforced upon it from outside, but the inspiration was always present within its own ranks to tighten up and revive the religious spirit when need arose. One of those who excelled at this difficult task was Louis Calco of Milan.

Louis was born in Milan in 1669, of a wealthy and pious family. His father was a senator, and a man of great charities as well as civic importance. Baptized Louis Marie, the boy was to follow in his father's charities, if not in his work. When he was very tiny, he would sacrifice food and toys for the poor, and, at the age of ten, he ran away from home to become a Dominican. The fathers at the convent of Modena were much impressed by the bright little lad who wanted to join them; but, when they learned that he was the son of the senator, they hurried him back to Milan. They told him he could come back when he was a little older, but, all things considered, they did not think he would. However, five years later he appeared at the convent of Our Lady of Grace, in Milan, and this time there was no reason to refuse him. He received the habit, keeping his own name in religion.

The young friar applied himself with great energy to his books, and was sent for further studies in Alexandria, Ravenna, and Rome. Ordained and equipped with degrees, he returned to Alexandria to teach, in 1695. He taught in Ferrara, and he was master of novices and almoner in several places. His zeal for regular observance had caught the eye of the bishop, and while he was prior in Cesena, he was given the delicate task of reforming religious observance in the diocese.

Louis would dearly like to have gone to the infidels, but instead he was sent to tell his own brethren where they were slipping in their observance of the rule, and what they should do about it. In spite of the unpopular position in which obedience had placed him, he was beloved by his own brethren, and he managed to effect a great change both in their religious observance and in the religious tone of the whole diocese. He always traveled on foot, ate next to nothing, and owned no superfluities—even as the bishop's visitor. He was a perfect example of what he preached to others, and his preaching had real effect.

Louis Calco died in 1709, surrounded by weeping brethren, and leaving the memory of a holy and honest man. Many miracles of healing were recorded at his tomb, and his cause for beatification was proposed in 1921.

BLESSED FRANCIS OF POSADAS
(1644-1713)

Few Dominicans have had more difficulty getting into the Order than Blessed Francis de Posadas, and he was one of the glories of the convent of the Scala Coeli, in Cordova. It is embarrassing for us to read that the reason for his exclusion was plain and simple snobbery on the part of the superiors of the convent of St. Paul, in Cordova.

Francis was born of a poor young couple who were war refugees, and who had been shunted from place to place until, when Francis was very small, his father's health failed, and he died in Cordova. The young widow tried several types of work, and finally she was reduced to selling eggs and vegetables at a street stand. She tried to educate her child, for she knew that he was very talented, but, without money, it simply was not possible to send him to school. She encouraged him to go to the Dominican Church of St. Paul, and he served Mass there every morning from the time he was six or seven years old.

While he was still a very tiny child, he used to gather the other children together for Rosary processions or other devotions. The smile of God seemed to rest upon him. For all his poverty, he was a very happy and attractive child, liked by everyone; and he was a natural leader among his fellows. Twice during his childhood, he was miraculously saved from death. This fact, and his undoubted piety, should have seemed sufficient reason for admitting him into a religious order. However, by the time Francis was old enough, there were two reasons to make his entry difficult: his mother had remarried, and the step-father would not permit him to enter. The Dominicans, moreover, would not have him. They said that they did not want the son of a street peddler.

Francis had friends in the Order, but the prior of the house he wished to enter took a violent dislike to him. It was several years before the young man could overcome the resistance of this man, who, having some influence with the provincial, was stubbornly determined that Francis should not be allowed to enter. Even when the fathers in the convent of Scala offered to take the boy and train him in Latin—so that he could qualify for clerical studies—the vindictive dislike of the prior followed him and almost prevented his acceptance.

Francis was finally accepted, made his novitiate, and gradually overcame all dislike and distrust by his charming manner and his unquestioned talents as student and preacher. After his ordination, he was sent out to preach, and he earned the reputation of being a second St. Vincent Ferrer. His talents as a preacher were rivalled only by his gifts as a confessor. He not only could read hearts and discover sins that had been wilfully concealed, but sometimes he was called to one place or another by an interior spirit and shown someone badly in need of the sacraments.

Francis hated the thought of holding authority in the Order. When appointed prior of one of the convents, he remarked that he would much sooner be sentenced to the galleys. He twice refused a bishopric, and he skillfully eluded court honors.

Several remarkable conversions are credited to Francis Posadas. His last years were a series of miracles wrought in the souls of his penitents. People followed him about to hear him preach, regarding him as a saint and miracle worker. One of his most noted converts was a woman more than one hundred years old—a Moor—with no intention of deserting Mohammedanism.

Francis of Posadas was the author of a number of books which he wrote to assist him in his apostolate. One was a life of St. Dominic, and several were biographies of other saintly people.

After a life filled with miracles, Francis died in 1713. Being forewarned of his death, he made private preparations, but to the last minute he was busy in the confessional before dying suddenly. By the time of his death, not only the Dominicans of Cordova, but the people of all Spain were happy to have him as fellow countryman. He was beatified a century after his death, in 1818.

ARTHUR MacGEOGHEGHAN AND COMPANIONS
(d. 1713)

Out of the hundreds of Dominicans—in all four branches of the Order—who died in Ireland during the years of persecution, a group of about a hundred has been suggested for possible beatification. The group is made up of individuals who died at different times and places. According to the usual custom, the group is classified under the name of the individual whose death occurred early in the persecution, and about whom a fair amount of information is available.

It must be remembered that, due to the nature of the persecution in Ireland during the sixteenth and seventeenth centuries, very few records have been left intact. Our best sources of information are the personal records written by priests who were themselves in exile. These men knew personally the martyrs they were describing, but they may have been inaccurate in the matter of dates, or other details, because of the circumstances of the martyrdom.

Father Arthur MacGeogheghan, for whom one group is named, was educated in Spain. He joined the Order there and for some time was stationed in the convent of the Rosary, in Lisbon, which kept up communication with the exiled Catholics. He was sent from this convent to Ireland, in the hope that he could discover and aid religious vocations there. He was captured while passing through England, and he never reached Ireland at all. Brought to trial for the crime of returning to England after being educated abroad, he boldly proclaimed that he was a Dominican, that he was on his way to Ireland to obtain more young men to be trained as Dominicans, and that he was quite ready to die for the faith. He was promptly hanged and quartered, and the affair was widely publicized as a warning that all such "traitors" would be harshly dealt with.

The crown did the Order a favor, though not intentionally, when it proclaimed the mission of the martyr. The Irish, few of whom had ever laid eyes on Father MacGeogheghan, responded with alacrity to the challenge. As soon as the news of his death, and the cause for which he had returned to Ireland became known, eligible young men from all over Ireland said goodbye to their families and set out for Spain and the Low Countries, risking death in leaving the country in order that later, as priests, they might come back and die as martyrs. The college and novitiate, which the young priest had planned to restock with students, became a seminary of martyrs, and the cherished goal of the youth of Ireland.

Another outstanding member of this illustrious band of martyrs was Father Peter O'Higgins, prior of Naas. An extremely popular man, and one who had been famous for years for his charities to the poor, he was left at liberty until he was well advanced in age. Finally, he was put in prison on a charge of treason, and condemned to be hanged, drawn, and quartered.

The commander in charge of the affair was personally fond of the Dominican, and he tried every expedient to delay the arrest. That failing, he tried arranging to get the prior out of jail. He assured Father O'Higgins that if he would just make a brief statement retracting his position, he could assure him of safety. He said, moreover, that no one really wanted him to die, for he was a venerable old man and had done no harm.

Father O'Higgins considered this for a few minutes and then told the commander that it sounded like a good proposition, but that—since his beliefs were well-known—it would be well to have the retraction just as public. He would like to see the whole transaction in writing—both the request and the retraction. These could be read publicly at the scaffold.

The commander swallowed the whole incredible story without a flicker. He was delighted with the way things had turned out, and he arranged to have a great deal of advance advertising for his triumph over the Dominican. He had the demand for retraction written out in detail and, as Father O'Higgins had requested, presented it to the priest at the foot of the scaffold. Father O'Higgins bowed graciously to him on receiving the document. He read it in a loud voice, so that all might hear. Then he said: "I was condemned on a charge of high treason, and there has been some confusion as to why I am dying. Now that we all understand quite clearly that I am giving my life, not because I am a traitor, but because I am a Catholic, let us not waste time." Tossing the document back to the startled commander, he cheerfully mounted the scaffold. He, and others like him, did not make life any easier for the soldiers of the Commonwealth.

Not all the sufferers died. Father O'Mannin lived—after being tortured until his back was broken. And he returned to the ministry. His was the slow martyrdom of hiding and preaching in secret places, of watching the young men die while he crept about in pain, hardly able to keep alive. Father Boyton became blind after torture. He worked as a cowherd for a Catholic nobleman who acted as go-between for people wishing to receive the sacraments. He carried on his difficult and dangerous apostolate for many years without being discovered.

At one time, there was just one Dominican priest left alive in Ireland, and he was ill in a remote spot in the mountains. Aware that he was dying, he begged God to let him live until another Dominican should come to take his place, so that the Order might not vanish completely from Ireland. To the sorrowing people praying around his bed, this prayer seemed to require a miracle, for the nearest Dominicans were in Spain. Yet, before the old priest died, there was a knock at the door, and the young man who rushed in to kneel by the bedside assured them that he was a Dominican priest.

It would certainly add a colorful and glorious chapter to Dominican history if the acts of these martyrs could be assembled with any completeness. Then we could read the full story of their faith and courage.

ST. LOUIS MARIE GRIGNON DE MONTFORT
(1673-1716)

Louis de Montfort was born in a little town in Brittany. His parents were poor, hard-working people, and he was the oldest of eight children. In the normal course of events, he would have learned a trade and helped to educate the younger children. But there were early, quite evident signs that he was cut out for only one career—the priesthood—and, at the pleading of his mother and his teacher, he was allowed to begin his studies.

As a very small child, Louis had organized Rosary societies, preached sermons, told stories of the saints, and led the Rosary with groups of neighbor children. He was particularly devoted to Our Lady, and he took her name in confirmation. As a student with the Jesuit fathers, he continued his devotions; he joined the sodality, and became an exemplary member. When he had completed his studies with the Jesuits, he left for Paris to enter the seminary. He walked the 130 miles in the rain, sleeping in haystacks and under bridges, and, on arriving in Paris, he entered a poverty-stricken seminary in which the students had scarcely enough to eat. On the verge of ordination, his funds were withdrawn by his benefactor, and it looked as though Louis would have to return home. He was taken in by a kindly priest, however.

Louis was ordained, and, after saying his first Mass in the Lady Chapel of St. Sulpice, he was sent as chaplain to a hospital where mismanagement and quarreling were a tradition. He endeared himself to the patients, and he angered the managers of the hospital. Consequently, he was sent away, but not before he had laid the foundation of what was later to be a religious congregation of women known as the "Daughters of Wisdom."

This rebuff was not the first Louis had to suffer; in the seminary, his superiors had exhausted themselves in trying his patience—making him seem to be a fool. All his life he was to meet the same stubborn opposition to everything he tried to do. Many of the clergy, even some of the bishops, were infected with Jansenism, and they fought him secretly and openly. In his work giving missions, his moving from one place to another was occasioned as often by the persecution of his enemies as it was by the need of his apostolate. Going to Rome, he begged to be sent on the foreign missions, but he was refused and sent back to France. He returned in his usual spirit of buoyant obedience, even though he knew that several bishops had already forbidden him to set foot in their dioceses.

For the rest of his life, Louis gave missions in country parishes, some of which had been without the care of a priest for generations. Ruined churches were repaired, marriages rectified, children baptized and instructed, and Catholicity rebuilt. He joined the Third Order of St. Dominic, and, everywhere he went, he established the Rosary devotion. People who came to his missions out of curiosity, remained, and his preaching did much to renew religion in France.

His enemies were as busy as he was, however; they gave false reports to the bishops, drove him from place to place, and, in one case, succeeded in poisoning him. The poison was not fatal, and it had an unlooked-for result. While he recuperated from its evil effects, he wrote *True Devotion to the Blessed Virgin,* which he himself prophesied would be hidden away by the malice of men and the devil. After nearly two hundred years, the manuscript was rescued from its hiding place, and, only a few years ago, it was given the publicity which it so long deserved.

Louis was the founder of two religious congregations: the Missionary Society of Mary—a group of missionary priests—and the Daughters of Wisdom.

Louis Marie Grignon de Montfort was beatified in 1888. In 1947, Pope Pius XII declared him a saint.

BENOITE RENCUREL
(1647-1718)

There are several things in the story of Benoite Rencurel which distinguish her from the many ecstatics and devout women of her century. She was, first of all, a Dominican Tertiary. Secondly, she was a stigmatist, and a mystic of such repute that her cause for beatification was introduced at one time. Most interesting, however, is the fact that she was one of the people chosen by the Queen of Heaven to be a messenger of heavenly things, and a builder of a world-renowned sanctuary of Mary. The visions which guided this undertaking took place over a period of more than fifty years, probably the longest single series of apparitions in history.

Benoite was born in the province of Gap, in France, in 1647. She was delicate and poorly cared for. One of a large family, she lost her father when she was very small. All the children had to work as soon as they were big enough to find jobs, and Benoite was eight years old when she began caring for the sheep of a neighbor. This meant, of course, that the little girl would have no more schooling. She knew the Our Father and the Hail Mary, however, and she could say the Rosary, as her mother pointed out. Her life is a homely demonstration of the lengths to which a devout soul can go with no more than this simple prayer.

Benoite's early years were full of toil—the crushing misery that always haunts the very poor. She seems to have accepted, without complaint, a life that was hard in the extreme. By the time she was seventeen, she had two jobs. She worked for her bed at the home of a woman who was very nearly as poor as she; and the money she earned herding sheep helped to feed the children of her landlady. On days that were especially bad, she did not eat. But she did not forsake her devotion to the Rosary.

One day, when she was herding the sheep in the valley of Laus, she sat down in the ruins of an old building to say a Rosary and eat her meager lunch. At the very time that she was wishing that she had something to drink with the dry bread, an old man appeared and spoke to her. He told her that he was St. Maurice, patron of the mountain, and that there was a spring of fine, cold water nearby. Benoite discovered that he was right, although she had never seen it before; in fact, she was sure that it had not been there before. She accepted the venerable visitor's suggestion and drank the water. When he told her to pasture her sheep in a certain valley so that she would "'see her heart's desire," she resolved to do so. The next day she went to the other valley, and there, for the first of many times, she beheld the Lady who was to direct her life, and bring people from all the world into this remote valley.

The Lady was very lovely, and she had a beautiful baby. She did not speak, even when Benoite, stammering in the presence of a Lady of quality, asked her if she had come to buy lime at the nearby kiln. The Lady only smiled, then disappeared. The next day Benoite went back, on the remote chance of seeing her again. There she was, lovely, smiling, and silent. Benoite's lonely life was brightened by a new and unheard-of thing—a friend.

It is strange to read of the apparitions of the next two months. The little peasant girl and the Queen of Heaven met almost daily in the lovely, lonely valley, and neither of them said a word. Finally, the neighbors precipitated action. Some busybody had noticed that Benoite took her sheep to this valley, and it was one that had always offered poor pasturage. "She is neglecting your sheep," they told her employer. He told her to take them to another pasture, and then he forgot about it.

Benoite came to him in tears a few days later, and she said: "I tried to do as you said, but the sheep will not obey me. They go there anyway." "Nonsense," said the man. "I will take them myself tomorrow." After an exhausting day in which the sheep persisted in entering that valley, no matter what he did, he was ready to conclude that Benoite was right; they would not go anywhere else. "Pasture them where you please," he said wearily. "They are as fat as anyone else's sheep."

But the neighbors were not satisfied. "She goes there to meet someone," they said. Benoite admitted that she did, and she described the vision, but, of course, she was unable to name the person she saw.

At this point the civil authorities stepped in. The magistrate, who was a good man, suggested that she go to confession and Communion, and then, prayerfully armed, enquire of the Lady who she was and what she wanted. He had his suspicions of her identity. These were entirely justified when Benoite did as she was told. The Lady's answer was quite plainly stated: "I am Mary, the Mother of Jesus, and I wish to be honored in this valley." She asked for a procession. It speaks well for the reputation of Benoite and for the piety of the parishioners that the pastor took immediate steps to organize a procession.

It was not all to run smoothly, however. For some weeks, while Benoite ransacked her conscience for guilt, the Lady did not come. Then one day, unexpectedly, Benoite was once more face to face with the heavenly visitor. She had gone into an old chapel to say her Rosary, and she was hardly conscious of the ruinous state of the place until it was suddenly flooded with light, and Our Lady appeared over the altar. Benoite hastily picked up her apron and tried to dust the altar, murmuring an apology. Our Lady smiled, telling her not to worry, that soon there would be nothing lacking there for the worship of God, and that Benoite herself should direct the building of a church, and also the devotion that would bring people to pray. "Many sinners will be converted," she said, "and my presence will always linger here."

One does not usually choose an unlettered shepherdess of seventeen to direct the building of a church. And no one planning to build a great church for pilgrimage would choose this almost inaccessible valley for a site. The only stone suitable for building was miles away, at the foot of a steep trail. No one had any money. And France, at that time, was hypersensitive about visionaries. Yet, with all these obstacles, the project got under way. Who suggested that each pilgrim carry a stone to Laus when he went there on pilgrimage? Who, indeed, informed these people from the isolated valleys and hamlets that the valley of Laus was a place chosen by Mary, that sorrows of body and soul would be cured there, in this blessed place, where a perfume always lingered on the air? No one can say. But the first few pilgrims became a few dozen, then a few hundred; in an incredibly short time, there were thousands toiling up the steep trail—singing, praying—each carrying a stone to Laus. Everyone seems to have accepted the direction of Benoite without any question. The building of the church was itself the first visible miracle of Our Lady of Laus.

In order to be near the work, Benoite had built a little hermitage close to the church. She became a Dominican Tertiary, and everyone called her "Sister Benoite." The troubled and the sick from faraway places came to ask for her prayers. She played a leading role in the particular work of Laus: the calling of sinners to repentance. In and around and above all her daily activity was the almost constant presence of the Blessed Virgin. Exactly how many times she appeared to the favored shepherdess we do not know, but the visions extended well over half a century.

One might expect, of course, that such a favored one would suffer. The devil tormented the girl; people in authority persecuted her; and bodily illness reduced her to a walking shadow. Once, she was refused Communion over a period of some months. Another time, she was put in jail for two weeks. Jansenistic church authorities nearly ran her out of the country. The church was utterly destroyed twice in her lifetime and the work had to begin all over again. The stigmata appeared in Benoite's hands and feet, and this favor was the occasion of a fresh hue and cry against her. Yet, the pilgrims flooded in, pushing past the barricades when the Jansenist custodians of the shrine tried to keep them away. And sinners, kneeling in the church of Laus, came back to God in uncounted numbers.

Sister Benoite died in 1718. She died alone in her hermitage, in a season when the bad weather kept pilgrims away. Then who told the people of the distant valleys that she was dead? No one knew. But a great mass of people arrived for her funeral, and they wept as she was laid under the altar of the church that she had built.

Benoite's inner life is shrouded in mystery. She wrote nothing, seldom talked about herself, made no close friends. She had savage enemies among the Jansenists of the time, and they did their best to blacken her name. They could not make people forget her, though. Eighty years after her death, some workmen, doing repair work in the church, accidently broke in the top of her tomb. Upon examination, it was found that the body was still perfectly preserved, and that there was fresh blood flowing from the face where the broken stones had hit it. At this time her cause was proposed to beatification. She still had enough bitter enemies alive to destroy most of the records, however, and that delayed the process indefinitely.

Benoite is listed among the stigmatists of the Order, and even in her lifetime she was popularly called "The Blessed One." The shrine which she built —Our Lady of Laus—is still a popular place of pilgrimage—still a place where sinners come back to God. It received Church approval during her lifetime; a bishop who was sent there to investigate, was himself the witness of a major miracle.

Even now, on certain days, a strange and lovely perfume drifts through the valley of Laus, and those who love the place assure one another that Our Lady is keeping her promise to the little shepherdess, and that some poor sinner is receiving the grace of conversion in that blessed place.

BENEDICT XIII
(1649-1730)

Pope Benedict XIII reigned at a time when the papacy was in a very difficult position. We can see now that if his ideals had been more carefully followed, and if he had had a few more years in which to put them into practice, he might have been one of the most influential popes of all time.

Peter Francis Orsini was born in 1649. He was heir to one of the greatest names and fortunes in Italy. Before his birth, an old Dominican friar had prophesied that he would become a Dominican, and would be one of the glories of the Order. As a small child, he showed a great interest in the Order, but, because of his position, his mother refused to take seriously the thought that her son might become a mendicant friar. At the age of twelve, when he was already a student of remarkable attainments, his father died, and he became duke of Orsini.

A brilliant marriage was arranged for the young heir by the elder members of the family. Young Peter had ideas of his own, however. At the age of eighteen, he applied at the convent in Venice for admission into the Order, and, since it was evident that he had a true vocation, the Dominicans gave him the habit, and the name Vincent Mary. This news set his family into a rage. His mother wasted no time; she went straight to the pope and demanded that her son be returned to her. Pope Clement IX called her son to court and questioned him closely. Then, instead of sending him home, he gave the lad a special dispensation to take his solemn vows after six months, thus precluding an attempt by his family of removing him by force. With a remarkable talent for right-about-face which she possessed, the Duchess Orsini quieted down and accepted her son's vocation. Eventually, she piously ended her days as a Dominican nun.

The young Brother Vincent made rapid progress in the religious life and in sacred studies. On his ordination, he hoped to depart on a course of preaching like that of his famous patron St. Vincent Ferrer, to whom he had great devotion. The papal court however, had not forgotten this talented young son of one of Italy's greatest houses, and, to his utter dismay, he was made a cardinal within a few years after ordination. Shortly after this, he was made archbishop of Benevento.

For thirty-eight years Vincent was the archbishop of Benevento, and he became the model of charity and discretion for all in his diocese. Two great earthquakes occurred during these years, leaving vast and terrible destruction and great suffering among his people. The archbishop was tireless in relieving the distress of his flock. He was dearly loved by his people. At an advanced age he went to Rome for the conclave, after the death of Pope Innocent XIII. When it became obvious that the choice of the cardinals was settling upon him, he tried to convince them that he was not worthy of such a high office. He was elected, nevertheless, and he took the name Benedict, in honor of the last Dominican pope.

It is hard to imagine a worse time to take over the papacy than during those troubled years. There was so much corruption in high places, and so little virtue where one had a right to find it, that a pope with high ideals would hardly know where to turn for help. It was a time when diplomacy and intrigue were apparently more of a necessity for a churchman than any other qualities, for church dignitaries were pitted against the most accomplished schemers of the secular courts. Against this background of colorful intrigue, the figure of the new pope stood out in somber colors; he was a Dominican friar first and last—committed to the care and the instruction of the poor and the ignorant, and to the furtherance of truth. Quite naturally, the poor loved him. Quite naturally also, the rich and the powerful, to whom he was a reproach, did not.

Benedict insisted on walking about Rome unattended; he chatted with children and beggars as he chose. He walked in and out of hospitals unexpectedly, checking on the quality of food that was served to the poor, and making changes in administration when he thought it advisable. He insisted upon going into the prisons to administer the sacraments and instruct the prisoners. One day, when no one could find him, he was discovered in one of the confessionals, where he had been hearing confessions for some time. One did not expect the pope to do such things, and most of the cardinals were upset and disapproving, although even his worst enemies admitted that he was probably a saint.

Pope Benedict XIII lived for six years, and his term was marked by great charity and the Christlike observance of all the virtues. He was in the forefront in the battle against Jansenism, which was just gaining a good foothold in France. He sent aid to the missions of the Far East and America. He canonized a great number of saints, among whom were Sts. John of the Cross, Aloysius Gonzaga, Stanislaus Kostka, and, the Dominican, Agnes of Montepulciano.

In February of 1730, a plague was raging in Italy. Despite the fact that he was eighty-two years old, the pope continued his usual—or perhaps we should call it unusual—program. He contracted the plague, and he died on February the twenty-first, leaving the memory of a vigorous and Christlike man, who walked amid corruption untouched.

MARY ROSE GIANNINI
(d. 1741)

It is difficult to imagine a more active—or a less private—life than that lived by this Neapolitan Tertiary. For forty years she was at the beck and call of the sick, the poor, and the troubled of heart; someone wrote of her that she almost seemed to live entirely in public, with no time for herself. Yet, this woman was one of those favored by our Lord with the stigmata; and she became a great mystic, in spite of her confused surroundings.

Mary Rose was born in Naples. We know nothing of her family, nor her early training. She appears first in our records as a Tertiary, living at home. From the accounts, one would think of her as a sort of dynamo of prayer and good works, serving all people, regardless of class or condition. She had a gay and happy disposition, and, of course, she was dearly loved by all her friends. Apparently, she brought a note of gaiety into the lives of the people for whom she worked so hard. It is recorded that what you remembered about her was her smile.

We do not know exactly what her position was, or why the rich and poor of Naples should have beaten a path to her door. She probably was just one of those people to whom one instinctively turns for help: the good manager, the rock of sense, the source of prayer, who always knows what to do. Naples, in her day as in ours, had ample room for people who would spend their lives helping the poor and the afflicted. People were helped in every kind of distress; spiritual and material needs fell to her lot. The miracle is not that she accomplished these things, although that in itself would be a tremendous work, but that she accomplished everything without in the least disturbing her own peace or her constant awareness of the presence of God.

Like others whose devotion to the Passion was noteworthy, Mary Rose received the sign of her dedication to Christ in a ceremony of mystical espousals. She received all of the extraordinary favors one commonly associates with the mystical life, and, during her last fifteen years on earth, she attained a union so perfect that she seemed one step beyond the visible phenomena of mysticism. According to her biographer: "The memory and all the other interior powers of the soul were utterly purged and purified from all sense of sensible images. She saw God in her soul and loved Him so much the more perfectly as her love was the less sensible. It seemed indeed that her contemplation was continual and uninterrupted, and whatever she did she referred all to God and did all for Him."

She acquired such a habit of recollection that nothing could separate her from the presence of God. Before going into the church or oratory, she made a distinct effort to put off and leave behind her the cares of her apostolate. She comments: "How can the mind be free from images and distractions in prayer if it busies itself in unnecessary affairs? I would go to prayer without any of these *noises* in my soul if I avoided conversations which do not concern me."

Mary Rose Giannini died in 1741. Her cause, which was opened some time ago, is still active. Perhaps some day this woman, who so well understood the necessity of prayer in the active apostolate, will be raised to the altars of the Church.

MOTHER MARY POUSSEPIN
(1653-1744)

Dominican annals list a great many founders and foundresses among the members of the Order. These are people who founded Dominican houses or provinces, or people who founded institutes under Dominican direction. Few, if any, of these worthy people tried so long or so earnestly to make a Dominican foundation as Sister Mary Poussepin. And then she saw her efforts fail in the end. She is remembered today as the foundress of the Dominican Sisters of Charity of the Presentation, an institute which only within the past century has been recognized as a part of the regular Dominican sisterhood.

Mary Poussepin was born in the diocese of Versailles in 1653. Her well-to-do family had a reputation for both sanctity and sound business. She was a gay-hearted and generous girl, well liked by all her friends. Her gifts of mind and judgment were far beyond her years. She might have entered religion earlier, but the illness of her mother required her constant care. When Mary was twenty-two, her mother died, and the girl took over the management of the house. She had the consoling thought that as soon as the shock of her mother's death had worn off, she would approach her father on the question of becoming a cloistered nun. In the meantime, she busied herself with the care of her young brother, and all the pious works she could do in a day. It soon became apparent that her plans for contemplative life would have to be revised, for her father fell ill, and she was needed to care for him.

Since her home was situated conveniently between the hospital of the Sisters of Charity and the church where the Dominican Third Order regularly met,

Mary Poussepin soon found herself involved in the charities of the one and the spiritual life of the other. She became a Tertiary, and she placed herself under the guidance of a Dominican confessor, who was to watch over her for nearly half a century. Working with the Sisters of Charity, she was constantly aware of the needs of the sick and the unfortunate, and she began to dream of a Dominican community in which these works could become a part of the apostolate. Not until after her father's death could she set about making this dream a reality, but, from the records of those intervening years, it is clear that she lost neither time nor opportunity in either charitable works or spirituality.

Mary Poussepin was thirty years old when at last she was free to follow her heart and begin the institute that she had so long dreamed of. It is a little hard for us to see why she should have had such difficulty in making the ideas attractive to higher authorities, for in America we have a proud tradition of Dominican sisters doing the various works of charity which she espoused. At that time and place, however, it was evidently a novelty for Dominican sisters to care for the orphans or the poor, the insane or the wayward. Reading between the lines, moreover, one is quite certain that the bishop with whom most of her negotiations had to be made was a man who heartily disliked Dominicans. It is impossible now to know with certainty the reasons for the things that occurred. We can only record the facts, and presume that the reasons at the time were ample.

Mary Poussepin began her institute of the Dominican Sisters of Charity in Angerville. She started with high hopes and one companion, and postulants soon came to fill the ranks. The sisters wore the colors of the Order—quite probably they were not permitted the same form of religious habit as that worn by the regular communities of Dominicans. They had a Dominican director, and—everyone agrees—the Dominican spirit. But when it came to obtaining affiliation with the Order, they were blocked by the bishop's refusal and—probably in view of this—by the reluctance of the Order to force their claims. The people of the town called the sisters "Jacobines," an allusion to the Dominican fathers; but, for nearly two hundred years, that was as near as they came to regular affiliation.

After several false starts, which necessitated moving and beginning again, the community prospered. It cared for schools, hospitals, kindergartens, and homes for the aged, the insane, and the delinquent. Their houses spread over France and were recognized, both civilly and ecclesiastically, as a religious institute with all the rights and privileges except the one for which the foundress had struggled for a lifetime: official acceptance into the Dominican family. At the age of ninety, as she lay on her deathbed, her hopes seemed ruined forever when she received word that all affiliations with the Order—even the solemnizing of the feast of St. Dominic—must be abandoned if she did not wish the rights of her institute taken away completely. All that she had striven to establish had come to nothing. Accepting the will of God, she commanded her sisters to remain spiritually close to the great Order she loved, and she died with no assurance that they would ever realize her desire.

Half a century after the death of Mary Poussepin, the French Revolution broke upon the country. Dispersed, and wearing secular clothes, hiding and working in dangerous places, the sisters took advantage of the occasion to resume the first habit and all the customs from the primitive days. A few years later, more Dominican privileges were granted, and the sisters pressed the question of affiliation. Not until 1897, two full centuries after the foundress first began her project, was her community allowed to use the full title "Dominican Sisters of Charity of the Presentation of the Most Blessed Virgin Mary."

Sisters of Mother Poussepin's foundation have been in Near East missions, Mesopotamia, and Kurdistan, as well as France, Spain, and Italy, for the past century. They also have missions in South America, and they have been in the United States, in Fall River, Massachusetts, since 1906.

BLESSED PETER SANZ AND COMPANIONS
(d. 1747-1748)

What are we to do with these men? Their lives are certainly irreproachable; even in prison they convert men to their opinions, and their doctrines so seize upon the heart that their adepts fear neither torments nor captivity. They themselves are joyous in their chains. The jailors and their families become their disciples, and those condemned to death embrace their religion. To prolong this state is only to give them the opportunity of increasing the number of Christians.

(Viceroy of Peking, speaking of the five martyrs)

This first group of Tonkinese martyrs to be beatified by the Church included two bishops, Peter Martyr Sanz and Francis Serrano, and three priests, Joachim Royo, John Alcober, and Francis Diaz. All were from the province of Spain. They were beatified by Pope Leo XIII, in 1893.

Peter Martyr Sanz was born in Catalonia in 1680, and made profession in the convent of Lerida at the age of eighteen. He was ordained in 1704. He volunteered for the Chinese missions and was sent to Manila in 1713.

After two years' study of the language, he was ready to attempt the dangerous adventure of entering China. In this perilous situation, he spent thirty-one years in apostolic labor among the Chinese people before he was finally captured and executed. The persecution in which he eventually lost his life was already in full cry when he received word that he had been named vicar-apostolic of the province of Fuekien and bishop of Mauricastro.

Francis Serrano, the second bishop, who received his appointment after the death of Bishop Sanz, had twenty years of work in China behind him when he was caught and imprisoned. He was a resourceful, cheerful person, who easily adapted himself to the gypsy life the missionaries had to lead. He became adept at scaling walls and hiding in chimneys, and once had himself carried in a sack on a man's shoulders, as he wrote, like meat being taken to the butcher—a grim joke that seemed to amuse him.

John Alcober was, like Father Serrano, a son of the Granada convent, and they were great friends. They had planned on going to the Chinese missions together, but some delay in sailing had marooned Father Alcober in Lorca. Here, while he was waiting for a chance to cross the ocean, he busied himself with preaching, and he developed a fine reputation as a popular preacher. In fact, he was beginning to forget about China, but the Lord reminded him. While preaching one day, he chanced to use the words, "How long, ye sinners, will you remain hardened?" His crucifix spoke reproachfully to him, saying, "And thou, John—how long?"

He sailed to Manila with forty-three religious in 1726, and he was ready to go to China in the following November. Here his life was very difficult; he had to hide in uncomfortable places, and, once, he was smuggled in a coffin to anoint a dying man. Sometimes disguised as a water seller, he moved around the city. On one occasion, he was far from any shelter, and he climbed into a tree to spend the night. Piously intoning the *Miserere* before going to sleep, he was startled to hear another voice answering his, and, to his great joy, realized that his old friend Father Serrano was roosting in the same tree. One of his last acts as a free man was to baptize a sick woman to whom Our Lady of the Rosary had appeared. The new Christian was so beautiful after her death that pagans crowded in to see her. Father Alcober's presence there became known, consequently, and led to his capture.

Father Joachim Royo was born in 1691, in Valencia, and he entered the convent in his native city. At his earnest request, he was sent to China when he was twenty-three, and was ordained there. At the time of the persecution he was the companion of Bishop Sanz.

The youngest of the group was Father Francis Diaz, who was born in Ecija, in 1713. He always claimed that he owed his vocation to the fact that he played truant from school one day. A religious dressed in white appeared to him, and his curiosity would not rest until he found out who and what the Dominicans were. When he talked of entering the Order, his father tried to persuade him to accept a benefice that belonged to the family instead of living the austere life of the Dominicans. Francis refused, and years later, when the news reached Spain of his martyrdom, his old father recalled his son's determination to serve God as a Dominican and to die in China. He arrived in China in 1738, and he had worked only eight years before being captured and martyred.

The five men, bound together by their vows and their work, were brought more closely together in their capture and death. Fathers Serrano, Alcober, and Diaz were captured first, and tortured to reveal the whereabouts of Bishop Sanz. They would not reveal anything, even under the most terrible tortures, but the bishop and Father Royo, hearing of the affair, surrendered in the hope of sparing their brothers' suffering. The five priests were dragged in chains to the emperor's court, where they were subjected to frightful torments. All of them, with a catechist named Ambrose Kou, were sentenced to death in December, 1746. During the long imprisonment, a Dominican, Father Thomas Sanchez, managed to get in to see them. He brought them some clothes and a little money, and all the news he could find.

On May 25, 1747, Bishop Sanz was beheaded. Even the pagans were impressed with his gentle demeanor as he was led out to die, and a fellow prisoner who had been converted in prison, followed him closely through the mob, openly proclaiming his sanctity. As the headsman prepared to swing the axe, the venerable bishop looked at him and said, "Rejoice with me, my friend; I am going to heaven!" "I wish I were going with you!" blurted the unhappy man. Laying his head on the block, the bishop preached his last sermon: "If you want to save your soul, my friend, you must obey the law of God!" Pagan friends of the priests scurried through the crowd, gathering up relics which they saved for the Christians. Many of these people, including the executioner, were later baptized.

The remaining four priests were branded on the face as criminals about to die, and then they were left to languish in prison for another six months. Father Alcober wrote a letter to his brother, who was a Carmelite, saying that they were all in good spirits, but they hoped it would happen soon, as they were eager to shed their blood. In prison, Father Serrano received the letters appointing him successor to Bishop Sanz—a position he could never occupy. Late in November, the four priests were all strangled one night in their prison cells; the authorities believed that this was the best way of solving the problem of their apostolic work among the jailors and soldiers. When the executioners returned the next day to dispose of the bodies, they were terrified to see that the faces were not only serene, but shone with an unearthly radiance—a phenomenon indeed for someone who had died by strangulation. Afraid of being punished for not carrying out their duty, they covered up the shining faces, but the Christians followed them anyway, making certain to save the relics when the chance offered itself. The mandarin's soldiers had already had trouble with the question of relics: those of Bishop Sanz had resisted burning and various other kinds of destruction. Thanks to this marvelous preservation, the harassed Christians had relics of the five martyrs.

CHARLES-RENÉ BILLUART
(1685-1757)

Charles-René Billuart was a tireless champion of St. Thomas in the troubled eighteenth century. His whole life was given to making the great doctor's work available to the students of his time.

Charles-René Billuart was born in Revin, in the Ardennes, in 1685. He was given a good education, and he had completed college with the Jesuits before entering the Dominican Order in his native town, in 1701. After completing his novitiate in Lille, and finishing his studies in Belgium, he was ordained in 1708, at the age of twenty-three. Two years later he was appointed professor of philosophy in Douai.

Douai had served as a rallying-point for English Catholics all through the past, troubled century. When young Father Billuart took up his professorship there, it was a center for Catholic thought, as opposed to the followers of Jansenism and Calvinism. Charles Billuart threw himself into the heart of the controversy with enthusiasm, but also with a reserved and careful exactness that made his writing and his preaching of great value. He was regent of studies in Douai when the Catholic mayor of Masstricht invited him to Holland to preach on the Real Presence.

Charles Billuart preached brilliantly on the doctrine of the Real Presence during the octave of Corpus Christi, and, afterwards, he conducted a public disputation with the Calvinist ministers. His authoritative presentation of the doctrine was of great help to the Church in Holland, where the revolt against Spain had muddled politics and religion so badly. The Dominican from Douai was unperturbed by the attacks of the ministers;

he silenced them all with his capable presentation of truth and his knowledge of Scripture and theology.

In 1732, when he was preaching a course of sermons in Liege, Charles Billuart was given the task of writing a monumental work on St. Thomas. He spent nearly fifteen years on this work. It was for the use of students of theology, and it was done with orderliness and precision. He included valuable materials which the ensuing years had made available, producing a thoroughly practical work which aided greatly in popularizing St. Thomas among theologians outside the Order. It ran through thirteen editions in his lifetime.

A gentle and silent man, unless called upon to preach or engage in controversy, Charles Billuart was beloved of his brethren, and he was respected by scholars of his day, as he is in ours. His writings, of which there is an imposing list, are all theological works written in Latin, with the exception of several shorter tracts that he wrote in French. He published a series of sermons which have been reprinted within the past century, in France, but most of his works remain in the sphere for which they were first intended—the training of theologians.

Charles-René Billuart died in the town of his birth, in 1757.

JOSEPH GALIEN
(1699-1783)

Our array of famous Dominicans would be incomplete without at least one experimental scientist who, in the tradition of St. Albert the Great, propounded theories that astounded his own times and could be judged only by the future. Such a one was Joseph Galien, who is called simply "Galien" by those who are familiar with his work. Galien, in the unseasonable year of 1755, actually went on record as saying that it was quite possible for man to fly. There had been a number of people before this who had made this silly suggestion, from the ancient Greeks on through St. Albert the Great, Roger Bacon, and Leonardo da Vinci. A Portuguese Jesuit had suggested a sort of balloon made of copper back in 1628. But the enlightened folk of the mid-eighteenth century knew for certain that these were all ridiculous fancies and that flight through the air was impossible.

Joseph Galien, who said it was not, was born in 1699 in the south of France. He entered the Dominican convent at Puy and made his studies at Avignon. After his ordination, he taught philosophy at Bordeaux, and later taught both philosophy and theology at the University of Avignon.

Just when he got interested in the subject of electricity we do not know, but he had the example of that Dominican master of the Middle Ages whom all men called "the Great." Joseph published a learned and surprisingly practical treatment of the subject of electricity, and in 1755 followed it with a work on meteors, hailstorms, and aerial navigations. Storms he had never dreamed of broke about his head; he was openly accused of witchcraft. Joseph insisted that the work was just a sort of hobby, an amusing thing, and he did not mean anything by it. His contemporaries, who felt that the way to deal with an incendiary book was to burn the author, were affronted by his boldness in suggesting, among other things, that it was even possible, let alone practical, to fly.

Joseph Galien responded in a way that should endear him to modern Americans—he laughed. If his readers wished to be stuffy, it only amused him. While people looked askance at him and made veiled remarks about witchcraft, he revised his book, added a few dashes of what we today would call science-fiction, and published a second edition. It finally became apparent to those of his contemporaries who had a spark of humor that he was enjoying himself very much, and that they had been definitely taken in.

It was left for our own times to see that Joseph Galien was not the impractical dreamer that he was thought to be, and that he was not a fraud. For his times, the machine he suggested was quite modern. It was to be a large cube-shaped vessel made of two thicknesses of strong canvas, waxed and tarred and covered with leather. He gave dimensions, specifications for the ropes and riggings, and pointed out that it would have to rise to the altitude of the hailstorm atmospheric strata, since—he quite sensibly observes—the atmosphere is much lighter there. The ship was too large to be practical—he planned to use it to transfer an entire army from Avignon to Africa—but he was at least a shrewd guesser of future developments.

It is hard to sort out in his work the suggestions that he made seriously and the witty gibes at the ponderous folk of the time; there is no question at all that Joseph Galien was a wit, and that he deplored the stuffy people his century was full of. His object seems to have been to deflate skillfully his intellectually proud neighbors, who were so certain at that time that everything in nature would yield to the intellect of man.

Joseph Galien died around 1783.

NINETEENTH CENTURY

CATHERINE JARRIGE
(1754-1836)

This "angel of the underground" was born near Mauriac in 1754 and spent her whole life within a short distance of her birthplace. Yet her adventures read like something out of a dramatic movie. The youngest of seven children, she passed a happy childhood, working on the farm and dancing at festivals. She was fantastically fond of dancing, yet townspeople from her early childhood nicknamed her "Catinon Manette"—"Catherine the little nun."

Sobered by a series of family tragedies, Catherine decided to become a Dominican Tertiary at the age of twenty-two. She accepted the rule of life in its entirety and promptly reordered her life to conform to its highest ideals. Employed as a lace maker, she used all her spare time to work among the poor and the sick. She was thirty-five when the French Revolution struck in all its horror.

In this unlikely circumstance, Catherine found her vocation. Gifted with a peasant shrewdness and a courage that was second to none, she set up an underground for the hunted priests, and for the whole of the Reign of Terror she was a lifeline to all the priests who passed through that part of France. Her plans were ingenious, and they worked by wholly unorthodox methods. She set up headquarters in a forest which had been a robbers' hide-out until it got too dangerous for robbers. Here, in hidden huts and barns, she concealed the priests who passed through the country. She provided them with food, shelter, transportation, and, when necessary, forged papers. To these hidden places she brought babies in need of baptism, and from them she conducted the fugitives to sickbeds and confessions. How many priests she saved from the guillotine no one knows; she lost only one, and that was hardly her fault.

He was a very young priest, and was fleeing to Spain when he had a change of heart and went under cover in Mauriac. One of Catherine's informers told her that he was hiding out in a barn. She tried in vain to get him out of the barn to a place of safety, but it was too late. He was captured and sentenced. Catherine marched beside him to the guillotine the next day, and after the execution, it was she who summoned a blind man to touch his eyes with the martyr's blood. His sight was restored, and so was that of a blind baby whose mother fearfully followed Catherine's bidding.

The "sons of the Republic" were demoralized completely when the headman screamed, "I am lost, I have killed a saint, I am lost!"

The revolutionaries made many attempts to capture Catherine. They brought her in for questioning time after time and never could convict her of anything. Once when they locked her up, the townspeople made so much commotion they had to let her go. The only time she was near to being convicted, they asked her point-blank if she had not been associating with priests. Catherine looked around, trying to think of some way to answer without telling an out-and-out lie, and her eyes fell on an apostate priest who was seated with the judges. She shrugged her shoulders indifferently and answered, "Associating with priests? No more than I am right now!" They roared with laughter and released her.

The most colorful episode occurred when she and the former prioress of the Dominican house in Mauriac went to a neighboring village to get two priests who were hiding in a root cellar. She brought peasant clothes for them to wear, and red mob-caps like those worn by the revolutionaries. Then when they were dressed to her satisfaction, she doused them with liquor and told them to stagger along in front and let her do the talking. On their way back to Mauriac they met the revolutionary leader who was known as the "butcher of Mauriac"; he was out hunting for two priests he had heard were in the neighborhood. Thanks to Catherine's wit and the cooperation of the two disguised priests, they got past him. In fact, Catherine let loose on him such a tirade that the revolutionist finally confided to the nearest priest, "Citizen, if I had a wife like that I would take her to the nearest river and drown her!" Once past the group of revolutionaries, Catherine and her charges ran for their lives. She kept these two priests in Mauriac for nearly two years, within inches of those who cried for their blood. The entire religious life of the district devolved upon her capable shoulders for several years, and she was proud of the fact that no one had died without the sacraments, and no baby remained unbaptized.

Catherine was an irresistible beggar. The only thing she ever asked for herself was a large pair of leather pockets to wear on her petticoat, as she was tired of the cloth pockets which wore through with all the lumpy things she carried in them. Some wealthy benefactor had the pockets made for her, and for more than thirty years she kept them filled for the benefit of the needy and the hunted. She even begged from some of the revolutionaries, but no one ever refused her. A prominent free-thinker, a lady of some wealth, was one of her greatest benefactors, and once shared a jail cell with Catherine when the authorities had caught them dispensing charity.

When the revolution was over, Catherine continued her works of charity. She went in and out of prisons at will, and no jailor would think of stopping her. She helped her friend Sister Frances to get the hospital in working order again after the revolutionaries had partially destroyed it; she supervised the restoration of the parish church after the revolution, and secured vestments and ornaments for it; she organized processions, saw that marriages were regularized, and arranged for children to receive their instructions.

Catherine finally ceased her labors at the age of eighty-two. Still anxious to keep busy, she was unwilling to realize that she could not move another step. In her few last days her friends gathered around her, sorrowing, and some of them dressed her in a Dominican habit, which made her very happy. She died quietly in 1836. Her cause, which has been kept alive in her own diocese, was little known in other countries until 1949, when it was proposed to Rome.

BISHOP EDWARD DOMINIC FENWICK
(1768-1832)

Ohio today, with its million and a half Catholic population, is a far cry from the wilderness of 1822, when Edward Dominic Fenwick of the Order of Preachers was made bishop there in the third largest diocese in the world.

Edward Fenwick was born in St. Mary's County, Maryland, in 1768. His father was a colonel in the Continental army, and both he and his young wife died during the Revolutionary War. Young Edward was sent to England to study, probably before the war. He remained in Europe nearly twenty years. A student at the English College at Bornheim, Belgium, he grew very fond of the Dominican Fathers. Several of his relatives became Dominicans, and several joined the Society of Jesus when it was reorganized after the suppression. They were a pious family, and it was no surprise to anyone when Edward entered the Order in 1787, taking the religious name Dominic. That he did so with the express hope of bringing the Order to America was well understood by his superiors.

Edward Dominic Fenwick was ordained in Ghent in 1793. The horrors of the French Revolution were already approaching the borders of Catholic Belgium, and shortly after his ordination the young priest found himself in a very uncomfortable spot. Belgian, French, and Spanish Dominicans were forced to flee to England, leaving him in charge of the Bornheim convent on the slim chance that the revolutionaries would respect his American citizenship and leave the convent alone. It was a vain hope. He was taken prisoner, and only escaped by what he considered the miraculous intervention of the Blessed Virgin. For ten years he lived with the English fathers, teaching in their college and planning for the time when he might return to his own land. Not until 1803 would he be able to arrange for this decisive step.

When the American mission was finally arranged, Father Fenwick sailed for the new land, planning to locate his Dominican house in Maryland, where he could count on the help of his brothers. When he arrived he found that Archbishop Carroll did not want him to settle in Maryland, but in Kentucky. Without any help, a total stranger to the country he was to evangelize, he set out for the Kentucky wilderness.

For the remaining thirty years of his life, Father Fenwick lived in the saddle. A missionary on horseback, he still managed to found a Dominican novitiate and college at St. Rose, Kentucky, against odds that would have discouraged most men. Riding up and down the new land to help the scattered Catholics, trying to establish the Order and the Church in the wilderness, he had to work against opposition from an unexpected source: his fellow priests of Kentucky. It is easy to see, now, why differences of policy would prevail between the English-trained Dominican and the French-trained Belgian secular priests. People flocked to the Dominicans to confession because they were not so harsh as the Belgian priests, who had unwittingly taken on some of the ideas of the Jansenists. Much hard feeling arose which made progress difficult.

In 1816, Father Fenwick moved on to Ohio. Here in the wilderness a few scattered families of German Catholics had settled, and were praying desperately for a priest. They wrote to Archbishop Carroll, begging for spiritual help, and Father Fenwick was sent to find them. As he rode through the forest, not knowing which way to turn, he heard the sound of an axe. He followed the sound until it led him to the small clearing where a devout German family had been besieging heaven for a priest. Quite naturally he seemed to them like a gift from heaven. This family was to provide the nucleus of the great Catholic advancement in the state of Ohio; the farmer donated land near Somerset for the first church.

Around this rallying point, as the years went on, a vital Catholic center grew up. The Dominican college was moved there from Kentucky, and as the state was opened up to settlement, more priests were trained to care for their needs. The nephew of Father Fenwick joined his uncle in Ohio

507

after his ordination in 1818. Three years later, four more Dominicans arrived in Somerset to aid in the good work. It was a mission that would have delighted St. Dominic, made up as it was of men who were zealous religious in the finest European tradition, and sturdy, hard-riding pioneers in the fashion of the New World.

In 1822 Pope Pius VII appointed Father Fenwick bishop of Cincinnati. Although he might have expected that the position would fall to someone who was experienced in this difficult mission, Father Fenwick had never thought of himself as the likely candidate, and he was terrified. He fled into the wilderness in the vain hope that it was not true at all, but shortly gave up his human fears and returned to accept his responsibilities. He was consecrated at St. Rose's church in Kentucky, which he himself had erected. Since this was only the second time in history that a bishop had been consecrated in the great west beyond the Alleghenies, it was an occasion of great joy and some curiosity to the scattered Catholics. Kentucky Catholics were not anxious to lose their beloved missionary, whom they had always hoped would return to them. But they were very proud of this sign that Kentucky was growing up spiritually to the point where they could furnish a bishop for another state.

Bishop Fenwick said the first Mass in his See city in conditions of dire poverty. The bishop and his party had slept on the floor in an empty house, and the Mass was said in the tiny church the next day. It was obvious to all those who witnessed the ceremony that the new bishop was a holy man and a very poor one. He was rich in courage and also in opportunity; the papal bull of appointment had given him jurisdiction over Michigan and the Northwest Territory. Only two other bishops in the world could boast of a wider field of endeavors. Being a realist, Bishop Fenwick set out as soon as he could for Europe, to solicit funds and priests.

God gave him ten years to build in the wilderness a living church that would be the future glory of a great country. He built a seminary in which he enrolled two young Indian boys as students, thus becoming a champion of an oppressed people and the first man to take practical steps towards a native American clergy. He also enrolled a number of Indians in trade apprenticeships, to help their people. He began America's first Catholic newspaper, the *Catholic Telegraph,* in 1829. Zealous for the development of his own Order, for which he had founded a novitiate and a college, he was equally zealous for the advancement of other Orders and of the secular priesthood. Until 1827 all but two of the priests laboring in his vast vineyard were Dominicans, but by the time of his death he had increased the diocesan clergy and was attempting to bring in enough native-born American priests to staff the seminary as one step towards building a native clergy. He brought in Sisters of Charity and Dominican sisters to begin the vast job of educating the children.

He could say a well-earned "Nunc Dimittis" when death found him—on the road, where he had spent most of his life. Ill with cholera after tending some victims of an epidemic, he rode up to a little hotel and rented a room because he was too sick to ride any farther. There, in a borrowed bed, like St. Dominic himself, he died the following day, September 26, 1832.

IGNATIUS DELGADO AND COMPANIONS
(d. 1838)

> This stranger, who was introduced clandestinely into the kingdom, spends his life in the study of things of the heart and in meditation on what is incomprehensible. . . . (From the death sentence of Bishop Ignatius Delgado.)

Continuing the saga of the martyrs of Tonkin, nearly a hundred years after the death of Blessed Peter Martyr Sanz and companions, two more Dominican bishops died for the faith. They were Bishop Ignatius Delgado and Bishop Dominic Henares. With them a tertiary catechist died, Francis Chien, and the group (beatified in 1900 by Pope Leo XIII) also includes a Spanish priest, Joseph Fernandez, Father Augustine Schoeffler of the Paris Foreign Mission Society, who was a Dominican Tertiary, and twenty-one native confraternity members.

Of the early years of these martyrs we know little. Both were born in Spain, Bishop Delgado in 1762 and Bishop Henares three years later. From the sentence of condemnation itself we learn that Bishop Delgado had labored for nearly fifty years in Tonkin, which argues that he must have been a resourceful man as well as a zealous one. In 1838 the two bishops and the catechist were captured, in a persecution recently stirred up by the mandarin. The prelates and a young priest had been hidden in the village of Kien-lao, and were accidentally betrayed by a little child who was cleverly questioned by a pagan teacher searching for the foreigners. Alarmed at the sudden activities, the captors of Bishop Delgado put him into a small cage which was locked around him, and then put into jail with criminals.

Communism has made us familiar with the type of questioning that Bishop Delgado had to face. A copy of his trial, which still existed a few years ago, showed that he answered truthfully and fearlessly where he himself was concerned, but that no amount of questioning or torture could make him reveal the whereabouts of his companions. A young priest in another place had taken to his heels when the alarm of the bishop's arrest was heard, and was still at large. There was no proof that Bishop Henares had been caught, nor the catechists who worked with him. So Bishop Delgado, an old man of seventy-six, endured the tortures rather than give any slight clue as to where they might be found.

The death sentence was passed on Bishop Delgado, and he was left in the open cage under the summer sun, to exist in misery until it should please the mandarin to kill him. Pagans jeered at him and threw refuse in his face, and he was deprived of even the simplest necessities. Worn out by suffering but still silent as to his companions' whereabouts, he died of dysentery before the mandarin was ready to behead him. The enraged soldiers cut off his head when they found that he had died, and threw the remains into a swift river. Fishermen promptly set about the dangerous business of rescuing the relics.

Bishop Henares was captured with a companion at the same time as Bishop Delgado. He had hidden himself in a boat, and the nervousness of the boatmen gave him away. Five hundred soldiers were detached to bring in the two dangerous criminals, the bishop and his catechist, Francis Chien. They too were questioned endlessly, and kept apart from Bishop Delgado. Two weeks after the death of the first bishop, the second was led out and beheaded in company with his catechist.

The relics of all three martyrs were recovered in part, and were honorably buried by the next Dominicans to come on the scene—Bishop Hermosilla and his companions, who would, as they knew, also be the next to die.

We have no information of the twenty-one members of the Confraternity of the Rosary who are honored with the three martyrs of 1838, nor about the Spanish Father Fernandez. Father Augustine Schoeffler of the Paris Foreign Mission Society should likewise hold a place of honor among Dominicans, as he was a Tertiary. Many of the records of these brave men were lost or deliberately destroyed, and many of them—we hope—may still be found in various neglected spots which war and trouble have caused to be overlooked.

MOTHER ANGELA SANSBURY
(d. 1839)

Several thousand American Dominican sisters are direct spiritual descendants of a valiant little lady who helped to plant the Dominican standard in the Kentucky wilderness. Her name was Maria Sansbury, a name reverenced today not only by the communities that claim her leadership, but by the whole Church in America.

Maria Sansbury was born in Maryland about the year 1800. Her parents were English Catholics who had emigrated to keep their faith. Maria and her sister, Frances, grew up in Kentucky, and were probably educated in Maryland, as many Catholic girls of the time were.

The first Dominican fathers to enter the Kentucky wilderness were Fathers Wilson and Fenwick. They painstakingly carved out a novitiate for the brothers in the new land, and then faced the desperate need for sisters that afflicted the entire country. On one Sunday in February, 1822, Father Wilson made the need for sisters the subject of the day's sermon. One wonders if every sermon he preached reaped such fruit, for at the end of his impassioned plea, nine young women came to him and said in effect, "Here we are, Father; what do we do next?"

The nine young women were all Americans, women who had lived all their lives on the frontier of the new land. They were well educated, as education of the time was reckoned, and no one can say that they lacked good will. Father Wilson took them under his instruction and taught them for a few months. By Easter he was convinced that the time was ripe for action. He prepared the girl whom all regarded as their leader to receive the Dominican habit in a public ceremony.

After the Mass on Easter Sunday, Maria Sansbury was given the habit of St. Dominic and the religious name of Sister Angela. She was the first of uncounted thousands of American girls to choose this garb and this profession, but she could hardly have known it then. Later on the same day, Father Wilson clothed the rest of the girls in the habit in a typically American setting, a log cabin. They had, of course, fixed it up; they had given it the name of St. Mary Magdalen's chapel—but it was still a log cabin, and even at Easter time the wind whistled through the chinks between the logs and reminded the girls that the new venture on which they were deliberately embarking was not going to be a pleasure trip.

Thousands of miles from the nearest convent of Dominican sisters, the young women of Kentucky set about learning the wealth of tradition and custom that the years had made their heritage. Father Wilson acted as novice master, and after a little while it was decided to get a dispensation for Sister Angela—who had not yet worn the habit quite a year—so that she could be their superior.

The new community now acquired not only a superior, but also a house of their own. Sister Angela's father gave them a piece of land with a cabin, a creek, a mill, and a still-house. The cabin they joyfully turned into

St. Magdalen's convent, with the aid of the only tools at hand—brooms and a bucket of whitewash; it was quickly divided into three parts—chapel, refectory, and workroom. They slept in the dark little dormer under the roof, going up and down by means of a ladder. They cooked in an open fireplace. There was no furniture, which made housekeeping quite simple and left plenty of time for prayers and gardening. The gardening was a necessity. One had to eat.

It is not quite clear how the sisters got through their first winter, except that the sheltering hand of God always guards the shorn lamb. People were kind, and the sisters were resourceful, unselfish, and doggedly stubborn. The following year, they decided it was time—since the motto of the Order was to give to others the fruits of contemplation—that they should begin a school. They began it, in the still-house, an original fate for a Kentucky still-house, to be sure.

Just when things seemed to be getting off to a good start, Father Wilson died. It was more than a tragedy for the little community. Their best friend and their kindest father was gone, and they were left alone to face the wilderness and a debt that was all but overwhelming for a small group with no resources. For the next few years the sisters had trials enough to discourage anyone. They prayed and they worked—a simple answer. Eventually it paid off, and their financial affairs took a turn for the better.

More girls came to join the sisters in white. When a call came for sisters to go to Ohio, Sister Angela sent them, although Ohio seemed as far away as Australia to the Kentuckians. The new group settled at Somerset, and soon carved out a place for themselves in the hearts of the whole region. Sister Angela herself went to Somerset to help in the new foundation.

One of the charming and unexpected touches we find in the story of Somerset is the tale of Christopher the tinker. God works in various ways to accomplish His ends; this time He sent an old man to knock on the sisters' door and ask for a meal and lodging in exchange for mending their pots and pans. The sisters gave him the lodging and the food, but explained in some embarrassment that they had so few pots and pans, and really they did not need mending. . . . Christopher went on the road again, mending other people's pots and pans. When he had acquired a little money, he brought it back to the sisters. This shabby old tinker provided the sisters with occasional very welcome bags of money, which he would toss in when he returned from his wanderings. They never quite got rid of Christopher (one does not wish to get rid of an angel, even one in disguise) as he stayed near them for the rest of his life. He lives on today, in the prayers of the sisters to whom he was so devoted.

Sister Angela, or Mother Angela as she is remembered in the communities which stem from her first gallant little band of pioneers, died in Somerset in 1839. Today there are several American communities comprising thousands of members which claim Mother Angela as their foundress.

PAULINE MARIE JARICOT
(1799-1851)

The inscription over the tomb of this servant of God reads: "HERE RESTS PAULINE MARIE JARICOT, FOUNDRESS OF THE SOCIETY FOR THE PROPAGATION OF THE FAITH AND OF THE LIVING ROSARY," but this does not even begin to tell the amount of great works packed into one lifetime by this delicate woman. For Dominicans, however, the chief interest lies in the fact that she was a devoted member of the Third Order and one of the most untiring propagators of the Rosary in the past two centuries—all this in spite of the fact that, for sheer difficulty, her life has few equals. It is doubtful whether anyone else has been so systematically persecuted or lied about in a long time.

Pauline, the pretty and pampered daughter of a silk weaver of Lyons, was born in 1799. Her father was a wealthy man with a rare and beautiful interest in his workmen, an attitude which probably laid the foundations for Pauline's social work long before she was aware of it. Lyons, during his lifetime and hers, was to be a recurring battlefield for the social upheavals bequeathed by the French Revolution. In 1793 M. Jaricot had narrowly escaped death at the hands of the Commune. At least four times Pauline was to endure the horrors of mob fighting under her windows in late flare-ups of the revolution. It was a restless, disillusioning time to live in France.

Pauline as a small child was unaware of strife; she was loved and pampered until the wonder is that she was not wholly spoiled. Her father never refused her anything, and it pleased him to see that his daughter, who was growing to be the prettiest young lady in Lyons, had a kind heart and loved the poor. For Pauline, who found it very pleasant to be alive, the days were a succession of amusing occupations. She danced through a pair of slippers at her sister's wedding, established the hair styles for all the young ladies of the social set, and carried on a whirl of activities that gave no hint of the depths beneath the attractive surface. She took her mother into her confidence on this, and a surprising fact emerged: Pauline wanted to enter the convent. The idea alarmed her father and troubled her mother, and the girl tried not to think about it. She became engaged to a young man who seemed an excellent match for her. Only at rare moments, when she had time to think about it, did she hear an insistent voice calling her to give her life to God. Then one day she suffered an injury that put her to bed for a year of intense suffering. She reviewed her life and soberly evaluated it. At the end of a dreadful year which took her mother, her health, and most of her light-hearted friends including her fiance, away from her, Pauline was ready to listen to the voice of God.

Family and friends were unbelieving when they heard that the fashionable Pauline had given away her pretty clothes and gone to work in the hospital, wearing an unbecoming purple sack of a dress and a ridiculous hat. Unkindly, they considered it what we would call a "publicity stunt." Even her father begged her not to be quite so eccentric; people would think the long illness had affected her mind. But Pauline had embarked on a road that had only one ending, a cross on a hilltop. Bit by bit she stripped away the vanities that held her to secular life. It was not long before all the beggars in Lyons discovered the miracle: a wealthy lady who gave them what they needed and did not, in doing so, offend what fragment of dignity they had managed to salvage from life. Pauline, whose whole life was to be spent in a struggle with money, and who would suffer her most terrible agonies at being considered a spendthrift, understood early and well exactly where money fits into the human plan.

"God will make use of you for his glory, and will use you to accomplish the designs of his mercy." This revelation was to sustain her through many trials. Pauline, who felt a responsibility towards the factory girls of Lyons, began her work with them. It was first of all a social betterment program, without any of the unpleasant connotations of that title. She worked personally with the girls, setting them up in the business of making artificial flowers so that they could support themselves decently. She taught them the neglected truths of religion, stood by them in crises, instructed them, and gave them always a friendly court of appeal. Out of this association with the factory girls of Lyons would grow the first of her controversial works of world-wide charity, the Society for the Propagation of the Faith. It came about naturally enough because of her own love for the foreign missions which she communicated to the girls. They wanted to help, and since they had not much to give, they gave little. Her fine sense of organization made that little effective, because she made each one a promoter who would contact others. Each gave only a *sou* a week, a tiny mite; but the circles widened like circles in the water, reaching out further and further.

The trouble came about through what to us looks remarkably like masculine jealousy. One churchman bluntly told her that "no woman could think up a plan like that." Pauline did not care what people thought of her, or whom they credited with beginning the Society. She made no protest when the direction of the Society was taken out of her hands—by people who took care to wait until success was assured before allying themselves with it. It was God's work, she insisted; if God wanted someone else to run it, why not?

It is unbelievable to read today the lies that were told about Pauline Jaricot, and to reflect that some of them were repeated by highly-placed churchmen who should have known better. "She was an adventuress. She was seeking to defraud the poor factory girls. She lived in luxury while the workmen who furnished her fortune starved." Her friends could produce proofs against every accusation—but no one ever asked them to. When one of the promoters whom Pauline had trusted managed to escape from France with all the Society funds, she was even accused of being in league with him. Her devoted brother, at St. Sulpice studying for the foreign missions, cheered her with reports of how the Society was spreading. Her fellow workers loved her loyally, and all the poor of Lyons were her friends. But from unexpected quarters, even from the pulpit, she heard daily the wounding accusations. "Pride! Who does she think she is, usurping the offices of older and wiser people? She acts against the Church itself; she has no permission, she has stolen someone else's plan, she is not clever enough to think it up herself—she is only after our money!" The effect on a girl with delicate health was inevitable; Pauline fell dangerously ill.

Once again illness was a milestone for Pauline. Her spiritual director bound her to give up all active works of charity for three years, to take no part in anything outside her own home, to give herself entirely to prayer. She loved to pray—her favorite haunt was the Church of Our Lady of Fourvière nearby—but she thought her heart would break at having to abandon her charities. However, she did exactly what she was told, and out of these three years of contemplation came the second great and lasting work of her life, the Society of the Living Rosary.

It began as a plan to distribute rosaries and inexpensive books to poor missions in France, and the Rosary was the spiritual backbone of it. It was built on the same plan as the Society for the Propagation of the Faith; the "sou a day" was in this case a decade of the Rosary, and the units were organized in groups of fifteen so that all the mysteries would be said daily in each little circle. It spread even faster than the mission society had, and in a short time the troubles that rained down upon Pauline were no less than phenomenal. "She is making a great deal of money with the fees—they make great profits on the books and rosaries they sell for the missions; let her try to get Rome to grant permission for such a thing, started by a mere girl!" Spite and jealousy had a holiday at her expense, but the Dominican

Order, traditional preachers of the Rosary, accepted the direction of the Society and soon became enthusiastic about it. Rome, too, showed unmistakable signs of approval.

Pauline was resolutely building a permanent center for the Living Rosary by setting up a sort of hospice, which she named "Nazareth," near the Church of Fourvières, where the business of the Society could be carried out, when she received sad news. Her priest brother, too delicate for the missions, had been her loyal helper in all her projects. And now he was dying, actually poisoned by someone who hated her. Pauline assisted at his holy death and returned to the work at hand. Several young women joined her at the hospice, and helped to disperse her fortune among the poor of Lyons. She began to dream of welding them into a religious community permanently dedicated to the work of the Living Rosary.

This was still unformed when a flare-up of the revolution struck Lyons. The house of Nazareth was directly in the line of fire. When pieces began falling off the roof, the inhabitants finally left it to take refuge in a cave in the garden. Pauline was ill of a fever, so ill that she could not stand up. They put the tabernacle beside her on the mattress and dragged it to the cave shelter. Here they were besieged for three days—cold, ill, and frightened. They had no food but the daily stock of a baker who had taken refuge with them—along with an actress, a butcher, and several of the other neighbors. When the fighting was over, they resumed their charitable and spiritual work as if nothing had happened.

By 1835 it became imperative that Pauline should go to Rome and get some permanent approbation for the Living Rosary Society. Without direct action from the pope, she could never be sure that the people who had thus far interfered with her mail and suppressed the privileges of the Society in France would not find some even better way to wreck the work. So, with one companion, she left for Rome. She was desperately ill, and when she arrived in Rome she collapsed completely. When the day came for her appointment with the pope, she could not stand up. Gregory XVI, who had heard a great deal about her from her friends at Rome, sent an astounding message: since she could not come to him, he would come to her. He spoke to her in the little room at Trinitá Dei Monti, where she was in the care of another holy foundress, Mother Madeleine Sophie Barat.

During the remaining sixteen years of her life, Pauline was to accomplish much for the spread of the faith in the missions and its restoration in France. She suggested the organization which we in America know so well as the Association of the Holy Childhood. Her last venture, had the times been less troubled, might have been the greatest of all, for she had envisioned no less than a community of Christian workmen with a sort of cooperative industry to sustain a living wage and a religious motivation which would counteract the savage and godless teachings of Communism. Unfortunately, she chose unwisely when it came to selecting a manager for the cooperative experiment, and a smooth-talking thief succeeded in making off not only with all of her own fortune but also the investments of others.

Reduced to dire poverty, she set about her last task, to pay back the money invested by others. In this effort she went to the director of the Society for the Propagation of the Faith to ask for recognition as the Foundress so that she might have their assistance in paying off the debts. They curtly refused to recognize that she had ever had anything to do with it or had any claim on their help. Gregory XVI was dead, and there was no one to speak for her to the new pope. Lies flew back and forth over the head of the dying woman who saw her works being stripped away from her one by one—the three Societies she had founded, the group of devoted women at Nazareth she had hoped to make into a religious society. She died in abject poverty, having given every cent of her vast fortune to the poor and every breath of her last years to pay off debts she had not contracted. Not until she had been a year in the family tomb was the last debt shamefacedly wiped out by people who should have seen, long ago, that this woman was a servant of God and had not a shred of personal interest in the money.

Pauline Jaricot had many saints among her friends, and many zealous founders and foundresses besides Mother Barat. The founders of the Marists and of the Viatorian Brothers used to consult her. Frederick Ozanam wrote in her defense, and prominent English converts, members of the Oxford Group, sent her funds, as did the royalty of Germany and Austria. Her most famous friend was the Curé of Ars, who shared many opinions with her. But not all of her friends put together could stop the relentless pressure of gossip and jealousy that shaped her soul through a long lifetime into something fit for heaven. Perhaps this is her last and greatest lesson to an evil-tongued world, to accept even such persecution as this as part of God's plan.

JOSÉ DIAZ SANJURJO AND MELCHIOR GARCIA SAMPEDRO, MARTYRS
(d. 1857-1858)

"I am going to Heaven. I take pity on you who must remain" (last words of Bishop Sanjurjo).

The group of Dominican martyrs beatified in 1952 is made up of Dominicans of the First and Third Orders who died in 1857 and 1858. There were two bishops, Jose Diaz Sanjurjo and Melchior Garcia Sampedro; two Dominican priests of the First Order, two Dominican Tertiary priests, and nineteen lay members of either the Third Order or the Confraternity, of whom seven were fathers of families.

José Sanjurjo was born in Lugo in Spain in 1818. Being a promising student with literary talents, he was marked for a career in the world, and his parents were not too happy about his decision to be a Dominican. Because of their opposition he stole away from home by night and entered the Dominican novitiate at Ocaña, the training ground for missionaries for the Philippines and the Far East.

Melchior Sampedro was born at Cortes in Asturias in 1821. He was a prayerful, serious boy, contemplative by nature and especially fond of the Rosary. Since his parents were too poor to provide him with an education, he set about working his way through college by teaching grammar to younger students. His parents looked forward hopefully to the time when he would raise them from poverty. It was consequently a sacrifice when he left for the Dominican novitiate at the age of twenty-four. The two future missionary martyrs were trained in the same school of sanctity. They were not to meet, however, until they reached the Philippines.

Father Sanjurjo went to Cadiz on making his vows and sailed for Manila, a 120-day voyage. Each day on board the ship he led the Rosary with the passengers. He arrived at Manila on the Feast of the Holy Cross and was assigned to teach at the University of Santo Tomás for six months until he should be assigned to the missions. Father Sampedro arrived in July and begged for immediate assignment.

Only the best and staunchest missionaries were sent to Tonkin because of the desperate dangers on every hand. Even the way there was perilous. As though the perils of crossing the ocean were not enough, they had to run the risk of being killed by the soldiers of the emperor of Tonkin, who watched the ports. The missionaries could only enter the forbidden kingdom in native dress—a short native tunic, loose-fitting trousers, and turbans. Even this was not a good disguise, for most Europeans were much taller than the natives and had heavy beards. They must travel by night, fleeing through woods and swamps, going without food, sometimes hiding for days in a boat half under water, the prey of insects, fever, and exhaustion. Nevertheless, the Dominicans who voluntarily took on this difficult mission fasted and abstained and kept the rule in its entirety.

Into this desperate life the two young Spaniards fitted themselves with enthusiasm. Their companions fell exhausted trying to keep pace. Father Sampedro writes:

Drenched from head to foot, covered with mud; with neither coat nor clothes for change, we deemed ourselves happy, so much, that the Vicar Apostolic and Vicar Provincial of the Eastern Province could sing in a poor hut, with the greatest joy, and I forgot the pains of my feet to praise the Lord. I have no fear of exaggeration in saying that rarely do we have greater joy than during the strongest tribulations.

Shortly after they arrived in Tonkin, the Holy See divided the territory into two vicariates and Father Sanjurjo was appointed vicar of the central one. Father Sampedro was appointed coadjutor with right of succession. Their predecessor had been martyred a short time before. The appointment of the two new bishops came just in time to meet the full fury of the new persecution.

In spite of their care and disguise, the two Europeans were hard to hide in a land of little men who spoke another tongue. The Christians guarded them carefully, but one of the soldiers traced Father Sanjurjo and caught him in a surprise raid. He was taken to prison for two months, where his great charity did much to preach the meekness of Christ among the people who saw him bearing no grudge against the man who had betrayed him. On July 20, 1857, he was led out to execution. Chained heavily, he was marched in a long procession bright with pageantry and loud with oriental music. The emperor's elephants dressed in glittering trappings, and the banners of the various military groups, gave vivid color to an occasion of terrible torture for the foreigner who had dared to invade the ancient kingdom. Bishop Sanjurjo was beheaded and his body thrown into the sea.

Bishop Sempedro was undaunted by the fate of his companion, though he realized that his own would be the same. He even wanted to come out of hiding and make a public proclamation to prove that the priests were not afraid, but was dissuaded by the Christians who pointed out that his time would come soon enough anyway, and in the meantime they needed him. It was only a short time until a trap was laid for him and he was ambushed and captured. He was put into a small cage, a particularly terrible torture, and, along with two native laybrothers, taken to the same prison where his predecessor had been.

Almost a year to the day after Bishop Sanjurjo died, Bishop Sampedro was led out to execution and taken along his route to Calvary, pelted by mud and stones. Finally he was laid on the ground and stretched out like the figure on the cross which the mandarin hated, and hacked to pieces bit by bit. His only response was to repeat the Holy Name until death claimed him. The laybrothers were tortured and beheaded at the same time. After their death, their remains were thrown into a ditch, and the king's elephants were led to trample over them. The beasts knelt down and refused to step on the spot where the martyrs lay. Eventually some of the relics of both of the bishops were recovered and treasured by the Christians.

Beatified in the same group with the two bishops are twenty-three others of every state in life. They died at different times and places, but since all were connected in some way with the Order, they have been grouped together. There were four priests, all natives. Father Dominic Mau and Father Joseph Tuan, who was far advanced in years, were priests of the First Order. Father Dominic Cam and Father Thomas Khuong, the son of a mandarin, were Tertiary priests. All died gloriously after long tortures. The laymen, members of the Confraternity, included men of all social classes. One was the wealthy Dominic An-Kham, who at the age of eighty was the prior of the Confraternity. He died with his son and several other wealthy members of the Confraternity who were killed for protecting missionaries. There were also two poor fishermen and two farmers who had been asked to trample on the cross and refused to do so. A doctor, a judge, a tax collector, and several independent farmers, of whom most were the fathers of families, all gave up their lives joyfully in the cause of Christ.

FATHER CHARLES DES GENETTES
(d. 1860)

In reading the history of the consecration of the world to the Immaculate Heart, one is bound to come across the name of Father Charles Des Genettes. Few Dominicans realize his close connection with the Order, or the fact that he was himself a Dominican Tertiary.

Father Charles Des Genettes was appointed to the half-ruined church of Our Lady of Victories in Paris in 1832. The revolution had driven out its Augustinian guardians, and the building had been used for the bestial ceremonies of the revolutionaries and then turned into a stock exchange. When the young priest came to try to rebuild his parish there, he found himself up against terrible difficulties. The indifference of the people was as solid as a stone wall. In December, 1836, Father Des Genettes was saying Mass in an almost empty church, and his heart cried out with discouragement. For a few minutes he was too miserable to go on with the Mass, and suddenly he heard a voice saying to him, "Consecrate your parish to the most Holy and Immaculate Heart of Mary." The very thought of being a visionary terrified him, but he decided to do as he had been told, and set about it by beginning a Confraternity of Our Lady. Ten people heard him announce at Mass that there would be Vespers of Our Lady that afternoon, and an explanation of the Confraternity would be given at that time. Four hundred people, most of them men, appeared for Vespers. Our Lady had worked her first miracle in his behalf. From this small beginning the Confraternity and the parish of Our Lady of Victories took new life, and began to revivify the world with its dedication to the Immaculate Heart.

During a visit to Rome, Father Des Genettes met Lacordaire, and was fired by his zeal and by the project of bringing the Dominicans back to France. He felt that he was too old to become a Dominican himself, but he promised to do everything he could to help in the good work. When Lacordaire came to Paris, Father Des Genettes threw open the facilities of Our Lady of Victories church to him, and it was here that the first chapter of Dominican Tertiaries in France was organized.

In January, 1844, the first convention of Dominican Tertiaries met at the church to be given the cincture marking their admission to the Order. Father Des Genettes, who was at the altar as assistant to Father Lacordaire, began to have scruples. "I have no business here," he told himself; "this should be a place for a Dominican. I do not belong here." Lacordaire came back from the communion rail where he had given the cincture to the Tertiaries, and the old priest knelt in the sanctuary and begged that he too should be received as a Tertiary. With great emotion, Lacordaire received him as the first priest-Tertiary of the Order in France.

For the remainder of his life, which was marked by the holy intervention of Our Lady at every crisis, Father Des Genettes continued his benefactions to the Order. The Tertiaries continued to hold their meetings in his church until they outgrew it, at which time he secured a chapel for them at a little distance from Our Lady of Victories. It was sometimes impossible for him to go to the Tertiary chapel on account of his age and infirmities, but he always carefully sent word to the prior where he was and why he could not come. When the Tertiaries needed a manual of prayers, he found a printer for them and paid for the printing.

After the First Order convent was established in Paris, the venerable old pastor of Our Lady of Victories always attended the feast day Masses there. He was asked to preach on great occasions in the new Dominican church, his principal joy being to preach on the Feast of St. Dominic. Even when the Franciscans sang the Mass on this day, Father Des Genettes preached.

At his death in 1860, the Tertiaries wanted him to be buried in the Tertiary habit, but out of deference to his flock, who had known him longer than the Dominicans had, he was buried in priestly vestments, with habit and cappa folded at his feet.

JEROME HERMOSILLA AND VALENTINE BERRIO-OCHOA AND COMPANIONS, MARTYRS
(d. 1861)

The persecution which had taken the lives of Bishop Delgado and Bishop Henares was still raging when, in April, 1841, Father Hermosilla was consecrated bishop of Tonkin. It was a position that was practically synonymous with martyrdom; several of the bishops appointed for Tonkin had not even lived to be consecrated. However, Bishop Hermosilla was to have one of the longest careers of these men who ordinarily lived such brief and glorious lives. He was to work for twenty years in this perilous field and, only after suffering all that the missions could offer, would death come to him, together with Bishop Valentine who came to China many years later.

Of the early years of either of the two bishops we know nothing. The fact that they were chosen for Tonkin is implicit information that they were men of splendid courage and resourcefulness, probably fluent at languages and skillful about the small details of getting from place to place. They must also have been men with no fear, for it was almost certain death for a European to enter Tonkin, and death by such horrible means that we today cannot even read about it without getting slightly ill. Bishop Hermosilla made it his first task on taking over his difficult episcopate to gather up the relics of the two bishops who had been martyred just before he came. Bishop Delgado had been thrown into the sea, but some of the relics were recovered by a fisherman. These and the remains of the other martyrs Bishop Hermosilla had carefully preserved, and it was he who wrote the account of their martyrdom as told to him by those who had watched it happen. It is an astounding picture, that of the young Spanish bishop carefully recording the terrible tortures that he knew quite well were waiting for him.

The twenty years of Bishop Hermosilla's life in Tonkin were made up of constant heroism, constant flight, and unswerving faith. He had to hold his flock together, while some of his finest helpers fell at his side. His work must all be done in secret. There was always the gnawing uncertainty as to whether the recently converted Christians, some of whose families were still pagan, could be trusted not to betray the hiding place of the priest or whether, if captured themselves, they could hold up under torture. It was a weak Christian who finally betrayed Bishop Hermosilla and Bishop Valentine and led to their death in 1861.

The two bishops had been hidden on board a ship, en route to a place where they were needed to give the sacraments to a group of hard-pressed

Christians. The betrayer told the captain the identity of his two passengers, and the captain summoned the soldiers. Even so, a number of courageous Christians tried to rescue them and almost succeeded. They were betrayed a second time and placed in chains. Three hundred men were sent to escort them to the capital.

As they approached the capital they saw with horror that the soldiers had laid a crucifix in the road where they would have to step on it to proceeed. Heavily manacled and weak from their torture, the two men fought so vigorously against this sacrilege that the soldiers finally had to remove the cross. The martyrdom was not long in coming. The bishops and a number of native Christians, as well as two other Spanish Dominicans of the First Order, were led to die in a triumphant procession. The prisoners were placed in cages and half-carried and pushed to the place of execution, surrounded by the screaming crowds and the elephants and other beasts of the emperor's stables. Christians who watched them said afterwards that the prisoners seemed rapt in prayer to the point where they were almost unaware of the noise around them. At the place of execution they were bound and tied to stakes on the ground, and then beheaded. After death they were guarded for several days so that the Christians could not come and take away the relics.

There were several other Dominicans who died at about the same time and are grouped together with the two bishops. One of these was Father Hyacinth Castagneta. There exists an affecting account of his voyage to Tonkin which tells of the letters he wrote home to his mother, of the serious mouth infection which he picked up on shipboard, and the forty-eight days of seasickness crossing the Atlantic. He gives an account of the march across Mexico and the embarking on another ocean; of the storm, the pestilence, cargo thrown overboard, the arrival at the Marianas with spoiled food and everyone sick on board the ship. Manila he found in the hands of the English; he and the other passengers were abandoned with their luggage by the terrified ship captain and had to wander around for months before locating the Dominicans. Hyacinth was ordained in the Philippines. Another sixty-six day voyage stretched between him and Fo-gan, where the memory of the martyrdom of Peter Sanz was still fresh. Hyacinth was captured and tortured, and once deported from Macao. He finally died by beheading.

At the trial of Vincent Liem, a native Christian who is honored with the same group, two criminals were present. One cursed and one begged for his prayers and one of the onlookers cried out loudly: "Why doesn't the Lord of Heaven come to deliver them in order that we may believe?"

The others included in this group are Francis Gil de Fredric, Matthew Alonzo Leziniana, and Joseph Klang. Pope Pius X beatitfied them in 1906.

Due to a number of miracles, the cause of Bishop Valentine Berrio-Ochoa has been separated from that of the group, and since 1952 the honor of canonization has been sought for him.

HYACINTH BESSON
(d. 1861)

The dearest friend and confidante of Lacordaire was a young artist who portrayed with his brush the spiritual beauty that the great preacher so well expressed in words. His name was Hyacinth Besson.

John Baptist Besson was born in his grandfather's chateau near Besancon. His father was killed in battle before the boy was born, leaving a young and beautiful widow to care for the delicate child. Mistress of the chateau was his mother's aunt, who had been driven out of a cloister during the French Revolution. It was a wealthy and pious establishment where the little boy first became aware of the world; but when he was still quite small the master of the house died, the fortune was lost, and his mother had to go to work.

The gentle Madame Besson was not accustomed to the hard work that now became her portion. She was annoyed by people who thought she should marry again, and by many dangers to which her beauty exposed her. Once, she confessed in after years, the only thing that kept her from throwing herself into a river was the thought of her little boy. Given such circumstances, the bond between mother and son was bound to be closer than usual. She did consent to John Baptist going out to school, but would not allow him to go to the seminary.

The young John Baptist was a competent though not an eager student. He was forever in trouble with his teachers for drawing pictures of them or of his classmates. By the time he was seventeen it was fairly obvious that he should be trained in art. He was sent to art school and soon was involved in the disturbing world of free-thinking young men that France harbored at the time. John Baptist himself never gave up his faith, though several of his close friends did so. The contact with such unhappy people had the effect of making him even more fervent in his religious beliefs. He and a devoted friend set out to counteract the godless behavior of their fellow artists by living a complete Christian life.

Study eventually called John Baptist to Rome, and he took his mother with him. He set up shop in a tiny apartment near the Capuchin convent, the only adornment of his house a lovely old medieval Madonna statue before which he kept a light burning. He had been in Rome only a short time when, inevitably, he met Lacordaire.

Longing to join the great man in his work of bringing the religious back to France, John Baptist knew it was for the time impossible. So he and his friends organized, under Lacordaire's direction, an artist's guild, dedicated to St. John the Evangelist—"because he was foremost among all the Savior's disciples to penetrate the mysteries of divine love and beauty, which are the eternal objects of contemplation to all true artists." The guild professed as its aim the sanctification of art and artists, and pledged to lead the Christian life and to pray for the conversion of artists. Its members dressed simply in black, white, or gray, kept a crucifix and a Madonna statue in their studios, and made a special effort to guard its younger members from irreligious influences. The guild included not only artists and sculptors but also architects and musicians. One of its earliest members was the composer Gounod.

In 1840, John Baptist was sent by Lacordaire to the Dominican house of Viterbo, to paint a copy of the tile of "Our Lady of the Oak" which would be placed in the first French convent. While he was painting the picture, he made up his mind finally and irrrevocably that he would have to be a Dominican. Now there remained only the task of telling his mother. Close as they were, he knew it would be a mortal blow, and he stalled it off as long as possible. Finally he told her. Madame Besson had known it was coming; she reeled under the blow, but responded, "I only ask to go where you go; if you are happy, I shall be happy too."

When Lacordaire went to Santa Sabina to begin his work, stating frankly, "Brothers, we are gathered here to pursue a work appalling in its difficulties," John Baptist Besson and his two best friends, an artist and an architect, were among the volunteeers. There were also the tall young Abbé Jandel, who had come to Rome to be a Jesuit, and a convert Jew. They began their work with great enthusiasm, and were barely started when the group was broken up and sent to two separate novitiates. The word to disband came on the very eve of their reception of the habit. Lacordaire, his heart broken, told them that they were still free. No one left him, though all were saddened as they took out a slip of paper with their religious names, and heard their assignment to another house. John Baptist was to be Brother Hyacinth, and was to make his novitiate at Bosco.

During that difficult year of novitiate, Brother Hyacinth's two best friends died, both of tuberculosis.

Why Brother Hyacinth decided never to paint again is not quite clear; he evidently regarded painting as a rival to his vocation. He resolved in beginning the major studies for the priesthood that he would never paint again unless obedience told him to do so.

Hyacinth Besson was the first one of Lacordaire's little group ordained; he said his first Mass on Rosary Sunday, 1843, with Lacordaire at his side. When Lacondaire returned to his preaching, Madame Besson was there in the crowd at Notre Dame, listening to the great preacher and praying that her son would return to France. The first French house was indeed opened that year, and the tile her son had painted was hung as its central treasure; but Father Besson was not one of the pioneer band to return to France. Not until two years later did he come. Then, for two happy weeks she visited with him and with the other brothers, all of whom she had long since adopted. After the brief and happy vacation, she returned to Paris, where she took care of other young art students, and there she died suddenly of cholera a few months later. Her own son was far away, but other Dominicans buried her and sent the sad news to Brother Hyacinth.

Busy with missions, retreats, and spiritual direction, Father Besson had no time for art. When cholera struck again, he went out to nurse the sick, and spent weeks in imminent danger of infection without catching the disease. Once, when making a patient's bed, he tipped over the lamp and got so covered with oil that someone had to put him to bed and wash his habit. From the quiet but thoroughly Dominican life he was leading in France, Father Jandel summoned him to Rome to be prior at Santa Sabina.

Father Jandel was now master general and in the throes of rebuilding the Order, which had deteriorated during the years of revolution and war until observance and membership were at a low ebb. He was a firm superior, and he wanted another firm superior at Santa Sabina. Father Besson carried out his wishes there, and did much to re-establish regular observance. He was very strict both with himself and with others. Once, when funds were low and a creditor demanded money, Father Besson sent the bursar to the chapel to pray to Our Lady for help. When a man walked in and gave the bursar a sum of money that would pay half the bill, he came out and consulted Father Besson. "Perhaps the baker will take half the money and wait for the rest?" he said hopefully. "Do you think the Blessed Virgin does things by halves?" demanded Father Besson. "Get back in there and pray for the rest of it!"

Father Jandel again called Father Besson to the work of the reform, this time as a painter. He was to do a series of murals in the chapter hall of St. Sixtus. Here, with one laybrother as companion and occasional model, he was to work for the next two years. Once, he was so engrossed in his painting that he did not even notice a carriage arriving, nor see the white-clad visitor who watched him for a long time. Only when the embarrassed laybrother came up after him did he awaken to the fact that Pope Pius IX was looking over his shoulder.

If he was busy with painting, he was even more busy with the care of souls. His days were always in pieces, as he went here and there to help with confessions, or took time to advise some eager soul in the spiritual life. Even after he had moved into the deserted convent of St. Sixtus, where he lived in the cell of Benedict XIII, his time was never his own.

In 1854 he was again made prior of Santa Sabina. At this time he painted a complete life of St. Dominic in murals. He took great interest in the archeological discoveries made at this time when the banks of the Tiber were excavated behind the convent. From this work he was summoned to go to Armenia to help on the missions.

The Dominican missions of Armenia have a tradition going back to the "wandering brethren among the pagans" of the thirteenth century, but in the mid-nineteenth century, even the re-established missions were in serious trouble due to political uprisings among the Turks. The Chaldean ritual made continual trouble for Latin missionaries, and Father Besson's first hope was to establish a Chaldean branch of the Order that would bridge over this difficulty. Before anything could be done in this regard, the plague struck Armenia, and he found himself in the midst of tending the sick, recognized by Christian and Moslem alike as a doctor. Nestorian priests and native chieftains lined up outside his door waiting for his treatments, and he did great work in breaking down prejudice by his kindness and capability. When he returned to Rome, he found that he could not forget the East and its needs; his hands itched for a brush to express what he had seen there, and his heart longed to reach out salvation to them.

France at the moment needed him worse than Armenia did. The French province was divided between the advocates of extreme severity and those of modified observance. In settling the trouble, which he managed to do, Father Besson found himself between Lacordaire and Jandel—an uncomfortable position, to be sure. Keeping the friendship of both, he resolved the trouble, and returned to the East.

He was secretly hoping for a martyr's death, for affairs had worsened in his absence and missionaries were in danger. However, the death that awaited him was that of illness. He died of typhoid fever in May, 1861, at a time when all of his brethren were too ill even to bury him. His last rites were lovingly performed by Chaldean monks, who regarded him as their good friend, and he was buried in a land that his brothers were soon to be forced to abandon. When the news reached Lacordaire that Father Besson was dead, he wept uncontrollably; he himself would die in a short while, his heart heavy for the loss of this most gifted son in Christ.

HENRI DOMINIC LACORDAIRE
(1802-1861)

In listing the greatest preachers produced by the Order which bears the name of "Preachers," one man who most certainly should be near the top of the list is Henri Dominic Lacordaire. After the original three great preachers, St. Dominic, Blessed Reginald, and Blessed Jordan, it would be hard to find any man who influenced so many people by his preaching. To Lacordaire, also, must go much of the credit for the rebuilding of the Dominican Order in its hour of need.

Henri Dominic Lacordaire was born in Burgundy in 1802, one of four sons of a doctor who died when the children were very small. Being delicate in health, Henri was left in the country when his mother went to the city to work, and he grew up among peaceful and beautiful surroundings, far from the turmoil that was agitating France at that time. He was a lively, intelligent boy with a gift of oratory, and soon became the favorite of a teacher who was intellectually gifted but spiritually disturbed. For ten years the brilliant lad wandered outside the Church, unwilling to abandon it, but unable to reason his way back. Finally, at the age of twenty-two he returned to the sacraments at the cathedral of Notre Dame and, constitutionally unable to do anything by halves, threw over a promising career to become a priest.

At the Sulpician seminary he discovered that his impetuous and argumentative nature was a definite handicap. The Sulpicians were conservative and suspicious, as well they might be in a country still riddled with Jansenism. They finally sent their brilliant and uncomfortable student off to study theology in Paris. Here he was ordained in 1827, to the tremendous surprise of his friends and in spite of the doubts of the clergy. The Archbishop, who had ordained the impetuous young man against the better judgment of all the wise and prudent, temporized by sending the young firebrand to teach catechism to thirty school girls at the Academy of the Visitation. It was hard to see how he could get into trouble there, but he did; the sisters reported, regretfully, that he was too intelligent.

Bursting with zeal and with ideas of what to do with it, the young priest decided to go to America, which was desperately in need of priests. He was offered the post of superior of a seminary in the new country, and one can only wonder what American Catholic history might have been had he not, at the last minute, met a brilliant and misguided man who was to change the course of his life and that of thousands of others. This was the Abbé Lamennais, a twisted genius whose ideas of spiritual and social reform sounded excellent to the zealous young Father Lacordaire.

Lacordaire's association with this man was to last a year and to bring him to the brink of disaster. They worked together publishing a paper that set all France aflame with new religious energy and which did not, at first, show its anti-clerical bias. They planned together for a new religious order. And then the Abbé Lamennais took issue with Church authority, and when the battle lines were clearly marked, his young friend had to turn sorrowfully away from him rather than defy the Church himself. Lamennais went from disaster to disaster and finally died outside the Church he had served so brilliantly but so imprudently. Lacordaire, to whom friendship was the most sacred thing on earth, had to pick up the pieces of his life and start over. The archbishop of Paris, who might well have penanced the young priest for his indiscreet zeal, acted upon inspiration and offered him the pulpit of Notre Dame for a series of Lenten sermons.

Lacordaire's success was phenomenal, his preaching causing a sensation that no one before or since has ever produced in Paris. His opening conference at Notre Dame was preached to 6000 people, mostly men; the numbers increased until there was "standing room only" for hours before the sermon was scheduled to start. For two Lents he packed the cathedral with people and preached to them on Christian doctrine. Then, on his last Sunday of the second series, he made an announcement that rocketed through Paris like lightning; he was retiring from the pulpit. He was going to Rome. Rumor added the incredible tidings that he planned to become a monk.

The religious orders were banned from France, and if Lacordaire became a monk he could never return, the ultimate sorrow for a Frenchman. Once in Rome, he thought over the situation, prayed about it and studied the rules of all the orders; then he came up with the most dazzling idea so far—he would become a Dominican, and bring the Order back to France. It took courage, persistence, and daring, qualities to which he added a flair for the dramatic. His enthusiasm was contagious as always, and he and his companions went to the novitiate. The weather was cold and miserable, and they were foreigners among people who did not share their enthusiasm. Still, in spite of illness and drastic misunderstandings, the group persevered.

This first group of disciples is worth a second glance. They were all young men—Lacordaire's appeal was always to the young—all happy and doing well in their professions. Two were artists, one an architect, one a lawyer; Alexander Jandel had come to Rome to be a Jesuit, and there was a young Jewish convert among them. Two of the most promising members died of tuberculosis while in the novitiate. Still, the group survived, and the day came when Lacordaire set out for France, wearing the forbidden habit and carrying an old soutane which a friend had forced upon him in case he should have to wear it outside his habit. He struck Paris like an atom bomb. Some hated him, some thought he was another Elias; no one could possibly ignore him.

Once again the archbishop of Paris displayed the courage of his convictions, and though even he wondered about the wisdom of it, allowed Lacordaire to go into the most famous pulpit in the world wearing a religious habit that had been outlawed in France. The king argued with the archbishop, anticlericals marched; the great preacher remained. Lacordaire preached for seven years in the pulpit of Notre Dame, and became so much a part of that edifice that his name will always be synonymous with it to men of his country.

Lacordaire's attempt to bring the Dominican Order back to France was successful, even though it moved more slowly than he liked. He first of all organized Third Order groups, then opened houses of the First Order. When these were firmly established, he rebuilt the ruined monastery at Prouille, abandoned to the weather for nearly a century. His was a tempestuous approach to spirituality, that of an enthusiast. But, as he says plaintively in one place, "What is difficult is to carry the cross each day, the cross which is not bloodstained but which bruises the skin a little without making it bleed, and which is composed of restraint, tediousness, and languor. If one could only mount Calvary once and for all, and give one's body once and for all to the executioners, what pleasure! But no, the torment is in detail; a little cut of the whip, a little slap in the face, a little humiliation."

Père Lacordaire was occupying three positions when death caught up with him; he was provincial of France, headmaster of the boys' college, and founder of the Third Order teaching fathers, each of these a task which made endless demands on his strength. A few months before he died he was made a member of the French Academy, the highest honor his country could bestow on him, but those who saw him receive the honor wept without restraint, for the signs of death were on his face and in his slow movements. He fell victim to a paralytic stroke while saying Mass, and died some months later, in November, 1861, mourned by his country, by the Order, and by the world.

DOMINIC CANUBIO
(1804-1864)

Bishop of Segovia in Spain during the troubled days of the persecutions in the mid-nineteenth century, Dominic Canubio earned an eviable place in the hearts of his fellow men.

Baptized Dominic Luke Peter of Alcantara, Canubio, he began life in 1804 well equipped with both names and wealth. More importantly, his parents were pious and charitable. His father used to take him to visit the Carthusian monastery when he was still a very small child. His mother, determined to keep him humble, sent him to bring water from the village well as if he were the son of a poor man. Dominic responded readily to such pious upbringing, and at the age of fourteen entered the Dominican convent at Jerez.

Two years later, religious persecution broke out in Spain. Convents were plundered, and were hampered on every side by laws which forbade them to accept new subjects. All those having less than twenty-four members were to disband, and the convent of Jerez was forced to close. Dominic had finished his philosophy course and was beginning his theology when he was obliged to return home. After a year, the arrival of French troops changed the status of religious houses once more, and many of them reopened. Dominic returned to Jerez, made his solemn profession, and was ordained in Seville in 1827. Here, until the next revolution, he taught at the College of St. Thomas. In 1835, the convents were once more invaded by a hostile government, and many religious were killed. Dominic returned home again, this time with gratitude, for his parents were very old, and both of them died while he was at home with them.

Living was precarious for priests. Many left Spain and went to the Far East or to America. Father Canubio, who had been director of a convent of Second Order nuns, was put in charge of a boys' school, and shortly after this, in 1848, he was appointed bishop of Segovia. The diocese was in process of reorganization after the revolution, and everything was in a formidable snarl of red tape. He set out to do what he could to untangle matters. It was not an enviable position.

The sixteen years of his office as bishop of Segovia were noteworthy for the religious aspect of his work. He rebuilt churches and schools, revised the system of education, and proved himself an able administrator; but one can do all these without attracting any love. Bishop Canubio's flock loved him. Down to the smallest child in the poorest village, all were convinced of his personal interest in their welfare. His spirit of poverty and mortification were evident, though he made no show of them He took personal care of his sick servants, faithfully attended choral exercises at the cathedral, made visits to the country parishes, and listened sympathetically to the problems of the people there. It was his personal concern that endeared him to them. Re-establishing the complex machinery of a modern diocese in a disturbed country was a great feat of administration, but he built even better in the hearts of his people.

One of the proudest tasks of Bishop Canubio was to announce to his diocese the papal proclamation of the dogma of the Immaculate Conception. Spain had been the first of many countries to establish a feast in honor of this privilege of Our Lady, and devotion to the Mother of God was traditional among Spaniards from apostolic times. Consequently, it was the crowning glory of his life for the good bishop to be able to announce that Our Lady's Immaculate Conception had been recognized as a dogma of the Church. He had the occasion celebrated with great solemnity, and started a great revival of devotion to Our Lady in the diocese.

During a late flare-up of the revolutionary troubles, Bishop Canubio had to move his entire seminary into the mountains for safety, and to put in safe places several relics and shrines which he felt were in danger. There was hardly a day of complete peace in his lifetime, a situation which makes all the more remarkable his calmness of spirit and his firmness in observing the rules.

Bishop Canubio went to Rome for the canonization of the Japanese martyrs, some of whom were from his diocese. He was present at the election of Father Jandel as master general. At this time he was offered several dioceses which would have been much easier to administer; he refused them all, and returned to the work in Segovia.

Early in the year 1864, the good bishop realized that he was a very sick man. A cancer on his shoulder weakened him until he was unable to get out of bed, but he had himself brought to the shrine of Our Lady of the Palm at Cadiz. The Carmelites carried him on a litter to the feet of the miraculous statue, and he prayed earnestly that if it was God's will he would recover to complete the work in his diocese. For a little while it seemed that he was a little better. He rose, in great pain, to preach on All Saints' day, but the next morning he could not get up out of bed. He died a few weeks later, mourned by the whole diocese.

SAMUEL AUGUSTINE MAZZUCHELLI
(1806-1864)

The great apostle of midwestern America was born in Milan of wealthy parents in 1806. He entered the Dominican Order in Rome in 1822, receiving the religious name of Augustine. In that same year, in the far-off wilderness of Ohio, a diocese was being erected to serve the scattered Catholics. In 1827 the missionary bishop of this diocese came to Rome recruiting help, and an earnest young student, Augustine Mazzuchelli, listened eagerly to his stories of poverty and hardship, and promptly turned his back on a life of comparative ease to volunteer to go to Ohio. He sailed for the new land in 1828, while he was still a sub-deacon.

If anyone ever had a rugged introduction to American life, it was the young Brother Augustine. The voyage across the Atlantic was unusually stormy, and for several days the ship was blown back and forth helplessly in a hurricane. Still battered from this experience, Brother Augustine arrived on American soil and proceeded to Cincinnati. Here he was left alone for a few brief months while he studied English. At Christmas time he was sent to Kentucky, a trip which entailed a long train ride and then a thirty-eight mile trip on horseback. Brother Augustine had never been on a horse before, and at the end of the thirty-eight miles he prayed earnestly that he would never see one again. He was to return to Cincinnati in February, but the Ohio River was jammed with ice and he was marooned for some time at Bardstown. Finally, battered and bewildered, he arrived back in Cincinnati, still clinging to his English grammar, which he studied at every opportunity.

Brother Augustine made his final studies for the priesthood at the convent of St. Joseph in Somerset, and was ordained in Cincinnati in 1830. He had by now partly accustomed himself to this wild country where a priest might be summoned to ride ninety miles on a sick call or must go five hundred miles down the river to confession. But his first mission, to the island of Mackinac in the straits between Lakes Huron and Michigan, made fresh demands on the young recruit from Italy. Here his parishioners were fur-trappers and Indians. Five hundred French-Canadians, who traveled more than 200 miles to go to confession, greeted him with tearful enthusiasm. Starved for religious services, they were incensed by the activities of a number of Protestant missionaries who were going about among the Indians and in the settlements, preaching against Catholic beliefs. Father Mazzuchelli found himself obliged to plan a series of sermons dealing with the bigoted charges of these ministers. He was still only a very timid beginner in the English language, and it was a difficult assignment. However, he arranged a series of instructions to which he invited both Catholics and Protestants. Two Anglicans and a Calvinist, curious to hear this brash missionary, came to the instructions and were converted.

It was hardly reasonable to expect one man to accomplish what he attempted. But his efforts were so successful that he was able to shape the settlement of Mackinac Island into a smooth-running community that was actually laying plans for building a church and rectory before he rode on to other fields. He converted an entire Indian tribe at Green Bay, and worked among the Menominees and their neighboring tribes.

He, whose introduction to horseback riding had been so drastic, now found himself committed to a lifetime in the saddle. He learned to make himself perfectly at home in his portable cloister, and his lively mind found much food for prayer and meditation in the rich wild land around him. Picking his way cautiously through a swamp or along a wet woodland trail, his hands guided the horse and his busy mind prepared sermons—dogmatic sermons, which required a great deal of thought as a bulwark against the Protestant teachings with which his people were surrounded, a task further complicated by the necessity of delivering them in English.

Some day someone may make a special study of Father Mazzuchelli's use of language. Whether he had the gift of tongues would be hard to say, but his contacts were remarkable. In all his mission work of thirty years, he rarely met anyone who spoke his Italian tongue; the French-speaking trappers and the English-speaking Americans were only a part of his vast flock. Frequently his mission was among the Indians, and every tribe of Indians had a separate language, completely unrelated to any other. Sometimes when he came to a new tribe he had time to learn enough of the language to preach fluently in their own tongue, or took time to have a prayerbook or catechism printed in the language (if there was a printing press within reach). At other times, he learned enough to hear confessions and give necessary instructions for the sacraments. When really pressed for time, he had to use an interpreter.

Pioneer mission work was dangerous in the extreme, even from a physical standpoint. One morning Father Mazzuchelli woke up to find a large rattle-snake looking him coldly in the eye. Another time, when he rose after an hour's chat with a sick Indian, he discovered that a rattler had been coiled up asleep under his habit. On one occasion, he recorded laconically, he "killed and ate a bear" in the course of his journey from one mission to another. He had, of course, no house of his own, but lived wherever there was a spare corner in sacristy or church, or in someone's attic or barn. In March of 1838 he had to cross the Mississippi on a sick call. Floating ice damaged the canoe and it began to fill. Kneeling in the freezing water, he cried out, "Lord save us, we perish!" and kept on paddling until the canoe reached land and promptly sank. The only thing that seemed to trouble him about this precarious sort of life was the deprivation of confession. Twice a year he went down the river five hundred miles to St. Louis so he could receive the sacrament. He regretted that he could not go more often.

Father Mazzuchelli earned the title "Builder of the West." He built the first church in the little village of Dubuque, where 250 people gathered around him at its consecration on the Feast of the Assumption in 1835. All through the rich lands of the midwest he did the same work of organizing parishes—acting as architect and builder part of the time, as dynamo all the time. Part of the time he *was* the church, his pocket being the only tabernacle where the Lord could rest in the vast wilderness. He said the first Mass in Iowa City in 1840, in the home of a German mechanic, and preached a sermon the next day in the hall of the town's only hotel. His next Mass was in the cabin of an Irish family ten miles away. In this bleak wilderness, who but the tireless friar would dare to dream of a church and school? Broken in health, but borne up by his plans for the future of the Ohio country, he sailed for Rome in 1843. After medical treatment and a great deal of enthusiastic salesmanship, he returned to America with permission to found a college and a new province of the Order. The college, which he named for St. Thomas, failed after a few years, and the province did not materialize. But he sowed the seeds that were to germinate after his death into a fruitful harvest. It was too soon, in 1843, to hope for a college in the Ohio wilderness. But he began a work at Sinsinawa Mound that was to carry on his name as builder and dreamer. Here the Third Order sisters were to light the torch of Dominican education in the new land, and in helping their establishment among the pioneers he guaranteed the future of the Church in the states of the midwest.

Father Mazzuchelli was one of the first map-makers to show the central United States in detail. He had covered almost every mile of this vast country, and recorded his findings in neat little drawings with Italian and English names and comments.

The apostle of the midwest died in 1864, after a lifetime of fruitful labors of which both the spiritual and the physical results would be far greater than even he could dream. His last years had been spent in pain, but he had not thought to complain about it—he was too busy building the kingdom of Christ in the wilderness.

It seems a shame that America, who honors her heroes so magnanimously, should have overlooked this man who brought to our New World the finest gifts of the old, and whose hand is so evident in the carving of our central states out of the wilderness.

MOTHER MARGARET HALLAHAN
(1803-1868)

Margaret Mary Hallahan was born in 1803 in London, of Irish parents. Her mother and father both died while she was small, and Margaret at the age of nine became a servant in the house of a French lace merchant. The woman was sharp-tongued and unsympathetic and left the orphan child to her own spiritual resources. Margaret, warm-hearted and lonely, turned to God and his Blessed Mother for the help that human friends did not give her. It was to have a strengthening effect on her character for the difficult years to come.

At the age of twenty, Margaret went to work for the family of a prominent doctor, and for five years she traveled with them and cared for the children. When the family took up residence in Belgium she went with them. Here, for the first time in her life, she saw what it was to live in a Catholic country. The open and sincere piety of the Belgian people came to her like a breath of heaven. She began to long for the time when such public devotion would be possible in England. Already bending her steps to this goal, she took a vow of perpetual virginity, and then sought entrance into a religious community. She was received as a laysister in an English community at Bruges, but less than a week's trial convinced her that this was not her vocation. She returned to the doctor's family and adopted a program of prayer and work that would daunt the average person.

Margaret's day was so full that it is hard to see how she stretched the time to accommodate all her activities. She put in a full day's work in the house; she begged food for the Poor Clares and money for poor seminarians, visited the poor of the city and did endless small tasks for them. Of course, she got an early start: she rose at four o'clock in the morning. In the evenings, her friends dropped in for the Rosary and the litany of Our Lady; only then, when she had shut the door on everyone else, did she complete her private devotions.

In order to tie in this apostolate with an established group, Margaret begged her spiritual director to let her join the Third Order of St. Dominic. For some reason he did not want her to do so. He forbade her to speak about it. Margaret was always vigorous about her prayers and never one to give in weakly. She obeyed her director and did not speak to him about it; but she went on a pilgrimage to a shrine of Our Lady, walking all the way, and begged Our Lady to do something about it. Our Lady did. The director withdrew his objections, and Margaret was received in the Dominican Third Order on the Feast of St. Catherine, 1835.

Margaret was now more eager than ever to enter religious life, but this her director completely forbade. He felt that she was fitted to do some special work for God, which as yet had not been revealed to her. He did not want her taking another false step. So, worried and anxious that she accomplish God's will somehow, she had to endure with patience his opposition to everything she suggested. Only after several very frustrating years, when Margaret felt that she was doing absolutely nothing, did he agree on a plan. An English priest had requested that Margaret come back to England and begin to work for a revival of Catholic life. She could start by teaching in his school in Coventry.

Coventry, in the Middle Ages, had been a center of English devotion to Our Lady. Destroyed during the Reformation, it was desolate physically and spiritually. Margaret, fresh from the Catholic land of Belgium, thought she had never seen such desolation. Dr. Ullathorne, who had called her to this work, was pleased with the progress she made among the poor and the unlettered of the town. She soon had two hundred girls under her care, and she had contacted many of the older people of the parish.

In two years' time, Margaret's hopes began to bear fruit. She and several other young women of like ambitions were given the Dominican habit and permission to wear it openly. Dr. Ullathorne took over the instruction of the little community, and he was a strict master. On the Feast of the Immaculate Conception, 1845, this first group of Dominican Third Order sisters in England made their first vows. Margaret was now Mother Margaret, superior of the new community, and the one on whom the responsibility of building a community in a hostile atmosphere pressed heavily.

Mother Margaret's greatest joy was that she had helped to re-light the sanctuary lamps of England. On her return from Belgium, it appalled her that the Catholic chapels and churches were in such a state of neglect; their fittings were not only shabby, but ill kept, and even in Dr. Ullathorne's church there was no sanctuary lamp. Margaret herself bought oil for the lamp, and lighted it on Rosary Sunday, 1842. "Never let it go out, dear Lord," she prayed. "O, never let it go out again!" She devoted her considerable energies to building a new church; someone complained that it was silly to build such a fine church where there was not "one respectable person." Margaret's reply was that the church is God's house, and God is always respectable.

God's Mother, too, came in for Margaret's most devout attention. Public processions had been forbidden since the Reformation and were, in fact, still officially forbidden. Margaret had a statue of Our Lady which had been given to her in Belgium. Always the little Madonna had presided over her evening devotions when the poor and the lonely came to say their Rosary with Margaret. Now she made up her mind that it was time for public devotions to return to England. She did not receive much encouragement, but she did get the bare permission necessary. In May, an outdoor procession was planned, and her little Madonna made the rounds of the parish grounds, the first Lady procession in England since the sixteenth century.

A practical and very militant Catholicity was Mother Margaret's most striking characteristic; her deep humility and complete trust in God balanced what might otherwise have been a too "active" life. Long years of sorrow had taught her to pray, and she could never quite forget that she was a servant and had—according to her own estimate—no right to head a religious community.

Mother Margaret's life was always shaped by pain. So familiar was she with it that she almost learned to ignore it. An injury to her spine gave her constant recurring infections which caused excruciating pain. Finally, in 1868, the disease became so bad that she was bedridden for six months of frightful pain before her death. Suffering in union with Christ, she came nearer and nearer by painful stages to the point of detachment from earth and union with God.

When Mother Margaret's death became known, the vast extent of her charities, hidden by her humility, was made manifest to the world. Her own community had prospered under her guidance and built new foundations; it had increased so that a large family was left to mourn the passing of their good mother. But the poor of England and the Catholics of England had each a separate debt to her, and her memory lives on even today as a courageous and good woman and—if God wills—a saint.

FATHER JOHN JOSEPH LATASTE
(1832-1869)

Father John Joseph Lataste, who died in 1869, is remembered as the founder of the community of Bethany. It is not commonly known that he also has another claim on our interest; he offered his life that St. Joseph might be named Patron of the Universal Church.

Père Lataste was born in 1832 in Southern France and was christened Alcide Vital. From the time he was very small he looked forward to becoming a priest, but he had a fear of being unworthy of so high a vocation. Finally, when he was a young man the fear so obsessed him that he gave up the whole idea and got a job in a tax office.

He became engaged to a good Catholic girl, and his life seemed to be falling into an ordinary pattern. His parents disapproved of the girl, and their attitude caused him to pray much about the engagement. He begged

God to let him know what he should do, because he wanted only to accomplish the will of God. The answer was abrupt and final; the girl died. Convinced that God was calling him to the priesthood in spite of his unworthiness, he resumed his studies and eventually entered the Dominican novitiate at Flavigny. Here he received the name of John Joseph.

During his time at the house of studies at St. Maximin, Père Lataste developed a great devotion to St. Mary Magdalen, who was specially honored there. He firmly fixed in his mind the thought that great love can atone for great sin, and adopted Mary Magdalen as a special patroness of his future work among sinners.

After his ordination in 1863, Père Lataste was assigned to mission work at Bordeaux. In the following year he was sent on what looked like a fruitless mission, to preach to the women prisoners in a nearby reformatory. Here he shaped his whole retreat around the idea that had so intrigued him at St. Maximin: that Mary Magdalen atoned for great sin by even greater love. Waxing eloquent on the subject, he saw that his hardened audience was listening closely. On the closing day of the retreat he saw three hundred and forty out of the three hundred and eighty prisoners receiving Holy Communion. The idea came to him that here would be the nucleus for the society he had envisioned, a community of religious women made up of rehabilitated prisoners.

The prisoners were enthusiastic about the plan; the archbishop was not. For some time, Père Lataste worked it over in his mind and discussed it with people who were interested in the project. It took a long time. Eventually, the obstacles were overcome, and he had the very great happiness of seeing his dream realized. Three sisters of a regular congregation assisted in the beginning, and their first two postulants were received the day the convent was opened. They called it "Bethany" to carry out the idea of the friendship of Christ.

Père Lataste set about getting a rule and constitutions written and approved. The life of the sisters at Bethany consisted in prayer, public recitation of the Little Office of the Blessed Virgin, the exercise of penance, and work in common. The house was to be characterized by endless and limitless devotion to Christ; the great love that would atone for great mistakes.

Just at this time, when he must have wished most to live, Père Lataste wrote to the pope offering his life that St. Joseph would be declared Patron of the Universal Church. The pontiff remarked to the master general, who had given him the letter, that he had received more than five hundred letters asking this favor, but only Père Lataste had offered his life in exchange. God took him at his word, and he died on March 10, 1869. A year later, St. Joseph was declared Patron of the Universal Church.

The work of Père Lataste had prospered with the foundations from Bethany. The constitutions of the Order were confirmed in 1931. On the anniversary of his death in 1937, the process was begun to raise John Joseph Lataste to the altars of the Church.

RAPHAEL CAPTIER AND COMPANIONS
(d. 1871)

It would be hard to find a clearer example of brutality than the massacre of Father Raphael Captier and companions by the Paris Commune on May 25, 1871.

Father Raphael Captier was one of the first four recruits for Father Lacordaire's new community of Third Order teaching priests. He had been very close to Lacordaire in life, had assisted at his deathbed, and was devoted to carrying out his ideals of teaching the youth of France in a thoroughly Christian and thoroughly modern way. Two years after the death of Lacordaire, it was Father Captier who was sent as superior to the new school for boys in Arcueil, the College of St. Albert the Great. Here for several years he had the joy of seeing the school develop and flourish. Then, with the Franco-Prussian war, came disaster.

With Paris under siege, the fathers had no choice but to send the children home and turn the building into a hospital. Several members of the faculty went into the ambulance corps, and spent the siege in searching the battlefields for the wounded and in caring for the sick and dying. They were within range of the German guns, but at least the enemy respected the Red Cross flag that flew over the temporary hospital, and the French army professed itself grateful for the care of their sick.

After the war, the boys came back and the school reopened. It had hardly resumed its work when the Commune took over, and again Paris was in a state of war, only, this time, civil war within her own ranks. The fathers brought out the ambulance once more and hunted for the wounded.

They were up against a foe that recognized neither their work nor their immunity under the Red Cross. A day came too soon when one of the most irreligious and cruel of the leaders of the Commune descended upon the building and had everyone in it arrested, from the superior down to the servants. One of the teachers managed to conceal the few children, and two of the older boys who were arrested with the teachers were later released. The sisters, who had done nothing more wicked than take care of injured soldiers, were carried off first and threatened with all the horrors their captors could invent—none of which, fortunately, were carried out. The women servants were next taken off to prison and frightened half to death. Then the priests and teachers were lined up and made to march off to prison. The group consisted of Father Captier, the superior; Father Bourard, a priest of the First Order who was chaplain to the school; four other members of the teaching Third Order, a young clerical student, a secular priest, four laymen, all members of the faculty, and twelve other employees of the school. They were put in prison along with a number of priests of other Orders, a journalist, a banker, and several police officers.

For the first few days of their miserable imprisonment, the fathers attempted to reach the authorities and insist upon a trial. No charge had been made against them, no information was given them as to their fate.

At last they got a statement from an irritated official that they were not being held for any crime at all, merely as witnesses. This uncertain state continued for a week of freezing nights on damp straw and days loud with the insults of soldiers. As they had been led to prison, a woman remarked, "There goes Jesus Christ with his disciples to Jerusalem to be crucified again." But first they had a week of maltreatment at the hands of soldiers no gentler than Pilate's. At the end of this time, they were moved to another prison and treated to the sight of an execution. After one brief moment of hope when they thought they might be released, all the captives composed themselves to die.

In the late afternoon of May the twenty-fifth the door of the prison was flung open and they were summoned to go out, one by one, into the Avenue d'Italie. They were shot down as they emerged into the street, without trial, without crime, without chance to defend themselves. The Commune's official, sitting in a carriage with a woman, watched the massacre calmly. He made no comment as the soldiers looted the bodies, mutilated them and tore off their clothes.

The next morning, a priest in disguise happened to pass through the Avenue d'Italie, looking for anyone who might need him. He recognized the Dominican habits in the trampled carnage in the street, and managed to get the bodies of the martyrs for burial. They were buried in a common grave at Arcueil. After peace was restored, a monument was erected to them at the school where they had served so well. Their cause for beatification was opened in 1924 and was still active in 1955.

ALEXANDER VINCENT JANDEL
(1810-1872)

The able administrator who restored the Order to regular observance under the inspiration of Lacordaire was Alexander Vincent Jandel. Baptized John Joseph Alexander, he was born in Lorraine in 1810. His mother had a reputation for Christian valor reaching back to the terrible days of the Revolution, when she had gone into the prison to say goodbye to her own mother, who was awaiting execution. She had been tireless in her assistance to priests in the troubled years after the Revolution; her son was always afterwards to credit this courageous devotion for his religious vocation.

In 1822 Alexander went to the College of Nancy to study philosophy, and from here went on to the seminary. His health was delicate, but he rigidly adhered to the rules of the seminary and kept a monastic silence. Before he was old enough for ordination, fresh political troubles hit France, and the seminarians were sent to Switzerland. Here he cultivated not only theology, but his only bad fault—he said himself that he was too fond of walks! A pardonable fault in beautiful Switzerland, it probably saved the life of the frail student. He was ordained in 1834, and began his priestly life by teaching in the seminary at Nancy.

The problem of a religious vocation now began to concern him. First he made a retreat with the Jesuits, and made up his mind that he would join their Society. Because of his delicate health, the Jesuit superiors put him off for two years. In the meantime he met Lacordaire, and felt drawn to follow him. Consulting his Jesuit confessor, he was told to be a Dominican and help to restore the Order to France. Still troubled, Father Jandel made the trip to Rome to see if he could settle the matter. He spoke to the pope about his indecision. The pope, looking in some amusement at the tall young priest, assured him that whichever order he chose, he could become a "big saint."

When Lacordaire finally organized his followers at Santa Sabina in 1840, the young Father Jandel was one of his aspirants. He was given the name Vincent in honor of St. Vincent Ferrer, and at the dispersal of the group was sent to Viterbo to the convent of Our Lady of the Oak. Having finished his novitiate, he rejoined the others in Bosco and was sent with the first group to France. For the rest of his life, Father Jandel was to be almost continuously in office. He was appointed the first superior in the convent of Nancy, and prior at the new novitiate at Flavigny.

In 1850 Father Jandel was summoned to Rome, under strictest secrecy, to become master general. The Order had fallen to the lowest point it has ever reached in its seven centuries of existence, and the pope felt that nothing but a firm and saintly leader could build it up again. He also felt that the power of rejuvenation lay within the Order itself, and so it was a Dominican he appointed to rebuild it, and not an outsider. Father Jandel was appointed vicar by Pope Pius IX.

The new vicar began his reform in Rome, setting up the convent of Santa Sabina as a house of regular observance. "We are the children of saints," he said. "We reap glory from our fathers. Let us, however, beware, lest, being no credit to them, we be numbered with those whose glory is turned to shame. For as a degenerate son is a shame to his father, so is illustrious ancestry a dishonor to unworthy descendants, and the old nobility in that case becomes nothing but an empty title and the shadow of a great name." He had no intention of allowing the members of the Order to succumb to this fate. His reform measures were vigorous, but they were also effective. A tide of new life flowed back into the Order in a new surge of good vocations.

Members of the Order were uncooperative at times during the early months of the reform. Fantastic rumors were spread about, telling how harsh and unreasonable the new general was. Until all the members of the Order had met him personally and discovered for themselves that this was not true, there was tension and trouble. In 1855 the fathers of the general chapter elected Father Jandel as general. Pope Pius IX complained mildly, "When I appoint him they say it is a hindrance to the working of the Order; now, when I want to make him a cardinal, they choose him themselves!"

Father Jandel was especially noted for his kindness to novices and his understanding of their problems. Much of what he wrote was for their use, and every free moment he had he spent with them. He reunited the Spanish province, which had been isolated by government interference for a long time, and sent visitators to South America. He rebuilt the English province and had the satisfaction of seeing it on its way back to its former glory. When Father Lacordaire came to him with his request to found a group of Third Order priests who would teach in the schools of France, he gave his hearty support. In 1870, he publicized the miracle of St. Dominic in Soriano, and gave great impetus to devotion in the Order.

Father Jandel died in 1872, mourned by the entire Order, who recognized in him a saintly leader and a builder in the spirit of St. Dominic.

MOTHER AUGUSTINE NEUHIERL
(d. 1877)

More than 6,000 American Dominican sisters of the Third Order Regular trace their lineage back to the cloister of the Holy Cross in Ratisbon, Germany, through a little band of four pioneers who came to America in 1853. Of the four, the one of whose personality and achievements we know most was Mother Augustine Neuhierl.

Little is known of the four pioneers before they came to America. Sister Josepha and Sister Augustine were choir sisters, and Sisters Jacobina and Francesca were laysisters, all members of the community of the Second Order at Holy Cross in Ratisbon. They came to America in answer to a plea from a Benedictine of Latrobe, Pennsylvania, who had placed the sad plight of German-speaking American children before the kindhearted prioress of Holy Cross. A Bavarian mission society paid part of their expenses of travel, and the four who made the trip had the promise that they might return to the cloister at Ratisbon if the American venture did not work out.

Sister Augustine was of noble birth and had been accustomed to wealth and convenience before her entrance into the cloister. She was very happy at Ratisbon, and enjoyed the great privilege of peace and prayer which was, at that time, growing so rare in Germany. When an angel appeared to her and asked her if she would like to go to America, she answered with a very definite no; she was happy where she was. Again she was visited by angels and asked the same thing. Even when the Holy Infant appeared to her and asked her if she would like to go and be a missionary, she told Him she would rather stay in Ratisbon—but added that if He wanted her to go to America, she would go. Shortly after this, the Benedictine from America appeared at the grille with his request for teachers for the German-speaking children of his country. Sister Augustine volunteered, and, once having made the step, went into the project wholeheartedly.

The four sisters traveled in secular clothes, not knowing what situations they might encounter on their long voyage or in the new land of which they had heard such strange things. They arrived in August, 1853, in New York, and looked about eagerly for the Benedictine who was to meet them and escort them to their new mission field. After all the crowd had disappeared, leaving them alone on the dock, they realized that the Benedictine had not come for them and that they were left to their own resources in a strange land, knowing nothing of its geography and speaking not a word of English.

One of the letters of introduction which they carried was addressed to a Redemptorist in New York City. It was probably one of the ship's officers who put the four strangers in a carriage and sent them to the Redemptorists. These good priests, having no place to house four sisters, contacted a friend in Williamsburg and established them there. He had been looking for teachers for his school, and rejoiced that he had benefited from the Benedictine's error.

The adaptability of sisters is traditional. Within a few weeks they had the school in good running order, and half the pastors in the state were clamoring for more teachers. Their first answer to the multitude of such requests was to the pastor of St. Nicholas church on Second Street, New York. Three sisters went there as soon as it could be arranged. Sister Augustine was sent as superior of the new school, with a teacher and a laysister as helpers. Here was built the nearest approximation to the Ratisbon cloister that America would have. When it was laid out in 1860 on the plan of a European monastery, the sisters were still cloistered and the fields around the building were empty of dwellings; today tall buildings encroach on every side around the tiny old convent which has for many generations been a school.

Mother Augustine died in 1877, prophesying that the Dominican Order would spread and prosper in America. She had seen the beginning of that growth; in 1869 the novitiate moved from St. Nicholas at Second Street to a new site at Newburgh, New York. The Brooklyn convent had grown from the tiny germ of Williamsburg into a thriving community which would send out branches to California and Kansas within a few years. Sisters from the Newburgh foundation began missions at Caldwell and Blauvelt in New York, Adrian and Grand Rapids in Michigan, and Nesqually—now Seattle—in Washington. Caldwell in its turn sent out missionaries to Akron, Ohio, and Washington. In all, twelve communities grew out of the original band from Germany, spreading in every direction in the United States, Cuba, Puerto Rico, and Santo Domingo. A separate foundation at Racine, Wisconsin, came out from Ratisbon in 1862, making a total of thirteen communities mothered by the convent of the Holy Cross, surely an exceptional mission record for one Dominican cloister.

MOTHER AQUINATA LAUTER
(1815-1883)

To attain a reputation as a teacher in an Order that specializes in teachers calls for extraordinary ability. Mother Aquinata Lauter, who died as prioress in Augsburg in 1883, extended her ideals of good teaching not only among her sisters in Germany, but into the newly evangelized country of Africa.

Waldburga Lauter was born in Bavaria in 1815, and educated by the Dominican sisters of Augsburg. At the age of twenty she entered their novitiate and received the religious name Aquinata. Her first twenty years in the Order were typical of the lives of many Dominican sisters; she was in charge of the convent of St. Ursula when she was summoned to Wettenhausen to help establish the community there.

The convent at Wettenhausen was very old, dating back to the time of Charlemagne. It was first burned by the Hungarians in the eleventh century, and had survived through many troubles since. The canonesses of St. Augustine, who occupied the convent until the mid-nineteenth century, withdrew from it at that time, and it was given to the Dominicans of Augsburg. Sister Aquinata, whose talents as teacher and administrator were well known by this time, was put in charge of the house. Her zeal for regular observance and her gift for teaching made her a logical choice for mother general, and she was elected to head the community in 1859.

The reputation left at her death by this zealous woman is an enviable one; she was not only an outstanding teacher who thoroughly understood her work; she was also a real mother, not only to the sisters and the children, but to the poor and the troubled who came to seek help at the convent gate. She was responsible for the great educational and religious development of the community in Germany, and her personal devotion to the Blessed Virgin flowered in all those with whom she came in contact. For twenty-six years she occupied the position of top responsibility in the community and brought it to great perfection.

Perhaps the most interesting feature of her work was the foundation of the missions in South Africa. The dark continent was opened up to trade just at this time, and the few scattered missionaries who had braved its hardships to work there were begging for help. Some one of these beleagured missionaries laid his case before Mother Aquinata, and in 1865 she sent the first mission band of sisters to begin work near the Cape of Good Hope. The seven nuns in the first band reached the Cape after a five week journey, and plunged into the physical and spiritual jungle of South Africa. North Africa had been Christian since apostolic times, but South Africa had no such heritage; it was wild and pagan, and overrun with gold-hungry Europeans who stirred up the natives and generally made things difficult. The stamp of Mother Aquinata's teaching must have been very deep in those pioneer sisters to enable them to set up in that wilderness a boarding school, an orphanage, and a school for poor children. Soon they were specializing, with a school for deaf-mutes and classes in technical arts for boys and girls.

By 1889 the spiritual daughters of Mother Aquinata were busily carrying out the Dominican ideal in various parts of South Africa. In Natal, where a motherhouse was eventually to be established, they taught in English and Zulu, and did not seem to be nonplussed by the bedlam of languages they had to learn. They worked with the Jesuits on the Zambesi, and built hospitals in the bush, where the sisters lived in tents for a year at a time and used a trunk for an altar. When a tornado blew the tent away, they built a little hut and kept on dispensing charity to the sick and bewildered natives.

In the mission among the Kaffirs, the sisters one day discovered to their distress that all their scapulars had been stolen off the clothesline. Not wanting to stir up war, they waited uneasily for a few days, until the chief and his bodyguard appeared in all the splendor of fur and feathers, each wearing a white scapular. They brought back the sisters' scapulars and apologized for keeping them so long; they had just wanted the pattern.

For many years Mother Aquinata directed the fortunes of her daughters at home in a politically-troubled Germany, at the same time as she was heeding the calls for help from her daughters in far-off lands with names she could not pronounce and among wild tribes who struck terror to her heart. She finished a fruitful life in 1883, leaving a splendid heritage of Dominicanism-in-action to people of two continents.

FATHER TOM BURKE
(1830-1883)

The Dominican priest who was never, except on the most formal occasions, called anything but "Father Tom" was an irrepressible Irishman whose preaching talents are still remembered nearly a century after his death.

Nicholas Burke was born in Galway in 1830, the only child of a poor and hard-working family. His father was a baker, and a fellow conspirator with the witty and gay-hearted little boy. His mother was the saint of the family, a woman determined to shape her son into a pious mold if it killed both of them. Nicholas was a talented mimic, a lively and impulsive youngster who was always into mischief. His mother believed in spanking, and she always invoked the Holy Spirit before laying hands on the culprit. Young Nicholas maintained that the longer she prayed the harder she spanked. "When I saw my mother enter the room, make the Sign of the Cross, and solemnly invoke the light of the Holy Ghost to direct her, I knew I could expect no mercy," he related. "I never got such a thrashing as those directed by the Holy Spirit."

To the Brotherhood of St. Patrick fell the task of channeling the boy's abundant energies. Nicholas was an exceptional student, but among his gifts was a special talent for keeping the class in an uproar. Teachers who had a sense of humor saw early that he had a vocation for the priesthood; others felt that such a mischievous rascal could come to no good end. An attack of typhoid fever at the age of fourteen sobered him considerably, and the famine of 1847, which brought such disaster to his homeland, turned his thoughts to the serious side of life. In that same year he left home to enter the Dominican Order in Italy. He received the habit at Perugia, and was given the name Thomas in religion.

The young Irish novice was rarely out of penance, but everyone loved him. He could never remember to keep silence, and his gay whistle or a burst of Irish music was always paving the way to trouble for him. That he made tremendous progress in the matter of controlling his high spirits is indicated by his appointment only three years later to the convent of Woodchester. Brother Thomas was at Santa Sabina when the master general, Father Jandel, sent him to England as an example of how the Dominican rule should be lived, and appointed him novice master there, although he was barely twenty-one years old and not yet ordained.

Father Burke's trip to England is an epic. He was, he said, dressed more like a smuggler than a friar. When he got to London he ran out of money, and was stranded in the station without food or transportation. A sympathetic porter gave him a herring and a bit of bread, and he finally recollected that there was an Oratorian father in London who might loan him the money to get to Woodchester. Nevertheless, he had to walk the last few miles, and when he arrived at the convent where he was supposed to be the pattern of observance, the porter took him for a robber and would not let him in. When finally admitted, it was not with enthusiasm, as the local prior resented the notion that his house needed any fine examples from Rome, especially an Irishman. Nevertheless, Brother Thomas was soon loved in the English novitiate as he had been in Rome; no one could long resist his goodness, his friendliness, and his irresistible gift for making people laugh.

In 1852 Brother Thomas was ordained a deacon, and began timidly on the career of preaching that was to be his most memorable work. His first sermons were carefully written out and delivered with his eyes shut.

After his ordination in the following year, he was sent back to Ireland to open a novitiate there. Here, as he preached around the countryside, his gift of oratory developed almost in secret. Those who heard him felt that he was inspired, but his sermons attracted no notice until he went to Rome to the convent of San Clemente. It gradually became noised about in the Eternal City that there was an Irish Dominican with a charmed tongue who was the most convincing preacher the Order had had since the great Lacordaire himself.

In 1869 the remains of Daniel O'Connell were buried with great ceremony, and Father Tom Burke was asked to deliver the address. Fifty thousand people listened in rapt attention to a sermon that all recognized as a masterpiece. After the ceremony they looked in vain for the preacher; he had rushed off to the hospital where an old woman who was dying had begged for him to come and hear her confession.

Father Burke attended the Vatican Council as theologian to one of the Irish bishops. While there, the possibility was discussed of making him co-adjutor bishop of San Francisco. The bishop who had brought him to the council undertook to give him some fatherly advice, to the effect that he would have been a bishop long ago if he was not quite such a tease. Father Burke was hugely amused at the thought, and replied, "If your reverence had taken *my* example, and had a bit of fun, you wouldn't be burdened with a bishopric, either!"

It is not possible to keep track of all the sermons preached by this untiring son of St. Dominic during the years of his greatest work. In 1871 there is record of 172 sermons and 21 retreats; this adds up to around 760 sermons for one year, nearly two a day for every day. The following year he came to America, and no record was kept of his fantastic schedule. His trip to America was typical of the way he worked; he chose a ship with a large proportion of steerage passengers, and spent most of the voyage with them. He heard more than 300 confessions on the way across, and frightened immigrants had the luxury of listening several times a day to the most famous preacher in Europe. In America, he worked through Kentucky, Ohio, and New York. For a year and a half he preached in the eastern cities, refuting anti-clericals, defending Irish nationalism, presenting Catholic truths. For hours before he was scheduled to speak, the church would be packed to capacity with men and women of all nationalities and types. Sometimes he could barely push his own way into the church to preach.

All this activity would have taxed a man of good health, and Father Tom was never strong. At the end of his American tour, he remarked about himself, "Tired isn't the word; I can only compare myself to Ned Burke's dog during the famine; they had to support his back at the wall to enable him to bark." Weary as he was, he loved America with all his heart; "Here I am a free man, and will speak my soul!" he said. Nevertheless, on his return to Ireland he was a very sick man. From this time until his death ten years later, he was never to be without pain, sometimes so agonizing that he could neither speak nor stand.

In spite of the increasing agony of his illness, the final ten years of his life were filled with priestly duties. He was a severe spiritual director, yet his confessional was always busy. He preached as long as he was able to stand up to do so, and pain never robbed him of either his eloquent speech or his unshakable humor. The famous sermon he preached in the Jesuit church, beginning with "To hell with the Jesuits!" was delivered at a time when he had just rallied from an ulcer operation and when, according to his own account, "he hurt everywhere but his eyebrows." A deep and tender love for Our Lady was evident in all his sermons, and people could rarely listen to him speak on the sufferings of our Lord without tears. An old Spanish crucifix at the novitiate in Ireland was his best-remembered tonic for a bout of pain, "What have I to complain about?" he would ask, looking at it.

A few months before his death, he forced himself to go to England where a new novitiate was being erected. So dearly did he love novices and the whole matter of religious vocation that nothing could keep him away. As he lay waiting for death, he roused himself for one last sermon when someone told him that 5,000 children in Donegal were starving. Perhaps remembering his famous namesake who died on the road, Father Tom made the trip to preach in behalf of the little ones. He returned to his convent to die on the Feast of the Visitation, 1883, at the early age of fifty-four.

JOSEPH SADOC ALEMANY
(1814-1888)

In the year 1840 the famous Daniel Webster registered his disgust with California by saying, "What can we *do* with the West coast—3,000 miles rockbound, cheerless, uninviting, and not a harbor on it?" In the same year, the Church, with more foresight than the great lawyer, appointed the first bishop of the Californias—Upper and Lower—a Franciscan, Father Francis Garcia Diego. Ten years later, when the harbor of the Golden Gate had shown the importance of San Francisco Bay, the episcopal See was moved to Monterey. The man appointed to the care of the vast and largely unexplored diocese was a Dominican, Joseph Sadoc Alemany.

Joseph Alemany was born in Catalonia in 1814. The piety of his family can hardly be questioned, since all seven of the children became either priests or religious. Joseph received his early training from the fathers of the Oratory in his native province, and at the age of sixteen entered the Dominican Order at Vich, receiving the religious name Sadoc. He made his studies in several of the houses of Catalonia, and finally went to Italy to complete them, since persecution had broken out in Spain and a decree of the government had forbidden the wearing of any religious habit.

He studied in Viterbo and was ordained there in 1837. After finishing his studies at the convent of the Minerva, he was faced with a hard decision. Spain was still in a disturbed political state, and he could not return there for an indefinite time. While he was considering going to the Far East, a plea came from a bishop in America with a need for priests just as desperate as that of China. Young Father Alemany set out with two other Dominicans to work with the bishop of Nashville, Tennessee.

Bishop Miles met his new recruit in Cincinnati, and decided that the young man had better have a chance to learn English before tackling the problems of Tennessee. He sent him to the Dominican house at Somerset, Ohio. After a year spent in learning English, Father Alemany was sent to Cuba to try to collect funds from Spanish Catholics there to help with building St. Joseph's church in Somerset. His mission was not successful, as Cuba was seething with political troubles. A bout with yellow fever did not help the situation, and he returned to Ohio somewhat discouraged, a condition he soon remedied by hard work.

The bishop of Nashville, who had started his labors four years before with no priest but himself to cover the 42,000 square miles of rough country, had just opened a seminary when Father Alemany arrived on the scene. He appointed the Dominican to direct the seminary, which meant teaching most of the classes and caring for nearby missions. Three years later he was appointed pastor in Memphis. Here he set about the task of becoming a naturalized citizen of the United States. The Dominicans had by this time established a novitiate at Springfield, Kentucky, and they were anxious to get the talented Father Alemany back into the Order's affairs again. They replaced him at Memphis and made him novice master at Springfield. From this it was a natural step to elect him provincial.

When, in the course of official business, he visited Rome in 1850, he was appointed by Pope Pius IX as bishop of Monterey in California. It must have seemed to the new bishop that his life so far had been only a succession of beginnings, and here was another and more startling beginning, in a land farther away and more primitive even than Tennessee.

At the general chapter which had called him to Rome, the new bishop of Monterey prevailed upon a fellow Spaniard, Francis Sadoc Vilarrasa, to go with him to California. On December 7, 1850, Bishop Alemany landed at San Francisco. Used to the beauty of European architecture, he must have been appalled at the ugliness of the rough little port where gold miners came to buy supplies and where as yet there was no hint of the great metropolis it was one day to be.

There were three churches in San Francisco and two others in the diocese. Territorially, the diocese was immense; most of the area had not even been surveyed, and some of the most disruptive elements known to man were on hand to keep it in a state of ferment. People were pouring into the state by the thousands, lured by the hope of gold. There were no homes, no hospitals, no schools, and the Franciscans, who had done such excellent work with the Indians, had been exiled fifty years before. Bishop Alemany, faced with a tremendous task, set about it with energy.

As early as 1853, plans were laid for a cathedral, and the bishop, whose see city was Monterey, foresaw that the place for the cathedral was the booming village of San Francisco. As if in reply to his faith in its future, in July of that year he was made archbishop of San Francisco.

One of the problems inevitable in rough frontier country was the question of mob violence. San Francisco teemed with lawless people drawn from the whole country, and citizens who called themselves the "Vigilantes" organized a volunteer police force. Their methods were quick and effective, but not always just. Archbishop Alemany had once to go to the scaffold with two men who were victims of Vigilante justice. He also had to quell a riot that had broken out in the gold country between national groups. In 1861 an even greater cause of trouble loomed; the country went to war. The Presidio of San Francisco was in charge of an officer with southern sympathies, who was quietly replaced at the outbreak of the war. The archbishop wrote hurriedly to Baltimore to ask the archbishop there what he should do if California should secede from the Union, an event which fortunately did not occur.

In 1868 a severe earthquake struck California, inflicting great damage. Archbishop Alemany sent out a circular letter, saying among other things that possibly the earthquake was a sign of God's displeasure with a state that taxed churches and orphan asylums while it allowed free rein to places of immorality.

In 1870 Archbishop Alemany was summoned to the Vatican Council, which declared on papal infallibility. One of the bishops present noted: "In my estimation, the shrewdest man in the council is a young bishop from California, a native of Spain but brought up in America, a little man with broad shoulders and a compact head like that of the first Napoleon. He never speaks above a few minutes, but he hits the nail on the head invariably." In 1884 the talents of the "shrewd bishop from California" were called upon to help prepare the *Baltimore Catechism*. In Baltimore as a member of the Third Plenary Council, Archbishop Alemany was made chairman of the episcopal committee that drafted the catechism.

In 1884, a coadjutor was appointed to San Francisco. Archbishop Alemany, whose health was failing, resigned his See. He said his last Mass in San Francisco in May, 1885, and waved goodbye to a huge crowd of people for whom he had labored for thirty-five years. He returned to Spain, now free of persecution, and took up residence in the convent of Valencia, where he died among his brethren three years later.

FRANCIS SADOC VILARRASA
(1814-1888)

The founder of the province of the Holy Name and one of the builders of the great state of California was Francis Sadoc Vilarrasa, a native of Spain. He was born in the province of Catalonia in 1814. When he was fifteen years old, he entered the convent of St. Catherine in Barcelona, where he received the religious name Sadoc. For four years he studied peacefully, and then religious persecution broke out in Spain. Mob violence flared in several provinces, and the convent of St. Catherine was attacked and burned. Eighteen Dominicans perished in the brief and dreadful persecution, and all the students were hurriedly sent to other provinces. Brother Sadoc was sent to the convent of Viterbo in Italy, where he finished his studies and was ordained in 1837. He was appointed assistant novice master at Viterbo, and two of the novices who came under his care were to do great things for the Order: they were Henri Dominic Lacordaire and Vincent Jandel.

With the exception of a year at the Minerva to get his lectorate, the young Father Vilarrasa remained at Viterbo until the plea of a fellow Spaniard,

Father Alemany, turned his thoughts to the far-off land of America. He sailed for the New World in 1845, in company with two young Italian volunteers for the American missions and two American lectors en route home from Rome. The young Spaniard described his journey simply: "After forty-eight days of sailing and without having encountered any danger, we landed at New York, thank God. We disembarked on January 3, at midday. On the ninth, in the afternoon, we arrived at Somerset, which is, one might say, built in the middle of the woods." He described feelingly the last two days, which were made up of "continual running and bumping in the stagecoach." Somerset in 1845 was a far cry from the cloisters of Barcelona and Viterbo.

For four years Father Vilarrasa worked in the Ohio region, being novice master, pastor, and preacher as the occasion demanded. In 1849 he attended the general chapter in Naples, in company with Father Alemany, who at this time was appointed bishop of Monterey in California. Bishop Alemany made haste to secure the help of his young countryman for his huge and far-off mission. Father Vilarrasa agreed to go if he might devote his time there to building up a Dominican province.

Never having seen California, he was still a good salesman; he convinced a young novice, Mary Goemare, to go with them to California and begin a community of the Third Order there, instead of making profession in the Second Order in Paris. He also secured the services of two French sisters who were bound for Ohio; in Ohio he exchanged them for two American postulants, and in this way built up a small expedition. On December 7, 1850, Father Vilarrasa got his first glimpse of California as they sailed in through the Golden Gate. Then began a love affair that was to last until his death; he could never say enough of this beautiful, fertile land that to others seemed a howling wilderness.

Father Vilarrasa's first assignment in the new country was at the old Franciscan mission of St. Charles Borromeo at Carmel, which had fallen into ruins since the Franciscans were sent away a half-century before. In February of 1852, which was little more than a year after his arrival, he opened a novitiate at nearby Monterey. He gave the habit to six young Spanish novices, two of whom were to be among the builders of the new province. Also at this time he established the regular Dominican life. In the observance of the rule he was never to waver, although even he admitted that "it causes serious inconveniences at times." The first convent was a complex of two little frame houses. There was no money and no regular supply of clothing.

Two years later it seemed better to transfer the novitiate to Benicia, where in addition to poverty they acquired a large debt. The people of Benicia proved to be heroically generous, however, and a humble convent soon rose. In 1857 the first Dominican ordinations in California elevated Brothers Vincent Vinyes and Dominic Costa to the priesthood.

In 1863 Father Vilarrasa noted that San Francisco was "rapidly growing into a very noble city," a roseate view indeed of the little wooden village on the bay. He purchased ground for a convent there, and also, with an eye to the future, made arrangements for the students of the province to study in England until there should be enough of them for a California house of studies.

In 1866 Father Vilarrasa attended the Second Plenary Council of Baltimore, and his hand is evident in much of the Order's legislation during the next few years. However, he was a quiet builder, not one to overlook the foundation; the fine superstructure he left to be erected by his successors. One of the greatest things he saw accomplished in his lifetime was the blessing of the Dominican church of St. Dominic in San Francisco in 1873, as this marked the permanent establishment of the new province of the Far West, and was a foretaste of the great apostolate to come.

Father Vilarrasa ruled the Order in California as commissary general until the day of his death in 1888.

MOTHER FRANCES RAPHAEL DRANE
(1823-1893)

Augusta Theodosia Drane was born near Bow in East London in 1823. Her father was the manager of an East India mercantile house, and his home was filled with exotic trinkets which very early became a part of her life. Augusta was the youngest of four children, and she grew up happily in an atmosphere of wealth and adventure. She was, she afterwards claimed, a naughty child who hated arithmetic and grammar, but loved poetry and history, and especially geography. She made a resolution very early to go to the strange places on her father's maps.

The Drane family were Anglicans in varying degrees. They were all very kindly Christian people, but saw little sense in arguing religion, a practice which Augusta took up in earnest after she was sent away to school at the age of twelve. In some of the family's travels, she met a nephew of the poet Coleridge who was an Anglican curate with Catholic ideas. They talked long and earnestly of religious questions which the Oxford movement had brought into prominence. Augusta made an earnest attempt to shore up the failing ramparts of her Anglican beliefs, and found that they all crumbled when she went to Mass in London. She made the very acute observation that "the Anglican churches in the country were so very lovely, but in the cities one could see so clearly that they would not do." It was a wrench for her poetic nature to turn from the exquisite country churches to the ugly and overcrowded city buildings.

When Augusta was twenty-three, a number of things happened to make the final step inevitable. Her friend, the Anglican curate, had gone over to Rome, and she herself had made several drastic attempts to go to confession in the Anglican church and had been rebuffed. She felt the desperate need of confession, and became convinced that she was outside the Church of Christ and must do something about it. Her mother's death brought all her painful ideas into focus, and she talked over the situation with another Anglican curate who was involved in the Oxford movement. She made a strangely prophetic suggestion to him at this time, as she had given a good deal of thought to the matter of what she would do after entering the Church. "I see a religious Order," she told him, "where there would be the three vows and a separation from the aims and habits of the world, a devotion to the poor, work for souls, charity—a bond of union for persons working in the world who are not able to go to the cloister."

The young clergyman looked at her curiously. "It already exists, you know," he said, "among Roman Catholics, and they call it the Third Order of St. Dominic." Augusta went home and wrote in her diary, "Some day I shall be a member of the Third Order of St. Dominic."

The first of many published works by this gifted woman was written while she was still an Anglican. Newman quoted from her pamphlet, which somewhat startled her. On July 3, 1850, having withdrawn from the Anglican school where she was teaching, Augusta was baptized conditionally in the Catholic Church. The priest who baptized her, feeling that she had come a long way already, was more than surprised when she demanded to be allowed to enter the Dominican Third Order. He managed to hold her off until she was confirmed the following year, but her eagerness was too great to be denied. The bishop sent her to ring the sisters' doorbell and get her first glimpse of a Dominican sister. She was received as a Dominican Tertiary shortly after this, and went happily to work in her new apostolate.

Two years of the active apostolate convinced her that she should now go one step further. In Rome she had gone to confession to Father Besson, Father Lacordaire's right-hand man in the Dominican revival. She said of him, "He listened in silence and then, taking every one of my words, he unwound them as if he had been unwinding a tangled skein of silk." After making a private retreat under his direction at the chapel of the Mater Admirabilis, she returned to England and applied to Mother Margaret Hallahan for admission into the Third Order sisters.

Mother Margaret realized the great literary and spiritual gifts of the new aspirant, and did a great deal to cultivate them. She left the young Sister Frances Raphael free for writing whenever she could, which inevitably led to a lifetime of being "Sister Stop-gap." It was a trial all her busy life to feel that she never had a regular assignment in the classroom, that perhaps she was not doing a full day's work. No one but herself worried about this, as books began to glide in a steady stream from her gifted pen. Her first work in the Order was a translation of the life of Lacordaire; then she wrote a history of England. Made novice mistress in 1860, she continued her writing, but changed now to lives of the saints which would be useful in training novices, and legends which they would find amusing at recreation.

Sister Frances Raphael suffered all her religious life from a sense of frustration which we find surprising in view of the facts. She wrote once, "I wish I could contrive to be of some use to *somebody,* but I must spend my life writing books." In season and out, in days of inspiration and days of dryness, she kept at it steadily. At one time she suffered a long stretch of spiritual dryness when she felt that prayer was utterly impossible, and that her mental processes had simply stopped for good. She took to saying the Rosary almost incessantly—not, she admitted, out of devotion, "but simply to make sure I was doing something"—until the darkness passed and things were normal again.

In 1861 Mother Margaret Hallahan died, "The fall of a giant oak in the forest." Sister Frances Raphael was made prioress of Stone. Here, for a space of twenty years she wrote steadily and capably, doing her research amidst great difficulties. In 1881 she was elected mother provincial.

Prioress for twelve years, Mother Frances Raphael was a capable and beloved superior. The travels to far-off places which had been her childhood dream were to be realized only in the sisters she sent to Australia in 1883, thus extending Dominican influence to yet another continent. At her death in 1893, she had to her credit nineteen books, which were in steady use in the training of young Dominicans, and a long history of kindness among her sisters.

MOTHER DOMINIC CLARA MOES
(1832-1895)

We are all aware of the great revival of the Dominican Order in the nineteenth century and are apt to think of two names only, Lacordaire and Jandel, when we recall the instigators of it. One Dominican who played a tremendous but completely hidden part in this revival was a little girl from Luxembourg whose cause for beatification has recently been introduced. The details of her life come as a complete surprise to most Dominicans, who owe her so much without realizing it.

Anne Moes was born in Luxembourg in 1832, and if we are to believe the records, miracles surrounded her from the day of her baptism. One is not required to believe all that is said to have occurred, but certainly her life was filled with extraordinary things.

What we do know is that the child Anne suffered intensely from the age of four: first from an eye infection, then from a series of physical ailments that included smallpox, a throat infection, and a general weakness which gave her parents reason to suppose that she would not live more than a few months. Oddly enough, instead of increasing their love for her, her illness made them very impatient and caused them to neglect her. Anne was of an affectionate nature, and it is hard to imagine a greater suffering than the neglect and scolding of her parents.

It is a strange picture, indeed, the little girl whose eyes were nearly blinded, huddling in dark corners alone and unloved. Unloved? No, that was Anne's secret; the motivating force of her whole life, to a degree that we find almost terrifying, was her love for Christ Crucified. As though she were not suffering enough from her various afflictions, she used to scourge herself with thorns and nettles, go without sleep at night, and pray for long hours at a time. At the age of six she made a vow of perpetual virginity. It is obvious that Anne was a victim specially chosen by God for some great mission, and that she was given both the grace and the suffering as a part of His plan. Exactly what her mission was, Anne was not to know for many years. But she knew from her earliest years that God had chosen her for a special purpose and that when His time came He would tell her what He wanted her to do. Finally, it was revealed to her that it was her mission to suffer and to pray for the revival of one of the great religious Orders of the Church.

The Dominican Order, to which the prayers and sufferings of Anne Moes were to mean so much, had reached a very low point in its history. The friars had been driven from France, and in all the intellectual circles of Europe their influence was weak. Two men—one a preacher and the other an administrator—were to be the instruments of the needed reform: Henri Dominic Lacordaire and Vincent Jandel. At the time of their crusade to revive the Order, neither of these great men knew of the existence of the girl in Luxembourg who was praying for them and offering her sufferings for the success of their venture.

To make it even more mystifying, Anne Moes had never seen a Dominican and did not know that such an Order existed. Impelled by the urgency of her prayers and revelations, she made several attempts to find out the identity of the Order for which she was praying. None of the local clergy could or would tell her what she wanted to know. Lacordaire and Jandel must fight their battle in the full light of the public eye. Anne worked in the dark.

When Anne was thirteen years old, the clergy of her town began to take an interest in her. She was obviously a pious girl, and they thought she ought to enter a convent. For several years she was bothered by their suggestions and criticisms. Several times definite plans were made for her, without her consent, to enter this community or that. Sisters of Christian Wisdom and Carmelites both were puzzled by this girl who refused to enter the community after the pastor had made all the arrangements. Desperately, Anne tried to explain to her spiritual director that God was asking her to pray and suffer for an Order—she did not know what Order, nor where—and that she couldn't enter a convent until He said so. The confessor scolded her soundly and made arrangements for her to enter the Nursing Sisters of St. Francis. At this moment, when Anne probably felt that she had all the trouble she could manage, our Lord appeared to her and told her that He wanted her to found a monastery of Dominican sisters. Surprisingly enough, when she explained this to the confessor, she managed to convince him that she was telling the truth, and he decided to help her.

The confessor could give her little information about the Dominican Order, but he managed to get a few books. He insisted that she should not try to found a Second Order cloister, but a Third Order group which would be more acceptable to the city at the moment. He even helped her to get recruits for the community and to find a house at Limpertsberg. This, according to her description, "had a roof like a sieve and looked like the hide-out of a group of bandits" rather than the peaceful home of a group of women who wanted only to serve God.

In religion Anne Moes took the name Sister Dominic Clara, a name soon changed by her companions to that of Mother Dominic Clara. For the remaining few years of her life her convent at Limpertsberg was to be the battle ground—and the word is well chosen—where she would fight the powers of darkness. The story of that struggle is difficult to follow; it is one more demonstration of the mystery of God's methods. All the forces of criticism and calumny were loosed against the new foundation. Even the Church would not recognize the house, and Mother Dominic Clara herself had to undergo a long and gruelling examination to prove that she was neither crazy nor a heretic.

She decided that her mission was to erect a Second Order cloister. The members of the Dominican Order, for whom she had suffered and prayed during her extraordinary lifetime, were not at all anxious to receive her as a member. Ill health, poor eyesight, spiritual desolation were her daily lot, and she suffered almost all that any one person could suffer in the way of reverses, criticisms, and rebuffs. When the new community was finally affiliated with the Order and the cloister erected, establishing Limpertsberg as a regular house of the Second Order, it seemed nothing short of a miracle to anyone who knew anything about it.

One might think that with all the disturbances of the founding years, Mother Dominic Clara's house might lack both peace and regularity. Such was not the case. It was a house noted for silence and regularity, famous for the precision of the chant, and radiant with peace and happiness.

Mother Dominic Clara died in 1895, at the end of a long and extraordinary life.

MOTHER THERESE CHUPIN
(1813-1896)

Her official name was Mother Vincent Ferrer, but those who knew her called her "the good mother." She was an almost unbelievable character, but, it seems, a remarkably holy one. And her road to heaven, like so many roads leading that way, was not an easy one.

Victorine Therese Chupin was born in Brittany in 1813. The family was poor and of deep faith; their very poverty had protected them from the horrors of the revolution so recently past. Six girls and three boys made up the Chupin family, and Victorine made friends early with that poverty which shaped the lives of the people among whom her life would be spent.

At the age of twenty, Victorine went to Paris to stay with her brother, who was a medical student there. She had thought seriously about the matter of her vocation, but had reached no decision. Her confessor bade her go to Paris and told her God would make His will clear. The first indication that God was taking a hand in her activities came when the parish priest engaged her to take charge of the Society of the Holy Childhood. Here, she met for the first time the girls of the big city, girls who were poorly instructed and who walked always on the brink of trouble. She went at the work with such vigor that she soon had the Society functioning almost like a religious community. So well did she succeed that people talked about it, and word of her ability was brought to the commissioner of police. Victorine was asked to take on the incredibly difficult job of supervising the women's prison of St. Lazare.

The job did not appeal to her in the least. She was a girl who valued purity and the spiritual life so highly that the very thought of contact with the vicious and unprincipled inmates of the infamous old prison was repugnant to her. She hesitated, prayed; and Our Lady appeared to her, reproaching her. Victorine gave in.

The huge prison of St. Lazare had had a varied history. It began in kinder days as a leper hospital; various religious communities had managed it for a number of charitable purposes in the long years since its foundation in the twelfth century. The revolutionaries drove out the Lazarist fathers, plundered the buildings of all valuables, and turned it into a prison. Now, when it appeared that no one could manage the women of the prison, one dared not bring religious in to take charge of it. Victorine, whose personal purity and innocence seemed almost that of a religious, was a desperate choice. She walked in calmly, as though she had been managing a prison for all of her twenty years, and in a short time had the hardened inmates in the palm of her capable hand.

For twelve years Victorine worked with the prisoners of St. Lazare. It was the prisoners there who first called her "bonne Mére"; a good name, for she could not help mothering everyone who needed it. It was they who, when the Commune made an attack on the prison, saved her from death. And in the face of almost certain failure, she succeeded in the work that she thought the Blessed Virgin wanted her to do—instructing the prisoners, seeing to it that they received the sacraments, even—to the utter amazement of the authorities—arranging retreats for the women. In 1848, when it seemed safe to bring religious into prominence again, the prison was given over to the care of the community of sisters, and Victorine was free.

It was the women prisoners themselves who led her to her next step. Some of them had been released from prison and found that life on the outside was too full of temptations for people who had no roots. One day a group of them surrounded "bonne Mére" on the street and begged her to take them in—somewhere, anywhere—and let them be under her spiritual care. They told her there were more than eighty girls who would come to her then and there if she had a place to put them. While she was still wrestling with the problem of where to set up her refuge, a Dominican father of the Lacordaire congregation sent her a young girl who needed help. Here was immediate need, with no time for elaborate discussions. Victorine borrowed some money and rented a flat.

For the rest of her life she was to be an embarrassment to the laws of economics, for there was never enough room or enough money, and always she made it stretch to reach. Her first refuge was in Paris, and God cared for it as He cares for the sparrows. The girls lived on the brink of destitution, sometimes utterly without food or fuel, but always, in the nick of time, the needs were supplied. The first permanent refuge was blessed in having the first Mass said by Father Bourard, a Dominican who was to die a martyr to the Commune in a few years. From this flat, "the good mother" (bonne Mére) moved her children to a large house on the outskirts of Paris, a huge place with no beds and no water. She set up a sewing business for her girls here, so that they might earn enough money to live. However, with the best of luck, and some miraculous assistance of Providence in the matter of lamp-oil and fuel, they still had to steal the potatoes from the pigs for more than one meal.

"Bonne Mére" and her several companions became Dominican Tertiaries in 1854. She took the name Sister Vincent Ferrer, but no one ever called her anything except "bonne Mére." It was this casual and loving attitude of the girls towards their "mother" that made difficult the next step in the long road to organization. Bonne Mére did not want to be tied down by rules that would tell her how many girls she could help, and when. She wanted to be free to help all who needed it, and viewed the whole notion of joining the Order with suspicion, dearly though she loved her Dominican friends. When it was finally pointed out to her that the future of her work would suffer from too casual an organization, she submitted, but not too willingly. The whole thing was settled for her by a visit to Pope Pius IX, who blessed her and her institute "until the end of time." That, to her, spelled a permanent organization. She went to see the Dominican master general and received his assurance that she and her companions would be given the Dominican habit when she had drawn up her rule and made arrangements for the training of her novices.

In 1865 the sisters were given the Dominican habit. A sister from the community at Langres came to train the sisters of the refuge in the religious life, and bit by bit the community was fitted into regular Dominican life.

"Bonne Mére" never lost her individuality; she remained somewhat of a "character" to the end of her holy life. She never could quite see the sense of silence, if speech seemed called for. She chafed under the somewhat rigid rule of the nun from Langres, though she humbly appreciated her talents. "Bonne Mére" could never quite forget that her business was being a mother, and that everything else came afterwards.

Who but this amazing woman would have thought to approach Alexander Dumas and point out to him that, since his books had led to the downfall of many of the young women in her care, he ought in justice to use his pen for their benefit, and write some copy that would bring in some badly needed funds to the refuge? It is a tribute to "bonne Mére's" charm that the great writer did exactly as she had asked him to do, and that he always remained —a little uncertainly, perhaps—a friend of the refuge.

"Bonne Mére" died in 1896, leaving her work well established and already sending out branch houses. This was most likely the result of her prayers and good will, for she was not an organizer. Her approach to life is best expressed by a priest who worked with her at the refuge: "He who wishes to do good must not search too keenly into the lives of the miserable; he must first relieve their misery and provide for their wants."

TWENTIETH CENTURY

HENRI DIDON
(1840-1900)

This golden-tongued orator whose eloquence is still remembered in France was a man of many talents. Born Henri Didon in a little village in the French Alps in 1840, he rose from the ranks of the unknown to be a household word in his country.

At the age of sixteen, Henri finished a brilliant course of studies at the minor seminary in Rondeau. He had already been drawn by the magnetism of Father Lacordaire to desire the Dominican life, so he applied in 1856 to the novitiate at Flavigny. He was happily received because of his brilliant scholastic record, but his frail health gave great cause for worry. Lacordaire had already lost some of his most promising young aspirants from tuberculosis, and the young Henri Didon did not look as if he would live long. However, he proved that he had a strong will and a dogged determination to survive. He knew what he wanted: to be a Dominican. So he went after it in the way that seemed most direct, by toughening himself and trying to improve his health. He forced himself to take long walks and other exercises designed to strengthen his body.

The young Brother Henri was sent to the convent of St. Baume and made infirmarian. He succeeded admirably in entertaining the sick when he could not think of anything else to do for them. He could always make them laugh, which made him very popular among them. There was a large community at St. Baume, and he loved the experience of being in a big house. He especially loved the liturgy, and used to chant loudly and with great gusto. Unfortunately he was tone-deaf, and no amount of practice seemed to help him.

The day that the sad news reached St. Baume of Lacordaire's death, Brother Henri planted a weeping willow tree in his memory. Every day he tended it and watched over it. "I want to make a giant out of it!" he explained. A curious young man altogether, his companions must have thought.

There was at this time no hint of the gift for oratory which was one day to bring all France to his feet. Father Didon was ordained in France in 1863, after taking his lectorate at the Minerva. As an ordained priest he was expected to preach, and he did work at it. But his style was cold and logical, lacking any warmth or any touch with his audience. He was not a "born orator," to whom the gift was presented on a silver platter.

He attacked the problem of preaching just as he had gone after the matter of his health, or the weeping-willow sapling. When he was assigned to Paris in 1867 no one expected much of his preaching, but they were electrified to hear his opening sermon on the Blessed Virgin and St. Hyacinth. His long hours of practice and his dogged determination had paid off. By the following year, when he was preaching Lent in Nancy, his sermons had to be transferred to a larger church because so many thronged to hear him.

In 1877 Father Didon was appointed prior at St. Jacques in Paris. He planned to make it a student center with a series of religious instructions to be held regularly. Someone took exception to his course on marriage and reported it with exaggerations to the cardinal. The cardinal, who apparently did not hear any of the sermons himself, suggested that Father Didon had better give them elsewhere, or change the subject, or just stop preaching. No definite prohibition was given, however, and the following Lent his series was mobbed by the people who wished to hear him. The master general, who wanted no trouble with the cardinal, sent Father Didon to Corbara in Corsica.

Corbara was a stern and comfortless house set in a desert, not far from Napoleon's exile, and much less comfortable. Father Didon, who had done nothing wrong, could well have wondered why he was being penanced to this bleak exile. It must have been a shocking change from the busy stir of Paris to the silence of Corbara. Yet Father Didon was greater even in exile than he had been at the height of his fame. He lived for twenty years in exile on Corbara, studying Scripture, writing his beautiful *Life of Christ,* always prayerful, and uncritical of whatever error in judgment might have placed him there.

In 1893 he was returned to France and made a preacher general. He was put in charge of the boys' school at Arceuil, where he was regarded as being "much too fastidious" because he put in bathrooms and playgrounds. He was on his way to Rome when death surprised him at Toulouse. He died with the brethren around him, content and at peace, in 1900.

CESLAUS VON ROBIANO
(1829-1902)

Ceslaus Von Robiano was one of the eager young men who helped to set the world on fire again with a revived Dominican Order at the time of Lacordaire. He was the restorer of the Order in Germany after the long bleak years of war and political unrest had caused it to dwindle down to nothing.

Alfred Count Von Robiano was born in 1829 in Brussels, of a noble and wealthy family. He was one of the recruits sent to the novitiate of Flavigny by Lacordaire in 1856. His older brother was a Jesuit, a man of quiet, even disposition. Alfred was an impulsive and very active person, full of enthusiasm for the wild plans of the young Abbé from Paris. He was given the name Ceslaus in religion.

After his ordination, Father Ceslaus was sent by the master general to restore the Order in Germany. Once a thriving province and the nursery of saints and scholars, the German province had all but disappeared under the long strain of political trouble and, due to war, the lack of contact with other provinces. It is a matter of note that the revival of the Order, led by a Frenchman, was so soon to find an echo in Germany.

Ceslaus built the convents of Berlin and Dusseldorf, and of Venlo in Holland, which became the house of studies of the province. He was prior in Berlin during the difficult times of the Kulturkampf, and managed to keep the province not only in operation but in a state of steady growth when other church institutions were plowed under.

Personally, Father Ceslaus was charitable to the point of imprudence, always ready to help anyone no matter how little they might deserve it. A high government official said of him in retrospect, "If you wanted to talk to Father Ceslaus, you had to pose as a terrible sinner." His confessional was always busy, his pockets always empty. He is still remembered in that part of Berlin as "our saint."

A man of prayer, of vision, and of charity, Ceslaus Von Robiano died in the convent at Dusseldorf in 1902 at the age of eighty-two. He had lived to see his province built up to where once again it was an important unit of the Order.

HENRY DENIFLE
(1844-1905)

One of the most scholarly of Dominican historians in recent times was Henry Denifle. He made it his life work to set straight the records of the early years of the Order.

Joseph Denifle was born at Imst in the Austrian Tyrol in 1844. At the age of nine he was left an orphan, poor and homeless, but with a fine intellect and an engaging personality. Someone directed him to the Canons of St. Augustine, who educated him well.

As a young man he read the letters of Lacordaire and was enthralled with the idea of being a Dominican. In 1861 he entered the novitiate at Graz in Austria, and took the name Henry in religion, in honor of Henry Suso.

After his ordination in 1866, the young priest was sent to the Minerva to finish his studies. Here his masters saw the first evidence of the historical talent that was to lead him to the top in that field. Sent to Hungary to teach in the house of studies, he went back to Greek originals for his information; there seemed no barrier of language that would stop him. As a young student at Imst he had saved his money to buy not new books but *old* ones—the older the better. Now, plunging into St. Thomas, he decided to write a critical commentary on the *Summa*, for which he would go back to the sources.

Always interested in his personal patron, Henry Suso, Father Denifle was appalled at the misinformation that clung to his name and the false impressions in literature concerning the German mystics of the fourteenth century. He embarked on a study of this matter that was to bring him to open battle with some of the most learned historians of the times. He directly attacked the legend of the lay "spiritual directors" who were supposed to have led the spiritual revival in the Rhineland in the time of Suso, those nebulous and controversial "friends of God," whose obscure remarks and shaky theology had been adopted uncritically by so many historians and had caused Protestant writers to list Suso, Tauler, and Eckhart as the first Protestants. He worked relentlessly back to the manuscript sources, and hammered at them until they yielded up the information he sought: some of the people most quoted as "fourteenth century mystics" had never even existed; the quotations which had so long cast a shadow over Dominicans of the time had been carefully taken out of context and changed to suit this or that writer's purpose. He fought valiantly for the reputation of his brother Dominicans who were then 500 years dead. Prominent historians soon discovered that Father Denifle was a fearsome opponent—he never advanced a statement until he could prove it, and his proofs could be devastating to some of their prettiest theories.

This work set the pattern for the whole life of Henry Denifle. Always he was the tireless seeker for truth, the uncompromising historian who wanted not handy theories but facts. Pope Leo XIII set him to work on a new edition of St. Thomas, a work which necessitated his traveling all over Europe to gather material. He preached as he went, a series of Lenten sermons in Vienna, retreats in Holland and Paris. In Paris he decided that the history of the University of Paris was badly written, and made a resolution to come back and do it properly when he had finished his present commitment. Everywhere he went he delved into the oldest books, demanding manuscripts that other people had never heard of or did not correctly value. He went to Spain, Portugal, Berlin, Paris, and Oxford. His position in the Vatican library was established—Father Denifle could use anything there, any time. True to his promise, as soon as he had finished his works on St. Thomas, he hurried to Paris and wrote, not only the *History of the University of Paris,* but a history of all the medieval universities, a five-volume work.

Dominican history had always tempted him, and it infuriated him to find inaccuracies. He found an important Dominican document in a Cistercian abbey in the Tyrol in some of his travels; a study of this gave new information on the *Primitive Constitutions,* which led to his *History of the Dominican Constitutions from 1228.* Dominican studies led him to do biographies of St. Raymond, Blessed Jordan, and John the Teutonic; branching out into other Orders, he wrote a history of the Carmelites in the thirteenth and fourteenth centuries, and a history of the Franciscans.

Research in sixteenth century German history convinced him that the whole story of Luther had been twisted, dressed up, and dramatized in the interests of Protestant history. Never one to avoid trouble, he buckled on his literary sword and went to work on the hero of the Reformation. As expected, his work drew the fire of every Protestant historian alive. "Nobody knows less of Luther than present-day Protestant theologians," he snapped back at them. Furiously, the Protestant historians fought back trying to prove their statements; delightedly, like a hound on the trail, Denifle followed them up each wrong path and abolished their arguments with irrefutable proof. Many years after his death, the most capable Protestant historians acknowledged their debt to him for forcing them to look for true facts; but during his last years they did everything possible to discredit him. It did them little good, as he was a careful apologist, and never adopted a position that he could not hold.

In 1903, Denifle suffered a severe stroke. "Luther has finally killed me," he said wryly. He rallied, however, and worked for two years more; sick and failing, he was still a formidable adversary to the angry writers he had challenged. In 1905, he was on his way to Cambridge where he was to receive an honorary degree when he was felled by another stroke. He died at Munich from the effects of the stroke, and on his deathbed received a blessing from Pope Pius X, who had watched his work with interest and appreciation for years.

ARNOLD JANSSEN
(d. 1909)

That the founder of the Society of the Divine Word was a Tertiary Dominican—and very proud of it—is not too well known, even by those who admire his work and the mission of the Society he founded.

Arnold Janssen was born in a small village of Holland, one of eight children of a pious farmer. Arnold's mother was a holy and sensible woman and a careful mother. Once, when she had prayed a long time at her night prayers, one of the children told her, "Mama, if you pray any more you'll pray yourself right through heaven!" She replied, "Anybody who has eight children has *got* to know how to pray, my dear!"

Her husband conducted family prayers, which sometimes seemed overlong to the restless children. Though they sometimes tried to shorten his devotions, his sons loved their father, and his devotion to the Holy Ghost was carried on in the Society founded by his son Arnold.

Arnold finished high school and worked his way through the University of Bonn, majoring in natural sciences. He took his degree the same year that the *Origin of Species* was published, and was so affronted by it that he made up his mind to fight the doctrines of the evolutionists in defense of Catholic science. He began by writing essays on the subject when he was teaching his first class in high school. One of his essays won him $50, and he spent the entire sum to bring his father to the city and give him a wonderful two days of seeing the city sights; the older Janssen had never in his hard and monotonous life had such fun as he had on this one and only vacation.

Arnold was at this time offered a better teaching post, in Berlin, but he had decided to become a priest. He studied at the diocesan seminary of Muenster and was ordained on the Feast of the Assumption, 1862. For a man who had dreamed of taking up the sword against Darwin, his first assignment was dampening; he was sent to teach mathematics at a small Catholic college, where he remained, in the words of one biographer, "a slave of the blackboard for twelve years." On weekends he went out to assist in nearby parishes as curate. His help was welcome, but his singing voice was terrible. It was said that the only acknowledgment he made of the notes going up or down was to raise or bow his head. After a few notable disasters, he was relegated to the role of perpetual subdeacon.

Out of this uneventful life he was rescued by a Jesuit who was looking for a director for the Apostleship of Prayer. The Jesuit had no idea that

Father Janssen had talents in this line, but he proved to be the ideal director. He eventually was released from other work so that he could go on the road to sell the idea to the whole diocese. "If we had prayed as much for Protestant Germany as we have railed against her, we would have converted her long ago," he said bluntly to those who enquired about his methods. In order to propagate his apostleship, he started a little magazine, *The Little Messenger of the Sacred Heart,* a missionary venture. In order to be free to write, print, and distribute this magazine almost alone, he asked for a post as chaplain to a community of sisters.

The magazine was begun during the worst days of the Kulturkampf, when no one with any caution at all would have initiated any new work. Priests were banished, Catholic Germany was in its darkest hour; and a young priest with no following whatsoever began, not only a magazine—which was bad enough—but agitation for a mission seminary to train priests for China. He looked in vain for someone else to found the seminary, it is true; but anyone with any ability was afraid to try anything so foolhardy. Not a single volunteer came forward either to join or to found the seminary.

He decided he would found it himself, but he could not very well be the student body. So he plodded on, telling his dreams time after time to an audience that admired his sanctity, but openly doubted his sanity. The children who lived next door used to slip out into the yard after dark to watch him praying—sometimes he forgot to pull the shades; they and most of the neighbors felt that Father Janssen was a saint. But the exasperated remark of one of the bishops he approached was echoed again and again among a hardpressed people: "We live in a time when everything is tottering, and you come along and want to start something new! There are heathens enough on the banks of the Rhine if you want to work on heathens!" In all the discouraging business he got no help at all. Finally, two small contributions came in, one from a convent of Poor Clares and one from a servant girl.

Battered but undaunted, Father Janssen bought an old tavern just across the Dutch border, where he could draw upon German resources and still be out of reach of the savage laws then in force. His first volunteers finally came in, a Dutchman, a German, and an Austrian—a priest and two students. They set up business in the old tavern with no beds, no furniture, no dishes, and, of course, no food. Their housekeeping thus took very little of their time, and they were free to study and practice poverty in the grand manner. St. Francis of Assisi would have been blissfully happy in the drafty old tavern where only the rats were well fed.

From this unpromising beginning an almost incredible growth has come to enrich the world. The first ray of sunshine was a brother who was a master-carpenter. He promptly took in hand the many infirmities of the building and soon had it shipshape. Then the brother of Father Janssen came along to help out; he was a better beggar than his brother Arnold, and he managed to get the community finances into reasonable solvency.

The community was slow to begin its growth; at one point, when Father Janssen wished to adopt the Dominican rule in its entirety, two of his three companions left him. He was himself a Dominican Tertiary, and he deeply admired the spirit of the Lacordaire fathers of France. He wanted to add to the Dominican Tertiary rule a distinguishing mark of the Society of the Divine Word, a study of natural history. This would not only perpetuate the battle against Darwin, but would cultivate a body of trained scientists in the Church who would use their knowledge of primitive people as a means of illuminating the faith.

Today, on the site of a ramshackle tavern with its four half-starved occupants, a city of 1200 brothers—priests and laybrothers—carry on the ideals of Father Janssen. His preference for the Dominican rule was modified, though they carried into their own the Dominican missionary spark that had animated the Order from the beginning. At the time that the mother-house of the Society was uprooted by the Nazis, it possessed one of the finest printing presses in Europe, equipped with the best of modern equipment and run by trained brothers, who turned their professional knowledge to the vast needs of the missions. Carpenter brothers were the first in the world to make prefabricated houses on any scale; these, too, were needed in the missions. And today's foremost authorities on the religions of primitive peoples are the sons of the dreamer who started a society for the missions when no sensible man would have tried anything of the sort. In place of the four first members are thousands of zealous missionaries who work in every country in the world, carrying the flame of the love of God kindled in the heart of their founder in the darkest hour of the Church in Germany.

In 1942 the cause of Arnold Janssen was proposed for beatification. We should pray that the cause will proceed smoothly and that the name of this valiant man will soon be added to the roll of the saints.

DOCTOR AGNES MacLAREN
(1837-1913)

America is well aware of the work of the Medical Mission Sisters, and very proud of this group of trained women who are bringing the Gospel to India by means of medicine. Dominicans, to whom the missions are always dear, rejoice in their progress in this new and very modern apostolate. But few Dominicans are aware that the woman who first dreamed of this unique answer to a desperate problem was a Dominican Tertiary.

Agnes MacLaren was born in Edinburgh in 1837. Her father, a wealthy and politically active man, brought into their big hospitable home all the thinkers and doers of that time of great social ferment. His friends were idealists, and they wished to alleviate the conditions that then prevailed in shops and factories. Agnes, little more than a baby, sat and absorbed the ideals of social justice that were discussed frankly at her father's table. As soon as she was old enough she joined in the discussions herself. It was a set of circumstances unusual for a young lady of the nineteenth century, and it was to shape her whole life and work.

The MacLarens were Presbyterians, solidly Christian people who took the Gospel seriously and thought of sensible ways to apply it. Agnes and her large family of brothers and sisters learned early from their father the power of legislation and the necessity of political consciousness, and from their kindly stepmother the practical and personal aspects of charity. In maturity, Agnes was to realize that they had taught her well to deal with injustice and poverty, both in the abstract and the concrete. But, broad-minded though they were, they balked when, at the age of twenty-seven, she told them that she wanted to study to be a doctor. Not only did nice girls not study such things, but it was a fact that no university would accept a woman as a candidate for medical college.

Agnes was not her father's daughter for nothing; she set out to batter down the walls. She lectured and campaigned and talked to officials, and ignored the jeers and the cold contempt that met her ideas. Several of her friends who had succeeded in getting into the University of Edinburgh were being booed and annoyed by the men students. Agnes joined with them in public debate on the touchy question, studying long hours to make her arguments as telling as possible. At length, failing to make any impression on the universities of the British Isles, she went to France with a letter from Cardinal Manning.

Agnes knew that the great English convert cardinal was interested in the social reforms that so intrigued her, but she had never met anyone quite like the French prelate to whom she presented her letter. It was her first conscious contact with the Catholic Church, and she was deeply impressed. Through the help of this churchman she was enrolled in the University of Montpellier, and after a long and gruelling course of studies, during which she nearly worked herself to death, she emerged with her medical degree. And she had something else—a deep love and respect for the Hospital Sisters of St. Francis with whom she had made her home as a student.

The splendid example of these good women was to bear young Doctor MacLaren through many trials. Never obtrusive, never scandalized, never critical, always cheerful, they cared for the lady doctor and gave her happy memories of the Church. But it was to be twenty years before the independent Scots doctor would seek baptism. Nothing ever came easy to Agnes MacLaren.

At the age of forty-one, Doctor MacLaren began practicing medicine. She loved her work, and she gave every ounce of energy to it. She felt no spiritual lack that she could define, but once in passing through Lyons she talked with a Catholic priest. No, she did not want to be a Catholic; she was too independent, she did not want to surrender one jot of that independence to an authoritarian Church. Nevertheless, she wrote to the priest and asked him if he would give her a retreat. She made it—an excellent retreat, she said—and emerged as staunchly Protestant as ever. And each year, for nearly twenty years, she returned to the same priest for a week of retreat which never seemed to dent her Protestantism. Then, one day, the gift of faith came to this hard-working and zealous woman whom her friends considered a saint, and Agnes MacLaren was received into the Catholic Church.

Long delayed, Agnes' acquaintance with the Catholic Church was rapidly filled in by her meeting with some of the most unusual—and to her, most understandable—features of the work. She was barely baptized when she met up with the work of Père Lataste, and had the great happiness of visiting his house of Bethany and finding in it a profound realization of his great ideal. She would like to have joined the sisters and remained there forever, within reach of the cave of St. Mary Magdalen which had so moved her, and close to their work of rehabilitation. But she was sixty-one years old, and very independent; it would be difficult at that age to fit herself to a totally different way of life.

There was nothing, however, to prevent her from joining the Third Order of St. Dominic. In this excellent group she would be able to pursue her own work with the added impetus of prayer and sisterhood. She was received into the Order with a great sense of having reached, at last, a definite goal.

Because she felt that it was time to begin planning for her old age, Agnes purchased a comfortable home, and spent a good deal of time and thought in furnishing a chapel in it. Her plan for getting a chaplain was simplicity itself; she would search out priests who were tired or ill, or at any rate in need of a rest, and give them the freedom of the whole lovely seaside home, in return for which they would say Mass in her chapel. The plan was well received by bishops and priests alike. Soon she had a steady stream of applicants for this unique form of clerical vacation. It was one of her visiting priests who opened her eyes to the last and greatest work of her life.

He was from India, and his tales of the missions there were enthralling. It made her blood boil to hear of the injustice, the poverty, and the hunger —she was always a campaigner for social justice. But the good priest told her that the key to the whole question of the conversion of India was a trained corps of women doctors, preferably religious, who would reach the women and children of this land now shut off by prejudice from ordinary medical and sanitary care. Agnes was astounded, and deeply moved. If she had been twenty years younger there would be no question at all about what she ought to do: she would go herself, and build a hospital staffed by women, and open the gates of bodily and spiritual health to the women of India. But at sixty-one, with failing health, one did not go trekking off halfway across the world. Still, there was one thing she could do about it; she could interest others in building and staffing a hospital.

The remainder of her life was to be spent in this effort, and it took every ounce of her strength and every bit of her ability. There were three things she had to do: to get together the money for the building of the hospital, to convince sisters to take up the work, and—hardest of all—to break down the solid wall of prejudice against the question of sisters studying medicine. The first took endless contacts, letterwriting, public appearances, among people of all walks of life. The second called for writing to and interviewing all the sisters she could contact, and persuading them that this was Christian work, an apostolate crying for help. For the third, she trudged endless miles of Roman streets and wrote letters to bishops and missionaries. The Church was conservative and Rome was slow to act. And Doctor MacLaren had so little time.

Only when she was virtually on her deathbed at the age of seventy-six was she to see a glimmer of hope. A young Austrian girl, Anna Dengel, a girl with a great heart and a vision of medical help in the far missions, wrote to her to ask about her plans. Miss Dengel had youth and strength and courage; Doctor MacLaren, racing against death, poured out in letters her hopes and dreams, and—for she was a practical woman always—the ground that had already been broken.

Anna Dengel would not have to fight, as she had, for the right to study medicine. She would not have to build the hospital, nor interest good lay-people in the cause of Indian women. She would not even have to walk the endless streets of Rome, pointing out to one bishop and cardinal after another that this was Christ's work. Miss Dengel could build on the foundation so long and painfully laid by the valiant Scotswoman she had never seen. Resolutely, she set about accomplishing her part in the plan, of becoming a sister-doctor who would make the work permanent. Tired and ill, Doctor MacLaren thanked God for the joy of knowing that the work would not die with her. She planned a meeting with the young girl from Austria who was to make her dream come true, but the meeting never took place, for on April 17, 1913, Agnes MacLaren died.

One never knows how much of any work can be credited to the labors of any one person. Many personalities, acting upon a project, give it the impetus of their particular gifts. But both the Medical Mission Sisters who carry on their great work in India, and the Dominican Order of which she was so proudly a member, can well afford to thank God for the work that Agnes MacLaren accomplished, even though she herself never had the joy of seeing how abundantly her plan was to bear fruit in the years since her death.

SISTER SUSANNA AND COMPANIONS, MARTYRS
(d. 1914)

One would expect to find a sixteenth century date on the heading of a group "martyred by the Turks"; it is a little surprising to note that the date is twentieth century. Sister Susanna and her companions, who were killed in Seert in Armenia just at the beginning of the First World War, were not at that time Dominicans formally recognized as a community; they were Tertiaries living together under the title of "Catharinettes," and wearing, instead of the full habit, a modest dark dress in which they were inconspicuous in their hostile environment. The community was well liked and had done excellent work, not only in Seert, but in several other towns.

Sister Susanna, the superior at the Seert school, was sixty years old at the time of the massacre. She had joined the first group of Tertiaries organized by the French Dominicans in 1896, and she had spent the intervening years teaching in several schools. Sister Regina, who was forty years old at the time of her death, was the cook and laundress in the group; she had come of a pious family and was also one of the first Tertiaries. Sister Anna and Sister Seidy were both natives of Seert and had taught there for several years. They and Sister Warda were in their early twenties. Sister Wareina, the only one to survive the massacre, was also the youngest. She was just twenty-one.

Shortly after war was declared, the Dominican fathers and the Sisters of the Presentation, all of whom were French, were hurriedly deported to France. Turkey, as an ally of Germany, might be expected to take this step; but there was no reason to anticipate the appalling slaughter of the Armenians which shortly began. The sisters out at Seert watched and waited, and in June, 1915, the terror broke in their own town. Shouts in the street, the screaming of women—then a horde of hysterical refugees began pouring into the school, with the shocking news that the Turks had taken every man in Seert, from young boys to old men, and shot them.

The sisters tried to keep order among the terrified women, and to feed and console them. They knew that their turn would soon come, and they prayed desperately for strength. Some one advised the sisters that they would be safer dressed as Moslems, so they dressed in the long veils of the Moslem women and waited for their orders. The Armenian women were called out first, and began their death march. A few days later it was the turn of the Chaldean women, among whom were the sisters. The hardships of this march are almost beyond description. Some 600 women with their children were forced to march all day for twelve days under the hot sun across the desert, while their soldier guards rode in comfort, berating them for their stupidity and punishing them when they lagged through weariness.

Concealed among their relatives and hoping to escape notice, the sisters plodded along with the sorry caravan. Sister Susanna and Sister Regina were guarding a group of orphan girls who had lived with them at Seert. On the second day of the march, Sister Susanna collapsed and it was obvious that she could go no farther. A soldier stripped off her clothes, to be sold later, and shot her as she knelt praying. The caravan moved on.

Sister Warda was trying to help her sister-in-law, her mother, and her old grandmother. When the grandmother fainted, a soldier killed her, and then craftily told Sister Warda that he would lead her little group to safety if they would trust him—that is, if they had money to pay him. They gave him all their money and fled with him by night. The next day the slow-moving caravan came upon their bodies on the desert.

Each evening the soldiers took care to camp within sight of a Moslem town, so that good Mohammedans could delight in the sight of suffering Christians. They could also, if they were skillful, steal girls out of the group for their harems; sometimes the girls were offered a choice, though few of them took it. Many were carried off by force.

At the end of twelve days the remains of the caravan reached a point in the mountains where it had been decided to end the frightful affair. The soldiers handed over to the townspeople the job of killing the women, while they climbed up on the hill where they could watch, only pausing to give orders not to waste ammunition on the victims. The women were marched up to the cliff overlooking a rocky ravine, and were killed with stones and clubs. The clothing was carefully salvaged for resale, and the bodies thrown into the ravine.

Sister Wareina was still in the company of her women relatives when they were led up to the cliff. A young Turk offered her freedom if she would go with him to his harem. She refused, and the rocks began to fall as she cried out the Hail Mary. She plunged over into the ravine and rolled down among the rocks. Hours later, she recovered consciousness to find herself stripped and wounded badly, lying among the dead.

She pulled a dress from one of the victims who still had clothes, and was frightened to see an elderly Moslem coming towards her. He had come to help, however; he took the suffering girl to his home, where he had lodged a number of Christian refugees, and cared for them in the face of his neighbors' disapproval, until they were able to travel. By then, a complication had arisen; he had fallen in love with one of the orphan girls who had somehow escaped the massacre. He refused to give up the girl for all of Sister Wareina's pleading, until he fell seriously ill and the Blessed Virgin appeared to him in a dream and told him to let the girl go free.

The sixth and last of the martyrs, another Sister Regina, was taken by the Turks from the school in Dzejirah, and killed with a dagger.

Both Sister Wareina and the orphan girl lived to see their little Tertiary group, shattered by war and martyrdom, joined to the Dominican Order.

The cause of the six Tertiaries was proposed in 1929. We may hope that they will someday be honored as martyrs for the faith.

HYACINTH M. CORMIER
(1832-1916)

A master general of recent times who did much to restore the primitive fervor of the Order was Father Hyacinth M. Cormier. Henry Cormier was born in Orleans on the Feast of the Immaculate Conception in 1832. All his life he treasured the thought that he had been born on Our Lady's day, and therefore he should be especially devoted to her. His father died while he was still a small child, so Henry and his only brother, Eugene, went with their mother to live near his uncle, who was a priest in Orleans. The two boys entered the new preparatory seminary at Orleans. The following year Eugene died, leaving Henry alone and grief-stricken.

Henry continued his studies for the priesthood at the major seminary of Orleans, and was ordained in 1856. At this time he fulfilled a desire that had been growing on him for some time; he went to Flavigny, where Father Lacordaire had opened a novitiate of the Order, and begged to be admitted. He was accepted, a little dubiously as he looked so delicate, and given the name Hyacinth.

When it was time for Brother Hyacinth's profession, the doubt had grown into a certainty; he had had several hemorrhages, and the community, which had already lost some of its most promising members from tuberculosis, was afraid to profess him. The master general, Father Jandel, took him to Rome as secretary and asked the pope for a special dispensation to allow him to make profession. The pope responded that if he went for thirty days without a hemorrhage he could make his vows. Young Brother Hyacinth tried hard—once he got as far as 29 days—and did not quite make it, but he fell seriously ill and was anointed. In the belief that he was going to die in a few days, he was finally allowed to make his profession. But at this point he recovered, and he served the Order vigorously for fifty years.

In 1865 the old Province of Toulouse was to be re-established, and Father Cormier was sent as the first provincial to build up the Order there. His ability for administration was so marked that the pope wanted to make him a cardinal; only the hostility of France towards religious kept him from doing so.

When Father Cormier was elected master general in 1904, it became necessary to replace him in some of the work he had been doing so that he could devote more time to affairs of the Order in general. It was then that his brethren found out what a load he had been carrying. Teaching and writing should have kept him busy; but he also was regular confessor to eight large convents and extraordinary confessor to several more. In spite of all the activity, he spent hours of every day in front of the Blessed Sacrament. He had a universal reputation for the soundness of his spiritual direction.

As master general, Father Cormier turned his attention first to the novices. Many of his writings had been for young people, and he always loved the novices on whom the future of the Order depends. As gentle as a child in his manner, but as inflexible as a Gibraltar in a matter of principle, he quietly demonstrated the policies that he wanted followed in the Order. He founded the Angelicum, the international house of studies at Rome, and supported other educational projects of the Order.

Father Cormier wrote incessantly, mostly devotional works or instructions for novices. Some of his works have been translated into English, but not by any means all of them. He wrote biographies of many eminent Dominicans, including Blessed Raymond of Capua and Father Jandel. His pen helped to make permanent the work done by Father Lacordaire and his companions in re-establishing the Order in France and in the world.

Father Cormier died in Rome in 1916. In 1945 his cause for beatification was introduced. Examined during the course of this process were 171 printed works written by this zealous apostle.

MOTHER MARY WALSH
(1850-1922)

The foundress of the Dominican Sisters of the Sick Poor, who now do such excellent work in the large cities of the United States, began her work in a very humble way, and the long road to accomplishment was paved with suffering. Mary Walsh was born in London of Irish parents in 1850, and left an orphan when she was a baby. Her grandmother came from Ireland to claim the baby, and took her home to Limerick. Mary had a happy childhood; she attended a national school, and her grandmother taught her to work around the house. When she was eighteen her grandmother died, and an uncle came from America to take the twice-orphaned niece to his home in Philadelphia. It soon developed that he was merely looking for an unpaid domestic, and Mary was not happy with the arrangement. After she had paid off her passage money she said a polite good-bye and went to work in New York City.

Mary knew how to work, and she soon had a thriving little business doing fine laundry. She was pious and devout, and her employers liked her cheerful and efficient service. But one hot morning on her way to work, she tossed aside the small security she had made for herself and found herself face to face with destiny. The cause of it was a child crying in a doorway, whom Mary's kind heart could not pass by. The weeping child led her upstairs to where there were three more children, a very sick mother, and a dead baby. Mary gave up her job to help the shattered family.

Word got around among the poor and the suffering, and before long Mary had more patients than she could well manage. Another young woman, sent by the parish priest, helped her for a while, but it soon became evident that they needed some kind of organization. They kept two rooms on the top floor of a house in the Paulist parish, where they could do laundry for three days a week and devote the other days to the poor. Both the Paulist fathers and the Dominicans praised their work, but it was several years before the Dominicans received them as members of the Third Order.

From 1876, when she found the child crying in the doorway, until 1910, when her little community was finally affiliated with the Dominican Order, the life of Mary Walsh was a long crucifixion. The poverty and hopelessness of the people among whom she worked would have been bad enough, but nearly every imaginable barrier rose in the way of the organization that she felt would help them. Orphaned children were left in her care, lovingly tended, and lost in death just as they grew old enough to join the group of workers. Several of the most promising sisters died of tuberculosis, and there was no way even to house them decently to ease their discomfort. For years helpers came and went, and at the end of ten years Mary Walsh was left with but one helper, who was ill herself.

It took heroic courage for anyone to join a group which worked against such odds. One postulant arrived to find everyone in the house sick in bed and five tubs of clothes soaking, waiting to be washed. There was no one to tell her what to do, so she rolled up her sleeves and began on the clothes. "I couldn't just walk out and leave the clothes there unwashed, now, could I?" she asked. She was one of the first postulants to stay with the work, and fifty years later could still vividly describe the poverty and desolation in which Mother Mary Walsh persevered in her ideal for years and years of trial.

Worse than illness or death was a misunderstanding that arose among the sisters concerning her ideals. There is always a troublemaker to be found, the gifted and glib-tongued person who hoodwinks the clergy and everyone else. God did not spare Mary even this, and for several years she was an exile from the community she had founded. When the imposter was finally unmasked, Mother Mary returned to her work, tired and ill, but determined that her hopes for the sick poor would be fulfilled if it took every breath of her body.

Under advice from the Dominicans, Mother Mary planned to send a postulant to a regularly established novitiate for training, then to erect the group into a branch of the Dominican Third Order Regular. By 1907 she had seven companions, and had chosen a promising member for the novitiate experiment. The girl collapsed, too ill to travel, and it was discovered that she, too, had tuberculosis—that secret enemy which had already stolen so many gifted and generous volunteers of the Sisters of the Sick Poor. With this disaster, the representative of the master general suggested that they disband. Mother Mary begged for another chance, and began suing for permission to wear the Dominican habit instead of the simple black dress which all had worn at that time. Also, she made the astonishing request for *all* of her little group to attend the novitiate. In the face of such determination, no one could hold out long. In 1910 a sister was sent from St. Mary of the Springs in Ohio to be novice mistress to the band of good angels from the New York slums. Mother Mary Walsh had been working for thirty years to shape her helpers into a religious community, and only her courage and the grace of God had held it together a good deal of the time. Yet, now she was the humblest novice of all, making no attempt to press her ideas on anyone.

With the endurance which was a special gift of God, Mother Mary had a fund of Irish wit and that faith with which members of her nationality always face calamities. There was never a disaster so terrible that she could not pray and expect it to get better, and sometimes her sense of fun brought the tragedy to a happy conclusion. Once when there was no food at all in the house, she was clowning to keep the sisters from crying, and she began to crow like a rooster. It was a good imitation, since it roused an irate neighbor in the next flat. He knocked at the door and handed her some money, begging her to "get rid of that rooster and let a man get some sleep." Another time she found a quarter in the snow and presented it for a sack of coal. Another customer noted the smallness of the sack of coal, and gave her a fine supply when he heard the story of their need. God always watched over the community, but He never seemed to spare them any type of suffering.

The community which grew out of these appalling hardships differed from its fellow Dominican groups only in the field of its apostolate. The regular life, silence, prayer, and meditation they had in common with the groups of sister teachers and nurses all around them. But their work was to go into the broken lives of the poor and make them whole again when sickness or other trouble had forced them into a state of catastrophe.

The religion or race of the people concerned made no difference, and their only requisite for the loving attention of the sisters was to be needed. The sisters could travel alone if need be, and in years to come, each sister was a graduate nurse with professional training in all the routines that would ease the miseries of those too poor to go to a hospital. Over and above the work shone Mother Mary's unflinching pledge of fidelity: "The faithful observance of the holy rule, according to the letter and the spirit, is the magnet which attracts to the Order and preserves it always in fresh vigor." In 1910, the little group was incorporated as "The American Congregation of the Dominican Sisters of the Sick Poor of the Immaculate Conception," a new branch of an old tree which its founder would truly love.

The first branch house of the community went to Columbus, Ohio, where people were suffering from a flood. Mother Mary was planning a house for Denver, which had made a request for her sisters, when death stilled her busy heart on All Soul's Day in 1922. In the years that followed her death, new houses were opened in several large cities: Cincinnati, Springfield, and Dayton, Ohio; Detroit, Michigan; and Minneapolis, Minnesota. She who longed to reach out to help every suffering person in the world would have been grateful to know that these centers of charity are still functioning according to her original pattern. Eleven other cities and several foreign countries now wait their turns until the day when there will be enough trained sisters to fill their needs.

"Until I knew her, I never met any person who really loved his neighbor," was the remark made at the death of Mother Mary by one who had closely observed her work, and it forms a fitting epitaph to the life of one who lived entirely for others.

ALBERT MARY WEISS
(1844-1925)

One of the most eminent writers of the Dominican Order in the present century was Father Albert Mary Weiss, whose pen was dedicated to the spread and defense of the faith in the troubled years of German nationalism. Adelbert Weiss was born in Bavaria in 1844 of a well-to-do family of pious Catholics. His mother was famous for her charities among the sick and the poor. His father was a doctor who volunteered for the medical corps of the army fighting for the independence of Greece, and died of fever on the battle lines. After his death, his widow moved to Munich and put her three boys in the Benedictine school there.

At the age of seventeen, Adelbert entered the University of Munich for courses in natural science and oriental and classical languages. A growing interest in theology manifested itself, and in 1866 he became a candidate for the seminary for the Archdiocese of Munich. Since his theology courses were nearly completed when he entered the seminary, he was ordained after only a year there. Already marked for his special ability, the bishop saw him as a valuable addition to the seminary faculty, and the young Father Weiss found himself professor and spiritual director of the seminary very soon after his ordination.

Such a rapid rise to a position of authority did not go unnoticed, and it brought its own problems. The spirit of rationalism then rampant in the German universities had seeped even into the seminaries, and Father Weiss was deeply concerned with its position in theology. Getting deeper and deeper into St. Thomas as he taught theology, he became more and more uncertain of his former position of tolerance for the new rationalism. It took courage for a popular young professor to declare himself openly and admit that his opinions had been wrong. The situation was even more difficult because he knew no one who could give him any help on the position he had adopted; there were no Dominicans in the vicinity, and Thomism was not a popular trend.

The definition of papal infallibility was the signal for an open break on the part of some talented German intellectuals who had been anti-clerical for some time. A group calling themselves the "Old Catholics" went into schism and refused to accept papal infallibility. Some of Father Weiss' old professors were among the ones who left the Church at this juncture, and very probably they hoped to take him with them. With deep pain, he saw that he could not take up arms against papal authority, no matter who else did. Heartsick, he plunged into working for his doctorate, and began the apostolate of the pen which was to occupy him so thoroughly for the rest of his life. Since the authority and orthodoxy of the Church were the points most at issue, these were the themes upon which he chose to write.

In 1872, Father Weiss joined the Third Order of St. Dominic. It was as near as he could get to the Order at the time, for he was having a fearful battle with himself on the question of religious vocation. On the Feast of

St. Dominic in 1875, he begged our Lord to give him some sign of what he was to do about the matter. The next day, as he was in his room studying, the door opened and in walked the Dominican historian, Father Denifle, the first Dominican Father Weiss had ever seen. They talked at length, and the young priest told all his hopes and his troubles to the friar. In the following year, Father Weiss entered the Dominican novitiate at Graz in Austria, receiving the religious name Albert, to which he added Mary.

In 1883 Father Weiss was made lector in the house of studies, and was later summoned to Rome to work on the Leonine edition of St. Thomas. In 1889 he was appointed to the chair of social sciences in the newly-erected University of Fribourg. For the rest of his life, his name was to be associated with this university. From here he sent out a stream of valuable apologetic and polemic writings; works on the relationship of modern science to the Catholic Church, on Gallicanism and the freedom of science, a defense of the Christian faith on a historical basis, the psychology of Lutheranism, and other works both scientific and popular. Though his subjects covered a wide range and gave testimony to the diversity of his knowledge, his motive was always the same: to explain and defend the truths of the faith and to expose the heresies which opposed it.

Father Albert Mary Weiss died at Fribourg in 1925.

PIERGIORGIO FRASSATTI
(1901-1925)

Piergiorgio Frassatti, who died of polio in 1925, was a young man of our own times, a handsome, gay-hearted, intelligent lad who loved life and was loved by his friends. He looked forward to a happy marriage and a family, but he was one who lived an ordinary life extraordinarily well, and his cause for beatification has already been brought to the attention of the authorities. A Tertiary of St. Dominic, he exemplified to a heroic degree the meaning of the words "Catholic Action."

Piergiorgio Frassatti was born in Turin in April, 1901. His father was the owner of a successful newspaper and made a very comfortable home for his family. Though because of their circumstances they might have had almost any luxuries they desired, Piergiorgio and his sister were brought up very strictly by a pious mother who used to train them to make sacrifices when they were little more than babies. Consequently, the children grew up accustomed to strict obedience, to self-denial, and to the consideration of others less fortunate than themselves.

Piergiorgio was healthy, happy, and bright in school, and he made many friends because of his cheerful disposition and his firm character. He excelled in sports, he was extremely handsome, and he had an excellent home. All this, or even much less than this, might have spoiled him and made him selfish and thoughtless of others. It did not; and here may lie the secret of great virtue, that true poverty of spirit which is so rare and beautiful in the modern world.

The years of Piergiorgio's youth were those of reconstruction in Italy, the postwar years when so many young people were drifting away from the ancient faith and joining various socialistic or atheistic societies. On the Feast of St. Dominic, 1922, Piergiorgio entered the society that he felt would best combat this evil influence and better his own spiritual life, the Third Order of St. Dominic.

He had been quietly moving in this direction for some time, though his friends were not aware that under his gay exterior was a soul that had already set its sights on perfection. He had been a daily communicant for years, a fact which was phenomenal enough in a young man who lived such an active life. At the university he had quietly formed a nucleus of Catholic thought and morality around which his friends gathered for discussions of worthwhile things. Looking back, his friends all agreed that they should have seen that he was dedicating himself to the life of a Tertiary; but Piergiorgio never made a fuss about the good things he did, and he never talked about himself.

Now began a more intensive spiritual life for the young man who faced every day the problems of university living, who entered with enthusiasm into sports and games, and who still kept one eye on heaven. He realized that "to bring to others the fruits of contemplation" made a positive demand on people who were in a position to spread the truth. He worked through the medium of what we now call Catholic Action, in a club made up of young people who, like himself, were fond of mountain climbing. He never preached, to them or to anyone else. But the example of a young man who, having every material attribute for enjoying himself in this world, gave such sober thought to the next, was tremendous. His unselfconscious goodness and his habitual virtuous reaction to the affairs of life exerted a strong influence for good among those who were beyond the reach of any other type of teaching.

Not until his death did the extent of his charities become evident. It was known by all his associates in the St. Vincent de Paul Society that Piergiorgio was first to volunteer for any mission to the poor, that he was endlessly patient with tiresome people, and that every cent of his own money went to relieve the needs of the poor. But they had no idea how many people, rich and poor alike, regarded him as a spiritual guide. The people who passed weeping beside his coffin were a cross-section of society, displaying every possible type of trouble, and he had personally tried to help each one of them.

His university career drawing to a close, Piergiorgio was asked what he planned to do with his life. His major was engineering, and he loved his work. He had an urge to go to some far country as a lay missionary—a state of life which was not well known in the early 1920's—where he could combine his professional skill with the lay apostolate. He planned to get married, and was very definite about the qualities he expected of his wife. Sometimes he said, half-jokingly, that when he came into his inheritance he would use it all to build a home for the destitute old people of Turin, since he was young and strong and well able to work for a living. But it is a truism that death loves a shining mark; at the end of June, 1925, Piergiorgio fell suddenly ill for the first time in his life. Since the family was already deep in grief for his dying grandmother, he tried not to let anyone know how much he was suffering. When he collapsed on the day of his grandmother's funeral, the disease was already well advanced, and the best doctors in Turin could not save him.

Piergiorgio Frassatti died July 4, 1925. Within a few years after his death, the young men of neighboring cities were coming in groups on the anniversary day of his death, receiving Communion and making a day of retreat out of it. The epitaph over his tomb says as well as any other brief statement just what was Piergiorgio's greatness:

> At the age of twenty-four—at the very end of his university career—handsome, strong, good-humored and beloved—he reached unexpectedly his last day on earth—and as ever, welcomed it serenely—as the most beautiful day of his life. The purity of his life and his charitable deeds bear witness to his religious faith. Death transformed him into a living standard held aloft before the eyes of Christian youths.

MOTHER ALPHONSA HAWTHORNE
(1851-1926)

Few Americans who read the works of Nathaniel Hawthorne realize that the favorite daughter of this New England Protestant became a Catholic and a Dominican, and was the foundress of a congregation devoted to a particularly appealing charity, the Dominican Sisters for the Care of Incurable Cancer.

Rose Hawthorne was born in Concord in 1851, the youngest of three children. Her father was at that time working on his books, *Twice Told Tales* and *House of Seven Gables,* and the hospitable Hawthorne home overflowed with literary notables: Emerson, Melville, Thoreau, and the Alcotts, who lived next door, among them. Rose grew up in an atmosphere of literature which was made even more vivid by the family visits to Europe, where her father patiently pointed out the sites of action in the cities of the stories she loved to hear him tell.

Nathaniel Hawthorne, who had discovered that writing is not the way to fortune, took a diplomatic post in Liverpool when Rose was small. They found England cold and depressing, and welcomed the warmth of Portugal when his duties took him there. Good New Englanders though they were, they fell in love with the people of Portugal and Italy and found themselves discussing Catholicism and its warmth and vigor. In Rome, Rose was walking one day with her mother in the Vatican gardens when she catapulted into Pope Pius IX. He smiled at the small red-headed dynamo and blessed her. She never could quite forget it. They returned to America still thinking of Rome.

Hawthorne died suddenly in 1864, leaving his family dazed and desolate. Unhappy at remaining in Concord, they returned to Europe, and a few years later Mrs. Hawthorne died and was buried in England. The three children, all grown, were now on their own, and Rose very shortly met and married a young writer named George Lathrop. They returned to New York in 1871, leaving in England the older sister, who planned to be an Anglican nun, and the brother who was in college.

Five years later, Rose's only child was born. He was a beautiful little boy, and for the short span of his life he held together his parents' tottering marriage. However, when he died at the age of five, they drifted apart. Both were grief-stricken over the loss of the little boy, and they sought different ways of soothing their grief. George turned to drink. Rose, who had entered the Catholic church with him in 1891, turned more and more to religion as her sorrows grew heavier to bear. Both of them were writing and publishing, but it was not an interest that could hold them together. Two years after they became Catholics, they separated permanently.

Adrift and uncertain, Rose fairly stumbled into her life's work. A little seamstress who had often done work for her was afflicted with cancer and died alone in the hospital for the poor while Rose was out of town. On her return, she was horrified to hear that her friend had had such a lonely death. She began investigating the needs of the cancerous poor, and on rereading some of her father's books discovered the compassion that he had felt for the afflicted. With no very clear idea of how she was going to go about it, she decided that she would do something for these poor people, since nobody else seemed able to. She enrolled for a short course of nursing at the New York cancer hospital, and then, with what little funds she had, rented a couple of rooms in a poor part of the west side. She cleaned and painted them, but they were still drab, and there were stables on three sides of the building and unceasing bedlam from the street. Her literary friends were either amused or horrified, and the neighbors were doubting but curious. Yet, one by one, the people who needed her sought her out and found that she was kind and careful, and that she regarded them as human beings.

One of Rose's first companions was a Salvation Army lassie whom she converted. A curious Dominican who had heard of her from a sick penitent came to see what the strange red-haired lady was doing in that unsavory neighborhood, and shortly after sent her a young lady helper. A gay little Irish grandmother, dying of cancer, was her first patient to come and stay in the makeshift clinic. One day Rose was called to the city hospital where George Lathrop was dying. She stayed with him until he breathed his last, and returned to the clinic knowing that her last tie to the world was broken.

City officials tried to put a stop to the whole thing, and found that the red hair was not a vain adornment. When they said, superciliously, "But my *dear* Mrs. Lathrop, what difference does it make whether the poor are *happy* or not?" she told them very clearly what difference it made. To gain a little money for the needs of her patients, Rose began writing again; she was probably one of the most talented beggars ever to turn her pen to the cause of Christ, and people who had no idea of becoming involved found themselves helping her with tears in their eyes.

Through the efforts of the Dominican visitor, Rose and her companions were persuaded to put off the "daughters of the puritans" costume they had worked out for themselves and apply for admission into the Dominican Order. By 1899 they had taken the preliminary steps to affiliation. Six sisters were given the Dominican habit, and Rose took the name Sister Alphonsa. Their greatest joy was that they were privileged to have the Blessed Sacrament in their tiny chapel, and their greatest sorrow was that if one more patient applied, they could not possibly take her. So, entirely without money but with a great trust in Providence, Sister Alphonsa began searching for larger quarters.

Someone sold her a large drafty house in Westchester County which un-doubtedly had room—the sisters had to run miles to look after the patients—but which also had leaks in the roof and a faulty heating system. Perhaps the very perversity of the decrepit old house helped them to survive the first winter in it. Its state of imminent collapse pressed upon Sister Alphonsa the need for a new and comfortable building not, she insisted, for the sisters because sisters were very durable, but for the patients. They were God's poor and they deserved the best. She turned the magnetism of her gifted pen on the task of getting the money to make this dream come true.

On the night before she died in 1926, Mother Alphonsa posted the last of her begging letters behind the statue of St. Joseph before confiding them to the U.S. mail. Her last twenty years had been an unceasing succession of such endeavors, most of them successful. All sorts of people helped her to accomplish her dream, Catholics and Protestants and Jews alike.

She had remarked that when they moved out of the original two rooms in New York to the house in Westchester County that it was like moving out of a mousetrap into the catacombs. Their move into a large, fireproof building which the charity of her friends made possible was like moving into heaven. The Christian Brothers, neighbors who had watched the old house anxiously every time the wind blew, were unceasing in their kindness; doctors, literary friends, the hospital auxiliary, and total strangers, all contributed to this first complete hospital for the cancerous poor. Old and very tired, Mother Alphonsa could take one quick look backwards before she died and see great accomplishments in her short lifetime; a new congregation of the Dominican Order set firmly on its feet: a provision made for the most neglected of Christ's poor.

Mother Alphonsa died quietly in her sleep in 1926.

BARTOLO LONGO
(d. 1926)

The world-renowned shrine of Our Lady of Pompeii came about, as Lady-shrines do, through the intervention of the Mother of God. But, humanly speaking, the instrument used by Our Lady in this work was a Dominican Tertiary, Bartolo Longo by name.

Bartolo was a lawyer of Naples, and in 1872 he went to the valley of Pompeii to settle some business concerning his wife's property there. He had been seriously ill and had also just returned to the sacraments after a long time of dalliance with spiritualism and other upsetting beliefs. The desolate valley, which had never recovered from the volcanic eruption of 2,000 years ago, was depressing enough to a healthy man. Bartolo found it almost intolerable. His confessor had suggested to him that he expiate his many years of infidelity by propagating the Rosary there. In his first appraisal of the wilderness where he must remain for a time, it seemed to him there was hardly a living creature to whom he could talk about anything, let alone the Rosary. He began, then, by saying the Rosary himself and trying to deepen his own appreciation of it.

Pompeii had become a robber's roost. The land was hopelessly poor, the people drained of hope and ambition. The little church was in ruins, and no one used it anyway. The lawyer from Naples began to see that here were people who had worse trouble than his own. He tried to talk to them, but failed to interest them in anything. The only spark of response he got was in the matter of prayer for the dead; some ancient reverence for death survived among them, and they did not like to bury their dead without any prayers. He formed a confraternity to attend funerals and to pray for the dead.

He begged of the pastor to know what he could do for the people. "They like raffles," said the pastor indifferently. Bartolo went to Naples and secured great quantities of medals, rosaries, and junk jewelry. He scheduled a huge raffle and religious rally for the Feast of the Rosary, and brought in a preacher at his own expense. The people cheered up at the idea of a lottery and so many small prizes, but there was a hurricane the day of the feast, so nobody came.

Bartolo was not discouraged. He began planning for the next year's feast. This time he prepared for months ahead, and sent out a woman with a loud voice to cry out the fair when the time came. Quite a crowd assembled, and they had a lovely day. But when it was over, Bartolo faced the fact that it *was* over; he had done nothing to make the Rosary devotion stay with them.

For this he determined to establish the Rosary Confraternity. He began teaching catechism; he organized the parishioners to clean up the church and paint it. After diligent work, he had a class ready for confirmation. With heroic efforts they got ready for the event, for he planned to get the bishop's permission for his confraternity at this time and—if he was lucky—to collect a little money so that he could build a Rosary altar. The bishop came and was very pleased, but he quietly upset the applecart with his reply to the lawyer's request: "Build an altar? Build a church!"

It was a lovely idea, but there was no money. Bartolo began doggedly to collect a penny a week from the poor families, though he knew that it takes a remarkably long time to build a church that way. In the meantime he managed to get people very much interested in the Rosary Confraternity. Finally, since the feast was coming around again, he got permission to go ahead with the Confraternity. The priest informed him that he could not do it without a picture of Our Lady of the Rosary—an oil painting, not a print. Bartolo had no money for an oil painting. He set out for Naples, hoping that he might beg one from some affluent friend.

In the selection of this picture it would seem as though Our Lady went to extreme lengths to point out to us that it was only an instrument of her grace. It is hard to imagine a picture with such an uninspiring origin. Bartolo finally obtained the painting, after tramping the streets until he was tired, from a sister who had stored it in the convent attic because the sisters could not bear to look at it. Someone who had paid twenty-eight cents for it at an auction had given it to them just to get it out of circulation. Even when new, it could not have been worth framing; the madonna was fat and ugly, the baby poorly drawn. St. Dominic looked positively stupid, and there was no good reason why St. Rose should be in the picture at all. Time had faded some of the paint and torn the canvas in places. A large piece had been removed from one corner, and the whole was dirty and cracked. Even at twenty-eight cents it had been no bargain. Still, Bartolo was desperate. He took the picture and gave it into the care of a neighbor who had come into Naples with a farm cart. He did not think to enquire what the friend was taking back in the cart. As a consequence, the picture of Our Lady rode into Pompeii bouncing casually on top of a load of fertilizer.

The priest was horrified when he saw the picture, and would not allow it to be hung in the church until it had been repaired. A wandering artist who did scenes of the ruins of Pompeii for tourists set about repairing the picture, but his efforts were no improvement. A later artist with a historical turn of mind painted St. Rose over into St. Catherine, and touched up the faces a little. Cleaned, the picture was still no beauty. But it was hung in the church and became the focal point for the Rosary devotion.

All this time, Bartolo kept hard at work collecting money for the church, but it was beginning to look like a hopeless task. The bishop had chosen the land for the church, but its owner wanted an exorbitant price for it. In the midst of his troubles, Bartolo received a telegram saying that his mother was dying. He went to her bedside and found that she was indeed in her death agony, and that she was unable to receive the sacraments. He prayed desperately to Our Lady of the Rosary, and his mother not only was able to receive the sacraments, she very shortly recovered. A priest friend of his, in almost exactly the same straits, likewise recovered.

Encouraged by this heavenly help, Bartolo and his assistant in the work, a pious countess, renewed their efforts to collect the money. It was the countess who precipitated another miracle. Going into a wealthy home to beg for the church, she found the daughter of the house dying in convulsions. "If you will pledge your help to Our Lady's new church at Pompeii, she will be cured," said the countess. It was a daring and desperate promise, but Our Lady made good her word: the young woman was cured.

At last the long trials seemed to be over. Miracles rained down on all sides, and with them came a flood of pilgrims to the desolate valley. Money poured in. The church which finally rose, in this place which was too poor to buy an oil painting, was one of the loveliest in Italy.

Today the poor old picture is superbly framed and surrounded by glowing lights and candles which are kind to the artist's mistakes. The surface of the old canvas is studded with diamonds, clinging to it by no means anyone can see. And the flood of pilgrims which began with the cure of the young woman of Naples has never diminished.

Bartolo Longo died in 1926, still in the shadow of the great church he had helped to build. After a troubled lifetime, he was at peace through the love of Our Lady's Rosary.

JOHN THOMAS ARINTERO
(1860-1928)

The man who was the prime mover in the Spanish revival of mystical theology in the present century was the Dominican, John Gonzales Arintero, who is known to Americans by his recently translated work, *The Mystical Evolution in the Development and Vitality of the Church.*

John Gonzales Arintero was born in Leon in 1860 of pious parents. Little is known of his childhood. He received the Dominican habit and the religious name Thomas in the convent of Asturias in 1875. Here his progress in philosophical studies was so promising that he was sent to complete his studies at Salamanca, where he made a special study of chemistry and physics as well as theology. He became acquainted there with the future master general of the Order, Hyacinth Cormier, who was a student in exile from France at the time.

Father Arintero's first assignment as a priest was as professor at Vergara. Here he built up a museum of natural history which was unique in its field and which gave evidence of the trend his studies were to take. Teaching the physical sciences, he delved deeper and deeper into the current theories of geology and anthropology which in the secular universities were being used to attack religion. It was to be his work to combat these false theorists, and in order to do so with authority, he had to make himself a master in the field of natural sciences. His companions always wondered how he could manage to read so much, but to him this was the only possible way of arming himself against a clever foe.

In 1898 Father Arintero was assigned to teach fundamental theology at St. Stephen's in Salamanca. In Valladolid he restored the ancient college of St. Gregory, which had suffered seriously during the political upheavals of recent years. In Salamanca he helped to found the Academy of St. Thomas. In 1920 he was called away from Spain by his old friend of student days; Father Cormier, concerned with the restoration of regular observance in Rome, summoned the talented Spaniard to help him in the work. After only one year he was obliged to return to Spain, as he had lost his hearing and was no longer able to teach. Shut away now from the world of preaching and teaching, he began writing in earnest.

All his zeal and his great knowledge now poured into his works in defense of the Christian position on evolution and creation. At a time when most Christian teachers were embarrassed by the weight of natural evidence which had been wrongly interpreted by the godless, Father Arintero's works, backed up by a lifetime of solid study and irrefutable argument, were a breath of hope. People who had felt that Christian philosophy had nothing to say on the subject of profane sciences were surprised to find how *much* he had to say and how well he said it. He devoted his pen to showing that religion did not have to accommodate itself to anyone's theories, nor need Christian philosophers feel unscientific because of their faith.

While writing in the field of natural sciences and evolution, Father Arintero began to delve earnestly into mystical theology. He found it fascinating. Soon, in spite of the handicap of his deafness, he was launched on the apostolate of reviving the spiritual life through a deeper understanding of mystical theology. He wrote much for the direction of sisters and earnest lay people, and founded a magazine on the spiritual life which served them as guide and inspiration. He was a great defender of the "oneness" of the spiritual life, and an avowed foe of the idea that only a select few may aspire to mystical union with God.

The vast array of his knowledge was placed at the service of the Church and the Order, both in his own works and in the inspiration he was to others. He was the one who first inspired Father Garrigou-Lagrange to devote his great energies to the cause of the spiritual life. Scores of other priests, both of his own Order and others, were led by him to join the modern trend back to the mystical theology that is part of the heritage of the Order. Magazines, books, pamphlets, correspondence flowed from his busy pen. At his death in 1928 he was one of the best known spiritual directors in Spain, and since his death some of his works have been translated into other languages, so that his direction is now available in many other countries.

The cause of Father Arintero's beatification was proposed in 1949.

BEDE JARRETT
(1881-1934)

One of the most popular preachers and most widely-read authors of the present century was Father Bede Jarrett. Because his preaching duties brought him to America, he is well known here and his books are a part of every Dominican library.

Cyril Jarrett was born in Greenwich in 1881, and baptized by the famous Dominican preacher, Father Wilberforce. His father was a colonel in the India service, and when Cyril was two years old, his parents returned to India, leaving him and his five brothers to be educated in England. As soon as he was old enough, Cyril entered Stonyhurst, the Jesuit school which had trained his brothers. Here he soon became a general favorite, a boy who was intelligent and fun-loving, good at games and usually the center of action. Even at an early age he showed a love for literature which was to color all his writing.

At the age of seventeeen, when it was supposed that Cyril, like his father and brothers, would go into the army as a career, he announced his intention to be a Dominican. He entered the Order at Woodchester in 1898, and received the religious name Bede. The revival sparked by Lacordaire was in full swing at Woodchester, and several remarkable men were stationed there. All of them left a mark on the eager young Brother Bede, but the most influential was Father Vincent McNabb, his confessor and theological advisor. It was Father McNabb who taught him the exact scholarship that was to make his future writings so valuable, and who guided him in the early studies of St. Thomas. Bede, the gentle historian, was a fine patron for the man whose style was to reflect so many of his qualities, above all his gentleness and simplicity.

Brother Bede launched into the field of writing with his *Life of Cardinal Howard*. The dreadful homesickness that he endured both at Woodchester and at the house of studies in Hawkesyard, the difficulties bound to trouble an eager young student in the time of reconstruction of a province, all these had left no stain on his clear and readable style. Encouraged by Father McNabb and by Father Hugh Pope, whose field was Scripture, he plunged deeply into the studies that would be the necessary background to his work. All his life the friendship of these two priests would prove vital streams pouring into his writing. "Friendship made is forever," he said, in speaking of the influence of friends on one another.

Father Bede Jarrett was ordained in 1904 and almost immediately was sent to Oxford for medieval studies and political and social theory. From the studies begun then were to proceed some of his best-loved books: *Saint Antoninus and Medieval Economics, Social Theories of the Middle Ages,* and his *History of Europe.* In 1907 he was sent to Louvain to continue his studies, and in the following year he was appointed to the London priory. Here he was to have a first-hand look at the social maladjustments he had been studying. "The social injustices are crying for remedy," he wrote sadly. "Soon they will be crying for vengeance."

Few men have demonstrated as clearly as Father Bede Jarrett the flexibility of the Dominican rule or the width of its apostolate. He made use of the modern tools and of modern situations to make his preaching effective. He used to claim quite modestly that "the only reason he preached so much in London was that he simply couldn't sing, and one had to do something to help out." The fact was that he had a genius for popular preaching, and a faculty of getting into the hearts and minds of his listeners of all classes. He voluntarily took on work with the Catholic Boy Scouts and busied himself with their needs and problems. He himself had said, "It is the Mass that makes the priest possible; it is the confessional that makes him necessary." He spent a vast amount of time in the confessional, occupying himself with the problems and the direction of all.

In 1914, when he was prior in London, war was declared. "The old order has gone down before our very eyes," he said sadly, as he organized the work of the friars for war time. War brought him personal grief, for one of his brothers died at Gallipoli and another in Flanders. Busy with a course of St. Thomas for lay folk and with the writing of the life of St. Dominic, he was thrust into even greater responsibility in the midst of the war by his appointment as English provincial. He was at this time thirty-five years old, and in charge of the seven English houses and the possible missions that would follow colonial expansion. Singularly enough, all of his projects for foreign missions failed; he proposed to found missions in the West Indies, in India, Persia, and Afghanistan, only to see them fail after years of red tape and other involvements. Only the one at Capetown, South Africa, ever became a reality, and his visit to the Cape to establish the house almost broke his heart. He was not first to cry out at the injustices done to the Negroes by white colonists, but he was one of the most eloquent. In 1925 his South African mission became a reality, and he devoted his attention to the return of the friars to Scotland and Wales, which he finally accomplished three years before his death.

Father Bede Jarrett loved to see things accomplished, and was enchanted with American "know-how," which he had seen at close quarters on a lecture tour in 1918 and again just before his death. American drive upset him, but he said in admiration that "the American people are a great people, alive to the fascination of machinery and sensitive to art." It was due to an American benefactress that his dearest dream came true, to bring the Dominicans back to Oxford, which he did in 1929.

These were difficult years in the English province, for all branches of the Order were in process of rebuilding and revising, of beginning over again the work that had been interrupted at the Reformation. Father Jarrett worked diligently to unite the Third Order sisters in England and perfect their legislation. He was editor of *Blackfriars* and also responsible for revising the First Order constitutions. *The Religious Life, No Abiding City, The House of Gold,* and *The Life of St. Dominic* are among his well-known books.

So busy that he really did not have time to stop, he was laid low by a stroke while giving a retreat in 1934, and died soon after at the early age of 52. The gentle self-effacing priest who hated fuss and ceremony was by this time so famous in England that seven bishops were in attendance at his funeral, and his fame had spread to every corner of the English-speaking world.

PETER FRANCIS MANDONNET
(1858-1936)

Père Mandonnet is known to Americans principally because of his historical notes on St. Dominic, which were published a few years ago in English. His stature as a historian is better known in Europe, where he held an enviable reputation in his own field.

Francis Felix Mandonnet was born in Beaumont in 1858, and received his early education from the Christian Brothers, for whom he always cherished a great affection. While he was still a student at the brothers' school, he became acquainted with Lacordaire through the medium of his books. Lacordaire himself was dead, but his ideals blazed like a beacon through his written works, and young Francis Mandonnet could not resist them. He went to his parents with the idea of becoming a Dominican, and they gave him a flat refusal. He entered the major seminary at Clermont, and finally in 1882 gained his father's permission to enter the Order. He received the habit and the religious name Peter in October, 1882. Since the French provinces were in difficulties at the time, he was sent to make his novitiate at a Spanish house, then to Austria for his studies.

Father Mandonnet was ordained in 1887, after completing his studies at the convent in Corsica. After a year of apostolic work in France, he was returned to Corsica to teach in the convent of Corbara, which was a rigidly penitential house. It was not a promising place for one's talents to become evident, but nonetheless word reached the master general of the abilities of young Father Mandonnet in the field of history. He was summoned to the University of Fribourg, where the faculties of Church history and theology belonged to the Dominicans. Here he was to teach for the next twenty-seven years, building up a reputation as a fine preacher and teacher, and as a capable and careful writer.

During the First World War, Father Mandonnet set aside his studies and devoted his time to the organizations which worked in Switzerland for the care of prisoners and displaced persons. His work with these suffering people demonstrated that he was not a single-minded bookworm with no interests in humanity, and he himself treasured the opportunity of working with people of so many needs.

After the war, Father Mandonnet returned to his teaching and his writing, but had to leave Switzerland because of illness. He was one of the founders of the *Revue Thomiste,* and his research on the Dominican rule and constitutions became the occasion of much further interest in Dominican history among others. He wrote *The Dominicans in the Discovery of America; St. Dominic, the Man, the Ideal, and the Work; Siger of Brabant and Averroism; Dante, the Theologian; The Authentic Writings of St. Thomas;* and many other topics of historical interest. Ill and working in retirement in the infirmary in Paris, he turned out more scholarly manuscripts than most well people could.

In 1927, France had another anticlerical upheaval, which necessitated his moving again, this time to Belgium. Here he lived until his death in 1936, a man of vast and specialized knowledge and of great simplicity, who could discuss abstruse questions with the most erudite, but who enjoyed chatting with the young students. He was an honorary professor of the University of Fribourg, held an honorary doctorate and the Dominican degree of master of sacred theology. He was also an officer of the French Academy, indicating that France, Switzerland, and the Dominican Order had given him their highest honors.

PRAXIDES FERNANDEZ
(d. 1936)

A holy woman whose son is a Dominican priest was proposed for beatification in 1953. She was Praxides Fernandez, and she died in Spain during the Communist regime of the Civil War.

Praxides Fernandez was married in 1914 to an electrician who was killed in a train accident six years later, leaving her with four small sons. Working to bring them up in the fear of God, she was obliged to put in long hours of hard work and often suffered from the work and the poverty. Nevertheless, she became an angel of mercy to the townspeople, who learned to call upon her in every need. She cared for the poor and the sick, saving most of her food for them. Every day for years she gave away her breakfast and her supper to the poor, eating only one meal, and on Friday none at all. Poor sick people, even those ill of contagious diseases, she brought into her home and cared for. Doing her housework in the night hours after a long day of work, she meditated on a large crucifix which she carried about from place to place.

Every day, this remarkable woman managed to make two hours of meditation. She was a Dominican Tertiary, and she not only lived the rule in its entirety, she added mortifications that seem unbelievable. She once branded herself with the names of Jesus and Mary with a red-hot iron. And rain or shine or soldiers or disaster, she attended Mass; even when the Communists came into the little village of Sueros where she lived, she and a couple of relatives dared to go through the lines and walk the long distance to another village to daily Mass and Communion.

One of her sons died, like his father, in a train accident. A second was killed in the Civil War. The third son was a Dominican novice when the time came that she should suffer her passion. She had predicted that he would be ordained in 1941, that she would not be at his first Mass, and that he would be a missionary. In 1936 the village of Sueros was under siege by the Red Army, and when Mrs. Fernandez became ill of acute appendicitis they refused to allow a doctor to leave the lines and attend her. Her friends tried frantically to get medical help for her, but failed. She died of acute appendicitis, and in spite of protests, her body was thrown into a truckload of dead soldiers and buried in a common grave. No priest was left in the little village, and there was no funeral. The young Dominican student was far away and could not come to her.

One might think that this good woman would be soon forgotten, with nothing to mark her grave and no publicity. Her friends did not forget the holiness of her life and her ability to help all who called on her. They began to pray to her, and she answered their cries for help. In 1953, in the cathedral church of Oviedo, a pontifical Mass was celebrated to mark the opening of her cause for beatification. Twenty-five priests were in the sanctuary, and the archbishop of Foo-chow celebrated the Mass, and also preached. Two thousand people assisted at the Mass, and saw the cause of the woman who had seen so much suffering in this life started upon the path to per petual honor and magnificence.

FATHER TITUS HORTEN
(1882-1936)

One of the causes for beatification introduced in 1948 is that of the late prior of Vechta, in Germany, who died in a Nazi prison hospital in 1936. His case is a pertinent illustration of the fact that tyrants of all times will sooner or later come into conflict with the truth, and that good men must die under every regime. It is the pride of the Dominican Order that every century can produce men who will die for the truth, in the same spirit as St. Peter Martyr and the other martyrs of the early centuries.

Francis Horten was born August 9, 1882, at Elberfeld in western Germany. His father occupied a position equivalent to that of supreme court judge in this large industrial city, and later held positions of honor in Frankfurt and Leipzig. His family was well-to-do and cultured, and the children were given an excellent education. Francis and his brother Timothy were sent to the Dominican prep school in Venlo, Holland. Here they studied law and modern languages, and here also both had their first lasting contact with the Order that both were later to enter.

There are few anecdotes about the childhood of Francis, although it must have been a happy one. He was an intelligent and likeable child with good intellectual powers, a friend of everybody. His sister speaks affectionately of his early years when his first Communion was an outstanding spiritual landmark and when the members of his family realized that this child was destined for something unusual. His charity to the poor was evident, even in childhood, a time when many young people are selfish; when he grew to young manhood, it became his outstanding characteristic. People around him always seemed to know that whatever their difficulty he would somehow help them.

Outwardly there was nothing exceptional about the university career of young Francis Horten. He attended the Universities of Leipzig, Munster, Grenoble in France, London, and Bonn. During the difficult years of study, when he was preparing his doctoral dissertation, he still took time to help people. He found jobs for them, guided them to spiritual directors, suggested good reading, listened to their troubles—all activities which took time out of a busy schedule. His friends said of him that they never knew him to be impatient or to refuse to go to the help of someone who stopped him in his work. Busy people who find it hard to remember other people's needs should find it inspiring to remember this young man, whose by-word was, "Oh sure—right away; I *always* have time." One time when he was particularly hard-pressed, someone came to him with a request which looked very trivial. Even his mother, who was virtuous enough to appreciate her son's charity, remonstrated with him. "Why don't you excuse yourself? You have so many things to study." Even her remonstrance did not stop him from his charities. It is not surprising that a life of such exceptional charity would sooner or later flower into the religious life. At the close of a brilliant university career, Francis Horten entered the Dominican novitiate at Venlo in 1909, and was given the religious name Titus, to which he added Mary.

In the Dominican Order the young brother found everything he had been looking for. He was faithful and persistent in the practice of holiness, and a model of humility in his studies; not all of his companions, naturally, were possessed of a doctorate and a background of five major universities. He took the regular course of studies from the beginning, in spite of his superior background. He completed his studies at Dusseldorf and at Rome and was ordained in Rome, February 27, 1915.

Returning to Germany shortly after ordination, Father Titus was set to caring for wounded soldiers in a military hospital. When the war was over, he became professor of foreign languages at the Dominican school in Vechta, beginning his association with the foreign missions which would eventually be the cause of his arrest. He was made prior of the convent, and for the remainder of his life would have the responsibility both for the press he had founded in 1922 to disseminate truth, and for the foreign missions of which he was procurator.

Because of the many activities and interests of Father Titus, it is difficult to give a brief account of those busy years between two wars, when his country was disturbed politically and financially and when he had such fine opportunities for exercising his charities. One can distinguish two principal lines of action in his work, that of the spiritual director to whom hundreds of people—priests, religious, and laity—looked for help, and that of the immensely practical man who somehow fed the thousands who came to him during the lean years and sent money to the hard-pressed missions of China. If he aspired to be "all things to all men," he certainly succeeded. Life was not easy for this talented man living by a difficult rule in the midst of political chaos. He was a man of great soul and of high idealism, of great personal asceticism and humble trust in God. He was also a man with a fiery temper, who fought with himself every day of his life, and who during those years of financial and political imprudence among his countrymen, had to learn to hold his peace and choose the wisest path. He was passionately stubborn about justice, over-generous, and always ready to believe in people. Having detached himself from everything that could hinder his own union with God, he was apt to think that everyone else was moved by the same high idealism.

The reason for his final arrest by the Nazis was ostensibly his infraction of the law about sending money out of the country. His work with the Catholic press and his militant Catholicism had long marked him for destruction. As procurator of the Chinese missions, he felt there was nothing else he could do but continue the support of the missionaries in spite of the unjust law. He was arrested on this charge and put in prison at Oldenburg. We do not know the full story of the ten months he spent in prison; he himself never complained of the treatment, but since he was suffering from heart trouble even the confinement was a torture. During his last few days, when it was evident that he was going to die soon, he was sent to the prison hospital. Here the windows were barred, and it was dark and lonely. He was in the care of a Protestant deaconess, who did her best to ease his last hours. Here he died on January 25, 1936, attended by the guards and the Protestant nurse.

When his body was returned to Vechta for burial, a surprising thing happened. The laws forbade any gatherings, but 6,000 people appeared for the funeral. During the hours before burial, thousands of people streamed in to touch their rosaries to the body of the priest whom they called "the father of the poor." In spite of special government regulations, people kept coming to his grave to pray, and letters poured in to the Dominicans telling them that Father Titus was still helping the hungry, the sick, and the jobless.

It soon became obvious that something would have to be done by the Church authorities about the man who was being called "the saint of Oldenburg." On July 30, 1948, the bishop of Munster began the preliminary work on the cause of Titus Mary Horten, who we hope may become recognized as a saint of our Order in due time.

MOTHER CATHERINE ABRIKOSOV
(1882-1936)

Anna Abrikosov, later to be known as Mother Catherine, was, so far as we know, the last Dominican sister of the Third Order Regular in Russia. She died in prison under the Red regime, and because of present restrictions on information there is still a good deal that we do not know about her. However, what we do know is enough to make us very proud that she wore the Dominican habit and carried in a darkening land the torch of truth.

Anna was born in Moscow in 1882, the daughter of a wealthy family, and was sent to England for her education. At Oxford she met Father Bede Jarrett, who was to be a lifelong friend and guide. When she returned to Russia in 1903, she was already enquiring about religion, but her immediate attention was taken up with the marriage which her parents had arranged for her with a cousin, Vladimir Abrikosov. On their wedding trip to Switzerland, Italy, and Paris, the young bride encountered the works of St. Catherine of Siena. The impact on her eager mind was tremendous. She and her young husband threw themselves into the study of the Catholic religion, and by 1909 both had been received into the Church.

They decided to remain abroad where they might exercise their religion and, in audience with Pope St. Pius X, asked for permission to transfer to the Latin rite. The saintly Pope did not grant the permission; he told them to study the Eastern rite and remain faithful to it.

Returning to Moscow on business, the young couple looked around for a way to exercise their apostolic zeal. Out of admiration for St. Catherine of Siena, both became Dominican Tertiaries, and they began their active work among the young people of their own circle in Moscow. These were the young intellectuals, confused by the chaos of political and social teachings all around them and by the breakdown of their old beliefs, aware of the coming storm but without any faith with which to withstand it. Anna and her husband decided upon an unusual course of action. Returning to Rome, they asked permission of the pope to take vows of chastity and devote their entire lives to the apostolate among these troubled young people. He blessed them and encouraged them in their work, and gave them the necessary permission.

They returned to Moscow and began definitely organizing their followers into a religious community. Vladimir began his studies for the priesthood. Anna established six young women in her home as Third Order sisters; she had barely begun the process of legal organization when the revolution was upon them and Russia was bathed in blood and terror.

Vladimir was ordained a priest in the Eastern rite on May 29, 1917. He was to have only five years to work among his needy flock, for in 1922 he was captured and condemned to death. Later the sentence was commuted to exile and he was sent to Siberia. Probably he died there among the other exiles; we do not know.

Anna was faced with a different problem; she was the center of a very active apostolate, which accomplished incredible things in the very shadow of death. Her young disciples were nearly all well-educated and talented people; most of them had academic degrees which gave them entree to the intellectual circles of the struggling country. They translated books into Russian, conducted study circles and discussion groups, and some even gave lectures at the university—on Dante, on scholastic philosophy, on dogmatic theology, on the theology of the Eastern Fathers of the Church. This daring program, begun before the revolution, transferred its activities to the underground when it became necessary. When they could no longer travel about freely to contact groups of young people, they still managed to reach them in smaller groups in private homes. The new regime was contemptuous of women to the point where they completely ignored this valiant band. If noticed at all, it was for the hardly punishable activities of caring for the aged and the sick, or teaching the children.

At the time of Father Vladimir's arrest, there were twenty-four sister professed, calmly going about their business under the very noses of the G.P.U. Anna, who was Mother Catherine now, realized that the sands were running out, and that it was only a matter of time until the new masters of Russia would wake up to the presence of their organization and liquidate it. Letters from her faithful friend, Father Bede Jarrett, brought strength for the trial that she knew lay ahead.

Mother Catherine at this time was given an opportunity to escape. England, far away and at peace, looked very attractive; so did Rome and its lovely memories. She knew that in those days of terror an opportunity to escape was a miracle and should be utilized. Yet she refused, electing to remain and do what she could for her beloved country now groaning under tyranny. On a November night in 1923, the soldiers burst in upon the community and arrested Mother Catherine and several of her companions.

We are unhappily familiar today with what happens to prisoners of the G.P.U., and nothing was spared Mother Catherine. After endless questioning and accusations, she was sentenced to ten years in prison as an enemy of the revolution; her accusers were too stupid to realize that it was she, not they, who was conducting a revolution.

Five of her prison years were spent in Siberia, in the bleakest exile on earth. Here Mother Catherine had no chance of any spiritual contact with anyone, and no spiritual help except what she carried within her own valiant heart. She was moved to a second prison camp, then finally to the Moscow prison.

For thirteen years she was in prison, shut away from all relatives and friends, deprived of all letters and newspapers, unaware of what was happening to the world or to those she loved. She who had been a daily communicant had no opportunity during those years to receive Communion. Yet, deprived of all consolation, she refused to be crushed by the situation. She made use of every chance that came her way to tell the sad and disillusioned prisoners that God still loved them and there was reason for faith and hope.

In 1932 Mother Catherine was discovered to have cancer and was taken to the Moscow hospital for surgery. Four years later she died, alone in prison, carrying to the end the torch of truth.

MARIE-JOSEPH LAGRANGE
(1855-1938)

A controversial figure to whom scholars of the future will be forever indebted was Father Marie-Joseph Lagrange, who founded the Biblical School of Jerusalem and who, almost alone, pioneered in Catholic scriptural studies in the light of modern archaeological research.

Albert Lagrange was born near Autun in 1855, a frail child who gave every evidence of an early death. When he was three years old, his mother took him to Ars, where the saintly Curè blessed him. Whether it was this blessing or the intercession of Our Lady of Autun that restored the little boy to health we do not know, but he recovered and set out early on the path of study.

The young Albert Lagrange had a varied career before becoming a Dominican. He studied law for five years and received his law degree, then spent a year in military service before entering the major seminary as Issy. While there, he decided to become a religious. He went to the Dominican convent of St. Maximin near Marseilles, and received the habit and the religious name Marie-Joseph. The day after his profession in 1880, religious orders were once more expelled from France. Brother Joseph was sent to finish his studies at Salamanca, where he managed to get in extra work in Hebrew. By the time of his ordination in 1883, his superiors were well aware of his gifts, and he was sent to Vienna to study oriental languages.

In 1890 the young Father Lagrange arrived in Jerusalem and began his life's work of founding a school of biblical research on the site of the martyrdom of St. Stephen, in an undistinguished old building which had belonged to the Dominicans for some time. His head full of plans, he looked soberly at the material he had to work with: a building which had once been the city slaughterhouse, and a library consisting of the two books he had brought with him—a Bible and a guidebook of Palestine. Preliminary investigation disclosed that a great deal of archaeological work was going on in the neighborhood, and that Catholic scholars had not yet taken it into account. He set out from practically nothing to build up a school that would have no apologies to make.

A vast amount of exploring and scientific work had been done, mostly by critical and unbelieving scientists, who used their information to tear down traditional faith in the Bible and to attack Christian beliefs. Father Lagrange had only one objective, to make the Bible better understood. The means to be used were the modern ones of scientific research methods unknown to scholars of former times. In order to do his work, a thorough knowledge of the ancient peoples of the Bible was vital—their history, customs, language, and religious beliefs. His law training was of great help in the study of the ancient law codes, and he rejoiced at the discovery of the code of Hammurabi and other material remains of ancient civilization. He made long tiring trips by camel-back to explore the sites of biblical events, and soon began raising a cloud of opposition by his critical analysis of both time and place in Scripture. He had the blessing of Pope Leo XIII, who as early as 1892 approved the research of the Biblical Institute. When they began, in the same year, to publish some of their conclusions, there was a murmuring of excited disagreement from traditional scholars, but the Holy Father approved wholeheartedly of the plan. The same pope who gave his enthusiastic backing to the new translation of St. Thomas and promulgated the study of the prince of theologians wished for an equally authoritative study of Scripture.

It is difficult for anyone not a Scripture student to follow the work of Father Lagrange. Scholars of all nations and of all faiths have come to value it, and we who are of his family should be proud that the man who opened the way for scientific scriptural studies was our brother. He had nothing but contempt for those timid scholars who were afraid to evaluate scientific discoveries for fear they would testify against revelation. His writings soon gained him the name of being a "dangerous radical," a label that Dominicans have worn with distinction since the day when a young priest from Spain laid his idea of a preaching order in front of Pope Innocent III. The controversy which raged over the head of Father Lagrange saddened him at times, but never embittered him. At one time, several of his Old Testament studies were listed as "forbidden" to young students in seminaries, which was not a condemnation. Pope Pius X did not always share his predecessor's trust of Father Lagrange, and the fact that he listened to the detractors of the great scholar was brought up adversely at the canonization process, indicating that Father Lagrange had been completely vindicated by time.

After forty-five years in Jerusalem, Father Lagrange was forced by ill health to return to France. He had been a warrior for historical and scientific truth all of his long life, and it was not easy to settle down to a quiet life in the cloisters of St. Maximin. That he did it, and so humbly and unprotestingly, was a great edification to all. The pen that had swiftly and accurately produced an almost unbelievable array of scripture studies was still active for the remaining three years of his life. On the day before his death, he was sitting up in bed correcting proofs of his latest book, his keen mind undimmed and his fighting spirit unpacified. While one critic shouted that he was "too conservative" and another thundered that he was "too advanced," he serenely finished his last article for the *Revue Biblique,* and said peacefully, "I abandon myself to God," and murmured "Jerusalem, Jerusalem"—as he passed into unconsciousness. He died on March 10, 1938.

Father Marie-Joseph Lagrange was the recipient of many professional honors; he was made a member of the Legion of Honor and of the Order of Leopold, and the Dominican Order had very early named him master in sacred theology. It is the considered opinion of scholars that he had done for biblical criticism what St. Thomas did for Aristotle, and that his foundation of scientific research is the basis for all further study. Students trained in his spirit are dealing today with the "Dead Sea Scrolls" which were found a few years ago, and fearlessly making use of the truths that their study will reveal. Were it not for the courageous and brilliantly scientific methods of the Dominican founder of the Biblical Institute, Christian scholars might today be just beginning truly scientific studies of the Bible.

ERIC GILL
(1882-1940)

One cannot omit from any list of distinguished Dominicans the great Tertiary artist and writer, Eric Gill. His impact upon the art world of our time is something that is not even yet fully appreciated, and his desperate concern with the apostolate of truth makes him a particularly vital member of the Order.

Eric Gill was born in Brighton, England in 1882, the second oldest of thirteen children. His people were religious in an experimental way, and several of his near relatives were missionaries in the South Pacific. Eric himslf grew up mildly agnostic and not too impressed with their beliefs; he had a fair education which he refused to take seriously. His whole family became Anglicans when he was fifteeen, but Eric had by this time begun to be repelled by some of the externals of religion which he thought were both morally and artistically bad. A slightly disgruntled youth, he went to London and was apprenticed to a church architect.

As a serious young art student he ran into most of the rebellious young men of the time, and heard what they had to say about organized religion. He was familiar with the Gospels, and alert enough to see the gap between theory and practice which was causing so many churches to be ineffectual. He became furiously interested in the working man and in the whole question of social justice. Finally, having investigated and found wanting a number of religions, he invented one of his own. After practicing it for some time, he was embarrassed but relieved to discover that he had "invented" the Catholic Church. He and his wife and three children were baptized Catholics in 1913, when he was thirty-one years old.

In the field of art, Eric Gill was winning an enviable place for himself. He gave various reasons for choosing stone-carving as his medium, and he has no peer in the perfection to which he brought the art of lettering on stone. He carved a masterly set of stations of the cross for Westminster Cathedral, and had just reached this point when he was conscripted into the army. He afterwards stated that his army stint was "a monstrous and momentous experience." It had given him a lifetime interest in the problems of people he had hitherto known nothing about. Returning from the army, he looked about to find a place where it would be possible to set up a sort of medieval guild, not simply because he was a great admirer of the Middle Ages, but because he sincerely felt that this was the only way for an artist to work. He and a number of other like-minded young artists gravitated together and set up some communal equipment, including a press. At this point, they felt that there should also be a spiritual organization and a rule of life. Reading and investigation led him to the Dominican Third Order, and it was to become one of the greatest forces of his life.

Joining the Third Order, Eric Gill met up with St. Thomas. His reasoned and clear presentation of the great truths of religion pleased Gill artistically, as he himself strove for a clear and honest presentation of artistic truths. Across the centuries he became a close friend of the medieval friar whose great intellect has guided so much of our thought.

After a long career of artistic merit, Eric Gill died during an air raid, though not as a result of it, in 1940. Most of the principles for which he had written and spoken for decades were flouted by the Second World War; he was a vigorous believer that war settles nothing, and that the only way to peace was social justice. He called himself a "Christian revolutionary," and maintained that poverty was a justifiable goal. In his own words is a statement of his principle of action:

> This is the circle of human politics. When we have accepted poverty, there will be peace among men. Only when we make peace shall we become the children of God. Only when we love God shall we love our fellow men. Only when we love our fellow men shall we have peace. When we have peace we shall have poverty, and when we have poverty we shall have the kingdom of heaven.

VINCENT McNABB
(1868-1943)

As much a part of London as the Marble Arch that marked the site of his preaching was the eccentric little friar whose name was Vincent McNabb, and whose reputation ranged from "mad as a hatter" to "the saint of Hyde Park." For fifty years he lived and worked in the heart of a great modern city, a piece of the Middle Ages thrust down into the twentieth century.

Joseph McNabb was born near Belfast in 1868. His father was a sea captain, his mother a good and far-seeing woman of great faith; Joseph was one of eleven children. This had the advantage of providing him with a gang of big brothers who could help to ease his way in the world during a delicate childhood. What he lacked in physical strength the little boy more than made up for in his gift for argument. He also developed a spirit of prayer that was unusual in such a small boy and which, of course, did not go unnoticed by his mother. She nursed him carefully through the recurrent migraine headaches that plagued him even as a child, and prayed in secret that God would call her son to the priesthood.

At the age of eighteen, Joseph McNabb was received in the Dominican novitiate at Woodchester. He was given the religious name Vincent. He asked two of his Dominican friends to explain this move to his parents, for he had begun his studies at the secular seminary and was none too sure how they would take his change of plans. His father, who was an independent character, reacted violently to the explanation of the vow of poverty. It was some time before the visitors could sell him the idea. As a matter of fact,

Captain McNabb himself became a Dominican Tertiary in his old age and was buried in the Dominican habit.

Brother Vincent completed his novitiate and was sent to Louvain for his studies. He began a long career of teaching at Hawkesyard. For most of his life he was in authority somewhere, and his main work of teaching would never stop. The public disputations for which he became famous began after he was stationed in London in 1920. Officially he was there on a regular assignment to preach and teach, which he did. But he was always an enthusiast, passionately determined to convey his intense idealism to others. The enthusiasm of the time was the land movement. He went at it so intensely that it became almost an obsession; he insisted on having the material for his habit woven from wool raised on the near-by land, and his boots hand-made by a craftsman. He declared war on such modern inventions as typewriters, and for a time even refused to use a fountain pen on principle. His sermons were startling, and his enemies—of course he had them—insisted that he was undignified, and that his manners in the pulpit were theatrical. But those who knew him best were drawn to him and to his message precisely because he was not theatrical, but terribly sincere.

The brethren who saw him at close hand admitted that he was eccentric, but that has never been a reason for an Englishman to blush. If he was argumentative and prone to lecture on his pet enthusiasms, he also possessed the basic sweetness of a child. None but the brethren knew how exactly he practiced what he preached, for they alone knew what his cell looked like—a bare comfortless room containing a bed which he never slept on, but used to store books under, and a chair he never sat in because he preferred either to stand or kneel when studying. No one made any claim that Father McNabb made a great contribution either to Catholic thought or to the Church, but he certainly reached a lot of people with his message of God's love.

If he was not an original thinker, he was the salesman par excellence of the Gospel message at a time and place where such a message would perhaps not have been accepted from a more conventional preacher. His literary output was amazing; nearly ninety books and pamphlets and several hundred articles are credited to him. All were written forcefully and hastily, with that sense of urgency which made one friend say of him that "the written word was the enemy of Father Vincent, because it was too slow to express his lightning-swift thought processes." Some of the finest devotional books of the last century are from his pen, and some of the best translations from prayers of the Eastern liturgies. The simplicity of his expression is startling to people who are accustomed to "pretty" writing; it has the rugged directness of the odd-looking little man who tramped through the London streets for half a century, persistently wearing his habit in public because he said that Englishmen needed to remember about God. He championed a great many causes in the course of his long lifetime, and his touch was sure, either in spoken or in written argument.

Two quotations from the brethren who lived with him and observed his work at close hand are revealing of the inner man. One said, "If all this represents a grim and repellent picture to your imagination, dismiss it at once; he was the happiest, least depressed member of the community, and he was the life and soul of merriment when the time for recreation came. Renunciation meant for him foregoing lesser joys for the sake of the supreme real joy." And another said, at his death, "Father Vincent has shown that St. Dominic is up to date. The true contemplative is always contemporary. The contemplative applies eternity to his own time." When Father Vincent died in 1943, the brethren went to lay him out as he had requested; he had even designed his own coffin. They found that his whole side was calloused from sleeping on the floor. He had left definite orders that his funeral was to be simple and the burial even simpler. It would have surprised him greatly to have known of the mobs that crowded around to touch his coffin, reverently certain that this odd little man who had been their friend was also a close friend of God.

WALTER FARRELL
(1902-1951)

One of the outstanding American Dominican theologians of the present century is without a doubt Father Walter Farrell, who died at the early age of forty-nine with a whole series of projected books unfinished, but with a lifetime of accomplishment behind him.

Raphael Anthony Farrell was born in Chicago in 1902, the youngest of four boys. He began his formal education in the parish school of St. Columbanus, and it should be a consolation to slow starters to read that he was promoted on condition from the second to the third grade. The facts seem to be that he was rather a frail child, dreamy rather than ambitious, who sometimes got into mischief in school, but who was always easily forgiven because of a quality of charm which he possessed even as a small child. His angelic appearance was a great pride to his mother and his teachers, who possibly envisioned him as a priest long before he thought of it himself. He became an altar boy as soon as he was old enough, and here felt himself

drawn closer to the altar. Sisters and priests who remember him at that
time remark that he was always unobtrusive, never forward, yet he was always on hand to "'serve the six" before the priest arrived in the sacristy;
sometimes, indeed, the priest had to waken him, as he had fallen asleep
waiting. When a visiting Dominican came for a mission, the parish priest
made the initial step by presenting him with young Raphael and remarking,
"Here is a boy who would make a good Dominican; why don't you work
on him?" The news of his religious vocation was a bit of a shock to his
family—to all, that is, except his mother—as by his own admission his abilities
were limited at this time to a splendid talent for baseball and gave no hint
of anything much else.

However, the idea of the priesthood had become fixed in his mind, and
he set his eyes on the high goal and never lowered them again. If the priesthood required good studies, then he would study; he set at his work with a
diligence that astonished his teachers. In September, 1920, at the age of
eighteen, he presented himself at the Dominican novitiate in Somerset, Ohio,
and received the Dominican habit and the religious name Walter.

Religious life was difficult for young Brother Walter. He was very frail
in health, a thing he would never admit nor allow to mitigate the stern discipline then in force at Somerset. He was also in the charge of a novice
master who believed that stern measures were best, and who had some
vague notion that Walter Farrell needed to be taken down a peg. He worked
industriously at the taking down, and the young student, sensitive and affectionate by nature, suffered agonies of bewilderment. At one point he was
ready to give up and go home, and only the intervention of his pastor (and
probably his mother's prayers) kept him at the task. The cold of Somerset
was a particular trial to him, and one bitter winter left him with deafness
in one ear and sinus trouble that would plague him all his life.

Somehow, with the grace of God, he survived the stern novitiate and made
profession. His fluency in Latin, which had caused him to be the target of
some sarcasm in his early days, now became an asset in his studies. He
still claimed that his principal talent was his ability to play baseball, for the
students were very proud of their team. At the end of a fine course of studies
he was ordained in Washington, D.C., in 1927. His thoughts were set on
China, where he hoped to go as a missionary, but he was sent to New Haven,
Connecticut, until the following year, when he was assigned to finish his
studies in Fribourg.

Here the fine mind that was to prove an instrument of grace to so many
began to shine in its reflection of eternal truth. St. Thomas was his first and
only love, and to many who know St. Thomas only through Father Farrell's

work *The Companion to the Summa*, he very nearly *is* St. Thomas. Under the capable professors at Fribourg, he delved happily into the profundities of theology, emerging with a dissertation on *The Natural Moral Law According to St. Thomas and Suarez*, which was rated *summa cum laude*, and an examination which gained him a *magna cum laude*. Yet Switzerland had not been kind to his health, and the sinus pain had more than once kept him walking the floor at night. He was ill and tired at the early age of twenty-eight when he returned from Europe and went to his post at Somerset to teach the young students.

For the remainder of his life, except for his years in the Navy, Father Farrell's days were to fall into a similar pattern. He taught to the limit of professional capacity, and in the remaining hours of the day he wrote, gave retreats, and helped out in parishes. He drove himself unmercifully, and had little patience with those who had entered the Order to find an easy life. As the years went on, he acquired more and more penitents who came to him for spiritual direction. He had serious ideas on this subject, too, and was unsparing on people who wished to make spiritual direction an occasion for self-gratification. Like Christ Himself, he was rarely if every severe with women, as the hundreds of sisters who came under his care testify. But he had the highest ideals, and he expected serious Dominicans to aim at them.

In 1933 Father Farrell was appointed to the house of studies in Washington, D.C., where he was regent of studies until 1945. In 1940, the Dominican Order conferred its highest scholastic honor upon him with the master degree in sacred theology. His work in Washington was close to his heart, for it entailed not only teaching the students but also the beginnings of theology for the sisters and for the laity, a project on which he had decided views. The Washington climate was not kind to him, however, and he suffered continually from sinus and respiratory trouble. The several enforced vacations and even a short rest under the loving care of the Dominican sisters from Adrian, Michigan, who had taught him in grade school, did not relieve the pain or the continual distress, and the hot, muggy summers in Washington were a genuine trial.

When America went into the war, Father Farrell began agitating for permission to take a chaplaincy in the Navy. His superiors were reluctant to let him go for a dozen good reasons, including his health. However, he finally managed to persuade a doctor to pass him in his health examination, and in 1942 he studied the arts of war among Navy officers to whom he was a good friend, but something of a puzzle. The Navy assigned him to the aircraft carrier "Yorktown," and for two years, until he was invalided out of the

Navy, the man of peace was surrounded by the worst that war could provide. Among men who were proud of their toughness, in a business that was tough in the extreme, this gentle soft-spoken priest found his place and became a valued member of the closely-knit personnel of the Navy carrier. He never left the flight deck while the planes were in the air, and was on hand when the fighters came home, some of them to crash-land and leave him with the sad business of giving the last rites to someone he had talked to an hour before. Every death was a personal loss to him, and every boy who did not come back to the Yorktown was sure of the earnest prayers of a devoted priest.

In his Navy days, Father Farrell dreamed of a future where, as he said, he could say Mass in a nice clean chapel where nothing would blow away while he was about it, and where sudden death would not rain down on those who were in his care. But his own failing health which forced him out of the Navy left him precious little time for any relaxation. His series of lectures for lay people on St. Thomas were succeeding marvelously in interesting the ordinary Catholic in extraordinary sanctity, and he planned a whole series of books popularizing Catholic truths. This he saw well begun, but he never lived to complete it. In 1947 he went into the hospital for lung surgery, and the remaining four years of his life were a losing battle to recover his strength.

Father Farrell died in his sleep, in November, 1951, in his home city of Chicago. The works he had begun have been carried on by men whose enthusiasm was lighted at the great fire of his love of God. A quiet man who found it terrifying to have to start a conversation, he was a religious who understood the beauty of union with God, and who continually referred to his pet thesis of the happiness of those dedicated to God: ". . . the profound happiness that is our personal right as religious is between ourselves and God, and invulnerable to any outside action." In a lifetime that had led him through many kinds of suffering and the tragedy of war, he had himself preserved that citadel of interior joy which he poured forth in his writings as the birthright of religious.

GERALD VANN
(1906-1963)

Father Gerald Vann's death, on July 14, 1963, is too recent to permit looking about for incidents in his life that could be used in an informal book of this kind. Since, however, he was known and loved by many people, either through their associations with him, or through his lectures and books, the following tributes to him may offer some tangible record of the regard his Dominican brothers in the English province had for him.

The first is the panegyric preached at his funeral by Father Sebastian Bullough, O.P., on July 18, 1963. (People who are not acquainted with Father Vann's writings should be informed that the titles of many of his books have been woven into the text and are italicized.)

We are gathered here this morning to honor a friend, and with the rites of the Church to pray for him. For Gerald Vann was a friend to many people: and in many ways. In a distant way perhaps, he was a friend to the thousands who read his books—yet he had a way of writing, so strong and personal, that he made the reader feel—and indeed still makes him feel—that he is speaking close to him. In a closer way, perhaps, there were other thousands, both in this country and in America, to whom his voice spoke by wireless—and many of these words which had vanished into the air, were afterwards presented in permanent print. Still closer were those who listened to him preaching or lecturing, with that voice of his, not strong, but clear and forceful. Many of these discourses have similarly been preserved in print.

But closer than these were the many of us who became his personal friends. We knew him well, and knew not only the clear and forceful voice, but we knew the merry laughter and the whimsical jokes, the little unfinished sentences and yet the love of the pattern of words, the glance of the eyes and the nod of the head.

Among these friends were especially his own Dominican brethren, who lived with him and often saw him every day, worked with him and sometimes under him. We knew his ways and we knew his weaknesses, and we knew that he knew them better than he knew his successes. We knew his affection for the brethren and that affectionate mockery only possible among friends who are brethren, which he knew so well how to receive and also to give back in return. We also knew something of the battle that went on as he pounded his little typewriter next door at night.

Closer still to him, perhaps, were those who heard from him the whispered words of the priest, the words of consolation and encouragement which we learn to expect from the good and wholehearted priest. But among these are also included the many who received guidance and strength from his silent

605

words lying upon the printed page. The encouragement they received was first of all an encouragement to be themselves. Not for nothing was his first book, written when he was 26, called *On Being Human*.

All his writing was a struggle with this problem, and perhaps it is typically Dominican to be concerned with how things are, and how they should be, if they are to realize themselves in the truth of the whole of creation. In the whole of creation there is perhaps no deeper mystery than *The Heart of Man*, with its love, its joy, and its pain. For thirty years Father Gerald preached the ideal of man's love and compassion for man, modelled on *The Divine Pity*, that makes a man fully human.

Just before the war of 1939 he became much occupied with the problem of world peace and his book *Morality and War* placed him among the leading theologians who at that time were tackling the problem—an uncomfortable one for the public conscience of those years—and then a great sadness weighed him down, when almost at once he saw the world again rent with strife. Most Christian men suffered in spirit during those grim years, but it was perhaps Father Gerald's lot to be saddened more, because he had thought about this aberration of human behavior more deeply than most Christian men.

There was a sadness about Father Gerald beneath the genuine gaiety and the fraternal bonhomie which his brethren knew and enjoyed so well. Perhaps it was just this—that his own personal understanding brought the pain upon him, an understanding not only of the problem of war, but of the whole problem of mankind's hunger for love, or of mankind's self-satisfaction without it, or contentment with the false love that is selfishness. Gerald Vann saw these things and felt them deeply, and he also saw that he was powerless to help, beyond remaining a voice crying in the wilderness and having compassion on the multitude. He saw that the problem could only be solved by obedience to God, that man's hunger for love could only be satisfied by understanding God's love of mankind, and that only thus could man be led away from selfishness and led to the true human love of other men. And in his humble wisdom, he saw himself among the starving multitudes who had need of this compassion.

Perhaps this is why his preaching and writing—his moral teaching, if you like—had a personal effectiveness; for he spoke to mankind of their needs, having seen the same needs within himself. And the pain that followed upon this realization was, in his own words, *The Pain of Christ*. The relief of this pain, the deliverance from *The Seven Swords* that transfix the heart of man, lay for himself and for the multitudes on whom he had compassion, in the merciful hands of God.

We, his brethren, saw this working out in his obedience: for more than half his active life he was a schoolmaster, not by choice but by obedience; and obedience kept him there because he did it so well, not by choice but by obedience. So, as with any other Dominican, his preaching and writing—or sometimes, as with any other Dominican, his silence—was the fruit of obedience. For a person of outstanding gifts—and his gifts were not only in literature and rhetoric, but also as a teacher, as a critic, as a linguist, as a conversationalist, as an organist—for a person of outstanding gifts, his obedience and faithfulness to the end, dying in his narrow monastic cell at the Newcastle Priory, became all the more noticeable, and to his religious brethren formative and encouraging.

It was a battle, as it is for every vowed religious, and for Gerald Vann with all his gifts, the consecration of them was a victory which he allowed God's grace to win for him: for *His Will is Our Peace.*

For Gerald Vann it was an arduous battle to preach God's love to mankind and for thirty years to call for God's love to be reflected in the love and passion of man himself. It was an arduous battle for him who felt the battle so deeply in himself and in the world, not only because he saw how man becomes so easily entangled in human passion, but also how man so frequently entangles himself in regulations and scruples which hold him back from the true human love which is free and sublime. Father Gerald felt passionately the tragedy of a spirit, tied down, as the Pharisees tied men down, to a legalistic view of life, as if there were no *Divine Pity* looking down upon them. Sometimes there were those who perhaps misunderstood him here, not knowing of *The Water and The Fire* through which he went, as he saw men going through the pain. Were they to be given *Stones or Bread?* Father Gerald was ever anxious to give them the bread of love and consolation.

A preacher upon his lonely watch tower is inevitably a solitary man. He cannot share his rostrum with anyone, nor his sacramental seat of judgment and healing. As Father Gerald preached the gospel of love, he became almost inevitably more of a solitary. The celibate man has a solitude that is a singular thing, yet it enables him, in a way no other can, to have compassion on the multitude starving for want of true love. This battle in the desert, even if surrounded by brethren and friends, remains a struggle in one man's heart.

Yet it is a simple thing, this gospel of love. Among his early titles Fr. Gerald turned to the Gospel of St. John, the lover: *Of his Fullness* was published in 1939. After that his pilgrimage took him through many paths. Early he turned to St. Thomas Aquinas, every Dominican's master and guide, and his study of the Angelic Doctor, published in 1940, is one of his finest books, though less well known. Two later titles show him turning to Dante. In 1950 with *The Seven Swords* he was finding the answer in his devotion to Our Lady. And in his last book, in 1961, he turned back to St. John, with *The Eagle's Word.* "Being human" had come full circle to the humanity of the Word made flesh.

Here Father Gerald's maturest thought came closest to the synthesis that can only be found when we *Awake in Heaven,* where those who hunger and thirst after justice shall have their fill. Last Sunday the restelss search, purged with pain, came to an end. May the rites of the Church which we are performing today, and the loving support of his brethren and friends, bring him to the place of rest, where "God shall wipe away all tears from their eyes; and death shall be no more, nor mourning, nor crying; nor sorrow shall be any more, for the former things are passed away" (Apoc. 21:4).

In September, 1963, *Blackfriars,* a monthly review edited by the English Dominicans, published a tribute to Father Vann. It was written by Father Gerald Meath, O.P., and *Blackfriars* graciously gave permission to reprint it here.

Gerald Vann was a preacher, lecturer, broadcaster, and writer of international fame; yet the most vivid memory he leaves is of a deeply loving person. For all his great success in the public eye he cultivated no personality, projected no image; he was simply himself, Father Gerald. In this respect he lived what he preached: What you are is more important than what you do. He received his Dominican training in the context of the humanism of the 'twenties (*On Being Human* was the title of his first book published before he was 30). It is scarcely surprising that the sinewy character of his thought was concealed in a gentleness that sprang from a lifelong attempt to display the goodness of God's human creatures. And when he became the center of controversy it was from the same cause: the desire to find the reflection of the Maker in His image, and to feel something of the tenderness of Christ towards sinners.

The readers of *Blackfriars* will be familiar enough with his thought and style both as writer and preacher. I wonder if it is widely known that for twenty years he wrote his books, lectures, sermons during an extremely arduous life of school teaching. Twenty-five classes a week, innumerable "preps" to correct, and all the usual routine chores of a schoolmaster: out of this came *The Heart of Man, The Divine Pity*, etc.

He was a true son of St. Dominic in that he never spared himself and was always alive to the needs of others. He who wrote so eloquently of pain suffered bitterly in his last months and grew even sweeter. Only shortly before he died he apologised to the young priest who had to change his bandages: "I thought I should have been dead before you had to do this." He died in his priory cared for by his brethren. If that priory seems emptier for his death so does the English province which has lost not so much a teacher and preacher as a loving brother. May God give peace to his gentle soul.

Chronology of Father Gerald Vann

1906: Born August 24 at St. Mary Cray, Kent.

1919-23: At Hawkesyard School.

1923: September: received the Dominican habit at Woodchester.

1929: June 11: ordained priest.

1930-31: Fourth year theology at Angelico, Rome.

1931-34: Studies at Oxford University.

(1933 first published work: *On Being Human*).

1934: Assigned to Laxton prep school (till 1952: 18 years).

1948: Appointed headmaster at Laxton.

1952-53: Assigned to Cambridge house of the Order.

1953-56: Assigned to Edinburgh, Scotland.

1956: Assigned to St. Dominic's Priory, Newcastle.

1963: July 14: died at Newcastle.

Visits to America

1948: Lecture tour.

1951: Lecture tour.

1956: Conferences, lectures.

1959-62: Lectured for the second semester of four successive years, in the Department of Education of the Catholic University of America, Washington, D.C.

BIBLIOGRAPHY

BIBLIOGRAPHY

Acta Sanctorum: Edited by the Bollandists, 1653 and following. Antwerp. 64 Volumes (microfilm).

Allies, M. H.: *Three Catholic Reformers of the 15th Century.* Burns, Oates and Washbourne, London, 1897.

Alvarez, M. R. P. Paulino, O.P.: *Santos, Bienaventurados, Venerables de las Orden de los Predicadores.* Edit. de el Santisimo Rosario, Vergara, 1920. 4 Volumes.

Andre-Marie, Le R. P. F., O.P.: *Missions Dominicaines dans l'Extreme Orient.* Librairie Poussielgue Frères, Paris, 1865. 2 Volumes.

Année Dominicaine: X. Jevain Imprimeur-Editeur, Lyon, 1898. 12 Volumes.

L'Année Dominicaine: Bulletin Mensuel de l'Ordre de Saint-Dominique. Librairie Poussielgue Freres, Paris, 1859-1913.

Anstruther, Godfrey, O.P.: *The Venerable Robert Nutter, O.P.,* in Archivum Fratrum Praedicatorum. Institutum Historicum Fratrum Praedicatorum, ad S. Sabinae, Roma, 1957.

Antoninus, Sanctus: *Chonicon Sive Summa (Historialis) Tertia Pars.* Bale, 1491.

Antony, C. M.: *In Saint Dominic's Country.* Longmans Green & Co., London, 1912.

Antony, C. M.: *Saint Catherine of Siena, Her Life and Times.* Burns, Oates and Washbourne, London, 1915.

Antony, C. M.: *Saint Pius V.* Longmans Green & Co., London, 1911.

Aron, Marguerite: *Saint Dominic's Successor* (Translation by Wilmar Shiras). Blackfriars, London, 1955.

Attwater, Donald: *Eric Gill, Workman.* James Clarke & Co., Ltd., London, 1941.

Aumann, Jordan, O.P., *Summa of the Christian Life;* Selected Texts from the Writings of Venerable Louis of Granada, O.P. Translated and Adapted. Herder, St. Louis, 1954. 3 Volumes.

Bayonne, Le R. P. Emmanuel-Ceslas, O.P.: *Vie Du B. Réginald de Saint-Gilles.* Librairie Poussielgue Frères, Paris, 1872.

Beata Innocentius PP V. Studia et Documenta. Prefatio Fr. M. S. Gillet, O.P. Mag. Gen.: ad S. Sabinae, Roma, 1943.

Bignami-Odier, J.: *Les Visions de Robert D'Uzes, O.P.,* in Archivum Fratrum Praedicatorum. Institutum Historicum Fratrum Praedicatorum, ad S. Sabinae, Roma, 1955.

Boardman, Anne Cawley: *Such Love is Seldom.* Harper & Bros., New York, 1950.

Bonne Mère: Translated and Slightly Abridged from the French by the Dominican Sisters of Portobello Road, London. Herder, St. Louis, 1932.

Bonniwell, William R., O.P.: *A History of the Dominican Liturgy*. J. F. Wagner, Inc., New York, 1944.

————: *The Martyrology of the Sacred Order of Friars Preachers*. Newman Bookshop, Westminster, Maryland, 1955.

Bremond, Antoninus, O.P.: *Bullarium Ordinis FF. Praedicatorum*. Roma, Typographica Hieronymus Mainardi, 1729. 8 Volumes.

Burke, Very Rev. Thomas N., O.P.: *Lectures and Sermons*. P. M. Haverty, New York, 1872.

Burton, Katherine: *According to the Pattern*. Longmans Green & Co., New York, 1946.

————: *Difficult Star*. Longmans Green & Co., New York, 1947.

————: *Sorrow Built a Bridge*. Longmans Green & Co., New York, 1937.

Butler's Lives of the Saints: Thurston and Atwater, Compilers. Burns, Oates and Washbourne, Ltd., London, 1912. 12 Volumes.

Bzovius, Abraham, O.P.: *Annales Ecclesiasticus (1198-1228)*. Barri-Duçis, Ludovici Guerin, 1870.

Campana, Pier Tomaso: *Storia de S. Piero-Martire de Verona*. Milano, 1741.

Capes, F. M.: *St. Catherine dè Ricci; Her Life, Her Letters, Her Community*. Burns, Oates and Washbourne, London, 1911.

————: *St. Rose of Lima*. R. & T. Washbourne Ltd., London, 1913.

Cartier, E.: *Life of Beato Angelico da Fiesole*. Translated by a Member of the same Order. John Philip, London, 1865.

Cartulaire Au Histoire Diplomatique de Saint Dominique: Ed. Bureaux de l'Année Dominicaine. Paris, 1893.

Casey, Hyacinth, O.P.: "Saint Albert the Great," in *Irish Ecclesiastical Record*, Vol. 39. Brown & Nolan, Ltd., Dublin, 1932.

Cassidy, Rev. James: *The Great Father Tom Burke*. M. H. Gill & Sons, Ltd., Dublin, 1947.

Castillo, Hernando de, O.P.: *Historia General de Santo Domingo y de su Orden de Predicadores*. Valladolid, 1612.

Catherine of Siena: Dialogues. Newman Bookshop, Westminster, Maryland, 1943.

Chocarne, B., O.P.: *The Inner Life of Père Lacordaire*. Translated by Augusta Theodosia Drane. R. T. Washbourne, Ltd., London, 1917.

Clark, James M.: *The Great German Mystics: Eckhart, Tauler, and Suso*. Basil Blackwell, Oxford, 1949.

Clerissac, Humbert, O.P.: *The Spirit of Saint Dominic*. Burns, Oates and Washbourne, London, 1939.

Cochin, Henri: *Le Bienheureux Frà Giovanni Angelico de Fiesole* (*1387-1455*), Librairie Victor Lecoffre, J. Gabalda, Editeur. Paris, 1924.

Coleman, Ambrose, O.P.: *O'Heyne's Irish Dominicans*. First published Louvain 1706. Reprinted by W. Tempest, Dundalk, 1902.

Constantius de Urbeveteri, O.P.: *Legenda S. Dominici*, in Monumenta Historica S. P. N. Dominici, Fasc. II. Ed. H. C. Scheeben, O.P., Roma, 1935.

Constitutiones Antiqu Ordinis Fratrum Predicatorum: Ed. H. Denifle, O.P. in Archiv Für Literatur-und Kirchengeschichte des Mittelalters I. Graz, 1955.

Conway, Placid, O.P. (Translator): *Lives of the Brethren of Gerard de Frachet*. Blackfriars, London, 1955.

Cormier, Hyacinth M., O.P.: *Blessed Raymond of Capua*. Translated by J. Dillon Trant. Marlier & Callanan, Boston, 1900.

Crombie, A. G.: *Augustine to Galileo; The History of Science A.D. 400-1650*. Wm. Heinemann, Ltd., London, 1952.

Curtayne, Alice: *Saint Catherine of Siena*. Sheed and Ward, New York, 1938.

D'Amato, P. A., and Others: *Le Reliquie di S. Domenico, Storia E Leggenda Ricerche Scientifiche Riconstruzione Fisica*. Pontificia Accademia Della Scienze, Tipografia Luigi Parma, Bologna, 1946.

Darcy, M. C., S.J.: *St. Thomas Aquinas*. Oxford University Press, 1938.

Dawson, Christopher (Editor): *The Mongol Mission*. Translated by a Nun of Stanbrook Abbey. The Makers of Christendom Series, Sheed and Ward, New York, 1955.

De Ganay, M. C.: *Les Bienheureuses Dominicaines 1190-1577*. D'Apres des Documents Inédits. Perrin, Paris, 1913.

De la Fuente, Vicente: *Historia Eclesiástica de Espana*. Libería Religiosa, Barcelona, 1855. Volume III.

Devas, Raymond, O.P.: *The Dominican Revival in the Nineteenth Century*. Longmans Green & Co., New York, 1913.

De Villard, Ugo Monneret: *Il Libro Della Peregrinazione Nelle Parti d'Oriente di Frati Ricoldo Da Montecroce*. Instituto Storico Domenicano, ad S. Sabinae, Roma, 1948.

Diacchini, P. Raimondo, O.P.: *Vita del B. Domenico Spadafora, Domenicano*. Foligno, Stabilimente Tipografico Guiseppe Campi, 1921.

A Dominican Artist; Père Besson: by the Author of "Tales of Kirkberk." Kelly Piet and Co., Baltimore, 1871.

Dominicana: Publication of Dominican Theological Students, Washington, D.C. June 1900-June 1955.

Drane, Augusta Theodosia (Mother Frances Raphael, O.P.): *History of Saint Catherine of Siena and Her Companions*. Longmans, London, 1915. 2 Volumes.

————: *The Life of Saint Dominic and a Sketch of the Dominican Order*. P. O'Shea, New York, 1867.

————: *The Spirit of the Dominican Order.* Benziger, 1910.

Dyson, Thomas Austin, O.P.: *The Life of Saint Pius the Fifth.* D. & J. Sadlier and Company, New York, 1887.

————: *Lives of Some of the Sons of St. Dominic.* D. & J. Sadlier and Company, New York, 1883.

————: *Saints of the Rosary.* D. & J. Sadlier and Company, New York, 1897.

————: *Stars in Saint Dominic's Crown.* D. & J. Sadlier and Company, New York, 1890.

————: *Within the Golden Gates.* D. & J. Sadlier and Company, New York, 1893.

Fages, Le Rev. Père, O.P.: *Histoire de Saint Vincent Ferrier, Apotre de l'Europe.* Maison de la Conne Presse, Paris, 1893.

Farrell, Walter, O.P.: *A Companion to the Summa.* Sheed and Ward, New York, 1945-1948. 4 Volumes.

Ferrara, Orestes: *The Borgia Pope, Alexander the Sixth.* Sheed and Ward, New York, 1940.

Fitz-Patrick, Wm. J., F.S.A.: *The Life of the Very Rev. Thomas N. Burke, O.P.* Benziger, 1886. 2 Volumes.

Five Dominican Martyrs in China; (Pamphlet) Catholic Truth Society, 10 Paternoster Row, London.

Gallen, Jarl: *La Province de Dacie de l'Ordre des Frères Prêcheurs.* Institutum Historicum FF. Praedicatorum. Ad S. Sabinae, Helsinki, Roma, 1946.

Galvanus de la Flamma, O.P.: *Cronica Ordinis Praedicatorum ab Anno 1170 Usque ad 1333.* Ed. B. M. Reichert, O.P., Rome, 1897.

Gardeil, Thomas, O.P.: *Gifts of the Holy Ghost in the Dominican Saints.* Translated by Anselm Townsend, O.P., Bruce, 1937.

Garreau, Albert: *Saint Albert le Grand.* Desclée De Brouwer & Cie., 1932.

Gastoué, A.: *Un Dominicain Professeur de Musique au Treizìeme Siècle: Fr. Jerome de Moravie et Son Oeuvre.* Archivum Fratrum Praedicatorum; Institutum Historicum FF. Praed. Ad S. Sabinae, Roma, 1956.

Georges, Norbert, O.P.: *Blessed Diana and Blessed Jordan of the Order of Preachers.* The Rosary Press, Somerset, Ohio, 1933.

————: *Meet Brother Martin.* (Pamphlet) Blessed Martin Guild, New York, 1940.

Gillet, Martin S., O.P.: *The Mission of Saint Catherine.* Translated by Sister M. Thomas Lopez, O.P., Herder, St. Louis, 1954.

Grabmann, Dr. Martin: *St. Thomas Aquinas.* Translated by Dom Vergil Michel, O.S.B., Longmans Green & Co., New York, 1920.

————: *The Interior Life of St. Thomas Aquinas.* Translated by Nicholas Ashenbrener, O.P., Bruce, Milwaukee, 1951.

Gregory, Padraic: *When Painting Was in Glory*. Bruce, Milwaukee, 1941.

Guerin, Msgr. Paul: *Les Petits Bollandistes, View des Saints*. Bloud et Barral Librairies, Paris. 17 Volumes.

Guglielmotti, P. Alberto, O.P.: *Memorie delle Missione Cattoliche nel Regno del Tunchino*. Nella Tipografia Salviucci, Roma, 1844.

Guiraud, Jean: *Life of Saint Dominic*. Translated by Catherine de Mattos. Benziger, 1913.

Hanke, Lewis: *Bartolomé de las Casas; Bookman, Scholar, and Propagandist*. University of Pennsylvania Press, Philadelphia, 1952.

————: *The Spanish Struggle for Justice in the Conquest of America*. University of Pennsylvania Press, Philadelphia, 1949.

Hansen, Le P. Léonard, O.P.: *Vie de Sainte Rose de Lima*. Librairie Catholique, Perisse Frères, Paris, 1894.

Herbert, Lady: *The Life of Don Bartholomew of the Martyrs*. Translated from The Portuguese. Thomas Richardson & Son, London, 1880.

de Herrera, Antonio: *Historia General de los Hechos de los Castellanos en las Islas y Tierra Firme del Mar Oceano*. Madrid, 1726-1732. 8 Volumes.

Hesselio: *Historia Beatorum Martyrum Gorkomiensium*. Lovanii, 1867, Typis Caroli Peeters.

Hibernia Dominicana: Coloniae Aggrippinae, 1762, ex Typographia Metternichiana sub Signo Gryphi.

Hinnebusch, William, O.P., D. Phil. (Oxon): *The Early English Friars Preachers*. Dissertationes Historicae Fasciculus XIV, Institutum Historicum FF. Praedictorum. Ad S. Sabinae, 1951.

Histoire du Monastere de Notre Dame de Prouille: par un Religieuse du même Monastere. Grenoble, 1898.

Histoire des Ordres Monastiques, Religieux, et Militaires, et des Congregationes Seculiers es de l'un et de l'autre sexe, Qui ont Establier Jusqú a Present. Ed. Nicholas Gosselin, Paris, 1715. Volume VIII.

Hughes, H. L.: *Piergiorgio Frassatti*. Translated and adapted from the Italian of Antonio Cojazzi. Burns, Oates and Washbourne, London, 1933.

Hughes, Philip: *A History of the Church*. Sheed and Ward, New York, 1947. 3 Volumes.

Humbertus de Romanis, O.P.: *De Vita Regulari*. Ed. J. J. Berthier, O.P., Rome, 1888. 2 Volumes.

————: *Legenda Sancta Dominici*, in Monumenta Historica S.P.N. Dominici, Ed. A. Walz, O.P., Fasc. II. Rome, 1935.

Jacobus de Voragine: *Aurea Legenda Sanctorum*. Lugdunum, 1514.

Jarrett, Bede, O.P.: *Saint Antonio and Medieval Economics*. Herder, St. Louis, 1914.

————: *The English Dominicans.* Burns, Oates and Washbourne, London, 1921.

————: *The Life of Saint Dominic.* Burns, Oates and Washbourne, London, 1934.

————: *The Religious Life.* Burns, Oates and Washbourne, London, 1939.

Jordanus de Saxonia, O.P.: *Libellus de Principiis Ordinis Praedicatorum,* in Monumenta Historica S.P.N. Dominici, Fasc. II. Ed. H. C. Scheeben, O.P. Roma, 1935.

Joret, F .D.: *Dominican Life.* Sands, London, 1937.

Kearns, John C.: *Life of Blessed Martin de Porres.* Kenedy, New York, 1937.

Kirsch, B. et Romain, H. S.: *Pèlerinages Dominicains.* Societè Saint-Augustin, Desclée De Brouwer & Cie., Paris, 1920.

Lacordaire, Henri-Dominique, O.P.: *Vie de Saint Dominique, Précédée du Mémoire Pour le Rétablissement en France de l'Ordres des Frères Prècheurs.* Paris, 1844.

Life of Blessed Louis-Marie Grignon de Montfort: by a Secular Priest. Benziger, 1892.

Loenertz, R., O.P.: *La Société des Frères Pérégrinantes; Étude sur l'Orient Dominicain.* Instituto Storico Domenicano. Ad S. Sabinae, Roma, 1937.

————: *Manuel Calecas, Sa Vie et ses Oeuvres.* D'Apres ses Lettres et ses Apologies Inédites. Archivum Fratrum Praedicatorum, Institutum Historicum FF. Praed. Ad S. Sabinae, Roma, 1947.

MacCarthy, Sister M. Stanislaus: *Life of Blessed Emily Bicchieri, O.S.D.* Dublin, M. H. Gill & Son, 1902.

Mandonnet, P., O.P.: *Guillaume de Moerbeke, Traducteur des Economiques.* In Archivum Fratrum Praedicatorum, Institutum Historicum FF. Praed. Ad S. Sabinae, Roma, 1933.

————: *Saint Dominic and His Work.* Translated by Sister Mary Benedicta Larkin, O.P., Herder, St. Louis, 1945.

Mann, Rt. Rev. Msgr. Horace K.: *The Lives of the Popes in the Middle Ages.* Herder, St. Louis, 1929. Volume XV.

Marchese, D., O.P.: *Painters, Sculptors, and Architects of the Dominican Order.* Translated by C. P. Meehan. James Duffy, 7 Wellington Quay, 1852. 2 Volumes.

————: *Sagra Diario Domenicano.* Naples, 1676. 4 Volumes.

I Martiri Annamiti e Cinese 1798-1856. Tipografia Vaticano, Roma, 1900.

Massetti, Pio Tommaso, O.P.: *I Martiri Giapponesi Domenicani.* Tipografia di Bernardo Morini, Roma, 1868.

Mauri, Revmo. Mons. Egidio: *Vita Della Beati Diana d'Andalo, Cecilia, et Amata.* Translated into Italian from the French of P. Hyacinth Cormier, O.P., Roma, Tipografia Poliglotta, 1892.

Menzies, Lucy: *The Revelations of Mechtilde of Magdeberg*. Longmans Green & Co., New York, 1953.

Mezard, P. Denys, O.P.: *Etude Sur Les Origines du Rosaire*. Couvent de la Visitation, Caluire, 1912.

Miss Agnès McLaren Du Tiers-Ordre de Saint-Dominique, Docteur en Médecine. College Angélique, Roma, 1915.

Monro, Margaret T.: *A Book of Unlikely Saints*. Longmans Green & Co., London, 1943.

Mortier, Henri, O.P.: *Histoire des Maitres Generaux Ordinis Praedicatorum*. Paris, 1903. 8 Volumes.

Morçay, Raoul: *Saint Antonin*. Librairie Gabalda, Paris, 1913.

Mothon, Le R. P. Joseph-Pie: *Vie du Bienheureux Jourdain de Saxe*. Société Génerale de Librairie Catholique, Paris, 1883.

Murphy, Richard T., O.P.: *Père Lagrange and the Scriptures*. Translated from the French. Bruce, Milwaukee, 1946.

Newcomb, Covelle: *The Broken Sword*. Dodd-Mead, New York, 1955.

O'Daniel, Victor F., O.P.: *The First Disciples of Saint Dominic*. Herder, St. Louis, 1928.

—————: *The Dominicans in Florida*. Herder, St. Louis, 1930.

O'Reilly, Miles: *Memoirs of the Irish Martyrs*. Catholic Publication Society, New York, 1869.

Osende, P. V., O.P.: *Vida del Beato Juan Masias*. Imp. "Artistica," Lima, 1918.

Palmer, Raymond, O.P.: *The Life of Philip Thomas Howard, O.P.* Thomas Richardson & Sons, London, 1867.

Pastor, Dr. Ludwig: *The History of the Popes from the Close of the Middle Ages*. From the German, edited by Frederick Ignatius Antrobus of the Oratory. Herder, St. Louis, 1898. Volume VI.

Petrus Ferrandus: *Legenda S. Dominici*. In Monumenta Historica S.P.N. Dominici, Fasc. II. Roma, 1935.

Pio, Gio. Michele, O.P.: *Delle Vite de Gli Huomini Illustri di S. Domenico*. Bologna, 1620.

Pochin-Mould, Daphne D. C.: *The Irish Dominicans*. Dominican Publications, St. Saviour's, Dublin, 1957.

Pieto, Fray Juan de la Cruz, O.P.: *Proceso de Beatificación de Fray Martin de Porres*. Palencia, 1960.

Quetif, Jacobus, et Echard, Jacobus, O.P.: *Scriptores Ordinis Praedicatorum*. Paris, 1719. 2 Volumes.

Razzi, Fra Serafino, O.P.: *Vita de I Santi, E Beati, Cosi Huomini, Come Donne del Sacro Ordine de Frati Predicatori*. Milano, 1777.

Reeves, John Baptist, O.P.: *The Dominicans*. Macmillan, New York, 1930.

Revue Thomiste, T. XIV (Nouvelle Series) No. 65, Mars-Avril 1931: "St. Albert le Grand."

Richardson, M. H.: *Materials for a Life of Jacopo da Varagine*. The H. W. Wilson Co., New York, 1935.

Roze, R. P. Marie-Augustin: *Les Dominicains en Amérique*. Librairie Poussielgue Frères, Paris, 1878.

Ryan-Ripperger (Translators): *The Golden Legend of Jacobus de Voragine*. Longmans Green & Co., New York, 1941. 2 Volumes.

Saint Dominique, Son Esprit Ses Vertue: d'Après les Témoins Oculaires de sa Vie et de sa Mort. Librairie Saint-Thomas d'Aquin, Saint Maximin, 1923.

Sandrini, Fr. Domenico Mària, O.P.: *Vita di Caterina Dè Ricci*. Florence, 1747.

Savignol, R. P. Marie-Joseph: *Les Martyrs Dominicains de la Chine au XVIII Siècle*.

Scudder, Vida: *Saint Catherine of Siena as Seen in her Letters*. E. P. Dutton and Co., 1905.

Schwertner, Thomas M., O.P.: *Saint Raymond of Pennafort*. Bruce, Milwaukee, 1935.

————: *Saint Albert the Great*. Bruce, Milwaukee, 1932.

Serres, l'Abbé J. B.: *Catherine Jarrige*. College Angélique, Rome, 1904.

Sighart, Dr. Joachim: *Albertus Magnus*. Translated from the French Edition by Rev. T. A. Dixon, O.P. R. Washbourne, London, 1876.

Stegmüller, Friedrich: *Meister Dietrich von Frieberg Uber Die Zeit un Das Sien*. Archives d'Histoire Doctrinale et Littéraire du Moyen Age. Librairie Philosophique, J. Vrin, Paris, 1942.

Stephanus de Salaniaco et Bernardis Guidonis, O.P.: *De Quatuor in Quibus Deus Praedicatorum Ordinem Insignivit*. Ed. Thomas Kaeppeli, O.P., Roma, 1949.

Taurisano, P. Innocenzo, O.P.: *La Beata Osanna da Cattaro, Domenicana*. Collegio Angelico, Roma, 1929.

Theodoricus de Apoldia: *Vita Beatissimi Patris Dominici*. In Historiae Seu Vitae Sanctorum (Surius). Turin, 1877. Volume VIII.

Thurston, Herbert, S.J.: *Surprising Mystics*. Ed. J. H. Crehan, S.J. Henry Regnery Co., Chicago, 1955.

Touron, A., O.P.: *Histoire des Hommes Illustres de l'Ordre de Saint Dominique*. Chez Babuty, Paris, 1743. 6 Volumes.

Touron, A., O.P.: *La Vie de Saint Dominique de Guzman Avec l'Histoire Abregée de ses Premiers Disciples*. Paris, 1739.

————: *La Vie de Saint Dominique de Guzman Avec l'Histoire Abregée de ses Premiers Disciples*. Paris, 1739.

Ureta: *Historia de los Santos y Predica de Antiopia*. Juan Chrysostomo Garriz., Valencia, 1611.

Valdez, Jose Manuel, O.P.: *Vida Admirable del Bienaventurado Fray Martin de Porres*. Huerta Y.C. Impresores-Editores, Lima, 1863.

Valentine, Ferdinand, O.P.: *Father Vincent McNabb, O.P.; The Portrait of a Great Dominican*. Newman Bookshop, Westminster, Maryland, 1955.

Vaughan, Roger Bede, O.S.B.: *Life and Labors of Saint Thomas Aquinas*. Chas. Van Benthuysen & Sons, Albany, 1874.

Vicaire, M. H., O.P.: *Histoire de Saint Dominique, un Homme Évangélique*. Les Éditions du Cerf, Paris, 1957.

Vignato, P. Giuseppe Bart., O.P.: *Storia di Benedetto XIII Dei Frati Predicatori*. Antoniazzi Editore, Milano.

Vincent Ferrer, St.: *Treatise on the Spiritual Life*. Translated by T. A. Dixon, O.P., Newman Bookshop, Westminster, Maryland, 1944.

Walsh, James J.: *Thirteenth, Greatest of Centuries*. Catholic Summer School Press, New York, 1907.

Walsh, William T.: *Characters of the Inquisition*. Kenedy, New York, 1940.

————: *Isabella of Spain, the Last Crusader*. R. McBride & Co., New York, 1930.

Walz, Angelus M., O.P.: *Saint Thomas Aquinas: A Biographical Study*. Translated by Bebastian Bullough, O.P. Newman Bookshop, Westminster, Maryland, 1951.

————: *Compendium Historiae Ordinis Praedicatorum*. Herder, St. Louis, 1930.

Wilberforce, Bertrand, O.P.: *Memoirs of Mother Frances Raphael, O.S.D. (Augusta Theodosia Drane)*. Longmans Green & Co., London, 1923.

Wilms, Hieronymus, O.P.: *Albert the Great*. Translated by Adrian English, O.P. and Philip Hereford. Burns, Oates & Washbourne, London, 1930.

————: *Lay Brother, Artist, and Saint*. Translated from the German by Sister M. Fulgence, O.P., Blackfriars, London, 1957.

Woodgate, M. V.: *Père Lacordaire, Leader of Youth*. Herder, St. Louis, 1939.

Wykeham-George, Kenneth, O.P.: *Bede Jarrett of the Order of Preachers*. Blackfriars, London, 1952.

Zeller, René: (Translator) *Blessed Imelda*. Herder, St. Louis, 1911.

ALPHABETICAL INDEX

ABOUT THE AUTHOR

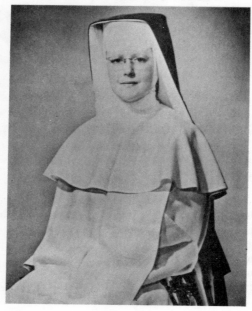

Sister Mary Jean Dorcy, O.P.

Sister Mary Jean Dorcy was born in Anacortes, Washington, the youngest of nine children. After she finished high school, she enrolled in the University of Washington. At the end of her freshman year, Sister Jean became a member of the Dominican Sisters of the Holy Cross by entering the novitiate at Everett, Washington. (The motherhouse has since been moved to Edmonds, Washington.)

After profession, Sister Jean returned to college at the Jesuits' Gonzaga University in Spokane. She received her Bachelor's degree from Gonzaga, and three years later earned a Master of Fine Arts degree from California College of Arts and Crafts at Oakland. She is justly famous both as an artist and an author, enjoying both media of expression to an equal degree. Her beautiful silhouettes have been used in her own books, but also have been reproduced on magazine covers, Christmas cards, holy cards, and even on church walls. *Saint Dominic's Family* is probably her most ambitious undertaking. At present, Sister Jean is stationed in Seattle, Washington.

Other books by Sister Mary Jean Dorcy include: *A Crown for Joanna, Army in Battle Array, Carrying of the Cross, Fount of Our Joy, Hunter of Souls, Mary, Mary — My Mother, Master Albert, Never the Golden City, Our Lady of Springtime, Our Lady's Feasts, St. Dominic, Shepherd's Tartan, Shrines of Our Lady,* and *Truth Was Their Star.*